PENGUIN BOOKS

CHANCE WITNESS

Praise for Matthew Parris:

'Thank heavens for Matthew Parris. A voice of sanity in our dotty world' John Mortimer

'No talent, darling' Peter Ackroyd

'Matthew Parris has the highest strike rate of any living sketchwriter' *Observer*

'An absolute shit' Alan Clark

'I am sure I have only slightly less high an opinion of Matthew's literary abilities than he does himself' Alan Lomberg, English teacher, school report

'Unreliable' Alastair Campbell

'A sophisticated pen, finely honed by years of writing some of the most exquisitely crafted parliamentary pieces' David Mellor

ABOUT THE AUTHOR

Matthew Parris worked for the Foreign Office and the Conservative Research Department before serving as an MP. He joined *The Times* as a parliamentary sketchwriter in 1988, a post he held until 2001. He now writes as a columnist for the paper, and in 2011 he won the Columnist of the Year Award at the British Press Awards. His acclaimed autobiography *Chance Witness* was first published by Viking in 2002.

Chance Witness

An Outsider's Life in Politics

MATTHEW PARRIS

PENGUIN BOOKS

PENGUIN BOOKS

Published by the Penguin Group
Penguin Books Ltd, 80 Strand, London WC2R ORL, England
Penguin Group (USA) Inc., 375 Hudson Street, New York, New York 10014, USA
Penguin Group (Canada), 90 Eglinton Avenue East, Suite 700, Toronto, Ontario, Canada M4P 2Y3
(a division of Pearson Penguin Canada Inc.)
Penguin Ireland, 25 St Stephen's Green, Dublin 2, Ireland (a division of Penguin Books Ltd)
Penguin Group (Australia), 707 Collins Street, Melbourne, Victoria 3008, Australia
(a division of Pearson Australia Group Pty Ltd)
Penguin Books India Pvt Ltd, 11 Community Centre, Panchsheel Park, New Delhi – 110 017, India
Penguin Group (NZ), 67 Apollo Drive, Rosedale, Auckland 0632, New Zealand
(a division of Pearson New Zealand Ltd)
Penguin Books (South Africa) (Pty) Ltd, Block D, Rosebank Office Park,
181 Jan Smuts Avenue, Parktown North, Gauteng 2193, South Africa

Penguin Books Ltd, Registered Offices: 80 Strand, London WC2R ORL, England

www.penguin.com

First published by Viking 2002
Published in Penguin Books 2003
Reissued with a new Epilogue 2013

001

Copyright © Matthew Parris, 2002, 2013
All rights reserved

The moral right of the author has been asserted

Printed in Great Britain by Clays Ltd, St Ives plc

ISBN: 978-0-241-96829-1

www.greenpenguin.co.uk

MIX
Paper from
responsible sources
FSC C018179

Penguin Books is committed to a sustainable
future for our business, our readers and our planet.
This book is made from Forest Stewardship
Council™ certified paper.

ALWAYS LEARNING   **PEARSON**

To my family, and Julian

Contents

List of Illustrations

A worried Alastair Campbell (*by permission of the* Guardian *and Martin Argles*)

Moonlighting as a television pundit (*by permission of NI Syndication*)

Paxman's jaw drops (*by permission of* Newsnight *and BBC Worldwide*)

The most dangerous gay man in Britain? (*by permission of the* Pink Paper)

Skydiving over Hawaii

Chased by bloodhounds

With horns

And without (*by permission of Alexander Caminada. Copyright* © *Alexander Caminada*)

With my llamas (*by permission of NI Syndication. Copyright* © *Richard Willson/Times Newspapers Limited, London 2002*)

On top of Mount Illimani

On Desolation Island

With Julian Glover

Planning the next adventure (*by permission of NI Syndication*)

Acknowledgements

Almost all my friends have agreed with a cheerful shrug that stories which might embarrass them should not, on account of that, be omitted. Instead I've camouflaged identities where these are unimportant but left the essentials untampered with. One friend alone, however, begged me to omit an entire tale in case anyone guessed he was involved. Naturally I complied. So let me sour the courtly politesse which custom requires of this page in a book and say to him: cowardy, cowardy custard. To all the rest, thank you.

To my successive editors at *The Times* – Charles Wilson, Simon Jenkins, Peter Stothard, Ben Preston, then Peter Stothard again, Robert Thomson, James Harding and John Witherow – and at the *Spectator* – Frank Johnson, Boris Johnson, Stuart Reid and Fraser Nelson – my thanks too. What more can a man ask than to be supported when he asks it, encouraged whether or not he asks it, and otherwise left alone? In the *Times* room at the House of Commons nobody was ever other than friendly, kind and patient with me. I cannot name them all so I will name none, but they know as well as I do how many of my best ideas have come from colleagues, and how many of my worst have been diplomatically strangled by colleagues at birth.

A particular word of gratitude for sub-editors – the whole breed. Columnists love to moan about subs but I must speak for myself: time and again the subs have saved me from errors in my journalism, some of them real howlers. They have cut and left no scars. They have spotted mistakes I had no right to hope anyone would check, and tactfully hinted when the argument was not clear. Editing cannot always be felicitous nor can every headline hit the target, but I decided early that these people were much, much better at it than me and I would leave them to it. I've never regretted that approach.

My dear secretary, Eileen Wright, is praised in the pages which follow. She is one of many whose research, advice and support I've relied upon. Facts have not always been my forte, and anyone who has been part of my team in writing and broadcasting knows that the square bracketed '[MATT TO ADD THOUGHTFUL END-ING]', familiar in our joint efforts, is only partly in jest.

In the preparation of this book, my agent, Ed Victor, cheered me, and at Viking, Tony Lacey, Keith Taylor and Zelda Turner bore cheerfully with my hesitation, delay and general disorganization. Gerry Taylor at News International found from the archives every-thing – and it was extensive – I was looking for, and David Prosser and Nick Angel read and improved my drafts. Copy-editing, Bela Cunha undangled my participles as she has done for so many authors before me. Julian Glover, my best friend in everything I do, steered me and the book from start to finish.

And it wasn't just what these people did which has mattered to me. What has been sublime has been the knowledge throughout – an assurance on which I've been able to lean all my professional and personal life – that I am travelling with people who are on my side. I am a lucky, lucky man.

Introduction to the First Edition

I started writing this book on the sub-Antarctic island of Kerguelen, so named after Yves de Kerguelen, a French adventurer who sighted the windswept archipelago in 1772. Two years later Captain Cook, the first man to set foot, called it Desolation Island.

I was there for nearly five months in the year 2000, a sort of willing exile. The archipelago, which belongs to France, comprises the most isolated habitable islands of any substance on the planet. Habitable but virtually uninhabited. Port aux Français, the French base and only settlement, housed some fifty souls. We were thousands of miles from anywhere and tens of thousands of miles from home: some 2,000 miles from Cape Town and a similar distance from Perth in Western Australia. India, to our north, was twice as far.

The latitude put us in the path of the Roaring Forties and as I began to write a ninety-mile-an-hour westerly gale shot-blasted the window of my cabin with hail. There was no way to get away but by boat and the passage, over mountainous seas, lasts more than a week. I was cast away on Desolation Island.

But if it was Desolation it was a serene desolation, full of light and life, although there are no trees – the wind blows away all who try to put down roots and the insects have lost their wings. The island has immense mountains, snowy glaciers, green marshes, black rocks and volcanic peaks, all beneath mighty skies and a silvery-grey light. The sea, by turns angry or quiet, seems almost to glitter as white horses chase each other across the bay. The weather changes as often in a day as in England it might in a month: rain, sun, sleet, hail, wind, snow and calm.

Every animal came from the sea and was preparing to return there for the southern winter as this book was started, for the ocean would soon be warmer than the land and full of nourishment. Birds of all kinds, from huge albatrosses to tiny diving petrels, elephant seals as big as sofas, hundreds of thousands of penguins lining every beach . . . all of them were, not 'tame', but blithely unafraid of man – almost unconscious of us, as though we were ghosts from another dimension.

True, the elephant seal wears an expression of mild alarm tempered by sloth; but he does not panic. Panic is perfectly pointless when you are tremendous and have no legs. True, the baby albatrosses on their nests, each hundreds of yards from the next, as big as a goose and as daffy as a day-old chick, snap their huge beaks with a soft snap–snap and stare goofily up from their raised mud thrones; but they know no ill of us. True, the penguins huddle busily together and peer a little sharply in your direction as though you were about to be the subject of a public protest meeting; but the meeting will break up without reaching any determinate conclusion: purposive yet without purpose, penguins, like politicians, experience decisions rather than make them.

I walked 500 miles over that archipelago. There were no roads and no paths, and we yomped, clambered and climbed in small groups for our own safety, sheltering the nights in caves or tents, once fearing for our lives as a gale flattened our tent and the water from melting snow rose around us, inundating our sleeping bags.

Once there was a shooting – a terrible accident in which our base doctor shot our radio technician dead when he slipped on the ice with a loaded, cocked gun. I learned much about death in small groups, about human stigma and human guilt, from that episode.

I tried on foot to circumnavigate the highest massif and failed, forced after three days to turn back. I fought with seasickness and sailed round the south of the island beneath the great black cliffs with water tipping from their rims and blowing upwards into the air and the Southern Ocean lashing their base. I struggled to improve my French but still found myself an alien, kindly treated but understanding only in part the society I had joined. And in between I wrote, reams and reams about my life and times, some of it nonsense on re-reading, some of it surviving into the pages which follow.

Why did I go to Kerguelen? Almost since I was a little boy at my infants' school in Cyprus – the school at the end of the track where I fell and smashed my arm – this was my ambition. I saw this island on a map, it looked big, nearly as big as Cyprus, and not so polar as to be mere waste – and nobody seemed to know anything about it. The longing grew with the mystery.

When, forty years later, I wrote about it in *The Times*, scores of readers added to my knowledge and urged me on. And in the end I got my chance: a television documentary paid the bills. That, however, is less than the whole truth. The truth is I was feeling stale and looking for an excuse to make a change.

Everybody, every busy man or woman, must have experienced the urge to drop everything. Moments of fatigue, moments when the workload or the routine – the sameness of things – feed an impossible daydream. For most it's never more than a whim: wild, fanciful – and passing. Yet the persistence with which something so foolish returns, seldom to wrestle us to the ground but instead tug hesitantly yet persistently at our sleeve, must signify something.

A sense of duty bids us ignore the tug. So instead we dream; we dream that, like Dorothy in *The Wizard of Oz*, some version of a tornado will scoop us up and transport us to a new existence.

I was trying to organize the tornado – and I could call it journalism, could tell myself it was in the line of duty. Career *and* adventure: a new chapter, a clean slate to write it on, and yet a record unblemished by waywardness. Many of us on Desolation Island were in the same case: dutiful as far as we could be – but, glory be, placed by our jobs in a new world. Besides, I was lucky. No wife, no family, no children, no dependants of any sort. A freelance job from which I could justify a sabbatical.

I needed it. Passing fifty, I was feeling weighed down, in a rut.

I have, you see, no sense of unrealized achievement to keep me keen. Especially in my world, which lies along the curious frontier between creativity and observation, many men and women are teased and invigorated by a sense of potential still unfulfilled. Some are sure they have within them the great novel, the great column still unwritten, the epoch-making proposal for television or radio, the idea or theory which might change the world.

I never have. Working at the limit of my abilities and extracting from my work a better income, more credit and greater attention than I deserve, I know I am good at what I do, but also that it is all I can do, a voracious stealer of other people's ideas, jokes, even phrases; a magpie with fitfully keen powers of discrimination and some talent to mock or amuse.

Leafing through one of my books one night before my journey to Kerguelen had seemed possible, I found inserted a scrap of paper on which a friend, presumably after some drunken evening, had scrawled:

'Piss off, Parris, you overrated bastard.' That's not far from the truth, and seemed like a sign.

Then – my good luck again – it arrived, in the shape of Desolation Island. I would piss off. This would be my chance not only to get away, not only to explore, but to write.

'Autobiography' is such a grand word, and 'memoirs' too precious. Besides, my achievements so far have hardly been on a scale that demands an account for history's benefit. The British Library are unlikely to be bidding for my papers. Though the chapters ahead brush me up against people and circumstances that do matter, most of my tangles with history and skirmishes with celebrities have been of an incidental kind. In no case am I the major player, and often I am uninvolved: on the scene but not of the scene – a chance witness.

There are, too, accounts of a more personal kind. Some of these were deeply felt, some embarrassing and some instructive; a few – almost – titillating. None would I be setting down if I did not think them of possible interest, but what in the end do they amount to? Only the experiences, commonplace or occasionally exceptional, which anyone may have.

So why me and why now? Me because it has all been such a strange rollercoaster, and I think I can interest you in some of it. Now because, possessing no 'papers' of any sort, and appearing in nobody else's, I might as well try doing it from my head while there's time, while it's still there, and before things which can never be retrieved start slipping away. The time and place – a spare season in sub-Antarctica – seemed an ideal place to start.

The only records useful in writing this book were in newspapers. Having written an almost daily column now for thirteen years in *The Times*, and hundreds for the *Spectator*, there are stories told already (in some cases I fear more than once) but which seemed worth including. I don't flatter myself that newspaper readers commit my columns to memory, but if occasionally a paragraph seems familiar to some, forgive me. After-dinner speakers know the agony of deciding whether to bore the handful who have heard a story before in the hope of entertaining the larger number who have not. On the whole we shrug our shoulders and opt to entertain.

And if this fails to entertain, it fails you. But if it does no more than entertain it will have failed its author.

Nothing – neither music, nor art, nor writing – means much to me if it lacks shape. I need form, tune, spine, a map. And yet I dislike form for the sake of form. Pattern repeated for the pleasure of pattern soon bores me and I find the baroque tedious. Sounds must go somewhere; a picture must tell you something and so must a sketch in words. Colour alone is not enough. Even as an infant I would kick at my soft toys as my mother read 'And the *medium* sized bear said, "Who's been eating . . . ?"' – oh cut the crap, Mum; what *happened*? The twirl of drumsticks, the plumes on horses, the folderol of folk dancing, the simpering repetition of religious litany, men in medals, women in hats, costume of every kind . . . everything tra-la-la in human communication or entertainment I have hated since an early age with a fiery passion.

For me a book tells a story, a picture speaks to our intelligence, music is a song – or they are nothing. What then should a life be, or do, or say?

Memoirs of public figures often contain a short and apologetic account, or no account at all, of childhood. They read as though the adult walked into the world as he walks into a meeting: shirt pressed, tie knotted, briefcase in hand, minutes of the previous meeting read and agreed – and now for the main business: my life. But that is not how we arrive, and when career starts the freshest part of our life is already over.

So I offer quite a full account of my youth with no sheepish grin. An autobiography should look outwards, of course – should be about what a person did or saw. But as you call your author to the witness stand you do still need to get to know him for you will be looking through his eyes.

We cannot be known in isolation from our youth. It is then that we felt most keenly, hoped most fervently, feared most anxiously, learned most quickly, absorbed most deeply, and took it all to heart. Prejudices and convictions, ambitions and tastes were rooted then. This is when our blind-spots were formed and also our sensitivities; our determination to see the world in certain ways.

I have the footings of a theory of childhood but (being no Piaget or Skinner) no competence to build on it. Thinking about sexuality is what sparked these ideas, but they go wider. I shall hit you now with five paragraphs which the journalist in me knows should be removed at once because they will lose readers. Skip them, but indulge me the satisfaction of seeing them in print.

Cars, circuit-boards and pizzas start their lives at the carcass stage, adaptable to a range of applications. A 'universal' carcass permits fitting out further down the production line when later decisions on end-use are taken. Car carcasses (car-makers call them platforms) are adaptable for soft or hard top, left- or right-hand drive; surface-mounted plastic boxes have dummy-holes to be punched later, depending on where the wiring is to enter; cardboard carding is supplied with fold-lines and perforations offering a choice of final shape.

The mind, I believe, enters the world like this: not so much a blank slate as a carcass, adaptable later and in light of circumstances to a wide but not infinite range of applications. Each adaptation pre-empts a clutch of others so scope for further change shrinks fast and exponentially as the consciousness matures.

As bats send out squeaks into the dark, as babies fumble with the air, and as mangrove trees shoot down adventitious roots in search of moisture, so we learn by what we bounce or echo off, grasp or lock on to. Other human beings we detect before we are properly conscious of ourselves as one of them. *We begin to see ourselves as an example of others we have seen, and not the other way round.* Others are our first mirror. Emotionally this is also true, and some poor children are like glow-worms flashing in the dark, their flash fading as they find no answering light.

The answers fix our own position. Others are the template. Others describe us to ourselves. We begin a relationship with ourselves which is modelled on our relationships with others: we watch ourselves, talk to ourselves, like, dislike, bore, amuse, love and fear ourselves. We are, from infancy, two people and the life which follows will be a continuous conversation between them as they explore the world together.

Their exploration soon makes a map. As the Ancient Greeks saw bears and hunters in the night sky, so our two adventurers arrange the numberless stars – points of light, sound, colour, smell, touch, taste and also emotion – into constellations: their patterns of the world.

I have found writing an autobiography hard. Most lives – mine, anyway – are not a song. Unforced, a life tells no story. There is no denouement here, few revelations, no clear moral, and the author is of passing interest. Sometimes I have felt what John Peyton in his autobiography *Without the Benefit of Laundry* describes as reaching back into memory as we reach into a tank of bright tropical fish – and withdrawing one's hand to find it full only of sand and seaweed. The living memories slip through my fingers. My tale has no plot.

But perhaps it is readable. This introduction, like most, is written after what it introduces and, casting my eye over the scenes which follow, I can reach no better explanation for the shape these chapters take than the conclusion George Eliot set out in *Middlemarch*:

An eminent philosopher among my friends, who can dignify even your ugly furniture by lifting it into the serene light of science, has shown me this pregnant little fact. Your pier-glass or extensive surface of polished steel made to be rubbed by a housemaid, will be minutely and multitudinously scratched in all directions; but place now against it a lighted candle as a centre of illumination, and lo! the scratches will seem to arrange themselves in a fine series of concentric circles round that little sun. It is demonstrable that the scratches are going everywhere impartially, and it is only your candle which produces the flattering illusion of a concentric arrangement, its light falling with an exclusive optical selection. These things are a parable. The scratches are events, and the candle is the egoism of any person now absent – of . . .

. . . Of myself, for instance.

L'Avenc, Catalonia, June 2002

1. Falling to Earth

The thing is, it was a new bike. It was my first bike. It had been a birthday present, it was shiny-blue and it had pump-up tyres, unlike my little brother Roger's, which was red and smaller and had solid tyres and was not (I had told him) a real bike but more of a toy. Mine was a proper boy's bicycle. So when I wheeled it too near the cliff and it began to slip there could be no letting go. I held on.

Scorched into memory is falling. A head-over-heels confusion, all arms and legs and bicycle tumbling through the air. I don't think I cried out, and cannot remember hitting the ground at the cliff's foot, but only the stillness afterwards, the bare earth and the Cyprus heat. Then the pain began.

The worst pain was from the least injury. My ribs and stomach were skinned and bleeding, and though superficial the wound hurt horribly. How this had happened in such a fall escapes me for the cliff was not as high as in a small child's imagination it seemed – a dried-up river bank twenty feet high perhaps. I only say cliff because that's how it felt.

It doesn't matter, does it? Nor does it much matter how a sure-footed little six-year-old, champion climber of olive trees, came to misjudge.

I know why I would have been there, though. I loved the river – more a series of half-stagnant ponds than a river – teeming with the frogs and tadpoles I tried to catch and keep, next to my caterpillar collection. I loved outdoors, anything outdoors; the very word 'indoors' was heartsinking, still is. Show me the inside of a room and I would be straight to the window, looking out, climbing out if I could. Show me a room with no window and I'll show you a prison.

I must have walked the bike too close to the edge and then, when it slipped, held on. The great fall marked me and my body indelibly, though I had no notion of that as I picked myself up, needing help.

There was also something else.

I claim this not as a virtue – it has led to acts of stupidity – but only as inescapable for me: I knew what happened next was up to me. I must do something, immediately – *I* must, and it did not occur to me to wait for help. Everything depended on me. That sharp companion, personal responsibility, put his hand on my shoulder for the first time I remember. He was to stay for ever.

I left the bike behind – not wanting to but the ribs hurt too much and all at once the bike didn't seem to matter.

Our house was about half a mile away, a new bungalow on the outskirts of Nicosia, rented from an overbearing Cypriot landlady with fleshy arms who pinched my cheeks, which children hate. I tramped through the dust. There seemed such a lot of blood. It had been my secret hope to see blood ever since Dad had given Roger and me a warning talk about Cypriot terrorist bombs planted against the British, and how we must never kick discarded pipes and cans. We never did but I always hoped someone else would, so we could watch the explosion.

Now bombs were far from my mind. The dull ache was getting worse. A young Cypriot man came down the track. When he reached me he glanced down and a look of fear crossed his face. He walked straight past and away, quickening his step. Pain and fear are different and I had not been afraid before. It frightened me now how frightened he was.

I glanced down too, and looked where he had looked.

Part of my right arm seemed to be hanging off. The forearm and hand were drenched in blood, still trickling fast into the soft dust and leaving a trail behind me. The top of the arm seemed all right. What was wrong was the elbow. The elbow did not look like an elbow, but a gristly knuckle, bone sticking right out. This, then, was the cruel dull ache, the one beneath the sting of grazed ribs, the ache which would dominate the nights and months ahead.

After that, memory goes blank for a bit. There is a gap – oddly, no memory of my mother, who seems so important in a host of other childhood memories – but only, when the picture returns, of my father.

Dad, always Dad when it was really serious. It had to be serious when Dad came into the foreground. I was sitting on his knee in Mr Farmer's Land-Rover. This was in itself unusual as normally Dad would drive – he always drove, we believed he was the best driver in the world. But now he had asked Mr Farmer to drive and sat me on his knee.

This was even stranger as Dad did not much like us to sit on his knee even though we always wanted to.

And – strangest thing of all – he did not seem to mind about the blood.

He was wearing his good suit and he did not have many. My father was always careful, in a practical not finicky way, about possessions: about not spoiling things, about taking care not to break or waste or abuse or mark them, about not leaving things out in the rain, putting things away properly at the end of the day. Now blood was dripping all down the front of his good suit and soaking into the top of his trousers and I wanted to move so the blood would go on to the floor.

I felt sure this must bother him. For once it was me not wanting to sit on his knee, and him wanting me to. I remember my bewilderment so clearly, more clearly even than the injury, and remember trying to work it out. And the only answer I could find was 'this must be serious'.

And now I recall falling again: this too is scorched into memory. Shooting like a rocket through thick, warm African air. I was the second stage of the rocket, the first being the vehicle which served as launch-pad and had just hit the ground. This, my second airborne experience, began with a Land-Rover in Cameroon.

At twenty-three I was in my first year of failing to apply myself to a postgraduate degree at Yale. With friends of like-minded adventurousness I had planned for that summer an overland trip from England to East Africa. Our Land-Rover was called Stanley.

The Atlas mountains had proved no obstacle and from every sandpit in which we had stuck in the Algerian Sahara we had extricated ourselves. Niger was hot and Nigeria sticky but both were survived without mishap. Now we had reached Northern Cameroon, an open green, gentle, hilly, grassy place, quite well-populated with African herdsmen and farmers as friendly as their life was primitive, working almost naked in the sun.

After the desert Cameroon seemed like some kind of Eden. Our only anxiety was Brent's driving but he insisted on doing his share. At the wheel he was of uncertain judgement and too fast, but nobody liked to say so. He was driving when we rounded an unexpectedly sharp bend with an adverse camber on a corrugated dirt road.

I remember it was a left-hand bend, and Brent's jaw jutting with a fierce and slightly asymmetric determination. Odd – about Brent's jaw and the bend being left hand – because I cannot remember much else about Brent: whose friend he was in the first place, for instance, or where he came from or why he had wanted to join us.

Brent miscalculated. Fearing that if he held the curve we might overturn he chose to veer from the road at a tangent. At about 40 mph we plunged across the tussocked earth. Then a great donga, a mini-canyon about ten feet across and five feet deep, scooped by erosion, yawned before us.

I was on the roof. On the roof is a marvellous way to travel and to be recommended except in an accident. Sitting at the front of the roof-rack I stared down for a horrified instant at the intervening donga, and gripped the rack with both hands as tight as I could. That must have been what dislocated my shoulders. But it kept me on board for the cross-donga leap. The opposite bank must have been lower, so we did not crash into the donga but flew over it, all four wheels in the air.

We hit the other side. We hit so hard the chassis cracked (though we did not discover this until Nairobi), all the side-windows fell out – unbroken – and above the four inside passengers the impressions of the tops of their heads were stamped into the roof.

I was not on the roof for long. Impact with the ground brought Stanley to an abrupt halt, but not me. Like an unbroken stallion Stanley rammed into the earth then bucked. I was launched in parabolic flight, upwards, then in an arc down. I hit the bare earth about twenty feet forward.

Every second of that flight stays with me. It seemed slow-motion. There was time to regret letting Brent drive, and to reflect that this at least would make the point without our having to tell him, about his driving; and to notice some African women labouring in a patch of maize near a thorn tree, staring up in wonder at the descending European space-traveller.

I landed crumpled at the foot of a tree. Lying there I wondered if I still existed, then, remembering Descartes, reminded myself that to ask was to answer.

I made as if to get up. The most awful pain ripped through each shoulder. Worse than from my elbow seventeen years before. But there were no wounds, no blood. Guessing what might have happened – I had seen dislocations before – I managed to lunge myself to my knees, then rise. Clapping, the African women broke into shouts of 'ah! ah! ah!' which right across that great continent means Bloody Hell, in a sympathetic sort of way.

Only then did my friends emerge from Stanley. None was much hurt.

In the greetings and relief which followed I temporarily forgot, but was soon reminded of, my shoulders. Nobody knew how to relocate somebody else's shoulder in the medically approved manner, but I had read somewhere that if you are alone then the job can be done by swinging from the top of something like a door. There being no door I tried the thorn tree. Scrabbling my fingers up the trunk I could raise each arm to a stump above my head, then drop my weight on to it. The pain was intense. It worked.

I could hardly speak. The most abrupt and immense depression fell upon me. I could not summon the will to walk or speak, and sat down under my thorn tree, staring into space. This I apparently did for about an hour, stunned by the whole world, monosyllabic to the point of speechlessness, perfectly useless, alone with myself, my best friend. These are important times.

By evening, Cameroon had renewed its charm. Everything seemed on the mend. We pitched camp, and repaired to the tin-shack bar of the village near which we set our tents. We drank a great deal of beer.

This tour of the bars of Central Africa was becoming a pleasant habit which led some days later to a bar night in the Central African Republic on the edge of the great Congo forest. I had quite recovered my spirits, and gulped some disgusting banana gin, too much – and became rather drunk. I must have been, because I danced with a pygmy. She was tiny but dynamic. She gyrated wildly, so wildly that in an enthusiastic attempt at counter-gyration I dislocated my right shoulder again. Soon fixed – there was a door.

Who cares about a few dents and scratches? I love scars. I love all witnesses to survival. I love a rusting corrugated iron roof. I don't mind a lined face, wind-beaten skin, worn steps, frayed collars and peeling paint. If there were a paradise I should wish to turn up there

with all my lines and scars, and my crooked elbow, and, having bored
you about each injury, bore St Peter too.

From the earliest age I have enjoyed being sat on. I would try to
worm my way under the cushions of an armchair or sofa, wait for
someone to sit down, and savour the sensation of being pinned to the
under-springs and almost crushed beneath the weight of the adult
above.

I'm fairly sure of the cause. I blame Maggie. I have often wondered
what Baroness Thatcher would make of my admission that the most
important Maggie in my life was black, a Zulu lady who called me
Sinkwe – bushbaby – and carried me strapped tightly to her back for
almost the first year of my life.

We often talk in our family as though that South African sojourn
after my parents' marriage in 1947, so short that I was just a year old
when we left Johannesburg to return to England in 1950, is explained
by my father's job as an electrical engineer. This took us all over the
world. In South Africa he worked for the Transvaal Light & Power
Company. Next, with British Insulated Calender's Cables we moved
to Cyprus, Southern Rhodesia, Jamaica and Franco's Spain. I went to
seven schools.

Yet South Africa was different from those later postings. They were
all with a British company, and postings. Nobody posted Dad to
South Africa. I never quite grasped this as a child but my parents had
upped sticks and meant to emigrate to South Africa for good. They
were a young couple. My father, Leslie, was not long out of the Royal
Navy. Theresa, my mother, had met him in 1946. If things had gone
as they had planned I would not have been British at all.

As my parents remember it, the United Kingdom was a drab,
pinched, depressing place after the war: food was rationed and accommodation hard to find.

Grandpa dearly wanted his only son to take over Parris Family
Butchers ('High-Class' Butchers, said the sign in the window in
south-east London) and, when his son insisted on trying to make it
alone, offered to find him instead a job in his chosen career, electrical
engineering, through Grandpa's friends in the Freemasons. Dad
refused this – he wanted to make it alone.

Grandpa was a shy man but cherished some hopes of modest social position and a commercial family dynasty, buying a big American Ford before most people thought of owning a car, joining a golf club and even in his years of retirement driving a top-of-the-range Mini called a Riley Elf, with a special grille, stunted wings and a walnut-veneer fascia. They owned Gower Lodge, a fine, mock-Tudor detached house in Sydenham Avenue near Crystal Palace park, with a lawn, croquet and a copper-beech tree, and Grandpa was a Conservative. But as a couple they could never quite follow it through, mostly due to Grandpa's, but more particularly Grandma's, blind terror of socializing. They had been known to hide when neighbours knocked at the door. What they loved best was gardening. Their names were Francis and Frances.

The Littlers, Leonard and Alice, my mother's parents, were different: poorer, perhaps a notch down on the social scale in Francis and Frances's eyes. Yet my mother, Theresa, had had high hopes as a girl: she wanted to be an actress and had obvious talent. At sixteen she won, on audition, a Shakespeare scholarship, fully paid, to study at the Royal Academy of Dramatic Art. Her mother refused to let her go. Nana was a kindly, chatty, anxious, houseproud woman who lived on a different level from her husband whom she adored without understanding. Mum never went to RADA, a bitter and abiding disappointment I think.

She shared with her father a love of learning, reading and the arts. Grandad loved Dickens. He became increasingly absorbed in Eastern religion and mysticism, and was sometimes strangely withdrawn, though he had a gentle but pointed and sardonic sense of humour.

He was a humane man, though. Years later, when in retirement he had become a proofreader for the Oxford University Press, he took me as a boy for walks in the grounds of the Oxford colleges which he loved. A raggedly dressed man sitting on a bench by an ornamental pond struck up conversation. He assured Grandad that all the dewdrops on the lily-pads were really diamonds and he could demonstrate this – and would Grandad like to ask him home for tea so he could explain further. He added (this must have struck me) that he would not take up too much of our time and would certainly leave when requested to; and that he had better clothes than these to wear, if he was invited.

Grandad pondered for a moment (I think he was wondering

whether to say yes) then said perhaps another time, most politely. When we recounted the story to Nana she said the man was crackers and what was Len doing talking to such people, particularly with her grandson to look after, and if he had any ideas of bringing tramps home for tea she would clock him one. Grandad said nothing, but I had noticed his courtesy to the man, the way he gave him a hearing, and did not speak ill of him, to Nana or me.

Grandad's special bugbears were vicars and insurance salesmen, whom he regarded as being in the same business. He knew well and could quote the Bible but had a hatred for ceremony in organized religion: 'Incense and idols are for idiots,' he told me. In the face of all insistence that ours is an unusually godless age I must report my suspicion that none of my four grandparents, all born in the nineteenth century, had any abiding belief in a deity: it was just that in those days you did not say so. When, near the end of Grandma's days, I made some polite grandchildish remark to her about the next life, she stopped dead on the pavement in Margate along which I was assisting her, glared at me, and said, 'You don't think I believe in any of that, do you?' She reminded me then of Queen Victoria who interrupted a courtier comforting her with the thought she would meet her dead baby 'in the bosom of Abraham'. 'We shall *not* meet in the bosom of Abraham,' she said.

Grandad was an RAF officer who worked his way up from the ranks to the position of squadron leader. He had the unsmart tastes of a self-educated Edwardian man: besides Dickens, Grandad knew most of *The Rubaiyat of Omar Khayyam* by heart and would recite long passages from 'The Jackdaw of Rheims' (John Major's favourite poem) and favourite Victorian books such as *The Gravedigger*. He often played his 78 rpm recording of the famous duet from Bizet's *The Pearl Fishers*. He read to his eldest daughter, to whom he was devoted.

She, in turn, must have spent thousands of hours reading Dickens to me as a child once I had graduated from her other favourites: Beatrix Potter, *The Wind in the Willows*, and A. A. Milne.

It was always darkly hinted Leonard Littler's father, my great-grandfather, had killed himself. I never liked to ask more. Few of us did. Grandad was a direct man: upright and correct in dress and manner and possessed of an enormous and natural dignity, but with no time for gentility and impatient all his life with the niceties. I wouldn't have dreamed of asking him to tell me more about how his father died.

Our great-grandfather, ran one rumour, had been chief signalman at St Pancras station on the Midland line to Derby. The railway company had brought in a system of written examinations for senior staff. Our great-grandfather never had a proper education and feared he would fail. The company offered him an alternative job as a station porter. Humiliated, he shot himself, leaving a destitute widow and eleven children, ten of whom died the same year in a measles epidemic. Grandfather ended up in the railwaymen's orphanage in Derby. That was the gist of the family story.

Years later I decided to try to investigate its truth.

My great-grandfather did kill himself: not with a gun but by hanging, from the top of the washhouse door at 30 Amersham Grove, New Cross, South London, on 6 July 1896. His name was Septimus George Littler. He was thirty-nine. His little son, Leonard, was a year old. A neighbour found him.

He did not have eleven children, but only one, my grandfather. Nobody had died of measles. Septimus George had worked not for the Midland Railway but for the South-Eastern Railway. He was not a chief signalman but an ordinary signalman. His post was at London Bridge station, not St Pancras. He had been downgraded not to porter, but to ticket inspector. But the shame was still real. He took his demotion badly, fell into acute depression and in the summer of 1896 ended his life. His widow, Lydia Littler, my great-grandmother, became a single mother.

She worked as a lavatory attendant by day, sewing men's shirts by night. She seems to have been almost destitute. When her son Leonard was seven she decided to send him to an orphanage. Leonard was sent to St Christopher's in Derby: the 'Railway Servants' Orphanage'. Lydia told the little boy his late father had helped as a volunteer collecting funds for the orphanage. I suppose it was her way of assuring him the family had paid for his education.

It is too easy, now, to assume the orphanage was a last resort, a sign of Lydia's desperation. But study of the records of St Christopher's suggests it may have been a proud institution offering Leonard a better schooling than a penniless widow's son could expect in New Cross. The orphanage had some 200 children; there was central heating, separate asphalt playgrounds for boys and girls, a proper sanitary system, and scripture taught by vicars. This must have been where Grandad got his lifelong hatred of them.

'It was most encouraging,' said the orphanage chairman, Christopher Bailey, at the AGM in the year my great-grandfather died, 'to see that the institution could turn out boys who could make progress in the world on leaving.' The boys were 'trained up morally' as well as educated. After the AGM 'an entertainment was given by the children, consisting of songs, dumb-bell exercises, figure marching etc.'

My grandfather, my aunt Irene Littler discovered, 'had wooden floors to scrub before breakfast, and dripping sandwiches to eat. But he cannot remember a time when he could not or did not read, and brought himself up on Dickens and Sherlock Holmes.'

When in 1978 I was interviewed for the Conservative parliamentary seat of West Derbyshire and was asked whether there were any family links with the county, I claimed my grandfather had roots in Derby. It is reassuring now to know the claim was substantially true.

My parents left South London for South Africa in 1948. They loved the freedom, Mum says. My nanny Maggie became quite a friend and was proud of her employers and her swaddled bushbaby.

Maggie was illiterate but one evening, when my parents had to return unexpectedly shortly after leaving the house, they saw in an armchair Maggie (who was babysitting me) arranged conspicuously at the living-room window, all the lights on, the curtains open (my mother had shut them), a pair of spectacles on her nose, and holding out an open book as though reading.

There was much in South Africa, including Maggie, that my parents loved. But politics began to upset this. They were troubled by a general unkindness of whites to blacks, and what seemed to be a hardening of attitudes. The year they arrived the Afrikaner-dominated Nationalist Party won a general election and apartheid started. It was to last nearly half a century. My parents had to decide whether this was where they wanted to make their family's future. Dad had just been offered a manager's job with Transvaal Light & Power. But they decided to cut their losses, return to England, and start again.

They travelled back by sea, driving to Durban to join the Union

Castle Line ship. Maggie was inconsolable. As we all drove away from the cottage, Mum says, she ran behind the car, calling and weeping.

We moved to North Yorkshire, to a tiny village by the North York Moors called Newsham. I remember the cold, always the cold; the rural bus journeys in single-decker buses with isolated solo-cabs for the drivers; and Mrs Patterson at Hill Top Farm, where I used to collect eggs, which I hoped to incubate. 'How was I as a toddler?' I asked when I visited her recently, by then in her eighties. 'Temperamental,' she said.

Yorkshire. Yes, I remember much about those dawning years but as before the sunrise, for there is something I cannot remember in Yorkshire. Light. The blinding sun. The baking earth, the squinting at a hot sky, the horizon as wide as the world itself and the knowledge of other worlds to be discovered on the horizon's other side. Whoever sees anything large in an English moor is small. Whoever calls Scafell Pike a mountain has never stared longingly from Nicosia at the blue-purple haze of the Kyrenia mountains in Cyprus, their great ridge shimmering distantly under a hot sky, or climbed that ridge, as I was to do, and seen the mountains of Anatolia fifty miles away across the Mediterranean, in Turkey. Whoever finds English sunshine bright has been living in a cave. Everything, *everything* from that time comes back to me cramped, in a sort of half-light, and it is always raining, and I am impatient to get out, and walk uphill, always uphill, towards some imagined crest in the heather, on my own.

'You never enjoy the world aright, till the sea itself floweth in your veins, till you are clothed with the heavens and crowned with the stars; and perceive yourself to be the sole heir of the whole world and more than so, because men are in it who are every one sole heirs as well as you,' wrote the seventeenth-century mystic Thomas Traherne.

I do not feel inwardly a jot different from that little boy in Yorkshire. He seems to me to be me in every respect, clear and formed: an unbroken line from there to here.

I remember, too, Mum cleaning the stone floors downstairs at the back near the door, or struggling with the portable lavatory that had to be emptied over the hedge, and singing in a sad voice. For this was the time when things went wrong because of her health, or possibly the other way round: a shadow over the whole of my childhood.

She was never miserable and always fun. But in Yorkshire my

mother was pining. Roger had been born after her return. The warmth and sunshine and freedom of life in South Africa had come to an abrupt halt, and there she was in the English rain with two tiny toddlers – the first of six – in a cold, damp, terraced cottage on the edge of a bleak moor, dreams of the theatre fading, husband often tense and often away in his new job. I cannot say why but with my mother ill in bed upstairs I formed the childish impression she was a prisoner, that Dad had imprisoned her upstairs and wanted to stop anybody, even her sons, seeing her. For a while we thought she had tuberculosis. Then rheumatoid arthritis set in (she was only in her mid-twenties) and has never left her but never defeated her either, and mostly she has been able to keep walking.

It receded most and for longest in the wonderful years which came next. My parents left Yorkshire for Cyprus, where my father's company had found him a position, hoping a drier climate might help my mother. I was four and it was 1954. We always thought of England as our country, but I did not return to live until I was nineteen.

As we set out for Southampton docks I doubt I fully grasped what this was about: a second try at a new life abroad. There were few backward glances.

We travelled to Cyprus by sea. We must have stopped at Athens on the way because I have a crazy recollection of trying to get to the Acropolis, fast, in a Greek taxi. The Acropolis I forget entirely but the taxi was a pale green Ford Consul with smelly leather seats and straps you could hang on to, and had to.

Arrival at Larnaca in Cyprus is literally burned into my memory. After four years in Yorkshire we had forgotten about the sun and couldn't really believe we had to stay out of it or cover ourselves in cream. The ultra-violet struck. We retreated to the Ledra Palace Hotel in Nicosia where many days were spent in agony. I had never before and have never since been sunburned like that. I couldn't lie down, I couldn't sleep . . . it seemed to an uncomprehending infant that Cyprus must be some kind of hell.

It became, for all my family who were born there and for Roger and me, one of the happiest times of our lives.

Yet this was a violent time for the island. The four years from 1954 when we arrived saw the slow rise towards apparent invincibility of

Colonel Grivas and the EOKA terrorist movement, agitating for 'Enosis' – union with Greece. They never achieved union with Greece (Greece was scared of war with Turkey) but they obtained independence from Britain, to the dismay of one jingoistic little chap who, having recovered from his sunburn and Sand Fly Fever, found Cyprus an outdoor boy's paradise and didn't see why it should not always be what I was learning to call 'ours'.

Cyprus was among the first colonies to go in that great postwar wiping-away of swathes of red from the *Daily Telegraph* wall maps of the world: maps on which I had spotted and become intrigued by the French island of Kerguelen but on which I would also proudly calculate what proportion of the surface of the globe was British, pleased Mercator's Projection flattered the empire by magnifying Baffin Island and the Northwest Territories of Canada, and a little vague as to what a 'dominion' was anyway. 'Ours'?

Yet this was the 1950s and things were changing. The received wisdom about the period is wrong: that the fifties were dull, unoriginal, suburban, a sort of prim prelude to the Beatles. The era was the real turning point, when modernity arrived. The swinging sixties were merely flamboyant, a giggling reaction to the immense postwar social, moral and economic change which the fifties ushered in. The new world didn't begin with the Magic Bus and 'Yellow Submarine' but with 'Think Formica', the Ford Zephyr, the Martini cocktail, suntans, crooning, the word 'contemporary', radiograms, babysitters, Noel Coward reinventing himself in ruder form, Frank Sinatra, the open discussion of adultery, and the French kiss.

To my parents, this world was still strange. But not to David and Yvonne, my (unrelated) 'aunt' and 'uncle', also living in Cyprus, and in whose house I spent much time. Yvonne was a modern woman. She had bright, light, bouncy hair, wore marvellously bold swishing cotton-print frocks, and smoked, with a cigarette-holder. She laughed a lot, throwing her head back. She was not demure. She and Uncle David had fun, drank cocktails, and sometimes they would cover my ears jokingly when the conversation was – as they might have said – risqué. They had a recording of a song by Noel Coward called 'Alice is at It Again' which I did not understand. The song was to appear on a record called *Noel Coward at Las Vegas* picturing the debonair entertainer in a tuxedo, holding a cup of tea in the midday sun in the desert.

This was the record my mother tried to smash, years later. That may seem out of character for she was usually anything but censorious, but Mum was very clear about one thing: 'dirty' language. Her record-smash failed. Being of the new vinyl type, this LP wouldn't. I remember her jumping on it pointlessly on the doorstep.

Modern people did modern things. We had modern expectations in the 1950s. We believed in electricity almost as a creed: Dad would have nothing to do with gas. We believed in science and we believed in nylon. The very word 'scientific' sanctified the supposed fact or argument upon which it was bestowed, as, in a previous age, a religious benediction might have done. Later I had for years on my bedroom wall a poster distributed by the Colonial Office of Information with colour photographs of all Britain's new nuclear-power stations, including Dounreay, waves smashing against the beach as its bright dome beckoned us towards a smokeless, coal-less future.

The people in the Dan Dare strip-cartoons in my *Eagle* comic seemed to us to live as modern people one day would, perhaps quite soon, perhaps in unisex tinfoil suits and paper underwear, eating pills instead of potatoes. There would be rockets: there almost were already, for was not the new British Comet plane to be jet-propelled and didn't the big Vickers Viscount, just introduced, on which we now travelled home for holidays in England, have 'turbo-prop' engines? Better than the bumpy old Dakotas we started with.

More and more people were getting divorced. Some of the American rock 'n' roll songs hinted that sex before marriage was unexceptional. I cannot recall that anybody much went to church, or, if they did, would have been seen as superior because of it. I read in the *Daily Telegraph* that it might not be long – perhaps the end of the century – before almost everything would be disposable. Suits and ties would soon be outmoded.

All this was just around the corner: a new world, freed from superstition, of which we were the first generation, the pioneers: and maybe even a new world government one day. On those children's wall-charts of the history of mankind since the Stone Age, the estab-lishment a decade before of the United Nations was marked as some kind of culmination.

All this existed behind a façade of conventional pieties and routine lives. We were not revolutionaries in the fifties. But there was an unmistakable excitement in the air: the feeling of a tribe which had lately discovered new gods; and even a small boy could tell.

In the mind's eye I can see our little house. It was in the middle of its plot – not, like English houses, shoved forward on to the street. It was always in the sun, or so it seemed, its walls so white you had to squint to look. You did not look at the sun as you could in England, but could steal only a momentary glance, and it always seemed to be there, always high, always hot – and tiny, not big and spoon-faced like in England, but a small point of dazzling hot white light.

The Greek Cypriot couple next door, who were especially friendly, turned out later to have had a bomb factory in tunnels under their chicken run – and this in the shadow of a huge British army camp just at the end of the road. I supported the British of course, but I loved the idea of bombs. Bombs meant holidays. Bombs meant the announcement on the wireless of 'States of Emergency' – and schools shut. In our bedroom I had proposed to Roger, who was a year younger but much graver, that we blow up my aunt Christine, and she had overheard just as Roger squeaked 'Not a bomb! Not Aunty Tine!' He was always a spoilsport. Tine, my mother's teenage sister, lived with us and we loved her – mostly. But an explosion would have been fun.

Every afternoon in summer we would drive over the Kyrenia mountains, sometimes picnicking at St Hilarion's Castle, and swim at magic little beaches on the north coast. Unable to manage more than a dog-paddle on the surface I became an ace underwater-swimmer. Ever since, I have preferred swimming underwater, with my eyes open, even in salt water. I would hunt starfish and coloured rocks, and, on land, flying insects and butterflies, on which I was determined to become an expert. All these creatures I would take home and try to keep, but they always died.

My parents did not go in for family-planning – no moral objection but they were haphazard – and two more children were born in Nicosia. Deborah's arrival made Dad as happy for an evening as I have ever seen him: he called Roger and me into his and Mum's bedroom – Mum was in the clinic – and exploded with the news. We found this levity in Dad at least as interesting as the arrival of a sister. I was from the start quite hard on Deborah, believing in my tiny way that as my even tinier sibling she should do as I said. She was resistant to this. We fought a lot in time, and I pushed her around when we were both a bit older, causing her anxiety and causing both of us to lose sight of how much I loved her. I saved up for a year to buy her a bicycle. I have always been good at big generous gestures: it's the patient kindness I have trouble with.

Then, a couple of years later, came John. John was sweet, more compliant, then later in his life, difficult (he would say the same of me). I tried hard with John too but, between trying to dominate and trying to patronize, never found the way through to being a useful older brother. Later he became angry at being compared with me.

All the childish tension between Deborah and me has long gone and we are relaxed and loving friends, though she is the readiest of all my brothers and sisters to scold me. Roger and I still know how to niggle each other but we are close; we have been as long as either of us can remember. John and I love each other and are fitfully angry with each other.

Besides having children Mum had a job. We always knew more about her jobs, only part-time, than Dad's. But he must have been pretty capable as he kept being promoted and paid more, while often seeming to dislike his work. Dad hated paperwork (at which he was good) and hated meetings (at which he apparently excelled) but by now had four children and could hardly start a new career.

Any aptitude I ever developed for creative writing was nurtured by my mother, but my father played a bigger part than he realizes in my development as a writer. He could write a splendid, sparse report of anything, getting straight to the essentials. He wrote the best minutes I have ever read. On an envelope he could write instructions or directions – for wiring a toaster, repairing an engine or finding a road over the mountains – which were crystal clear. He once helped me with a project to describe on one sheet of foolscap, for the benefit of someone with no acquaintance with bicycles, how to repair a puncture. His assistance in this was brilliant and made a strong impression on me: the use of English to convey information or an argument.

Mum became a 'continuity announcer' (we would say DJ now) for the Forces' Broadcasting Service in Nicosia.

By all accounts she was an instant star. Theresa had become Terry, and Terry Parris was voted by the troops 'Miss Pussy-Voice 1957' (I think the term was more artless in 1957) and, known by her voice alone (she was usually too pregnant for photo-portraits) she became a forces' sweetheart. She did all the request programmes, wincing at having to play hits she disliked, such as 'Don't Give Daddy Any More Whisky' and 'Don't Roll Those Bloodshot Eyes at Me'. Roger and I laughed at her and teased her with snatches from her least favourite numbers.

It was never suggested in our hearing, but occurred to me later, that she incurred a real risk with this job. A British forces' wireless announcer and newsreader would have been a shrewd target for an EOKA assassin. Mum did say she had an armed army driver to accompany her to and from the studios, but he usually seemed to be about seventeen and more nervous than she. Odd that, though the facts about the 'emergencies' were known to all including Roger and me – we received plenty of 'security' lectures – no feeling of crisis or insecurity ever communicated itself to us.

Cyprus, our Cyprus, was good to us. The people, the island, the very air had a sort of generosity, an enchantment, which defied the comparative poverty of the place. One day we visited the village of a Turkish Cypriot friend of my mother, Mr Pantelis. First, a long, dusty road, with a poor little hamlet at the end of it. And then a great effusion of delight, hospitality – and food. It was almost embarrassing. We were plied with food and drink, offered the best fruit afterwards, and treated in every way as honoured guests. In all this bustle none of us heard someone opening our Morris Oxford's boot.

Having managed to persuade our Turkish hosts we really could eat no more and must return to Nicosia, we set out. But it was not until we reached the smooth tar road that Dad heard a thumping from behind the back seat. We stopped and opened the boot. Mr Pantelis's family had filled it with more food, and added a goat.

All this was in the middle of what the newspapers reported as a grisly terrorist war – and certainly people, among them British people, were shot in the street, including Ledra Street down which my father had to walk to work most days; but this somehow did not seem to affect the spirit of the island or the friendliness of the people – Greek and Turkish Cypriots – to us.

I was always busy and absorbed, usually in a solitary but seldom an unhappy way, with one great project or other: a tree house in some olive trees over the road; an attempt to fish without bait – Roger and I thought bent pins on strings might be enough; a series of prototype sailing boats made out of half-logs and shoebox lids whose failure taught me the elements of hydrodynamics; and a labyrinth of tunnels in a giant heap of builder's sand on the waste ground over the road, inspired by a pyrites mine I had visited in the mountains, where a little ore-train I yearned to ride emerged from a hole in the hillside.

At that time my parents believed I was bound to become a scientist or engineer. I was forever conducting experiments, with a special bias towards dams and channels, tracks, roads and tunnels, or anything involving fire. I melted and moulded lead, invented slow-burning stoves involving paraffin and sand, and cooked inedible biscuits made of flour and water over fires of bamboo, above them elaborate constructions on which to hang old saucepans. Our garden was littered with the remains of small conflagrations of bamboo, and Mum's pots and pans covered in paraffin soot. For the future, Dad put me down for Dulwich College, a boarding school in London with a good reputation for modern education (his company would have paid), but I never went.

While I was carrying out some remedial civil engineering in my sand-heap tunnel system, news reached me of my baby brother John's near-death. I had left outside and within a toddler's reach a drinking glass half-filled with paraffin, for one of my many experiments with fire and sand. John had drunk it – all. Mum had caught him too late but in time to realize what had happened. Poisoned, John collapsed.

Crying, Roger came to fetch me. I knew it was my paraffin John had drunk and felt a strange, disgraceful curiosity about what might be the effects on an infant of paraffin ingestion. And I felt resentful at my parents' anger with me because I had not meant him to drink it. John lay silent in my distraught mother's arms, his eyelids half down as though drunk. A doctor arrived, John's stomach was pumped, and he recovered completely. Petroleum attacks the lining of the respiratory system and the patient often dies of pneumonia.

Most of my hobbies and games were happier: wonderful afternoons on the beaches beyond Kyrenia. They, and the days that brought them, seemed never to end. We always appeared to be dancing along the tops of dry ridges in the Kyrenia foothills, singing 'walking-along-the-dragon's-back!' or bowling down a hot tar road in the Morris

Oxford, Roger and me shrieking 'Good job Daddy's a good driver!'

With these trips went other treats. There were visits to a farm near Kyrenia where an English lady and her husband, who was a dwarf, kept a tea-room, with scones, jam and real cream. I think my parents were quite friendly with them. One day the lady died. After that, her little husband's eyes were red with crying whenever we went there, and I think the tea-room closed.

We drove to a famous mosque where we were told Mohammed's Aunt's Rock could be visited. This was apparently a levitating rock, hovering a foot or so above the plinth beneath. The imam told us only holy men were allowed to witness it. We could look at the curtain behind which the rock hovered if we wished but not see the rock. My parents were respectful and said nothing as we drove home. Dad knew Mum thought you should not undermine other people's beliefs.

For my part I thought the whole thing ridiculous. The rock, I thought, if there were a rock at all, was most certainly *not* hovering because if it did then millions of people would come to look, not just us and Nana (who was visiting); and any imams would have been proud to display it; second (I thought) it was a trick to say 'only holy people' could look, because holy people would be part of the trick: they had an interest in this miracle being believed. Poorer and more ignorant people would admire them more, and give them more money, and be more likely to think they must indeed be holy. Professional conspiracies are the same everywhere and I had just spotted my first.

The big event of the year was Christmas – not only because it was then the postal-orders came, five shillings for each child from Nana and Grandad, and £1 from Grandma and Grandpa – but because that was when the Governor held his party. 'The Governor's Party'. The title thrills me still. Every Christmas our diminuitive Governor, General Sir John Harding, invited all British children on Cyprus to Government House.

Not everyone could come but hundreds did. We would crowd into a huge reception room and around the window, watching for the famous helicopter. When it landed – Father Christmas emerged! We knew it was the Governor because Father Christmas was little more than five feet tall.

One Christmas I arrived with my head bandaged (one of my innumerable cycling or climbing accidents) and Sir John came over to me, bent down worriedly and said *to me*: 'Been in the wars, my boy?' I explained about the accident and he looked relieved. He thought I had been attacked by terrorists.

Sir John was a popular figure among British colonials in Cyprus: you were always hearing him praised. He was a proper military man, his brief being to corner and eliminate EOKA, and he and our troops were believed to be doing an effective job – winning even. But it was a wonder the couple were never assassinated for you could always spot them in a crowd: two tiny, middle-aged people, one in a well-cut suit and the other dressed like a real lady in something slightly too hot.

I remember one such day. It was a blazing summer in about 1955. We were outside on some sort of park ground, the warm air screeching with cicadas. Everyone was English and everyone was wearing too much. These colonial occasions managed triumphantly to overlook the fact that most people in Cyprus were Greek or Turkish Cypriots, who were nowhere to be seen.

Lady Harding was in a huge hat. Sir John wore a trilby. The gubernatorial couple were flanked by two gigantic, big-boned young security men, both at least a foot taller than their charges, in plain-clothes and trilby hats – but with strangely bulging pockets – hugging the Hardings' sides as though ankle-shackled to their legs. They made a bizarre little posse.

London, though, was losing interest in holding on. General Sir John was later replaced by a civilian governor, Sir Hugh Foot (brother of Michael Foot and later Lord Caradon), whose brief (it was indignantly rumoured) was to give in gracefully to the terrorists.

I think it was. Sir Hugh began at once by cancelling the Governor's children's party at Christmas. I sometimes wonder whether my life-long instinctive support for colonial powers fighting terrorist wars was not forged in anger at that dastardly anti-children action by Sir Hugh and my consequent preference for the pro-children warrior, Sir John, who had talked to me.

For me as a child there were two tremendous horrors. I did not believe in ghosts, but I was terrified by skeletons. And I was haunted by the idea of being cut by a circular saw. Living skeletons – the very idea would send me under the blanket. Saws made me cry.

This next chapter of my life was stalked both by skeletons and by the circular saw. The cause was my fall over the cliff, holding on to that birthday bicycle.

The operation that followed had been bungled. The Nicosia hospital had informed my parents that, after the fracture caused by falling from the cliff, my elbow joint would never bend again. So my parents had decided to send me to Great Ormond Street Hospital for Sick Children in London, to see whether the joint, now knitting up, could be rebroken and made to work.

On our flight to London was a man who became very drunk. As a small boy I had no idea who he was, but my dad did. He had a posh accent. He had been unpleasant from the minute he boarded the plane. This came as no surprise to us because he had been in our airline limousine to the airport, already the worse for alcohol and furious at the diversion to collect us as he had wanted to travel alone to the airport and resented sharing his car with a father and an injured boy. On the plane he drank more. To the other passengers and the aircrew he was vile and foul-mouthed. Dad told me this oaf was Randolph Churchill, Sir Winston's son, but the name meant nothing to me.

Falling off a cliff, smashing up my elbow, spending months in a plaster cast down to my waist – and enduring constant pain, syringes, ether, men in masks, everything, without much complaint – I developed an almost hysterical terror of the circular saw at the hospital which was to remove the plaster. Nothing could allay it. Memories of a stretch of childhood which ought to be dominated by the fall, the blood, the flight to England, the care of grandparents and the novelty of being a boy with plaster from his waist to his neck, pale by comparison with the one overriding anxiety, its approach counted off fearfully, day by day, on Grandma's calendar: that Great Ormond Street circular saw.

I already knew about saws before they re-operated at Great Ormond Street. The plaster in which my arm had arrived from Nicosia had had to be removed. I felt a blind terror at the circular saw. I remember yelling almost madly. I can still hear the noise of the saw – just a screaming sort of hum until it bit the plaster. The impending moment seemed like the fall of the executioner's axe. After the operation they put me in a new cast, and this one encased my whole torso as well as my right arm, which was cantilevered out on a strut. Grandma knitted me special jerseys and comforted me when I got biscuit crumbs down inside my plaster. We tried to fish them out with a coathanger.

Great Ormond Street was a nice hospital: it must have been if the memory of the nurses and the games and Grandma's and her daughter Joyce's visits and presents, and the toys, is – as it is – positive apart from the saw. The circumstances were not. My parents were gone and I missed them terribly. I was in a grim building whose balcony was caged in with cross-hatched wire so sooty that when I pressed my face against it to see out over the chimneys of London I returned to the ward with a cross-hatched face, and all the nurses laughed.

But there was television: a new experience for we did not have that in Cyprus. Grandma looked after me at Gower Lodge when I came out of Great Ormond Street in my massive plaster cast and with her I loved to watch a children's programme called *Rag, Tag and Bobtail* (*Bill and Ben* I thought a bit silly, though I liked Weed). And I got to know Aunty Joyce, my father's older sister, married to a struggling, stammering 'modern' artist, Uncle Don. Joyce played Snap with me, the only card game I have ever enjoyed, helped me fly balsa-wood gliders (in which I became an expert) and assisted in the tree-nursery I started near the rhododendrons. Tree seedlings and trees (not flowers at all) began to entrance me and to this day I tend and cultivate them. Grandma and Joyce were my early tutors, and every night Grandpa would sit on the end of my bed and answer my childish questions about science, the world, and the reasons for things, just as he had done for my father and Joyce and as my father did for me. I cannot express how much these five-minute talks meant to me.

Poor Joyce. She was utterly in love with Don, and remained so all her life. About forty years later, I wrote this in *The Times*:

Since the death of my artist uncle, Donald Young, in 1990, my Aunt Joyce has dedicated herself to cataloguing the 600 paintings and drawings her husband left behind. Rooms are stacked with them. Each must be photographed, listed and numbered, alongside the often quirky titles Don found for them.

Joyce is past seventy now, and though she has been unwell, she throws herself at the task with the commitment she showed Don through all their long married life. For decades she supported him by teaching while he paced his studio at home with the obsessive dedication he showed each work. In her cataloguing, Joyce has now reached 490 of 500 paintings.

Don was, in my view, an artist of genius, and from his earliest days at the Chelsea School of Art his work has been a *succès d'estime* with those who have seen it.

The trouble is, too few have. Don would never have anything to do with publicity. Most infrequently he could be cajoled into an exhibition, which he would attend awkwardly, hating any discussion. Don was a shy man, with a stammer, who disliked the prancing around of the world of the fine arts, and preferred to stay at home, smoking his dreadful pipe, listening to his old jazz records and playing chess with Joyce and their small circle of friends. They were not rich and they had no pretensions.

For an unusual but unshowy painter of the exhibitionist school, whose work lay outside the postwar mainstream, Don's refusal to posture was fatal. Joyce was trying to promote an artist who simply wouldn't play the fine art game. Living in Beckenham, unable to drive, and no habituée herself of London's artistic salons, she has worked hard: but it must have been discouraging.

Four years after I wrote that, Joyce too was dead. It was June 1999. I had sat with her on her last afternoon, in a small hospital ward in south-east London, the early summer trees swaying in the breeze outside as they had when she had looked after me that summer in England, when I was a child. She was drifting in and out of consciousness, and reason.

Sometimes she confused me with her late husband, Don; sometimes she called to him. Once she called out, 'Not long now, Donald, not long now.' Then reason would return and she would talk, as had always been her habit, in an entirely practical way. She knew she was dying. As she was giving me instructions I had the excuse to take notes. This is what she said:

'It's the one thing you can do for me. Exhibit Don's work. I want posh people to go. I want you to ask someone famous, someone *known*, to write the introduction. It's what my life has been for. I want people to see I wasn't barmy – to go out to work and support a strange young man with a stammer; and staying at home and filling my house with paintings nobody bought.

'But I believed in him. I knew he was a great artist. I know he *is* a great artist. It's a strange story, like Van Gogh. Now they may not *like* it, but I want them at least to come and see his work, then I'll know I've done what I was on earth to do. To support Don.

'Without me, none of these paintings would be here. All those fifty years, that has been what I was here to do. I want his work to be known. It wasn't barmy.'

These were among Joyce's last words. After telling me this, she asked for water. Then she said, 'Pick me up.'

'What do you mean, Joyce?' I said.

'Lift me, hold me, like Don.' So, half-embarrassed, I leant over the bed and picked her up as you would a sleeping child, left arm under the knees, right arm under the shoulder. She weighed almost nothing – she who had always been a bit chubby. I sat on the bed holding her like this, and she went to sleep. She was breathing peacefully when I left. Two old friends arrived to sit with her. She died that night.

Six hundred of Don's paintings are now stored safe and dry and away from the light in my brother Roger's cellar. I am troubled by my promise to Joyce. Some of Don's work strikes me as profound: witty and well-crafted. I simply do not know if he is a great artist; nor do I know what we can do to bring his work to public notice. I cannot forget Joyce's friendship in my childhood.

Only once did I see my mother and father really fight. They bickered a bit from time to time, of course, and Dad was often irritable and sometimes surly and wordless, but nothing worse. But one night I saw Mum standing in her nightdress, shouting at Dad. She shouted the word 'damn' – the most awful oath we ever heard her utter. I have no idea what the argument was about and somehow suspect it was not in itself important. Dad seemed to have taken cover, and was sitting, cowed. 'But Terry . . .' was all I heard him say. He hardly ever used Mum's name.

I crept back into my bedroom, crawled under the sheets and sobbed, quietly and for a long time. Who was there to comfort me if she was what had frightened me?

That time in Nicosia must have been a period of strong and

confused feelings of many sorts, for a recurrent difficulty I had as a child with getting to sleep became acute. I just couldn't get to sleep at night. Insomnia caused anger – I would storm about the house in the small hours, slamming doors and kicking things – and this prolonged the insomnia. The problem must have been intense and persistent because my parents – who no more than me are great believers in drugs – took me to a doctor who prescribed sleeping pills which for a while I took. My parents were not enthusiastic about this and I soon stopped taking them, have never taken sleeping pills since, and never will.

I was not unplayful or friendless, but restricted in my friends. I had the friends who would have me. I was from the start an inept gang-player and unconfident of myself with other boys and girls as individuals and friends – but not as audiences. The awful habit grew of turning social occasions into performances. The phrase 'give-and-take' – 'must learn more give-and-take with classmates' – began creeping into school reports. Why this should have been is a mystery. It has marked my life and cramped companionship.

And then we left Cyprus. It was winter 1958. Dad had been promoted and we were to live in Southern Rhodesia.

Let me try to paint a picture of the family preparing to set sail for Africa. We were excited because we were going to a new place, happy because we would go together – moving around had already made us all each other's best friends in the world – and confident in the leader of our expedition, Dad, surely the best salesman of electric cables in the world, who we knew would do well. If my mother had a moment's quiet regret that her own career in broadcasting seemed always to be cut off just when it was taking shape, that was never expressed and never for a second occurred to any of her children.

Who numbered four. John was still a baby. Deborah was a square-rigged toddler with an easily pink face and a sort of undeclared determination which exasperated her oldest brother. Roger consented to be led and vented his own insubordination in a sideways manner. And Matthew, who was eight, was finally able to pronounce his own name, which had been Mashew for the early years.

He was quite solitary except when he was trying to be in charge, and impatiently strong-willed. In criticism it can be said he showed off and was too fond of the sound of his own voice. Worse than that, he had completely failed to absorb his father's constant and wise advice: that it is always possible to withhold comment. How often he failed to remember that, and how I wish he could have learned it. Further, he was often heedless of the sensitivities of others, facetious, too much in a world of his own, lacking in team spirit, over-confident of his own judgement, unwilling to take correction, and quick to boss his younger brothers and sister around in what he thought were their own interests. He was at best a pace-setter, not a leader.

It was at about this time I began framing the idea that I should perhaps become Governor of an important British colony, and give Christmas parties for the English children, and invite some of the native children too, if they were good, and emulate my hero, General Sir John Harding.

2. Rhodesia

Take no notice of what my parents say: the Holland–Africa Line was dreadful. The British lines such as Union Castle on which they had sailed to and from South Africa had been slovenly, with surly, unionized staff. On our return by Union Castle from South Africa the crew had pilfered on an epic scale. By contrast my parents loved that voyage out in the Dutch *Jagersfontein* because the ship was fast and clean, the food good and the service honest and conscientious. And also because there was a nursery for children: compulsory for under-tens during daylight hours.

I deeply resented the well-scrubbed Dutch concentration camps into which all four of us were dragged after breakfast. There was no deck (too dangerous for kiddies) and only a small porthole to see out of. Worse, there was no pleading with parents for release because banishment to the nursery was, Dad said, 'ship's rules'.

It was maddening. I wanted to explore the ship, every part, and stand on the bow to search the horizon for land, and it seemed to me evident no general rule should forbid this so long as the child was trustworthy, which I was.

But to the nursery we went after every breakfast. A voyage which seemed like months (it was about a fortnight) was spent trapped with mewling toddlers and ridiculous soft toys, supervised by large Dutch ladies. I have never forgiven the Dutch people for this outrage; the very word Netherlands still lowers my spirits.

There was some relief. All were allowed out for celebrations around the pool when we crossed the equator, and a fancy-dress competition was held. My mother, whose literary imagination tended to run a little ahead of the populist herd, decided on the theme of Dickens's *A Christmas Carol*. I was Christmas Past; Deborah (I think, but trussed up in string and crêpe paper it was hard to be sure) was Christmas Present; and poor Roger was Christmas Yet To Come. I don't know what we did with John. It was not even Christmas.

I say 'poor' Roger because Mum got it into her head that the best figurative representation of the future-unknown was nakedness. Roger was forced to appear nude before the entire complement of passengers, our captain, and many of the officers. It is a great mistake to think a six-year-old has no sense of personal modesty. Shame in the young can be intense. Now fifty-one Roger still blushes at the mention of the episode. I did not object to my own costume, though it included a nappy – probably the ship's bath-towel, Mum never having been an ace dressmaker; even my safety-pin caused her (and me) difficulties. But then she always was inclined to treat a jolly party as though it were avant-garde theatre or an artistic sketch.

The other relief was of my own devising. It struck me that if we shed messages in bottles in sufficient profusion all the way from southern Portugal to Cape Town, one or two would surely find their way back to me. The lucky recipients of these messages all along the African coast would, assuming the natives had stamps, be needing an address for me so I wrote the name and address of the hotel where Dad thought we would be staying when we arrived in Southern Rhodesia. I think about twenty bottles were dispatched in this way.

I don't know whether anyone involved in the management of the Highlands Park Hotel (outside what was then Salisbury, now Harare) is still around; if so they may remember my repeated inquiries – long after we had left the hotel – for news of communications from beachcombers in Morocco, the Spanish Sahara, French and British West Africa, the Belgian Congo, the French Congo, Gabon, Portuguese West Africa, South West Africa and South Africa – or possibly any of the associated islands – anxious to inform me of the receipt of a bottle.

It was a slow but sad let-down. Each bottle had been lovingly sealed and, en route to the dreaded nursery, thrown into the Atlantic personally by me, always on the port side of the *Jagersfontein* as that was the way the bottle was to go.

From all that long voyage, only two images from deck stay in the memory: both of mountains.

The first were the mountains of Madeira, where we anchored. I had only to look at the hazy purple-green massif soaring behind the port to remember the Kyrenia mountains seen through the eyes of an even smaller boy from our veranda in Nicosia, and the mountains of

Anatolia seen from the ridge of St Hilarion's Castle, and to long to leave the *Jagersfontein* and begin the exploration of Madeira.

What is it about land seen from the sea? Madeira from the Atlantic; the Horn of Africa from the Red Sea; the great dry ramparts of the Gulf of Aqaba; Djibouti from the sea; the flat, hazy coast of East Africa from Zanzibar; the mudbanks, marshes and islands of the Thames estuary as one arrives up the Channel from the Atlantic; Shetland, Rhum, Harris, across the water; Scotland from Ulster; Blue Mountain in Jamaica, floating across the Caribbean; the mountain peaks of Cuba, 200 miles across the sea from the summit of Blue Mountain; the ice-cliffs of Antarctica from the Southern Ocean; Cape Horn from Drake's Passage; the volcanic peaks of La Réunion from the Indian Ocean; and now, as I write, the massive black cliffs, tipping waterfalls and snowy peaks of Mount Ross in Kerguelen, seen across the Gulf of Morbihan in the white spray of the Roaring Forties in the Southern Ocean . . . how can these fail to excite? They excited me. They were to excite me all my life.

I was allowed out for the last day of our voyage, when Dad said we should try to spot Table Mountain. I was determined to be the first person on the *Jagersfontein* to see Africa. I wasn't quite, but was in there with the leaders. Ever since, Table Mountain – the barest outline – has appeared to me as a sort of cipher for adventure.

Arriving by ship meant a four-day journey of some 1,500 miles with all our belongings, from Cape Town, through Kimberley and Johannesburg to Mafeking, then across what was then Bechuanaland – along the edge of the Kalahari desert to Francistown – and into Southern Rhodesia: Bulawayo, then Salisbury.

It came alive for me as we left the relatively domestic landscapes of the Cape and headed past Joburg into the desert beyond Mafeking. Bechuanaland always had a good feeling about it and Botswana still does. Here the locomotive was steam and I lay in my bunk at night, window open, listening to the distant chuff of the engine (there were eighteen carriages) and watching the thorn trees and stars rocking by outside and the occasional fire and kraal of huts sway and rattle past. A missionary travelling out from Europe to Bechuanaland died of a heart-attack on that train: news passed among the passengers.

Then memory goes blank again: just misty snapshots of a golfing hotel, the Highlands Park, with little outdoor lamps at knee-level among the shrubbery, low hills – and twice-daily inquiries at the reception desk about my message-bottles.

After a few months renting a small house surrounded by exciting elephant grass higher than my head we moved into our new home in Denham Close – the last drive, at the end on the left – in the posh Salisbury suburb of Highlands, bought by Dad for £8,000. There was soon a sign at the end of the drive, 'L. F. Parris' (Dad refused to have a fancy house-name). We had a triangular acre of rough lawn, a paw-paw tree, two avocado-pear trees, a small gum tree and a fruitful mulberry. Along the edge of the plot was a high hibiscus hedge, behind which were the *kayas*: little cabins where our nanny, houseboy and gardenboy lived. Dad soon fitted them up with electric lights, which were not at that time thought necessary for Africans, candles being included in the weekly rations of tea, jam, *sadza* (mealie-meal or rough corn flour made into porridge), sugar and 'boys'-meat' (all bones and gristle).

Their wages, which were average for the time, were £5 per week for the houseboy, something similar for Lorna, the grumpy nanny, and £3 10s for the gardenboy, Linguan, from the neighbouring country of Mozambique which we called Portuguese East Africa.

Dad put the wages up to £6 10s and £4. Mum said this was more reasonable. Ever the little prosecuting counsel I said they might think they were being fair but in fact they were letting white society do their dirty work for them by setting low average wages, which they could then better and look generous by comparison. I was a severe child, and from the start thought a certain kind of liberal wants the best of both worlds.

My parents, however, were finding that Southern Rhodesia did seem, as they had been told to expect, far less unpleasantly racist than South Africa. There was no theoretical apartheid or white brutality on the South African scale, and many whites (and later blacks) in Southern Rhodesia were working for a gradual betterment of the lives of Africans and integration of the races. My mother, though, and many of her friends, were impatient with the pace.

Within weeks of settling in Denham Close Mum decided we should try not to say 'boys' but 'servants' though these servants rather unhelpfully kept calling themselves boys and the habit of addressing Dad as 'master' and Mum as 'madam' proved ineradicable.

'TRUTH CONQUERS' said the grey-and-yellow crest sewn on to my grey school cap at Borrowdale School. Government primary schools for European children in Southern Rhodesia took you all the way from 'kindergarten' (KG 1 and KG 2) through Standards I to V when, at about twelve, you went on to secondary school. All the classes were streamed according to performance, 'a' and 'b'. I entered Standard IIa. Our teacher was Mrs McLeod.

Mrs McLeod was a good teacher for me and for my intellectual self-confidence. By the same token she will have discouraged those to whom scholarship did not come easily. Some of the best teachers, I suspect, as remembered by the kind of people who write newspaper columns, may be remembered in the nightmares of the kind of people who do not.

Mrs McLeod was a Scot of the Jean Brodie variety whose educational philosophy was that school was where a teacher put things in rather than drew things out, and the standards by which she judged quality in a scholar – good spelling, good manners, good grammar, good elocution and a preparedness to raise your head, open your mouth properly and *project* (I can hear her saying it now) when you spoke – were narrow, but she liked and encouraged me and approved of my educated English accent and facility at spelling. In return I tried my best to please her, and when the weekly tests were totted up at the end of term I was almost always Top Boy in her class.

My only fault in her eyes was my handwriting.

The fears and regrets of a child – skin on custard, bones in fish, circular saws, skeletons, being scolded about untidy writing – are discounted by the adult he or she becomes, pushed to the side as though they never mattered. But my bad handwriting caused me as much misery in my schooldays as anything in my life ever has. Maybe it came from having been taught too many styles in too many schools; but whatever the reason, I just couldn't get it right. As yet another teacher would turn on me and moan 'Your *writing*, Matthew' I would inwardly scream. Now I type and it is forgotten. How it mattered then.

In many ways Borrowdale was a better school than one had any right to expect of a state primary school in a country where learning was not venerated. Our headmaster, Mr Walters, set a high tone, though more by pose than by anything he did. Ruddy-faced and short with thick hairs like unicorn horns down the crest of his nose, he adopted the air and dress of an English countryman, ambling round the school's enormous grounds in twill and tweeds and pausing often to repose on what he called a shooting stick: a sort of portable, folding leather seatlet on the blunt end of a spiked metal pole. He had married, rather late in life, a much younger and beautiful former actress. They made an unlikely couple.

I remember too a small bird of a man with a heavy continental European accent. Crumpled of dress, figure and face, he had found work with the ministry of education as a sort of roaming introduction to the delights of classical music. He went from school to school – his visits to Borrowdale were annual – carrying his violin and a portable record-player. He entertained us in our tin-roofed hall. We would sit on the floor cross-legged after assembly as the little chap strutted up and down the stage, going through his practised routine.

You think I mock? He was brilliant. Bubbling with enthusiasm for music and particularly the violin, he was funny, diverting and truly instructive. He demonstrated the pizzicato and slide, and made animal noises with his bow and strings. He would play familiar tunes, first well and then – on purpose – badly, making us howl and hiss. On his gramophone he would play snatches of classical music, explaining what they were and how the music was produced. He kept the attention of young and old throughout. Everyone looked forward to his visits when they were announced, in the manner of a florid music-hall maestro, by Mr Walters, reclining rakishly on his shooting stick which he also used indoors, pock-marking the lino floors.

Looking back on this travelling musician what might you have seen? Someone who had once been a young music scholar in Europe but had never quite made it into a proper orchestra; had travelled out to southern Africa in hopes of pursuing a professional career; and had finally been reduced to tramping round from primary school to primary school in a philistine country, with his little suitcase of stage props and his violin, doing his nut in the African heat to entertain crowds of kids in overgrown Nissan huts of school halls with corrugated iron roofs. Graham Greene could have turned him into a tragic figure.

He was a noble figure. Maybe he himself believed that to have attained the level of second violin in a provincial orchestra would have been preferable. In his own bleaker moments he might have judged himself a failure, even ludicrous. I suppose he told himself this was better than nothing. But I think it was better than almost anything. He had something important to do and he had learned to do it really well. Think of all those children's hearts in which he must have stirred some dawning interest in classical music. He did in mine.

Nobody talked much about 'politics' at Borrowdale, the routinely abusive way in which white children spoke of Africans hardly counting as politics: it was life. So the subject which one day would become my metier was never in the syllabus and hardly spoken of in the classroom, teachers skirting round it, out of a fastidiously old-fashioned professionalism. Politics had not yet become interesting in Southern Rhodesia. My own family's liberal ideas about what we would have called multi-racialism were way out of line, but, equally, the hardline reactionary white supremacism of Ian Smith was not yet upon us; 1950s white supremacism was not angry but gently assumed, no ism at all.

What you might call the polite, educated, British view had been expressed by a previous governor, Sir Godfrey Huggins, who had spoken of a 'partnership' of white and black in the territory: 'the partnership of the rider and the horse'. This, in the context of its era, was not as insulting as today it sounds. It illustrated the belief that African society was not to be derided but a long way behind in its capacity to govern, run things, work things, or take charge of affairs; and so for the foreseeable future the white man would remain in charge and keep the privileges which went with authority.

Some Europeans, especially urban people, believed this would not be for ever. Education, improvements in living conditions and the spread of Western values would by a gradual inevitability 'lift' the Africans closer to 'our level' and lead eventually, perhaps, to the assimilation together of all the races in Central Africa in an equal 'multi-racial future'.

The real white settlers – second and third generation – tended to be of the sceptical view. Disproportionately they lived on the land, out in the bush, farming and mining. Brilliant pen-portraits of this breed are provided in Peter Godwin's memoir *Mukiwa – A White Boy in Africa*. Godwin knew the countryside, and the rural Africans too, in a way I never did. At worst the white people he describes were brutal, at best patronizing towards the blacks, but they did live with them, among them, work with them, and after a fashion know them. They had sunk their future in this land.

Urban whites were different. There were really two classes in Salisbury. My family belonged to the professional class, sometimes expatriates, often families who meant to stay, but linked by an umbilical cord which had never been cut, to Europe; specifically Britain. This class included many quite liberal people, and a few seriously left-wing progressives.

Then there were the post-Second-World-War white immigrants. These were many but did not live much in Highlands, Greendale, Avondale, Borrowdale, Mount Pleasant or Chisipite, the leafy suburbs where we were. They lived in new bungalows on smaller plots in Hatfield and Cranborn and tended to be of working-class or lower middle-class background, and it was among them – the poorer whites – that the most virulent racism was often encountered. A disproportionate number of these people seemed to be Scots. African servants did not like to work in the poorer white suburbs where they were paid less and were more likely to be abused, and called 'kaffirs'.

Unlike the bush-Europeans, these people were almost completely ignorant of the Africans they despised. They were really the core-constituency upon whose support the racist Rhodesian Front – the party Ian Smith finally led – grew to a governing party.

My mother's strong instinct to believe in people, particularly African people, seemed to me uncritical and always irritated me. I chafed against it and persuaded myself she was optimistic in her hopes of the imminent emancipation of the black population in Southern Rhodesia: I had absorbed, I suppose – and have not entirely renounced – something of the settlers' conventional wisdoms about the deep-rooted 'otherness' of African culture, and its distance from our own. But I was without hesitation on our family's side in our key belief: that it was always wrong to insult or exclude anybody on account of their colour.

How much of this state of affairs was apparent to a boy not yet ten? The answer is almost all of it. Even at fifty-two I have not really developed my key ideas much beyond it. I know this because I recall a long and animated discussion with myself while walking one weekend morning back from Borrowdale School, where I had some 'goons' (ball-bearings used as marbles) to collect from under a root.

It was about a mile home. With Roger I must have cycled or walked that mile thousands of times. We knew every blade of elephant grass. On the outward journey you cycled the length of Denham Close, passing the Scammels' house (Mrs Scammel was a charming Danish ex-model, Mr Scammel eventually became involved in Ian Smith's police and surveillance operations), past the house on the left where the old lady, who disapproved of my parents' allowing their children to play with black children, later informed against us . . .

Then you turned right into Burnham Road, a shady, tree-lined small hill, up which you had to labour, and carried on past the end of Orange Grove Drive where people of real position such as the Holdernesses lived; and past Andrew Waddington's house. Fair, curly-haired Andrew, always smiling, reminded us of a junior Liberace, was no good at sport and was much teased.

Burnham Road turned sharply right into Northend Road, and on the right you passed first the house of a man who was said vaguely to have something to do with 'security', and afterwards the Madisons' house. I could get through the verbena hedge in the corner of our garden into their plot. The Madisons were Irish Catholics, relaxed, warm, untidy and different from other European families; for a while I worshipped their elder son, Patrick, who tolerated me kindly and kept a white rat.

Then there was a long, straight, flat half-mile bowl along Northend Road, passing the Borrowdale racecourse on your left (we never went; Mum disapproved of betting) and a big patch of open veld, long yellow-brown elephant grass with a meerkat colony in the middle. On a bike, racing along the smooth, winding paths of bare earth made by Africans, you could cut across this to the big Dombash-awa Road where the shops were and where eight years later Dad was to teach me to drive Mum's 1952 Morris Minor.

If you were going to school you stayed on the Northend Road to the end, meeting another main road on which you turned left, carrying you to Borrowdale School, into which you turned to the left.

And it was walking back from the school among the trees along this path one day that I consulted myself – how old at the time? Nine? – on my own beliefs about the emancipation of Africans in Southern Rhodesia. Odd to mention the *msasa* trees but they are linked in memory with the internal conversation. It was between one who believed in justice and understood the colour bar to be unfair, and one who personally found the Africans he knew strange, unreliable and impossible to gauge: deeply and I thought irremediably other.

News of a pay-rise for Dad – leaked by someone to us, for Dad was always private about money – alerted us to what we had never known: his salary. It was now £2,000 per annum, a good salary in those days. Our Humber Hawk was two-tone (white roof) with a special sun-visor and we had three servants where many had only two.

My sister Belinda, my parents' fifth child, was born when I was twelve. She was named at my suggestion because nobody could think of another name after the rest of the family had vetoed Mum's proposal of 'Rose' (and then, worse, 'Cherry') with such vehemence that uncharacteristically Mum buckled. I named her after Belinda, the little girl in the Pookie Book series who wore a patched dress, lived in the forest and kept Pookie the Flying White Rabbit in a shoe-box. Pookie's adventures at the North Pole when he met the North Wind, a giant made of icicles, had so excited me as a little boy (I kept the book beneath my pillow to frighten myself) that they stayed vivid in my imagination. But for this book, Belinda would not be called Belinda and I would never have set out across the Southern Ocean to live on the island of Kerguelen in the sub-Antarctic.

The new baby girl was the first (I suppose) who seemed to present no imaginable rivalry for my parents' attention, or intrusive nuisance into an established sibling's life; I was now grown-up enough to delight in a tiny sister and loved Belinda from the start, making her my special project and saving up (when she became a majestically grumpy toddler) to buy her a little outfit which was very early sixties: black PVC boots, red tights and a black jacket. We remember her scowling in this gear: somewhere on the cusp between sixties dolly-bird and hell's angel.

Besides Belinda and us my mother had also had two miscarriages and was to have one more, and (much later) another boy, Mark, eighteen years younger than me. That makes six. We could have been nine.

The bigger the family got the more we liked the numbers, taking pride in how many we were. Mum said nothing was ever such a strain as the early years of having two small toddlers, Roger and me, and no help in the house. Now the older children looked after the younger, and there were servants. The idea of ever returning to England faded imperceptibly though it remained (I suppose) our official destiny. The English abroad always talk of 'going home', though many of them never will. We, however, hardly talked of it, and never adopted the British expatriates' habitual litany of invidious comparisons between the place where they are, and the country they say they're longing to return to, and never do. We loved the place where we were and couldn't imagine going back to the rain.

Our holidays in Africa were often adventurous. We travelled to Beira, the nearest seaside in Portuguese East Africa, swam in the Indian Ocean and sipped the confusing mixture of Portugal and Africa, blended and diluted with a hefty measure of poverty. There was no racism in Mozambique, just secret police and fascism mitigated by friendliness, Mateus Rosé, potholes, ignorance, inefficiency and hot piri-piri sauce.

One year we and some friends rented a huge Chevrolet station wagon and drove the thousand-odd miles down to Natal in South Africa, bound for a seaside holiday north of Durban on an immense surf-lashed coast called Umhlanga Rocks. In the Transvaal a wheel came off and rolled past us in the dust, stranding us in Pietersburg for three days: my first in-depth experience of the stifling dullness of Afrikaner provincial life.

Visits to South Africa were epic. Leaving Salisbury you would soon be on the 'strip' road to Fort Victoria. These roads consisted of two parallel strips of tarmac just wide enough for your nearside and driver's-side wheels. The rains tended to erode the ground between and to either side, so the strips became like raised planks; the car would come off with a sickening lurch – and had to, to pass any oncoming vehicle. Each would take one strip, which was easier said than done at 60 mph. A game of chicken would be played between approaching drivers vying to come off the crown of the road at the last possible moment.

Rhodesia was divided into the highveld, the middleveld and the lowveld. Highveld was the most productive land, much of it reserved for white agriculture. Here were great swathes of tall yellow elephant grass, dotted with occasional low thorn and *msasa* trees. At around

5,000 feet altitude there was less malaria and the winters were cold, frosty at night. It was grand country but I found it tame. As you descended gradually into the middleveld the weather got warmer and the earth drier; there was less grassland and more scrub.

But it was the lowveld I loved. This began after Fort Victoria and continued for many hours' strip-road driving to the border at Beitbridge over the Limpopo. Here it was always hot, always flat, and yet there was always a prospect of very low hills somewhere on the horizon. It was too dry for scrub, weed or thick long grass and the ant-peopled earth was often quite bare beneath the endless thorn and baobab trees stretching away, it seemed, for ever. Few blacks and no whites lived here.

The baobabs were monumental – vast, thick, soft, pulpy trunks as wide as an African hut, with stark and stubby branches like a baby's fingers, usually bare and sometimes dangling with peach-sized hard green pods full of seeds surrounded by a delicious sticky white powder not unlike sherbet, and used for making cream of tartar. Often there were great hollows in their trunks and every big baobab had an ancient sense of mystery about it. You knew you were in the lowveld when the baobabs started, and my endless attempts to get them to grow in Salisbury always failed.

There were smells in the hot, dry air down here. Wherever there was water (and there was little) all kinds of vines and flowering plants would grow and every mudbath seemed to contain a family of hippos. Because the trees were not thick but spread savannah-like across the landscape, you could walk for hours – days – across the lowveld, all the way to Portuguese East Africa and the Indian Ocean if you knew where the rivers were. It was, strange to say, a kind of parkland, unseen by human eye, unkept by human hand.

The rivers were tremendous gashes of mudflats and sandbanks marching from nowhere and into infinity, dry at most times of year with just tadpoley green hippo pools to remind you of the violent flash-floods which could sweep down in the rainy season. The road – the only road – crossed them on Dexion-like steel-girder bridges we called Bailey bridges, or long, low causeways cheaply constructed of concrete and culvert and regularly washed away.

This lowveld cast a spell over me from which I will never be free. Something about the emptiness and heat, the dryness, the night perfumes, the thorns and the lavender-purple prospect of distant hills fills me with excitement and magic, even as I write. For me, night will never be night without the sound of frogs, nor day day without the cheep and screech of singing insects.

When you crossed the Limpopo it began to change. The human side of South Africa was always a bit nasty, a bit mean, a bit officious and a bit tense. We didn't think the Africans hated us in Southern Rhodesia but in 'the Union' as (still a British Dominion like Canada) it was then called – and later 'the Republic' – they assuredly must. Also the Afrikaners hated the English and the English looked down on the Afrikaners. There were poor white people here, and the police were brutes. Polite customs officers, European and African, in white colonial uniforms on the Rhodesian side of the bridge were quite unlike the surly, ruddy-faced, toothbrush-moustached characters on the South African side, who looked at you angrily if you spoke in English rather than Afrikaans.

South Africa was alien territory and grew more alien as you left the veld and skirted the wrecked and populous landscapes of the Witwatersrand, industrial, sterile, littered with cyanide-ridden mine dumps, flat-topped and eroding by the highway; wretched African townships sprinkled about, and the scrappy bungalows of the whites in clusters. But there remained a treat in store as you veered east down to Natal past the ordered town of Pietermaritzburg: the Drakensberg mountains. These really were mountains, like few I'd seen before. To the right of the road great dark crags, rock battlements, tremendous peaks loomed high above us, a sort of Gothic kingdom in the sky. There too I wanted to tread.

But soon the road was winding down among sugar-cane fields and the air was hot and sticky. You were in coastal Natal. This was 'tropical' in the English sense, all banana and palm trees and afternoon storms. Fun for a while – body-surfing on waves so big they could crush you into the shingle was a treat.

I liked the seaside – what boy doesn't? – but our best beach holiday by far was in Nyasaland (now Malawi), near a village called Salima on the shores of Lake Nyasa. We took the malaria pills, kept clear of the swampy bits where the debilitating disease called bilharzia lurked in the snails on lily-pads, and played on a white-sand beach lapped by breaking waves and clear, fresh blue water, hundreds of miles from any seashore. By day I would stare at the mountains over on the other side in Portuguese East Africa – a wild region I longed to explore – and by night I would dive under my net to escape the mosquitoes and listen to the slow thump of the ancient long-stroke Lister diesel generator which provided our hotel's electricity: I loved this generator. I used to go and sit beside it, watching it bang through the hot night.

Nyasa was my favourite water, but it was for the lowveld that I hankered. The lowveld! Why couldn't we just stop at the Sabi River and have a holiday there? My parents couldn't see the point.

The nearest we came was game reserves. There was the Kruger in the Northern Transvaal. You got blasé about the game itself – once you've seen thirty giraffe the thirty-first loses any special appeal – but the nights in the lodges were magic to me. From my memories of drinking Fanta on big verandas and watching animals come down to the waterhole at sundown, I've derived many a parliamentary sketch.

Once, in the Wankie game reserve in Rhodesia – Wankie was, unfortunately, its name – Dad had stayed at the lodge for a siesta and Mum was driving the Humber with most of us in the back, polite after-lunch piano music on the car radio, when we rounded a bend on a wide dirt road and drove almost straight into an elephant. Humber steering-wheel gearsticks are not the easiest to deal with when reverse gear must be rapidly selected, and Mum had one of those short driving panics which seem, when a full-grown African bull elephant is lumbering towards you, bellowing and flapping his ears, to last for ever. But she found the gear and we screamed off backwards, zig-zagging up the road. I just remember the advancing elephant, the set of Mum's jaw, and the piano tinkling daintily in the background.

The best holidays of all were in the Eastern Highlands: Inyanga. Occasionally in Africa a hot, dry and dusty region throws up from its midst a highland area of lush greenery and cool blowing cloud. There is always something miraculous about such places. The mountains of Ethiopia, for instance, Kilimanjaro and Mount Kenya, the Zomba plateau in Malawi . . . They are a sort of sky paradise.

My parents encouraged Roger and me to accept an invitation from a friend of our mother to stay for a week with his family in their African village in the bush, far from Salisbury. This was an unusual thing for

Europeans, particularly unaccompanied children, to do. It turned into an important experience.

Not because anything happened. We could come to no harm in that quiet, remote place, and the family, unsure what to do with white boys, gave us mattresses on the hard earth floor and shared their food with us. I knew what Africans' food was like, haring shared it with our servants. Boring but edible.

No, what was memorable related not to our friendly reception or our personal comfort, but the near impossibility for a white boy of accepting that here was life, here were lives, in which so little happened. I have never since then believed anthropologists who say tribal life is just as crowded with incident as a New York street, although incident of a different sort. It is not true. The people in that village simply did less. They were not lazy but, such was the way life was organized, there was less to do. People sat around. The women cooked, squatting by fires which were kept smouldering all the time, and the men talked, or prodded at cattle from time to time, moving them on. The sun rose and fell, rose and fell, babies cried, chickens clucked, dogs yapped.

To a white boy, life was astonishingly communal. Every night, most of the village would drift into one of the round mud huts and sit around the fire. Huts had no chimneys and so the smoke had to escape slowly through the straw thatch of the roof. This meant that the interior of the hut was full of woodsmoke. It almost choked Roger and me and made our eyes water so it was only with an effort of will that we could stay inside. Our friend said this kept the insects out. Thus was explained to me what I had never understood: the strange, acrid smell of many Africans: everything, clothes, body, sweat, hair, was infused with woodsmoke.

On one of these evenings everyone present offered the group a performance. Soon fingers were pointing at us. I sung a hymn. Roger did a wild dance. My reception was polite; Roger's ecstatic.

There was a significant kopje (flat-topped rock hill) a few miles from the kraal and I asked our friend's bright cousin of my own age, who had learned English at school, how long it took to get to the top. He said he knew of nobody who had ever tried; further inquiries confirmed that nobody had climbed it: there was no point as cattle would not go up there to graze. No *point*? I was baffled.

There was an old car parked by one of the huts; it was of some potential value because of its age; it would be a priceless vintage now. The tyres were flat but, on inspection, there seemed nothing much wrong with it. I asked why it was abandoned and learned that this was because it had 'stopped' many years ago. It now belonged to nobody in particular. It was not for any individual to take it into his hands to alter the essentially parked nature of this object. It was not for any individual to take it upon himself to penetrate without reason the essentially virgin nature of kopje. It was not for any individual to get it into his head to do anything different, or think anything different, from what the generality thought and did already.

In relating this one begins to sound like those white settlers with whom my parents were always arguing, who would claim 'your African' has no sense of time or pressing need, and if taught how to double his harvest will simply take every second year off from bothering to cultivate crops. But I am sure it has nothing to do with 'your African' or 'your' any-other-race, but with a culture instilled from birth. There is no new insight in that, of course; but what surprised me was how far this culture was from my own and how deeply it seemed to be imbued.

In particular I noticed how tribalism – really only an anthropologist's term for an extreme form of communitarianism – seemed to have dinned the individualism out of people, so nobody cared or dared to take a lead or differ notably from the others. Some people will tell you tribe (or village, or community) humanizes, brings comfort and security. I thought it was stifling, and brutal in its way.

I began to understand why eyes looked brighter and steps lighter in those areas where a missionary was at work. Because Christianity teaches a direct personal relationship, bypassing hierarchy and tribe, with God, it can represent a release to those oppressed by their tribe and its panoply of brooding and often vengeful spirits. I do not myself believe in God but can still see how Christian monotheism can act to liberate. I think we sometimes sentimentalize tribe. In my experience it was bound up with conformity and with fear, crushing the individual. Tribe flattens.

An early hero, Francis of Assisi, had better luck or a more attentive providence. My first cat got cat flu and died. My second cat, Jilly, was run over and suffered a broken hip which, though fixed by Dr Sugden, our lady vet, turned her grumpy, and my affection thereafter went unreturned. My tortoise escaped: I had not realized they can burrow. My hedgehogs died.

Mum let my canary go because she felt sorry for it. I explained that robin redbreasts thrive in snow, as Christmas cards testify, but this unlucky canary would now freeze to death in the African winter. Mum was only superficially repentant, the thought being what counts with my mother. It was certainly a beautiful thought. I hope the dying canary appreciated that.

My silkworms thrived on the mulberry tree but something went wrong with their cocoons. My tadpoles always perished. My chicken never laid an egg, and finally expired. I never despaired and was forever searching the 'pets offered' column in the *Rhodesia Herald* in hopes of new horizons for animal husbandry. One day I saw a cageful of white mice for sale, with all accessories.

Thus began a long love affair with mice. They were fascinating. From about ten to about twelve I became Central Africa's great child expert on mice. My bedroom smelt abominably. Mum ceased coming in. I didn't just keep these creatures, I studied them, watched them for hours, planned their pregnancies, succoured their little blind, pink sausage-like babies with strings dipped in milk and sugar when the mothers got low, and even looked up journals on breeding to see how, from a black and a white mouse I might achieve piebald mice (little chance), and what might be the chances of my prized honey-coloured mouse having some honey-coloured offspring (better). I experimented with the introduction into the cage of a few caught wild-mice (disastrous) and then the introduction of caught wild-mouse babies into domestic nests – and was distressed to discover the importance of genetic as against learned traits, in mice at least.

There were embarrassments. My mother was broadcasting a series of children's stories on the radio at the time, *The Johnny Stories*, based on the daily life of my little brother John. In an instalment one afternoon I was horrified to hear my mouse-keeping had been broadcast to the nation – without prior consultation with me. Worse, I was said to have named a new mouse-arrival 'Twinkletoes'.

This was pure invention on Mum's part. My mice had proper names such as George and Susan. You may imagine the derision which greeted me on arrival at school the next morning. Mum seemed only mildly repentant. I had learned an early and searing lesson about irresponsible journalism.

One day I came home from Borrowdale School, racing up the drive and past the line of scarlet cannas on my bike (navy-blue, Raleigh, 24-inch wheels, no gears, a prized possession even after I outgrew it) to find my mother in tears at the door. She had no great feeling for mice but she did for me. Jilly, my grumpy cat, had entered my bedroom and overturned the cage. A complete massacre had taken place. Not one mouse had survived. I cried for the rest of the day.

My best friend and co-expeditionary was Peter Marshall. Only later looking back do I realize he came from a more working-class background than mine – his father walked around their bungalow out on the Dombashawa Road in a vest – but even at the time he and I both knew we were different types.

Peter was a quiet, tallish, slim, very blond boy and a good sort. I know why I wanted to be his friend: he was pleasant, good-natured, adventurous and practical, and put up with me when we went camping on the great granite hills at Dombashawa rocks, and designed, built and tested to destruction a variety of extremely fast go-karts using wooden boxes and bicycle wheels. But I never knew why he wanted to be mine.

Some years later (we had parted company when he went to the technical college) he came over unprompted to see me, on a 500cc motorbike. I was riding my mother's Honda 50 scooter at the time. I suggested we went for a spin together, which he must have found painful. Early variants of a rocker and a mod, we both realized we had nothing to say to each other, and both felt a bit sad, I think. I still do. It was nice of him to come to see me.

The closest thing I ever had to a permanent boyfriend thirty years later was also tall and thin and called Peter, and also (and in the end unsurmountably) different from me. But he's still one of my best friends. So, in my mind, and though I shall never see him again, is Peter Marshall.

Almost all the other children at my school talked with a Rhodesian accent (a milder version of South African) and my British accent got me off to a bad start. 'Limies' (or pommies) were presumed until they demonstrated otherwise to be 'weeds', 'drips', 'runts' or 'saps' – the words still sting. Far from demonstrating otherwise I reacted by accentuating all the qualities I was accused of. Being a 'kaffir-lover' didn't help but I must not pretend to have been some kind of human-rights martyr; politics was just one element in the picture built up of me, and which I then helped spin, of being a boy who couldn't fight, disliked sport and thought himself superior to other boys.

When unpopularity upset me, my mother would tell me that it was better to know that one was right than to be liked by others; that courting popularity was cowardly, and that 'moral courage' was more important than being good at fighting. I *think* this was the right advice but it did help me to glorify my own isolation instead of ask how much of it was necessary, and verged on encouraging priggishness in me. It is impossible to know, I suppose, in raising children, how far they could or should fit in with others. I cannot regret how or what I am, but would have liked to have learned earlier the art of just stringing along with other people.

By now I had left Mrs McLeod's class. Sport was becoming a problem: I hated games and did not see why I should be forced to play them. Every afternoon became a misery. So determined was I to have nothing to do with what the other boys thought was cool that it was to be years before I realized I was a good athlete.

And years before I realized I was really not a good actor. But it got me away from the miseries of school. At about nine I was a boy-star hit as a Babe in the Wood in the Salisbury Repertory Company's production of that show. I was not really acting, just playing it straight, and besides what brought the handkerchiefs out was to Dad's credit, for he wrote me a tune where '*sings*' was all the script specified. Dad loved and understood music, especially classical music, and taught me to love it too. His song, sung when I was lost in the forest, was touching. I remember the beautiful, sombre blue and green set, and the blue footlights, and not being able to see the audience but hearing somebody sob. That feeling of power!

This dramatic debut was followed up by an even bigger success as Louis, the sailor-suited son of the governess Anna, in *The King and I*. Though sadly I no longer have a sailor-suit, I can still sing 'I Whistle a Happy Tune' fetchingly, with all the movements, the whistling and a little dance. But one is seldom asked as an adult.

It was touch and go whether my parents would allow me to join the cast of *The King and I*. This was because someone said that, according to the *Rhodesia Herald*, the producer had been acquitted of charges of indecent assault involving another man. Indecent assault in this context meant a homosexual advance, as my parents tried euphemistically to explain. This I had to explain to my friend Glenn, who had thought it meant swearing in public lavatories.

There was an earnest discussion between my parents. Its gist was that the man had, after all, been acquitted. So I was allowed to accept the offer of the role of Louis, and was never importuned. But Mum and Dad had had a talk with me about being careful, avoiding being alone with the man, and letting them know if anything worried me. I remember the shudder. To this day I have a horror of being seen myself in that light.

In Standard IV the bullying and the unhappiness reached some kind of a low point. My handwriting was worse than ever and I had a recurrence of the insomnia which had plagued me in Cyprus, and even earlier, as an infant in Yorkshire. I started to read, so voraciously it alarmed even my father, who would come into my room in the small hours and turn off the light which I had surreptitiously turned on, to finish yet another book.

I read anything and everything, and was tired and thin-tempered during the day, lashing out at brothers and sisters and getting into a bad relationship with my young class-teacher, Miss Huxley, herself of a nervous disposition and a stickler for good handwriting.

A doctor suggested as a sort of therapy a school term at a special boarding school called Vumba Heights. My parents must have been worried because they really don't believe in this sort of thing – yet they agreed.

At Vumba Heights I came under the influence of Mrs Morrison.

Old ladies are the finest flower of their sex. Old men fade. Old ladies blossom. Mrs Morrison was probably hardly seventy but to the young everything beyond fifty is old and her wrinkles and white hair made her so to me. She was Scottish, spirited, ordered, strict, kindly, energetic and certain of her opinions on everything to do with right and wrong. If (as we must assume) there had ever been a Mr Morrison, he was long finished and never mentioned, for she was self-contained and created her own world around her. I think she liked me because she was an educated woman in a fairly rough place, and I spoke without a Rhodesian accent, liked reading, and liked her.

Trying to piece together the memory of Vumba Heights I remain stumped as to what it was and why. The institution was situated in an area of the Eastern Highlands not far from Inyanga called the Vumba: a place of high, gentle hills, ferns, forests and mist – always mist – and the soft, light drizzle, more spray than rain, we used to call 'guti'. It was always cool, always damp and often cold there; and our school was not far from the highest mountain in those parts, Castle Beacon (about 8,000 feet), from whose summit you could see a hundred miles.

I know it was damp because I remember the mildewed smell of the books in the school's tiny library – little more than a bookcase. By the time I left there was not one book unread: *Little Men*, then (reluctantly) *Little Women*, then *Vanity Fair* and dozens more besides, mostly nineteenth- and early-twentieth-century novels but also a two-volume encyclopaedia dated about 1910: I read every page.

The smell of damp book, along with the smell of Wrights Coal Tar Soap and dry pink toothpaste-cake, still takes me straight back to Vumba. It was where my appetite for reading – reading *anything* – really hit its stride.

Later it died. I read more books for pleasure between the ages of ten and fourteen than I have read between fifteen and fifty. Much of my present knowledge of classic English literature, especially the novel, was acquired then. It follows that my adult acquaintance with the great writers of the English language is with a body of work filtered through an early adolescent's understanding. I am a bad case of arrested literary development. But an attentive teenager can get the sniff of things pretty well.

There were drawbacks to this pre-pubescent taking-by-storm of English literature. I read *Animal Farm* at Vumba (George Orwell was about as modern as the library got) without having the least knowledge of modern Soviet history, or indeed knowing anything about George Orwell. So, ignorant of the epoch *Animal Farm* allegorized, it never struck me that this tale was about post-revolutionary Russia. I just thought it a delightful and finally sad story about the animals taking over. But the lessons are no less true for that, and I absorbed them.

Reading, though some of it jumped the gun, consumed me. And happily there was little organized sport. But if my parents had supposed

Vumba was a specialist institution for 'highly strung' boys and girls then they overestimated the likelihood that Southern Rhodesia's small white population would sustain such a place. The school was full of misfits and (a lesson so obvious you might think it has by now been learned, but it hasn't) there is no reason misfits should fit together. We didn't. Yet the place hurt nobody. Vumba was an educational refuge: some of the children had learning difficulties, some had behavioural problems, and some were ill.

Just below the school was a patch of real rainforest. Deep and dark, with high trees and upper canopy and monkey-ropes dangling down (hanging vines so strong you could swing on them), this exciting world was inhabited by troupes of baboons. In the night you could hear them bark. I learned to imitate the noise – still my most accomplished animal impression.

It was not the fauna, however, but the flora which absorbed me. I wanted to learn about trees but nobody at Vumba could help. Total lack of interest in the native environment – even a certain hostility towards it – was a feature of white English urban society in Southern Rhodesia. People spent their retirement in Salisbury proudly cultivating herbaceous borders from seeds sent from England, and would remain as unable to identify a local tree as they were ignorant of even the rudiments of the local African language. Their attitude to native vegetation was to beat it back.

As the Africans were equally uninterested in their native flora and fauna except as a source of food, medicine, danger, or good and evil spirits, their overriding attitude to their environment being wariness, you may say Africa has been sadly uncherished by her inhabitants.

'Camp in the bush?' an African once said to me. 'But animals sleep there, not people.' I was to notice the contrast between Africa, where most native peoples are uninterested in, and tend to fear, the wild, and South America, where the Indian people I encountered loved and respected their environment, thought it beautiful, and well understood (as Africans often cannot) why strangers would travel to see it. 'Para conocerlo' ('to know/acquaint myself with it') is an acceptable answer to a South American Indian who asks why you have come to his lands. To a rural African it was not.

In our library, however, was a textbook about ferns. Within a month I became an expert not only on types but on propagation (very complicated with ferns); and such an enthusiast that on leaving Vumba Heights I embarked upon a huge school project on ferns, and returned to Vumba to collect and press specimens.

As well as fern-hunting in the forest, there was climbing. I climbed Castle Beacon again and again, even persuading my father to climb with me when my parents visited for the weekend and took me to the Leopard Rock Hotel for tea and a swim in a huge round pond. (The excitement of seeing your parents' car coming up the school drive! What visit since can compare?) It became a habit with me to stay as long as allowed on the summit of Castle Beacon, trying to identify distant landmarks. One sundown I managed to spot the granite ramparts of the Chimanimani mountains, and the glinting arc of the Birchenough suspension bridge over the Sabi river right down in the lowveld.

For the first time in my own life I was left to shape my days and, though I was desperately homesick and overjoyed when my term there was over, the whole strange episode must have been important for it has left a handful of stunningly vivid memories: of Louis, the Afrikaner boy I befriended, in the forest lying by a fallen tree and having an epileptic fit; of the baboons in the night and the tiny arc of Birchenough bridge; of the smell of damp books, the obsession of the whole cast of *Little Women* with dressmaking fabrics (and, of *Little Men*, with chopping wood); and Wrights Coal Tar Soap . . .

There was another incident. It was in the night, a cold night, in our dormitory, and baboons were barking in the dark forest beyond. Awake, I heard Bill Compton, the toughest of us, say he wanted to be sick. 'Well go to the toilets then,' called Frank Kremer, who used to pull the skin of one testicle through a hole in his trouser-pocket and pretend it was chewing-gum.

'Would anyone come with me?' asked Bill. The truth, we knew, was that he was scared to go alone. After lights-out everyone was scared of the dark corridor down to the ablution block. The generator was switched off at quarter past ten and there were no lights, although we had torches. Nobody volunteered.

'Please,' said Bill, his voice faltering in an uncharacteristic way.

And, you know, I remember so clearly not just my decision but the act of coming to it. I thought: All right, Matthew, you aren't *really* scared of the dark, just of the dark, are you? I felt sorry for Bill because, though he had no opinion of me, I liked his manliness; but something else occurred to me too. I thought: This is your chance. The others are more scared than you, all these boys who think themselves tough. This is a chance to show them. Take it.

'I don't want to go on my own,' repeated Bill. To myself I thought that as I was hesitant about going the best way to make it happen would be to say the words 'I'll go with you' – and then there would be no backing out.

'I'll go with you,' I said.

There was no backing out. I had not naturally sprung to Bill Compton's aid, but made a calculation and then acted on it. And as soon as I was out of my bed, holding the torch, and walking down the corridor with Bill, it was easy. He was very sick. I waited, not in the least scared now, then we walked back. Before we did, while we were still in the toilets so he could not be heard by the others, he said – these were his exact six words – 'You were brave that time, Matthew.'

This made me proud. I lay in the dark repeating the words silently to myself. In the years that followed they have been repeated a thousand times. Many, many years later I saw on a professor's desk at Yale a translation of (I think) Aristotle from the ancient Greek: '*It is by acting bravely that we become brave.*'

This put into words an idea whose core appeared to me in the ablution block with Bill: if a desired human quality does not seem to be coming naturally then the answer may be to stop fretting about how we might get it and instead ask what things we would do if we already had it; and then do them.

Home in Salisbury there was school to face. Worse (or so at first I thought), Miss Huxley – bane of my life – had come to live with us as a lodger. Mum had invited her. Mum did such things. In between writing and recording a marathon series of children's stories for the Rhodesian Broadcasting Corporation, creating radio plays and teaching at a little school for African servants' children my mother had with others set up, Mum did some supply-teaching at Borrowdale and had become friends with Miss Huxley. She was a sharp, tactless woman: the expression 'highly strung' comes to mind. We two probably had more in common than we thought and stopped fighting.

Later she married a Rhodesian policeman with hairy legs and became lower strung, happier and less interesting.

As for me, however strung, I began at last to settle in at Borrowdale. By the time I left primary school I could read very well, add up better than most and write untidily; and had gained much useless information about the corn triangle in the United States, the industrial infrastructure of the lowlands of Scotland (to the effective elimination of which as a parliamentarian I was one day to add my vote) and the reason why people have silver teapots (I was reproved for writing 'snob-value' on my test paper; the reason, of course, is that shiny surfaces lose less heat). I had collected a shelf of books awarded as prizes for being Top Boy in various classes, and suspected I really was a top boy.

At home Roger and I were firm friends and co-expeditionaries. On the wildest of my ventures it proved impossible to persuade him to come: I decided to cycle to Rusape, which was 100 miles down the road; and, amazingly, did, in eleven hours. This mad cycle ride was a solo journey. But Roger came with me to camp the weekend at Dombashawa.

Dombashawa Rocks was a group of massive solid granite hills, about ten miles north of Salisbury. Roger and I cycled there with tent and cooking equipment strapped to our bikes. We walked over the summit and pitched camp not far from a great overhanging rock in which, centuries before, Bushmen had once lived. The rockface was covered with their pigment paintings of giraffe, buffalo and birdmen.

Next morning as the sun rose, we walked out over the rock. Cresting one great slab we confronted an amazing scene. Absorbed in their game, a small troupe of baboons had not seen us. Silently we flattened ourselves against the granite to watch.

Some of the younger baboons had hit on an idea. They had found wishbone-shaped pieces of dead branch and, dragging these to the top of a rock slope, had discovered they could ride this primitive sled down the slope, sitting on the crux of the wishbone, and sliding. The game was in full swing. There were only two or three sleds and the young baboons were squabbling for a turn on each. As each ride was finished, a new baboon would drag the sled back up the slope, sit on it, and push off. The older baboons sat on the side of the hollow, watching the very young at play.

It is easy to anthropomorphize: to load those animals' behaviour with significance and invest in them feelings only humans have. But I doubt we were mistaken here. These young baboons were simply playing; they were doing it for fun. The adults were amused to watch.

And our own feelings, watching them? I am at a loss to explain this, but I was terrifically moved. It was one of those rare, spine-tingling moments which come to us strangely and suddenly, and depart as unaccountably. I knew I was watching something of immense significance. My sense of that has never departed.

Some quarter of a century later I was with a friend in the Tassili n'Ajjer mountains in the Algerian Sahara. Here too the Bushmen once lived. Their paintings are everywhere among the waterless rocky moonscape of this extraordinary region: paintings of animals which can only have lived in a fertile savannah such as the Sahara must once (and not so long ago) have been.

We stopped by the track to look at a particularly impressive over-hanging rock. It was covered in paintings; the same paintings I remember from Rhodesia. Intriguing, of course; but even more intriguing was a section of rock covered in small clusters of dabs in the same pigment. How were these explained?

My friend, himself a painter, jumped in the air, arms upraised, easily able to touch the upward sloping rock ceiling with his fingertips. We saw that if you had dipped your fingers in the pigment you were painting with, you would have left precisely such dabs on the ceiling we observed.

The Bushmen, having paint to spare, had organized a game: who could jump the highest, leaving fingerprints as proof? Smaller than us, only their champion jumpers could have reached this height – and here was the record. Some say their art was functional, designed to capture the spirits of the animals they hoped to catch. Maybe it was. Not so the finger dabs. These were just playing. In that moment I felt a link to those people more powerful than anything provided by an appreciation of their art. It was the same link I had felt with the baboons in Rhodesia. It is in the knowingly pointless gesture, made for fun that we see, in perfect form, the expression of pure intelligence.

When primary school ended, Mark Ross-Smith, Martin Enoch, Dinah Holderness, Amanda Proudfoot, Peter Marshall and friends were scattered to the winds of different schools and now, I imagine, different countries, and I had to start all over again.

Whatever else he expected of life, Barry Gibson will not have expected to feature in this book. He may not even remember me. I remember him. Barry is the ember glowing among the ashes of my two futile years at Oriel Boys' High School.

This was a low-point of adolescence upon which it is better not to dwell for long, not because there is anything to hide but because there is so little to say. Oriel was a Rhodesian government secondary school for white boys, and in retrospect there was really nothing wrong with the place. True, the real passion of Mr McGrath, our headmaster, was for rugby; but he wanted Oriel to cater for the less sporty types too, and neither the staff nor most of the boys were a particularly rough lot.

I expect the problem was me. My accent was still British, my handwriting seemed to be getting worse, I loathed sport, made hardly any friends and no good ones, and seemed to switch off school as an institution altogether. Worse (something which had never happened before), my schoolwork began to suffer. This did alarm my parents.

And the bullying began. People used to wait for me in groups and spring out at the bottom of the big hill on my two-mile cycle home. I was a good runner and fast cycler and could almost always escape, but one day an older boy started to cycle after me and – though I pedalled until my lungs were bursting – he finally started gaining on me. In panic I dropped my bike and climbed a tree – which was pointless – then burst into tears. Seeing what he had reduced me to my assailant simply stood at the bottom of the tree, laughed, and cycled off. The incident was deeply humiliating; worse than being beaten up. I felt it keenly, and to be honest still do; so much so that as I come to write this down it is proving difficult. As if it mattered now. Quite absurd.

So perhaps this is the moment to write the thing I'm finding it hardest to make myself record from this unhappy period: hardest because it's more than a matter for embarrassment, but for shame.

There was a boy in our class called Colin. I thought it a beautiful name and was drawn to this winsome and lonely lad, who, being no sportsman and lacking swagger, seemed to lack friends. He was as isolated as me, but less resilient, and I was much the stronger. I did my best to befriend and protect him and invited him home a few times. He began to gain in confidence; people talked to him. After about a year of being friends with me (and whether or not this owed anything to me) he seemed to be finding his feet.

One day he was with a circle of other boys when I passed. The others shouted something out, something routinely derogatory, but I was used to that. But then Colin shouted something too – 'drip', 'sap', 'creep', I forget what, nothing original – and the others laughed and slapped him on the back.

It felt like an arrow through my heart. I turned and called, 'No wonder your father committed suicide with a son like you.' And it was true; Colin's father was known to have killed himself.

What I had said was an awful thing to have done. I knew that immediately. Silence fell upon the crowd. There were no repercussions and Colin continued to make friends and settle in, but I reproached myself from the moment my bitter little voice had died away, and I have fretted about it for all the years since. Anyone who could say such a thing must have a sour and nasty streak and the incident has seemed to me to stain my character in what it says about me. You may smile to know I've put this passage in and taken it out half a dozen times, because it so shames me.

Equally embarrassing to recall, let alone record, but no cause for shame at all, is my secret infatuation with Barry Gibson.

Perhaps for everyone there is someone who first triggers sexual longing so unambiguous it has to be acknowledged. It must be inherently unlikely I had altogether lacked sexuality until Barry's big hairy thighs loomed into view, but when they did something registered which for the first time I can remember noticing.

Barry was head boy and besides being brawnily handsome was also intelligent and decent. My embarrassment at proving quite so susceptible to something quite so obvious has since been softened by the discovery that one of our schoolmasters was equally struck and – unlike me – did not succeed in keeping his feelings to himself.

Unless one is careful one writes of these times and people as though one were a novelist relying upon imagination; but the imagination here is memory. These things happened; there were other witnesses, and many of the people will still be alive. I wonder if Barry is. Has he any idea what he stirred in me? Just by being, Gibson invaded, and for most of my two years at Oriel occupied, my adolescent imagination. There were others, too, who followed, though always a few paces behind.

Barry was dark with curly black hair whereas Dougal was blond; both were quite stocky and manly, but Colin was slight, softer, slimmer and quite delicate; all they had in common was that none of them were girls. Allowing for this important exception it must be said that from the first I swung – within the compass of a gay pendulum – both ways. My tastes were catholic.

But not indiscriminate. It was only ever a few. Then no more than now can I discern any pattern in this discrimination, but discrimination there was. Most people never attracted me physically. Most repelled me. The exceptions were not always apparent to me at first sight, and often attraction grew slowly. Some (like Barry) were obvious; others anything but. Between these objects of desire I can find no common thread. The attraction was mysterious.

It was also unconsummated, without hope or intention of consummation, secret and unashamed. Sometimes we do best not to tender explanations lest they distort the theory we want them to fit. Best sometimes just to lay understanding aside and give the report.

The realization I was gay did not arrive for me (as it seems to for some) either in a blinding flash or in a reluctant coming to terms with an awkward fact. Why should it? Is the realization we have two legs, or enjoy cricket, or hate cold, something with which we 'come to terms' or which is revealed to us in a moment of truth? For me sexual attraction was just a fact. When I began to feel it there was no mistaking this fact; therefore no agonizing, no problem about the definition, no seeking of a second opinion, no struggling with the admission. I never felt physically attracted to girls; the first and only physical attraction I experienced was towards boys.

So this was how I was. No use denying it; no difficulty in recognizing it: plainly Barry was not a woman. Not much point in regretting it. This was me. This, it seemed, was how I was. Being on pretty favourable terms with myself, we – myself and I – would from now on just have to take this as read.

Question number one – 'What have we here?' – found a ready answer. As did question number two: 'Is this acceptable?' Is a cloudy

day, a Roman nose, the fact I don't have wings or do have keen
hearing, acceptable? How can a fact be unacceptable? It never for one
moment occurred to me that feeling a sexual attraction, any sexual
attraction, could be a matter for guilt.

What to do about it was another question, and one with which I
was to struggle mightily. But never once did it occur to me to discuss
the struggle with my parents. In later years I had no doubt my mother
had guessed and would have liked me to talk to her about it. But I
never wanted to — not with either of them. I have no difficulty
explaining this. I loved them and they loved me. I knew they would
not be shocked, or not for long. I knew their attitudes were modern
and that, though they might worry a bit, they would not disapprove.
But I thought it unlikely they could suggest anything which would
not already have occurred to me and that their response would be,
overwhelmingly, one of sympathy. This I could not bear. Even anger
would have been preferable.

So I kept the knowledge to myself for a simple reason: pride.

The 1960s hit Rhodesia from the outside, a manufactured import,
and to our perspective felt odd. No doubt the view was similar from
Mississippi. Television finally reached Rhodesia and commercial radio
was already with us. Southern Africa's equivalent of Radio Luxem-
bourg, LM Radio, a pirate-like station, beamed Dusty Springfield
and Cilla Black across the subcontinent from what was then Lourenço
Marques in Portuguese East Africa (and is now Maputo in Mozambique). We learned to say 'fabulous', 'trendy' and 'grotty', and call
girls 'birds'; and in time even white Rhodesians realized it was no
longer cool to say 'super': things were 'fab'.

So all the sixties fashions in design, music and colour, in pop-art,
clothes and slang — and even (in a superficial way) fashions in ideas
too — hit us as they hit Britain, but usually about six months behind.
In *Mukiwa* Peter Godwin mentions the old Rhodesian joke: 'In
ten minutes we shall be landing at Salisbury airport,' says the flight
announcement on the recently introduced Boeing 707s and Vickers
VC 10s, 'where the temperature is 82 degrees and the local time is
1950.'

The joke made its point sharply but the truth was more confused.
Salisbury looked modern, more modern than most English towns.

Like Perth in Australia it was a clean and generously planned city, with wide streets lined by glorious flowering jacaranda and flame trees, with good drains, and even with small skyscrapers. As in Western Australia too, attitudes were relaxed and informal, people were free-and-easy, there was no standing on ceremony.

Arriving in Salisbury in those days you might for some time think you had reached a culture which had embraced modernity not with less but with more enthusiasm than postwar England. Mobile, adaptable, gadget-conscious, car-centred, leisure-oriented, we whites in Africa were living in some ways more as people would in the future in Europe. Whites had less time for class distinctions among our own race. We drank out of cans, used deodorants and shopped in shopping-centres before these things became common in England, and we were quick to abandon suits and ties. White Rhodesians were cleaner than the English in England – everyone bathed or showered every day. Everyone had a telephone. Women were more emancipated than their English sisters – servants already playing the liberating role which washing machines, non-iron shirts and instant food were to play in England. A 'modern lifestyle' we certainly had and much enjoyed.

Yet the sixties – if they included a progressive approach to education – bypassed Southern Rhodesian white schools. Oriel's educational philosophy was fairly well summed up by our oddity of a chemistry teacher, Mr Murphy. Despite his name, Mr Murphy was a Scot. He was short and wizened, with a strong Scottish accent, and his approach to imparting scientific knowledge was beautifully simple. He adopted the philosophy we apply to the teaching of multiplication tables and applied it to the acquisition of all scientific knowledge.

Mr Murphy made us chant – literally chant – the facts. The facts – chemical valencies, the elements, properties of chemicals, etc. – were plonked on to the blackboard without explanation while we made notes. Then Mr Murphy would declaim the first half of a phrase in whose second half an important fact occurred. His voice would rise up to the point where the phrase was left hanging, so to speak, in mid-air. He would break off. Our job was to chant the missing fact in unison, thus completing the sentence.

'An acid plus a base,' Mr Murphy would chant, 'gives . . .'

'. . . a salt plus water!' we would chant back.

'As blood circulates round active muscle, oxyhaemoglobin is converted to . . .'

'. . . CAR-boxyhaemoglobin!' we chanted. To this day I pronounce (to myself) all those elements and chemicals Mr Murphy
taught me by rote, with a Scots accent. Haemoglobin becomes 'Hey,
McLobin!' and I have to stop myself burring the r of 'carbon' and
turning 'dioxide' into 'di-awkcide'.

This communal chanting completed the group-learning experience. To test individual learning the whole class was arranged in a
semicircle, shoulder-to-shoulder, around the outside of the labora-
tory. Mr Murphy stood at his desk, surveying the semicircle, which
was ordered numerically from one (on his left) to thirty-eight (on his
right). Mr Murphy would then repeat some of his half-chants, adding
extra ones from previous lessons; but instead of requiring the whole
ring to take up and complete the chant, he would point – theatrically,
just as his voice quavered into expectant silence – to the boy he
wanted to finish the phrase.

If you got it right, you moved up a place; if wrong, down. And
whenever the class reassembled for another choral test, we resumed
the positions we had occupied for the last. Thus during the course of
the term an order of ability was gradually established, and used for our
school reports at the end.

From time to time progressive journalists from Britain or America
would arrive with the intention of showing us up as Neanderthals
living in the past, and hoping to find the whites lumbering around on
ox-carts, whipping natives and dining by paraffin lamp. In the best
traditions of journalism such reporters seldom failed to find what they
had been commissioned to report, but they had a struggle and usually
made things up. Outwardly, white Central Africa did not seem to be
falling behind its times.

So at least on the surface the sixties did not catch us unreceptive.
Mini-skirts were accepted with little struggle (a country where some
men wore shorts to work and boys wore shorts until we were eighteen
could hardly have reacted otherwise) and we kids all dyed our T-shirts
purple.

The Beatles encountered early resistance but, within a year or two,
were embraced too – in the end enthusiastically. The Rolling Stones
met greater hesitation but won. In England they started to dance the

Twist, and within a year people at barbecues in Salisbury were doing the Twist too.

But these were appearances only. The sixties were received passively by whites in Africa, like a product: we had played no part in their creation. Separated but not cut off from our European base, we whites were consuming a cultural shift without properly understanding what else was changing in Britain and America to cause all this. So we embraced the outward signs without comprehending the internal causes.

We were subject to another big cultural influence: South Africa. Within white culture there Afrikanerdom was much entwined. Here was an influence not only unsophisticated but anti-sophisticated, and behind the times in the obvious as well as the subtle ways. Sexual attitudes were fundamentalist, manners crude and a sort of relentless populism ruled public taste. Favourite music was country and western; Pat Boone took a long time to yield to Elvis Presley and Ricky Nelson, and Presley and Nelson in their turn put up a prolonged rearguard action against the Beatles. And through all these battles, Jim Reeves remained vastly and perennially popular. Anything country did. Hits such as 'Crying in the Chapel', 'The Chapel of Love' or 'Why Do the Birds Go on Singing?' which spent their allotted weeks in the charts in America and Europe and then sank, rode the airwaves in southern Africa for months – years.

Attitudes to the United Kingdom were torn. Like all Britons abroad, white Rhodesians loved to complain about the place where they were; but as the sixties got into their stride the home country looked more and more like a potential enemy to white supremacy in Rhodesia. I watched as sentiment changed, slowly at first but faster as those who really did incline towards Britain went back there (as the hardliners sneeringly urged us to do). The liberals peeled away, as liberals tend to. In the end Britain (or 'the UK') became a by-word for everything the remaining whites feared and disliked about the rest of the world and the threat it posed: a place full of communists, shirkers, queers, malcontents, kaffir-lovers and ignoramuses.

But we kept on buying Beatles records, giggling at the mini-skirt and crowding to Salisbury's drive-in cinema to see the latest 'Carry On' film. White South African culture was all very well, Johannesburg was Babylon – the big city, and exciting – but Calvinism, *boerwors* and

Boer 'music' were not the English-speaking white Rhodesian's idea of his cultural future.

Our future was cloudy and we knew it. Something had happened at the beginning of the sixties which cast its shadow over the five strange years which remained before Ian Smith was to yank us all into the political wilderness; and it helps explain how he was able to. The affair is almost forgotten in Europe, except perhaps in Belgium. The Congo, the giant Belgian colony which composed Africa's heart of darkness, collapsed at independence and the white population, especially from the province of Katanga, fled for their lives.

The easiest land route out was through neighbouring Northern Rhodesia, then south to Salisbury. I do not know how many thousands of panicking white Belgians came through Salisbury on their flight south, but the *Rhodesia Herald* gave the impression the numbers were huge. We were all urged to volunteer food and shelter, and many Rhodesians did. The paper was full of pictures of arriving white families with as many of their possessions as they could carry piled on to the roof-racks of their cars.

The story was a gift for local journalists and for the alarmists' horror stories about the prospects for black majority rule. Upon a relatively small white population such as Rhodesia's the effect was shattering. Reason flew out of the window. The tremendous irresponsibility of domestic Belgian politicians and Belgium's decades of selfish neglect of her colonial responsibilities in Africa were brushed aside, as white supremacists insisted this was what must happen everywhere, 'once the blacks take over'. After Katanga it became impossible to join any argument about black majority rule without someone muttering 'Belgian Congo'.

The experience may have affected me. Though shunning the racist majority I never could take the final step to join my mother in her optimism – practised as well as felt – about a harmonious future for all the peoples of Central Africa. She and Dad were learning chiShona, the language of the largest tribe in Southern Rhodesia, while Mum was increasingly active in the movement for African education.

They were not starry-eyed idealists; what my father really believed I have never known; but my mother's instinct was to bypass arguments about ideology, in which she never felt at home, and simply act as seemed right. Reading George Eliot's *Middlemarch* recently I came upon Dorothea's description of her life's purpose: 'That by desiring what is perfectly good, even when we don't quite know what it is and cannot do what we would, we are part of the Divine power against evil – widening the skirt of light and making the struggle with darkness narrower.' This was not only how my mother thought, but what she was and is: a widener of the skirt of light.

To her it seemed right that servants' children should be educated, and as she was a teacher and there were thousands of servants in our suburb it seemed right for her and friends to start a small school for them. They built a hut on some unused land and taught there. Mum did not need to think her way through to a policy for African education generally, to be sure this was worth doing.

I admire people whose nature it is to behave like this, but I could never think like that, not now and not at thirteen. The African peoples of Rhodesia seemed to me so far in their minds from where we were in ours, and there were many millions of them. There were only 250,000 Europeans in the whole country whose first and (to me) natural wish was to educate their own children in their own culture. Next came an obligation to educate Africans. We needed to decide what for, to what level, and with what resources. We needed a policy. Mum did not have a policy: just a blackboard and chalk. I did not think this was enough.

Yet I was proud of my mother: we all were. When, a few years later, Ian Smith's Rhodesian Front government closed her school down and Mum came home, cut out sheets of cardboard for placards, bundled my sister Belinda (about four) and little Amos (the gardener's boy, about five) into the car, drove to the parliament building for the opening of the session, and stood outside with Belinda, whose placard said 'I have a future' and Amos, whose placard said 'I have no future', we were more proud of her than we could say. Ian Smith, the Prime Minister, entering the building, *ran* past my mother, so scared was he of any confrontation in front of cameras.

The news article and photograph were censored from the next morning's *Rhodesia Herald* whose brave editor used to leave blank spaces wherever the official censors ordered the removal of columns; so there was just a blank space on the front page. To build up a picture of what was happening in Southern Rhodesia you didn't join up the dots, you joined up the blanks: a useful lesson in many areas of life.

The sixties crept in sideways, through the blanks in the *Rhodesia Herald* and through friends. These I was beginning to find outside school – or among fellow-refugees at school. There was Trisha Swift, a few years older, at first just a friend of my mother but soon of the whole family. In her origins Trisha was a real Rhodesian but she was more: a real individual who ended up more radical than any of us. Small, noisy, intelligent, good-natured, funny, decided in her opinions, Trisha was fun. She and I fought constantly – still do – because she's usually wrong; but she's sometimes right in her judgement of people. Those adolescent years in Salisbury would have been meaner without her.

Her family kept a smallholding on the outskirts of Salisbury, with pigs. Her grandmother chewed willow-bark for headaches. I would help Trisha, driving their old VW Kombi round the hotels and restaurants early in the morning, collecting pigswill. One of our mutual friends was Diane Haeslop, a beautiful, willowy blonde art teacher at Oriel; mischievous and arch, pursued by handsome and mysterious boyfriends – one with a sports car even. Diane helped us make batiks (all the rage) of our white T-shirts, and dye every other garment purple or orange. The colour purple, the smell of hot wax or a splash of orange can still take me straight back to those times; a sort of excitement went with the sounds and colours of the sixties.

We thought ourselves terribly daring. One day we – Roger, Diane, Trisha, her brother Don and I – read in the *Rhodesia Herald*'s Entertainments section an offer from the management of the cinema. For the opening night of the film *Day of the Triffids* free entry would be permitted to all customers dressed as triffids.

We set to work with crêpe and old sheets and orange and purple dye, and turned up early because we supposed hundreds of others would be taking advantage of the same offer. This may have been the sixties but we had reckoned without Rhodesian conservatism. The cinema was packed but everybody else had paid. There was no other triffid in the auditorium. Our plant posse had to put up with abuse as we rustled down the aisle. In the dark, persistently, throughout the performance, somebody pulled my fronds.

What possessed me to join the Boys' Brigade, the paramilitary wing of the nonconformist churches, let alone the local Presbyterian church to which our BB company was attached, I cannot say. I did not believe in God or knots, particularly knots. Yet somehow I found myself on Saturday mornings polishing brass buckles and learning semaphore, whiting my sash with tennis-shoe paste and studying huge tracts of the Old Testament for examinations of the severest kind. Sundays found me singing treble (at first) in Mrs Begley's church choir, and even solos to a large congregation, some dabbing their eyes, whether with pain or emotion I am unsure. The parallels with the young Tony Blair are too painful to contemplate.

Why? Partly it was a reaction against my family's new enthusiasm for Quakerism. Good people, the Society of Friends, genuinely good. I couldn't stand them.

Joining the Salisbury Friends was my mother's idea. More than other churches, I think, they would for her have answered two needs. First, they believed in things of the spirit (what my mother, to my adolescent fury, called 'the inner light') without the dogma, rigmarole, social display and general prancing around towards which – following my grandad's oft-repeated and principled objections to incense, dressing up, women in hats, vicars and insurance salesmen – all my family maintain a certain suspicion. Quakers do not proselytize. They have no form and no ceremony. Their meetings have a sort of calming serenity and the silent hour passes quickly.

The Society of Friends in Southern Rhodesia had another attraction. Its members were actively opposed to racialism. This cannot be said of much of the Christian church at the time. Whatever official pronouncements might have been made at episcopal level or back in England (and though brave missionaries and educators working among Africans stood against the tide of the times in white Africa) the churches serving respectable European congregations were feeble. The sound of their trumpet was not certain.

The Quakers did their best to attract a multi-racial congregation and, more important, seldom failed to raise their voice against the now fast-running drift towards an official government policy of white supremacy.

White supremacy was becoming an ideal to be maintained and if necessary promoted. Those who had always professed a belief in gradualism were forced off such ground – either towards Ian Smith's 'never in my lifetime' or towards taking a stand against him. Most were joining him.

Quakers took a stand against him. I say nothing which might call into question the respect which these brave people are due, beyond recording the fact they irritated me. They seemed smug. Most had a severe sense-of-humour failure.

Their own lives were comfortable enough – they were disproportionately cultured, educated types, some quite rich, who saw little threat to their own positions from the policies they supported. Few were really tied to the African soil; most could leave; most in the end did. They were arguing from a comfortable fantasy, shutting their eyes to the clash of interests, the clash of cultures, the gulfs in understanding and philosophy, which pointed so clearly to the likelihood that race and land and tribe must dominate African politics for the foreseeable future, the question being only which race, which tribe, whose land.

Quakers were forever travelling to conferences and fellowship-weekends. If one questioned the usefulness of all this costly and time-consuming fellowship one was regarded pityingly as someone whose inner light was faltering; Quakers would fly or drive thousands of miles to agree with each other in person. Their refusal to evangelize was admirable, but such obsessive communing seemed inward-looking – even self-congratulatory – in a subcontinent where an air-ticket would have bought a good quantity of blackboards and chalk.

Yes, I too am at heart a liberal. But it won't do; liberalism won't do; there are things in heaven and earth undreamed of in a liberal's philosophy and many of them are found in Africa. As a boy I did notice that, and while much of this raging against nice people may have been an adolescent reacting against his parents, not all of it was. There are some bleak truths in conservatism and I was dimly sensing them.

I used to talk about these things to an untypical Quaker, Ernest Delgado, a very old man who from his accent (and despite his name) seemed continental European. He suffered from Parkinson's Disease and was deteriorating. At Quaker meetings he and I had started discussing philosophy, and I began visiting him in his small flat. He explained David Hume's sceptical view of miracles (the miracle required to believe in a miracle is a greater miracle than the miracle itself) and Descartes' 'I think therefore I am' and Bishop Berkeley's proof that we cannot know objects exist. These puzzles and conjectures gripped me. He said I should study philosophy at university. In the end I did.

By the time I left for boarding school, Ernest's hands were shaking so much he could not lift a cup, and not much later he died. Visits to the old man had become more of a duty, now he trembled so much and could not speak clearly. I have some faint and guilty recollection of slackening in the last months, just when I should have kept up my calls.

At home I bickered and lashed out at my brothers and sisters. I had almost no friends at school – my shy brother Roger was more popular – and sport, especially rugby at which Oriel excelled, had become a misery.

And I had begun slacking at school. Always capable of passing exams without working much, I worked less, dropped down the league tables to which educationalists at the time were addicted (it seems to have come round again) and stopped bothering with homework. I read, and read, and read, and kicked around a bit with Trisha and friends. It was a low time with many bright sparks. I must have been looking for something, something missing.

That may explain the Boys' Brigade. All this Protestantism, semaphore and knots must have mystified my parents but they never discouraged me. I have no idea where I thought I was headed. Fuming at the Quakers, I sang simplistic hymns at the Presbyterian Church, hymns whose words I knew to be untrue, square-bashed with the Boys' Brigade – never promoted beyond the rank of private – distinguished myself in Bible knowledge and disgraced myself at marching and morse, fell in love (from afar) with young Lt Moxon, liked the camaraderie of the other boys and the kindly, patient endeavours of our BB leaders, learned how to pitch a tent and every verse of the BB hymn: 'Will your anchor hold in the storms of life?' which, trite as it was, was not without meaning. The truth is, I was adrift. I was fourteen.

But I did enjoy much of it. Camping at Inyanga, for instance. And there was Olly. Oliver was our NCO, dark-haired, quiet, assured, and a few years older. He was the kind of boy all the other boys admired: never boastful, always steady, a natural leader.

Once on a camp in the Inyanga mountains he got his penis stuck in his zip. It happened as he was dressing in the tent I was sharing with him and others: an easy accident while zipping jeans too vigorously, lying down. Olly yelped and tugged but the zip would budge neither up nor down. At some cost to his dignity he asked me to try, but, anxious not to hurt him, I was too tentative. Everyone tried. Nobody succeeded. Matron was called from her tent – a real climb-down this.

In she crawled through the entrance, grabbed Olly's trousers, grabbed the zip and yanked. There was a scream of pain from Olly, but it worked. He was exceptionally quiet for the rest of the camp.

We carried on admiring him but after that it was never quite the same. Insignificant as this incident had been, Oliver had lost his limitless command. He knew what we had seen, and we knew he knew. And I understood that, though entirely beyond a person's control and not their fault at all, one memorable occasion on which they are seen to be ludicrous breaks a kind of seal. Arse-over-tit in the shingle on Brighton beach many years later, Neil Kinnock suffered Olly's fate.

3. Swaziland

Waterford School, my mother said, was new. This was its first year. It was a boarding school, in some eyes an 'experimental' one: open not only in theory to boys of all races, but dedicated in practice to being so. About a third of Waterford's first-year intake was African and the rest were either white, or Indian or 'coloured' – meaning of mixed race. The headmaster, Michael Stern, had quit a smart white boarding school in Johannesburg to pioneer multi-racial education in one of the few places in southern Africa where it was legal for people with white skin and black skin to be educated together.

The school was in Swaziland.

I realized what my parents were suggesting: a huge step. Swaziland, a tiny, landlocked country wedged between the top right-hand corner of South Africa and the bottom left-hand corner of Mozambique, was nearly a thousand miles away. A British protectorate, the territory was in practice governed by a British governor, and the King of the Swazis, Sobhuza II. Its capital, Mbabane, was a small town nestling in high, steep green hills, and on one of these was Waterford School. There was no airport – just a bad road.

I would be exiled to a Swazi hilltop, three days by train from my family. But I must have understood things were going wrong for me, and agreed to think about it. I was anxious.

We decided to make the journey there to see the school for ourselves. I set out with just my parents, in the Humber – now upgraded from Hawk to Super-Snipe: Dad was doing well. Heading down through my beloved lowveld and over Beitbridge, we turned east in the Northern Transvaal and I saw for the first time the mighty skies and immense, cool, windswept, rolling plains of the Eastern Transvaal, a place few tourists visit. Crossing the border into what was still directly ruled British territory was a strange sensation: for us, as I have said, the Republic of South Africa (as it had become) always had a tight, oppressive atmosphere; Swaziland's back-of-beyond feeling, its windy hills, blowing mists, its dripping wattle plantations, its underdevelopment and its complete lack of tension made a total contrast and you could sense as much within yards of the tiny frontier-post staffed by surly Afrikaners half-reluctant either to let you out or, once out, back in.

What can you know of a school from a morning's visit? It rained throughout. I talked to some of the boys there and joined a Land-Rover slithering up some muddy tracks to collect wood; my parents were impressed with Michael Stern's energy; and we came away reassured at least that this was a viable school, not a crackpot scheme. If I went I would be the first from Southern Rhodesia.

There were some written tests, but exams, especially written exams, were never a problem for me. I had already decided to say yes to Waterford. This decision, my parents' idea, redirected the rest of my life.

We took a short holiday before going home. We stopped for a picnic near the Drakensberg mountains and while my parents unpacked food I walked in the wind through deep grass across a hill and understood this mattered. I was fourteen, and would join the school in only its second year of existence: a pioneer.

Breyten in the Eastern Transvaal can feel on a winter dawn like the coldest place on earth. There has always been something beguiling for me about vast, bleak landscapes and small, bleak towns, but there is no denying Breyten lacked the more obvious charms. And if Breyten shows an icy face to its rare visitors, its railway station is icier still.

This was the railhead for Swaziland. From here onward to Mbabane a sort of lorry service – the lorries carrying small passenger compartments behind the cab – was operated by the South African Railways Road Transport Service.

The slow, overnight steam train from Johannesburg left all the Waterford boys coming this way at Breyten before sunrise. The heater in the train had frozen up and we were already shivering as we were set down. With a hiss the big black engine and ancient iron and wood carriages went rumbling off into the Transvaal grey. The white boys had travelled in a different carriage, of course, from the African students. For some this was not their first term, and the whole Waterford contingent found each other and gathered on the platform, I with them. Our lorry would not leave until after dawn, in over an hour.

That we had travelled separately had not seemed shocking. Segregation on trains and buses was so much part of life in South Africa you hardly noticed it. But now came an embarrassment which you could not overlook. Breyten station was a small, shabby place; there was only one waiting room; it had a coal fire burning; it was for whites only.

Naturally it was for whites only. What else did one expect in the Eastern Transvaal? We could have counted ourselves lucky it was not for Afrikaners only. But for the first time in my life, racial segregation meant more than being in a different position from that of black people: it meant walking away from half the people I was with, comrades, and leaving them out in the cold while I took refuge before a coal fire in a warm room into which they were not allowed.

We all felt awkward. Some of us made a half-hearted stand and stayed outside to freeze with the Africans, but they were not impressed, and told us to stop being ridiculous and go in. One rather loud black boy – I came to know him as the school show-off – told us he would not hesitate to leave *us* out in the cold in the new era which was coming, when the boot would be on the other foot; and this dampened feelings of solidarity.

The rail journey from Salisbury had taken three days. I had left without emotion on the Rhodesian Railways overnight sleeper for Bulawayo. Mum, however, had cried. She had warned me not to drink water before going to bed in my train bunk, in case I woke in the night wanting a pee, forgot where I was and, half-asleep and in the dark, walked out of the carriage door and fell under the wheels.

I laughed. I only cried when, our diesel engine roaring in front through the starry highveld night, I opened for the first time the case Mum had packed and discovered she had placed a New Testament on top of my new school uniform. It didn't matter crying because nobody else going to school was in the compartment with me, only a travelling salesman.

At dawn in Bulawayo I marvelled at the world's longest railway platform – there is only platform 1 – and boarded the train for Mafeking. There being then no direct rail-link with South Africa, I had to travel through Bechuanaland. This took all day, all night and half the next day. At about 30 mph we swayed along the same single-track my family had travelled up on from Cape Town when I was eight. Again the dry bush not far from the Kalahari desert, again the chuff of the distant steam locomotive, the interminable stops while it took on water, or waited to pass an oncoming goods-train. Again the Africans at every station selling live birds and bushbabies, baby monkeys and wooden carvings of *tokoloshies* – strange little man-cats with spotted markings, potent troublemakers in the spirit world.

Then, the following day, hours to wait in Mafeking, truly the end of the world, for a South African Railways train to Johannesburg where I changed the same night, for Breyten. For an apprehensive boy anxious about leaving home, missing trains, or being detained at customs if I told the South African officers Waterford was my destination, this was quite an adventure.

Such worries were minor compared with one which had nagged me since the decision to go to boarding school. Communal showers. I laugh to think of it now but the worry haunted me for months beforehand. What if I got an erection?

Within days of arriving at Waterford this worry dissolved. The water was freezing. Fear of an erection in the showers was fast replaced by a more practical anxiety: to *get* to the showers before the short-lived dribblings of tepid water from the small wattle-fired boiler gave out, and the passion-killing icy deluge began.

We felt the winters at Waterford. Despite the exotic name Swaziland was no tropical sunpatch. The mountainous small territory enjoyed warm summers and misty, gusty, frosty winters. And it always seemed colder indoors. The dormitories and halls had been designed for us by an idealistic Portuguese architect from Lourenço Marques, Pancho d'Alpoim Guedes, an eccentric and philanthropic genius of extravagant imagination, whose organic-looking concrete creations hugged the Swazi hillsides belly-down, like cubist caterpillars, their corridors following the slope with shallow cascades of steps.

There was no wood, no carpet, no cosiness, and wind whistled up the corridors past our little sleeping compartments where foam-rubber mattresses were laid on concrete slabs and slatted-glass windows wouldn't close tight and mildew developed between the foam-rubber and slab, and the cistern in the urinal down all those stairs at the end of the passage drip-drip-dripped in the night, each hollow splash echoing up the concrete corridor . . . but we were all in this together and the camaraderie was good. And in the summer the armies of small grey-green wattle trees came into bloom together, the wind died and the whole hillside was enveloped in the pale yellow haze and the warm smell of their blossoms. Strong, strong memories.

If you ask for the sharpest recollections of school I could recite dates and babble about events; but cutting through trophy-memory like a living flame through dead certificates is the aroma of wattle, the cold, lonely lavender sunsets, the drip-drip of the cistern echoing up the concrete corridor at night, the diesel generator hammering, and the smell of mildewed rubber.

I did well from the start, but not as well as Stephen. He was popular, he was intelligent, he cut a confident figure, he was good at exams, good at athletics, good at football and very good indeed at cricket. Nobody ran a faster 220 yards. He was the captain of cricket, captain of athletics and captain of heaven-knows-what-else, including, of course, captain of school. He was a founder member.

Stephen was not one to throw his weight around. He did not bully, he did not have to. Stephen was no less than an excellent boy with a proper and circumspect sense of how to distribute his favours. Let me not carp: it is a healthy instinct in a young man to incline to the winning side. In later life he proved a good man.

But he hit me. Hard. He smashed me in the jaw during the washing-up in the kitchens after lunch one day. Probably I was being annoying, perhaps (as so often) more annoying than I intended or realized. Some kind of horseplay had been going on and I think I had tossed a washing-up cloth at him. Perhaps it stung him, but all at once mischief turned to anger and he strode right up and hit me, in front of all the others.

This was hard to take. I was not badly hurt – just a nosebleed – but the blow made my eyes water suspiciously like crying and I beat an ignominious retreat. Overcome by self-pity I took cover in my dormitory for some hours, and never forgot.

That evening I walked over to fetch schoolbooks from what we called 'the rondavels': the original classrooms housed in round huts. It was a half-mile walk over the fields and back, crossing a stream; always a lonely trudge and tonight lonelier than ever. I never got over homesickness at school – never entirely did at university – and just after sunset and just before dawn were times when the African sky would fill me with thoughts of home and I would stare out in the direction where I had calculated Salisbury was.

Swazi sunsets are inexpressibly sad. Bleak, as remorseless as the sound of French horns. The sky loses all warmth, leaching to the palest yellows along the western horizon and washing into a vast, cold lavender above. I remember that evening, cold lavender, pale yellow and that great purpling sky, and I always will. The sky tore at my heart. I stood quietly. Defiance inhabited me. Then I gathered up my *Latin Grammar* and my *Zulu Dictionary*, and walked on. I resolved to forget neither the attack, nor the sky, nor the colours, nor the moment. I had not forgotten, some months later, when the school gathered on the main road for the annual hill-climb.

Waterford was set about 500 feet above the valley leading into Mbabane, down which the main road from Johannesburg ran. From this you went down the dirt road to our school, past the mud and straw huts of some Swazi kraals, crossed a stream, then zigzagged steeply up through the wattle trees to emerge on to a flattish shelf where Waterford was situated, with two higher hills, 'Tom' and 'Kelly', behind. Every year the whole school joined the race from the main road to the main block. Shortcutting the zigzags the distance must have been about two miles, and winning times were in the region of twelve minutes.

I was in my mid-teens. I had never entertained the least idea of being any good at running, or, beyond a determination not to be last, pushed myself in any race. But running had always come easily and I thought I had noticed others tended to run out of puff before me. Anyway there was no getting out of the hill-climb. It had been held in the school's first year, this was the second, and Mr Stern – whom we called the Boss – wanted it to become a tradition.

Another nascent tradition was that Stephen would win. He had won easily the first time and nobody had proved anything like his equal at running. This year the finish was to be watched by Pancho Guedes, the architect – and his beautiful daughter, Lonca, whom we all believed to be Stephen's actual or hoped-for girlfriend. She would see his victory. It was to be a touching moment.

But something about Stephen's frame, his very sturdiness, told me he wasn't really a long-distance runner: just confident, strong and fit.

The starting gun was fired. Off we all trooped down the dusty road, a tight group at first but increasingly straggling as the taller and keener (like Stephen) took advantage of long legs for the downhill stretch, and pushed to the fore. With my shorter stride I fell behind and by the time we crossed the bridge, left the road and began labouring straight up the footpath which climbs direct, I was well behind the leaders; I couldn't see Stephen and supposed he must have streaked ahead. I settled into the steep climb – head down, ground in front of you, short steps, keep jogging, *don't walk*, don't lose the rhythm, dance on one spot if you must, try a sort of dancing plod, breathe hard but even, and bob your way up.

Soon I forgot the others and fell into a sort of steady, upward bounce.

Then something new happened to me. The effect was like a drug. A sort of mindless, regular beat took me in its grip. I was running – it was more than a plod – but it had the dogged, bit-between-the-teeth, from-here-into-infinity feeling every plodder recognizes. My breathing was coming deep, fast and regular with a rhythm matching short, springy steps. I could feel my heart pounding but with resolution, not panic. Under my breath I beat out a melody from some simple tune stuck in my brain, a single phrase, repeated over and over. Everything – lungs, legs, heartbeat, swing of the arms, the beat of the song – seemed to have meshed into gear together; clunk: a low, powerful, crawler-gear; locked on to something sustainable.

Then I passed someone. I had no experience of passing people. He was in trouble. I wasn't. It was wonderful. And I thought: You can do this. You can keep this up. You're not going to die.

It was then I saw Stephen's legs. Bandy, hairy, pale, you couldn't mistake them, far enough ahead, but not *that* far ahead, not as far as I had imagined. Above and beyond, perhaps half a mile away, was the outline of the school buildings.

And I thought: What if?

And I thought: Yes!

And I thought: You still have something left.

I gave a small, measured twist to the throttle, stepped up the breathing, slightly lengthened the stride; and watched those bandy legs getting closer. Now we were within a few hundred yards of the finish. I could hear people cheering.

And I thought: You can get him.

I passed Stephen. Even in my exhaustion his shock registered. I heard his breath rasping behind me as he quickened pace. He was making a last-ditch effort to regain the lead. He drew up beside me on the path, just by my left shoulder, and began, slowly, to pass.

And I thought: No you don't.

And I thought: I still have something left.

And I thought: This isn't for ever now; it's just a couple of hundred yards. For this short time you can take any punishment because in a few seconds it will be over. Lowering my chin I threw everything remaining into the race.

Stephen never passed me. After fifty yards I felt his presence receding behind. From the crowd came bewildered cheers as I crossed the finishing line, a clear winner. Seconds later Stephen did. He was very sick. In front of Lonca.

From that year on I won every hill-climb. When my brother Roger joined me at Waterford he came second. This, from the point of view of my perspective and of family pride, was the ideal outcome.

What I shall write next would have hurt an old man and a great one, Michael Stern, to whom I owe a great debt and Waterford owes everything. But I do not think our school did achieve what he had intended.

It came close. Mr Stern's hope – it was really the *raison d'être* of our school – was to make a living demonstration of the possibility of racial harmony, realized through a community of teachers and young people learning and teaching together, and living together. In the obvious sense that experiment succeeded.

Nobody at Waterford liked the word 'experiment' because it suggested doubt was possible, but, seen as an experiment, this test of multi-racialism seemed neatly contrived. It is true our teachers were almost all white, but among the boys there was a sizeable contingent from almost every race in southern Africa and we were drawn from half a dozen countries.

We were taken from our home environments and placed together in a situation which was, for all except the minority of Swazi boys, conveniently distant from the influences Waterford hoped to shake off. We were isolated on a hillside out of town. Few of us returned home except for the holidays. All started with a presumed shared intention of making the idea work, but (most of us) without any big political axe to grind. If it didn't work, we could have admitted it.

We knew what our enemies said: white children had to be taught and treated differently from black. Africans and Europeans were incapable of learning or living together and Waterford School would collapse in a confusion of cross-purposes, hostility and misunderstanding. Some thought the whole school a communist plot.

These suppositions Waterford exploded completely. Most of us knew they were ridiculous before we started; any doubters were quickly convinced when they saw the results. The results were good. We lived and worked contentedly together. There was no gang warfare or racial persecution. Examination successes placed us ahead of most other schools and even the slower boys made progress.

So why do I hesitate now, and why did I hesitate then, from calling the experiment a success? Because the truth is we didn't really *mix*. I'm far from sure this was just because of skin colour. *Language* is consistently overlooked as a major divider of peoples. But I'll offer no final judgement on the reasons we didn't mix much, but simply state the facts.

They were these. In everything which could be imposed from above – who slept in which dormitories, who was promoted to be prefects or sporting captains, who was selected for which team – the staff took care to ensure a good mix of races. But in social groupings which could not be imposed the races stuck together. Even the African tribes tended to prefer their own tribe where possible, and, where not, joined a more pan-African grouping. The Indians maintained their own groups (with complicated internal divisions) but did mix with the whites too – and hardly mixed with the blacks at all. The 'coloured' boys more or less joined the whites. And the Chinese maintained courtesies but beyond that scarcely mixed with anyone. In southern Africa nationality was secondary, except that everyone from Portuguese territory formed a sort of subgroup based on language.

So, viewed from the middle-distance, Waterford worked, and in a most important sense this was what counted for we showed there was no good reason to segregate schools. But take out the binoculars and you might have noticed a less encouraging reason why racists were wasting their time segregating schools. We segregated ourselves, without prompting. From my four years at Waterford I can remember a fair measure of inter-racial goodwill, many friendly exchanges, a good spirit and no serious problems. This seemed important. And I can remember not a single 'best-friend' relationship which spanned the races. This also seemed important.

Fernando Honwana, by being nobody's best friend, came closest to being everybody's: the exception to what I have just written. He was quite in sympathy with everyone, and not completely with anyone, and part of no racial mainstream.

Fernando was very black. His father was long gone even when I knew him, his mother, who had many children, had been left without resources in Lourenço Marques; but his brother, who was blind, had become an admired poet and story-teller in Portuguese. Fernando (through the help of Pancho Guedes's family) had been awarded a bursary to study at Waterford, arriving the year after me. Within a few terms his English was perfect.

I don't know what it was about Fernando but most people felt it. He was different. In appearance he was spare and good-looking with classic Bantu African features, bright, humorous eyes and clear, almost luminous skin. In character he was an utterly reliable comrade. Quick-minded, unforced, considerate and a good listener he had that most potent of qualities: he could convey sympathy without indicating an opinion of his own. Fernando managed to reserve judgement on many things, yet he gave no impression of indecision and his mind never seemed unformed.

He was a wonderful actor, particularly in parody. He could clown more cleverly than any of the rest. Yet he never seemed to give offence or take it. Once though, when each of us had to recite a text of our personal choice, and everyone expected Fernando to be funny, he chose a poem about African liberation, sharp and angry, and delivered it with quiet passion. Everybody noticed and remembered.

In his person – not in anything he ever argued, for he didn't argue – Fernando Honwana came the closest of anyone to embodying the spirit of what Waterford School had been meant to achieve. In this he was unusual.

Many years ago, while still a Member of Parliament, I received a message from the Foreign Office. Fernando Honwana wished to renew acquaintance. He was in London with the President of Mozambique, Samora Machel. When I rang to ask more, the chap at the

FCO confided (so far as a civil servant ever does confide in a politician) that Mr Honwana was more than his official position, aide to the President, would suggest. Not only because his English was flawless but because (a tougher test than language) he seemed to be able to communicate with Mrs Thatcher, he had proved an astute go-between while Samora Machel helped the British government in awkward negotiations with Robert Mugabe in Rhodesia.

We arranged to meet. Our meeting was genial enough. But drinking tonic in the characterless foyer of a modern hotel jarred, and the twenty-year lapse made a gulf, and half an hour was not enough. But we did (I think) both realize we still liked each other a lot – funny how immediate that sort of recognition is – neither of us really knowing what more to say. I asked if he remembered being served tea in our beds by a black servant in a sunny room in the house of a British colonial administrator of Swaziland, all those years ago. He did.

Not long afterwards he was killed with Samora Machel in a mysterious plane crash in South Africa which excited speculation about murder. Otherwise I think he would one day have become President of Mozambique, but, more important, a great and perhaps salvationary figure in the politics of the African continent. I have seldom felt so sure of so large a speculation. The death of Fernando Honwana was a greater loss than that of his chief. He was the closest I came to having a real African friend.

My best friend was Charles Long, a shy, spotty, painfully sensitive, impossibly fair-haired boy of unusual intellect: an artistic genius, a whizz at maths, with a goonish sense of humour and absolutely no ambition. His mother, Sadie, whom I loved, was tiny and Swedish and his father was Government Secretary, which in colonial language seemed to mean Deputy Governor.

I stayed many weekends with this family, in Mbabane. Fernando was friendly with Charles too, and one weekend joined us. He and I were put in the big guest room. On Sunday morning we were awoken by the Long's house servant, with a tray of tea and biscuits for each of us. As the black man placed Fernando's delicately set tray by his bedside and, with a deferential but puzzled nod at the black curls on the white linen pillow, departed, gently shutting the door, I whispered from my own bed: 'Don't you see the attractions, Fernando?'

He grinned. Fernando, exceptionally, could cope with the divide.

You didn't have to crack a five-minute mile to be a good miler in Swaziland, and a two minute eight second 880 yards put you into the athletic elite. For the first time in my life I enjoyed not being hopeless at every variety of sport. And though I was still not particularly popular, I had started to be promoted – to sub-prefect first.

Mr Stern – the Boss – was too professional a headmaster to dote on favourites, but he had them, and I was one. I admired him and was a helpful boy. Cheeky rather than insubordinate, I still had the natural conservative's instinct to throw my weight behind order rather than chaos. At Waterford I tried to do this in an intelligent way. The Boss did everything to help and sponsor me. My whole subsequent career turned on this, though I did not then know it.

Schoolwork went fine. Each week a running total indicating the exact position and percentages obtained by each boy, subject by subject and overall, was posted on to the notice-board. Regular interim positions would be posted at certain times in the year, and the yearly position formed a central part of the school report. There was keen interest in these league tables by the cleverer and more ambitious boys, and constant jockeying for position. I was never far from the top. It never occurred to me to wonder whether the spur this proved for the front runners might not act as a discouragement to the rest.

A stroke of good fortune came my way. There was a wave of marijuana-smoking among some of the older boys. Marijuana was easily available – at the bottom of the hill for instance, where the Swazi kraals were – but I'd never even smoked tobacco and had only the haziest idea what marijuana was. That some in my class and the class below would slope off down the road in the late afternoon and return rather less sharp than they set out, pretty much escaped my attention.

The Boss found out, of course – the Boss always did – and a number were expelled, and even more demoted.

Expelling Swazi boys was always a delicate matter. The King had about a hundred wives; Sobhuza II had been crowned in 1922 and like all kings of the Swazis selected a new wife every year at the 'Incwala' rainmaking ceremony, when Swazi virgins danced before him in a stadium. It followed he had innumerable children. It was once said that one could not throw a brick in the English Home Counties without hitting the niece of a bishop; one could certainly cast no stone in Swaziland without hitting a prince. Every second adolescent whose surname was Dlamini turned out to be some kind of prince. You had to be careful whom you expelled.

But in this case the Boss decided to make an example of the affair. Quite a swathe of potential prefects and sub-prefects lost their predominance. At the age of eighteen I became head of my house, captain of athletics and captain of school. I was already chairman of the debating society. I was the Boss's choice. After the expulsion an anonymous chorused hiss of '*Judasssssss, Judasssss*' greeted my arrival at assembly, but this died away; I was not violently unpopular, just one of the Boss's men. I had not grassed on the smokers.

We prefects had irresponsibilities of our own, though. A boy called Richard attended the Inter-Protectorates Athletics in Bechuanaland and came back claiming to have slept with a prostitute, which was almost certainly not true, as close cross-questioning tended to confirm. Pedro Guedes kept puff-adders under his bed in a box (until discovered) and boiled sections of a dead horse in quicklime in a row of 44-gallon drums to construct a horse-skeleton (until the smell, not least of Pedro, halted the project). I helped him.

I'd like to report some after-lights-out hanky-panky in the dormitories, of the kind that is believed to happen quite routinely in boarding schools. Unfortunately it did not in this one. One of my friends used to pummel me in a way I greatly enjoyed, not least because it was secretly affectionate, but I embarrassed him by saying so and it stopped. Where all this rampant boarding-school homosexuality happened I cannot say. Not in Swaziland, though in South Africa Waterford was rumoured to be a hotbed of inter-racial perversions.

I hitchhiked from Rhodesia to Mbabane many times (with permission, remarkably, given), getting lifts with missionaries, drunkards, homicidal maniacs, Afrikaner businessmen, even in a chauffeur-driven Rolls-Royce, once. Standing in the heat of the day by an empty shimmering strip road in my beloved lowveld, going home, with no hurry, no rain and cold night to fear, no worry about sleeping the night by the roadside if no car should come . . . what pleasure can compare?

And I rode my mother's two-gear 30cc Honda scooter (top speed

28 mph) the thousand miles from Salisbury to Mbabane. And once I took my (now) undersized blue Raleigh bike on the train from Salisbury to Bulawayo to Lourenço Marques by the Indian Ocean, then cycled across the bottom of Mozambique, through the Swazi lowveld and up to Mbabane, much of it on dirt roads, eating only Nestlé's condensed milk and camping in a leaky tent half way.

My most ambitious project, almost reckless, came in my final year. It seemed a fine idea that our school should send an expedition into black Africa – East Africa – to climb Kilimanjaro. The Boss agreed; and agreed to come. It was difficult to organize. By then Rhodesia was largely cut off, isolated by international economic sanctions after Ian Smith had made his unilateral declaration of independence. Northern Rhodesia was now called Zambia and in its usual state of chaos; and the road from Zambia to the Tanganyika coast was a wreck-strewn mud strip called the Hell Run, along which Zambia was trying to run all her exports of copper and imports of everything else.

We took the school's elderly blue twenty-seater Mercedes bus. We got there, all seventeen of us. Twelve of us reached the top, Uhuru peak – the Boss being sick and crawling on hands and knees for the last hour. Three of the black members of our expedition were sunburned on lips and nostrils, something none of us had thought possible; as miraculous as the day it snowed in Swaziland and all the people came out of their huts and clapped and marvelled. This Kilimanjaro trip was my first big expeditionary success requiring organization. I have climbed that mountain in every decade of my life since.

Somewhere in the yellowing archives of the Foreign and Commonwealth Office at King Charles Street in Whitehall will be a letter sent from Swaziland or Rhodesia – typed, surprisingly, given the correspondent was only a schoolboy – and inquiring about prospects for a career in the colonial service. The inspiration for this letter was Sir Francis Loyd's Daimler, with a crown instead of a number-plate.

As a senior boy it was one of my duties to meet and greet famous people who came to unveil foundation stones, cut ribbons, open science blocks, present prizes or cheques, or just look at us. A series of these faced my adolescent attempts to be brilliant and respectful at the same time.

The King at least was spared an address and treated to an awkward bow. He arrived clothed – waist-up – in formal British black top-coat and hat, and in a leather skirt waist-down. He made a point of being an hour and a quarter late, and of speaking exclusively in Swazi through a halting interpreter whom he then continually interrupted, angrily correcting him in perfect English, to the huge delight of all the Swazi boys.

Contained within that performance is a difference between the African and European attitudes to leadership. A favourite (and apparently true) story about King Sobhuza related how he had been driving in the lowveld when he passed a Swazi tribesman hitchhiking in the heat of the day. He ordered his chauffeur to stop the Rolls, and held open the door, in a cloud of dust. The tribesman clambered in, delighted. The Rolls pulled off. 'Well?' said the King to his subject. Only now did the tribesman realize whom he had flagged down . . . and at this point the African tale parts company with its likely European equivalent, in which the King offers tea from a Thermos to his grateful subject, who then gives an interview to the *Daily Mail* declaring that the monarch is 'really down-to-earth' and a great bloke who wants to share the ordinary citizen's experience of life . . .

'Stop!' King Sobhuza shouted to his driver. 'You see who I am, now, don't you? Get out, you impertinent, brainless worm.' The tribesman was bundled out, bowing and grovelling and apologizing in his confusion and disgrace. The King laughed and drove on.

Swazis would tell you this story as illustrating what a splendid chap their monarch was, and how he loved practical jokes.

The King's attitude towards our school, which, now the territory's independence in 1968 loomed, was of growing importance to us, had always seemed ambivalent. A speech to us was scheduled. What, we wondered, would His Majesty say?

The King's speech as it unfolded seemed courteous but uncommitted. At the end, however, he ventured a personal remark. He had wished to visit us, he said, ever since he had seen boys wearing the school uniform in Mbabane; and in the words of the famous Swazi proverb 'When you have seen in the grass the body of the snake you become curious to see its head' – a remark whose exact purport baffled the audience and worried our headmaster.

In carefree mood King Sobhuza then decided to rename the school

'KaMhlaba', which apparently meant 'world', and which was ever thereafter suffixed to 'Waterford', double-barrelling us at a stroke.

Who knows what impression we made on King Sobhuza; he certainly made an impression on us, not least because of the behaviour of a retinue of Swazi men of different ages who arrived with him and stood apart from either the official party or the rest. When the King rose to speak – and before he could – they set up a great muttering and haranguing and exclaiming, in Swazi, into which the King broke, the noisy party falling immediately silent.

This was not a republican demonstration, it was what Swazi tradition demands before a monarch speaks: an excited babble of praise-poetry. For so great a figure to rise in silence before an unanimated audience would be thought as unpardonable as being given a slow hand-clap.

The experience stood me in good stead in 1999 at a banquet given by the Lord Mayor of London for the young King of Swaziland, Mswati III, Sobhuza's son. The Lord Mayor and his co-hosts looked momentarily panic-stricken to hear their distinguished guest treated to what looked like a noisy protest demo by a Swazi interloper in a leather coat. I passed around the whisper that all was well.

The day after the Lord Mayor's banquet the young King was an observer at the Commons and I wove the incident into a parliamentary sketch. Unfortunately *The Times* illustrated it with a photo of the Chief of the Zulus. Historically, the Swazis are in Swaziland to get away from the Zulus: the whole point of their separate territory.

But this lay three decades into the future for an acne-ravaged captain-of-school-elect, as he practised his bow to giggling school-mates, the night before.

I hope I didn't bow to Sir Harry Oppenheimer but it would not have been beyond me. I had practised my speech naked in the showers. On his visits our great school benefactor (and potentate of the De Beer diamond corporation) put up with my spotty face and egregious remarks more than once as I handed him the ceremonial key, or school history wrapped in a dust-jacket made from a Portland cement bag, as appropriate.

Poor Nadine Gordimer, the famous liberal South African writer, had to endure a welcoming speech in which, according to my brother, I said 'nay' – twice. I thought I was making a tremendous impression.

When, a quarter of a century later, she was in London to promote a
new book and *The Times* sent me to interview her she did not seem
to remember who I was. The tremendous impression had faded.

I startled the Governor. Or so one supposes, as he first saw me
bounding out of the bushes half way up the hill to stop his car, climb
in, and escort him to the place of official welcome. Sir Francis Loyd
was genial but of few words, and no doubt I gabbled away regardless
for I had planned our conversation – even practised some phrases –
and was determined to maintain at least my half of it.

But all the while I was admiring the car; more than the car, the
whole concept of being driven around the bad roads of a dusty country
in a shiny black chariot with a lion and a unicorn fluttering on a little
flag on the bonnet. Colonial government appeared to me to bring all
the attractions of good order, the rule of law, a proper regard for the
well-being of the masses and an efficient and uncorrupt administration,
without the messy and degrading business of having to seek support
from the mob. For reasons of my own I felt ambivalent about the
mob. I wrote to inquire about a job.

A polite reply from the Dependent Territories Department of the
FCO hinted without saying so that Britain's future as a great imperial
power, and mine within a great imperial power structure, might be
limited. I read the letter with disappointment, restless to widen my
horizons, and decided that one day I would try the diplomatic service.
At least I would then be able to travel.

An early chance came when the Boss decided to go on a fund-raising
trip to America and take with him two senior boys from the school,
one black and one white, as exhibits. Now captain of school, I was to
be the white exhibit, and my black companion a voluble and articulate
youth called Johnny Nchabeleng. Our headmaster's contacts in the
United States – and he seemed to know some influential people –
helped organize an itinerary for us and in the middle of the winter of
1968 we arrived in Boston in a blizzard, and at a smart reception
organized for us I drank my first whisky.

Johnny and I had to make short speeches, or answer questions, or
just be introduced to people, wherever we went. We visited and
stayed at an expensive boarding school, and were amazed at the deep
snow, waist-high, through which paths from the dormitories to
the teaching blocks were cut like canyons, and the stereophonic

headphones one of the American boys demonstrated, letting us listen to his rock record. These young men were East Coast aristocracy, I could sense that in the way they patronized us and in their politely blasé reaction to everything we told them. One of them in particular I remember fancying a quiet, authoritative youth. His name was Steve Forbes and he was about my age.

Somehow (it was Michael Stern's genius to swing these things) we were offered a meeting with Senator Robert Kennedy in New York. Only a short chat, handshake and autograph made a vivid and positive impression on me. Even at the time I realized there was nothing in this for him; he simply wished to be encouraging. Something – some kind of calibre and also goodwill – shone through. In Washington we were taken to more cocktail parties, and round Congress, so I had visited the American legislature before I ever saw my own. On return, the mud huts, green hills and wattle trees of Swaziland seemed even more of a backwater than before. My eyes had been widened.

First though there was the daunting business of passing exams, and getting into a good university – where? – and studying something there – what? – and persuading – how? – the British civil service to choose a colonial boy from an African school in Swaziland.

Michael Stern answered all these questions. Get first-rate A-levels and go to Cambridge, he said. That was where he had been. So I tried.

The night we celebrated the A-level results there were maybe half a dozen of us in the party. I had done well. My examination perform-ance had been helped by a literary critic, A. T. Lockwood, on whose commentary on D. H. Lawrence's *The Rainbow* I drew extensively in my answers, taking issue with him in what I think was a particularly cogent manner, and who did not exist.

The Boss took us out for a slap-up meal. Mbabane wasn't much: a town with two hotels, at one of which, the Swazi Inn, we celebrators dined. The Boss undertook to buy as much wine or beer as we asked for. I asked for too much of both. By the time we piled into his long-wheel-base white Land-Rover Safari to be driven home I was drunk for the first time in my life.

All at once, the challenging question of the meaning of life seemed to take on a particular urgency. 'I don't know,' I kept saying, noticing my words were slurring, 'I don't *know* I *don't* KNOW.' I sensed a feeling among fellow-passengers that I had made my point, but persisted.

Knowledge, I said, growing theatrical, was more like a rubbish heap than a jigsaw puzzle, and every year more things that didn't fit were piled on top. '*And I don't know,*' I declared for the last time.

After that I was sick.

4. Across Africa – Jamaica

Jeremy Thorpe was mocked for suggesting the British government should respond to Ian Smith's unilateral declaration of independence in 1965 by sending in the bombers, but he had a point.

If Harold Wilson thought his economic sanctions were a gesture of British support for white or black liberals in Southern Rhodesia, or for the stranded black government of neighbouring Zambia, he was wrong. They were a kick in the stomach. They hardened resistance, drove waverers into Smith's camp and polarized white opinion, reducing cornered liberals to an embarrassed remnant. The idiotic Foreign Office advice was that we should remain there, but how could my father sell British cables when Britain had imposed sanctions? How could you scour the supermarket for cornflakes sneaked in by sanctions-busters from South Africa and then declare over dinner that you hoped sanctions would bite? Smith's supporters called this treacherous and hypocritical, and it was hard to argue with them. Foreign Office fudges can look very clever in the elegantly balanced drafts borne by messengers down the marbled corridors of the old India Office at King Charles Street, but they create and bequeath the most murderous messes whose wrecked logic lives to stalk the decades that follow.

In the end most white liberals departed. Black moderates were left swinging in the wind, and whites who, like my family, stayed to stand our ground (as Wilson urged us to) found ourselves conscripted into the sanctions-breaking effort by the very fact of needing to eat, pay bills and fill the car with petrol.

Ingenuity was needed and the challenge was sometimes fun. Defiance and sanctions-dodging were exciting, but for all the thrill of that game Rhodesia was a sad place to go home to for holidays after 1965.

There was one big draw. My Morris Oxford. You could drive at sixteen in Rhodesia, and at sixteen Dad bought me an old car. Cars and engines interested me and Dad thought I might best learn mechanics by repairing and maintaining my own. We toured the showrooms until we found her: a 1958 model in the Traveller version, an estate car, £180. There were 69,000 miles on the clock.

'She's an elderly lady,' said the dealer.

The top-overhaul and new rings, the resprung springs, the endless polishing and the body-work repairs would bore you fast but they did not bore me. My Morris was a slightly later version of Dad's black Morris Oxford, KO12, in Nicosia. I loved that car, and in my final year at Waterford drove to Swaziland so I could keep her with me and walk up every day to see her parked near the staff block, and pick the bits of fallen wattle out of her sills, and polish her obsessively. Machines return affection to a degree of which humans are not capable. My Morris returned mine.

In Salisbury she was my best friend. Other friends – Trish Swift and her brother Don – were fun to mooch around with, and in their company I was beginning to grow up.

For our family as a whole, politics was unpicking many friendships, especially at the level of my parents' generation, because opposing Smith's government was simply antisocial to most whites: British sanctions had seen to that. Another baby brother, Mark, the sixth and last of us, had been born, while Mum kept up her increasingly be-leaguered efforts for African education, and carried on writing and recording children's stories for the (now renegade) Rhodesian Broad-casting Corporation, where the grip of Ian Smith's Rhodesian Front party was making her feel uncomfortable.

I would go with her there sometimes. One day we were down at the studios when Mum suggested I take a friend of hers, an African teenager not much older than I was, for a cup of coffee. He was a bright and friendly person with good English, we were both smartly dressed, so I suggested we went into a little café just opposite the RBC called the Flower Pot – very sixties, good coffee, and what passed for a bookish and bohemian atmosphere in the Salisbury of that era.

In my younger years in Southern Rhodesia before I went away to school there had been nothing like a universal or formal colour-bar in Salisbury and this café hardly seemed the sort of place to throw people out on racial grounds. My mother's friend and I sat down, ready to order.

A waitress came over and asked us to leave, explaining politely but quite unapologetically that the café was 'whites only'. We left quietly, covered in embarrassment.

The slightest of incidents. Its like must have occurred millions of times to innumerable people in millions of places. Heaven knows bigger racial injustices have occurred in history. But not in my history. I knew all about the politics of race, of course – we were in the thick of it – but nobody had ever asked *me* to quit a place for such reasons before. I've never quite accepted my mother's approach to right and wrong – that you just know – but this time I did just know. One could theorize about ideology until the cows came home, and pick holes in liberal optimism with great ease, and I did; but here was no debate, just an evident wrong.

When I hear friends on the intelligent right in Britain – friends like my fellow-journalist Bruce Anderson – affecting support for white supremacist government in Africa, I ask myself how they would have reacted to being asked to leave the Flower Pot, and feel sure they would have reacted like me.

It was one of those moments – like the 'whites only' waiting room in the freezing Breyten dawn – when a simple truth blasts its way through argument. I think the incident caused a small but critical readjustment in my approach to politics and for the first time I thought about getting involved. It's shaming that only when it happened to me did I wake up.

But now we were leaving. Sanctions had destroyed Dad's job selling cables. He and his company had successfully supplied the power lines for the great Kariba Dam project, and had been on the verge of signing a contract for the electrification of the entire Rhodesian railways system, when sanctions bit and the project was dropped. Gradually his job disappeared.

Before I left Waterford, BICC moved and promoted Dad again. He was to start and manage a new cable-making factory in Jamaica, and all the family were to move to Kingston. I was at school in Swaziland with a year to go when they left Rhodesia. It was as obvious in 1968 that they would depart by air as it had been obvious in 1958 that we would arrive by sea. Times had changed.

In 1969, school finished, I left Africa too. I decided to drive overland across the continent to Europe. We were leaving Africa in the lurch.

The idea of an overland trek appealed to my friend Trish too, and she asked to come. Then (as is her habit) she foisted upon me a friend none of us knew: could he come too? He did. Then my headmaster, Michael Stern, asked to join us (taking a few weeks' sabbatical from Waterford) and of course I agreed.

I busied myself with the preparations, visas, insurance and maps, but the truth is we started out with little idea how four people and all their luggage might travel north to Kenya in an ancient Morris estate car, and no idea at all of how we might continue north from there.

An irritating if only cosmetic problem with the car was that after ten years of African sun through the windscreen the heavy rubberized lip along the top of the dashboard was disintegrating. I had a five-foot python-skin and it occurred to me to cover the dashboard-top in this: the only Morris Oxford with a python-skin dashboard ever to hit the road. My vindscreen viper. All across Africa scales fell on to our laps.

Something terrible happened on our journey to Europe and in the glare of its recollection subsequent memories from the strange journey turn to ashes. Until this moment I have tried to avoid thinking of it and have never written a word down. Nor have I spoken about it, ever, to anyone; and an effort of will is needed now. It's a pitfall in autobiography that what we least want to talk about may matter.

Our journey had started well. In the heat the python-skin turned out to be incompletely cured but the pong was bearable. We reached Nairobi. Our hosts there were Waterford parents, a white couple. The father, formerly of the Kenya colonial police, now worked for a soda-pop manufacturer. Before independence he and his wife had been posted in a remote, up-country station during a particularly nasty period of killings by the Mau-Mau African nationalists, fighting for independence. The couple explained how much of this fighting had been inter-tribal, and many more Africans than Englishmen were murdered. Now the couple lived under the black rule which Mau-Mau had indirectly ushered in. It must have been a tough transition for them, but they seemed to have made it. They were kind hosts.

And we were grateful guests. The journey north had gone surprisingly easily as far as East Africa. Trish's friend was frankly odd, the Boss had been his usual maddeningly bossy self, and I was impatient to turn the page on this chapter of my life and begin the next, but we were all still friends, and so was my Morris Oxford.

After the general chaos of black African bush bureaucracy (post-colonial Africa was jettisoning all except the stupidest aspects of British administration), after the heat and dust of the Hell Run through Zambia, and after the hot hard slog which back-of-beyond 1960s Tanganyika presented any traveller, Nairobi seemed the sort of paradise it almost was.

The White Highlands had hardly started to fall apart in those days; the smart suburbs of Nairobi were cool, gracious and leafy, though strangely artificial: cut grass and cut-glass, singing birds and swimming-pools, a million miles from what most of Africa was and where Kenya was heading. The couple we were visiting had a long, shady ranch-style house, French windows giving out on to a huge lawn which sloped down to the flowering trees at the bottom of the garden. Our hostess, if no longer young, remained an elegant and commanding woman with fine herbaceous borders. The only intrusion upon her calm was what she saw as the slow-wittedness of the servant, Japheth, and the threat her pampered little snowy terrier posed to her neatly cut lawn edge.

We were sitting on this lawn one day in the cool of the late afternoon, drinking tea. The details imprinted themselves on my memory. Outdoor chairs and table were nicely arranged, the tea service was fine china, and there was even a little gingham tablecloth.

'Japheth,' called our hostess to her presumably and habitually uncomprehending house-servant, 'do hurry up with the sandwiches, or we shall *die* with frustration staring at the cake.'

She was in the middle of telling us about the Mau-Mau. I kept no note of her exact words but the drift is easy to reproduce.

It was a remote and lonely place, she explained, where her husband was stationed. As head of the police there he had complete responsibility for law and order in the district. 'You can imagine how impossible that was during the troubles. Blacks were killing each other all over the place. We were supposed to make every reasonable effort to identify the bodies.

'Snowy. *Snowy*. Leave those nasturtiums alone.

'There had been a particularly bloody battle away in the bush. News reached us of many deaths. My husband would take me with him when he went off into the bush – for company and to help, there were only the two of us – and because it seemed safer together, and we had not been married all that long; so the next day we set out together with a black sergeant in our short-wheelbase Land-Rover truck.

'Japheth! The *sandwiches*!

'When we got there everyone who could have given evidence had fled. Only the corpses were left . . .

'*Snowy* – not the marigolds either.

'. . . and they were beginning to rot.

'*Japheth*!

'Well, what we were supposed to do when we had a body was bring it back to the station for identification if possible, but it never was, and you ended up just taking fingerprints for the records. But there were half a dozen bodies and they were all over the place and there were only the three of us and I was expecting George at the time – or was it Adrian? – and anyway what was the point of carting decomposing corpses around the country? We could do the fingerprinting back at the station where we kept all the ink and special paper, but like fools we hadn't brought any of that with us . . .

'Snowy – *no*!

'So what to do? My husband always carried a bush knife, and the sergeant had his panga . . .

'Ah good, at *last* the sandwiches. Japheth just doesn't think in European time . . . they don't, these boys.

'So we set to work. It's a bit of a . . . mental effort at first, of course, and you know they're awfully difficult to get off, hands; you chop away, and still they hang on by bits of gristle on the wrist; but after the first hand you get into your stride and it's just a job like any other . . .

'Just put them down here, Japheth, that's it – no, the cucumber here, the ham there and the sandwich-spread separately. No egg and cress? Oh, Japheth, what am I to do with you? No, that will be all.

'And before we knew where we were we had half a dozen right hands, more or less neatly severed, *popped* into a bag. So much more sensible than humping all those bodies into the back, and me pregnant with Adrian – or was it . . .

'Oh *no*. Look how he's cut the cucumber. In great wedges. Might as well have put the whole cucumber between bits of bread. Thin slices, *thin* slices, how many times do I have to say it? I despair. They just don't listen you know. Snowy! Snowy? What's that dog up to now?'

We stayed longer in Nairobi than we had planned. The problem was the onward journey north. The Sahara had to be crossed, and could be, but getting into it looked impossible. Some kind of a war was going on, as usual, in the Sudan and the only other way into the north was to cross the Congo westward and then travel up through the Cameroons, Nigeria and Algeria. Nobody thought it sensible to try crossing the Congo in an ordinary saloon car; the tracks through the rainforest were said to be in a dreadful state. We hesitated and asked around.

In the end we did the sensible thing: drove down to the Indian Ocean to look for a cargo ship planning to round the Horn of Africa. We would skip the desert and hit the road again in northern Egypt, Jordan or Israel. But first a boat had to be found. We would begin inquiries in Mombasa.

All four of us and my Morris arrived at a pleasant, inexpensive beachside hotel some miles to the north of the heat and steam and stink of Mombasa. We were given individual beach-houses. In the morning we would drive into the old port where the shipping agents' offices were, to start the search for transport. That afternoon Trish and I would go off in search of mangrove swamps – something Trish had never seen.

We decided to take the car – not as yet unpacked; it still had the Boss's suitcase with all his belongings in it, and a briefcase full of papers and photographs from Waterford – and drive south on the coast road a few miles then strike down a track to the coast some way along from our hotel where the swamps were. You could see glimpses of this beach from the main road, but it could not be reached along the shore from our hotel.

Already in swimming briefs I didn't even bother with a shirt or shoes; Trish had a light summer dress and shoes. We drove the car as close as we could to the mangrove beach – a few hundred yards off, on a little hill above – then parked on the sandy track and walked. I picked my way barefoot over the broken coral. The mangroves were exciting and the sea was cool. It was almost sundown as we walked back.

I went ahead of Trish. As I breasted the hill I saw someone near the car: a big, tall young black man. He seemed to be breaking in. I shouted. He saw me and waved a knife. Hoping to give the impression I was the advance guard of a large party, I shouted back towards Trish, 'Come quick everyone, someone's breaking into the car.' She arrived. We both stood looking at him. He was quite unfazed. Perhaps he had been observing us. Neither thought it a good idea to run at him, he with a knife and I with no shoes.

'Let's go and fetch the others,' I shouted, hoping this would worry him. Trish and I ran back a little way down the hill as if to do so, and looked around to see if there were any way to run along the coast and fetch help, but there was not. We came back. He had gone. When we reached the car we saw Trish's handbag had gone too. The suitcase and briefcase were still there. Disconsolately we got into the car to return to the hotel.

It stuck in the sand. Wheels spun, digging deeper. We tried reversing out but it was no good. The more we rocked back and forth the deeper the wheels spun themselves in. We tried pushing too – one driving and one pushing – and putting clumps of grass under the wheels, but without success.

As we struggled a man came down the track: a big, hefty black man whom I half thought might be the robber: we were unsure. He inquired what was wrong and I explained. We asked if he could help us. Trish afterwards felt she had made the mistake of affecting girlish helplessness but I do not remember her using her femininity in any obvious way. He readily agreed to help push, allaying our suspicions about him.

We resumed our efforts, somehow the addition of a big man as strong as both of us put together – Trish is tiny and I was a weedy youth – seemed to make no difference. 'Watch out,' the black man said in broken English. 'This is a dangerous place. There are many *tsotsis* [thieves] here.' An African fisherman walked past with a basket on his head and our friend spoke to him. I assumed he was asking him to help with the car, but the fisherman hurried off.

It was getting dark. I decided we must abandon the car and suitcase and go back for help. The man said he would walk with us for our safety, and the three of us set out down the track back to the main road.

After a while the man said, 'Follow me down this side path. It is safer and faster. Too many *tsotsis* on the road.' Neither Trish nor I were at all sure this was wise; suspicion of this man began to return. Very, very stupidly, and lacking the local knowledge or confidence to act against his advice, we followed.

The path grew narrower and the bush thicker. The man turned on us and accused us angrily of being racists. Bewildered by this sudden change of mood we insisted in a still friendly way that he was wrong – even offered to show him some of the photographs of Waterford School in our briefcase, which I had brought along for safekeeping. He pulled out a knife, a big knife, from among his clothes. Though I was terrified, some presence of mind remained. Trish had shoes and could run; he and I were barefoot. 'Run for help, Trish,' I shouted. 'He can't chase us both.'

It was not a bad strategy. But Trish refused to run. 'I'm staying with you,' she said. She meant it too, and it was not a wrong response. But, barefoot I could not run. He bore down on me with the knife, grabbed me and held it to my throat. There was nothing Trish could do: it would have been crazy for her to try attacking him. He would have stabbed me or her. He tied my hands and then my legs together with black plastic from an old plastic bag, sometimes pushing the knife against my throat. I told Trish again to run but she would not. Holding the knife hard to my throat he tried to tie plastic across my mouth. I was petrified.

It would be easy for me, and it is tempting, to try to remember it differently, to reconstruct circumstances in which a man with a knife in one hand might be able to tie up another man despite the presence of a third person without the victim getting the knife; and maybe it can be done against resistance and maybe it can't. But the truth is he met no resistance. I was terrified into helplessness and had no will to struggle or try to use our potential advantage over him. Nor did Trish.

All the while he kept up an accusatory tirade about racists and racism. Then, rounding on Trish, he said to her: 'One trick and I will release you.' She knew what he meant. 'Don't look,' she said to me.

I didn't. It was silent and quick. Trish afterwards said she thought it was not exactly rape because she had 'agreed', but of course she had not agreed: she had simply been forced not to offer any physical resistance by the fear we would both be killed. When I did look, Trish was tied up too, and our assailant let us know that if we tried to leave he would see us and kill us. He then made off, back down the path we had come up.

We quickly got ourselves untied. It was by now dark. In our still abject terror we somehow believed he might be waiting for us or could see us, and we were afraid to go back down the path we had come up and along which he had returned, towards the isolated beach. I thought we might continue the other way but Trish was adamant she wanted to leave this path fast. I however had no shoes. She asked if I thought I could make it through the bush with her, barefoot. I agreed to try.

It was thorn-scrub and I was in nothing but briefs. I was soon badly cut and scratched but this did not seem to matter. The bush got thicker and thornier, it was pitch dark, and soon we were having to try climbing over the thorn-scrub, then when this failed trying to fight our way through with bare hands and arms. We could no longer see our way but I could hear a cement factory and knew it was near the main road, so we staggered towards the sound. Biting ants were everywhere. We were exhausted and wanted to rest but the moment we stopped they would swarm over us and begin to bite: the ants kept us going. I was bleeding.

Once I fell into a shallow pit and, being covered in bloody gashes and scratches by now, was at once swarmed upon by ants, biting me. It did seem a rather low point. But it was Trish I felt wretched about. Her ordeal had been earlier and of a different order.

Finally we made it to the road. We flagged down a truck. In the cab on the way back towards our hotel we agreed we would say nothing about the rape. Neither of us wanted anyone else to know.

The usual pointless police statements were taken later that night. We said we had been threatened, robbed and tied up, no more. The Boss helped dress my cuts and scratches. Next morning I found myself almost physically unable to return to the place where it had happened, but forced myself. The Boss's suitcase had gone from the car.

When we returned to the hotel his sympathy seemed to have switched to fury. He flew unprompted into a rage about his suitcase and blamed me for the loss. He started shouting about irresponsibility, and going on about the insurance, and what he had lost. I went for a walk by the sea as the sun set.

Not once in my life have I come seriously close to suicide, but that walk was the closest. I have never understood how any kind of practical problem, except perhaps pain, could make a man want to kill himself, but I understood then how shame could. I felt very, very ashamed.

Given the Boss did not know the worst of it, and I had been stupid to drive off to a lonely place without shoes and with his suitcase, his anger was explicable if harsh; but at the time – the root cause was probably remorse about Trish – I felt myself the victim of a monstrous injustice, resolved never to forgive him, and for the rest of that journey and many years to follow found it hard to. I'm sorry to say it was only when tragedy struck him, decades later – he had become an elderly father and his young wife died – that the last of the resentment really vanished.

And the feeling of shame? It has never gone. Over and again I have mentally rehearsed what I remember, and looked at it from every angle, and examined what has happened to others in comparable circumstances; and in my head I am now sure we did not react foolishly and I did not behave badly.

In my head. Not in my heart. This is odd because, though recounting this story now (as when we recounted parts of it at the time) I find it hard to explain plausibly why we were so passive, both Trish and I did understand. We understood so well that we never had to justify anything to each other though we knew our story sounded feeble. Apart from the idiocy of accompanying the man down a side path, I would not today advise anyone in comparable circumstances to act differently.

Yet I am unreconciled. My head says he was a big man with a knife, I could not run, Trish would not, she would not fight and I, though I would have tried, am a poor fighter. My head says people do resort to knives in Africa – very fast – and life would have been cheap to such a man. My head says the murder rate along the East African coast has always been high, and if we had split up one of us might have been killed; that if we'd tried to overpower him both of us might have been; if, if, if . . .

I know the arguments. I've comforted myself with them so many times. But at the end of the arguments a simple sum keeps coming back. There was one of him and there were two of us. A primitive truth also taunts me: I may only have been eighteen but I was the man and Trish was the woman and she was in some way my responsibility, and she was raped, and I was unhurt. I said to her afterwards I wished it had been me, and meant it, and not in any stupid camp way.

For as long as we stayed in that hotel, and because Trish said she wanted to be alone but was afraid someone might break into her bungalow, I slept outside her door for her.

Mombasa was where I had had my first birthday, on a Union Castle Line ship bound for the Suez canal and Southampton, when my parents were quitting South Africa. I could not remember that visit. This one I could not forget.

The Zim Line was an Israeli merchant shipping line. One of their vessels, sailing from Australia and bound for Eilat in the Gulf of Aqaba, was due at Dar es Salaam. We headed south down the coast for Dar and waited. The ship took a small complement of passengers but one had died at sea, leaving his widow to finish alone what had started as their retirement cruise. The mood among the group we joined was less than carefree.

So was ours. The Boss continued irascible, I was bitter and inward; of the three of us Trish stayed the most level. Except when she told me one day that she was definitely not pregnant, we did not discuss what had befallen her. We hardly have until I asked her recently what I might write.

We began arguing, she and I. I was struggling to contain, and did contain, a tremendous and quite involuntary urge to distance myself from everyone associated with the last few weeks of my life which had just passed. That included Trish – a feeling which could hardly have been more unjust but for which there is no point in apologizing as it simply overwhelmed me, and the imperative became not to let it show. I behaved correctly but was not the warm and comforting friend I should have been.

The Horn of Africa – cracked rocks, dry earth and baking mountains, trackless and uninhabited – had never looked more strange; the Red Sea had never felt more stifling; Djibouti had never seemed dirtier or more woebegone, the Gulf of Aqaba more forbiddingly biblical, the Israelis ruder or Eilat more crass, than they did to me that time.

The Sea of Galilee was exactly as I had supposed. Athens wasn't. I think I expected Socrates. I found a traffic jam of an intensity and violence of which a boy who has learned to drive on the left on the empty roads of central Africa in his mother's Morris Minor can have no inkling. I barely survived. The car was bearing up and so were we, but it was only on reaching Yugoslavia – it was now January – that the consequences of having a 'tropical' export-model Morris struck us with full force. We had no heater.

In midwinter, places such as Skopje and Split are cold. In a heaterless car whose doors and windows don't shut properly and whose wind-screen – on the inside – keeps freezing up with the shivering breath of the occupants, they are intolerable. This was a dismal contrast with the Africa we had left. But a python-skin dashboard, its putrefaction arrested by the intense cold, was a novelty in Split.

In Zagreb we stopped at a lonely and Soviet-looking public lava-tory, which both Trish and I made for. There were two signs, one above each entrance. One said something like 'Zhensky', and the other 'Musky'. We agreed 'Zhensky' sounded like 'Gents' so I took that door and Trish the other. We were simultaneously repelled from our chosen entrances, Trish by a yabbering man, and I by a yabbering woman.

Trish, born and brought up in Africa and new to Europe and men's lavatories, had never seen a urinal before and thought it was an ornamental waterfall designed in brutalist communist artistic manner.

Shivering, we reached England. There we split up, Trish to return to Rhodesia, the Boss to Swaziland, and me (for the Cambridge term did not begin until the autumn) to Jamaica to join my family. Some thirty years later I would stand among mourners, all white, at Michael Stern's funeral in Hampshire. He had been killed in his eighty-first year driving home from a weekend with me in Derbyshire, in my old constituency, in July 2002. I wrote his obituary for *The Times*.

But all that lay ahead. Nearly nineteen, I was returning to live at home for the first time since I had left on that night train on the Rhodesia Railways from Salisbury to Bulawayo, with the New Testa-ment my mother had packed in my suitcase on top of my new school uniform, and with tears in my eyes at her entreaty not to go sleepwalking for the lavatory, lest I fall on to the tracks.

I had been fourteen then. Almost everything had changed.

★

Maddeleina was agog. 'I saw them,' she said, 'I saw the John-crows.' Having no doubt she could not have seen them, nor any doubt she believed she had, I learned that day a lesson about miracles which has reassured me at wobbly moments ever since.

Maddeleina was our maid, a good woman and neither dim nor credulous. But when an astonishing rumour swept Kingston, Jamaica, almost entirely by word of mouth, she was one of thousands who wanted to see for herself.

John-crow is what Jamaicans call those huge black carrion crows you encounter everywhere in the tropics. The rumour was that three of these, almost man-sized, dressed in black tail-coats and top hats, speaking with upper-class English accents, and pushing a coffin on wheels, had set out on the main road from Montego Bay and were heading for Kingston. Maybe someone had misheard 'John-canoe' as 'John-crow'. John-canoes were humans – a kind of mummer.

Rumours of the John-crows' progress rumbled around the capital, until it was said their arrival in Kingston with their coffin was imminent. It was said that huge crowds had converged on the city centre downtown to witness their arrival. Maddeleina used her day's leave to catch the number 33 bus down from our house in Redhills overlooking Kingston. She departed in high anticipation.

She was not disappointed. The crowd had been enormous but she had managed to get a glimpse of the three John-crows and their coffin. They were just as everyone had said, top hats and all.

Maddeleina did not fabricate: we heard this from other sources too. Nor was there any pressure on her to report that the fabled birds had been real: a sceptical account would have found more favour. The excitement in her eyes and voice was real. Swept along by crowd hysteria she had persuaded her own senses she was seeing something which was not there. I never forgot the story, or what it teaches.

I never forgot another Jamaican crowd scene either: uglier, this. Coming from Old Harbour (my father's cable factory was there, and I was working for him), I drove into a flash-flood. A sudden downpour had left the main road cut by a big, muddy, angry torrent. It was still raining as I stopped the van short of the water and joined the crowds on the bank. Some, like me, were motorists waiting for the flood to subside, some were pedestrians; many had come just for the fun. The fun included a drowning dog.

The dog, a mangy-looking thing, had been caught in the current and dragged under, but was still fighting for its life. It came up, gasping for air. The crowd roared for its extinction. For a moment it seemed close to clambering on to a floating door. The crowd screamed with anger. The dog lost its footing and went back under. The crowd roared its pleasure. The dog came up one last time, its spine arched in impending rigor. The crowd went wild. By now it was being swept on down, soon lifeless. The crowd lost interest.

Linked in my imagination with this incident was the experience of watching films in Jamaican country cinemas. Audiences in smart uptown cinemas in Kingston were not unlike audiences anywhere in the sophisticated Western world, but in what in Jamaica we called 'the country parts' it was different. There, an audience yelled for whoever was winning a fight. The crowd would be excited by any violence – the greater the violence the higher the excitement – and, however cruel or unfair the fight, simply back the winner and bawl for blood.

This could produce bizarre dissonances between the film director's intentions and audience sympathies. With friends I went to watch *Wait Until Dark*, a psychological nail-biter in which a beautiful and vulnerable blind girl, played by Audrey Hepburn, is pursued through a house by a ruthless killer who can see. She tries to extinguish the lights and gain her advantage; he to get illumination back.

In the Jamaican cinema, the crowd were rooting for the killer throughout. When Hepburn turned the lights out, they hissed. When he got them back on again a huge cheer rocked the theatre.

Jamaica is an unhappy island, always was. Die-hard colonials (and many older Jamaicans too) will tell you it was independence which ruined what was once a Caribbean paradise, and it is true Jamaica has become a more unruly and dangerous place since 1962; parts of the country have become poorer; crime has worsened. But my family were there not so long after independence, and you could sense it then, and it is not a matter of politics. The troubled spirit of the island was rooted in place: envy and discontent breathed through the psyche of the island itself, through the trees and the wind and the water, through the spirit of its people. There were slave rebellions in Jamaica when other West Indian islands were tranquil; there were notorious excesses by plantation-owners, and violence between slaves as well as to them. There seemed to me (and this is no more than a hunch) more mental illness in Kingston than in any other city I know.

Is this some kind of revenge by the shade of the Arawaks, the island's warlike natives wiped out by European and African usurpers? Was the mix of West African tribesmen transported there as slaves a particularly volatile or troubled one? Was the island unlucky in the coincidence of a batch of unusually cruel British planters? Whatever the explanation I did not mistake the troubled spirit of the island's people today.

One of them I slept with, and I never even knew her name.

We – a young friend, David, and I – were in Negril, a long, beautiful beach at the extreme western point of Jamaica. In those days undeveloped, there was hardly a hotel but scattered beach-clubs, makeshift bars under the trees and straw shelters. Negril was a haunt for more adventurous pleasure-seekers, younger than the rich tourists who stayed on the north coast and in Montego Bay. There were Jamaicans too: some tourists themselves, some ganja-dealers (ganja was marijuana), and some just hanging around.

David and I had made our way from Kingston in a beat-up old Ford Escort with no clutch. It is tricky but possible to drive a car with no clutch.

After swimming we decided at sundown to join a small party beneath a thatched canopy on the beach. There was a nearby bar, and unlimited rum. Among our increasingly merry group was an American youth with a pony-tail, and a Jamaican woman in her early twenties. Of mixed race, she was pretty, flirtatious, and – increasingly – tipsy.

She seemed to have her eye on all of us. David eventually sloped away over the beach, blanket in hand, to sleep. Finally just she, the American boy and I were left. She fell into deep conversation with him. I decided to roll over on the sand and pull a blanket over myself. The sound of the waves on the nearby shore and the hushed low voices of boy and girl, lulled me to sleep.

I woke up – it must have been in the small hours of the morning – to the muffled sounds of two people making love. Opening an eye I saw the pair were lying on the sand beside me, under a blanket. A few quick, animal movements, and it was over. He rolled off her and was ready for sleep. She was not. She began kissing and caressing him, trying to arouse him again. He muttered he was tired, turned away and to all intents and purposes passed out.

She saw I had seen. Rolling over the sand towards me she put her hand under the blanket, and felt I was aroused. I lay still, neither resisting nor encouraging. Slipping down my trunks she tried pulling me on top of her.

I thought: No, this is not what I want. Then I thought: What the hell? Having never had sex with anyone I didn't much know what I was doing, but she did. I gritted my teeth. A few quick, animal movements, and it was over. Easy, really, and not unpleasant.

She wandered off in search of fresh prey. I walked quietly down to the sea and swam for a while, the water sparkling luminous around me.

There had been nothing to it. I doubt if I had proved this woman's greatest lover, but she will have had worse. I did not feel the overwhelming repulsion or disgust that afflicts some gay men when it comes to penetrating women.

The act was a mechanical one for which sentiment was not required. It was probably the sight of the American boy which had aroused me but, once aroused, the rest followed in a pattern which hardly seemed to involve me. I was left without any strong desire to do it again, or any particular disinclination to.

I was dimly conscious there are watersheds, and you really can go one way or the other. Though I could not choose to be a heterosexual, I saw I could choose to lead a heterosexual life. But the apartness of being gay had never seemed an unmitigated pain, and there was lonely pleasure in the thought that, though an invitation had been extended, I had declined to join the party. My rescuers from the home planet, if they ever came, would have been disappointed if I were to have gone wholly native on this one. But they would not have wanted it said I hadn't tried.

And my curiosity had been satisfied. 'Tried it once, didn't like it' runs the old joke, but the truth is I didn't specially dislike it either. I could take it or leave it.

I left it.

My mother had a particular friend in Kingston, a wealthy, middle-aged man whose special passion was the theatre and who every year produced and directed a Shakespeare play at the uptown theatre there. Paul Methuen designed gardens, sailed yachts, knew royalty, commuted often enough to England, and had been a friend of Noel Coward's when Sir Noel had lived on the north coast of the island.

Paul lived in a magnificent old plantation house, a wooden mansion, in Kingston. He was not a snob, he knew all kinds of people; his circle excluded no walk of life, but included the best people. His dinner parties were lively affairs for he was a bachelor and the society he kept was at the centre of his life. He was generous, witty and fun.

He produced me in *The Tempest* in which I played possibly the worst Florizel who ever trod the boards, the nadir of my performance being the love scene with Miranda in which I, a nineteen-year-old greenhorn, had to kiss a thirty-something divorcee passionately on the mouth. But though I worked with him, Paul and I did not get to know each other well and I recall no serious conversation, ever. So he will not have known it, but he became an example to me. Here was an ageing unmarried man who was neither sad nor lonely, leading a marvellous life. Paul seemed more sociable, better liked and less isolated than most of the married men I knew.

I could be like that one day, couldn't I? I saw that being somebody, doing things, knowing things, knowing people, going places, mattered. I saw too that, not for what it meant but for what it enabled, money helped. It occurred to me there were worse fates than to be a rich, old bachelor.

Jamaica was just one place among many where we lived. Quitting was not sad for me but leaving the island involved one wretched moment – leaving home. I had never conquered homesickness but until then there had been the comfort that, waiting for me back home, was my room. My room at home meant more than a reserved space, but the subliminal assurance that, wherever else I was, this – the school dorm, the tent, or ship, or youth hostel – was not it. I had a home and family, in a place to which I would sooner or later return. It mattered little where the place was: it existed and it was mine.

For no particularly logical reason, leaving Jamaica for Cambridge felt like giving up that pretence. No point, now, in keeping a place for me at 'home'. Home wasn't home any more, never would be again. After university a man sets up home for himself. Sadness took me quite by surprise, overwhelming me.

Yet I had been lucky. I had made a favourable impression on a generous man we met at a party in Kingston, who turned out to be the director of a shipping company which served Tate & Lyle's refinery at Silvertown in London. Hearing I was saving for my fare to go to Cambridge, he enlisted me as 'supernumerary' crew on one of his company's sugar-boats, bound (from the West Indies) for the Thames. I was to be paid a shilling.

Collecting all my belongings, my books and my LP records – even the Honda 50 scooter which I had once ridden for three days to Swaziland – I packed my trunks.

The departure was strange, dreamlike. My parents took me to a jetty at Milk River, a wide plain of sugar plantations and mills where pale green hills and flatlands of cane peter out along a formless coast into a muddy sea. Offshore, my ship was at anchor. It was dusk. A little launch carried me and my trunk away, and I clambered up a swinging ladder. It seemed unreal. Then our ship moved off and out into the ocean.

We sailed along the coast, passing Kingston at dead of night. I could see the dark outline of Blue Mountain towering behind, and all the stars and, at the mountain's feet the city lights twinkling. You could trace the streetlights climbing the hills behind the town. You could see Redhills. I thought I could make out the lights of our own house. My parents and family would be there. I could – as it seemed – see home, yet home was now so far away and departing for ever. I was helpless. A widening gulf of dark sea separated me from my youth.

Something more than distance was intervening. It was like looking in a photograph album, like watching through the thick round glass of an aeroplane window as friends wave goodbye from the airport terrace, themselves unable to see you: there they were, so loved, so familiar, yet beyond my reach, dwindling and fading. They didn't even know where I was. A wall of one-way glass had been interposed. Faces, people, move into another dimension. Thus it must seem to a ghost who revisits to say goodbye. That powerless feeling – I have felt it with friendships too – cut adrift and watching helpless as a slow current takes someone, or something, or somewhere, or part of you, away, is a melancholy thing.

And a lucky, lucky boy, with a place at Cambridge, a free passage to England, a loving family, every kind of security, a quick enough wit to live on, innumerable narrow escapes behind and many more ahead, sat in his quite ridiculously grand cabin, the 'owner's suite', and cried. I was at sea, and all at sea. I was to stay all at sea for longer than the voyage to England.

Which took three weeks. The ship's engines kept breaking down. In the August heat in a heaving and windless Atlantic, surrounded by whales, I discovered a loathing which I shall never shake off, for the stink of warm molasses.

5. Coming into the Cold

Late in an early autumn afternoon the boat from Milk River, Jamaica, entered the Thames estuary in a still, light, translucent mist. Banks and marshes, other ships, clouds and vapours drifted by to the throbbing of our huge diesel engines. I knew little of England and nothing of the Thames, and I could make little out beyond the blur of distant streetlights. There would be no one to meet me in London, no one to take leave of on this ship. A sad, soft, dreamy formlessness enveloped me.

We moored at Charlton buoys. Nobody bothered about immigration or customs and a small motor-boat took me ashore at Charlton – belongings to follow in the morning. It was raining. I would stay with my grandmother. Someone said you could get a bus. I stood in the dark and rain until the shape and sound of one of those old red double-decker buses I had seen in films loomed out of the shabbiness, the damp, dead orange streetlights, mean streets and cramped brick houses, which were beginning to form my idea of Britain.

It was September 1969. I sat alone on the top deck of the bus lurching through south-east London, wondering what Cambridge would be like. The last few years of my school life had been spent dreaming of this place. All my hopes had been invested there.

I had somehow got it into my head that the holy grail was over the water, somewhere elusive and exclusive and elitist: Cambridge. In the little round huts which served as some of our classrooms on our Swazi hillside, Michael Stern had spoken of the place in other-worldly tones. On this cultural mountaintop whose ascent it had become my teenage ambition to achieve, there must reside secrets, I decided, which once found would explain, release, unlock – and usher me into a new life. All this, Cambridge would do for me.

My boyhood and adolescence had been spent in conformist societies. Colonial life in Cyprus, the white settler culture of Southern Rhodesia, and a Swaziland boarding school old-fashioned in all save its multi-racialism, had left me aware these worlds could not be all;

that another must surely exist: a world of bold minds and independent lifestyles, a world I longed to know for myself. Where was this age of reason and liberty to be found? In England, surely, and above all at Cambridge.

These were, after all, the sixties. Everyone knew that at the surface level England was as swinging as anywhere got, but beneath the outrageous fashion, the mini-skirts, the long hair, pop music, drugs and the determination to shock, I imagined there must also be a deeper freedom.

Here I would meet the intellectual curiosity, the disregard of convention, the heady nonconformity which, because knowledge of such things had come through my parents, I assumed were common in the land of their birth. In England I would find myself. And Cambridge would be my natural home. My fellow-undergraduates at Clare College would be clever, certainly – perhaps cleverer than I was – but they would also be original: brave citizens of the new age which must have swept Europe even if it had yet to reach Swaziland.

In this mood of anticipation tinged with insecurity I set out with my suitcases from my grandmother's house in Beckenham, found my train at Liverpool Street, chose a compartment, and looked around. It was an old-fashioned carriage with closed compartments: green leather seats and dark wood. I got talking to the only other passenger there, a well-built, good-looking young man with fair hair, a year or two older. He seemed assured and experienced.

It turned out he was also on his way up to Cambridge, for his final year. He asked me all about myself and seemed most friendly and sympathetic. I confessed my nervousness about the new life starting, I thought, as we spoke; and told him how out of place I felt in the country which was really my native land, whose inhabitants looked, spoke and dressed as I did, and yet which seemed oddly cool and formal. I poured out the anxieties most undergraduates will feel on the first day, anxieties added to by feeling foreign.

To all this he listened in a kind and interested way, telling me also something about himself – he had just recovered from a serious bout of hepatitis. I believed I was making a friend. A good start, I thought, hoping it would all be like this at Cambridge.

Just before we pulled into that long, low, dismal, yellowbrick nowhereness miles from town which Cambridge calls its railway station, my new friend took a pen and paper and wrote out his name and college, asking in return for mine.

'There's a little group of us who meet quite often for coffee and biscuits,' he said. 'We're Christians, but don't worry: we don't sing hymns or handclap or anything like that.'

My heart sank. Women sometimes speak of their sense of insult on realizing the man who has been showing intelligent interest wants them only for their body. The evangelist wants you only for your soul. This is also insulting. I wonder whether Christians really understand how hateful are the kindnesses of those who would offer the same to any human being regardless of their apparent worth – and offer them because God wants them to rather than because they feel drawn especially to this individual?

In the end this fellow wanted us for our votes, too, for he turned out to be active in the university Labour Party, and decades later became an enthusiast for New Labour. I never contacted him. He visited me once, then gave up.

Bertrand Russell describes arriving at Cambridge as a new undergraduate excited at the prospect of meeting there the most brilliant young men of his generation. Though he soon had a circle of friends, however, none of them seemed to know the most brilliant young men of their generation. Where were these legendary creatures?

Then the answer dawned on him. He and his friends *were* the most brilliant young men of their generation. More modestly than Russell I would say that such self-confidence as I've ever managed to acquire has been based not so much on any conviction that I am clever as the suspicion that few others are either, and this I learned at Cambridge – for if the supermen were not here, where were they, and did they exist at all? Not at this university. Not anywhere then.

Cambridge, I found, was full of cliques. You could wear dressing-gowns till lunch and be rather fey; you could wear cravats and jackets with leather patches and go beagling and be rather hearty; you could get in with the rowing set and be rowdy. You could become a fearful egghead and spend all your time in the University Library and be perfectly dull or perfectly brilliant. You could join any one of many groups but if you joined no group you were as awkward and lonely as you might have been in Breyten.

There was a choral set, a college chapel set, a political set, a

God-squad set, a thespian set, and a let's-smash-up-the-Garden-House-Hotel-to-protest-against-the-Greek-Colonels set. And there was certainly a dope-smoking set, whose recreation was to freak out and listen to Bob Dylan or Joni Mitchell and tell each other that when you got out of this place you were going to smash the system, or work with the poor, or grow dope in Guatemala, or whatever.

It was even said there was a homosexual set who had their own group, or society, or something; or drank in the Still & Sugar Loaf on the market square, or cruised on a bleak expanse of grass called Parker's Piece . . . or something. For me it was always 'or something': a half-pictured world about which I did not quite like to inquire. The very thought of introducing myself to such people filled me with horror. It never occurred to me to find out more. I think I was afraid of being branded.

In that Cambridge offered a wider and more miscellaneous range of cliques than anywhere I had ever lived before, you could call the prospect liberating. But within each clique there appeared the uniforms and uniformity that go with cliques. Leaving one set of conventions, it seemed, you just joined another. Having thrown off school uniforms, we were looking for a uniform of a different kind.

I would fall in for a while with one group or another, attached – with varying degrees of indolence or passion – to some particular way of looking at the world; but I quickly found that my new friends never seemed much interested to hear anything except what confirmed them in their creed. They sought to distance themselves from what or where they came from, but they did not want to differentiate themselves from each other. They worshipped at the altar of the new – environmentalism, anti-racism, socialism, rowdyism, marijuana, lager or LSD – as slavishly as their parents might have worshipped at the altar of the Church of England. In the end, most of them would get married there. And these were the brilliant young men of my generation.

They would revert to type. In the meantime it was just fashion, all fashion, fashion, fashion, fashion. I hated fashion. These brilliant young men of my generation were going to be social workers, or radically reforming public servants, or aid-workers, or revolutionaries or something; and I knew none of them would. None did. Most ended up in Whitehall, conventional politics, the media, the professions or the City. They were all going to live alternative lifestyles and be freaky and free; and I knew none of them would. These brilliant young men of my generation were only briefly liberated and destined to return to their chains. One I remember – all long, greasy hair and radical opinions – finished as the groom at a Church of England wedding. You chuckle? I don't. Beliefs are not uniforms, to be worn for a while then discarded in favour of simpering Anglicanism.

An original in my college, James Lefanu, was a medical student. His head was a beehive of massed curls. Being freaky, however, did not imply being a new man, and James, returning from a party and spotting a stunning girl, called out, 'Hey hotpants!' in a wolf-whistling way. She turned out to be stunning in more than the metaphorical sense. She marched straight over the road and, with a single blow, laid James out in the gutter. He's the *Daily Telegraph*'s 'A doctor writes . . .' doctor now.

In the end I gained much and learned much from Cambridge, and in the end I was not lonely. But the three things I thought to find there in unfamiliar abundance – freedom, courage and originality – were missing. There were clever and ambitious people at Cambridge, few were original, few were brave, and we were, almost without exception, captive spirits.

Some students came round to visit me in my first week to tell me not to open a bank account with Barclays, because Barclays were involved in South Africa and of course no self-respecting undergraduate would want to be associated with that. I went straight out and opened my first account with Barclays. My motive was not support for apartheid, but perversity.

Out of similar perversity, and because there was something horribly, indefinably cool about public-school boys which set their clique apart, I fell in with a gang of mostly grammar-school boys at Clare. At least they weren't up their own arses. Our gang was led by my friend Martin Steibelt. Martin wore a Mickey Mouse costume to parties for fun; his girlfriend, Sally, wore a Minnie outfit when she came up for weekends. They held gnome-painting parties – bring your own paintbrush. We made the gnomes from plaster of Paris.

Martin studied chemistry, collected red plastic tomato-ketchup dispensers shaped like tomatoes for our corridor kitchen, and claimed to be writing a guide to Wimpy hamburger restaurants called *Eating Out in South London*. He designed and built an internal telephone system between rooms, linked by wires strung across the roof, and affected a particular dislike of God, trendy studenthood, lefties in Afghans, rich kids pretending to be cool and socialism. Our group was often joined by the studious David Cannadine, a sort of mascot and our pet swot, who had a wonderfully unfashionable Birmingham accent and became a famous historian. We wore our gowns to dinner in Hall (spurned by the smarter set) and sported suspiciously new straw boaters to go punting. We affected conservative attitudes to drugs, sex, politics and personal liberation.

And it was then I began to consider myself a Conservative. More than anything, I think, this was a reaction against what appeared to me the shallowness and progressive pretensions of my privileged generation in England. They wanted to be in an elite yet against elitism, unconventional but only in the same way as their friends, politically radical yet from the firm foundation of a prosperity and social order against which they liked to inveigh yet upon which they secretly depended and which, if we were not careful (I thought), could be damaged. And in the end they would all revert to type.

They have, every one of them.

In short, I thought the progressive left hypocritical. It was irritation, not conviction, which drove me into Conservatism. One joined *pour épater les chic*. I was hardly conscious of a positive Tory ideology beyond a certain limited belief in individual responsibility and a pretty strong confidence that as an economic system socialism must in the end destroy itself. The Tory Party itself was ghastly, and many of its members unspeakable; but it became mine.

I have never changed these views.

Nevertheless, I attended one mainstream meeting of each party, but the Liberals were obsessive and nerdish, Labour tribal and pack-minded, and the Tories snooty and dim.

I didn't like the Tories because I didn't like the people.

What put me off the Liberals, some of whom were sweet, was different: they had no appetite for power; for all its many and contradictory convictions, you could tell this was a cop-out party.

I had no serious thought of joining Labour anyway but even had I agreed with their ideology I would have been repelled by the organization: some of them were fine as individuals but when they assembled as a party a sort of dog-pack feeling suffused the group. They were deeply and incurably collectivist.

Active Tories at Cambridge were a dreadful shower, strutting careerists of distinctly mixed calibre, forever infighting, networking and elbowing their way through a scene which appeared more social than political. I never joined CUCA (the Conservative Association) though a rather slinkily plausible young man in a white polo-neck sweater called Keith Raffan, who now sits for the Liberal Democrats in the Scottish parliament, recruited me for PEST (Pressure for Economic and Social Toryism), a leftish sort of Tory grouping. I also joined the university Liberal Party.

But I never attended another party political meeting in all my time at Cambridge. I don't recall following national politics at all: Harold Wilson seemed contemptible and Edward Heath uninspiring. Heath was obsessed with the European Common Market, about which I felt ambiguous. Jeremy Thorpe was just an articulate and amusing card. One had the vague impression that, spurred on by the trade unions and a deadbeat business community, Britain was going down the drain, but needed to go down further before the nation woke up to its threatened fate.

So, apart from baiting the progressives at college meetings and pretending to be anti-environmental in order to nettle our Master, Sir Eric Ashby, Chairman of the Royal Commission on Pollution, I busied myself with other things. One of these was tending to lame ducks.

Ahmed was an Arab student I befriended in my first year. You would have described him then as a lonely and distrustful boy. By our second term he was hostile and suspicious. In our second year he was taken away to a mental asylum. He had become clinically paranoid. Trying to talk things through with Ahmed taught me lessons about the human capacity to see conspiracies which I carried with me into politics and journalism, and my own life too.

I remember him battering at my door in the night, shouting, 'Mr Matthews! Quick! It's killing me – come fast!' and seizing me by the arm and pulling me into his room. A distant porch-light shone through a hedge outside, just discernible through his tightly drawn curtains. 'Death-ray, Mr Matthews,' he said.

'Ahmed, that's not a death-ray. It's somebody's porch-light, shining through a hedge and your curtains.'

'Mr Matthews, *please listen*. If you wanted to kill a man secretly, would you make it *look* like a death-ray? Would you colour it blue and place it outside his window with big warnings written? – "DANGER! DEATH-RAY!" – no. You would make it look like something else – how you say? – "disguise". Camouflage. Make it so your friends would say, "Ahmed you are mad".'

Later he came to believe a conspiracy of Jewish dons was blocking his academic progress. Still later it was a conspiracy of black dons. Since there hardly were any black dons to be seen at Cambridge (of course there weren't, Mr Matthews, they were hiding), I gave up reasoning with him at this point, and not long after that they took him away. No doubt Ahmed concluded that the blacks and the Jews, having failed to kill him with the death-ray, had teamed up to put the word around that he was mad, and got him committed.

I thought of Ahmed years later as I listened to Tony Benn addressing a meeting in Battersea Town Hall in the early eighties. If it had not been for Ahmed I could have come under Mr Benn's spell: he was clever, funny, courteous, convinced and kind and I tremendously admired his willingness to give up an evening to talk to a hall full of angry and alienated nobodies who could do nothing for his own career. I wrote down what Mr Benn said and turned it into an article which I submitted to *The Times* – one of my first published:

'You read of different events in different parts of the world,' Benn told an audience of mostly young and mostly poor white and non-white people, 'and some of you think they are unrelated. A coal-miners' strike in one part of the country. Safety problems with a nuclear power plant in another. Cruise missiles in Berkshire. South Africa's President Botha at Chequers. Mrs Thatcher off soon to see President Reagan. *These things are all connected.*'

Calmly and in a rational voice, Mr Benn explained how nuclear power plants need uranium – from South Africa – and produce plutonium – for American nuclear weapons – and help the Tory government stockpile coal – to smash a miners' strike.

Benn's audience were hushed with wonder as he explained. Suddenly it was all so clear . . .

I remember thinking, as I watched Benn, of Ahmed's urgent rationality.

The young Arab was in my mind again in 2001 as a tiny Cessna bore me skyward over Hawaii. I was about to try a free-fall parachute jump, my first, and had been almost overcome with terror. In the moments before I jumped I managed to persuade myself this could be a plot to kill me, and a seamless theory of how that might be so had formed in my anxious mind. Utter madness, of course. I, however, was able to know this was paranoia, and hold on to my sanity. Poor Ahmed let go. I could not help him in the end.

I may have seemed a lame duck myself. A couple of English families were especially good to me, a rather lonely colonial boy.

Admiral Sir Alexander and Lady Bingley were the parents of my friend Lizza, a girl I had first met when she did Voluntary Service Overseas helping out at my school in Swaziland in the year I was head boy.

All the words I can think of for Lizza come out sounding wrong: 'good sport', 'jolly', 'clever,' 'capable', 'kindly' . . . an impression is given of a bouncy family Labrador, full of energy but safe to leave with the children. Lizza was all those things, but she also had a gentle intensity, an openness to other people, and real guts. She could talk to anyone, and, more important, she could get anyone talking to her because she really listened, as I so fitfully do. I remember her gouging herself – I forget where or with what – and being in terrible pain but managing to stay cheerful and make no fuss.

We had become friends at Waterford and stayed in touch. She and her parents asked me home for many happy weekends at their ancient and pretty home, Hoddesdon House, in Hertfordshire. The Admiral, a quietly impressive man, had retired. His wife, Juliet – outgoing, forceful, funny and a terrific organizer of things, people and charitable causes – made me welcome. They were not super-rich or snobbish; they were cultured and progressive, even left-leaning, in their opinions; but they were distinctly upper middle class. Through them, their friends and their house-parties I began to understand something of the English establishment and class system, the courtesies and rules of behaviour, the quietly observed distinctions, the subtleties and nuances.

These were not heard in barked commands or vicious judgements, but detected in the faintest grinding of the teeth, set of the mouth or working of the jaw. Elizabeth's twin brother William had a friend, I remember, who was not of their class, a bit of a lad, with a passion for customized cars. He was never spoken of unkindly and every effort was made to make him feel welcome at Hoddesdon House: but 'effort' is undoubtedly the word. He was killed in a crash.

The Bingleys had a couple living in an adjoining property who helped around the house and garden. I noticed the infinitely delicate way in which this couple were treated and described as friends of the family – and really were – but not in *quite* the way other friends of the family were friends of the family. Enormous care, however, was taken not to imply subservience. Likewise with the elderly of Hoddesdon, whom it was Lady Bingley's passion (and enormous labour) to help care for. They were known in the family as 'the oldies' and discussed as a sort of breed; we made jokes, always kind, about the oldies, one of our favourites being an oldy who insisted on referring to the incontinent laundry service she relied upon as the 'Intercontinental Laundry Service'.

There was nothing, I repeat, insensitive about the attitude at Hoddesdon House towards Lady Bingley's charges, and nor was Juliet some kind of amateur, do-gooding Lady Bountiful: this was much of her life's work and she had a professional command in the field of social and mental care-work. But still I sensed that the Hoddesdon oldies lived in another country, and not just because they were old.

Re-reading what I have written I see it is in danger of sounding oversensitive to the point of imagining attitudes which were hardly there. I can only say that that is how it seemed at the time to someone who had not been exposed to English life before. Possibly I misunderstood. Or possibly we become too much part of class distinction to notice how it pervades.

I remember the long caravanning holiday on which Elizabeth accompanied me and my family. My father loves caravanning and I had organized a trip around Scandinavia, up past the Arctic Circle, down into Leningrad and back. But however ambitious the itinerary, a caravan is a caravan and I could tell that the Bingleys thought the idea strange and that Lizza was making a telling sacrifice in summoning up enthusiasm for our mode of travel. Nobody had told me that the upper middle classes never caravan.

Lizza was keener on me than I think I was allowing myself to notice. I should have sorted it out. The trouble was, she was such good fun as a friend. When, later in my time at Cambridge, I invited her to be my guest at the Clare May Ball, and ended up drunk and dancing with the tent-pole of the marquee while Lizza stood quietly by, she perhaps began to accept what I think she had not allowed herself to notice. I had not consciously led her on but I had allowed it to happen. It was feeble of me.

My second foster-family was that of one of my best friends at Clare, Andrew Carver. He would invite me home for weekends in Shackleford, near Godalming, Surrey. Andrew's mother, Edith, was very different from Juliet Bingley. In class terms even grander, she seemed to me at first dauntingly conservative and reserved. Only on longer acquaintance did I realize how kind and constant and how capable she was. Edith Carver came in time to seem to me almost the model of the best of a certain type of upper-class Englishwoman. She reminded me of my idea of the Queen, and when, thirty years later, I met and talked to the Queen, the comparison held.

The Carvers and the Bingleys were my handle on English society. I liked the Carvers and the Bingleys but I was uneasy about the society into which I had been introduced and which I was beginning to move within. At the centre of my own anti-socialist universe were the ideas of effort and of merit, yet in the social stratum I was learning to explore – the heartland of non-socialist politics – there seemed to me only the most flickering relationship between merit and effort on the one hand, and reward on the other. The Carvers and the Bingleys were bookish and refined, but the class in which they moved was littered with well-born duds and philistines with cut-glass accents.

Most of Cambridge was middle class or grander; most of Cambridge was bright. If at first I had thought there was any natural link between these two, I was discovering that the same relationship did not apply in the England beyond my university. I was discovering that the key advantage a public school education gave a boy was a manner and a self-belief which shielded him from being found out too quickly. You often had to know an expensively educated Englishman for months, sometimes years, before you discovered he was thick. Fee-paying education was a sort of course in confidence-trickery.

Andrew's father was Chief of the General Staff and the family lived in a huge old Victorian rectory, with innumerable chimneys, long corridors and small rooms. Though cool and quite formal as a family they were good to me, including me in everything. They had a sort of *stature*, almost nobility.

I did once, however, detect human frailty. It was the family's habit to play croquet on one of their lawns. I learned to love the game and play it quite well. Liza Bingley was staying for the weekend too, and she and I teamed up against Andrew and his father. General Sir Michael Carver (as he then was) was proud of his technique and silently, fiercely competitive. Then came a disputed shot. The General insisted on his opinion, we on ours. Ready to climb down, as seemed best, I glanced at him. His eyes were brimming with tears. They were unmistakable. He was at the time on the verge of becoming chief of all three of our armed forces.

I was getting used to England. I was no longer lonely at Cambridge. People no longer seemed aloof as at first they had, and I have never since found my countrymen cold. Perhaps I was becoming cold too.

'Mr Matthew Parris from Clare College will make his maiden speech from the floor, in favour of the motion.' The pit at the bottom of my stomach gaped wide and deep. Ever since the debates I had organized and spoken in at school in Swaziland I had admired the Cambridge Union. Now it was time to take the plunge. I seem to recall the debate was about the class system, and I was against it. The rest is a dreadful blur from which only isolated moments start out at me in horrid clarity.

My plan had been to speak without notes. The speech would be short, confident and of astonishing lucidity. The force of this hitherto unknown young undergraduate's argument would take the Union by storm. Years from then, when I was – say – Prime Minister, biographers would note that even at my first Union debate I had astounded all who heard me by my poise and fluency. 'Parris spoke both from the intellect and the heart,' they would add, 'without a note.'

I was not confident such spontaneity would be possible without careful preparation. I would therefore write out my speech and learn it by heart, like a stage performance. A dozen or so beautifully crafted sentences – gems, I thought, each succeeding sentence following with impeccable logic from the sentence before it – were committed to memory and practised in my room. I had notified the chair of my intention to make a maiden, and received an invitation to a sherry party afterwards with the main speakers. It should be quite a thrill. These were the days when Arianna Stassinopoulos was making her way up the Union hierarchy towards the presidency, admired by many of the undergraduates for being Greek, and nothing to do with the hated Greek Colonels in temporary control of that country. That she was also rich was overlooked because she wasn't a fascist and she was beautiful. Tycoons in London sent helicopters to collect her for lunch. Undergraduates dubbed the hellenic heiress 'The Face That Lunched a Thousand Shits'.

I dressed smartly (as I thought) in the new grey houndstooth jacket I had had made at Ryder & Amies, but eschewed the cravat adopted by some of the more pretentious Union types. I should from the start make my name for simplicity of manner, dress, mind and prose.

The debate began. I tried to hear and take in the proposing and opposing speeches and their seconders, but a tremendous fit of nerves was beginning. In my stomach I felt the stirring not so much of butterflies as of giant fruit bats. Just remember the first sentence, I kept reminding myself, hold on to that in your mind. That will launch you. Once launched, the rest will flow.

After the principal speeches from the floor, the President called me. I walked noteless from my seat on to the floor, still parroting to myself that first sentence. I had indeed managed to hold on to it, and remember wading blindly in. The next thing I recall is realizing half way through this sentence that, though I could remember the second sentence too, a sort of mental blank had settled over the third.

Strange how in these life-and-death situations so much can flit across the mind so fast. You can have whole conversations with yourself, sometimes of a perfectly tangential nature, as the steam engine comes thundering down the track to which you are tied. Even as I spoke I thought, Now don't panic: if when you reach the end of the second sentence you still can't remember the third, then you can ad-lib, following the argument along, even if not in the prepared phrases.

But that was while I could still remember what my argument was. Somehow the very knowledge of how important it was to remember what I was trying to say – that now plan A was failing, the lifeline in plan B (to ad-lib) was the thread of the argument itself – caused some malign hand to cut the thread. I forgot my argument completely.

Why do we stymie ourselves in this way as though there were an enemy within? Why does the recognition of what would be the worst thing to say or do in the circumstances seem to prompt us to say or do it? It is like that weird urge when standing on the edge of a cliff, to jump.

Somewhere in the middle of the second sentence, I forgot not only the third, and not only the general drift of my own argument, but the subject of the debate itself. I could see my way to the coming full stop and everything else was a red mist. I wrestled with a rising panic, thinking, Only fear can stop you; quell the fear and enough wit will remain to make a passable speech – but as I wrestled, all else slipped away. Had anyone asked me my name at that moment I should probably have had a mental blank about that too.

The full stop seemed an age in coming. It approached like nemesis in slow motion, and the closer it approached the plainer it became that everything, *everything* had now fled my brain. Yet still that strange internal dialogue continued, as between a man and his mischievous alter ego. Should I go to the sherry party, I remember wondering, if all this collapses in disarray, as now looks likely? You would think a drowning man had better things to occupy his thoughts.

The sentence's end arrived, like the end of a life. In the pause that followed I had time to think, Just say something, *anything*, maybe that will break the lock. But when I opened my mouth no words would come out, none. My whole throat had tightened and I could not utter. I stood there, mouth agape like a goldfish.

How long I stood there I have no idea. Perhaps it was only twenty seconds or so. It seemed a quarter of an hour. People began to titter. Eventually the President suggested kindly that as I seemed to have wound up my remarks it would perhaps be a good idea to resume my seat. I slunk back miserably.

Gripped now by a mixture of shame and terrible pride, I reflected that to leave before the debate was over would be the final indignity so I would sweat it out. Nobody spoke to me, maybe out of embarrassment, and I sat silent in a sort of roaring internal confusion, staring at the benchback in front of me, until the end. Then, making a supreme effort, I went to the sherry party, of which I remember nothing except one kind, consolatory remark from the President, who reminded me that Disraeli's maiden speech had not been a great success either. I left as soon as my time there had been long enough for nobody to say of me that I had fled. Wild thoughts of going into seclusion to grow a beard, and not coming out until I was unrecognizable as the poor fool who had blanked at the Union, whirled through my brain.

I returned to my room, locked the door, and wept.

It would be nice to record that from this débâcle a great resolve to redeem myself was born, and that I returned to the Union to tough it out and try again. I didn't. I never spoke again at the Union – or not as an undergraduate. I did not make another platform speech for eight years.

Rarely since then have I ever spoken in public without experiencing at least once in mid-speech a flashback to the Cambridge Union, followed by the thought What if it happens again – now?, followed as often as not by the tiniest mental blank in which I whisper a get-thee-behind-me to the internal satan who has just reminded me he has not gone, but is just biding his time.

One morning I awoke late, weak winter sunshine filtering through the net curtains of the mean yellowbrick terraced house in which, in my second year, it was my fate to lodge. I had a thumping headache. Was this a hangover? I could remember nothing about the night before.

It was after 10 a.m. I had missed the morning's first philosophy lecture – Dr Lewy, I seem to recall, on logic: the crabbed old man in a mildewed gown with a middle-European accent and a biting tongue, the don who in an early lecture had glared at a goofy-looking boy in the front row, asked his name, and then offered as an illustration of an 'if/then' sequence, 'If Henry gets a first class pass in his Part One examinations, then I'll eat my hat.' Henry never came to lectures again. I heard later that Dr Lewy was secretly kind.

I hated logic. It was not what I had supposed philosophy to be about when I chose philosophy for my degree, but at Cambridge a sort of desiccated analysis ruled the fashionable approach. Ethics, which interested me most, was regarded as a subject properly in the province of French literature, but which had by some mischance strayed into the philosophy syllabus and must therefore be glancingly acknowledged as a peripheral irritant to our chosen discipline. At the centre of this discipline was a mission to scrutinize and understand the workings of our own brains and language. Mathematical logic and philosophy of mind ruled the roost.

To me the whole thing seemed so circular as to be virtually watertight, impacting hardly at all upon the world outside. Challenged on the relevance of so dry an approach to the questions real life poses, my tutors would protest that until we understand how we understand we could not hope to understand anything else.

I remained sceptical. I heard one professor drawl boastfully to an undergraduate audience that surely in everyday life one never encountered serious moral dilemmas, did one? The best and most redeeming mental anguish occurred in libraries – not shops, the battlefield or the factory floor. In all practical matters, ethical perplexity concerned mere facts rather than values, did it not? Students around me chuckled admiringly at the shocking boldness of the assertion.

I thought it crap. I thought it plain wrong. I thought it seriously degenerate. I thought it a silly, adolescent remark. The man needed a smack in the mouth. What kind of a pygmy-life could this fellow have led if moral choices had never baffled him? They baffled me all the time. I was puzzled at a body of scholarship in which intensity and effrontery of approach should be so admired when confined within books, yet have no consequences for life as we live it, where shabby tweed and a timid conventionality were the order of the day.

Our senior philosophy don at Clare and my director of studies, T. J. Smiley, was an acknowledged genius in his field: logic. Elizabeth Anscombe, the renowned Wittgensteinian scholar, was lecturing at the university and vastly respected – almost mobbed – for her insight. But both Anscombe and Smiley were Catholics. Catholicism is super- stition: this much was obvious to me. It did not therefore seem to me that the rigour of Anscombe's and Smiley's respective academic analyses could have leaked out much into their worldly lives. Here were two virtuous people who were unquestionably cleverer than I would ever be. My best friend, Andrew Carver, was unquestion- ably so. But Andrew was casting around unsure what to do, and Smiley and Anscombe were praying to the Virgin Mary. So maybe there was hope for me in the world, maybe I could, after all, get a grip.

Anyway, cutting that logic lecture was no loss. But the headache was getting worse. From my pre-war single bed I stared around the over-furnished small rented room on the first floor of a house inhabited by our elderly, lonely, kindly, tidy, nosey landlady, Mrs Fuller, and one other student, Jon Satow, who, like all Jons at that time, was remorselessly sensitive, listened to Joni Mitchell LPs all day and irritated Mrs Fuller by being too unfocused to maintain sustained conversation with her about the Second World War and lolling around in the house's only bathroom too long. Always an ingratiating youth I was Mrs Fuller's favourite. But the truth was I didn't like it there.

The ghastly green-striped Regency wallpaper seemed to throb.

Then a disgusting smell entered my nostrils. Vomit. For some reason I glanced across at the nasty glass-and-veneer display-cabinet near my bed, stacked with dozens of silly little cheap glass goblets, ornate, in assorted sizes. Except they were missing.

And it all came back: the staggering home, the feeling ill, the realization that Mrs Fuller was in the bathroom for her weekly bath which always took ages . . . I shut my eyes. Let the next bit be a dream; let this not be true. I opened them again. It was.

Beside my bed I had arranged all the goblets in ascending order of size, from the merest thimble on the far left to a fair-sized wineglass on the right, in a neat line. Then I had filled each – right up to the brim and almost brimming over – with urine. It was amazing how I had achieved this, for there seemed to be nothing spilt. Aim, judgement and concentration must have been minute. Finally, I had opened my fat Hospers's *Introduction to Philosophical Analysis* at page 100, laid it neatly open, square to the line of piss-filled goblets on the carpet, and been sick on it, right in the middle.

The arrangement was impressive, druidical in its geometry. It was a gesture of pure hate. I did recall filling the goblets, but the finishing flourish with Hospers took me by surprise. Some other Matthew had done this last night, but this morning's Matthew, though not responsible, understood and endorsed what he had done. I was not happy in my studies.

The vomit marked a turning point. In my stupor I had sent a message to myself calculated to be beyond ignoring. Cleaning up, I resolved to take heed. A lower second class pass in the preliminary exams at the end of my first year was to be followed (as it turned out) by an upper second in my Part One examination at the end of year two, but I did not want to carry on. At Cambridge you can switch disciplines between your Parts One and Two if they dovetail, and philosophy and law did dovetail. I decided to switch to law for my final year.

This was a good decision. Anyone with half a brain can understand English law. You just have to learn a few hundred landmark cases, many of them of a sensational nature involving women making love to Alsatian dogs and midgets being squashed by frightened elephants at a circus, and demonstrate a reasonable ability to extract from them the principles on which they have been decided. Like my father, who learned law late in life as part of his business career, took to it immediately, excelled at it, and secretly (I think) wanted me to become a lawyer, I am quick at distinguishing between the facts and the principles of a case. It is one thing at which I've found myself quicker than most of my peers. I can see before others where the logic of a decision leads, how this is related (or opposed) to other decisions, and how the reasoning could be extended into new cases with different facts. Thus one can anticipate trends and conflicts in public policy, and identify what are likely to be seen as precedents, thin ends of wedges – so the ability is useful. I cannot think why I find legal reasoning so easy, yet calculus so hard.

I cruised easily through my law course, not even needing to work much. Caught short of having studied much of my Smith and Hogan textbook, *Criminal Law*, as the Finals approached, I adopted the high-risk strategy of studying only half of it. Half was theft and the (then) new Theft Act; the other half was murder, rape, other sexual offences, assault and bodily harm. Theft was boring. I settled for the rest. In the Criminal Law paper which followed one had to choose five questions from about twelve, and just five of these did not involve theft. I was lucky.

Tort was easy, Contract an intellectual delight, International Law a great opportunity to waffle thoughtfully, and Jurisprudence (the philosophy of law) was to me gripping. The exams seemed to go well.

So when I jostled my way among hundreds of anxious undergraduates into the yard in front of the Senate House where the results had just been posted, and found the board on which the Law Finals were pinned, and searched ambitiously for my name among the Upper Seconds, and couldn't see it, and, lowering my eyes and expectations, scanned the Lower Seconds, and still couldn't see my name, and gulped, and steeled myself, and searched the Thirds with still no mention of my name, and walked around the court twice to settle my nerves and face the possibility I had failed, and, returning for a sneak glance, saw my name among the Firsts, it was in the immediate a fantastic surprise, but in an underlying way, not.

My director of studies and Tort tutor, Bob Hepple, who is as I write Master of Clare, congratulated me, but with a note of reserve in his voice. His favourite scholar, I think, had been a decent, clever, clean-cut youth from Canada called Paul Pearlman, and Dr Hepple had predicted a first for him. Paul got an upper second. 'The examiners,' Dr Hepple told me mournfully, 'must have found your ignorance refreshing.'

A don called Tony Weir gave me the news I had won the George Long prize for Jurisprudence. The prize was not enormous – £200 – but to be awarded it was an honour. Jan Christiaan Smuts, a former South African Prime Minister and hero of mine, had won it in his day. Then Dr Weir summoned me back and said the examiners had withdrawn the prize because it was expressly intended for someone in his third year of law and I was only in my first. Did I wish to appeal against that decision?

Grateful at what seemed undeserved success in the exams as a whole, I thought it might seem ungrateful to expect more. 'No,' I replied, 'let it drop.' Dr Weir looked doubtful, but I felt thankful to have a first, and we let the George Long prize go.

Years after, I regretted that. I have no ambition to collect honorary degrees: on accepting one later ('Sean Bean and some other local celebrities were yesterday awarded . . .' was the paragraph in the *Sheffield Star*) I found that these are meant well, but unreal. But I am still vexed by the loss of that one prize I really did deserve and so nearly won.

I could have been a decent academic jurisprude. I had, you see, an idea. I got it from my father. You may prefer to skip from here to the end of this section because what you may find a tedious rant follows, but I would let myself down if in this book I never mentioned one of the few clear, strong beliefs which has guided the way I think about human governance and which has made me – in so many ways a natural liberal – a philosophical conservative. At the centre of my creed is the concept of certainty.

I could have developed it as a don. I might have succeeded academically, not least because there has been so little competition in modern times. Practising English lawyers and even judges – great minds in practical ways – have for the most part a tenuous grasp of the skein of philosophical strands on which their disciplines dance. Formal English jurisprudence over the last half century has been weak.

I could have made some impact in the field. English judges and legislators (it is one of their strengths) seldom let ethical theory block their path: not because moral reasoning is a negligible force in legal decisions – it is powerful – but because it is primitive: those who fashion the law in England are usually content to let 'common sense' – the unexamined jumble of sentiments, instincts and prejudices we call popular morality – be their guide. Academic jurisprudence then becomes a matter of explaining to those who practise law where (logically) they're heading, where they've come from, where clashes and confusions are likely to arise, and why.

Still I could have tried to lay bare, and by exposing reinforce, one of the philosophical sinews beneath the surface of human regulation: the great human need for certainty. Let me explain.

In our relationships and dealings with other people we set much store by what we call consistency and what we call trust. You need to know where you are with somebody, and that he will not change with the wind. So far as those he must live and work with are concerned, consistency in an individual's nature is as much of a virtue as virtue itself.

It is the same with the law, or should be. First – and last – we need to know where we stand. As a conservative jurisprude I believe almost passionately in certainty: it is half the law's purpose. In an age in which 'natural justice' has become fashionable – no doubt as a reaction against a callous devotion to the letter rather than the spirit of law – the pendulum has swung too far that way.

The trouble with natural justice is that opinions about what it might dictate differ, and can change. Stick to the letter of the law and you cleave at least to what anyone can look up and read for himself in black and white. Resolve to alter or reinterpret statute and precedent as little and as infrequently as possible, and you minimize the occasions on which people will be confused about their rights and duties.

Try to guess the spirit of the law and your guess may conflict with that of others. I prefer certainty: the imperative that a citizen should know his position under the law and be able with confidence to predict what legal consequences will flow from whatever course of action he may contemplate. Deprive a citizen of certainty and you have taken away as important a right as any we may have to 'natural justice': you have infringed his right to understand how and where the law will protect him, and to know how others' arrangements will bear upon his, and his upon theirs.

Observe the training of small children or of animals, and you will see how from the start the individual craves consistency from his master, and is unsettled by its lack. Look at the strained, anxious face of a small child whose life has lacked security, unsure from where the blows will come. It may or may not be cruel to hit a child, but it is always cruel to hit him when he does not understand why, or how he can avoid being hit again.

Life for the small as well as the great is a sort of navigation. One man's natural justice is another man's shipwrecked confidence in his own bearings under the law. The ancient dispute as to which – equity or certainty – should trump the other, can be resolved. Equity trumps; but uncertainty is the greatest inequity of all. Partly because there have for some time been few great lawgivers to articulate this with any resonance, the claims of certainty have been rather overlooked in legal and political philosophy.

That is not so in economics, where the fight against inflation is driven by an appreciation of the need for certainty. We know that for markets and for individuals, uncertainty depresses business. This is the best argument for a single market, a single currency or a stable exchange-rate mechanism. Economists understand this well, lawgivers less so: sight of it has been lost in our headlong pursuit of natural justice and our increasing squeamishness about handing down hard decisions in hard cases. Whenever judges do so, the modern political and journalistic itch to call for a change is strong. So a great truth has gathered dust. It needs polishing.

To restore it to former brightness could have political consequences. I should have liked to try. I really am a Conservative; and Conservatism can after all be more than an irritable dislike of socialism, more than an affair of the spleen.

It might have been amusing to spend a life on the banks of

the Cam, harping on about the importance of certainty in public administration . . . But already you are bored. Anyway, luck led me elsewhere.

Being, then and now, a thin man, I was always interesting to plump girls. They appeared to find my scrawny build and buck teeth strangely attractive. This attention was not returned. But as men know, women are not much discouraged when a man takes no notice of the notice they take: in fact rather the opposite. And I have never understood the popular belief that the male of the species is the natural predator; experience points the other way. My experience at Cambridge certainly did.

First there was a girl called Eve. Alas I was no Adam. I had some good women friends but was forever distracted by my anxiety to stay friends without sending out any signal capable of being misread. My room-mate, Martin, would mischievously encourage every misreading possible. With a knowing smile he would give women friends information of my whereabouts and likely times of arrival. Most of these women will have had no amorous interest in me whatsoever – for all I know Eve had none – but Martin enjoyed stirring, and I was forever being ambushed.

One morning Eve arrived at nine. Martin (who was up and making tea) knew very well I was still asleep, but welcomed Eve warmly, told her I was pottering about in my bedroom and would be furious to have missed her, led her to my door, opened it and ushered her in.

As I did not wear pyjamas I was trapped. I had to make a show of light conversation from my bed. Meanwhile, Martin had hared down the corridor and fetched a few of our male friends, urgently informing them that here was one for the books: there was a woman in Matthew's bedroom – and before breakfast too. He encouraged them to come and listen at the door, to verify from the voices that this was so.

Martin told everyone in the college about it. That was probably helpful as, though uninvolved in national politics or political parties, I had thrown myself into student politics and done well, being elected secretary of our Junior Common Room after mounting a campaign based on a combination of humour and detachment from all ideological groupings: I was an early prototype of Pim Fortuyn: a right-of-centre maverick independent with outrageous opinions. I chose a few amiable and good-looking duffers as my henchmen, engineered a separation between ourselves (I renamed us the Clare College Students' Association) and the left-leaning university students' union, and managed to make a clearer separation from the college sports-clubs fraternity too, who were forever trying to corner an unfair share of funds for their endless playing fields, clubhouses, accoutrements, crockery-smashing dinners and booze. I wrote the CCSA's constitution, carefully entrenching the mass membership's position against ambushes by the left, who tended to be the only students to turn up at meetings.

I got myself a position in journalism, too: circulation and business manager of *Broadsheet*, a university-wide arts and entertainment magazine. The editor and his deputy were to the political left, but, being uninterested in the calamitous finances it was my job to sort out, left me to pursue an independent commercial policy. I recruited a team of subscription-salesmen to whom I offered incentives. Above a certain level of sales the salesman was allowed to keep up to half his takings. We more than doubled the circulation; advertising revenues improved.

Sales of subscriptions were boosted by an innovative approach I devised and implemented until we were warned it was called 'inertia-selling' and illegal. On the expiry of each annual subscription the subscriber was informed we would assume a renewal unless informed otherwise. When my team called later for payment, most just paid up.

. . . But we were talking of Eve. In the end Eve gave up, but was replaced by Maggie. This Maggie, after my African nannie the second of three big Maggies in my life, was a blithe, spirited and attractively rounded mathematician. But she was indefatigable in the chase.

Martin's and my rooms were on a staircase in a high loft looking out over the seventeenth-century roofs of Old Court at Clare. We were at the end – a dead end – of a long corridor whose floor would give a bit under the weight of those who walked along it. The bigger the visitor, the earlier the warning, and we could know as much as thirty seconds or so in advance of the arrival of the heavier sort of visitor. This was the case with Maggie.

One winter's afternoon at around tea-time my senses, ever alert, detected from that vibration the approach of a substantial woman. It was Maggie, we guessed, on another of her prowls. This one was not unexpected, as on the previous foray she had left a bag behind so we knew she would be calling sooner or later to collect it. 'Hah!' said Martin brutally. 'Your little friend I think.'

I panicked. There was no way out but back up the corridor she was coming down, running past her; there was nowhere in our sitting room to hide. My bedroom was back up the corridor too; a closed door to Martin's, which adjoined our sitting room, might have aroused her suspicions because he never closed his door. I eyed the window. It was a dormer window, giving straight on to the roof. The roof was not so steep as to deny me a safe foothold.

Maggie was on the last stretch of corridor. Thump, thump, thump.

Looking back on the episode what came next appears crazy, but I tore open the windows and, scuttled out on to the roof. I heard Martin closing them behind me as the knock on the door announced the arrival of Maggie. I heard him lock the window-catches. Bastard. I lay flat beside the dormer so I could not be seen. It was freezing out there and I was shoeless in only jeans and T-shirt. 'Oh hello, Maggie' – Martin's muffled voice was just audible through the roof-tiles – 'come for your bag? Matthew's just slipped out but he'd never forgive me if I let you go. Stay and have a cup of tea. Maybe he'll come back.' Then he gave her toast, too.

She stayed for the better part of an hour before giving up. Desperately, as the cold bit, I rehearsed in my mind possible airy explanatory greetings one might attempt while entering through the window from the roof, but none carried conviction. I could hide but I couldn't run.

Finally I heard the latch being undone. Teeth chattering I crashed back in through the window, cursing the cackling Martin as Maggie departed down the corridor. Thump, thump, thump.

A longer story and a sadder one was of my friendship with Lizza. Lizza just drifted away, or more likely I did.

Some years ago I was swimming with a friend off a beach in Venezuela. Up to my neck in water, I was suddenly aware of a strong current. Digging my toes in the sand, I could just resist it. My friend Rona was swimming some yards away, laughing. When I looked next, she was much further out to sea, trying to swim back, her laugh faltering. Every time I looked she was further, still facing me, still swimming, as it seemed, towards me. I let the current move me her way, but kept my toes dragging in the sand. Still the distance between us grew. She began to panic.

Although we both survived there is something nightmarish in the recollection. Facing one another, making for one another, we were being separated by something we could not see. That awful sense of invisible tide, the feeling of being swept, of watching, helpless, an onlooker to one's own drift. So it was with Lizza and me.

The truth is I was in a mess about girls and sex and cannot now think why a boy of my intelligence who was anything but indecisive and not always cowardly, should ever have got himself into the mess or shrunk from the choices which surely faced me.

It wasn't that I didn't know what I was: I had no doubt. It wasn't that I was tormented by moral or religious doubt: I knew Christian and Judaic attitudes to homosexuality were sheer superstition and was quite untroubled by others' silly moral attitudes to sex. It wasn't that I lacked the imagination to picture a coming world in which there might be a place for openly gay men: I knew gay men who were having not too bad a time in the existing world.

I could reason it all through, and did. I think I just lacked the guts to do anything practical about it for *myself*. It was an almost physical cowardice.

It is true I had set my heart on the Foreign Office and there really was a problem about being openly gay in the diplomatic service: I remember worrying about this. But what seemed to elude me was the obvious recourse which gay men had chosen through the ages: to cheat. I should have cheerfully sought clandestine sex, if only to experiment and see whether it was good enough to persist with. Instead I lay around drinking instant coffee and fantasizing along the lines of E.M. Forster's truly dreadful novel *Maurice* that someone would somehow climb up a ladder through my window, or that I would find true love with another student in exactly the same position as me. It should have occurred to me to ask how, if solo rumination over the Nescafé was the limit of our efforts, he and I were ever going to locate each other.

So I just looked.

There was, for instance, the winsome Steve Green, a pale, lanky youth with long black hair and a toothy grin, who came from the West Midlands, drank too much, seemed lonely and defiant, and possessed (among other marks of his rebellious sense of humour) a three-wheeler car, a Reliant Robin. Steve played the trumpet, and used (after partying) to punt down the River Cam along the backs of the colleges in the small hours of the morning during exam weeks, trumpeting awake other undergraduates who were awaiting important exams. After another party once, he went tearing up and down his staircase in his underpants. I liked Steve, and used to wonder . . . But I banished the thought, which was purely fanciful and encouraged by nothing I knew about him; and never did get to know him well.

A quarter of a century later our paths crossed again. I had just been sent for review a book by an ardent Christian anti-homosexuality campaigner and activist. The dust jacket described the author, S. E. Green, as a roofing contractor in South London, married with children. I thought it a ridiculous book, full of fatuous biblical quotations and offensive allegations about Aids.

Its author and I were both invited to join a television panel discussion. Yes, it was Steve, minus Reliant Robin but now with a beard. I couldn't help remembering him in his underpants. I couldn't help still feeling fond of him. We didn't talk about the old days. Steve maybe saw them as a time when he went off the rails. He thought he was back on the rails now. I thought he had gone off them.

There was an American student, a postgraduate. He seemed friendly and invited himself for a glass of apricot brandy. Over his second glass he suddenly blurted out that he was gay, and liked me.

I dropped – literally dropped – my glass of apricot brandy, in shock. He fled in the confusion. We never met again.

His action had been brave; my reaction was mean in its failure to respond, but caused by panic. I have tried to piece together what must have been my feelings, or presumed feelings, about homosexuality, for I never wrote anything down or discussed things, and if I talked to myself I cannot remember what either of us said.

I do remember thinking all sex absurd, no kind of human sexuality morally better or worse than any other, and my own inclinations (which I did acknowledge) not wrong but just a huge nuisance and likely career-embarrassment. With the Foreign Office in mind, I remember resolving to be celibate and thinking this would present no insuperable difficulty.

These conclusions seem to me now to have been stupid, unpercep-tive, unrealistic and – worst of all – cowardly. They were also an act of insensitivity and unkindness towards myself: it was a harsh way to treat myself and may explain the harsh view I took of others. I cannot justify the idiocy, and regret the missed opportunities; but nor can I hate myself or feel truly ashamed, for it was me and it came from the heart – what I had of a heart. Failure of nerve, betrayal or straight miscalculation are what cause me most to hang my head. This was none of those. It was a foolish notion by an ambitious young man that willpower alone could blast me through; and it was also a great physical shyness about sex.

At some time – in my final year, I think, but the unconscious mind has made a determined effort to blank this episode into a half-remembered dream – I went to see someone about being gay. She was some kind of social-medical worker in the town, to whom I had been referred (I assume) by the college chaplain or perhaps by my moral tutor, Dr Santer, now Bishop of Birmingham, though I cannot imagine approaching either don on such a subject. Her address was given me (I can remember that) and I walked into her consulting room and sat down.

Then I began to cry. That's all I can remember. I cannot remember what I said, or anything she said, except that she referred me to a psychiatrist in St John's Wood in London, and said the National Health Service would pay my train fare to visit him.

I was supposed to go regularly, nobody said why. The psychiatrist had a long, greasy white pony-tail and, beyond the instruction to talk to a gay undergraduate, not a clue, I think, what he was for. He certainly failed to communicate it to me. He just kept asking questions, stupid questions, such as Was I reluctant to go to sleep at night? He encouraged me to talk about myself but I had said I found other men attractive and beyond that I didn't see the point. He never offered any sort of action plan or even suggested what, for me, the optimal outcome of our sessions together might be. At no point did he indicate whether the object of these sessions was to stop me being gay or to make me better at it. My scepticism about the science of psychiatry grew.

Yet there I go – attacking *him*. How pathetically I was funking a perfectly manageable challenge even as I joined the confident elite of my generation. The realization checks me often in my habit of judging others as timid or berating them for being feeble. Many labour under greater difficulties than ever beset me. I know that.

I also know they need a bloody good kick. I did. I wish someone had given it me. I didn't need a psychiatrist. I needed a Gay Guide to London.

My futile visits to the man in St John's Wood soon ceased. I stopped turning up. I suppose it's all in some NHS archive somewhere. Presumably not an archive to which British intelligence had access. For while I had been sent to see a woman in one part of Cambridge, I had been separately (and by a different don) directed to see a man in another. He was an intelligence agent. I had it in mind to become a spy.

Anyone who has read those cheap thrillers in which Oxbridge dons with links to MI5 or 6 nudge likely lads in the direction of British intelligence, and thought, 'It can't really be like that' – is wrong. It is like that. I should not publish the name of the don at Clare who had advised and arranged my first interview, but I must assume this was the don of spy novels, sniffing out young talent for British intelligence. He had suggested a chat; and after the chat, in which he had warned me I must not expect spying to be all about sleeping with beautiful blonde women, suggested I go for another chat with a man from London who had installed himself temporarily in a room somewhere in Cambridge.

This chat too went fine. This man too warned me not to suppose spying was all about sleeping with beautiful blonde women, and suggested another chat. This chat was to be more formal: an appointment at another address, in Carlton House Terrace, near Buckingham Palace in London.

I went down by train to Liverpool Street and took the Underground, somehow fearful I might be being watched. On reaching Carlton House Terrace I rang the bell outside an unmarked door and a plummy young lady let me in and brought me my train fare in cash, coins and all, on a silver tray.

Another interview ensued, in which it was explained that spying was not about sleeping with beautiful blonde women. I said I was glad of that, but my interviewer missed the irony.

They offered me a job, conditional on my passing the preliminary general examinations for the civil service later that year, and upon a final interview still to come. And they wanted me to go ahead in the ordinary way with an application to join the Foreign Office.

Some would argue that my interest in being a spy was more compelling evidence of insanity than my visit to the counsellor to talk about being gay. There I was: twenty-one and in the running to be a spy while bursting into tears in counselling and being referred for psychiatric treatment in Hampstead. Few twentieth-century quips are better known than Groucho Marx's remark that he would not wish to join the sort of club which would accept people like him. I was to conclude that if our national security is guaranteed by a secret service which would offer employment as a spy to people like me, nobody should sleep easily in his bed. Twenty-five years ago they were scraping the barrel. God knows who was accepting these jobs.

For the spy novels are wrong in one respect. They suggest that the British intelligence talent scouts at Oxbridge scoop up the brightest and best, clever young men and women, possessed too of all the easy social graces: the kind who can slip unobtrusively into a wide range of social situations. Whatever talents I may possess, slipping unobtrusively into social situations was never one of them. I couldn't slip unobtrusively into a warm bath.

Undeterred, however, the people at Carlton House Terrace asked me to proceed with the ordinary civil service examinations. This suited me fine. My plan was to see whether either side or both offered me a job, and only then to decide.

I passed the civil service examinations. The next test was the Civil Service Selection Board. I cleared that hurdle too, but from Carlton House Terrace had gathered (though this was not said) that had I failed, this would not necessarily have been the end of the road as far as intelligence was concerned. I even wonder if they might have preferred me to fail, so the non-spook option would have been removed from me. This may have been a misapprehension, but if I am right then it was easier in 1972, not harder, to get into intelligence than into the regular civil service.

I had offered character referees: my tutor and Liz Bingley. Elizabeth's name came up when I was asked to report to another secret address in central London for a final interview. This took place at an oak table before an array of distinguished and mostly elderly gentlemen chaired by a retired military officer with such an unusual name that it could not possibly have been an alias. With much embarrassed clearing of the throat I was assured by this gentleman that all present were men of the world, and that there were a number of awkward questions, some of a personal nature – hoops, if you like – through which we would all have to go. He was apologetic about that.

He began with the first. 'I don't mind telling you,' he said, confidingly, 'that I have drunk too much on occasions. Others around this table may have drunk too much on occasions. You may have drunk too much on occasions. We do not need to know that.' But (more clearing of the throat) was I an alcoholic? If so, I would have to tell them. I said no. We moved to drugs.

'I'm a man of the world,' the chairman repeated, 'I read the *Daily Telegraph*. I know students experiment with drugs. You may have experimented with drugs. You may know people who have smoked marijuana. It may have been smoked in your presence. You may have smoked it yourself. We do not need to know that. But if you were addicted to any hard drug, you would have to say so now.' I assured him I was not.

With more clearing of throats, I was asked, most apologetically, about my character referee: Miss Bingley. 'Is she, er, a *friend*?'

My brain went laser-like to the likely purpose of this line of questioning. I stabbed him with a manly *glance*. 'A *good* friend,' I replied, giving the committee a knowing look. They smiled indulgently. 'A *very* good friend,' I said. They looked pleased. 'A very good friend *indeed*, sir.' I said, as significantly as I could. Relieved faces beamed at me from around the table. There were no further questions on this subject. Shortly afterwards, I was offered the job.

I turned it down. On reflection it struck me I was too unreliable to be a spy. I am not discreet, not self-effacing, not patient, not heterosexual and besides, there was, as Mrs Thatcher would have put it and probably has, 'something not quite right about that boy'. It's a matter for relief that I had noticed my unsuitability for British intelligence. It's a matter for concern that British intelligence never did.

Instead, I chose the regular diplomatic service.

The FCO were recruiting about a dozen graduate trainees every year to their administrative grade – a sort of fast track to the senior levels of the service. I was selected for the grade and place for which I had applied: administrative trainee. Such appointments were in short supply and hard to get. Yet I was still unsettled. I persuaded the Foreign Office to defer my entry for two years. I had turned down MI6 who had asked me nevertheless to keep in touch, which I did.

I chose America, as one of the Mellon Fellows sent to Yale by my college each year. Arriving in Chicago to visit some friends I purchased a beat-up old Ford pick-up for $150, five of whose six cylinders were still firing, and painted it bright green with some household enamel. The rust holes in the driver's door were so big that things would fall out en route. In this way I reached the town of New Haven, Connecticut, and was shown to my room. And there on the doormat was a letter endorsing me – a character reference from Sir Eric Ashby, the Master of Clare. The envelope should have been addressed to the Master of my new college, Berkeley, at Yale. By secretarial error it had been addressed to its subject.

. . . intellectually highly competent, but not, I would say, brilliant, Parris has been very active in student politics here at Clare. Small, and sensitive, and dedicated to the financial reform of the amalgamated sports clubs, Parris is altogether just the kind of young man we are delighted to be able to send to America.

My room was on the mock-Gothic third floor of a mock-Gothic tower-like block in a mock-Gothic campus near the middle of the town. I hate mock-Gothic. I liked Yale.

I liked America. I liked Americans. New England academia is hardly typical of the nation but wherever else I went too, in my vivid green Ford truck with rust holes, I found an easy rapport. I do not think we and the Americans are quite as different as it is our habit to suggest. I agree very much with Anthony Trollope who in his autobiography advised fellow-Englishmen that, whatever picture we might care to entertain of Americans, we should never suppose they are stupid.

Still, it was good to have a little band of Englishmen to hang around with, and the Mellon Fellows, of whom there were four, formed the nucleus of mine. Peter Clegg was an architect; Nigel Whittaker was a law student who lived in a single room with a huge Frigidaire painted in violent blue matt wall-paint, his girlfriend Joyce, his rock drums and very little else.

Then there was the fourth Mellon, Peter Ackroyd. Anything but the famous flushed and portly novelist and historian of London and Dickens that Peter is now, he was thin, pale and moustached. Then as now his voice was almost indistiguishable from Michael Heseltine's but then you could just hear (what is now quite submerged) a trace of London in his accent, and he sometimes spoke of his Cockney mother. Then as now he was brisk to the point of brusqueness, unaccommodating, severe in his judgements and unsentimental. He was also outrageous. I had never met anyone before who could so carelessly offend the proprieties or so unapologetically pursue pleasure, and I admired and envied him enormously, and traipsed along behind.

With his boyfriend Brian – a big, handsome, gentle, quietly spoken ballet dancer from the Bronx – Peter moved in the company of a weird assortment of literary wannabes, bohemian eccentrics and appalling tarts. Some sniffed cocaine, some sang, some danced, some were boastfully promiscuous, some seemed to do nothing at all – and everybody drank. It was very 'anything goes'. Andy Warhol used to come to their parties, though I don't think I quite understood who he was or why this was remarkable. Or was it David Hockney? One would see these weird or wacky people and know that some of them were famous, and others would be, and half of them were drunk and the other half stoned, and nobody seemed to give a damn. For me it was heady stuff.

We would go for tea, Peter's crowd, and move on to bourbon. Sometimes they came to my room. Peter spilt whisky on my ribcord bedcover and wrote a haiku about it, widely admired. Quickly bored and often drunk he would behave in an astonishingly offensive manner to people – such as the wife of the Master of his own college, Saybrook – whom one might have thought it unwise to offend. He laughed at her huge hats. He didn't care. He would make arrangements to join people and then simply not turn up. He didn't bother with excuses. Peter was horribly honest, in his way.

He would talk for hours about his ideas on philosophy, none of which I ever understood – and still don't. I just assumed he must be too clever for me – still do. He assumed so too – still does.

'D'you know your problem?' he once announced to me, loudly but in a straightforward way at a well-attended afternoon drinking session. 'No talent, darling.' Though I had by then achieved little success in life I did not think this a fair judgement. Now I have, I suspect he might be right.

Peter was pretty free in his diagnoses of my problems. 'D'you know what's wrong with you?' he announced, more than once. I said I didn't. 'You're a virgin.' Amid the laughter I reflected that, at least in Peter's sense, that was true.

And 'D'you know your problem?' he would repeat often, fixing me with that destructive twinkling stare. 'You find everything terribly *difficult*, don't you? You find being a person such a strain. You look strained already though you're only twenty-three. I think on your tombstone I shall arrange to have engraved Here lies Spider Woman. A *Difficult* Life. RIP.'

'Spider Woman' was Peter's name for me. It derived from an episode when, having drunk too much – I was drinking rather heavily at that time – I managed to lock myself out of my room after showering, and, with only a towel around my midriff, climbed out of the window of the student whose room was next to mine on the third floor, and spidered my way around the side of the building, clinging to the stonework. The towel fell off half way. Those walking below were amazed. I was particularly thin then.

Not that the abuse was wholly one-sided. There was one story with which it was possible to embarrass Peter. He and Brian once kept a dog in their room in Saybrook. It was their habit to take themselves off to New York for indeterminate periods. One Friday, they left the room locked, with the dog still in it, expecting to return soon. As it happened, they did not return for more than a week.

Peter says he arranged with a neighbour for the dog to be fed, but something went wrong. In any event, the dog starved – to death, according to one account, though others say it was rescued. In its desperate search for nourishment the dog appeared to have tried to eat most of the contents of the room, and chewed some of Peter and Brian's Beatles LPs. From then on, whenever we played *Revolver*, we had to remember, every few tracks, to stop and lift the needle over a track (I think it was 'Eleanor Rigby') which the dying dog's toothmarks had made unplayable.

I did tease Peter back. His habit was to insult senior members of the university, especially when drunk. A tea, given the previous year by the Mellon Fellows for the masters and (as they were called) masteresses of all our colleges, had been memorably wrecked when Peter had again started to deride the wife of one of the masters of one of our colleges. Peter claimed she was the woman on whom Edward Albee had based the female monster in *Who's Afraid of Virginia Woolf?*

I was determined that this year's tea, which it fell to me to arrange and hold in my own room at Berkeley, would not break up as that one had, in tears. But I was equally determined that all the Mellon Fellows should attend, and would not contemplate the obvious solution, that Ackroyd stay away (something he would anyway do, if he pleased). So I bought a bottle of cheap Scotch and placed it discreetly but visibly on the top of a wall cupboard by the window. 'Peter,' I said to him, before the other guests arrived, 'that bottle of Scotch says you're going to behave this afternoon. If you do, you can take it.'

He proved the soul of charm and tact throughout the occasion, even complimenting Mrs Henning loudly and without obvious irony, on her hat. From time to time his eye would stray cupboardwards. I let him take the whisky before he went.

He has not changed. A few years ago, after an evening with him at a West End restaurant (we were guests of the *Times* editor and his wife) he grabbed me by the arm in the street outside. 'Let's go somewhere. Anywhere. Some club or pub or something.' I pointed out it was nearly midnight, and I was going home to the East End.

'Ah,' he said, 'the White Swan then. That's convenient for you.' It was; and, this being Wednesday, it was Mr Amateur Strip Night at the White Swan. We grabbed a taxi.

Peter was not entirely sober when he arrived. Within half an hour he was not at all sober. He threw his jacket aside, lost it, and took on a predatory look. When an on-stage contestant began to dance and take his clothes off, Peter lurched at the stage, unbuttoning his own shirt. I begged him to desist. Soon the shirt was off and, not long after, trampled underfoot, for the pub was packed. But with the help of a couple of friends I did dissuade him from entering the competition – as a wild look in his eye seemed to suggest he had it in mind to do. One glance at his large fluffy torso suggested he was unlikely to have won. Body hair is out of fashion in gay circles. And he hardly needed the £100 prize money.

Confined now to the spectators, Peter was lunging about in only his trousers and eyeing people he did not know in too fixed a way. I feared for him and told him so. 'Spider Woman, you always were such a spoilsport,' he complained. He was now trying to dance. 'I'm having a marvellous time, go home, darling.'

I offered to hail and pay for a taxi for him but, indicating that the night was young (it was not) he declined. Eventually I gave up and went home, leaving this great, pale ball of none-too-sober fluff heaving shirtless around the floor, knocking over drinks. I felt guilty abandoning him.

At about seven in the morning my telephone rang. 'Hello? Spider Woman? It's Peter here, darling. I just rang to make sure you got home safely. I was worried about you. You were drunk.'

There was a woman at Yale who was haunting me at that time. Jane Hammersley came from Idaho, where her family grew potatoes. She was the sort of nice, unpretentious mid-western girl of whom there were few at Yale: quite unlike the girls who hung around with Peter's crowd. Jane tied her pony-tails up with coloured wool. It was my Englishness rather than me I think she really worshipped. Small offerings of tea-bags wrapped in crêpe and tied with ribbon were placed outside my door, as to a minor god.

One day she persuaded me to go to a college dance. I drank too much. She pulled me on to the dance floor. In a sudden and uncharacteristic display of anger, or possibly despair, I broke free, kicking her inadvertently in the shins, said, 'No, I'm going to talk to my friends,' and walked off. It was a nasty thing to do and I worried about it afterwards. I felt ashamed – not least because I was liked in my college – the most popular I had ever been anywhere.

This was the time of Watergate when Richard Nixon was on the ropes. Many were the arguments in Rudi's Restaurant in which I would stick confidently to my line that Nixon would survive; something few of my American friends took, as I did, for granted. I was making the mistake of bringing a British perspective to US politics. Some sort of a cover-up, however partial, would have been arranged if Nixon had been a British Prime Minister and he would have limped on. I simply had not reckoned with the American habit of pushing things to conclusions and I bet a friend $100 this President would survive.

I didn't bother with academic work at Yale and never took my degree. International Relations – the subject in which I had chosen to do an MA – was in the grip of quantitative analysis. People measured with rulers how many column inches had appeared in newspapers on an issue such as (for example) East–West cooperation, and how many inches on East–West non-cooperation; this was supposed to be a way of measuring levels of amity and of hostility. It was obviously absurd.

But at that time everyone in political science in America (having perhaps seen the word 'science' in their discipline's name and thought it might have something to do with science) was beavering away to show that important truths could be learned about politics through feeding data about the news into computers and establishing 'correlations'. Five minutes' reflection was sufficient to conclude this was unlikely to be the case: Yale graduate school looked set to spend five decades reaching the same conclusion. I left them to it.

Without the benefit of quantitative analysis I had learned an important truth: that academics, even very clever ones, fall easily into the grip of orthodoxies, become the slaves to fashion, and are spectacularly craven about speaking out against ruling nostrums.

There was one, and only one, moment of relief from a frustration which led to my downing tools academically. At a point of head-banging rage against quantitative analysis and all the pretentious waffle that went with it, I took a calendar – Phil's Barber's Shop Calendar, a simple wall-chart listing days and dates, circulated free at Yale – and wrote a book review of it, done in the house style of the university's political science people. Parodying the postgraduate essays one was supposed to write (*aperçu* was a favourite term at the time) I praised Phil's *aperçus* into the relationship between Monday and Tuesday, and his perceptive observation that, for instance, Sundays occurred with notable regularity, every seven days. I also commented on the subtle but important difference between Friday and Saturday – a difference which empirical if anecdotal evidence suggested was sufficient to make the whole of Congress pack its bags and go fishing.

I showed my review to the one spirit among the dons at Yale who seemed kindred: a mellow and sceptical don from the Southern States, Professor Fesler, rather older than the young thrusters among his colleagues and pleasantly detached. He had it published in an American quarterly magazine: my first published work, and a piece of political satire. I owe that man a lot.

I had begun some long-distance running and regularly went out road-training with a small group of American undergraduate friends. I even entered the Boston Marathon, having never run more than five miles, and finished – in four and a quarter hours. I started going often to the Payne-Whitney Gymnasium, a huge and marvellous building with a quarter-mile lap indoor running track and acres of steaming communal showers in which I could gaze longingly at what, for some stupid reason, I had decided was for ever out of bounds. MI6, surely, must be watching me? Crazy, but I genuinely believed they might. Even the smell of the Payne-Whitney Gym became a kind of addiction: the smell, and the squeak–squeak of my running shoes on the red shiny floor as I went endlessly round the quarter-mile lap. I would train there for hours, timing my laps. I got my mile time down to five minutes and two seconds: very good, for me. Finally I broke five, just once, alone – something I would never do again.

In the evenings I drank. Usually with friends, often in Rudi's Restaurant, sometimes with Peter's crowd, who tolerated this alleged virgin who wouldn't talk about sex but seemed to want to hang around with them. Then, feeling guilty before bed as my head spun, I would force myself to have long cold showers, even in winter, motivated by some mad idea the punishment would sober me.

I tried marijuana (which I had spurned at Cambridge) but it didn't do much for a non-smoker beyond causing coughing fits. I tried cocaine, which was good, but not as good as bourbon and much more expensive. Cocaine gave me a mildly and pleasantly aggressive, confident feeling – geed me up. But really I didn't need geeing up; as Peter kept reminding me, I needed geeing down.

I tried LSD. Someone gave me two little tabs of blotting paper, and said, 'Eat one.' I ate it. After ten minutes I felt nothing so I ate the other. Beginning to feel a bit odd, I decided on a walk. It was one of those beautiful, clear, sub-zero New England winter days: cloudless blue sky, yellow sun and still air. I walked down well-kept, wealthy avenues lined with bare trees to a little hill at the end of the town, at the foot of which was a small lake. We used to run there, and up the hill, training, but today I walked and lingered.

Something strange was happening to my senses. It was as if everything in this scene, nature itself, was going sharp and hard and cold, sharp enough to cut, hard and cold enough to make my soft flesh and messy humanity an untidy intrusion into a crystalline celestial world parallel to our own squelchy universe. If I reached out and touched that bare twig it might cut my fingers with its hardness. The sun hit the cold lake and shattered, streaming back in a shower of bright chips that looked to me like the cascade of sparks that pours from an oxy-acetylene lamp slicing steel. I wanted goggles to protect me from all this sharp brightness.

I turned to walk home. As I walked, I kept hearing my name called. These were real sounds – street-greetings between friends, walkers' conversations – but in them I kept hearing my own name. I knew very well this must be the effect of the drug, and so made myself ignore it, dismiss it as the mild paranoia it was.

Then I saw a tramp on a bench. He was filthy, ragged, swigging from a bottle. I felt an urge to kill him. When I say 'urge' I do not mean I had to restrain myself: I knew immediately that the very idea was absurd and there was no way I would have indulged it. But it was there: a hatred of this dirt like a hatred of excrement or vermin. He was a blot, a stain, a soiling of an otherwise pristine scene. I had not the least wish to hurt him – just a wish to rub him out, remove him, as painlessly as you like and without mess, from a picture he was spoiling. I winced and moved on. I had seen the roots of Nazism.

I made my way alone up the stairs to my room where there was a mirror. Staring out of this mirror was the face of a devil. It was my face, but with the impishness turned grotesque; the crows'-feet radiated from my eyes like a spider-web, and my eyes looked so harsh. Harsh towards myself. He looked an unkind man, unforgiving.

I went to the cinema to watch a pornographic film called *Deep Throat*, but it did not move me. I returned to bed. I had spoken to nobody all day. I slept. In the morning I felt normal again.

But I have never forgotten the scene. Never forgotten it because really I knew it already. It was a graphic reminder of the way the world sometimes looks to me and always has, and of the way I sometimes seem to myself, and always have. It was a caricature, an accentuation, a hideous parody, of something already there; and now, whenever I want to be reminded of it, and even when I don't, I flash back to that weird day in Connecticut.

6. Foreign Office – MI6

The *Queen Elizabeth II*, Cunard's new liner, was a new way to go home: $200 for a student ticket, steerage class and unlimited baggage. I trained on the deck, running back and forth from bow to stern, and was pursued through the lounge bars but not along the deck by a fat girl who wanted me to dance with her. In the end, on the pretext of moving away to buy her another gin and tonic I slipped out of the lounge and scuttled off away to my cabin to escape her. As a long-term or indeed middle-term solution to an unwanted suitor this wouldn't have been clever anywhere. On a ship in mid-Atlantic it isn't clever even short-term. I must have panicked. My mother did the same at a village hall dance when she was sixteen, having promised a man with a wig he could walk her home. On a ship it was madness. I spent the rest of the voyage trying to hide.

Academically, two years at Yale had been wasted. The best times had happened outside what was supposed to be the goal: study, for which I did not care.

The surroundings to this big hole in my doughnut had been full of incident. I had driven my old green Ford all around the eastern and southern states: up to Boston to run my first marathon at twenty-one; down to Baltimore to the home of my best friend, John Imboden, whose divorced mother lived in an enormous stone house with its own bar, a tiger-skin rug and an elk's head on the wall.

The rich and well-born in America struck me as surpassing, both in wealth and breeding, the English equivalents to which so many Americans for some reason looked up. Mrs Imboden was a gracious and quick-minded woman, combining delicacy with a sense of fun. There was more respect for learning, and (oddly) for courtesy among this class of American than at the same level of wealth and privilege in Britain; they lived better, knew more, travelled more, entertained in grander style, and seemed at greater ease with their own countrymen. Their lives were more interesting and their horizons broader. By comparison, the English upper classes seemed boorish, clumping around with their ignorant opinions, their rampant materialism, their bad manners and their dogs.

I had hitchhiked the Eastern Seaboard often down to Miami to fly home for holidays with my family in Jamaica. I had hitched a ride with a psychopath with a gun (we got on fine) on his way to North Carolina to shoot his wife's lover. I knew he was a psychopath because when he fell off the bar stool in the truck stop where he was drinking and I laughed nervously, he repeated the fall, exaggeratedly, twice, for the amusement of everyone else too. In the truck he showed me the gun he planned to kill with. I did not report him: as every hitchhiker knows, your lifts are your saviours.

Driving a Cadillac down from New York to Palm Beach for a car-moving agency I had myself picked up three delinquents on the run from their borstal in Massachusetts, and ended up lending one of them money to go home. I had to walk miles into the city to pawn my watch for the $5 I needed for the airport tax, and then, weak with hunger, walk back. At the pawnbrokers a Cuban was buying a gun. This America was a different place from England.

I had been arrested and fined for hitchhiking in Virginia, to date my only conviction: for 'begging rides'. Trying to hitchhike on a New York expressway at dead of night in mid-winter (never do this) I became so cold and exhausted I lay down and felt myself beginning to pass out. It was not unpleasant. Had the inkling something was going fatal not stirred me to get up and stagger off the highway and into Harlem – itself a dangerous recourse – I would have been found dead from exposure the next morning. This was for me the first experience of that careless feeling which steals over us as the body begins to close down; a reminder a few times since that in moments of peril and fatigue a sudden and irrational peacefulness can be a warning sign, not a boon. Death may be like this.

I had organized a Land-Rover expedition from Europe across the Sahara and the Congo to East Africa, dancing with pygmies, flying through the wind in the Cameroons and dislocating shoulders, all but losing one of my Yale companions down a broken sewer in Bangui in the Central African Republic (just in time I felt Brent's hand reach up as I plunged my arm down into the pit of sewage), climbing the Ruwenzori mountains, and stared into the seething orange of the Nyiragongo volcano.

There was something unforgettable about sitting on that volcano's rim. To my left the tiny lights of the town of Goma twinkled beyond the forest thousands of feet below; on my right an angry sea of lava, rock and ash hissed and crashed all night. Side by side, each place was hidden from the other. I between and the carpet of stars above – we saw both. When in 2002 that volcano blew up and spilled down, engulfing Goma, I leapt from my bed where I was listening in the small hours to the BBC World Service, and dashed off 700 words for *The Times*.

And I had run naked alongside 2,000 fellow-Yalies in a mass-streak past the house of the President of Yale, Kingman Brewster, who stood bemused at his door. Many years later, when Mr Brewster was US ambassador to Britain and I, a Tory MP, was introduced to him, I mentioned that the last time he had seen me I had been naked: a remark he took with the same heavy lidded dispassion he had displayed towards the naked mob on his front lawn.

I did not remind him of the time when, attending one of the Brewsters' occasional industrial drinks receptions for students I had noticed a pair of feet sticking out from under a long window-curtain. Drawing apart the curtain, I peeked behind. Kingman Brewster was standing there, very still, half-cut and bored rigid. He was hiding from his guests. He raised a finger melodramatically to his lips, in a silent shh. I smiled and replaced the curtain. I hardly understood then the urge to escape which had driven him behind the curtain. Ten years later, as a Tory MP, I knew it well. And he was looking at the reception room full of British parliamentarians with the same vast boredom, the same inner scream, as he had betrayed peering from behind his own curtains at his own student guests.

I had even tinkered with terrorism. My life's only attempt at personal intervention in the political process (one excludes being a Member of Parliament, which is perfectly peripheral) came when I tried to cause a bomb scare during an IRA fund-raising meeting in New Haven.

Posters had been stuck on to trees across the university and in the town, advertising speeches from IRA representatives at a local church hall. A collection would be taken afterwards. In those days I was rather an enthusiast for the Protestant and Unionist cause and anyway I was British and this was an outrage. Waiting until the meeting was nigh I

walked into a public telephone kiosk in another part of town, dialled
the emergency services, told the operator there was a bomb in the
hall, hung up and scarpered. The police took no notice and the event
went ahead. So much for direct action.

I had been popular despite, or maybe because of, too much Four
Roses bourbon and too much Schlitz, and made real friends. Nowhere before had I ever been a notably popular figure; but here I had
been considered a likeable eccentric Englishman. America had been
fun.

I had, however, gained no degree and must return to England to
take up the job held for me by the Foreign Office. They had kept in
touch, as had the chap from MI6. From both I had received very
British letters, inquiring politely about my health and progress. They
didn't seem to mind about my frittered years at Yale. I didn't tell them
about the failed bomb scare. I disembarked at Southampton with all
my suitcases in an English summer, in July, in the rain. I think I
thought this was the beginning of my life.

The scruffy Southern Region train proceeded, not very fast, to
Clapham Junction where I was to change for Victoria. I looked out.
What I saw was small. Small English hills which called themselves
'downs', small English fields with pylons planted in them, small
English roads and bridges with fussy restrictive signs, small English
industrial estates with dead-end streets and small corrugated asbestos
warehouses, terraces of small English townhouses with sagging net
curtains and small English gardens each with its dwarf tree and scattering of small plastic kiddies' playpools and small artificial rock-
gardens, and streetlights – streetlights everywhere, waiting gently to
stain the night with their low-watt orange glow. This small England
rattled by. Tawdry. Ungenerous. No scale. Nice, very nice. Tame.
Telegraph poles pulsed rhythmically past the grimy British Rail carriage window: pentameters, says Gore Vidal, in a blank verse tragedy.

But this wasn't big enough to be poetry and I wasn't brave enough
to be tragic. And this was going to be my life. This was England. I
didn't feel English at all.

Sometimes a street-sign, the sight of a particular front door, a voice,
a name, a face, says 'bad news'. A mental skull-and-crossbones flashes
on to the corner of the page. This is all the unconscious mind at short

notice has been able to retrieve: a quick, urgent, economical 'get out, fast' notice.

In 1995 I walked down King Charles Street in Whitehall and through the arch into the Great Court of the Foreign and Common-wealth Office. I was a journalist on my way for a cup of tea with Malcolm Rifkind who had just become Foreign Secretary. I glanced idly about at the dreary nineteenth-century façade: a scheme of architecture at the same time lifeless and overwrought, full of fussy emptiness.

A vast wretchedness flooded my soul, as immediate as it was unexpected: a great cube of grey granite had hurtled like an asteroid out of nowhere and thudded into my heart. This was the first time I had been back to the Foreign Office since I had left the place twenty years before. There was no other reason for the message flashing across my brain: *Get out, fast.* I quickened my pace, and drank my tea hurriedly with the Foreign Secretary. Momentarily I had revisited hell. My first job.

If you wanted to attach two or more leaves of paper together at the FCO, the first thing to know was that you did not use a paper clip. Paper clips were vulgar. Paper clips were what they used at the Department of Health and Social Security. No self-respecting diplo-mat would be seen with a paper clip, except possibly in the act of disposing of the item after it had arrived in an unsolicited letter from a member of the public.

The second thing to know was that you did not *staple* papers together. Stapling, after all, suggested finality – suggested the content and order of this sheaf of papers had been decided and a problem perhaps solved. Solved? As we well knew in the diplomatic service, there are no solutions. The shape of a dossier, like the shape of a problem, was a matter for continuing discussion and consultation. Everything at the Foreign and Commonwealth Office is under con-sideration and everything always will be.

In any case it would certainly be beyond the remit of a junior officer, a third secretary like me, to bring down a stapling machine on to any assembly of papers or arguments. My job was ever to 'put things up' for consideration at the next level, that of assistant (a second secretary) in the room next door. Once a dossier had taken some sort of categorizable shape it became part of a ring-file, the stigmata punched into its margin offering, if not immortality, then at least a claim to being what we would have called 'of more than passing interest'.

The third thing to know was that you did not usually *pin* the papers together. We did in our room admit a small supply of pins (quality pins, with round heads, like those on the better sort of gentleman's shirt in its tissue-papered box on a Jermyn Street shelf) but these were only for occasional use in circumstances when one was reluctant to invite even the finality of the imprint of a hole-punch on to a sheet of paper. We pinned only *in extremis*.

A very Foreign Office term, *in extremis*, bespeaking a classical education. 'Hurry' sounded cheap, while 'emergency' hinted at fluster and 'crisis' at panic. But we were allowed to find ourselves *in extremis* from time to time, especially as 'close of play' approached at 6.00 p.m. each day. Once you had decided on your first eleven, your twelfth man, your opening bat, your googlies, your straight bats, your lbws, your appeals to the umpire and your easy fours (we eschewed hitting anything for six at King Charles Street, there was a severe danger of breaking windows; hitting for six was the kind of thing they did at the Ministry of Defence, often with calamitous results), you were (if a cricket-hater like me) in such a spin that the long walk back to the pavilion beckoned, usually before tea.

But if, *in extremis*, you wanted to pin, there was a Foreign Office way of doing this. The sharp end of the pin must enter the top folio in its top left-hand corner, penetrating the whole sheaf and emerging from the final folio, across whose reverse side it should then proceed, heading broadly rightwards and away from the putative reader's finger, for about a quarter of an inch. It should then re-penetrate the sheaf, re-emerging from the top folio. Finally this sharp end should plunge back through the top folio, along whose reverse side it should travel for a further quarter inch, ending its passage sandwiched safely between the top and the second folio. Thus the pin's end would be sheathed, proof against any danger a head of department (or, worse, a Cabinet minister; or, even worse, a permanent under secretary) might prick his finger in handling the document.

I hated the Foreign Office. I hated it with a slow-burning, fiery passion. I hated the obsession with procedure, with polish, with process and with style, to the exclusion of anything but a passing interest in content. I hated the superb intellects and well-founded sense of superiority I encountered all around me: abilities always equal to and often greater than my own, but harnessed to what? Time and again (as it seemed to me) energies were bent not towards doing the right things or even giving the right advice, but doing things in the right way, advising in the right way, and protecting – if possible enhancing – one's own position.

We new entrants were sent to Brussels on a familiarization tour of the European Commission, and there I encountered what felt like the FCO on stilts: clever men in secure jobs whose eyes glazed over if you asked them what, in the end, they or their jobs were for. Language which, though on the face of it looked like English, you could read, reread and still wonder what any of it meant, what had usefully been conveyed. A cocooned feeling, so far from the peoples whose interests and anxieties it was the declared intention to serve. Circular arguments which, untouched by vulgar reference to democracy, all started from – and must therefore end by confirming – the premise of well-warranted self-satisfaction. No wonder the Foreign Office was (I thought) so slavishly uncritical of the Common Market and the self-serving way in which it made its accommodations. The European Commission had created the last word in an administrative class – and no silly questions from ignorant MPs to answer.

I hated Brussels. I hated it in my guts. I hated it instinctively. Almost within hours I found myself asking questions designed to torment the expressionless, Soviet-like officials shepherding us around. My reaction – I do not know where it came from – was so strong that to the amusement of my fellow-trainees I made an irascible nuisance of myself while there, and have never been able to forget it. Ever since, though the zealotry of the Tory Eurosceptics repels me and the argument for closer union makes all kinds of sense, I have never wanted to crusade for the European Union.

There in Brussels our diplomats seemed almost more at home than back in King Charles Street, so uncomfortably close to Westminster. Back in Whitehall I found myself, week by week, bridling more bitterly at the FCO.

Foreign Office drafts read sweetly, but was the advice good? If you asked that, people looked at you as if you were mad, or getting above your station, and suggested you'd better try your hand at elective politics. Colleagues cared less about the long-term wisdom of a document than about the prose style, its checkable facts, and its presentation. Intelligent as the whole ethos of the place was (it was frighteningly so) little was done, no opinion offered, no telegram dispatched, no minister briefed, without careful and methodical attention to procedure. Procedure trumped all; system eclipsed usefulness.

If an Old Testament prophet had returned to earth and offered the Foreign and Commonwealth Office his services in the prediction of wars, pestilences, famines, floods and revolutions, he would have been politely advised that the world was a big and uncertain place in which little we might do could make much difference anyway, while no serving civil servant mindful of his own career would want to be bothering anyone else's head with visions of the future or grand plans for the rectification of foreign policy. In a briefing-note's margin the initials of a Job or Jeremiah were just initials, no different in kind from the initials of a permanent under secretary – and the latter would still be there after prophets and politicians had moved on.

FCO hierarchy, our prophet would have been told, was a subtle and intricate thing. Guiding supple minds down nicely judged paths of consultation, ally-gathering and the protection of backs was what life here was all about. No raw intimation of the future of the universe could much assist with this.

However, our Old Testament prophet would have been advised, predicting contingencies *within* the Office as opposed to the world outside it, really would be useful, career-advancing stuff. So would he please nip over the corridor to the Personnel Operations or Protocol and Conference departments? Here they could undoubtedly do with a little foresight.

For the endgame was not consequence, but system, organization and career: here were a thousand clever, cultured, super-civilized people involved in a sophisticated machine whose operation time and again amounted to the fine-tuning of itself and its own workings. Ministers and politicians were treated with infinite care, courtesy and contempt; the country whose interests we were supposed to serve was not highly regarded; and the British people themselves were viewed with little affection – rather an embarrassment. It was as though the FCO had unfortunately found itself without a nation worthy of its talents.

A watershed for me was a bitter 'valedictory' – a final dispatch from a British ambassador for whom the post he was leaving was his last before retirement. This valedictory came from our man in Reykjavik. As third secretary I opened the envelope.

After a mostly affectionate review of his years in the service and finally in Iceland, our outgoing ambassador remarked that, beyond all the routine work that had had to be done day-in day-out, he reckoned he had offered important advice at critical moments to Her Majesty's Government on perhaps a dozen occasions. On many of these his advice had been good, as events had shown. A handful of times, however, subsequent events had proved him wrong.

Remembering those occasions and surveying his whole career, the ambassador did not suppose any single human intelligence in the FCO had ever noticed, let alone recorded, the score. Nobody would have cared if he had always been wrong, and nobody but himself would have known if he had always been right. By the time the wisdom or otherwise of advice had been established, everyone had moved on to new posts. The ambassador's progress had therefore depended on his competence in the immediately noticeable things – in everything, in fact, but the only enduringly important thing he had to do: to give what would later turn out to be the right advice.

The prevailing wisdom is otherwise: that it is politicians who cannot see beyond next week, while civil servants scan the distant horizon. But this ambassador's reflections planted in me an anxiety about Whitehall which has often surfaced since: that a mandarin's outlook is essentially short-term. 'Constraints' is among his favourite words; 'though less than ideal' usually precedes a recommendation; 'impatience' heads the deadly sins. He will not be punished for reading the future wrong. He will not be identified at all. His name is unlikely to be mentioned in connection with the future of the planet, and he will not be needing to submit himself to the Last Judgement of a popular plebiscite. So why look beyond the next gong? Politicians do care whether policies work. Civil servants don't.

The dispatch crystallized for me what I was beginning to suspect would always make this the wrong job. For a civil servant I was not sufficiently mindful of the importance of method and procedure, and excessively taken up with the wisdom of policies it was way beyond my competence to influence or question.

Nor could I look forward, as so many of my colleagues did, to the pleasures of a civilized and sophisticated life in the company of bright men and women in glittering locations all around the globe. The tales I heard of the diplomatic compound abroad appalled me. Who wanted a life of embassy parties? With my family I had lived all over the world, in – really *in* – the places where we resided: we had been part of them. Yet reporting-letters I was processing from even our younger and less hamstrung diplomats abroad suggested a life largely confined to base and to the company of other diplomats. And anyway, I reckoned, there would be no family life in which to take refuge; I would always be on my own. I felt myself standing outside the Office while working within it, and sensed the distance growing.

I should be candid, though. Plenty of my more contented colleagues were cleverer than I was. Had I been an instant hit at my job, ambition alone might have kept me there and made it more fun. But, while no duffer, I was not finding the ways of the place came easily. Shambolic in my methods (I was always forgetting to lock secret, top secret, 'penumbra' and 'umbra' material into our security safe, and cleaners would blow the whistle at weekends), I never really got the hang, the mental map, of the correct paths for information and advice. Lists of the people who needed to be consulted and arrows indicating the order in which they needed to be consulted, like the myriad arrows on those ghastly charts of military campaigns, never seemed to imprint themselves into the layout of my brain. Maybe there was something wrong with my brain. It was, in its way, a failure of intelligence: mine.

The only work for which I was consistently commended was the production of light drafts for the non-policy parts of ministers' polite after-dinner speeches. I was really good at these, especially when (as with James Callaghan, then the Foreign Secretary) my style suited my master's. My little jokes seemed to work well in his mouth, proposing toasts to generous hosts in Oslo, Copenhagen or wherever.

The Queen, too, used most of a longish passage of an amiable kind which I drafted for her when she had to welcome a Scandinavian Prime Minister, or perhaps monarch, to Scotland. But I noticed she (or her minions) removed one rather pointed joke about women's liberation.

So this was to be my fate: writing passable drafts for ceremonial occasions, with my jokes removed by private secretaries. In disgust I flung into the dustbin at home in my tiny shoe-box of a room in Primrose Hill (where I was now my old friend Elizabeth Bingley's tenant) my personal copy of a little green booklet of etiquette for diplomats. The document was 'Restricted' under the Official Secrets Act. One passage recommended the rules to be observed by a junior diplomatic officer who on a social occasion wished to sit down on a sofa but found the only available place to be (a) immediately adjacent to a senior officer; or (b) immediately adjacent to the wife of a senior officer; or (c) immediately adjacent to another empty place but in circumstances where, should a still unseated senior officer or his wife wish to sit down, either might be left with no option but to sit next to the would-be seated junior officer. I think the rule was Don't. I am breaking the law revealing this.

At dusk in Primrose Hill I would see, silhouetted on the cold skyline of the little park there, men, walking, lingering, loitering. They were looking for something.

For what was I looking? A life in diplomacy? I saw my way right through to the likely end of my career: as a medium-ranking ambassador or high commissioner in an 'outer darkness' (FCO-speak for 'not Europe, America or Russia') posting, penning an amused, whimsical but faintly sour valedictory dispatch from, say, Nairobi. If from the foothills you can already see the top of the mountain range you're tackling, you have time to ask yourself whether the peaks are worth it. For me they weren't. I wanted to stay my own man. I would never be an influential insider here, just a lightweight gadfly with a talent for after-dinner speeches.

Not that my work was fluff. The department to which I had been seconded (all trainees start with two years in Whitehall) was the Western European Department. My desk included most of Scandinavia, plus Italy and the Vatican. Italy always seemed in the grip of a political or industrial crisis, and this made work for us. For some weeks much of mine revolved around a chap called Pugsley, championed by a Tory MP of whom at that time I had never heard, Robin Maxwell-Hyslop, MP for Tiverton. His constituent worked (I think) for an Italian university.

Pugsley had not been paid for months. This was unsurprising; no one in such jobs had been paid. Italy was going through one of its occasional administrative paralyses. I drafted for my minister a thoughtful answer explaining to Mr Maxwell-Hyslop why HMG could not reasonably ask for special treatment for his constituent alone. My draft was put up in the usual way for approval by seniors.

It came back fast with a sharp marginal note: I was to see my superior at once. I did so. 'Re-draft,' he said. 'The Foreign Secretary himself will promise to do all he can for Pugsley.'

I expressed surprise. 'Never mind the logic,' said my head of department, 'this is an MP. And this is an awkward bugger of an MP. Maxwell-Hyslop makes a stink if he doesn't get satisfaction. Never lets go. He has no case at all but give him what he wants for his damned constituent.'

The outcome was that our ambassador in Rome, protesting mildly to Whitehall, was instructed to raise Pugsley's problem with the Italian Foreign Minister. Pugsley was paid. We heard he was almost the only man in his profession in Italy who was.

I learned my lesson. When much later I entered Parliament I soon spotted the Maxwell-Hyslops among colleagues on both sides of the House. To the awkward squad special attention is given by ministers and their departmental civil servants.

With me among the twelve graduate recruits to the Foreign and Commonwealth Office in my year was another secretly gay officer. Robin Chatterjie was one of the brainiest and most entertaining of the bunch, and he gave excellent parties. From conversation over too many Pimms at one of these I have no doubt Robin was gay, or wanted to be. I also have no doubt this was putting him under tremendous mental strain, not only from the career but from the family point of view. He died later from cancer.

Within some fifteen years, five of us twelve would be out of the service, or dead. My friend Dominic Lieven was one of the early leavers. Like me, he never quite got into the swing of Office procedure: once, handling from the FCO end the arrangements for a visit by the Queen to the Maldive islands, and apprised of the need for a last-minute change of plan, Dominic tried to contact the Queen directly, as this seemed the most logical way to make an eleventh-hour amendment to the royal schedule. I saw his point, but his boss did not. Dominic is now a very distinguished professor of history.

A good friend of both of us was Elizabeth Brimelow, the daughter of the permanent under secretary at the time, Sir Thomas Brimelow. She looked and dressed just like a younger version of Good Queen Bess, and was I think the cleverest of us all. She ended up in the City, working for an outfit called Blue Arrow. Blue Arrow was caught by the law. She had to resign, and for what seemed an age was in fear of prosecution personally, though this never happened. For years she lived in anxiety and sadness about this, though too reserved and dignified to talk about it or complain. I never tried to master the ins and outs of financial regulation in order to work out what her involvement in the infringements might have been. I did not need to. Grand utterances may be out of place in a book like this and mine here will be of interest to very few people today, but still I should like to put it on record that I had a pretty good idea of Elizabeth Brimelow's character and have absolutely no doubt she would never have initiated any disgraceful action; the worst she could have done was get caught in some terrible conflict of loyalties. I reckon she was made to take the rap for others. May they rot in hell.

I came close to lurching out of respectable employment myself in a more spectacular way. At the age of twenty-six I was nearly recruited by the Bulgarian secret service. The story reads like fiction but Foreign Office records will confirm it. I am perhaps the first man to be saved from treachery by halitosis.

One night in 1976 I went to a party given by a departmental colleague in her north London house. A friend had lent me his car: a rusting but lively green Alfasud. Lots of FCO friends were there, as well as a sprinkling of young foreign diplomat friends we knew professionally.

I spent some time talking to a young man I had not met before. He was a Bulgarian of about my age and rank, posted to London. Slim and pale with dark hair, he was – to me, anyway – intolerably attractive. His English was poor, but he seemed interested in me and my work. I forgot the other people at the party. I forgot the time.

So it must have been the small hours when I realized most of the others had departed, and it was time to go. He and I had been left locked in earnest conversation in a corner while Joan, our hostess, cleared up. It was now too late for the Underground, and my new Bulgarian friend asked if I would give him a lift into central London.

I lived in Clapham and assured him central London was not out of my way. Timbuktu would not have been out of my way.

As we drove in from Wembley, now alone together, conversation intensified. I became aware the Bulgarian was moving across the passenger seat, sitting closer and closer. As the car had bucket seats, this was not a natural way to sit. I have always been hopeless at spotting signs of interest from others, and tend to prefer any explanation to the obvious one. When even I realize someone is making a pass at me, they always are.

He told me he was unmarried. A nervous young man, I now became seriously worried. Nothing like this had ever happened to me in a car. What should I do? Prudence battled with another impulse. I tried to concentrate on the driving.

As we negotiated the Shepherds Bush roundabout, the Bulgarian leant so close he was breathing into my face. I could smell his breath. The other impulse died. Prudence reasserted itself. I had never smelt such breath. It was dreadful. How could such rottenness be concealed within such a beautiful head? Catching a whiff of an elephant seal's breath in sub-Antarctica recently I was taken straight back to that moment. Standards of dentistry in Sofia must have been abysmal. Quite involuntarily I flinched, jerking my head away.

He retreated immediately to his side of the car. Conversation died. 'Where are you going?' I asked. 'I'll drop you at your door.' But he would not tell me, insisting instead that I drop him on the Cromwell Road where my route crossed. This I did. I never saw or spoke to him again.

Could I have been seduced? Yes, on the spot if he had flossed his teeth. Would I have been compromised? Undoubtedly. Could I have been blackmailed? No, not if you mean how would I have reacted to a demand from Sofia that I betray British secrets on pain of exposure. I would have gone straight to my FCO bosses: I am not a communist. But there are subtler forms of influence and subtler ways of extracting information. Was this his plan? I rather think so, unless he was genuinely attracted to me, a possibility I fear we should discount.

A couple of months later, a chatty postcard arrived from him from Bulgaria, suggesting we might meet again sometime. Thus far I had not mentioned the incident to my superiors, but it did seem best to hand this card over to the security people at the FCO, together with a sparsely written account of the circumstances. It was received without comment.

I often wonder how my life might have turned out if someone had recommended this would-be Bulgarian agent an effective mouthwash. Are young British spies trained in dental hygiene? They should be. Upon the smallest things, destinies can turn.

At the same time as speechwriting for the Queen I was applying to London Transport for a job. On the bus home one day at the end of an unusually frustrating week I had seen an advertisement posted in the interior downstairs: London Transport were looking for apprentice diesel-fitters for their South London garages. No great level of education was required. Certainly no greater than Cambridge and Yale. And the pay was not bad.

I enjoy car mechanics. I had refitted, overhauled and maintained my old Morris Oxford for years and, instructed by my father, had always shown a reasonable aptitude for practical engineering. With my brother Roger I had since adolescence been trying in our spare time to invent what, ever since the Industrial Revolution, inventors had failed to come up with: a direct-drive infinitely variable gearbox (it eludes us still, though we recently got close).

Instead of mechanics as a hobby, I thought, how about bus mechanics as a career? My father had started as an apprentice too, and come up through business as a power engineer. I admired this and envied him his engineer's mind. Unlike him I lacked a real, hard skill; mine was just a life of living on my wits.

So I applied. I really meant it. London Transport turned me down. A decade earlier they gave the same response to John Major's application to be a bus conductor. Both of us, I suppose, are really just bus company rejects.

If London Transport had offered me an apprenticeship I would have taken it. Rejected, I returned to writing speeches for the Queen.

7. Old Queen Street

In 1975 Edward Heath was challenged for the leadership of the Conservative Party. I put ten pounds on Margaret Thatcher's chances.

The bet was with a bookmakers near Victoria station. The odds were heavily against her: seven to one. At evens William Whitelaw was the runaway favourite. I had never placed a political bet, or any bet, at a bookmakers before. What had prompted this had been a discussion of her bid in the Third Room of the Western European Department where I worked.

All the others thought she had no chance. She was a woman, which virtually ruled her out: how many women Foreign Secretaries had there been? But, worse, she was also a political outsider and not the kind of Tory whom diplomats associated with high office: Mrs Thatcher sounded shrill, prickly, combative, opinionated and bourgeois, everything they disliked. Nor did she seem to know much about the world beyond our shores.

That of course was pardonable. And remediable. Roy Hattersley, James Callaghan . . . these were Labour Party men who had had to learn to be Foreign Office ministers but now breathed easily in the air of civilized fatalism which hung heavy in the corridors at King Charles Street. Such men had been, as we would have put it, tamed. Some of the roughest were easiest to tame.

She was not rough; she was spiky. She did not seem to *want* to learn – and by 'learn' a senior civil servant denotes the process of becoming intelligently impressed by the compelling nature of events outside one's own control: a quality much esteemed in the Office and arguably the principal distinguishing mark of the wise. 'What is wisdom?' asks Ecclesiastes. 'Submission to destiny,' replies the diplomat. Thatcher was not wise.

My colleagues were not too worried, though. True, their near-certainty nobody would challenge Edward Heath had been surprised. I had assumed a challenge was likely because Mr Heath had failed: failed as Prime Minister and failed to win general elections. Losing things did not strike me as immaterial to his prospects. Fellow-diplomats thought he would sail onward. When he didn't they assumed his right-hand man, William Whitelaw, would succeed him, a seamless progress from officer to officer.

I pointed out that Mr Whitelaw was not in fact challenging Mr Heath. They said of course not, not in the first round; that would be vulgar. But if Heath were to be wounded then Whitelaw would challenge. It depended whether Heath stumbled in the first round. Decent chaps didn't do the tripping: a rank outsider like Thatcher might. But an insider would be the beneficiary and win.

Such was thought to be – often proved to be – the world of the political insider: like that of newspaper leader-writers who (in H.L. Mencken's imagery) wait in the hills until the battle is over, then come down to bayonet the wounded. Margaret Thatcher had fallen into the error of fixing her bayonet before the field marshal had fallen.

But I could see Edward Heath was finished. Unless his friends could see the same then for once it might not be an insider who dispatched him. I went out at lunch and placed my bet. My winnings when she triumphed were modest, but brought a big fillip to my confidence in my own political judgement. Owing both to her, I decided that to join her would be a worthwhile thing to try.

It may or may not be true that in affairs of the heart the first cut is the deepest. It's certainly true in politics. I embraced for a while – and will never wholly shake off – a certain kind of chippy, small-shopkeeper-style Toryism because I'd seen a series of British governments which we called socialist but which were really 'third way', 'social democrat', or 'mixed economy' merchants bugger things up so comprehensively that even to this day I am prey to sudden attacks of greengrocer-like right-wingery.

Harold Wilson's and James Callaghan's 1970s administrations were neither wicked nor possessed by any particularly mad dogma. I would hardly call them socialist. They were just without compass, confused and worn down by internal attrition. They had been kicked too easily into the habit of taking the line of least resistance. They just kept giving way. Edward Heath had fought and lost.

Plenty has been said since about the greed and stupidity of the trade union movement and I agree with most of it. But less is said about how British business more or less colluded. Lazy, careless and low-calibre –

insensitive to the point of being incendiary in their attitudes to their own workforces – the leaders of British industry lurched from the long lunch to the pointless scrap. Fat, weak-faced businessmen in badly made Jaguars divided their time between the golf-club where there was always one more tepid gin-and-tonic, the ill-natured industrial arbitration, the moan that Britain was going to the dogs, and the inevitable appeal to government for 'intervention', subsidy and yet another stay of execution. It was usually granted. We remember all this. Nobody who doesn't will ever understand.

Things were going crazy. The Alice-in-Wonderland quality of Britain in Harold Wilson's and James Callaghan's time eludes objective writing – almost eludes report. The defeat of reason hung in the air. There was a feeling of despair, rage and in the end resignation. The madness is best captured in a rereading of Bernard Levin's columns in *The Times*, railing against the Gas Board; or Peter Simple's parodies (in the *Daily Telegraph*) of the conventional wisdoms of the progressive order of the day. But even these lose accessibility to those who do not remember the teeth-gnashing, breast-beating why-oh-whyness, the banging-your-head-against-a-brick-wall-ness of mid-seventies Britain.

And there's something else that has been almost completely forgotten by those who call the Thatcher eighties greedy. It was a time, the seventies, of remarkable selfishness. There was no age of community-mindedness before her. A repeated refrain at the time was that 'I'm all right, Jack' had become the order of the day, and it was a reaction *against* this selfishness that helped sweep her into power. Her message as Opposition leader – I was to write it often enough – was that the Conservative Party would stand up for people 'who care about their country'. The message was not (as she later carelessly said and never believed) that there was no such thing as society; quite the contrary: it was trade unionists who were called anti-social.

Nor was it only the working classes who didn't seem to want to work, indeed the very term 'working' class was reminiscent of a time when gentlemen did not have to: an attitude many employers and professional people did not seem to have realized was no longer tenable in the mid-1970s. Along with some Tories they found it easy to blame everything on organized labour, but the malaise went deeper and trade unionists sniffed the air of defeatism and *sauve qui peut* which hung around British industry – the idea we were all going down the tubes anyway – and decided that in that case they might as well loot what they could from a beached economy.

We believed we were becoming a nation of jobsworths, clock-watchers and passers-by-on-the-other-side, heading down an easy slope towards the everlasting bonfire. It was a time in which individuals felt impotent against the spirit of their age: felt a kind of fatalism and a kind of fury.

I remember being introduced to a very senior figure in one of Britain's biggest docks. The industry was on its last legs almost everywhere in Britain, thanks to a thieving workforce, union obduracy, bad management and a head-in-the-sand attitude to change. Traditional docking was dying and the industry needed to change or die. A tough assignment, you may think, to try to lead the docks at such a time. I expected to meet a modern, keen, hard-headed, hard-driving, ball-crunching type of chap, absorbed – maybe to the point of tedium – in his task. I expected him to talk figures, and machines, and new technology. I wanted to ask him about them.

He really wasn't interested. Dressed in the shooting-set's weekend-smart uniform of greeny-brown tweed (three-piece) and over-polished brogue shoes, the fellow was in his mid-sixties and distinctly upper-crust. He looked and sounded utterly bored by his job. He told me the docks were completely shot and there was nothing to be done about it. I asked him about the new method of containerizing cargo. That was 'another world', he said, petulantly – and changed the subject.

He came, my friends whispered, from a good family. I thought he should go back there. The upper-class twit, a stock-in-trade of comedy caricature, was as valid a caricature of as familiar a spirit of the age, as the *Daily Mirror*'s working-class, work-averse cartoon anti-hero: the fag-on-lip, flat-capped Andy Capp. Both were to blame.

No doubt many dockers were a rascally and workshy lot; no doubt their short-sighted trade union leaders were much to blame for the industry's effective suicide over that decade and the next. But, managed by a waistcoated goose in shiny shoes, what did anyone expect? Unions and management deserved each other.

When in the mid-seventies the chairman of another of our great state industries was sacked on the grounds that his industry was not succeeding, the fellow (who had what people call an 'unblemished record' and had smoothly risen to the top) complained to the financial journalists of the day that his dismissal was an outrage. Nobody had accused him of fiddling the figures, he protested, and he was 'not a homosexual' – so why had he lost his job? It was indicative of the prevailing mindset. Reading his outburst, my father (quite uncharacteristically) snapped at the breakfast table that the remark was proof enough of the man's incompetence.

I felt not just Tory, but new Tory: one of those as impatient with the top as we were with the bottom. In fact I felt so Tory I will never quite recover. We had the sensation of witnessing the political version of a slow-motion road accident, and road accidents can be traumatic. You get flashbacks for the rest of your life. The metaphor of the 'defining moment' can be overdone, but whether you call it 'confined by' or call it 'secured by' those experiences, I will always be anchored to them: the kind of Tory who begins to grind his teeth whenever things go cosy.

I once at a formative time in my youth saw things sliding out of control under a third-way government for whom the cosy deal had become a reflex, splitting the difference a habit, and a slithering into compromise to live and fight another day, a way of life. It is the return of this – this evasion of the fundamentals – for which my political nostrils will for ever be a-twitch. I felt like Alice in Wonderland in a mad world. I read the speeches of Keith Joseph, full (it seemed to me) of brave and rigorous good sense, and cheered.

I asked to resign from the Foreign Office.

More than a few friends wondered and have wondered since whether some hidden disgrace was the explanation. I picked up the same whispers when, ten years later, I left Parliament between elections in the same sudden way. Was I being blackmailed, or about to be exposed for some appalling scandal? Would that the truth were so exotic. But on neither occasion was I in any personal difficulty. I just got fed up. In the unconscious mind decisions are weighed carefully and over long periods; evidence both ways is collected; and at a certain point a judgement is made, a switch is thrown, and we find ourselves acting – as it is said of us – 'precipitately'. But only on the conscious level is it sudden.

My move was certainly inconvenient. I had just been offered my first overseas posting: second secretary in Nairobi. To me this was a fascinating posting: just what I had wanted. Whatever my memories of Mombasa, Kenya was a beautiful African country with a language I could learn, poised at an interesting time politically. The High Commission was of modest size, so I wouldn't be lost in a giant machine. And within a few hours' drive, there was Mt Kenya, Kilimanjaro, the Rift Valley, and beyond it peaks, lakes and forests yet unconquered.

So why was I setting out for my Swahili lessons in Clapham with such a heavy heart? Because underneath I knew this was not my career; and if it was not, then something should be done about the situation at once. I hate misleading people. I hate shuffling around. I hate stays of execution. Were I a condemned man I would rush for the gallows. There was no point in delay.

More rational from my own point of view would have been to find another job before I told my FCO employers. But that seemed low-minded; nobody in the Office had done me any harm; on the whole I had been decently treated. So having made the decision to leave I fast began to feel guilty. I decided to lay my cards on the table. After a brief interview I wrote to the head of Personnel in January 1976 saying (because to say otherwise seemed ungracious) that I had no axe to grind against the service, but

I want to be my own man, or to have that prospect.

The highest ranks of the Foreign Office, were I to attain them, do not offer that. This was made clear, and was clear, to me when I entered the service. The realization that because of this my heart would not be in my job has grown since then, and I know that it will not pass.

I have decided to try and follow a political career. I cannot realistically expect to go far, or even to attain more personal independence than I have in the service. But when I fail, as I honestly expect I shall, it will be through failure of luck or ability, and not through failure of will. To stay in the service rather than try for what I really want would be a failure of will.

I found a carbon copy of this letter the other day. I do not remember writing it. I do not remember thinking it. Odd what we forget.

It is depressing too, re-reading that letter for the first time since I signed it a quarter of a century ago, to see there has since been no noticeable development since in my literary style: a certain ring, a confessional tone and a faint odour of sanctity, as though the writer is about to be burned at the stake.

It worked, anyway. Throwing myself on the mercy of the Personnel Operations Department, I asked to carry on until I found another job. They agreed to let me. That was kind.

So until June of that year I toiled away in the Rhodesia Department, answering letters from disgruntled members of the British public, almost all of whom were outraged that HMG were not supporting Ian Smith. But I bit my lip and kept my cool. It was the least I owed the diplomatic service.

I left Lizza's flat. It had not been a good idea to try to recapture our former closeness at Cambridge. I had been unhappy there. I felt left out. Poor Lizza had fallen for a chap who was interested in wild flowers. She had begun subscribing to a monthly wild flower magazine so she could make intelligent conversation with this man, inevitably called Tim. She did seem to pick 'em: the men not the flowers.

Having not wanted to be her lover as she may once have hoped, I now felt resentful of her friendships with the wild flower man and with her American fellow-social worker, our flatmate Jeannie, who objected to my running up the stairs to my broom-cupboard of a room above. She said it made a thumping noise. Lizza sided with her.

It was a miserable departure, each of us feeling we had somehow let the other down. Elizabeth asked whether I would be wanting to take the rocking-chair she had bought me for my twenty-first birthday, and which she very much liked. It had been in her bedroom because there was no room for it in mine. So I said, 'Oh no, you have it' – and felt immensely bitter about that, though I didn't really want the chair.

I have never been able to forget leaving. Many years later I went to visit Lizza in York. She had found a man nice enough to deserve her, married, had children, and settled down there. On a walk by the river she said she wanted to tell me about something which had caused her such anguish at the time that she had been unable to talk about it. I had replied to the invitation to her wedding, she said, with a two-line refusal letter written in the third person, saying Matthew intended to be in the Sahara at the time. This was true. And that silly rocking-chair was the cause.

On the banks of the River Ouse I almost told her, then felt quite cut-up about it, and bit my lip. Never refuse a present. Never take back a present you have given. There is something very deep about presents.

Leaving Primrose Hill I had found a flat in south-west London, just off the West Side of Clapham Common. Filling it with lodgers so I could afford the rent, I slept in the conservatory with a bathroom strip-heater on the ceiling to take the chill off winter nights and Kenny Everett on Capital Radio in the morning to make a new day worth facing. I stepped up efforts to storm the bastions of Conservative Central Office.

While I was working out my time at the FCO, my journey home from Whitehall on the number 88 bus entailed a walk over to the West Side of the Common. After dark I would see the silhouettes of men walking under the trees, or standing around. I skirted this area, keeping to the road. But I was fascinated. Then again, I thought, maybe MI6 were still keeping an eye on me? This would not be the way for a member of HM Diplomatic Service to behave.

Nor for the chairman of the West Side Branch of the South Battersea Conservative Association. Even before deciding to leave the FCO I had joined the association and become treasurer, then chairman of a small ward branch, Clapham Common West Side. I got on well with the Tory agent for the area, and even wrote to her asking for advice on training to become a professional party agent. She warned me this was not an appropriate route for someone eager to become an MP.

Nor was that short cut across the Common. I avoided both.

I tried other routes into the party. Richard Body was a Lincolnshire Tory MP on the right of the party, but a Quaker and determined opponent of the death penalty, who had met my family when visiting Rhodesia; they had found him sympathetic and I did. He promised to talk to the leader's office, but reported there was no vacancy for new staff.

Shamelessly I tugged the sleeve of any friend well-connected with the Conservative Party. Peter (Lord) Carrington, who knew the Bingleys, was helpful. I asked General Sir Michael Carver too.

Eventually I was invited for a strange interview with a man called Airey Neave. He seemed uninterested in my abilities but curious about my loyalties. He was (and for years remained) 'head' of Mrs Thatcher's office, but I could not at the time work out, and never subsequently did work out, what Airey's role actually entailed – apart from looking conspiratorial, spotting enemies everywhere, and worshipping the woman he told me was 'lucky'. Later I discovered that others in the office thought him rather a pest, but Mrs Thatcher wanted him there because he had been an early supporter, and that was that.

After he was killed by an IRA car-bomb in 1979 Airey ascended to semi-heroic status, as perhaps the manner of his death merited; but in those earlier days he was a faintly comical figure. One of Mrs Thatcher's colleagues told me that in the Second World War, during Neave's celebrated stay at – and break-out from – Colditz, his affectionate nickname was Dog, because he smelt like one. I never noticed this on his visits to the leader's office. I think she was just trying to find something for him to do. She never forgot those who took her side, and never forgave those who left it. Only later did the phrase 'one of us' become famous as the way she thought, but it was thus with her from the start, with Airey Neave almost wackily so.

I was unsure whether Airey concluded I was 'one of us'. I met the dark and significant glance which I was later to discover people always met. I don't think it meant anything. Finally I was invited to talk to Chris Patten, the director of the Conservative Research Department, to whom I had written once already, addressing my letter to D Patten Esq, without result. I travelled nervously to Old Queen Street where the Conservative Research Department occupied two adjacent Georgian houses in Queen Anne's Gate, each about two feet wide and five stories high and composed mostly of staircases.

My job interview was a casual affair. Chris wanted to know which columnists I read in the newspapers; why I was uncomfortable in the Foreign Office, and what I thought of developments within the party. It was very clear – you sensed it at once – that declarations of undying loyalty to the grand old Conservative Party and its inspired leadership were not being invited and would be met with the sharp, humorous, sceptical glance we all came to know so well at the Research Department. I did not sense hostility to Mrs Thatcher and her fellow *arrivistes*, just a good-humoured agnosticism.

There was time, visiting his office, to get a sniff of the place. The sniff was elitist, mostly in the best sense. The Conservative Research

Department was a low-lying island of old-fashioned Toryism waiting for the tsunami of Thatcherism, a faint perturbation on the horizon, to wash over and obliterate it. Thatcher predated Thatcherism.

The Conservative Research Department's function was to service the party, parliamentary and national, in all questions relating to policy. In practice this boiled down to two main jobs: helping develop new policy, and advising spokesmen, backbench MPs and the national party on existing policy. Manifestos, briefings for debate, position papers and pamphlets outlining policy and offering ammunition were the bread and butter of our work, while the cleverest among us (not me) huddled with the policymakers at Westminster to plan new directions. For most, however, it was more wank than wonk.

The department's determination to have as little as possible to do with Conservative Central Office was evinced not least by their dogged refusal to be relocated there in Smith Square, which was close and where there would surely have been space. But the Conservative Research Department was different. Macleod, Powell, Butler – political intellectuals, many of whom had been associated with it – were the ruling ancestral spirits at Old Queen Street. We were a world away from the bureaucrats and post-office mentality of the party machine, with its shiny-shoed functionaries, its ranks of little middle-aged men with toothbrush moustaches, counting up the money raised in raffles, and its direct links to that ghastly creature out there in the swamp, the Party-in-the-Country.

Most Conservative Research Department officers seemed to be young men, most Oxbridge, and all bright. The atmosphere was quite casual, as between equals. To me on that visit they were just a scattering of faces. I did not know or recognize any of them. Michael Dobbs and Bruce Anderson, both future friends, appeared only as a bluff, genial, ginger-haired rugger-bugger type, and a big, thin, rather intense Scot who liked to shock, whose shoes, which had never been polished, were falling apart, who lived (he claimed) in a rented cupboard in Stoke Newington and who used (he said) to be a communist. But Bruce was always more columnist than communist. These were the people I hoped to join.

Chris Patten's first letter had said there were no posts available but something might come up. His second said something had. Maybe it was the note from Peter Carrington. I was to start in July. I was twenty-six. It was just before then that my resolve to stay celibate cracked.

Heterosexuals don't 'come out' so why should homosexuals? I lurched out then scampered back.

Anyway I hate the expression 'coming out'; it's so cute, so pat, so precious; as if one could reduce the piecemeal and stumbling and mostly unwitting way we learn about each other to a series of charming little social ceremonies; as though every creep or stumble forward in personal development were preceded by a roll of the kettledrums and concluded with an implied round of applause.

It is as unlikely that the eternal messy struggle between honesty, privacy, pride and shame could be contained in this way as that a man's spiritual progress could be tracked by christenings, confirmations, barmitzvahs or the like. Nobody comes out. Nobody is out. Nobody is in. We are all more, or less, known; all seen in part, none completely; none quite sure what he has revealed; none wholly privy to what others may have guessed, or imagined, or presumed about him.

Having got that off my chest I must confess that much to my own surprise I came out first to my brother and sister.

Close family are often among those with whom one is least likely to discuss intimate secrets, or so it was for me. As my parents' oldest son, and older brother to all my brothers and sisters, pride, as I have said, was bound up in this, but it was not just pride. The more we are together the closer we are but, proximity being quite other than intimacy, the more raw we feel about unsuspected vulnerabilities, our own and others. Anyone who has journeyed in dangerous conditions with a small and close-knit group of comrades will tell you that the long nights together are not occasions for intimacies and secrets, but for retreat, each into his own world.

I should be as embarrassed to be taken into my sister's, or father's, or mother's confidence on anything painfully personal, as I should be reluctant to take them into mine. I don't want those I love most to 'open up' to me, any more than I usually want to open up to them. Somebody more anonymous – even professional – seems better suited to this role: a priest, doctor or psychiatrist.

Or an audience. I don't think I'm the only columnist able to talk more easily about inner feelings to 100,000 readers whom he will never meet, than to those who know him. From where the actor stands the glare of the footlights blanks out individual faces.

Yet it was the individual faces of my brother Roger and sister Deborah I saw across the table from me at a restaurant called the Hungry Horse in the King's Road in London. The faces were slightly unfocused as I had drunk too much. It was not my habit to get drunk with my brother and sister so maybe I had planned this and was working up the Dutch courage to go through with it; I don't know, I cannot remember.

All I remember is that neither seemed at all upset or shocked, and I felt loved, and I talked too much and too long and perhaps too loud, because all at once it was after midnight, and as we left I distinctly saw a young man on a nearby table give me a thumbs-up. It was tremendously encouraging. Then I said goodnight to Roger and Deborah who were travelling north, and decided to walk home.

I don't know why I decided to walk. It was about four miles to Broxash Road, SW11, across Chelsea Bridge and up across Lavender Rise to Clapham Common and . . .

It must have been after one in the morning. The Common was still, quiet, cold and very dark. But against the lights of the houses on West Side I could see the silhouettes, some moving, some motionless. I could see the glow of a cigarette in someone's hand, under the trees. I had sobered up somewhat by then. But I decided to take the short cut.

There is an etiquette of sorts about cruising, though I knew nothing of it. You walk, or amble, past people, and unless as you approach you have already seen enough to know the answer is No, you slow down a little as you pass, as, hopefully, do they. You do not stop, face to face, and stare. You do not speak. But if, having passed and having given yourself a few seconds to think about it, you think the answer is Maybe, you stop, turn and look back – or look back while walking on. If the other person has done the same then you're in business. If not – well, he doesn't even know you turned.

With luck though, both of you will have come to a halt, perhaps twenty yards from each other. One or both of you may now retrace your steps to meet. Alternatively, you may veer off the path and into the undergrowth, there to stand and wait until, you hope, the other joins you. When he does, few if any words are usually spoken, though a short conversation is not unheard of, especially if one or both would prefer that together you go back to the home of whomever lives closest, rather than grope and fumble in the dark and open air.

There were in those days three dangers to be on guard for. The least of these was the police. They did occasionally drive around the perimeter of the cruising area, sometimes with headlights on, sometimes off. Sometimes they would swing their panda cars to face the trees and bushes, then switch on their main beams. But on Clapham Common I never knew them to send plainclothes officers on foot to entrap, though they easily could have, and around pubs and clubs often did. The effect of their arrival in panda cars would anyway be a rapid evacuation of the area, sometimes running. I never saw them give chase or make an arrest.

More vexatious than the police were other gay men of either the voyeuristic or the 'Can I join in?' variety. A few gay men do like an audience, and a few prefer group sex. But couples would mostly try to repel boarders, a sharp word being sufficient.

More dangerous than either police or hangers-on were queer-bashers. They were rare but caused panic, and a friendly system existed to warn others of either police or queer-bashers: a whistle in the dark. Queer-bashers were almost always white and in groups, while gay men did not tend to cruise in groups, so the suspects could often be spotted; and their dress tended to be subtly different too. If you got close enough to a queer-basher of the skinhead variety his appearance and dress gave him away. Even more sinister than these was the very occasional type of those who were themselves gay – or ready anyway to join in – and would become violent later. I never encountered one of these, but others did.

Nothing of this, absolutely nothing, did I know when, as a 26-year-old novice, still slightly drunk, I veered off across the Common on a metalled pathway leading through the trees. A man passed me walking an Alsatian dog. Goofily I said to him, 'Hello. What do people here do?'

'You know. Don't be stupid,' he replied, and walked on. I passed a youth wheeling a bicycle who promptly got on it and cycled away. After a few minutes I was nearing the end of the trees, and the other side of the Common, the West Side. To make this walk for me had been hard, a sickening leap. I did not want it to end this way, in

Family Christmas in Rhodesia, 1965. Standing, from left: myself, John and Roger; front, from left: dog Tina, Deborah, my father Leslie, my mother Terry holding Mark, and Belinda

My first school photo

With tadpoles in Cyprus

With Grandpa
and broken arm
in Sydenham

With mouse in
Rhodesia

School play, with me second from left.
Mum couldn't make my ears stand up

Uncle Don's sketch of my
Aunt Joyce and me

With my brother Roger, on the right

For my first driving licence. I passed my test
aged sixteen in Mum's Morris Minor

Mum and Dad under the banana trees

At Cambridge after receiving my degree, to the surprise of my tutors

With Trish and beard. Trish came to visit me in Cambridge after we had travelled across Africa together

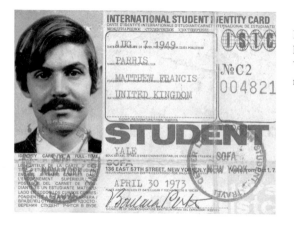

Peter Mandelson used to have a moustache too. What is it about young men who try them?

Posing as a drunk at a party at Yale.
Friends failed to realize I was in fancy dress

The leader of the Opposition presents me with my RSPCA award. This was before the dog tried to mount Mrs Thatcher's leg

Below: A front page which confirmed Mrs Thatcher's suspicions about my insanity

A poster from the 1979 general election, before London Weekend Television straightened my teeth

Below: Running the White Peak Marathon for the Matlock Athletic Club. Running was good for me politically

LADY MANNERS SCHOOL PARENTS' ASSOCIATION
BAKEWELL, DERBYSHIRE

Pour y Parvenir

RUN FOR A BUS

Help to raise money for a
SCHOOL MINI-BUS
by sponsoring
Matthew Parris, M.P.
in the London Marathon on
SUNDAY, 9th MAY, 1982
Distance 26 miles, 385 yards
SPONSOR FORMS FROM SCHOOL OR COMMITTEE MEMBERS

The Blue Chips, by Rose Cecil

From left to right: Robert Cranborne (seated), Michael Ancram, Matthew Parris,
Peter Fraser, John Major, William Waldegrave (seated), Robert Atkins, John Watson
(seated), Nicholas Lyell, Chris Patten (seated), Alex Pollock, Douglas Hogg (seated),
Tristan Garel-Jones (seated), Richard Needham, Ian Lang (seated), John Patten.
The portrait on the wall is of Jocelyn Cadbury

failure. I saw a fallen tree trunk lying by the path. I decided to walk over and sit on it, and stay sitting there until something happened.

After about ten minutes, something did. A nice-looking young man sat down beside me. I told him I had never done anything like this before. He suggested we go back to his flat, which was close, in Leathwaite Road: I can remember the number.

He told me his name and I told him mine, making in a split second a resolution from which I never subsequently departed: not to tell people lies about myself. His flat was unnaturally clean and tidy, and smelt of a rather surgical bathroom freshener. I felt nervous and unsure what to do. I sat on the sofa while he made a cup of instant coffee. He sat down beside me and, realizing how tense I was, reached for a photograph album and began to show me pictures of a recent holiday, sitting close. After this it got easier, and soon it came naturally enough, though I had not really wanted to be penetrated, and it hurt.

He gave me his telephone number and I gave him mine. After an hour or so he kissed me, rather perfunctorily, goodbye, and I walked before dawn the half mile or so to my flat. I left my watch by the bed by mistake.

I could tell you, I suppose, how I fell rather stupidly in love with this man though he had given me no reason to imagine I was anything other than a casual pick-up; how he dealt with me kindly but obviously wanted to shake me off; how he returned my watch but declined the invitation to stay; how I wrote to him a couple of times, then gave up; how I did subsequently see him once or twice – we still exchange Christmas cards – but was by then learning that it is, or was, a hard-faced world, the 'gay community'. I could tell you much; but it would be commonplace, the experience of millions, and led, for me, to no particularly blissful but certainly no tragic ending: no drama at all.

Perhaps best then just to say that as I walked through the cold damp air back from his flat to mine, I felt as though I were emerging from a dark cave, into the open. A stone had been rolled away. Before that day, my hands had always shaken. They have never shaken since.

It is hard now to look back on the Michael Portillo, the Chris Patten or the Michael Dobbs I saw then, and see them again as I saw them in the Conservative Research Department.

Michael Dobbs sat opposite me in our untidy little office at 24 Old Queen Street: like me, one of the Conservative Research Department's younger officers. His name was Michael but everyone called him Mick. It's a shortening he later dropped. His wife didn't like it. Mick was one of the most popular among us and the man with whom I was on the easiest terms. He was a Nice Bloke with an amiable disposition: perfectly bright and a good observer of others, but no edge: anything but driven, not even sharp in any way you would notice. That in a different era he was to go on to write *House of Cards*, create Francis Urquhart, coin the catchphrase 'I couldn't possibly comment', or see his political thriller televised to chime with Margaret Thatcher's fall was beyond my powers of observation. She had not yet won and few of us were confident she ever would.

But at least everyone knew Mick Dobbs. Michael Portillo stood out less.

Michael was recruited not long after I joined the office. Everyone immediately started to call him Porthole. The nickname was later dropped. He never cared for it.

Then there was Fluffy. Chris was no longer called Fluffy by the time he reached the House of Commons. Fluffy could hardly have been the name of the man who took responsibility for sorting out the poll-tax disaster, nobody ever called the Governor of Hong Kong Fluffy, and European commissioners for External Affairs are far too grand to be Fluffy: there's probably no French equivalent.

Chris Patten managed to combine freshness and youth with world-weariness and a sort of wink; pleasant, brisk and bright, unpompous, his only mark of pride being a certain intellectual impatience. Relaxed and informal as he was, Patten had the air of the commander about him even then: the young officer with whom all were on easy terms, but familiar only up to a point.

It was always and only ever up to a point, with Chris. Though very much on the inside, he was an outsider, and, for all his approachability, faintly mysterious. You were never quite sure where Chris had come from, or where he was going.

Did I spot the potential of these future stars? Did I spot their weaknesses? I'd like with the benefit of hindsight to claim so, but all I saw in Portillo was an ambitious young man, one of many, with a streak of ruthlessness about him, friendly up to a certain point but unreachable beyond it, and possessed of an air of mystery which he did nothing to disclaim. An attention-finder without seeming to be an attention-seeker, he attracted gossip from day one. And we could tell he was especially competent, no more and scarily self-contained. Nor were the baffling lapses of judgement which later tripped him evident then.

Despite Chris Patten's luminous ability, general niceness and serious claim to the epithet 'civilized', and the fact that as a very young director of our party's whole research effort his career was already pointing towards the top, I failed to spot what was to hold him back in the end.

I'd like to claim I suspected early that his fastidious reticence whenever lesser comrades were reaching for their blunderbusses might land him in – say – Hong Kong rather than Downing Street. But all I really noted was that Chris didn't like to play dirty and didn't encourage us to; and was too merciful towards some of the under-performers and old lags at Old Queen Street, for not everybody was equally ruthlessly raring to go.

During power cuts, for example, the head of our economics section had taken hours off work to return home daily to place her cats in her Volvo and sit there with the engine running and the car-heater on, warming them up. She had a critical role in drafting the party's 1978 pre-election outline of economic policy for government.

If too merciful, Chris knew where the problems were. He was a good boss with a light touch but a sharp eye and ear; and a stickler for quality. He did not miss much.

Ideologically speaking, though, he was no thruster. He did not just dissent from Thatcher's tone (to which his pained reaction was very plain) but from some of the core of what she was aiming to do. Chris, in those days, could be classified fairly simply as on the Tory left. I think he has been genuinely converted since, both to her personally and to the economic programme which at the time he and some of his Conservative Research Department contemporaries saw it as their job to temper. Ted Heath had not long ceased to be our leader and there remained a strong cohort rooted more in regret at his usurpation than enthusiasm for the alternative. Some wished he were there still. Others who knew there was no going back regretted he had not been replaced by somebody more centrist, somebody who had been (as they might have seen it) bred to Tory leadership.

There was no obvious contender. William Whitelaw, whom Thatcher had beaten, was widely admired but now a loyal lieutenant; and men such as Ian Gilmour, Peter Walker and Jim Prior had joined her readily enough and agreed to serve her. So to talk of splits or cabals in opposition would be inaccurate. Nobody I knew was plotting. On the whole – and it's about as much as you can ever say of a pack of rats like the Tories – we wanted our leader to win. But we were not sure she would, and, had she failed, there would have been no shortage of people to coo 'I told you so'.

At Old Queen Street the nickname for her was Hilda, her middle name. I regret to report that it was used by all, from our director down.

Hardly part of the Thatcherite vanguard, I was not among the smirkers at the Conservative Research Department either. I shared the ambivalence of one of my deskmates, Rob Shepherd, whose intensely argued pamphlets about the coming forces of 'globalization' we all regarded as politically deeply unsexy. Neither of us was a public school boy and neither of us shared her right-wing primitivism, but we loved watching her brutal interrogations swat away the woolly minded and defeatist stuffed shirts who infested our party. It is forgotten now that throughout the country and even among many Tories at the time, the question was thought to be, 'Is the Conservative Party capable of getting on with the trade unions?' This was considered a prerequisite for government. But not by her. I wanted her to win and was not as sure as some of my friends that this was unlikely.

My views anyway counted for little, for if we are talking of underperformers in the department, that probably includes me.

Nobody called me any nickname. I was never quite assimilated there. I was never really one of the fun people; never quite in the swim of things; never quite an insider. I just watched, and wrote unreadable tracts on defence, of which I knew little, and foreign affairs, on which I had a few liberal ideas about Africa and some growing doubts about Mrs Thatcher's tinny anti-Soviet rhetoric. My thoughts tended beyond my competence and my brief, and time and again my superiors brought me back to earth and my job, which was really to string together lists of quotes from party spokesmen, drearily bewailing Labour's 'craven folly', the 'dead hand of socialism' and Britain's 'weak' defence and foreign policies, 'under Labour'. To this day the words 'under Labour' make my spirits sink. I hate the hack prose to which too often I have resorted.

Fitfully though, Old Queen Street was a merry place. Michael Dobbs would return cackling from dreaded briefing sessions with Mrs T. She tended to brush aside earnestly intellectual advice and reach for the *Sun*, to see what the tabloid had chosen that morning for the two punchy, bullet-point editorials which in those days the *Sun* published on page two, opposite its big-breasted page three models. One day, Michael told us, she had plonked the paper down in front of the assembled male company, open at this spread, and said, 'What do you think of those two, eh?' She meant the editorials. No man present dared catch another's eye.

I had a dreadful immediate boss. Colonel Peter Joynes, head of the Defence and Foreign Affairs Section, took the term 'research' to imply a diligent hunt for anything the Conservative Party had already officially said about any subject, in order to re-hash it with lashings of quotation marks so party spokesmen could be prompted to say it again.

The Colonel had a wonderfully discriminating eye for any sign of originality or interest in a draft, which he would remove. I remember rushing into the loo, eyes brimming with tears, thinking that if there were any untraceable way of killing him I would do so then and there. I would have. He could scan a thousand words in a matter of seconds and light unerringly upon those few which might suggest to a shadow minister something he did not already know, or move the argument forward. These he would strike out.

What were those original thoughts excised by the dismal Joynes and so agitating me? They were hardly profound. I was worried that Mrs Thatcher, the drift of whose ideology on foreign and defence policy I usually agreed with, was adopting an angry and ungenerous tone in putting it across.

And she could rely too heavily on instinct. Over southern Africa, then a sore subject among Conservatives, many of our supporters, and I suspect her husband Denis, were disappointed we were not promising to send in the army to support Ian Smith against his terrorist insurgents (or even to lift economic sanctions against him). Peter Tapsell was one of the junior spokesmen on foreign affairs whom I served: well-connected, worldly and undoctrinaire as well as

knowledgeable about those parts of the world the Foreign Office used
to call the Outer Darkness. His pantomime-grand and florid manner
concealed a candid and reflective mind.

He needed little briefing. I agreed with Tapsell's advice to Mrs
Thatcher, insistently given however angry it made her: that a Conservative government would have to deal with black leaders and
former terrorists and we should steer clear of involvement with white
supremacists. There had been quite a panic too, when, with the visit
to Britain of the Israeli Prime Minister imminent, she had retorted
carelessly to her advisers that she would not shake hands with
Menachem Begin because he had once been a terrorist against the
British. She was calmed down. She did shake hands with him.

In the end she was forced to take Peter Tapsell's advice about
working with black nationalists in Rhodesia, but I do not think she
forgave Peter for giving it. She moved him to the Opposition Treasury
team, though he was an avowed Keynesian and rejected monetarism.
We knew he didn't want to go. It was said at the Conservative
Research Department that when he protested she had retorted that
she didn't care what Peter's economics were: she wanted someone to
beef up Geoffrey Howe's feeble efforts as her shadow Chancellor.
This calls into question the conventional wisdom that it was only
much later that Thatcher lost confidence in Howe.

Peter Tapsell took me under his wing. He showed me round his
merchant bank, James Capel. He told me Disraeli was right: as a man
gets older his thoughts turn to money; and he offered me a job.
Mercifully I never took it. Though I will never forget Peter's help
and confidence in me, I could not read a balance-sheet and would
have been useless in the City. I abhor cuff-links.

I had not been long at Old Queen Street before hearing gossip
about what everyone gigglingly called the 'Villa of Vice'. A number
of my Conservative Research Department colleagues, all male, had
taken to renting a villa in Italy for a few weeks every summer. Stories
from the Villa of Vice were whispered: tales of summer parties, tiffs,
assignments, sexual liberation, bedroom farces and handsome and
compliant Italian boys. An outsider to these romps, Bruce Anderson
(now a columnist) ran a book on which of our colleagues would end
up sleeping with which. There were some surprises. Only a select
handful of Conservative Research Department officers ever went, of

course, and who they were has conveniently slipped my memory. I was never invited, being considered of undetermined sexuality and rather a prude.

All this and more must have passed within Chris Patten's occasional earshot, but how much he heard, nobody knew. Even if he had heard there would have been no repercussion beyond perhaps the sort of friendly warning one might give a moth circling a flame. One of the nice things about Patten was that he combined personal probity and religious conviction with a tolerant uncensoriousness about others. We had the impression he enjoyed the stories: ready to hear though seldom to relay.

Did he know about another of our CRD colleagues, quite senior, whose habit was to pick up men in bars in the West End in the hopes of taking them home? This friend's problem was that he lived miles away from the centre of town, and was too stingy to call a cab. So he would board the night bus with his evening's catch.

The night buses' interiors were lit with fluorescent strip-lighting. It took the better part of an hour to get home. He was no oil-painting. The result, he recounted (to a general spluttering into our tea), was that in the harsh glare his new friends would take a second, harder, look at their would-be host, and, seized by panic, dive off the bus at intermediate stops all across London, if necessary to hitchhike their way back to safety.

Our colleague claimed to be losing catches at an attrition-rate of about two in five. One day he arrived late for work, speaking of an overnight burglary at his house – apparently a break-in through the bathroom window. We thought it might have been a break-out. Later, he did well in public life.

Did Chris know about the Tory punk-rock fans in Old Queen Street? Another young officer, John Wittingdale, used to slip off with me to punk gigs after work. John claims to have no recollection of this, but I seem to recall the two of us pogo-dancing along with the crowd at the back of the Lyceum in the Strand, as a group called 999 played. Stiff Little Fingers, I think, were on the billing too. Which of these bands was smashing out a number attacking the forces of law and order, as, along with the crowd, fists clenched, we punched the air and yelled along with the chorus – *Police oppression!* I cannot recall. John says he didn't punch the air.

John Wittingdale is shadow Secretary of State for Trade and Industry as I write. I wonder whether he remembers a man as assuredly on his way down in our days together at the Research Department, as John was on his way up. The shadow Foreign Affairs Secretary then was Reginald Maudling.

Maudling had been Home Secretary until personal disgrace, in the form of a business and property scandal, knocked him from office. Some of the financial impropriety alleged was never proved against him but on the kindest of readings he had been guilty of culpable negligence. Worse, there had been more than a whiff of greed.

Maudling had survived, however, as an MP and then in the new leader's shadow Cabinet. But he had lost credibility. Great was the laughter at Old Queen Street when it was reported that – on his feet and complaining from the Opposition front bench that, whereas it took German car workers an average of one and a half days to build a car, British workers took almost twice as long – he had been interrupted by a heckle from Labour's Dennis Skinner. 'An' 'ow long would it take *yer*, fats?' barked the working-class warrior, as Maudling floundered.

He had become lazy, and was rarely seen at Old Queen Street. I watched him from time to time in the House, where we officers would sometimes go out of curiosity or occasionally duty.

He seemed bored, lacklustre and tired, and was all out of tune with the new Thatcherite certainties gripping a party preparing for the possibility of government. But he also seemed wise: thoughtful and undogmatic in his responses. It is not unusual to find that men who have been touched both by power and also by some sort of disgrace, show towards the end a certain frankness, an impatience with certitude and a weary humanity. I like that, and admire it too.

Even though I was new to this game, very green and part (I suppose) of that new Thatcherite certainty – even though I had been impelled into the party by impatience at the old order which people like Maudling represented – I sensed that this type of politician and this type of politics were not all bad. Weariness, tolerance, proportion, and a feeling for the mutability of even apparent certainties, called only softly to me in those younger days, but I heard the call. I was changing.

As for Michael Portillo, I would have predicted great things for him, but not in politics. I thought of him as a future head of the Foreign Office, and perhaps of the whole civil service.

It was against a Whitehall backdrop I first encountered Michael. I was already at the Conservative Research Department; he was joining for a spell – possibly temporary – after graduating from Peterhouse College, Cambridge. He had still to make up his mind what permanent job he wanted and was attracted by a career in the diplomatic service. He had a fairly firm offer of a place there. Hearing I had recently left the Foreign Office, the new boy asked if we could talk over my reasons for doing so. I suggested a pub nearby on Victoria Street, the Albert. We walked over there together.

Michael was very young. There had been much excitement in the office, not all of it professional, about his arrival. He was strikingly attractive, cool and bright. He had a sort of presence about him. He kept his own counsel – not a common practice at Conservative Research Department. He dressed well – another novelty. He took some trouble over his hair – unheard of at Old Queen Street. He tucked in his shirt and polished his shoes. His sexuality was unknown.

A colleague whose office was just over the corridor from the washroom began to report that Michael could regularly be seen there tidying his hair and checking the mirror. But I would not call him vain, just uncommonly anxious that everything about him should be right. Of this he persuaded most of us, but never himself. 'I'll never be Prime Minister,' he used to moan, 'because I've got a foreign name.'

Over a pint or two of beer at the Albert, we talked. I described my own frustration as a trainee civil servant. He asked whether I thought the reasons which had led me to resign from the diplomatic service might apply to him too. I said I could not tell. Michael struck me as a better operator than I would ever be: more of an Office man, more contained, and anything but shambolic. That sort of quiet efficiency and personal command went down well in Whitehall. But I told him how little scope the job offered to initiate anything. I did not know how strong was his hankering for politics, and the Foreign Office was a more reliable route to an interesting and influential career close to the centre of power, and it paid better; but I left him with a sense (I think) of how the civil service can cramp.

He said nothing, but thanked me for my advice. He stayed.

Some two decades later he and I returned to the Albert for a second lunch. It was after Michael's agonizingly public loss of his Enfield Southgate seat in the 1997 general election. We had once been friends. We had fallen out over a sketch I had written when Michael was Secretary of State for Defence, making the annual oration at a Conservative conference in Blackpool, and seriously cocking it up with belligerent, boastful peroration and the quickly infamous 'Who Dares Wins' and 'Don't Mess with Britain' references to the SAS. That speech was not Michael at all, and we both knew it. I knew it as soon as I heard it, though the immediate reaction within the hall and among much of the media had been positive.

My sketch was abusive and he had pretty much cut me since. Tellingly, when a keen helper who told him at once he thought the speech ill-judged, bumped into Michael the next morning, Michael wouldn't even look at him, but turned on his heel and walked away. We all hate criticism but Michael's immediate response is to hate the critic too. This kind of thing is self-defeating and he is too clever a man not to realize this; I think he cannot help it.

By the time we had that second lunch at the Albert, however, he had plenty of opportunity to reflect. Over an indifferent fish-and-chips which probably gave Michael (a demanding diner) more pain than me, he thanked me for being honest about the speech. We shook hands.

Possibly his motivation was just friendly, possibly he hoped I would become an ally as a journalist. A relaxed dinner some time later (it was with Michael and his wife Carolyn and William Hague and his wife Ffion at the Portillos' house in Victoria Square) seemed to take away what was left of the chill.

But it did not affect my professional judgement of him as a politician. I've never been convinced by Michael as a potential leader, though he is capable and cultured, has a mind which runs quick and deep and that precious thing: stage presence. He is too impatient, too regularly prey to small, key errors of judgement. The conference speech on defence was an example. Were I Prime Minister I would have Michael as my Chancellor, but watch him like a hawk.

His hesitant disloyalty to John Major, having telephone lines for an HQ installed when Major invited challengers – then leaving it to Redwood to wield the knife – was not sure-footed. His restless search for attention while he was between constituencies was oddly impatient. His bizarre 'maiden' speech, later, as the new MP for Kensington and Chelsea – in which he held up a patent Australian portable, inflatable pillow called a Portillow and explained how the instructions recommended us to apply our lips to it and blow – escaped most press attention, but not that of the *Times* sketch.

And, just as I was never persuaded of Michael's right-wingery when he was (under Thatcher) on the right, so later I was only half-convinced by his conversion to 'inclusive' Toryism, under William Hague. I stick in Michael's case to first impressions at the Albert: of an unsentimental, undogmatic, 'can do' sort of young man, with exceptionally clean fingernails, well-read and cultured, unfailingly polite. A young man at root good and humane, but a young man on the way up. Michael's politics are explained by ambition, probably not ideology, and certainly not – God help us – compassion.

So I did not join his press claque as he might have hoped. During the election campaign of 2001 when Portillo, then shadow Chancellor, was trying to escape the press because his deputy, Oliver Letwin, had made some indiscreet remarks about spending cuts, I tracked him down to a rainy street in Leek, Staffordshire. Improbably he was visiting a knicker factory. I stood in the foyer beside his welcoming party. He walked in, shook hands with them, walked straight past me without looking at me, and stalked away. This kind of thing is terribly silly. Contrast it with Tony Blair, about whom I have always been unspeakably rude, who remains able to manufacture a matey grin when he passes.

Of Michael Portillo's bid for the leadership a few months later I wrote (as he launched his campaign) this:

In Africa yesterday there was a solar eclipse. In London, Michael Portillo launched his leadership campaign. Both events inspired wonder.

The second inspired perplexity too. To kick off his bid to reconnect the Tory Party to the concerns of ordinary people, Mr Portillo chose as a venue a millennial-chic bar restaurant – all glass tops, cherry veneer and recessed lighting – in fashionable St James's. Outside The Avenue (as it is called) was the establishment's logo on a purple (or, this being London, mauve) flag: a simple @ sign – ubergroovy or what? [This was] a swanky purveyor of small pieces of papaya and kiwi fruit on big white plates. The paintings were abstract, the pain was au chocolat, the scrambled egg came in pastry thimbles, the coffee in cafetières and the bacon in nouvelles butties.

I was tempted to ask for a cup of tea but feared being frog-marched from the place by young men in black with earphones. The decor screamed metropolitan elite. The mirrors were huge. The waiters were gorgeous. The place breathed self-regard.

Why, Michael, why? It was a small, key misjudgement of the type that has characterized Portillo's career. One recalled the time when he hired an entire cinema for a fringe meeting at his party's conference in Bournemouth.

And he came among us like a bridegroom at a wedding feast, walking from elegant table to elegant table and remembering first names. The aspirant leader had ensured that the guest list of journalists was leavened with camera-friendly political supporters to applaud whenever he spoke.

Francis Maude, happeningly jacketless, opened the meeting. The party needed, said Mr Maude, 'a big leader'; a man, he said, of 'high intellect' who would also have 'abundant energy' as well as 'deep convictions' and 'broad appeal'. Who could this colossus be?

Big, high, abundant, deep and broad, Michael Portillo stepped forward. He was also gruff.

'I want the Conservative Party,' he growled, 'to be four things!'

'Great,' I thought, 'abundant indeed. Actually, two or three would do. Or even one . . .'

'Not against things,' he continued. My heart sank.

In his book *Tory Wars*, Simon Walters paints a horrifying picture of skulduggery in the Portillo camp, heading a chapter on Michael's image problems with a quote from him: 'Everyone hates me; the *Sun* hates me; Matthew Parris hates me . . .'

This worried me as I do not hate him at all. Not long after, I saw him at a party chatting to the former singer Adam Faith. So I went up to the pair. 'Michael,' I said, 'Simon Walters quotes you as believing I hate you. I don't. I tried during the leadership election to give an honest assessment of your chances . . .' But I got no further. Michael inclined his head with a tight smile, and walked away. 'Charming,' said Adam Faith.

But all this is a long way from the Albert, a long way from the handsome, personable young colleague I met at the Conservative Research Department. At that first pub lunch we had talked about a choice between a possible career in politics, where he as yet had no place, and Whitehall where he already did. Had he but known it, he and I would have had more to discuss than that, and I wonder whether, with the career civil service in mind, he was wondering, as I had wondered, how much one would have to hide there, how much one could hide, and for how long.

I don't suppose we'll ever lunch again, or that if we did he or I would be any more certain than we ever were what this strange, troubled, valuable, talented, silly man should do.

I have a cheek to use a word like silly, for having downgraded myself from the Foreign Office I was shortly to downgrade again, moving to Westminster, where Margaret Thatcher was in need of a letter-writer. And this soon-to-be correspondence clerk to the leader of the Opposition – by day – was going home every afternoon to a South London squat, and by night cruising on Clapham Common.

My creepy landlord had given notice he wanted the flat back, so with my sub-tenants I had needed somewhere new to live. We looked at cheap flats for sale. The nicest I saw was in Gayville Road, SW11. I had come close to making an offer but changed my mind. There was no way I could live in Gayville Road, work in Old Queen Street, and spend evenings on Clapham Common. Instead we had moved into a sort of squat in a big, derelict house in a nearby street, Hillier Road, SW11 – number 27.

It was not the worst sort of squatting. We did not break in. The man who owned the place was afraid of hostile squatters and preferred to have friendly ones, so he arranged to leave the place open for us, warned us about the lack of gas or electricity, the leaking roof and the dry rot – and left us to it. We bought some junk furniture in a second-hand shop, and moved in.

I remember there that long, hot summer of 1976. It seemed it would never rain again. The baking air was filled with the sounds of Abba's 'Dancing Queen' and I was trying to raise a litter of newborn kittens I had found on a skip by dangling into their mouths a piece of string soaked in sweetened milk. Number 27 Hillier Road was so infested with rot that many of the floors were caving in and you had to be careful where you stepped or slept. Everywhere was the smell of the fungus, whose strange yellow flowers were bursting all over through cracks in the paintwork. One of my brothers, who was going through an alcoholic phase, was dossing down with us and all our bottles kept disappearing, but I was too fond of him to care about that. I kept canaries in a cage at the time – I don't know why – and he looked after them faithfully for me.

At night I would go up on to the Common. Not often nor for long at first. I was ashamed of the sordidness and anonymity, and a bit afraid, but told myself I might find true love this way, and besides it was the safest option. Which, short of celibacy, it was. Any of the known bars or clubs in Earl's Court or pubs such as the Union in Brixton carried the danger of being seen by people who both recognized me and who might not have been afraid to say where they saw me.

I have already described some of the ways of the place; and it was then that I began to learn those signs and warnings, and to understand the odd amalgam of a cold and predatory anonymity, with a shared sense of being all in the same boat together. But it was a hard place, inhabited by hard people, and its code, though there was a code, was almost without remorse. The saddest thing I learned was that lack of experience was regarded as contemptible, and a sort of heartless confidence was all.

When you talk to other gay men about their own reactions to cruising, they all say the same thing, record the same dismay. Everybody, it seems, just wants someone to cuddle; nobody ever really cared for the sexual jungle; nobody approved of anonymous sex. We all agree that 'partnership' is what it's all about. Cruising was a last resort.

So who are all these people, these people who never speak up around the dinner table, who want it hard and faceless? Or are they the same people, the same as those who protest their longing for tenderness and constancy – unwilling, away from the dim sodium light, the glow of a cigarette and the hiss of the wind in the trees, to admit to another side to their nature?

What a page it would have made in the *Daily Mail*: 'Thatcher aide in gay sex squat shock'.

8. Under Maggie's Stairs

I left Old Queen Street excited to be going where I thought I might be of use. Colleagues offered me their sympathies on what few considered a promotion and most thought a ghastly prospect: to Hilda's staff.

I was overjoyed. Better, I told them, to be a slave in Caesar's palace than a centurion in Gaul.

Caesar had her work cut out. She was pre-eminently and forever busy. There was no time in her life for sipping coffee, staring at the wall and wondering what it was all about. Busy-ness, a sense of purpose, was what impressed you first and always about her. You were struck by the bustle of her walk – small steps, like a partridge conscious of pursuit but unwilling to break into an undignified flap. You were riveted by the sudden swivel of her concentration as you spoke, her eyes locking on to fix you with an auto-focused glance, an intense beam, which said: 'Very well, you have fifteen seconds to deliver, fifteen seconds during which you will have my undivided attention. The countdown starts now: 15–14–13 . . .' It was flattering and unnerving at the same time.

Her attention, fiercely bestowed, could be brutally withheld. The very liberal Rabbi Julia Neuberger described to me the Thatcher handshake as offered to those in whom she was resolved not to be interested: the small hand proferred as though hanging lifeless from the wrist, said Julia, a bunch of limp fingers dangling like a dead fish, to be grasped or not, as you wished.

In her presence, men who knew more than she would ever know, men who were cleverer than she would ever be, turned into jelly.

I did. Whatever her defects, whatever her prejudices, however blinkered she may have been from worlds not dreamed of in her philosophy, Margaret Thatcher struck me from the start as a natural leader. She lacked for much, but never for this: certitude. She radiated it. I would not quite call it calm for there was a fierce alertness to danger under the surface: the cartoonist Garland gets it spot-on in the tiny flush he lends to her cheeks. But if we are to place our faith in a leader we need at least to believe she knows where she is heading. She did. She may have wanted your advice on how to get there, but the desired destination was never in doubt.

There has always been a false contradiction between the recollections of colleagues who say she wouldn't listen, and those who are sure she did. Both are right. Thatcher would take advice on how to achieve what she wanted but not on what she ought to want. She needed maps and diagrams. If you could show her instructions then she was all attention, putty in your hands. From the simplest tradesman to the most brilliant quantum physicist, she respected know-how. She would not second-guess a plumber, let alone a field marshal. Having decided on the ends she had humility as to the means, and was ready to call in the expert and take advice.

She would not, however, brook challenge on her underlying philosophy or her strategic goals. As Prime Minister she knew she wanted an independent nuclear deterrent in the same way that, as householder, she might know she wanted a dishwasher. The plumber was there to fit the dishwasher, not question its necessity. The military strategists were there to explain how the deterrent worked or supply examples of its potential usefulness, not argue about disarmament. On overall strategy she relied upon instinct, of which she was not short. The only objection to her ultimate goals which Mrs Thatcher would allow was that, however desirable, a goal might be simply unachievable. This, after much bridling, she would hear, and if persuaded (often after humiliating the message-bearer) accept.

Her certitude infused all the small staff at the House of Commons, as does a sense of siege. In the Opposition leader's office I joined in 1976 it always felt like a kind of siege. Siege from the impossible workload she and all of us faced. Siege from the press who, while not universally hostile, were incredulous and finding grave difficulty in taking the new leader seriously. Her disadvantage here was that her natural allies on the *Daily Telegraph*-reading right were inclined to be the type of Tory who found the idea of a grammar-school girl becoming leader of a party hard to take. They were later to pretend (they pretend today) that they were with her all along. They were not. They were with the doubters and smirkers. Her early stalwarts were the highbrow theoretical right, not the traditionalists. 'Disgusted of Godalming', later to become her core supporter, was at first disgusted that the Tories had elected a female to lead his party.

Sniping from this quarter was a cruel beginning. Siege from the government an Opposition leader must expect. I used to sit in on Prime Minister's Questions sometimes to watch her, willing her to be brilliant. She wasn't. Her performance was scratchy and thin. Jim Callaghan's government was coming apart in his hands but he was still able regularly to best the Opposition leader at the dispatch-box. The strength and confidence those who met her privately saw, turned edgy in this very public forum. She was facing the man for whom but a couple of years ago I had been writing mellow after-dinner speeches: wily, avuncular old Sunny Jim.

She would rise with a critical inquiry, perhaps a shade too shrill. He would reply that the Right Honourable Lady really must calm down: the Rt Hon. Lady had worked herself into a rage about something she did not entirely understand.

This would throw her into a rage. Her voice would rise and sharpen. He would reply that the Rt Hon. Lady must please stop shrieking, and would do best to go away and learn a little more about the subject before raising it in this House. She would subside, fuming. And return to her Commons office, and the quiet, undeclared siege from her own party.

All of us in the office called her (speaking to each other) 'Mrs T'. We knew they didn't care for Mrs T much over at Old Queen Street. We knew Conservative Central Office at Smith Square, though loyal, was dim. We knew various of Mrs T's colleagues were bad-mouthing her at smart dinner parties all over London. We had heard Julian Critchley rehearsing what would later be cast as his advice to readers: to write to 'The Prime Minister, c/o Dickins & Jones'. We knew half the party were waiting for her to fail. Lady Bingley laughed that she probably dressed at Cresta Fashions. And we knew our former leader, Edward Heath, was barely on speaking terms and in a storming and perpetual pout about her. She would not even hear his name among us and we were told to steer clear of the whole subject. 'No jokes,' Richard Ryder, her private secretary, warned us, 'best not to mention him at all; she doesn't see the joke.' She didn't.

Nobody should confuse the Sir Edward we observe (as I write) in the autumn of his life with the graceless former leader we faced then, still brooding over his old party; still troubling its spirit; still dividing the loyalties of our poor, faithful county activists unsure to whom they were supposed to be faithful; and still refusing to speak to his successor, struggling to find her feet as the new leader. Ted started it, not Margaret, and it was a serious problem at the time – and more interesting to the newspapers than any battle she might have with Labour.

If Mrs Thatcher learned from these early days a certain distrust of the male Tory establishment, a certain chippiness towards her own senior colleagues, and a tendency to appeal over the heads of those around her to a more natural constituency outside – press and public – then from my time among the young of the old guard before the old guard realized its day was done, I can testify that the provocation was not all on her side.

Though not seriously challenged, the Thatcher ascendancy had not secured itself within the party establishment. And nowhere was this more more keenly sensed than in the Conservative Research Department.

I have said Margaret Thatcher was little admired at Old Queen Street in the mid-seventies. Doubts did not cohere around any particular policy she promoted, although her tendency to be gung-ho about all of them grated. Europe was an irritant but not a defining issue. Her own views on Europe seemed vague, perhaps unformed.

Besides, even by pro-Common Market Tories, Ted Heath was suspected of having pushed his luck there, especially in the burning issue (now forgotten) of his alleged purge of Eurosceptics from Conservative Central Office's approved list of would-be parliamentary candidates. True or false, the legend of this purge became one of those old sores from which the bitterness of the Tory zealots who helped bring down John Major twenty years later can be indirectly traced.

No, Thatcher-scepticism was not a 'Europe' issue nor exactly an economic or libertarian or left/right issue. Among my peers it was felt to be more a matter of good taste. The patrician Tory left – the likes of Ian Gilmour – joined the traditionalist right in finding her vulgar. To their high-born doubt whether anything could actually be done in politics (or should be), there was a distinctly public-school snobbishness about her being a grocer's daughter from Grantham.

Few put it like this, and certainly not to her, but the occasions when she would go over to Old Queen Street for briefing sometimes became embarrassing. I had seen it from within. Now I saw it from without. She disliked that walk to the office and I'm not surprised. Small gatherings would be arranged of senior officers concerned with whichever subjects were for discussion: informal meetings at which she could ask questions of others, as could others of her. From Westminster I heard reports from both sides that these could be uncomfortable encounters with an undercurrent not unlike the testing of a brittle schoolmistress by a clever but insubordinate sixth form. Sniggers were heard, or almost heard. Questions would be put to her, between whose lines could be read an intention to make her look ignorant or silly. There was a laughing up the sleeve, a collective snigger.

I am sure this was not the rule – Chris Patten was never less than courteous – but I had the clear impression that, while any Conservative Research Department officer who went around bawling that the leader was an ignorant, populist witch would have been thought well out of order, anyone who declared undying adoration towards our new leader would not quite have been one of the boys. The cuff-linked and silk-tied young men in double-breasted suits who were to become so much the Thatcher youth-wing in the eighties were exactly the sort who were not there when she needed them, in the seventies. Thatcher-worship was to start in the press, not the Tory Party.

The office of the leader of the Opposition was a small suite on various floors connected by stairs, just behind the Speaker's chair. Though there were many rooms the impression lent by the fevered braggadocio of Barry's and Pugin's hateful, overheated neo-Gothic monstrosity, the Palace of Westminster, was of cramp and conspiracy. Can any public building ever have taken so much space to create so little grace? The architecture and interior decoration of such a building should breathe calm. They breathed obsession, trickery and distrust. But we were believers. Even when things were going adrift, we had faith in her.

My work was a labour of Sisyphus. The faster I answered letters to Mrs Thatcher the faster they seemed to come. It's a remarkable job dealing with an Opposition leader's public correspondence. Her entire mailbag was plonked every morning into my broom-cupboard of an office. She rarely received less than fifty letters a day. After she voiced a fear Britain was being 'swamped' by immigration she received nearly 5,000 in one week. The burden of opening all of them, referring on the small minority which were not 'general public correspondence', and dealing with the rest, was shared between two or three secretaries, a long series of emergency temps, and me.

There was willowy, blonde Caroline, who was rather glamorous in a supermodel kind of way, confident, energetic, rude and fun. Mark Thatcher used to hang extremely spottily around and find excuses to look in on her work – but Caroline was no more interested in him than in another young Tory hopeful, now an MP with innumerable children, whose complexion was even worse. Even if she had been keen, she will have known – we all did in the office – that Mrs T absolutely abhorred the tangling of politics with love; office romances were anathema to her. None dare speak in her presence the name of Jonathan Aitken, the young MP who had jilted her daughter Carol. Another secretary, much admired for her work, had had an affair with a married Tory MP and left under a cloud. Though often relaxed about people's private lives our leader took a dim view of women who had affairs with other women's husbands.

There was Sally: quieter and less volatile, and much liked. And there was Diane Stevens, whose husband, a member of the band Procul Harum, had written and performed the hit song 'A Whiter Shade of Pale' before dying in a haze of drugs, leaving Diane with a deaf and disabled son, to fend for herself.

I have no idea whether Diane was really a Conservative but she was a devoted member of our team. Her responsibility was to handle the 'poorlies' among our correspondents. These were members of the public who wrote not about policy or politics, but needing the help or advice an MP may give. Diane was well placed to understand some of the ups and downs and turbulent lives which leaped from the lined pages of that sometimes confused or semi-literate manuscript which anyone in public life who acquires a reputation for sympathy or influence is bombarded with.

I still worry about the gap between the time and attention you can devote to answering such pleas, and the time and anxiety which has gone into their expression. These days I get such letters sent to me on my own behalf. I cannot today, and could not then, come to terms with that gap, and live always in fear of brushing aside a last cry for help from someone with a genuine grievance and nowhere else to turn. If only these people knew in what haste and with what impatience their *cris de coeur* may be speed-read and binned. There is something infinitely pathetic about hope misplaced.

One of the nicest things I know about Mrs Thatcher was her attention to this. However little we could reasonably do to help, the poorlies were not to be answered with a 'thank you for your views'. When Diane and I would ask her to sign a personal reply to someone in trouble she never grumbled. We were never reproved by Margaret Thatcher for asking her to take some small trouble to help a nobody. She could be brutal in her rejection of a plea but she always insisted it be properly heard.

One such letter, I remember, was from a woman whose husband had just died. She confided in Mrs Thatcher that life was hard to bear, and she would find comfort in the knowledge that one day she might see her husband again. Did Mrs Thatcher, whom her correspondent so admired, herself believe in an after-life? Neither Diane nor I had any idea how to answer on the Opposition leader's behalf, so we placed this letter in the pile we would regularly leave in the evening for her personal attention, which we were never once asked to cut down in size, and which would be returned promptly, often the next morning, with notes and advice scrawled all through it in her bold, regular, unmistakable blue felt-tip script.

In this case Mrs T had handwritten her own reply. 'Christians,' she wrote, 'believe in an after-life, and I am a Christian.'

I was puzzled by this: struck that she should have been attentive enough to give the letter a special reply but that having done so she could not bring herself to answer with a simple yes. She was never a good liar.

I would often be required to draft articles which the Tory leader had been asked to write for newspapers, forewords to books and pamphlets, and messages to charities and organizations of which she approved. I rarely hit the style she liked, as I had usually managed to do with Jim Callaghan. She distrusted humour and was ill-at-ease with anything which sounded like musing, self-deprecation or reflectiveness. Her preference was for bold, simple statements of the obvious.

I once opened a letter addressed to her from the Cambridge Freedom Association, requesting a 'message' from the leader. This sort of request was always dealt with by her personally, but I attached to it my own draft message in case she should want some ideas to work on. It included this passage, a copy of which I kept:

Each of us wants to be free to do those things he considers harmless, enjoyable or useful. Each of us is happy to allow similar freedoms to others. Even a Stalinist would agree to this. But the acid test of belief in individual liberty is our willingness to allow people to do things we consider harmful, unpleasant or useless.

The draft was intercepted and removed.

I only once got it spot-on. An organization involved in supporting voluntary associations – I forget which – had requested a message of support from the leader of the Opposition, which she asked me to write. The point of the message I drafted for her was that human association should be for the purpose of action rather than for association's sake; that people find companionship best when they have a common purpose; and that, as Noel Coward put it, work is more fun than fun.

Mrs Thatcher was quite uncharacteristically delighted with this, enthusing in the margin that it was EXACTLY what she thought. The three-line underlining in her blue felt-tip pen made the emphasis clear. I had, just for a moment, found her voice, but I rarely found it again.

Curiously my work did not feel very political, except that it taught me that my countrymen, or those who wrote, sounded more conservative than any of the three parties between which they had to choose. By no means was it only Conservatives who wrote to Mrs Thatcher: Labour voters, angry at what was happening, wrote too. I began to understand, at the same time as distrusting, the power of populism. I saw the danger of ignoring it.

Our correspondents were not an especially charitable lot. There were marked regional variations. Londoners and the Scots did not write much. Essex did. Correspondents from Wales, even sympathizers, often chose a particularly vindictive and personal style.

Letters from Mrs T's colleagues, or anybody who sounded important or grand, went straight to Richard Ryder, as did any envelope containing money – even as little as a five-pound note.

It fell to me to organize all replies on policy. We had a letter from a man in the West Country who had lost his job because he had refused to join the closed shop in his industry (a practice, backed by law, according to which the trade union representing a workforce could force every employee, on pain of dismissal, to join the union, and stop employers from recruiting anyone who refused to). Our correspondent described his distress to Mrs Thatcher, and asked her what plans her party had, should she become Prime Minister, to remedy such injustice.

The Conservative Party had no plans – or none that any of us knew of. We sent the letter over to Old Queen Street where Jim Prior's man worked on employment policy. Jim was the Opposition spokesman on such things.

The letter came back with a suggested reply in draft. The burden of the draft, to be signed on Mrs T's behalf, was that she was most distressed to hear of her correspondent's problems; that the closed shop was a vexed and sensitive issue; that the party would need to consult carefully and at length with the Confederation of British Industry and with the Trades Union Congress before deciding, in government, how to proceed; and that meanwhile Mrs T wished her correspondent and his family the very best at this difficult time, and her thoughts were with them.

This was not the sort of thing she would want sending on her behalf.

I put the draft up to her. Back it came next morning. She had scrawled a big, bold blue diagonal line right through it. Beneath, she had written – and this was all she had written – 'I HATE the Closed Shop.' HATE was underlined, three times. I returned this amended draft to Jim Prior's man.

All hell, we heard, broke loose in the Prior camp at the Conservative Research Department. They were aghast, and I remember sympathizing with them. I cannot recall what reply was eventually agreed and sent; it was true the leader had strayed over the line and beyond agreed policy, and was making policy on the hoof. And yet, and in a deeper sense, it was we, not she, who had failed to understand.

*

On 12 February 1978 I was walking home from Westminster to Waterloo for a train to Clapham Junction from which it was a short walk to my flat. Later I was meeting an office-mate: young Alison Ward, one of Mrs Thatcher's secretaries.

It was a cold night and dark. I walked alongside the Thames in front of County Hall. The tide was high. Whipped by a winter wind the water was rough. I saw a little boy and girl weeping and staring into the river. I asked them what was wrong. 'Our dog is drowning,' they said. It had scrambled over the parapet and tumbled in. The little dog's head was visible in the swell, swimming in circles, unable to find the steps. It had been in for twenty minutes. I could see it was floundering. I did a stupid thing. I threw off my suit (I only had two) and jumped into the Thames.

Do not ever do this. I lasted a couple of minutes – just long enough to reach the dog (now swimming towards Westminster Bridge), start swimming him towards some submerged steps – and collapse just short of them. Hands reached out and grabbed me. It was as if I were a puppet and someone had cut my strings.

Be warned, should you ever mix with very cold water: you do not fade gradually, allowing time to get out. First the tremendous shock of the cold hits you. Then for a while you are fine and swimming strongly, and you think, 'Amazing! I can do this.' Then – snap – your muscles go. There is no warning.

I was lucky. People helped me up the steps. A council janitor got me into County Hall through a window and dried me with tea towels. I dressed. The children's uncle turned up. Dispatching the kids and the wet dog, he insisted on taking me to a pub called the Old Father Thames at Waterloo.

I asked if he thought I should have a stomach pump, but he bought me two double whiskies which was much nicer. Then I remembered Alison. I must postpone our evening. Finding a public telephone I tried to dial but my hands were shaking with the after-shock and I could not coordinate, so the uncle dialled for me. He gave me five pounds for a taxi home. I thanked him, said goodbye, pocketed the money and took the train, which was 32p.

Alison told Mrs Thatcher. I may have neglected to ask her not to. The uncle told the RSPCA. Mrs T called me in.

She looked at me, as she was to do so often in the years ahead, with an expression which said 'there's something not quite right about that boy'; it was, perhaps, her first intimation that I was mad.

She told me I had acted very foolishly in jumping into the Thames to save a dog, and should never dream of doing such a thing again. I remember clearly that this was not a 'You were stupid but . . .': it was a 'You were stupid.' It was only a dog, after all, she said. She added that the RSPCA were anxious to award me a certificate for bravery in a small public ceremony, with the press present, and she would be pleased (as they had asked) to attend and present it.

And so it came to pass that on a cold, sunny day in March 1978, in a short but moving ceremony on Westminster Bridge, and in the presence of the dog, called Jason, and the children, Patrick and Elizabeth Hanlon, and their parents, and the Mother Superior in charge of their school, and the late Sir Freddy Burden, parliamentary president of the RSPCA, and a small scattering of newspaper photographers, Mrs Thatcher squared up to the cameras to present me with a framed certificate citing my 'courage and humanity'.

Meanwhile, something dreadful was happening to Jason, or rather to Mrs Thatcher. The dog had caught sight of Mrs T's elegant calf (she had nice legs). The little pink sliver of Jason's penis emerged from its furry sheath. The dog lunged joyfully at the leg. Gripping Mrs Thatcher's knee with his two forelegs, he thrust purposefully at the hosiery.

Mrs Thatcher looked radiant in the photographs. So did Jason. His victim exhibited that marvellous ability which I saw in her then for the first time, and was to see so often subsequently: the ability to pretend something untoward is not happening. From her friendly smile to the cameras you would never have guessed the indignity which was occurring below. Happily (it would not happen today) the newspaper picture editors chose snaps taken before (or after) Jason's passionate encounter with the leader of the Opposition, so the headline in one of the following morning's papers – 'Hold on Jason' – spoke truer than its readers knew.

I watched, a while ago now, while Alison Ward, in emeralds, attended in the Lords chamber as her husband became Lord Wakeham. She had married John Wakeham after his first wife was killed by the Brighton bomb. The Baroness Thatcher of Kesteven was there in the

Lords too. Patrick and Elizabeth will have been grown up. Jason will have been dead.

Letters were coming in from the public faster than we could answer them. She would grab handfuls from my desk, and start reading them and suggesting replies – a practice we discouraged. So I started preparing for her an occasional report, summarizing the strands of opinion represented in the letters she was getting and giving her some idea of the numbers, and changes in numbers. It's a measure of how far and fast things have moved in the tracking of public sentiment that my idea was considered quite a novelty; office clerks had hardly bothered party leaders with such things before.

She liked these summaries. She always wanted to know 'what people are thinking'. When they were thinking what she thought they were thinking it seemed to buoy her a lot.

In making their assessments of Margaret Thatcher's great resolve then and later to stick to her course, historians should not overlook the way the private man is invigorated by the public temper. We really are not islands, though biography may see us so. Ted Heath, like Thatcher, had meant to 'stand up to' the trade unions and the defeatists in politics but the national mood – the force, as it were – was not with him. The force was very much with her. She had the great advantage of going with the national grain.

The temper of the times is the hardest thing to anticipate as a prophet, to record as a chronicler or to review as a historian. It is evanescent, the ghost in the room which, when the photographs are developed, does not show up. You can neither predict it before it comes nor measure it after it has gone; it arrives and departs without warning and leaves scant trace. But you can feel it in the now and it can be very strong. Through all Margaret Thatcher's trials – when colleagues were sceptical, when the unions were hostile, when the universities and newspapers and chattering classes were contemptuous, when even the polls looked dodgy and whenever things didn't work or went wrong – she will have been conscious of a fine lacework of British opinion, prejudice and sentiment, as flimsy and as persistent as gossamer, hanging in the late-twentieth-century air. It supported not so much her as her way of seeing the world. It sustained her. You might even say it created her. I could read it in all those hundreds of thousands of letters, and so could she.

I know she read my summaries carefully because they would come back with heavy underlinings beneath any opinion cited which was close to her own. Passages recording unwelcome views were left unmarked: a reaction mirrored in the way her face would blank over whenever anybody started to tell her something unhelpful. Mrs Thatcher had a well-developed ability to draw down the blinds. My llamas display a similar characteristic: if any aspect of the scene displeases them they simply look away. This refusal even to acknowledge unwelcome news is a trait I have noticed both in the very successful and the mad.

'Dear Mrs Thatcher,' began a letter in small, careful ink. It ran to many pages. I wish I had read to the end for it concluded 'and I have always admired you, Mrs Thatcher, and will be voting Conservative at the next election'.

I never finished the letter. It was late and I had been working flat out all day. This was not long after Mrs T's 'swamping' speech had swamped us – with letters – and the backlog lingered for months. I was told later that my successor in that job collapsed. I was working myself silly.

I was tired. And something about this letter irritated me. Our correspondent was complaining about her council house in Gravesend. Nothing about her house, or the estate in which it was situated, seemed to please her. The walls were too thin, for a start, and she could hear the budgerigar next door pecking its seed. Some neighbours had a child with Down's syndrome and she did not see why she should have to put up with the nuisance. She also objected to the presence of coloured immigrants on her estate; she did not see why such people should be in public housing near her.

I took against this woman. Council accommodation was vastly subsidized in those days and rents were low. There I was, struggling at the end of every month to pay the mortgage on my flat at 41 Bramfield Road, SW11 (my housemates and I had had to quit the squat) – and she was complaining about her subsidized council house. The recipient of support herself, she had no charity for those less fortunate than she.

In a moment of petulant self-righteousness I dictated this letter to Helen Senior, a quiet, talented woman whose dream was to become an actress:

. . . At Mrs Thatcher's request I am replying on her behalf to your recent letter. I hope you will not think me too blunt if I say that it may well be that your council accommodation is unsatisfactory, but considering the fact that you have been unable to buy your own accommodation you are lucky to have been given something, which the rest of us are paying for out of our taxes.

    With good wishes,

    Yours sincerely,

    Matthew Parris.

If I had only left that to re-read after the weekend. How could I have been so stupid as to commit such a spiteful little outburst to print? How could I have been so stupid as to think it in the first place?

    Reading it, I feel the same spasm of dislike for the writer as, reading the letter to which it was a reply, I had felt for the author of that. My reply was disgustingly prim; I did not know the woman or her circumstances; and there was no need to personalize. When I had finished dictating, Helen, who was overqualified to be a temp, raised an eyebrow. 'No,' I said, 'she deserves it.'

    And that was the last I thought of the matter – or the last I thought I would think. Overstretched as we were, the secretaries used to sign letters 'p.p.' above my own name, and Helen signed this one. Much later, some speculated that Helen had written the letter and I had nobly taken the rap. I regret to say that was not true. I wish it were.

    I should have recalled it, of course. I should have re-read it. Then I should have screwed it up, thrown it in the bin and started again, expressing sympathy for Mrs T's correspondent and gratitude for her offer of support. The letter we did dispatch was one of those we all write in our heads from time to time, and sometimes get as far as committing to paper; but which should thereafter be treated as therapy and jettisoned.

    Instead of being consigned to the bin, mine was sent on Mrs Thatcher's notepaper, embossed 'The Rt Hon. Mrs Margaret Thatcher MP' in blue, and (printed beneath my name) 'Private Office of the Leader of the Opposition'.

    I forgot about it.

*

My mistress would never have sent such a letter, though I think it represented her thinking better than it did mine. I was merely petulant. She really believed homeowners were hard done by. But one must be careful before spraying out generalizations about what Thatcher 'really believed'. There are two pictures of this woman and the organization which sustained her; one is at odds with the other; both are true, or were true at different times. From below stairs I saw glimpses of both of them.

In one picture she is calm, strong, convinced and utterly in control. This is the Thatcher some senior colleagues describe at the helm, able to speed-read an intricate brief and command the question at the dispatch box half an hour later. This is the Thatcher who, visiting the Falkland Islands after the conflict, had arranged to spend the entire journey by Hercules inside a medium-sized Portakabin which had been dragged into the fuselage of the cargo plane especially for her; and had emerged into the pale sunshine in Port Stanley to greet the adoring crowd unruffled and uncreased, immaculately made-up and her hair perfect – raring to go.

In the other picture her calm, like that of a sprinter meditating furiously before the race, is tinged with a panic she is managing not quite to betray.

In one picture she is the woman for whom first impressions on meeting someone are final – who knows at once – and who sizes up a problem and grasps the solution fast and decisively.

In the other her snap judgements are not a sign of strength or of calm, but of too little inner confidence to acknowledge error, see doubt as friend rather than foe, or think again. Unflinchingness can be a kind of quiet hysteria; he who thinks he knows at first sight may indicate not so much his intuition as a mulish disinclination to reopen the case.

She was not so confident as to think she needed no help. In spinning the deftly spun persona which served her so well, she came to rely more on professional advice than Tony Blair has ever bothered to do. A warm, funny, stylish man called Gordon Reece – champagne instead of morning coffee, a mane of hair, ostentatious cigars and a show-biz manner – was often with her, advising on almost everything. We believed it was he who organized the softening and lowering of her voice by half an octave in the late seventies.

We in her office saw and heard the result. Gordon deshrilled her. In the seventies barely a critical commentary about her was missing the word 'shrill'. By the mid-eighties nobody used it. Nobody would use it now. She had seen what people said, and made the necessary adjustments on the hoof.

In much bigger ways than that Thatcherism was always so much more of a seat-of-the-pants operation than the retrospective view — of a steady and relentless rise to ascendancy — would have us believe. It is sometimes remarked that Mrs Thatcher's administrations made up their ideology and programme for government as they went along; less often is it suggested — but I believe — that the young Margaret Roberts made herself up, also, as she went along.

One day, near the end of my time in charge of the leader's correspondence, I walked into the Shadow Cabinet Room to retrieve our papers from the great oak shadow Cabinet table, which we had been using as an overflow from our poky offices. The place was one of those big, gloomy, over-decorated rooms in which the Palace of Westminster abounds, with florid wallpaper and fussy window-frames. It was the day on which the shadow Cabinet met; and the shadow Cabinet were due soon.

As I entered I saw that the leader had arrived already. She was standing on a rickety chair in her stockinged feet. She had kicked off her shoes and, on tiptoes, was running her fingers along the top of one of the dismal oil-paintings which crowd the walls. She could just reach. The chair was wobbling. 'It's the way a *woman* knows whether a room's been cleaned *properly*,' she said. It is remarked that in her later years an element of self-parody (conscious or otherwise) crept into her performance, as brave demoiselle turned into *grande dame* and finally into pantomime dame. Less often is it suggested — but I noticed — that she *always* had a penchant for burlesque.

Cleaning, womanhood and good housekeeping were themes she loved to mingle. I was witness in 1978 to her attempts at roadsweeping in Battersea. As an officer in my South Battersea Conservative Association it was my job to help arrange the leader's visit to the Northcote Road. Elections for the Wandsworth Borough Council were imminent (I was a candidate) and it looked as though for the first time in years the Tories might be able to win there. The leader of the

Opposition was to stage a grand walkabout in the borough and everyone was keen she should make an impact.

Impact? She hit the Northcote Road like an electrical storm. It was the first time I had registered the manic quality with which she undertook these encounters with the public. She jumped from the car, handbag in hand, her eyes burning with that icy fire which seemed to inhabit her the moment she was on display. All was movement, this way and that – often setting off at a storming pace, she knew not where, but determined to keep moving; then, bouncing off some crash barrier or blind alley, storming back at the same pace until the next obstacle was encountered. Those battery-operated dogs which jerk and yap to the edge of their toy enclosure, hit the edge and ricochet off, still yapping, towards the other side, have the same mindless energy. She was a woman possessed.

An ageing Cockney radio star, Monty Modlin, part of the bemused entourage, tried to keep up, but had neither the banter nor the pace. 'Hello-how-*are*-you-my-dear-now-what-are-these?-tomatoes!-just-what-I-need-for-Denis's-breakfast-are-they-*British*-dear?' – and she would be off again, stallholders left floundering behind.

She spotted a council street-cleaner at the tiller of one of those motorized street-sweeping machines with big bags, like giant Hoovers. Without so much as a by-your-leave she grabbed the controls from him and went careering towards the market stalls aiming for a cigarette package by the kerb. 'Women know how to get into corners *men can't reach*!' she yelled above the roar of the engine, the swish of her brushes and the scribble of local reporters' pencils.

I do not know how we got from one end of the Northcote Road to the other, but by the time we did, what had started as a little group of Tories trying to stage a walkabout had become a civil commotion, she at the eye of the storm, hundreds of the uninvolved, drawn by the noise and energy, crowding around to see what was happening.

She was happening. She had an unerring sense of how to happen. There was never a hint of diffidence, of hanging back, of abashedness at the comicality. If this pantomime performance contained any trace of irony or self-parody on her part, she betrayed not a hint. She played it straight, and for all it was worth. I never knew how far her heart was in it, and nor I suspect did she.

Those paragraphs about the Northcote Road market almost write themselves, as might the next: 'lesser mortals pulled along in her wake . . . eyes blazing . . . colleagues flapping behind as she forced the pace . . . bewildered officials . . . hapless security men . . . despairing staff wringing their hands while the great lady tears up her itinerary and . . . loose cannon . . . force of nature . . . unguided missile' . . . How easily the phrases flow.

They aren't quite true. On the whole she stuck to her itineraries, doing violence only to the details. On the whole it was other people who devised and supervised them. On the whole she took their advice. The loose cannon thing was a bit of an act. A missile, certainly, but by no means unguided: the explosions were more calculated than sometimes they seemed. Kingsley Amis's remark 'Do you imagine that when a woman loses control, she loses control?' applies to Margaret Thatcher. After the shouting and broken china, someone would come in with a brush and dustpan and clear it up, the torn up position papers would be stuck together again, and she would read them.

I am as guilty as many other lazy journalists of feeding the myth of the Unstoppable Maggie. It was a shrewd way of selling her, the easiest way of explaining her success and the shortest way of accounting for her fall. But it was never the whole truth. The picture of a political and intellectual giant grabbing her epoch by the scruff of its neck and bending it to her will, relentlessly marketed, distorts. There would be a wary glance at the will of her epoch before she came anywhere near the scruff of its neck. You could even argue that the epoch grabbed her. I always thought her a confused person underneath, though that was not the quality of her leadership or the impression she so masterfully exuded.

She was full of contradictions. She enjoyed pomp and circumstance yet was contemptuous of stuffed shirts. She worshipped merit yet craved a seat in the Lords. Nobody I have encountered in politics had a firmer belief in doing certain things simply because they were the done thing – an instinct hard to reconcile with her root-and-branch radicalism in other things. Rarely did I sense that she enjoyed the Commons chamber or felt particularly at home there, but she respected it not because she respected anyone in it or much that it did but because, in an almost mystical way, it was to be respected. It was part of our ancient constitution.

Likewise in her approach to relationships with other people. She hardly ever showed any trace of being personally moved by the many letters she received from people in trouble but she was quite insistent they be sympathetically handled and was unstinting with her own time where personal replies were called for. She would not cut corners. It was as though she had read a handbook on how to do the right thing – and thereafter, however busy, and however little it came from the heart, she never spared herself the trouble. She was solicitous. Samuel Johnson remarked that it is possible to be kind by an act of will, but not to be fond. Perhaps she illustrated that – who knows what she felt. Perhaps a correct concern for others is more virtuous than an impulsive one. It is certainly more reliable.

Only once did I see Mrs Thatcher bettered by her own emotions. While I was at work on my pile of letters her son Mark joined a trans-Saharan rally and became lost in the Algerian desert. I had made the same crossing three times and knew well the track he had lost and the area where he had disappeared. I knew it would not be hard to find him though it might take a couple of days; and that in this short time little harm was likely to befall him if he stayed with his car. I went to see her to tell her this. She nodded her thanks through eyes swimming with tears.

I was pleased with the way we were keeping our heads above water in the correspondence section. All of us worked hard and I was taking sacks of letters home at weekends to work on too. Mrs T herself, Richard Ryder and her senior secretaries seemed pleased with my performance, Chris Patten told me he had heard good things of me, and, all in all – and though I was still paid much less than at the Foreign Office – my career seemed on the right track. The track, that is, to the House of Commons. In 1978 I had been adopted as Conservative candidate for a Labour-held council seat: Fairfield Ward in Wandsworth. Wandsworth Borough Council today, I thought, Westminster tomorrow.

I had nearly won, too. Fairfield was a two-councillor ward, and with an enthusiastic running-mate called Julian Dunlop I canvassed virtually every household, even the grim council blocks where old men in string vests shouted at Tories.

On one such estate I knocked at the door of an elderly lady. She looked fearful and frail. I was accompanied on this canvass by an old

Tory hand, veteran of many Wandsworth campaigns. He told the old lady I was her Conservative candidate.

'Oh good,' she said, voice quavering, 'I wanted to ask you something. My friend says that if Labour win they'll bring in compulsory euthanasia for old people. I can't sleep for worrying. Will they?'

I was about to assure her this was only a local government election, and anyway her fears were groundless, when my canvassing colleague pre-empted me. 'Madam,' he said, with the bedside voice of a Harley Street consultant with difficult news to impart, 'I must be honest with you. It isn't *in* their *manifesto* for Wandsworth. But it's just the kind of thing they'd do.'

This was the year the Tories first won Wandsworth. In my ward we doubled the Conservative vote. I got 1,313 votes, Julian Dunlop 1,312, the difference being the vote of a prostitute whom I had canvassed. She received me, mid-afternoon, in a pink frilly nightdress, and the pictures and decor of her flat left me in little doubt. She said I was the best-looking of all the candidates, as I backed towards the door. She said she would vote, but only for me. It wasn't quite enough: seven more votes and I would have won. The nailbiting finish, with final defeat, turned the night of the count into a bitter moment, for I had not entered this for the experience or as a line in a CV: I really wanted to win. How dreadfully things which may prove of little account can seem to matter at the time.

As apparently calamitous was failing to get the Tory prospective parliamentary candidature for Stockton-upon-Tees North.

I had been applying for every seat which came vacant and had, by dint of my job and my good record in Wandsworth, got myself on to Conservative Central Office's list of approved Westminster hopefuls. But safe Conservative seats in search of candidates rarely bothered to reply to my applications; while Tory associations in unwinnable seats, who generally did reply, did not seem to be shortlisting me.

I had scores of disappointments. To Caerphilly I promised to learn Welsh, to no avail. Kirkcaldy in Scotland, and even Vauxhall (a seat right next door to me in South London) were among those unwilling even to interview me for the role of Tory no-hoper at the coming general election.

Why should they? I was only twenty-eight with no family, no means and little experience. I had been born in South Africa and raised abroad. My position in Mrs Thatcher's office was lowly. Richard Ryder, her private secretary, who also wanted to get into Parliament, was ahead of me in the queue and there was no way the great woman would have put in a word on my behalf, even if she had cared to, before Richard was fixed up. And the Conservative Research Department cut little ice with most rural Tory associations, who nurse an ancient hatred of the party machine in London; if anything, this part of my CV heightened suspicions.

It looked unlikely, as the Callaghan government tottered towards its end, that I would find a hopeless seat to fight this time. But there was no hurry and I remained absurdly hopeful. When Stockton North decided to shortlist and interview just a handful, and included me, I was overjoyed. The seat was rock-solid Labour but I reckoned that if I did well I would be well placed to find a winnable seat in another five years' time, aged about thirty-three. And in the meantime Mrs T would surely take me to Downing Street, if she won, to handle the political side of her public correspondence.

For Stockton I wrote a good speech and learned it by heart, ludicrously exaggerating my links with the North. There was an extended passage about sitting as a child on Father Christmas's knee outside his igloo at the big department store in Darlington – and no mention of the fact we had left for Cyprus when I was four. I planned to give the selection committee the impression that to take up the Tory torch in Stockton would be tantamount to coming home. I don't think I had ever been to Stockton.

The speech worked, though the chairman, offering me a quiet word afterwards, let me know it wasn't necessary to suggest to association members that the Conservative Party could actually win this seat; they were not fools.

Five hopefuls, grimly waiting in the bar of a Conservative club outside, were summoned by an association office-holder relishing his moment of power, and informed that three of them could go straight back to Stockton railway station. And would Mr Robert Jones and Mr Matthew Parris stay behind as the committee wished to interview both of them again, before making their final choice.

Heart pounding I did my best, which wasn't bad. Jones did better. Back to Stockton station for the train to York. I cannot forget the hour spent shivering on the platform in the cold damp at York, late at night, with a couple of pints of consolatory bitter sloshing around unhappily inside me, waiting for the last train to London.

To get so close, and lose! And yet what a setback it would have been if I had won.

Confidence was knocked again by my debut as an invited Tory platform speaker. The invitation was to the Tottenham and Wood Green Conservative Ladies Association. Tottenham is not a hotbed of Tory activism, but the ladies had seen my name on Central Office's list of 'will speak anywhere, any time, on any subject' hopefuls, and asked me to talk to them about my work in Mrs Thatcher's office. I entitled my speech 'A Day in the Life of the Leader of the Opposition', wore my good suit, and took a taxi just round the corner from the Underground station to the Tottenham Constitutional Club where the ladies met, so that I should appear important.

They were five. Three of them were very, very elderly. One of them went to sleep while I was talking. At the end of my speech the four still awake applauded politely, then their chairman, thanking me, said: 'And now, ladies, to the main business of the day' – which was their raffle. The prizes were paltry. First prize was a small box of Black Magic chocolates. Second prize was five pounds of potatoes, donated by a local greengrocer. Third prize was a five and three-quarter ounce tin of Heinz baked beans.

Nobody claimed the beans. The chairman rose and said: 'Ladies, as these beans are unclaimed, and as our guest speaker, Mr Parish, is unmarried, terribly thin, and appears to have a terrible cough, I propose we give them to him.' Four kind old ladies nodded assent. The sleeping lady slumbered on.

It was – and for all I know still is – the custom of the Tottenham ladies to sing the National Anthem at the end of their meetings. I descended from the rostrum of the Constitutional Club holding a tiny tin of baked beans in my hand, to the strains of four old ladies singing God Save the Queen; and took the Tube home. It was a difficult moment in my personal campaign.

My feelings towards my boss, too, had grown ambivalent. We adored her, but my adoration was edged with hesitation about the strange flatness of her picture of the world. Of course a party preparing for government needed to be enthused, not bemused; simplicity, not depth, was the watchword and every successful leader needs to avoid too many shades of grey. But did she really divide those around us into friend or foe? Did she really think socialists were wicked? Did she really see the Soviet Union as a great Satan rather than (as I thought) a dangerous and sick bear with a sore head? Did she really understand how many of the poor and jobless were just unlucky, not workshy? Such were my doubts.

Success is a wonderful suppressant of doubt. When, to my amazement, West Derbyshire Conservatives shortlisted me for interview it was the autumn of 1978, I had worked for Margaret Thatcher for a year, and I was twenty-nine. My days working for her were drawing to a close.

Wind the reel on twenty years.

After the end of the (now) Baroness Thatcher's time in office, her former office secretary, Caroline, invited me to a dinner given in her honour. Caroline had become Lady Ryder, having married Richard, the private secretary. Richard had been Minister of Agriculture, then chief whip. He was now in the Lords.

The dinner was in a sort of tower at Mosimanns, a very grand restaurant in Belgravia, and was attended also by Denis, by Alistair McAlpine, a good friend to the Thatchers and now also in the Lords, and assorted Texans. I cannot think why I was included as Lady Thatcher feels towards me, I imagine, a sort of amused disregard.

She had just been seeing members of the Chechnyan government, visiting Britain. Alistair McAlpine was berating her in the way only a good friend dares. 'Margaret,' he protested, 'you yelled at them for half an hour. They don't speak any English and the room was unbelievably hot.'

'I had to get our point of view across,' she retorted. '*British citizens* are being kept as hostages there. It's appalling.'

'They're Jehovah's Witnesses,' someone murmured. Lady Thatcher's face clouded momentarily.

'Anyway, they're *our people*,' she insisted. '*Our people*. Hostages! It won't do. I had to ensure the Chechnyan government understood this.'

'But, Margaret, you did rather shout. For half an hour. And they didn't understand our language. And it was dreadfully hot.'

'I expect they got the message.'

'But, Margaret, we doubt the Chechnyan government knows where the hostages are. They've been kidnapped by rebels, not the government.'

'*Our people*, Alistair. *Our people*.'

After the soup and entrée, Caroline shuffled all the guests around at the table. To my terror I found myself next to Lady Thatcher for the lemon sorbet. She turned to me. 'Now, Matthew, what are you doing these days, dear?' she asked.

'Still writing for *The Times*, Mrs Thatcher,' I stammered, forgetting her peerage.

'But what else? You always have some grand plan, some wild and woolly expedition. What is it now, dear?' I described my intention to spend four months in the sub-Antarctic on the island of Kerguelen.

She interrupted me: 'I know what you'll be looking for. You always were. You want to go thousands of miles to some remote and dangerous place, and climb to the top of a mountain, and look up at the moon and the stars, and say, "Here I am in a wild and dangerous place, miles from anywhere, looking at the moon and the stars."

'You'll go all that way. And you'll succeed – oh yes, you always do. You'll see the moon and the stars. And it will be worth one newspaper article, or at the most two. And then you'll have to come all the way back again.

'Now take my advice, dear: don't bother. You can see the moon and the stars from Spalding.' She turned from me to converse with the person the other side of her. My interview was over. It had been meant kindly.

Wind the reel on into the next century: April 2002. I had been asked to make a short speech at a grand Foyle's Bookshop luncheon – their 692nd – at the Dorchester. The occasion was the publication of *Statecraft*, the Baroness's last book. I was seated between the German ambassador's wife (good of the couple to come, given the wild remarks Lady Thatcher had just made suggesting continental Europe was the source of all evil in history) and Carol Thatcher.

Carol must be as sick of being called a 'good egg' as I am of being asked to cast a 'wry eye', but she is a good egg. Lady Thatcher's daughter grew increasingly anxious as the luncheon proceeded. Her mother, after a series of strokes, had recently been advised by doctors to stop speaking in public. The reason given was that this endangered her health but I suspect the danger was that she might compromise her dignity; her short-term memory was going and she was beginning to ramble. In a speech not long before she had told the same story three times, her husband Denis mouthing 'repeat' at her to warn her. This time it had been agreed she would not speak, but she put on her spectacles and started to write notes.

Carol fussed around, trying to ensure she was discouraged. But at the end she did speak, and she did slightly ramble, but only very mildly, and it was short, and she made sense.

I had spoken a few minutes earlier, briefly, mindful of Richard Ryder's private office memo quarter of a century before: 'Mrs Thatcher does not like to listen to other people's speeches.' But she seemed to have liked what I said, and (sitting a few yards further along the table) leaned forward and gave me a little distracted wave and a sad, pale smile. I felt she was waving goodbye.

As I write now she is sinking. She will not read this. She was never one for reading books, except for a purpose, except when their subject was caught in the narrow beam of her attention – for 'tunnel vision' understates the confining quality of Margaret Thatcher's will. I regret this, for I would like her to know how important even one who has made a living from laughing at her thinks what she stood for was. Like fleas on a big cat's back we may have made it our business to irritate but we drew our life from the vigour of hers. Whether as agent or puppet of destiny, she stood for a great, collective, national digging-in of heels and she was, in that sense, a reactionary of the most glorious sort.

In this century her reputation, still restive, will settle down. Her role was that indicated by an old conservative in Giuseppe di Lampedusa's *The Leopard*: 'If you want things to stay the same things are going to have to change.' Thus are her revolutionary and her reactionary claims reconciled.

I have been bumping into her for a quarter of a century; worked for her as part of her small office for two years; served for seven as an MP in the party she led as Prime Minister.

Still I cannot say I knew or understood her personally. After years of speculating that this might be because the mystery was too large, I have come to the conclusion that it may be because it is too small. There may not be much to know. She branded a whole philosophy of government but the woman behind the brand may be rather less than the brand: definitive but, stared at from very close, and like all brandings, strangely insubstantial: a work partly of the imagination, ours as well as hers.

She did some amazing things. She said some amazing things and read many amazing scripts drafted for her by others. She presided over an amazing era. But as to what she *was* – the real Margaret Thatcher – we are left with countless anecdotes and many different assessments, and a collection of snapshots which never quite cohere.

The Blessed Margaret, Norman St John Stevas called her. The Great She Elephant was my backbench colleague Julian Critchley's nickname. Denis Healey called her Rhoda the Rhino, Clement Freud called her Attila the Hen, Ian Paisley called her Jezebel and President Mitterrand said she had the eyes of Caligula and the mouth of Marilyn Monroe. I got into trouble by describing her as a cross between a B52 bomber and a sabre-toothed tiger. The press called her the Iron Lady or just Maggie; the nickname at Chris Patten's Research Department was the Leaderene or, more insolently, Hilda. Denis Thatcher impersonators called her She Who Must Be Obeyed.

Tony Banks MP asked what we could expect from a woman he variously characterized as a sex-starved boa-constrictor or an ex-spamhoarder from Grantham. Jonathan Aitken remarked that she probably thought Sinai was the plural of sinus. Her former tutor at Oxford said she was a 'perfectly good second-class chemist'. Unconsciously echoing Walter Bagehot's assessment of Sir Robert Peel ('the powers of a first-rate man and the creed of a second-rate man'), Julian Critchley said she was a woman 'of common views but uncommon abilities' . . .

And she? She swung her handbag a couple of twirls and said nothing. She encouraged us to see what we chose.

Not that Mrs Thatcher was ever a fraud, or impostor, or negligible, or secretly meek, or in the end dull. She won her place fairly; she could be formidable when in determined mood; her word moved mountains; and as a famous personality she became a source of national entertainment. These were all true facets to her character. But when – of anyone who ever worked close to her or knew her well – it is asked, 'What was Margaret really like?', most respondents find it hard to give the sort of answer the questioner expects.

Readers of *The Wizard of Oz* are quickly absorbed in the quest by

Dorothy and her friends to reach the Emerald City and meet the great sorcerer whose marvellous accomplishments inspire such awe among his subjects. The build-up is intense, the encounter, when it finally happens, a disappointment.

... For they saw, standing in just the spot the screen had hidden, a little old man, with a bald head and a wrinkled face, who seemed to be as much surprised as they were.

... 'I thought Oz was a great Head,' said Dorothy.

'And I thought Oz was a lovely Lady,' said the Scarecrow.

'And I thought Oz was a terrible Beast,' said the Tin Woodman.

'And I thought Oz was a Ball of Fire,' exclaimed the Lion.

'No, you are all wrong,' said the little man meekly. 'I have been making believe.'

The Wizard of Oz, it turned out, came from Omaha, Nebraska. Margaret Thatcher came from Grantham, Lincs. He was bald. She had big hair. But in other respects there may be parallels.

Is she still big, was she always big – and is it, as she believes, just the pictures that have got small? Or was she never as big as the role in which providence cast and the electorate directed her? Looking back on it all now, looking back on my time under her stairs, I see there something of the Emerald City and its little emperor projecting a big voice from behind a screen. It worked for Oz and it worked for Britain. We wanted it to.

I left her office uncertain about her, and I am uncertain still.

Earlier in this chapter I described how Margaret Thatcher hit the Northcote Road market in South London in 1978. Nearly a quarter of a century later I was on hand as she hit Northampton market in the 2001 general election:

'She was so close I could see the white of her face powder.'

Some images, fleeting as they are, will stay with us the rest of our lives. Standing on a rubbish bin in the market square in Northampton yesterday I watched a tiny figure in blue brocade, a face so pale it was almost a death mask, mobbed by friend and foe.

She was almost at my feet. All around her was a kind of frenzy. Cameramen jostled, reporters scribbled, Tories cheered, protesters booed and an agitated crowd of the committed and the curious pushed and surged for a glimpse.

And she was still. Still, but not calm. She was the centre of all this furious energy. Nobody I have followed in this campaign – not Tony Blair, not William Hague and certainly not Charles Kennedy – has aroused such spontaneous passion.

She had arrived after noon in a Jaguar Majestic so blue it was almost black. Television crews and journalists had been positioning themselves there for most of the morning.

Supporters of Shailesh Vara and John Whelan, the Tory candidates for Northampton's two marginal seats, carried 'Save the Pound' placards and a life-size cardboard cut-out of Lady Thatcher, with handbag. The replica swayed sickeningly above the mêlée as the real thing pushed her way purposefully into the middle of the throng. Admirers shouted: 'Hurrah!'

One woman shouted 'Rubbish!' The Baroness, hearing this, moved not away from but towards the protester – who shrank hastily back to shout 'Rubbish' from a safer distance.

Like a dangerous animal suddenly attracted by the movement of a prey, Lady Thatcher fixed her eye on the brightly coloured tie of Central Television's Peter Hayes. Momentarily oblivious to the hands of worshippers reaching out to touch her, her expression said: 'Make my day sonny, ask me a question.'

'Why are you afraid of the euro?' asked Hayes.

'What a question!' she snapped. 'What a question.' Mr Hayes flinched. 'As' – she stabbed him in the chest with an index finger – 'a broadcaster' – she stabbed again – 'you should protect' – stab – 'the pound.' Hayes began to back away into the crowd. She pursued him! Then she grabbed his mike like some kind of trophy and brandished it in front of his own crew's camera. In much the same way the tribesmen of the Danekil in the Horn of Africa sport, on a necklace, the withered penises of the men they have killed in battle. She had finished with him. She turned her attention to a girl with Down's syndrome, who was clasped, a little boy with flowers, whose hand was held, and an old gent in grave danger of losing his stick, whose shoulder was gripped.

In a burst of sunshine I could see the gold lacquer in her hair, and the papery skin beneath.

Lady Thatcher began to move through the market. A karaoke girl-band sang 'Mama Mia'. 'I came face to face with her,' gasped one Northampton woman. 'She's so tiny!' From the fringes of the scrum a gaunt, angry Scot shouted: 'Show us your bank account.' The police pushed him back. 'She gets police protection and she's not even an MP,' he bawled.

'She's a baroness,' an indignant Tory corrected him.

'She's a pain in the butt,' snapped a stallholder.

Lady T spotted me and fixed me with a gimlet eye. I didn't know what to say.

'You seem to be attracting a lot of attention,' I stammered.

She glared. 'Are you surprised, Matthew?' I blushed. 'You should be ashamed of yourself, she said.'

'And you should be Prime Minister,' called an admirer. Thatcher leant over to me. 'Did you hear that, Michael [*sic*]?' she said to me.

Off she went, the riot around her backing and stumbling, a child's hand forced into its candyfloss in the confusion. 'We must move,' she explained. 'We're affecting their profits.'

Someone challenged her about the euro. The very idea, she harrumphed. 'We,' she added, as though completing the argument, 'have a much older history.'

As Lady Thatcher moved back towards her waiting Majestic, the girl-band sang 'Thank You for the Music'.

She paused at the car door, almost pinned to the side. So many faces – so much attention – pressing round. She seemed to hesitate. Something in her face said: 'I don't want to go. Ask me another question.' It was as though they were taking her away.

And she went. A Tory with a megaphone continued his harangue about the euro but the crowd drifted off. It had been the singer, not the song.

And her importance in history – singer, or song? I think it was the song.

9. I Win

Peacocks shrieked and deep gravel around the grand portico of the Hassop Hall Hotel scrunched beneath my untypically polished shoes as, weak with terror, I advanced, in an absurdly heavy camel coat (brand-new, Selfridges, £120), trying to look Churchillian and succeeding only in looking scared. West Derbyshire was a constituency accustomed to being represented by a gentleman. Approaching it was a frightened youth.

I owed my invitation for interview before the West Derbyshire Conservative Association's selection committee to the dog: Jason, whom I had saved from the river Thames.

A general election was coming, and late in the day this safest of Tory seats was looking for a candidate. Its MP, James Scott-Hopkins, had a place in the European Parliament too, and the party had twisted his arm to choose which Parliament to run for next time: Europe or Westminster. He had chosen Europe.

The constituency association was inundated with applications. They included mine, not because I had any serious chance of picking this late autumn plum, but because I applied to every seat going – safe or hopeless – as a matter of course. Here I would hardly have expected so much as a rejection note.

The selection committee decided to shortlist twelve, interview them all, narrow the field down to four, then hold a final selection meeting to choose their candidate. There were some eleven obvious names, and they did not include mine.

Mrs Mona Gillan, a respected local councillor and key member of the committee, saw my name on the long list; she recognized it. Mrs Gillan was a great dog-lover. It is said that she exclaimed: 'I read about Mr Parris in the paper. He works for Mrs Thatcher. More important, he rescued a dog. I should like to shake his hand. He looks different. Let's include him as our twelfth man.' And as nobody had any other ideas, they did.

When I received a late call from the constituency agent, Al Adam, asking if I could get up to Derbyshire for interview, I honestly thought I might be dreaming. I would have fought any seat that would have had me, however unwinnable. But this! I could not have asked for a more beautiful or gentle place.

Not that I was there yet. The shortlist was formidable. It included a brassy and energetic woman called Joan Hall who had already been an MP and made a good name for herself. It included two particularly bright and successful young aspirants already winning good opinions within the party. They were called Peter Lilley and Michael Howard. And as it turned out it was these three whom the selection committee at Hassop Hall shortlisted. I, the fourth on their list, had narrowly failed.

But I had spoken well. Too nervous to join the other candidates for a chat before each of us in turn was invited to perform and answer questions, I asked the motherly secretary keeping the door whether I might simply sit alone somewhere and collect my thoughts. This I did, but the request was mentioned to the committee members, who thought it odd though forgivable. When my turn came I gave the speech all I had. The questions afterwards were easy for one whose job it was to answer those from Mrs Thatcher's public correspondents.

I made one calculation which paid off. Everyone knew that the association now interviewing me had forced their sitting member out by making him choose; they had resented not him but his dual mandate. Other hopefuls, knowing this, had made no mention of Mr Scott-Hopkins for fear of upsetting his enemies or friends. But this is bad manners. Everyone knew Scott-Hopkins had been a genial and hard-working Member; there would be sadness about his leaving.

I also knew my own party. Tories will trip a colleague but, once he has fallen, praise him to the skies. It would be good Tory form, now that Scott-Hopkins had been dispatched, to praise him. I did so, the only aspirant to praise the outgoing Member, from a mixture of courtesy and calculation, and because praise was due. This went down well.

It went down well not least with the constituency's canny young professional agent, Al Adam. Al and I took to each other, and he had a hatred of stuffed shirts. Al had advised the committee to add a couple more names to their list of four, as reserves, in case any of the front runners should prove unavailable. The committee added my name as fourth man.

They had asked all twelve of us to telephone the constituency office later that night, after the committee had decided which three to invite back for the final interview. And it so happened that the third short-listed hopeful, Peter Lilley, failed to ring. There had been some kind of misunderstanding.

It would have been open to the chairman to wait and make attempts to get through to Mr Lilley the next morning. But Al told the chairman that he really should not have to do so; the candidate had failed to get in touch as requested, and should be struck from the list. When I telephoned I was told the office were still waiting for a call from someone else, and to ring again. When I did they told me the call had not come; I was shortlisted.

West Derbyshire is a green English rural constituency in the centre of the country at the southern end of the Pennine hills. About eighty miles long, the seat included dozens of picturesque stone-built villages; the market towns of Bakewell, Wirksworth and Ashbourne and the old spa towns of Matlock and Matlock Bath; hills, dales and moorland, and hundreds of square miles of pasture bounded by drystone walls. Much of the seat is within the Peak District National Park. Though in my maiden speech I called its beauty spectacular, it is not spectacular and it is not majestic, but it is lovely.

The north of England thinks Derbyshire is in the Midlands. The Midlands thinks of Derbyshire as being in the north. Eastern England is sure Derbyshire is over the other side; and the North West thinks the same.

I, meanwhile, had not thought about Derbyshire at all. I hardly knew where the county was. I had been through Bakewell once, tipsy, on a coach trip returning from supporting my college team in a *University Challenge* match against Manchester, which we lost. I had some distant recollection of hills. On the back of my brother's motor-bike I had revisited these hills again from Sheffield. Bakewell looked nice, but it had been raining.

And now I was on a shortlist of three to contest – which, for a Tory candidate, was to say win – this seat. As I so often have in my life, I awoke the next morning to wonder whether I was dreaming.

I wrote, re-wrote and polished the very best speech I could. It was gentler in tone than anything I had thought I believed when leaving the Foreign Office to be a Tory. It stressed the conservative rather than the radical side of the party's politics. The moment I thought I might actually be in charge, all the spikiness seemed to drop out of my opinions and, somewhat to my dismay, I found myself looking for things I could say with which nobody would disagree. But it wasn't just calculation; with success I began to feel more generous.

And I had changed. I was growing to dislike the raw side of the Tory appeal and the harshness of some of our supporters' views: working on Margaret Thatcher's public correspondence had taught me both the power, and the limitations, of populism. I was not sure – I could not know – whether moderation would chime with the West Derbyshire Conservatives; I simply hoped.

I practised that speech over and again, even deliberating where to pause, where to draw breath and what hand gestures to use. With friends such as Michael Dobbs at Old Queen Street I rehearsed questions and answers, anticipating the most likely gripes and inquiries and framing the best responses. I even committed individual phrases to memory, parrot-fashion. I learned all about the Common Agricultural Policy, and for a short period was able to walk, chew gum and understand Monetary Compensation Amounts and the Green Pound, all at the same time. Not even agriculture ministers can always do this.

In the lavatory on the train from London St Pancras to Chesterfield, I listed again in my head the questions I might be asked, and went through the answers we had prepared. And I practised my speech, twice. Passengers may have been puzzled by the noise of a raised voice and a stream of sub-Augustan prose emanating from the loo.

Preparing myself to impress West Derbyshire, I found little difficulty of principle with the emerging Tory manifesto of 1979. That manifesto was bland. My only big reservation about our stance concerned tone: I hate ungenerosity in a political voice and persist in believing it doesn't win votes either. This is a truth upon which, one day, a mainstream party leader will stumble, to his or her very great advantage.

As to particulars, only two issues bothered me, neither a matter of party policy. They were hanging and homosexuality. I was against one and in favour of the other. I'm ashamed to say I fudged both.

The death penalty was a huge issue at that time. I had and have no conscientious objection to capital punishment. Anyone who believes (as I do) that the state may kill large numbers of foreigners in defence not even of its citizens' lives but of their property or way of life, can hardly argue that human life is 'sacred' and that it must in principle be wrong to take one life in order to defend many. But that is a long way from saying that hanging people is a seemly or practical recourse for modern law enforcement, or that it works.

I was moving in my mind from indecision to doubt. I believed too that if the death penalty were to return we would have to make the repugnant move of taking murder cases away from juries. Modern jurors would increasingly acquit if the alternative was to write some-one's death warrant. But I knew that to declare myself opposed to capital punishment was probably to end my chances of selection, for I was the outsider in this race. Derbyshire is not a county of extremists, but in the English countryside of the 1970s, supporting the death penalty was not an extreme opinion: folk of all political allegiances were overwhelmingly in favour of capital punishment.

It seems strange to report this, but I cannot now remember whether I was asked. It does not matter. For me the important thing was resolving how to answer if I was: this was the moral decision, and in making it I would do the right or wrong thing. My decision was that, if the question were put, I would say I saw no objection in principle to the death penalty, if I could be persuaded it would save more lives than it took. I can justify this answer to myself, but it was not brave.

On my homosexuality I did not think anything should be volun-teered, unprompted. Without a shadow of a doubt this would have been fatal. But I agonized about what to say if asked. The question was unlikely to be put but if it were I could not lie, and would decide, as and when the moment arose, whether to say 'yes' or 'mind your own business'. If asked about policy I would reply that sexual prefer-ences, when unaggressive, should not be a matter for the police, and the age of consent ought to be lowered from twenty-one at least to eighteen. This is what I then believed.

I hoped the Derbyshire Conservatives would be too old-fashioned to ask a blunt personal question, and believed that they were unlikely even to ask about policy. I was right. The subject was never raised. Nobody even asked about girlfriends.

So I escaped. As an openly gay man would not have been selected as Conservative (or, indeed, Liberal or Labour) candidate in any

Derbyshire seat in the 1970s, I was lucky not to be cornered. But I was not proud of the way I was really gambling on the good manners of my inquisitors. So after an internal conversation I resolved that if by this plan I avoided the issue then the price of my cowardice would be to promise myself not to turn away from it later as a Member of Parliament, but to use my position to advance the cause of homosexual equality. This compact I made with myself quite explicitly, late in 1978; and it was not broken.

Re-reading this I am struck by the Jesuitical tone. The best I can say is that tortured logic – even hypocrisy – is evidence at least of a struggle.

I was met at Chesterfield station by a genial chap called Rupert Turner, and we drove in his old Land-Rover up the snowy roads over the moor to the village of Edensor, in Chatsworth Park. Here I was billeted in a grand house to await my turn before a large selection meeting composed of all the officers of all the two-score branches in the constituency. Each hopeful was waiting in a different house, and we never met.

My turn came.

The Edensor Institute, where the selection took place, was an imposing ducal version of a village hall, but I can remember almost nothing about it, nor about the audience, my speech or their questions – except for one inquiry, the decisive one. A small, thin, kind-looking and well-spoken lady asked me about my dog rescue. That woman was Mrs Gillan, my guardian angel.

Everybody laughed in an encouraging way. And now my words took wings. I could leave aside political pieties and stilted opinions, and tell them a true and exciting story. As the tale unfolded I could see people really listening.

Afterwards I heard that the other two candidates each put in a powerful performance. Joan Hall was plucky and boisterous. Her main difficulty was sexual prejudice: a minority were unhappy at the concept of a woman candidate in a North Midlands agricultural seat.

By common assent, Michael Howard made the best speech. He was charming and fluent. He was obviously extremely clever. He had gone to some trouble to brief himself about the constituency and its special problems. The skill with which he answered questions was little short of dazzling – but in a barristerial sort of way. His wife, Sandra, wowed the association. But a minority thought that he sounded rather too much the London lawyer; while a handful (no more) had been muttering about his being Jewish.

None of these prejudices was held by many; each, however, took the edge off one or another of my rivals' potential lead.

I am told my speech was well received but not the best; but that nobody in particular took against me. There was no 'Stop Parris' faction. I was almost everybody's second choice.

My cause had been done no harm by a rumour running round the audience, that a woman with a nice voice had phoned from London and left a message with the office shortly beforehand, asking the chairman to let me know urgently that it had proved at the last minute impossible for her to drive up to be with me; and that she was awfully sorry; and that she wished me luck.

My friend Anne Wroe denies that it was her so I must have remembered wrong. But somebody did it, and whoever she was, she had, like a true friend, understood what I could not ask. I had no more primed her to do this than I had thrown Jason into the river. But it helped.

And so I got through, with a little help from sexism, anti-Semitism, anti-intellectualism, Jason and the general dislike of lawyers. When the chairman, Max Turner, told me I had won I remember him asking why I didn't smile. I never do when I win, I just feel tense; and my instinct is against crowing, or even celebrating, lest I tempt fate.

I awoke the next morning in a four-poster bed in a huge bedroom in which a Stuart king was said to have slept, in Max Turner's house. A funny, forceful man and a widower, Max had made a fortune in pressure-sensitive washers and described himself as a geriatric playboy, but was shrewd and confident, with an independent mind, and good to me from the start.

He had been too good to me with the whisky the night before. With throbbing head and trembling hand I opened the curtains on Chatsworth Park spread before me, and thought: 'This is Chatsworth? And I was chosen last night as the future MP for West Derbyshire? Is it true?' And it was.

It was the dog rescue that did it. I did not reflect – how could I? – that the dog rescue was also Mrs Thatcher's first intimation of my recklessness. I was never to be offered a position in government.

I returned to London and bought a hit single played incessantly on the radio at the time. It was about goal-scoring, and called 'I Knocked It Off'. On my way home I called in at my brother Roger's house in Warwickshire to tell him the news, but he was out. So I left a scrawled note on his kitchen table: 'I won.' And so I had. I was twenty-nine. There was a distinct possibility in my mind that I should become Prime Minister, though I had told the West Derbyshire selection committee that the Home Secretaryship was probably my limit. I wanted to sound modest. Peter Lilley and Michael Howard had to wait two more general elections before they found a seat.

Politicians' memoirs include a chapter which is almost obligatory, describing their first election campaign. The tone is warm, jokey and nostalgic. The chapter contains a few jolly stories about canvassing, a warm reference to the devoted door-knocking team, some self-deprecatory small anecdotes about the candidate's doorstep blunders, triumph at the final count, and, at last, that nervous journey down to London where the MP takes his seat and feels 'like a new boy in school'. Spare me this. My memory is of fearfulness and unfamiliarity, a catastrophe which almost destroyed me, a handful of stalwarts who saved me, and a place where I was a stranger who felt throughout and even at the final victory more like an interloper than a conqueror. I had been taken on trust and was at any moment ready to be shown up, dressed down and thrown out. I had unlimited hopes and fathomless anxieties, and the mix ran me ragged.

My memory is of a small room in my agent's flat in Bakewell, and the sound of the church bell striking the hour early in the cold morning as I stirred in my sleep, remembered where I was and the tests which lay ahead, and, wondering what might go wrong that day, stared at the ceiling as the grey outside turned to dawn.

I had reason to worry. The *Daily Mirror* had got hold of that letter I had written to Mrs Thatcher's council-house correspondent, telling her she should count herself lucky to have a roof over her head provided at the taxpayers' expense. The woman had apparently given it to her husband, who had given it to his trade union shop steward, who had contacted the *Mirror*. The newspaper had sat on the letter a while as election fever grew. Then, on 30 March 1979, they published.

It was their front-page lead. It was all over their front page. There was even a small photograph of Mrs Thatcher in a headscarf saying how sorry she was.

I was tipped off only as the paper went to print. Though I had been selected as the party's 'prospective' parliamentary candidate I had not yet been formally adopted. With the election declared I would have to be. Usually a formality, this might not now be a foregone conclusion. Today's political image-merchants would probably have advised the leader's office to tell Conservative Central Office to tell the local association to sack such a candidate on the spot, before a 'Will the leader/won't the leader act decisively?' story starts running in the press. In those more amateurish days it was left to the local association.

Al Adam, the agent, rang me in London not long after dawn on the day of publication. 'It's lucky we chose you a few weeks before this news broke,' he said cheerfully, 'instead of the other way round. Because it wouldn't have happened the other way round.' Miserably I apologized for what I had written.

'Oh no,' he said, 'I agree with every word of your letter. Most of us in the constituency will. Some of them had been worried you were a bit of an intellectual. Now they've been reassured that's not the case.'

Al said we would have to handle things carefully in the constituency and he was drawing up a list of our best supporters in each council estate, to take me round and introduce me personally to tenants. As for the formal adoption meeting, he thought he could swing that with the officers of the association. He would tell them they would be playing into Labour's hands by making an issue of one silly letter.

Then I had to go into work and face Mrs Thatcher. I remember trying to shave, wondering whether it mattered which suit or tie I wore. I remember wondering for one glorious moment whether I might just run away to start a new life in Siberia, or somewhere. And I remember sitting on the bus to Westminster, the number 88 bus, and rehearsing my best replies to her likely questions.

There was only one question. 'Why?' It was the question I had asked myself repeatedly, and still failed to get a sensible reply.

As I advanced across what seemed an acre of carpet towards the dreadful presence which had departed her desk and placed herself in a favourite wing-backed chair upholstered in yellow, she inclined her head slightly to one side. Again I saw that expression, the one she adopted when congratulating me about the dog, the one which said 'there's something not quite right about this boy'.

'Why?' she said. 'Why, Matthew? Why? Why? *Why?*' I saw only horror in her eyes.

She did not shout. Her voice was steady, very level, hugely controlled. The tone combined genuine bafflement with the message that she was *not* going to shout, she was not going to raise her voice, she was not even *angry*: she was just terribly, terribly disappointed. It's the sort of tone nannies use.

I think I tried to explain but I could hear in what I was stammering out the obvious riposte: fine; so I hadn't taken to this correspondent. How many of our correspondents did I take to, for heaven's sake? Was that the test? Did I have to tell them when I did not like them?

'And what do you think I should do now?' she inquired. I resisted the urge to say 'sack me, of course'. I suggested we should publish the whole correspondence – the letter to which I was replying – so that people could understand the context.

Her response was unhesitating – again, that wondrous certitude. 'No,' she said. 'No, not at all. I have apologized already. I may say it was out of character for you. And then no further comment. Not from you, not from me, not from any of us. The less we say the sooner the story will go away.'

She was right. It did, quite fast, for her. I'm afraid the assassination, days later, of Airey Neave helped. His car exploded on the ramp up from the Commons underground car park. I rang my old team in the leader's office, about a hundred yards from the place of Airey's death. They said the bang was awesome.

The Labour Party had printed three million leaflets featuring a facsimile of the *Mirror*'s front page, and arranged for them to be delivered to every council property in every marginal seat in Britain. Plus West Derbyshire.

The lorry-driver delivering the leaflets to the Labour Party, whose headquarters were shared with the Trades Union Congress across the square from Conservative Central Office in Smith Square, muddled the address, but he knew it was Smith Square, so when he got there he examined his cargo in case there were any clues there as to its destination. He saw sheafs of letters with Mrs Thatcher's name at the top. So he delivered the leaflets to Conservative Central Office, who kept them, and kept quiet, for twenty-four hours to give time for urgent consideration of how to react, then sent them over the road to their rightful owners.

That Friday I had to travel up to Derbyshire to face the music. This was my last week in Mrs T's office. I went out for a drink with the women who had worked for me. They were worried about Helen Senior, whose name and signature had appeared above my own name in the *Mirror* and who was anxious people might think she had written it. We drank a bit and tried to console each other. A sad, embarrassed end to a happy job.

The train to Derby had closed compartments and bench seats. Alone in my compartment I stretched out on one of these, my head spinning from too much gin. We pulled away from St Pancras, the diesel-electric engine throbbing through the mahogany veneer, and I fell fast asleep, and dreamed of other things and places. Awaking, blinking and rubbing my eyes near Derby, I registered first the familiar accompanying signs of approach to the constituency for the weekend. This I had already started doing as prospective candidate. Then it hit me again: the reason for this trip. It was the opposite of the sensation when you awake from a bad dream to realize, with lifting heart, that none of it is real.

Memory of the heart-sinking moment returned years later after I had awoken to notice that my telephone was unplugged, then remembered why: I had said Peter Mandelson was gay on *Newsnight* the night before. And it came back in an infinitely heavier way when, a year ago, all of us on the island of Kerguelen learned that the doctor on our base, Joel, had shot dead his friend in an awful hunting accident. Joel too, I thought, will have awoken the next morning . . . and then remembered.

So of my blunder we should avoid words like 'tragedy'. But it was the most awful cockup, it was completely my fault, and I had been lucky, yet again, to escape.

The Conservative Association in West Derbyshire couldn't have been nicer. Not for the last time I saw the way political supporters will show a devotion to their leader which, if they but knew it, he hardly merits. I hate the way journalists sneer at party workers in all parties: good, civic-minded people with nothing to gain from their work. They deserve better than the leaders they get.

I was determined not to let them down again – though in the end I did – and, under Al's guidance, we redoubled our efforts. The Liberals made what they could of my discomfiture; the local Labour Party, whose candidate, Bill Moore, was in the best sense a rather high-minded man, scarcely bothered.

I became fitfully convinced that the Liberals were going to take successful advantage of surely the best chance they could ever have to unseat the Tory. I did not know I was to give them an even better one seven years later. But Al and Max steadied nerves, and I never let my panic show. The adoption meeting, when it came, passed without incident or challenge. And, slowly, memory of the whole thing faded.

For me the story would linger, and I had known it even as I staggered out of Mrs T's office. Richard Ryder, her private secretary, waiting for me by the door, opposite which there was a little kitchen, had reached for a bottle of brandy and, seeing no glass immediately to hand, grabbed a tin mug and half filled it. I gulped it down. He explained – kindly – that from me a period of silence, and, better still, absence, was now called for. Perhaps I would like to devote myself completely to the constituency, a little earlier than I would otherwise have had to do anyway.

'Oh,' he said, as I left, 'I may have to field inquiries from the press as to your future in this office. I'll say you never intended to stay beyond the election – don't you think? – and that you are no longer working here.'

In other words, 'You're fired', but he did not put it like that to me or the press. Had he told the newspapers I was fired I might not have survived my coming adoption meeting. Richard Ryder handled all this calmly, kindly and well. A less level man would have taken out his anger on the whippersnapper who had found himself a parliamentary seat before his senior and then dropped us all in it. I heard later that he had been vituperative about me in private. That was the place to be vituperative about me and I don't blame him. I deserved it.

I deserved the sack. It amused me more than twenty years later to see a minister, Stephen Byers, clinging on to a political adviser, Jo Moore, who had sent an e-mail in the hours after the September 11 destruction of the World Trade Center in New York in which thousands had died, announcing that it was a good time to bury bad news. It's just the kind of idiotic thing I might have written. I found it hard not to sympathize with Ms Moore.

I have a recurring dream in which I have been pulverized by some mischance into a sort of remnant, a core, just a kind of seed; and from this core I am rebuilding myself after the most appalling accident. It is a dream of convalescence. In this dream the superb feeling of fragility yet survival, and of returning strength, is impossible to describe. And, as in this dream, I came back from that catastrophe. But it made the worst possible start to my parliamentary candidature in West Derbyshire.

'How are we doing?' Conservative voters used to ask during that 1979 campaign. I would launch into a tense report of the huge problems posed to us by the Liberals, then see a blank look spread across my supporters' faces. They meant nationally, not in West Derbyshire. It's a mistake candidates often make: *their* future depends upon one count; their party leader's upon another. Almost everybody in the democratic process – even the ordinary voter – is more interested in the national result of a general election than a parliamentary candidate is likely to be. He has a contest of his own to think about.

There were special reasons for anxiety in West Derbyshire. The Liberal candidate, Peter Worboys, did seem to be breathing down my neck. That he was a local, a good man, and one who had fought this seat before – while I was a Southern carpet-bagger from London – didn't help. And then had come the business which, within days, we were simply calling 'The Letter'.

We did elections the old-fashioned way in West Derbyshire: megaphones, posters, blitzes of council estates, and forty meetings in forty villages across the constituency. Nobody came. That was not the point. It was necessary to show the flag, or people would say that you had not bothered.

The candidate's state visit to the village of Elton, near Matlock, was a case in point. Elton is situated about a thousand yards from nearby Winster. My meeting in Winster evinced little interest. At Elton there wasn't even a village hall so we pitched camp on the square of tarmac in front of the public house, The Duke of York. It was a freezing spring night. I had had my old Land-Rover, veteran of several Saharan adventures, fitted up with loudspeakers but for this meeting I adopted a hand-held megaphone.

I took my stand at the appointed time, Al Adam beside me. One, or perhaps two, curious villagers stood at a safe distance, not exactly *attending* the meeting, but pausing to observe it, as it were, in passing. I began my speech. The landlord stumbled out. Mr Bloor was a little the worse for drink.

The legendary Billy Bloor was rumoured to have been expelled from Tideswell school sixty years earlier for crouching by the outside loo and shoving a bunch of nettles up the gym mistress's skirt through the gap beneath the door. People claimed that in his upstairs bedroom stood the furniture – wardrobe, chest of drawers, and the like – just where it had been placed by the removal men, askew and in the middle of the floor – many years previously when he moved in. Enraged by complaints that he never put enough fuel on his snug-bar fire, he had banned from the pub a customer from the council houses who tried to smuggle in a lump of coal in a brown paper bag.

'We don't sell cigarettes. Bugger off,' had been Billy's reply to a man with an earring who asked for twenty Benson & Hedges. Someone asking for a gin-and-tonic was told 'We don't serve fancy London drinks here. Bugger off.'

'He had an earring, too,' Bill, who did in fact serve gin and tonic, had explained to me.

Visited by the police as he sat upon the upholstered ceiling inside his upside-down Rover 90 in the ditch of the A515 between Ashbourne and Buxton one night, Bill wound down (or up) the window. He had been drinking. He *was* drinking, from a hip-flask. 'Are you all right?' asked the constable, who knew Bill and had not been intending to take the matter further as no other party was involved (things were done differently in those days). 'Bugger off,' said Billy. So he charged him. He had not been allowed to drive since.

Such was the man who swayed across the tarmac towards me, a nervous first-time candidate with a megaphone and no audience. 'Give that thing to me,' he said. Grabbing the megaphone and addressing me, my agent, a couple of giggling villagers, the empty churchyard opposite and the darkening sky, Bill launched into a rambling quasi-political tirade, mostly about the Inland Revenue, the police and government meddlers generally. The conclusion of this address always

seemed in doubt, until we reached it: fortunately 'Vote Tory. Vote
for, er, Michael Parrish.' Then he went back in. He did not invite my
agent or me.

I remarked afterwards to Al that the visit to Elton had perhaps been
a mistake. 'On the contrary,' he said, 'it was a triumph.'

'But nobody came.'

'Word will reach them soon, will indeed be reaching them already.
Billy's friends will consider that you have been endorsed; his critics
will just feel sympathy for you. They'll say you tried.'

'But we could have had a joint meeting, in Winster, for both
villages.'

Al gave me his withering look. 'It would be better for your political
prospects in either village to have been lynched by the other village,'
he said, 'but more painful. You offered meetings in both, to which
nobody in either came. That is the ideal compromise. Everyone is
satisfied.' In the event I got a very substantial vote (you can tell at the
count, when the boxes come in) from both Winster and Elton.

It is a funny feeling for an outsider adopted as candidate in a safe
seat just months before an election. You ought to feel that this is your
own special candidature, your pitch for popular support; and that the
teams of helpers are your servants. But it's hard to shake off the
suspicion that the helpers – your local association – are your employers;
that you've been interviewed for the job and been lucky enough to
be taken on; and that now you have to prove yourself. Were they
lucky to have me – or was I lucky to have them? The business about
'The Letter' only made it worse.

I've never been very good at swagger. During that campaign of
1979 I felt and looked like a lost dog. All this scampering around and
tail-wagging aroused the protective instincts of the overwhelmingly
female army which manages the Tory effort in most constituencies,
and I made friends and got on well with almost everyone; but if and
when, the campaign over, I was sent back to Parliament as West
Derbyshire's MP, it would hardly be a victor's march to London:
more a meek trotting along. Watching some of the new intake of
Labour MPs in 1997, especially some of the women, I felt a sense of
déjà-vu. I felt like shouting from the press gallery 'They can't kick
you out for four years – don't waste it – this is your shout!' I wish
someone had yelled that at me.

Much of the male part of the constituency association seemed to consist of Al's drinking companions. He had one in every ward. My chauffeur for most of the campaign was a retired solicitor called Mike Brooke-Taylor. Like his cousin Tim, a member of the Goodies comedy team, who were famous at the time, Mike was a natural comedian. He was also a formidable drinker. Never quite drunk and rarely entirely sober he drove me, unbelievably slowly and not always in a straight line, in an atrocious Austin Allegro, the length and breadth of West Derbyshire. My speeches he avoided, taking himself to the local pub. There being three or four speeches a night, there were three or four local pubs.

There were a number of key opinion-formers, Mike, Al and Max told me, with whom it was most important to make my mark. They weren't necessarily *active* Conservatives, but other Conservatives respected them. They included a bank manager, numerous retired small businessmen and a chap in brake linings. They were all male. Somehow they all seemed to like a drink.

So we kept ending up in pubs or bars, and the conversation turned only occasionally and in a desultory way to politics. I hesitantly queried Al's certitude that he had in fact identified the political movers and shakers of the county. 'You don't talk *about* politics in rural Derbyshire,' Al insisted. 'But these fellows are respected. The important thing is for them to like you. Here, have another whisky.' When we got home every night, Al's long-suffering wife would look long-suffering.

He died recently, after splitting from his wife, moving to Scotland, and finally (I later discovered) into a caravan. I owe Al much. I couldn't have helped him but I should have tried.

And he did have a point. Before the campaign I had briefed myself extensively on not only the main points but the minutiae of the Conservative manifesto. We even had a policy on female circumcision. Nobody asked about female circumcision in West Derbyshire. Nobody much asked about politics at all. Farmers would invite you to NFU meetings for a ritual humiliation and shout at you (and not bother to vote anyway) and on doorsteps it was usually local or personal problems people wanted to discuss. The trick was not so much knowing the policies, as listening sympathetically and indicating some familiarity with the background. I began to realize that as a backbencher I could spend a whole life, and much of my intelligence, building up this intricate network of local knowledge. I was good at it and the task was pleasant. But even then, even at the very start, I was beginning to wonder why.

Women party members outnumbered the men – or seemed to because it was they who did most of the work, and who turned up. There is a lazy habit among political journalists talking about Tory activist women of referring disparagingly to 'the blue-rinse brigade'. This always gets an easy laugh. It is unfair. The blue-rinse brigade have not existed since at least the 1960s and when they did exist they were ahead of, not behind, the times. Women organizers are consistently more intelligent, energetic and up-to-date than their male equivalents among Tories, noticeably more humane in their opinions, more open-minded and more receptive to new ideas. The average woman Conservative enthusiast is, quite simply, kinder, gentler and less dogmatic in her politics than the men. Male commentators who seek nasty red-necked Tory activism should talk to some of their own sex rather than make cheap remarks about the women. Certainly such women were always good to me. In Derbyshire politics it was the men who were the gossips and stirrers.

At a meeting in Ashbourne a rather intense man asked me about Rollover Stock Relief. In my panic I latched on to the word 'stock'; my fevered brain told me this must have something to do with my most feared of all topics: agriculture. Maybe stock that had rolled over was what farmers called fallen stock – and entitled the owner to compensation? Maybe Rollover Stock Relief was a form of reimbursement for dead cattle – or 'beasts' as I was learning to say?

I told the intense chap that this was a complicated issue on which I would rather not give an off-the-cuff reply, but would write to the Minister of Agriculture for a background briefing. He looked puzzled. I later learned that he was an accountant.

In Wirksworth, a small, rather hard-bitten town nestling between hills and quarries, a woman asked about gas prices. But I thought she had said 'bus passes' and gave a learned discourse on that topic: public transport was a special interest of mine. Afterwards Al told me of my mistake. 'But they were just as interested in your views on bus passes,' he said. 'The important thing was that you seemed to have something to say.'

Wirksworth was unusual in West Derbyshire in being a mostly Labour town. Here in the town hall, just before the election, I was heckled and booed for the first time in my life. It is hard to describe the irrational fury an MP feels when voters don't like him – but it is strong. In their constituencies MPs feel more like minor monarchs than politicians, and come quickly to think they deserve respect and gratitude from everyone.

It should come as no surprise to a constituency MP that many supporters of other parties in his patch are never going to like him. But it always does. For whatever he knows in his head, in his heart an MP feels that by dint of a general election an entire constituency has gone over to him – to him personally, not necessarily his party – and attached itself to his cause. In return he gives all constituents his own loyalty and works hard for them, visiting prisoners, haranguing ministers, taking tea with senilely demented folk in urine-reeking private nursing-home lounges, bending over life-support machines in local hospitals and wiping honest tears from his eye when calling on the recently bereaved.

They are all, he feels, 'his' people – and you will often hear Members talking about 'my' farmers, 'my' teachers, 'my' garage-owners, and the like. Even if they did not all support him at the most recent election, he cannot quite shake off the hope that at the next, now that they have got to know him and he has helped so many of them, they all will.

Hostility, opposition, and – worse – insolence, come as a huge shock to most MPs and candidates. 'Wasn't that great!' Al said to me, as we left Wirksworth Town Hall after I had been booed and heckled. Al loved raw politics, and a contested meeting pleased him more than a docile one. 'Great!' I said, weakly. If at that moment I had had it in my power to visit upon the town a rain of fire and brimstone, and leave it burning like a modern-day Sodom or Gomorrah, I should have done so.

At that time I was riding a Honda 250 motorbike, bought from my brother Roger after a fabulous thousand-mile ride together over the Pyrenees to Spain. I also had an ancient Land-Rover called Suki. When not in Suki (with loudspeakers strapped to the cab roof) blasting the villagers with stupid music and brainless political slogans, I would roar around on the Honda.

We also canvassed sheep. It is a little-known fact that if you face a field of sheep with a loudspeaker and declaim, 'If you're voting Liberal, say baaaa!', they all bleat. The trick is not to try this substituting the word 'Tory' or indeed any other word.

Still, my strangest memory was of canvassing a smart new private housing estate near the village of Cromford. This was a follow-up canvass and I was doing a street alone while my helpers did another. A youth of about eighteen came out of the bungalow whose house-holders, his parents, had asked me to call, and explained that they were out. But he seemed inclined to chat with me a while about politics and the likely outcome of the election.

He was wearing a tracksuit. Though baggy, the trousers of a tracksuit can be unexpectedly revealing. As we chatted I noticed he was developing a real stonker of an erection. It was quite extraordinary. The more I talked about manifesto promises and prospects for taxation, the bigger it got. I made my excuses and left.

On the night of the count I stalked the floor of the Matlock Leisure Centre gulping at a flask of brandy Al had smuggled on to the floor where the telling was taking place, watching the votes from the towns, which came in first, pile up ominously in the Liberal cause, observing bitterly to myself that they had the edge, wondering why Al seemed so calm, then watching the votes from the villages coming in – great heaps of Tory votes, ballot-box after ballot-box – and beginning to relax.

We had won by some 10,000 votes, a solid victory and a few thousand more than the Tories had received last time – just like everywhere else.

I had prepared only a speech of defeat; though hopeful of victory it would have been tempting fate to anticipate it.

Winning, therefore, I spoke briefly and off-the-cuff. I have always been afraid of public speaking but when I have to it often goes well, and this did. It was a conciliatory speech for, more than anything, I detest crowing and 'pledging' things. It was also modest about the incoming Tory government's ambitions and prospects. Who knows what we actually expected – but it seemed the right thing to say.

I could not banish from my mind the disappointment of the Liberal, Peter Worboys, standing beside me. This was a bitter moment for him: his best, and last, chance to make it to Westminster, gone. Praising and commiserating with him, I meant to be generous. Probably I just sounded patronizing.

In the *New Statesman* the columnist Paul Foot wrote: 'Who will be the nastiest MP in the new House of Commons? I nominate Matthew Francis Parris.' In the *Spectator* Auberon Waugh remarked that, though he had never met me, he expected I was the kind of man with an unsatisfactory moustache. In the *Daily Telegraph* Frank Johnson wrote that one thing was certain: Matthew Parris would never be heard of again.

10. The Commons – the Common

'Darling,' shouted Spencer le Marchant at me, in the booming bark of a rutting male elephant seal, right across the crowded Central Lobby of the House of Commons where I was meeting a group of constituents just arrived from Derbyshire. All heads turned.

'Why are you such a cunt?'

Spencer, Conservative MP for the High Peak, was my regional whip. No doubt I had forgotten to vote again and this was his way of drawing my attention to the omission. The language was routine, even affectionate, for Spencer.

About ten feet tall, loud, grand, lush, kind and – in the words of one of his fellow-whips – mad as a snake, Spencer le Marchant included among his electors the struggling hill-farmers of the North Midlands and the residents of the old mill towns of the Peak District, tough, chapped little satellites of Manchester which straggle up the long slow hill from Stockport to Buxton. Their MP's efforts in support of the reopening of the Buxton Opera House and the establishment of the annual Buxton Festival – real achievements: he was a secretly cultured man who loved music – were received with scepticism by farmers and townsfolk alike, and his constituency agent once confided in me that he could understand only about half of what Spencer said, while few of his constituents understood a word but viewed their MP, rather like the strange and famous Blue John Cavern at Hope in his constituency, as a phenomenon.

Spencer was fun, unmalicious, generous, incredibly rude and a serious alcoholic. In the end drink killed him, and I am left with a sad mental snapshot (from Spencer's last days) of the once bull-like figure, now knighted, his skin yellow, his face sagging and his liver all but gone, at dinner in the Members' Dining Room during one of his final attempts to stay on the wagon. He had drunk only water, but ordered 'melon with port' for dessert.

Into the shallow depression left in the half-melon by the removal of the pips, they pour a couple of teaspoonsful of port. Spencer was desperately scrabbling in this depression with his pudding spoon, trying to recover the last drop.

I was one of his favourites among his North Midlands Commons flock and in his drunker moments he was very insistent that I should marry one of his daughters. At lunch at his expensive riverside flat he rounded on the fiancé of one of them, pointed at me, and in front of all the other guests bawled at the poor lad that he wished his daughter had found somebody worthwhile to marry, like me.

It was at the time when he was organizing a Members' horse-race, the horses in this case being the Members. Along with a handful of other Tory MPs rich enough to have real racehorses and boast personal racing-colours, Spencer had nominated a horse of his own – me – and was to supply me with an outfit in his colours. Other Members had chosen from among junior colleagues runners of their own, to be kitted out in comparable liveries. The racecourse was to be the perimeter of the Members' Smoking Room, round which was strung a range of sofas, armchairs and coffee-tables, and at one end the bar. This course was to be a sort of steeple-chase, the idea being for the MP-horses to race each other to complete ten circuits of the room's perimeter without touching the floor – jumping from sofa to bar to coffee-table.

All the arrangements were in hand, the chairman of the House of Commons Catering Committee had been squared, and Spencer had given his tailor my measurements, when the *Evening Standard*'s Londoner's Diary apparently got wind of the planned fixture. Naturally we all denied it when telephoned but Spencer's colleagues among the government whips thought it prudent to cancel the race, and it never happened. Spencer thought the cancellation a pretty poor show.

Le Marchant was one of those Commons 'characters' who find passing mention in dozens of parliamentarians' memoirs, as examples of what rollicking good fun it all was.

And sometimes it was. With every passing Parliament the Commons becomes a more sober place, but the Parliament I joined came just at the tail end of a different era, and many of its representatives lingered on. My secretary, who had joined the typists' ranks at the age of sixteen immediately after the Second World War, told me that in the fifties and early sixties few Tory MPs were always sober, many were mostly drunk, lunges by married MPs at pretty secretaries were absolutely routine and affairs were legion. A former Tory colleague of mine still in the House confessed to me, when at the end of the last century the innovation of morning sittings was introduced, that he was unsure whether he had ever made a speech in the House while entirely sober, and wondered what it would be like. 'I can't even reverse my car properly without a drink,' he added, 'I can't get my head round. A glass of claret loosens the neck. Alcohol has been a good friend to me.'

Such men have made their accommodations and live at peace. They are good company. Spencer was sometimes good company but he was not at peace. He could find no balance. He must have been a more tortured soul than his outward gaiety suggested. After he died I discovered that there had been, in the other sense too, a gay side to his nature, but pretty wretchedly indulged.

At the time, and as a young new MP, I would never have dreamed such a thing. Though a rogue beast, Spencer seemed a deeply establishment figure and was the doyen of the Members' Smoking Room. Any time after ten in the morning, only champagne was served in his office, and it was served only in half-pint silver tankards. A morning chat with the regional whip left you reeling before lunch.

I had many of these chats. For much of my time at Westminster I floundered and was forever in trouble with the whips. I wish I could claim this was due to independence of mind or a rebellious spirit; more often it arose from sheer disorganization: a failure to get into the Commons swing of things.

Oh I could tell you any number of jolly little anecdotes from the place, and lots of jolly books by Members and former Members do, and they're mostly true and all a good read. In preparation for writing this book I penned a list of anecdotes of my own, intending to work through it: 'the day I sat down at the chief whip's table, by mistake' . . . 'the day I ate dinner on the Labour side of the Members' Dining Room, by mistake' . . . 'the day I wandered into the chamber after too much wine at dinner and joined the Opposition benches by mistake' . . . 'the day I rushed, late for a division, into the wrong lobby as the doors closed – and hid in the gentlemen's lavatory so as to avoid voting with the Opposition' – and some of them might raise a smile or two.

I could tell you how in a crowded division lobby I would feel the feminine touch of the Prime Minister's fingers on the back of my neck, as from behind she turned down an upturned collar; or how she used to approach the clerks ticking off the list of Members voting and advise them of her name, in case they had forgotten it – and point it out to them on their list. 'Thatcher, M!'

These I could relate and the impression might be gained that it was all a bit of a romp, but it was not a romp: not for me and not for a great many other MPs then or today, Labour, Liberal or Conservative. Their testimony is seldom heard because they worked hard to get there and are privileged to be there, and don't have to stay there if they don't want to, and do not wish to sound sour.

They carry on willingly enough and they will stand again at the next election. But their secret story is that even after many years they haven't found their feet or ever quite worked out what they are supposed to be for. I sympathize with them. I never found my feet in the House of Commons.

My maiden speech, however, went well. It was one of the best received – perhaps the best received – of all the 1979 intake of new MPs. I waited for a couple of months, until the end of July, before making it, and chose a debate on Southern Africa, writing the speech carefully, polishing it well and learning it by heart so that I would not have to read. I kept the text in shaking hands, however, just in case of a mental blank. Once in the Cambridge Union had been enough.

The Chair is kind to new MPs with maidens to make, and does its best to put them out of their misery early. As it happened the Prime Minister was present in the chamber when I spoke.

What occasioned the debate was a critical phase in Britain's negotiations with Ian Smith and the black nationalist parties in the then decades-long impasse in Rhodesia. Smith's government was nearing the end of the road; African nationalist forces, principally Joshua Nkomo's grouping and that of Robert Mugabe were gaining ground. A peaceful way for the whites to yield – 'internal settlement' was the phrase – was being sought.

I knew about the subject, and cared too. But a maiden speech must begin with certain conventional tributes to the new MP's constituency and to his predecessor. I observed the convention . . .

I am grateful to you, Mr Deputy Speaker, for calling me this afternoon. It is the first time that I have spoken, and sitting on these benches waiting to speak it struck me that the term 'maiden speech' was an apt one. Similar to losing one's innocence in other ways, it is one of those things that we do not especially care to do, but we simply had to grit our teeth and plough through so that at least no one can say that we have not tried . . .

The Prime Minister turned towards me and smiled. I relaxed. The rest of the speech, which was about not promising too much in politics and about the need to understand the fears of both whites and blacks in Rhodesia, went very well.

The large numbers of congratulatory notes which reached me in the days which followed convinced me this speech really had been quite a hit. It was (as it turned out) the only really effective Commons performance I ever achieved in the seven years I was to remain there.

Not long after I arrived at Westminster, there was a series of votes on the death penalty. This, it was clear, was never going to return, but the motions (literally) had to be gone through if only to satisfy our constituents. I attended all the debates. My intention had been to vote for an early motion, recommending the principle of capital punishment, and then vote against the various practical proposals for introducing this. I had studied all of them and none was workable.

Any study of the original daily Hansards for the period, however, will suggest a more confused approach. In one division I am recorded as having voted in both the Aye and the No lobby. It appeared the MP for West Derby, Mr Robert Parry, was confused by the clerks with the MP for West Derbyshire, Mr Matthew Parris. The result is that in the division in question Robert Parry (an abolitionist) is not recorded as having voted at all. My name, however, appeared on both the Aye and the No lists. I did not struggle too assiduously to get this record put straight, though in the end it was.

I received letters from the public congratulating me on my abolitionist stance, and letters congratulating me on my support for the return of hanging. I did not reply.

So much for the jolly diary of a Commons new boy. For after my reprieve on capital punishment and my triumphant maiden speech, I began to tread water. Despite occasional blunders, blunders were not the problem. I just never hit any kind of stride. I couldn't really work out what I was there for.

I have mentioned that it is commonplace for MPs to compare their first days at Westminster with the experience of being a new boy at school. But it is much stranger than that. For a start, there is no prospect of mummy coming to take you home at the end of the day. And – though you do feel lost, and do have to ask where the loos are and whether there are showers and how you book a place in the chamber, or at Questions or in the dining rooms – you don't feel small. It's when you begin to understand your place in the British constitution that you feel small.

In fact at first you feel quite big: rather proud, and important, and equal. The *House* – as opposed to the government, or Opposition, or Commons timetable – is yours; it really is: you can go anywhere; the policemen know your name; the servants of the House are your servants, and treat you with the obsequious contempt which has characterized servants since servants were invented.

For a few days or a few parliaments you feel like a child with a new toy. You can call at the Table Office and table a question and – lo! – the Foreign Secretary will answer it, and the exchange will be printed in Hansard. You get your own embossed notepaper with a portcullis crest and your name across the top, with the letters ' MP' appended, and if you write to ministers on this they will sign the replies personally, often putting in a handwritten postscript indicating familiarity – which you can then send on to your constituents, and impress.

Only gradually do you realize that none of this is making much difference to anything. Only slowly does it sink in that though the world will doff its cap to you, and though you will always be on the top table at any local feast, and though the local newspaper will print your thoughts on any subject and even the letters editor of *The Times* will be inclined to let you jump the queue, and though your name will now be in *Who's Who* until you die, nobody is actually taking any notice.

You meet the whips. Your first encounter with these fearsome beings is with their vicars-on-earth, the whips' messengers. These are like barristers' clerks, only more respectful. Men of often humble backgrounds and unassuming manner, they man a little office – 'den' would be a better word – just off the Members' Lobby at the entrance to the chamber itself.

They know everything. They know when the divisions are really going to be, as opposed to when the printed whip – the piece of paper demanding MPs' attendance – says they are going to be. They know when there will not be a division at all, despite the whips' advice. They know their opposite numbers in the other parties' whips' offices, and they exchange information. They do not, however, dispense this freely or as of right. On the whole they're kind but on the whole they remain mindful that their master is the chief whip, and the chief must get the government's business through. The purpose of their office, and every party's whips' office, is so to arrange things as to smooth the road beneath the wheels of the onward-rolling party machine.

At the whips' messengers' office you are the supplicant. Tugging at the sleeve of the policeman behind the Speaker's Chair, who also knows the score and will deign to answer phone calls from you if you ingratiate yourself with him, you are the supplicant too. From this you rightly conclude that as a backbench MP you are lower in the pecking-order than a policeman or a clerk.

And then you meet the whips themselves.

The occasion on which Spencer had hailed me so abusively was probably after I had forgotten to vote on a three-line whip on the previous evening. I didn't care for Spencer's method of administering a reprimand, but I preferred it to Michael Jopling's. Jopling was the government chief whip: a great bullock of a man with hair usually in need of a shampoo and trim, who was said to be a serious motorbiker. Certainly one could imagine him as a superannuated Hell's Angel, leather jacket scuffed in many a brawl, and greasy black jeans under increasing strain at the waist. He it was (and not, as is wrongly believed, Alan Clark) who called Michael Heseltine the kind of fellow who bought his own furniture.

It took me a while to get the hang of voting – the right way, that is, and at the required time. None of this mattered in the least: the government then could rely on easy majorities at all times. It would have mattered only if my early indiscipline had been a sign of intentional cussedness rather than simple disorganization. It was not, and Jopling must have known that.

But he had also – plainly – picked up the impression that I would be easily frightened. Like all bullies, whips bully only the people they can bully, treating serious rebels with more respect. He called me into his room. He demanded an explanation for my erratic voting pattern. I gave it. It will have been obvious the explanation was sincere.

'Your life's in a bit of a mess,' he said, with a mixture of sneer and menace, 'go away and sort it out.' His glance suggested he had just said something rather clever and wounding.

This was the behaviour of an undistinguished assistant headmaster at a second-rate boys' preparatory boarding school. It wasn't even intelligent. At that moment I resolved not so much to become a consistent rebel – I never was or wanted to be – as simply to plough my own furrow, and let preferment come my way or otherwise, as it chose. I was not going to suck up to a man like this.

Willie Whitelaw, the Home Secretary, was more skilful. I had always seen him as the faintly comic figure of *Private Eye*'s 'Ol' Oyster-Eyes' lampoon. As Mrs Thatcher's letter-writer I had put up to her (without comment) a letter she had been sent by a mother of four declaring herself to be a keen Tory but wondering respectfully whether 'your Mr Whitelaw' (who, she said, was undoubtedly a very clever man) could be asked not to be on television before the 9 p.m. watershed 'because his face frightens my little girl, and she can't sleep'.

Such was the face which confronted me when, with a handful of fellow-backbenchers, I went to see the Home Secretary to explain our concerns about widespread telephone tapping by the security services, and our hope that this could be brought within the law.

Whitelaw poured us all, and himself, enormous whiskies. Then, looking each of us successively very straight in the eye, he told us that the anxieties we had were very much in his mind too and we were quite right to express them. He was glad somebody had. It strengthened his own hand in dealing with these matters.

He would like us to know, he said, that as Home Secretary he faced some most awkward and sensitive security questions. He had oversight of what the intelligence services did and was every day confronted with their reports and requests for authorization. And he had to report to us, in the very strictest confidence, that there were some very dangerous men indeed at work in the world, and in Britain; and that it was important we kept track of what they were up to.

We would understand, as colleagues, of course, that it would not be possible for him to reveal to us what he knew, and what the intelligence services told him. But as colleagues we would also respect him, he hoped, when he gave us his gravest personal assurance that no surveillance action would be taken unless he were himself absolutely convinced of its necessity. Would we forgive him – would we as men who understood the world – understand, if he left it at that?

We departed slightly giddy from the whisky and not a little giddy at the vast confidence our senior colleague had reposed in us by speaking so frankly.

He had, of course, sent us away empty-handed. Not one of us ever raised the issue of telephone tapping again.

A chat with Sir Edward du Cann was different again. The former chairman of the 1922 Committee and arch-conspirator who had moved from Tomorrow's Man to Yesterday's Man (and later to bankruptcy) via a controversial business career has been variously described as silky-smooth, duplicitous or slippery, but you will notice him popping up all over the place in biographies and autobiographies of the period, often in a quite significant role.

A transitional figure, he nevertheless dealt in more than confidence. Edward engaged naturally with and sometimes anticipated the spirit of his times. His diplomacy was famous ('What's the time, Sir Edward?' a junior once asked. 'What time would you like it to be, dear boy?') but the politesse, though it was at least precautionary, was more than that. Edward du Cann once cheered me up not just momentarily but – in a small way – for the rest of my life . . .

I was moping in the Commons Tea Room. The Matlock Mercury had printed some letters, obviously inspired by agents of the local Liberal Party, criticizing me, unfairly I thought. I long forget what it was all about but it seemed important at the time. Du Cann was sitting opposite. He noticed my long face.

'Downcast?' he said, kindly. I explained my woes and, as I explained them, realized how trivial they must seem. 'Of course when one has been in this game as long as you have, Sir Edward,' I said, 'I expect it's water off a duck's back and you aren't hurt any more . . .'

'Dear boy,' he said, '*nice* people are *always* hurt.' It was a cheering possibility.

I had not, on being elected, stopped going to Clapham Common. I did not cruise there habitually or often; it happened maybe no more than half a dozen times, after each of which I resolved never to return. But months would pass, and I would return. I cannot think why.

It was crazy. Why do we – why do they – do it? Why do MPs, and JPs, and DPPs, and VIPs of every type . . . why do public figures, of all people, take such risks?

When Oscar Wilde called it 'feasting with panthers' he meant seeking sex with working-class youths. But it's an apt expression for many sorts of adventure. It means hazard. It means foolish, reckless excitement. It means danger, secrecy and shame.

How we find it depends on us. Some will run up crazy gambling debts; some will philander, kerb-crawl, drink and drive; some turn to drugs; some will pursue boys, some girls. Some will pursue dodgy money in crazy schemes. Each to his own, but all have this in common: that if they are found out, the world says, 'Why? He had everything going for him. He must have known he risked ruin. And he seemed such a steady chap. Why?'

But the world misunderstands. The secrecy and danger are not a regrettable side-effect of the folly: they are the reason for the folly. They are the spice, the drug. That the visible part of a man's life looks respectable and safe should be no cause for surprise that in the shadows between the real and the imagined he has sought for himself a perilous other life. Crushed by decency, he embraces hazard as a means of escape. To regret that he could not find something safer is like suggesting to those who crave furtive lovemaking behind the shelves of busy supermarkets that they buy a container-load of cornflakes and recreate the Tesco backdrop in their own bedrooms. It misses the point.

So what is the point?

People have the impression that MPs take more personal risks than other citizens. Why this impression? Of course more publicity follows an MP's exposure, but I doubt whether that is the whole explanation. I think they really do take more risks. If the proportion of my ex-colleagues who philandered is true to the national average, then this is a feckless nation. If, proportionately, as many citizens are gay as MPs are, then homosexuality in Britain is rampant beyond even the wildest calculations of the militant queers. I suspect politicians of every bent do take unusual risks in unusual numbers, and the suspicion is reinforced whenever another is found out. He is almost never one of those I knew about.

Another misconception needs to be corrected. Miscreant MPs do not 'always get found out in the end'. I never was, and nor were most of the gay (let alone the adulterous) MPs I knew. The calculation is not between safety and certain ruin, but between safety and risk.

Why might a career in public life in the Commons and in the constituency dispose an MP towards such risk? First we must ask whether the risk-takers are self-selected. Are men with a weakness for surprising private behaviour especially drawn towards a political career? Second we should ask whether the job itself, once secured, turns previously cautious men into secret risk-takers.

The answer to both questions is yes.

Nobody without a gambling streak, a taste for uncertainty and a belief in his own luck would embark upon a Commons career. Statistically most must 'fail' within their own terms, which are (usually these days) the achievement of high ministerial office. The hours and conditions are arduous and the salary no more than what the majority of politicians could have hoped to attract in a career outside. For many it is less. You may sacrifice a career in the hope of securing a seat, for which you will not be extravagantly paid, which is on balance unlikely to lead to great fame, influence or money, and which you may at any time subsequently lose, without compensation.

However regular a guy a candidate may present himself to his electors as being, no unadventurous family man in search of security is likely to want a career in politics.

And there is something further which I believe self-selects men with a streak of exhibitionism, buccaneering or bravado. MPs are a miscellaneous bunch, but united by this: a craving for applause. They are attention-seekers. The job rarely offers real power or influence but regularly offers publicity. You may do little, but you are somebody. It is remarkable how few MPs' biographies reveal boys who were the 'rounded' type at school: popular enough, clever enough, good enough at sport – the 'balanced all-rounder' beloved of school reports. Nor will you find that most were great crusaders for causes they believed in. Instead you will find that many were just unhappy, awkward, lonely or unpopular.

Men often go into politics to prove something which they feared might be in doubt. 'One day I'll be popular. I'll be Prime Minister, and be driven around in a big car, and everyone will cheer.'

Thus the selection process attracts adventurers with more bravado than self-confidence, more exhibitionism than idealism, and more ambition than talent. Then it lands them in a dead-end job. What follows, follows.

You are a little monarch in your own constituency. In the House you are a smaller fish, but still you feel you belong to a most important – the most important – club. Your head swells. But your heart troubles you because you know it's not true. You know you are there only because your party association chose you and few have ever voted for you as an individual, or ever will. You know, too, that your power at Westminster is almost zero, the whips humiliate you privately and your influence in the constituency derives not from your skill or the real respect you command, but from the portcullis on your notepaper. You know you are a fraud and your position is a fraud.

It breeds an internal cynicism and an imperceptibly opening gap between your public life and your private, internal life. The latter becomes a world of its own in which you increasingly choose to dwell, all the while developing the skills you need to keep up appearances in the external world. The gap between these two worlds becomes, for some, almost unbridgeable. The gap generates fears and anxieties, yet they are invited.

Once in the constituency I had to deal with the problems caused by the closure of a mill which was moving out of Derbyshire to transfer to Scotland. I had invited a delegation of workers (all women) to come down to see the minister with me to try to stop this. The (Labour) leader of the county council had, like me, muscled in, and decided to accompany the women.

He and I shepherded them from the small mini-bus that had brought them, towards the minister's office in Victoria Street. Each of us was resentful of the presence of the other. Each of us was trying to impress the women with our own mastery of the situation. Both of us knew that nothing we could do would make the least difference.

One of the women turned to me and asked how I thought she should address the minister if he spoke to her. I looked at her and realized how completely genuine and how nervous but how timidly hopeful she was.

I suddenly felt a complete heel. Tears filled my eyes but, it being dark in the street, nobody was able to see this.

It is not surprising that MPs learn to despise, if not themselves, then the thing that they are pretending to be. It is not surprising that they sometimes try to escape this, sometimes in a manner which to the rest of us looks desperate. Being an MP feeds your vanity and starves your self-respect.

A couple of gay friends and I decided to call in at the Two Brewers on Clapham High Street, just over the Common from where I lived.

By then it was more of a bar and club than the pub it had once been, the management had blacked out the windows and, if you didn't know what kind of a place it was when you entered, you soon picked up the feel. The endless, mindless, high-energy dance music (so loud you had to shout), the atmosphere at the same time heady, tense and cold, the checked shirts and moustaches popular at the time – why did people escape from one kind of conventionality and conformity only to rush headlong into another? – and the hard stares and sense of predation hanging in the smoky air . . . there was no mistaking these places. But they seemed to be all there was – that or the Common, which on the whole I found a softer and more human place.

I didn't know many gay pubs. Earls Court, famous at the time for its gay scene, repelled me. Once when I was in the Foreign Office, before my first foray on to Clapham Common and so before I had ever touched or kissed another man, some friends had taken me to one of the best-known gay pubs in Earls Court, called the Coleherne, where there was some kind of a drag show. Drag bores me (as it bores most gay men) witless but for a homosexual virgin the thrill of just being in such a place with such people had been intense. I had been all but overcome with the excitement – so much so that on leaving I seemed to be treading on air, and walked into a lamppost, almost knocking myself out.

Now, however, I was more blasé, and both wary and weary of such places, weary even of the Two Brewers, and expecting little. I seemed forever to be plucking up the courage to risk a foray into the light, ever hopeful I might meet someone. I rarely did, being useless at chat-up routines and feeling wretched about one-night stands. I would return home disappointed, vowing not to bother again; but the resolutions never lasted.

This time I did catch somebody's eye, or so it seemed. At any rate he was looking rather fixedly at me. He came over. 'You're Matthew Parris, the Tory MP, aren't you?' he said.

Discovered. My blood ran cold. I nodded miserably.

'I'm a journalist,' he said. 'Don't you recognize me?'

I half thought I did. Through my mind was racing a series of defensive stories, all immediately rejected as hopeless. 'Just came in here with a couple of mates – had no idea what sort of a place it was . . .', 'researching for some work I'm doing on reform of the Sexual Offences Act . . .' No, there was no point. This mild-looking, fresh-faced little chap was obviously a hardened and brilliant investigative journalist.

'How did you guess?' I asked.

'I didn't,' he said. This was one of his local haunts, he added; he had hardly expected to see me there. His name was Martin Dowle; he was a lobby correspondent for *The Scotsman* . . .

As he continued, the obvious dawned on me. He was gay too. He was here socially, not to fit me up, or even to pick me up. He had not the least intention of exposing me and may have had worries of his own about being gay while working for a conservative Scottish newspaper. He was a rather discreet person.

Martin is now a friend. A quiet man, he ended up in charge of the British Council in Rio de Janeiro and was there when Peter Mandelson visited as a minister, staying with Martin. *Punch* magazine got hold of a tangle of tales about the visit and grabbed the wrong end of the stick: a story arose that Mandelson had clubbed until dawn as the guest of a high-living British official, and had been lent his boyfriend. The young man in question was called, said *Punch*, Fabrizio, but was known throughout Rio as 'Fabulous Fabrizio' and famous for the outrageous drag in which he danced in the city's most fashionable underworld clubs. And this blazing comet of the Rio gay scene had been the minister's for the night. Or so it was insinuated.

I realized at once that the true elements in this interesting tale were unlikely to be the interesting ones. It was easier to imagine Martin in reading glasses and carpet slippers than sequins. But the *Daily Telegraph* was poised to hit the story hard, though its editor was undecided and under pressure from Mandelson, who insisted the story was untrue, to back off.

I suspected the minister was right. I contacted the editor, Charles Moore, to tell him I knew some of those concerned and this did not have the ring of truth. Later I was able to speak to Martin. Fabrizio was not Martin's boyfriend, hardly fabulous and never a drag artist. Mr Mandelson had not clubbed until midnight, until dawn, or at all. Nobody had lent anyone to anyone.

If only. I wish being a gay MP had been more of a hoot for me or, I suspect, Peter Mandelson.

The panic my encounter with Martin Dowle at the Two Brewers had caused provoked a bit of reflection. Should I go right back into the closet? I reached the opposite conclusion. I must push harder. I ought to be able to enter a gay bar openly, if I was with friends, without fear; I would put up with the questions this would provoke, and resolutely refuse either to confirm or deny, insisting that this was private. In the end, I figured, the penny would drop with everybody, and I would have got from A (in) to B (out) without provoking any tabloid headlines on the journey.

As far as my political work was concerned, I would (and did) take a leading part in the Conservative Group for Homosexual Equality (I became a parliamentary vice-president) and take what opportunities arose to work for reform of the law and a change of public attitudes.

The plan looked fine on paper but it was not completely honest and it was less than brave. I was never comfortable with it. Every so often I would push the door open wider than the plan allowed, half-hoping I'd go beyond a point of no return.

One night, a couple of years after I was elected, after an early division then dinner at Douglas and Judy Hurd's home, I drove across Chelsea Bridge towards my house in Clapham, pretty sober – but short of petrol. I was driving an ancient Rover 2000 at the time – the car my rich and glamorous Austrian friend Marlen had given me in a rather dramatic gesture when she had telephoned me from a kiosk somewhere near the M3 and shrieked, 'Matthew, my car's on fire on the hard shoulder by junction 7. I don't want it any more, I'm taking a taxi. You want it? Come and tow it away' – and I had.

Half way down Lombard Road I ran out of petrol, but after stopping found a can in the boot, drained it into the tank, and carried on. When I reached the edge of Clapham Common I parked in one of the side streets, and walked out on to the Common. I stuck to a wide, paved path called The Avenue. It seemed safer. It was around midnight.

I saw two men walking towards me. This was not unusual. Perhaps they had just met, and were now leaving together. As they drew closer I noticed they were young men, and white – but it was too dark to see more. I walked on, moving a little to one side to pass them.

Suddenly I was on the ground, curled up, felled by a terrific blow to the jaw. I never saw the fist coming, never noticed the body language, never anticipated attack, never knew who first hit me, never remembered their faces. Now they were kicking me, hard, in the ribs and head. All this happened in complete silence, not a word spoken by the assailants.

How I got to my feet is a mystery. Had something frightened them, distracting them momentarily? Later, unable to remember how long the kicking had continued, I remembered only that somehow I had scrambled up, and begun to run.

They gave chase but I outstripped them. Soon I was at the edge of the Common, where the streetlights are – but for some reason I just wanted to keep running. Instead of returning to my car I ran down through the network of residential streets which lie between Clapham and Wandsworth Common – an area of whose Conservative association I had once been chairman – and kept running until I reached my terraced house.

Nobody was following and I knew this, but I felt, and ran, like a man pursued.

Fumbling for my key, I stumbled through the door, slammed it shut, deadlocked it and ran upstairs to the bathroom. I stared at my face in the mirror. I was cut and grazed, my chin was pouring blood, and blood soaked my white shirt.

But I was safe. Strange to relate, I stood there at the bathroom mirror, staring at myself for perhaps a quarter of an hour – looking as one might at a friend in trouble, full of sympathy and affection. It was immensely comforting, perhaps the most intense and comforting moment of companionship I have ever known.

These moments of desolation are important in a person's life. I am
no great believer in pivotal experiences – so much is cumulative – but
these are pivotal. At a certain intensity of pain or despair comes a sort
of calm: you collect yourself, steady yourself and see that it is up to
you. This was the same feeling I had had twenty-five years earlier as,
picking myself up from the hot Cyprus dust with my wrecked arm
bleeding, I had resolved to get myself home; the same feeling I had
had, head bowed, under the thorn tree in Cameroon in the warm
African sun when I had survived being thrown from the Land-Rover's
roof, and depression hit me, but also calm.

Strange to relate, it is sublime. We feel the universe wheeling
around us, *us*. We have been picked out. Just as much as triumph,
trouble, when it hits us, frames us and centres us. We have stepped
into some kind of searchlight. But I do not believe in God. It is
ourselves we catch momentarily in the beam, and the moment may
be – as it was just after that attack on Clapham Common which could
have killed me – a moment of desolation. It is chillingly personal.
Sometimes in the dead of night I wake to hear a blackbird singing,
and know that it is singing only to me, and that it is not. I am singing
to myself.

The bathroom mirror before me and speaking to myself, I resolved
to keep the shirt, find some way in the parliamentary years ahead,
however gradual, of openly acknowledging my homosexuality, and
resolved again to use my membership of the Commons to improve
Britain for other gay men. I washed as best I could – there was blood
in my hair, blood all over my face and blood on my hands and arms.
I lay on my bed, and passed out.

The next morning was a Friday. My ribs were unbelievably painful,
making breathing difficult. My jaw hurt so much I could barely open
my mouth. But my face and head, though cut, were not bruised or
swollen.

I knew I had a lunch in my constituency. I have never been one to
cancel things, so I took the train north. My agent collected me and
drove me to my lunch, which was at a giant yard where they made
culverts and breeze-blocks.

What to say, how to explain? I am not good at lying. When one
must lie it is best to keep the story as close to the truth as possible, and
to run through the invented sequences in the imagination beforehand,

as though they were happening, and then 'recall' that. So I recounted to myself the incident as it had happened, but changed the location to Lombard Road, where I described running out of petrol and said I had walked for help. This was then what I told others. My agent urged me to report it to the police.

At lunch I realized I could not open my mouth properly. It was agony. Later that afternoon the Derby Royal Infirmary confirmed that my jaw and several ribs were cracked but would heal without intervention, they said.

Returning to London I stuck to my version of events when I reported the incident at Battersea police station.

Sympathetic reports appeared in my local papers, small articles in national papers. Constituents were shocked and solicitous and scores of friends wrote cards of sympathy. Douglas and Judy Hurd sent a get-well card. Urged to make a claim before the Criminal Injuries Compensation Board, I thought better of the idea.

The affair was soon forgotten by everyone but me. I told almost nobody the truth, nobody found out, and if anybody guessed, they never let on. The whips cannot have known. When finally I left Parliament years later, I left, I suppose, with an unblemished record. Only in my own mind was there a gap between record and reality.

Some fifteen years later the gap was troubling me when the then Secretary of State for Wales, Ron Davies, ran into difficulties of his own on Clapham Common. This was the moment to tell my own story: it helped explain the difficulties a man might get into. Because of this *Times* article, *Newsnight* asked me to join a discussion of Davies's plight. That was when I mentioned that Peter Mandelson was gay.

Ron Davies's story was different. I have no idea what he was doing on Clapham Common. All I know is that his career was wrecked, and mine untouched. I was lucky. Most people are lucky. The stories I do know will surely be the tip of an iceberg of unknown size – for nobody ever found out about mine.

I never returned to the Common: fate I thought had given me a final warning. The secret stayed with me but I was not happy about this. When one's real past and present diverge from what others have been led to believe, and as new lies are needed in order to sustain old ones, a gap begins to open between the known and the private side of one's nature and, like two roads after they have forked, the gap widens. This gap becomes a source of anxiety, both practical and moral. But the longer it goes on the less good reason one can find for suddenly blurting everything out. The longer it goes on, the more has been built on a dishonest foundation. They say that the truth will always out, but that is not so. Mostly the truth does not out. Mostly people get away with things.

Washed as clean as could be managed I kept the bloodstained shirt for many years, to remind me of my luck, my secret disgrace, my muddled sense of shame and defiance, anger and self-pity, and of self-reproach. With considerable violence I had been singled out and knew I must do something – and that the something must not be to retreat – but beyond that, what? I was confused about what to do.

Come out? Improve the lighting on Clapham Common? Did I want a world where there was no shame in seeking anonymous sex in public places, or a world where homosexuality became a cosy and respectable variant of heterosexuality? Should I be working to liberate or to tame? What was, what should be, the issue: freedom, licence and anything-goes, or equal pension rights for same-sex partners?

The truth is that I did not know much about homosexuality. As my jaw and ribs healed and the bloodstains on my white shirt faded, all I knew was that dishonesty had been at the root of this. I was unsure how to frame the question but certain that honesty was part of the answer.

Some time before the 1983 general election, my first as a sitting MP, I was invited by the Oxford Union to propose the motion that 'This House would be glad to be gay'. I decided to accept.

In prospect my speech somehow became very important to me. I spent a huge amount of time and thought writing it, then typed it out and learned it by heart. It was impassioned stuff. Nobody hearing it would have doubted I was gay, or at least had had – like Michael Portillo – homosexual experiences, though I never said so in so many words.

All the way to Oxford in my old Rover 2000 I practised the speech out loud in the car, as I had practised my speech for the West Derbyshire selection committee in the lavatory of the train to Derby.

It was an enormous success. We won the vote overwhelmingly

but, as important, students kept coming up to me afterwards and congratulating me; a handful wrote to me later. Some people who were there have told me it was remembered for a long time, and by many. I had made an impact; I could tell that immediately.

The following morning, and the day after that, I waited for a story to break in the press. I kept a copy of the speech and had decided I would not comment any further, but refer journalists to the speech itself. I was braced to be called gay, and not to deny or confirm it. That may look timid now, but it felt brave then.

There was not a single inquiry, and no report.

Well, I reflected, at least I have not, after all, ruled myself out for a conventional promotion. More use, perhaps, a half-out rising star than an out-of-the-closet nonentity? A note had arrived from Patrick Jenkin, a capable, civil man of moderate views, in charge of a vast department of state. Mrs Thatcher's first Secretary of State for Health and Social Security, then Industry, then Environment Secretary, Patrick was just the kind of minister any backbencher would have hoped to start his career working for. His note was handwritten. Would I pop into his office for a chat? I did.

He wanted a parliamentary private secretary – a backbench aide – he said. Would I do it? Overjoyed, I agreed at once. A first rung on the ladder at last, and Patrick mattered. I would have been proud to work for him.

'Good,' he said, adding that he couldn't appoint me there and then but must first clear it with the whips. No problem was anticipated.

I went home and thought about it hard. Something told me that here was one of those forks in the road at which a decision, though it may seem to signify no big change in direction, leads you in time along a route quite distinct from the other you might have taken. If, even by silence, I lied now, it would become harder and harder to tell the truth as my career progressed and the years rolled by.

So I sent the chief whip a copy of the speech I had made at the Oxford Union, with a note saying that Patrick Jenkin was hoping to recommend me for the post of PPS, a post which I wanted very much; but that I had better start with the whips as I meant to go on, and so would like the chief whip to see the sort of speech I had been making outside the House, and might make again.

A note arrived asking me to call into the chief whip's office for a drink before supper.

The chief whip (I shall not say which) sat me down with a very large and very full tumbler of whisky. He thanked me for sending him my speech. 'Very good speech,' he said.

'Thank you,' I said.

'I wouldn't have made it.'

I stared into my tumbler and said nothing.

'I'm going to tell you something,' he said, 'which I've told very few other living souls. I haven't told the Prime Minister or the other whips. I haven't, in fact, told my wife. When being interviewed for the Conservative candidature in my constituency, I did not feel the need to tell the selection committee. And they did not ask.'

I sipped my whisky nervously.

'I don't believe in God.' He gulped his. 'But I don't shout about it. I don't feel the need to add it to my election address at general elections – special box, bold type: *Your Conservative candidate does not believe in God.* I don't address atheist conventions. When I go to church in the constituency on Remembrance Sunday I don't feel any urge to jump up on my pew in the middle of the creed and shout, "I DON'T BELIEVE IN GOD." It's a secret, if you like. It's private. It's between me and my . . . well, I don't believe in Him.

'See? See my point?'

This had not been said rudely, though it had been said brutally. In its way it was a fair and honest statement of whips' wisdom on such matters and I was, or should have been, grateful to him for giving it straight. I thanked him and left. The next day a troubled-looking Patrick Jenkin called me in and said there had been a problem, unexpected, and it pained him to tell me (and I could see it really did) that the job was no longer on offer.

I felt sad about this, but a little relieved. I had not shied at my first fence. Times, perhaps, would change?

There was another moment when I pushed at the door. Late at night on 25 October 1982 I was one of the few Members in the chamber when the Northern Ireland (Sexual Offences) Order came before the House. It was a liberalizing measure.

In whips' terms the thing was a non-event. They knew the measure would command an easy majority of those few who had bothered to stay. But for me this was going to be, I was sure, the most significant Commons evening of my career so far. Shortly after 11 p.m., knees shaking, I rose:

I wish to speak only briefly and not on those constitutional issues on which other hon. Members are more competent to speak than I.

The subject of the order is adult male homosexuality in the last major part of this Kingdom where it is still outlawed.

Seldom does so small a measure, debated in so short a time and brought at such a late hour, touch so deeply the lives of so many thousands of people in the United Kingdom.

I do not believe that homosexuality is morally wrong or necessarily harmful, although I accept the fact that many hon. Members think of it as an affliction. But surely we can all agree that it is an impractical interference in the privacy of adult life to brand such people as criminals, as we still do in Northern Ireland.

Hon. Members luckier than I may find that personal conviction gives wings to their argument – the more powerfully they feel about an issue the more powerfully they can speak. Unfortunately that is not so in my case. I can happily argue the toss, but where I feel as deeply, strongly and personally as I do on this issue, argument altogether fails me.

I support the measure with all my heart.

At the end of the debate Jim Prior mentioned my speech especially kindly. He knew what I had done, or thought I had done.

Strange to tell, another parliamentary colleague who seemed particularly to have noticed this speech was Enoch Powell. Enoch had spoken immediately before me in the debate.

When he had risen I had been momentarily cast down. I just wanted to get my speech over with. But at least (I thought) he would be interesting; and he would surely speak in a way helpful, or at least sympathetic, to my own argument. He had, after all, been one of the minority of Conservative MPs who voted in favour of the Wolfenden reforms for England in 1967.

Soon after rising, Powell reminded MPs of the 1967 vote (when he had been a Conservative) and added that in 1980 (Powell was by then an Ulster Unionist) he had voted for provisions in a Bill which extended the English reforms to Scotland – a measure adopted on a free vote, he said.

I have since checked this statement and found that Powell's memory may have been at fault. There was indeed a 'free' Commons vote (moved by a backbencher, Robin Cook) but Powell does not seem to have voted for it. He did later support the Bill as a whole (a much wider measure) but this was a government Bill, moved at Third Reading on a whipped vote.

I was only to discover that later. At the time it was his speech itself which dismayed me. Powell opposed the Northern Ireland Order. Other Unionists attacked the morality of the measure in predictable ways, but Powell avoided the merits of the Order and instead made a long and tortuous – and, I sensed, tortured – speech about the constitutional implications of extending the law to the Province in the form of an Order, in this particular way.

He found the procedure unwelcome, and would oppose the Order for that reason, he said. He objected to the shortness of time allocated to the debate, he said. Then he said his objection to the manner in which the government was proceeding was that this vote was whipped, whereas on previous occasions a free vote had been allowed on matters 'of conscience'. It was 'an affront', he said.

A Tory MP interrupted to point out that the vote was not whipped, as indeed it was not.

Powell then seemed to change tack, insisting that even if it was upon a free vote, the measure was advanced 'with the authority of the Government on a Government Motion' – and this was not the right way to proceed.

The reasoning was odd. The Scotland Bill had also been put forward as a government motion – and indeed whipped. But Powell had voted for it. It was on the genuinely free vote on the 'gay' clause for Scotland that he had not voted.

Powell said nothing about this, and the closest approach he would make to discussing the issue itself – homosexuality – was to say that 'it has hitherto been thought right' for different laws on moral questions to govern different parts of the Kingdom. I noticed how careful he was neither to endorse nor question that.

Instead, he began to criticize the European Court, which he said was imposing 'judge-made' laws on the United Kingdom. We were acting 'under compulsion'. It is true that we were being heavily leaned on but this hardly seemed sufficient reason to vote against a measure. Enoch did not suggest he always voted against measures Britain was under pressure from Europe to adopt; nor could he.

He spoke for a quarter of an hour (the House had only ninety minutes) and I kept waiting for him to express a view on the purpose of the Order. He never did.

Well, let me not mince words. I think Enoch Powell supported the reform: but his adoptive Ulster Unionist Party was opposed – violently – and I think his courage failed him. So he found other reasons to vote against the Order. They were not (for him) trivial reasons, but they were not his real reason. His was an unhappy speech. After I, too, had spoken he kept looking at me.

Between then and his death he twice buttonholed me and repeated, at length, and in the same tortured way, the reasoning behind his speech and vote that night. We were just about on Christian name terms but he did not know me well and I was surprised at this apparent anxiety to explain his behaviour to a very junior backbencher.

When, after Powell's death, a Church of England canon, Eric James, wrote to *The Times* to correct a *Times* obituary and disclose what Enoch Powell had asked him not to disclose until after his death: that an early love poem was not to a woman, but to another man, it helped me understand. Powell's reputation has not been well served, I believe, by the fact that his biographers have tended to come from the conventional moral (and Unionist) right. They would not welcome – they would be unwilling to recognize – the picture of a once-bisexual man, free-thinking and sensitive, seduced and finally trapped by the cheers of the mob: a free spirit cast in the role of populist bigot, condemned to end his political days among a party of boorish obsessives for whom his bookishness made him a kind of intellectual mascot for a world from which he was very, very far.

Towards the end, I passed him on a pavement and said brightly, 'You're looking well, Enoch!'

'The three ages of man,' he replied, sadly. 'Youth. Middle age. And "You're looking well, Enoch."'

I was once invited to interview him on stage for the right-wing Conservative Graduates group. I asked him whether he had not sometimes regarded the mass of his supporters, some of whom were racists, with a fastidious shudder. I had hoped he might say yes. He shook his head sadly and said that 'in politics, you take your support wherever it is offered'. It was a demeaning and, I thought, dejected reply.

After the debate on that Ulster Order, I ran home (I was training hard for the London Marathon) after midnight, heart still pounding, but with an immense sense of release. Maybe I had gone too far; maybe the tabloid papers would descend on me; maybe the telephone would be ringing already when I got home. But I had said it now and it needed to be said; and there was no unsaying it.

The phone was not ringing when I got home. The following morning one tabloid paper did telephone to ask why I had made the speech and what I had been meaning to say. I said, 'I have nothing to add to it,' and put the phone down. There was no report. Nobody commented. Nothing was said. Nobody raised the subject when I returned to the constituency that weekend. A weekly student newspaper, the *London Student*, described me as having come out but no other paper picked it up. Perhaps the old joke was true: if you want to keep something secret, make a speech about it late at night in the House of Commons when the press have gone home. But surely by now the penny had dropped?

Perhaps not with everybody. British intelligence were still in the dark. After I had left the Foreign Office they had stayed in touch, asking to meet from time to time to talk about my Conservative Research Department work, about my contacts in Eastern European diplomacy, and in particular about one East German diplomat whose job included talking to the Conservative Party. MI6 offered to pay for any hospitality I might offer him. I hasten to add that there was no suggestion I was some kind of a honey trap. Better honey is available, even to MI6.

I declined the money though I did brief them on our very occasional meetings. I think they thought that because he was sociable and liked England he was subvertible. I could tell – and told MI6 – that he was not: he had come from nothing (his father had been a railway worker), owed everything to his Communist employers, and showed no signs of discontent at all. Anyone could have told them that.

MI6 asked me to continue these conversations and to report them, after I became an MP. I met my MI6 contact once or twice, but reflected on the unwisdom of this not so much from my point of view but from that of our intelligence services. It was not as though I had anything worthwhile to report, and it really wouldn't do (I thought) for an outfit with its good name to protect, to be hobnobbing with gay MPs about Eastern European diplomats. So next time my contact came along to the House for a drink I took him out on to the Commons Terrace and told him that he and his office ought to know that I was gay.

After that I did not hear from them again. Even for British intelligence the penny had dropped.

Oh, hell, everybody *twigged*. But you can smirk about who twigged what until the cows come home: what was called for here was an open, matter-of-fact, so what? statement. To Chris Smith, the Labour MP who told a Labour conference he was gay a few years later, goes that honour. He was the first.

I think I sort of tried, though. It was harder in the early eighties and it was harder for a rural Tory. Not the whips, not my parliamentary colleagues and not the press, but anxiety about my constituency and all the good people there who had taken me on trust and worked for me: this was what in the end held me back from making myself plain – or, as the why-oh-why? brigade like to put it, 'ramming it down our throats'. I shall always regret not ramming it down their throats. I shall always regret my final hesitation, for I got so close. It might have finished me, but what a way to go.

A few years into my first parliament I found myself in a Commons lift with the man who had been my inspiration before I entered politics: Keith Joseph, then a Cabinet minister. He thought I was the lift attendant. 'Upper Committee Corridor,' he said to me. I bit my lip and pressed the button. 'What do *you* think of trade with the USSR?' he asked. 'Should we lock them into capitalist trade, and hope to influence them as partners; or should we use the lever of trade sanctions to try to force them to change?'

In the twenty seconds I had I attempted to answer. 'Most interesting,' said Keith as he stepped from the lift. 'We must continue this discussion next time I'm in your lift.'

11. Prince of My Patch

The youth looked about eighteen – pale, fair-haired and ill-nourished. His girlfriend, who was small and plump, looked even younger. They had been ushered by my constituency agent into the shabby office we hired regularly for the MP's surgery at the Imperial Rooms in Matlock.

'How can I help?' I said. The boy looked awkward, glancing at his girlfriend.

'Well, it's, er, like this. We can't get anywhere to live.'

I had not been an MP for long but already knew the ropes where housing was concerned. Housing problems occupied a good deal of a Member of Parliament's time in those days; almost half the population were tenants of the state. Elected local authorities administered most council housing and so an MP had no business interfering – this was a matter for local councillors – but woe betide a Member with a Liberal challenge to face who said anything was not his concern. Anything at all.

'You've applied for a council house?'

'Yes. But we're not married and we don't have a baby, so we don't get enough points, you see. We're on the list but at the bottom.'

'Don't you have parents to live with?'

'I don't get on with mine. Hers threw her out. We're living in a tent at that campsite near Riber.' It was mid-winter, 1980. 'And I can't find a job with no proper address.'

'In a tent? Aren't you cold? What can I do to help?'

'Well . . .' he looked again at her, embarrassed. 'We thought if we did have a baby, we'd get to the top of the list.' He paused. She looked at him, rather accusingly I thought.

Was my advice being sought? 'It's no business of mine but I don't think that's a good idea – to have a baby to get points – not if you're so young and can't really support children. Couldn't I write to the Director of Housing? I could put in a word . . .'

He interrupted. 'No, it isn't that. We've decided. She does want to get pregnant, don't you?' She nodded. 'Only she isn't . . .'

'Isn't what?'

'Isn't pregnant. We're trying, though. So . . .' Silence. They both looked at me for a response. 'We're wanting advice.'

'On what?'

'On how to get pregnant.'

I could just hear my agent snort from the other side of the keyhole. I was twenty-nine. Erskine May's magisterial work gives guidance on some of the most obscure difficulties a Member may face – but not on this. Nobody had mentioned human fertilization during the selection procedure which had plucked me from obscurity and set me on the 1979 general election campaign trail. Getting women pregnant was not one of my areas of expertise. I speculated, not aloud, that perhaps the intense cold in this couple's tent was the problem. What should I advise? Should I refer them to a doctor? Or the Citizens Advice Bureau? Or the nearest vicar? Or a camping advice centre?

I undertook to get them a leaflet about family planning advice clinics. I was unsure whether these gave advice only on how not to get pregnant, or whether they could help the other way too. I would deliver the information to their tent, I told the boy. The couple thanked me and left.

An hour later, over pints of beer at the Gate Inn up Bank Road, Al, my agent, and I were still shaking our heads and smiling. Al thought the misunderstanding might have arisen from the word 'surgery' in 'MP's Surgery'; my theory was that they had called on an MP because they couldn't think of anyone else.

The nearest clinics were in Chesterfield and Sheffield. I obtained a leaflet. I hope I found the right tent. We lost touch.

I was a good constituency MP from the start. I had learned that Robin Maxwell-Hyslop, whose dogged unreasonableness had moved even the Italian bureaucracy when I was an officer in the diplomatic service, was right: if an MP makes enough of a fuss, bureaucrats will bend the rules to make him go away. And it is not disagreeable to prance around as prince of a little patch of England to which the term 'my' can be attached – my district council; my teachers; my hospital; my farmers – and to minister, like some latter-day Lady Bountiful, to the needs of the poor and the aggrieved, on a salary, and with allowances, and commanding a level of deference, vastly in excess of what any properly trained social worker or priest could command.

Al and some in our Conservative Association had suggested I might want to rent from the Duke of Devonshire (our patron and president) a house on Chatsworth Estate, as my predecessor had done. But Tories have to watch out in these matters. The Liberals had mounted a strong challenge and this kind of thing played straight into their hands. The rural English are no socialists but a certain kind of populism can appeal, and the Liberals are good at that. Determined not to lord it around or try to set myself up as some kind of local squire (something which went against my nature and which I could not anyway have afforded to do) I decided that, though I had no money to speak of, I would look for a small house.

In the meantime I lodged in Bakewell with Barbara Carrington, a marvellous person who had been widowed and lived alone in a fair-sized house by the meadows near the river. She looked after me better than as a mere tenant I could have expected: fed me, laundered my clothes, and was a gentle, good-humoured companion. I could not have had a more pleasant start. In time I bought (for £9,000) an end-of-terrace stone cottage in the hilltop village of Elton not far away. With my humble house and the old Land-Rover, I was able to feel fairly detached from class in the constituency (not, anyway, a particularly class-conscious part of England). The West Derbyshire Tories have never been a snooty lot and my unassuming ways sat easily with them, I think. I was happy with Barbara, and then happy alone in Elton.

It is not disagreeable to be fêted in your local paper as a guardian angel of the oppressed; to barge in all over the place trying to disturb the delicately balanced priorities of cash-strapped public services; to be pictured in the *Matlock Mercury* handing over keys or ushering elderly folk on to the pelican crossing you have by your own noisy efforts secured, against police guidelines.

It is not disagreeable to be approached as though you were an oracle of wisdom and a sword of justice combined; not disagreeable to identify the queues and bottlenecks which an administration whose coffers are not bottomless will always create, shake the hand of the pushy or ingenious 1 per cent of the electorate who would ever dream of going to their MP for help in the first place, and, using your MP's headed notepaper, help them jump the queue in which the remaining 99 per cent wait. Your constituents will read only about the few you helped.

It is not disagreeable to sniff out the handful of hard cases which any rule-based system throws up, then use the office to which you have been elected to cut, for one or two individuals, the red tape binding everyone else (red tape manufactured by your own party in government), then issue press releases insinuating that, unlike the bureaucrats (whose labours you secretly know to be necessary), you, the MP, are human.

It is not, even, wholly disagreeable to burn the lamps into the small hours as you struggle to keep up with the swelling mailbag of human woes which your swelling reputation for sympathy and diligence has attracted, then tumble exhausted into bed, outwardly complaining about the workload but inwardly congratulating yourself on generating it.

There is a potentially infinite supply of this kind of work in the world. If constituents stop coming to you, you can go to them, touring avenues and estates, knocking on doors and asking if there's anything you can do to help. You can be sure there will be someone with a need or a gripe.

I enjoyed the role at the same time as being troubled by it. There is something slightly unbrave about covertly sustaining an administration and the rules any administration has to make and police, then seeking praise for one's efforts to bend those rules. And, as any MP in his or her cups will confess, your best weapon is not your intellect or understanding (you are in fact rather hazy about the labyrinth of procedure and regulation in which you claim to act as guide) but those letters 'MP' at the top of your portcullis-crested notepaper.

You tell yourself, of course, that it is not the casework which justifies your existence, but the insight this gives you into where government is failing, where the needs arise. Fine – in theory. But what do you, a humble backbencher, do with this insight? A speech or two, perhaps; a grumble to a minister; anecdotal evidence offered to a bored standing committee in the small hours on a long Bill. How much difference does any of this make?

The textbook theory which a new MP takes to Westminster teaches that from his constituency labours will come an accumulation of wisdom he can bring usefully to bear upon government. Learn the smaller picture then widen to the bigger one.

I honestly doubt that's how it goes. More likely the MP acquires a productive habit of getting steamed up about the small picture while leaving it to ministers to bother with the big one.

I wish I believed that all or even most of the thousands of small decisions I swung for people as a constituency MP were the right ones. Few caused any serious harm. I did from time to time get a complacent official off his backside, and some abuses I uncovered were real and a pleasure to correct. But mostly my influence was used to swing decisions which were much of a muchness in the first place. There are always plenty of these.

A decision I failed to swing troubles me still.

It was almost my first constituency surgery: one of the very earliest. This one was in Bakewell (I made it my habit to move my princely court from town to town and village to village so nobody felt left out) and held in the old town hall – now, I see, used for bric-à-brac sales. Al ushered in a middle-aged couple – not ignorant or uneducated, but humble people – carrying a bag. Their names were Ray and Juanita Downing.

They waited for him to leave. Then they tipped from the bag some unwashed clothes covered in faded old bloodstains. I stared at the clothes then at the couple.

'These are what our son was wearing when Wendy Sewell was murdered,' said the father. 'Look at them,' he continued, determined but polite. 'Examine them for yourself. You can see that there is not enough blood, or in the right place, for him to have done it. You're our new MP. The old one was not able to help us. Our son has been in prison for nearly five years now. We want you to get the case reopened.' He pushed the bundle a little closer to me.

What was I supposed to do? I had no knowledge of how to trigger a legal appeal, still less the forensic expertise to draw any conclusion from this bloodstained bundle.

We talked for a while. The case has since become famous and this is no place to rehash it. In brutal summary, Stephen Downing was a slightly but not seriously backward youth who had been labouring in a Bakewell churchyard around the time a woman some regarded as loose was bludgeoned to death there. Downing was detained in an improper manner at the Bakewell police station and subjected to a gruelling interrogation at the end of which he signed a confession. Later he retracted it, saying he had signed only in order to be allowed home.

There had been no other suspects in the minds of the police, although Stephen's parents and their supporters were suspicious about a number of names. He had appealed against conviction but lost the appeal.

I promised to write to the Home Secretary, William Whitelaw. The Downings put the clothes back into the bag and left. I felt enormously sorry for this small, polite couple whose family so huge a disgrace had struck, sure of their boy's innocence, unwilling to bang the table or make a fuss yet determined not to leave him in prison.

Al told me the Downings' fight was well known in Bakewell, and that some people supported them, others supported the police, and most did not know what to think. Al was in the third category. So was I. I still am.

I wrote to Whitelaw. The reply was that, there being no new evidence, there could be no new appeal. I was advised that this was correct, and had to tell the Downings so. They took it without complaint.

That was the last I saw of them until more than twenty years later when they came to the Court of Appeal. A change in the law now allowed re-hearings and the (recently established) Criminal Cases Review Commission had recommended this one. An editor of the *Matlock Mercury*, Don Hale, had taken up and fought the Downings' case with persistence and courage. I had written a column urging that the case be reconsidered. Now *The Times* wanted me to write a courtroom sketch of the appeal, which had become a *cause célèbre*.

When after a long and laboured hearing the appeal judges found Stephen's original conviction to have been unsafe, they found what I am not proud to say had been pretty obvious from the start. Unlike some, I never reached a settled opinion about who killed Wendy Sewell. I was never sure that Stephen was innocent, but his guilt had not been properly established – I could see that in 1979 – and he should not have been in prison.

I doubt a constituency MP could have done more for him then, but I am sorry I did not try harder. Watching his parents driving away from that court twenty years later – they, the vicar who had supported Stephen, the journalists who had campaigned for him and Stephen Downing himself, all twenty years older than we had been then, all grey, all wiser, some of our freshness gone – I compared the faltering 29-year-old who had sat in front of Stephen's parents in Bakewell town hall wondering what to do, with the assured hack I had become, but was pleased to see that I was still fretting about this case, still wondering what would have been then – and what would be now – the right thing to say and do. What was an MP really for?

In my seven years' constituency work I had a lot of fun. Four times I joined the judges at the Matlock Bath Pavilion to select Miss Derbyshire. I was pulled through small towns on floats, and had wet sponges thrown at me along with the best of them. But despite reports to the contrary, my time as a North Midlands politician did not involve transvestism. That, however, was the report in the short-lived occasional magazine *Scallywag*: 'Pooftah Parris Parties On'.

First, the truth. A regrettable gap in a life which has been so far too short to embrace the full range, is that I have never actually given a transvestite party. It's more a matter of oversight than conscious plan. Though I have no hankerings towards transvestism (and though I don't think I've even been to a transvestite party given by someone else, let alone myself), one should never be closed to new ideas. But a transvestite party was once held at my house in Derbyshire.

I was away in South America at the time. Two friends from London were staying. They decided to give one of those 'murder' parties, with a twist: all present were invited to cross-dress.

Much of the murder game took place outdoors. Not far from my back door is a spring, a covered stone arch, and around it a sea of mud. One of the clues in the game was, apparently, thought to be hidden under the arch.

At around that time an IRA list of target names had been recovered by police in South London, and mine was on it. That was odd. As an MP I had become doubtful about the Ulster Unionists, whatever my history of attempts to wreck an IRA fund-raising meeting at Yale.

I was asked to make special security arrangements at my Derbyshire home, to inspect under my car every time before I drove it off, and to expect occasional unscheduled visits from the Derbyshire Constabulary, to check I was all right.

What our security services thought was the chance of the IRA being just in the act of attacking me at the point when, about once a month, the panda car arrived, I cannot say, but the police followed their instructions faithfully. The whole thing spooked my friends more than it spooked me. I took it philosophically.

And so it was that, as Paolo, an Italian, in a tiara, screamed from the banks of the mud patch in front of the spring, while Mara, another Italian, her bosom gathered into a tuxedo, looked on, and a third guest floundered in the mud, his high-heeled shoes well and truly stuck, the headlights of a panda car from the Bakewell police station swung round the corner of my drive and illuminated the surprising scene. This was a side of rural England the two young policemen had perhaps (though don't count on it) not encountered before.

Apparently they paused for a second, their faces registering shock, then roared off in a scattering of gravel. Whatever they had stumbled upon, this was not an IRA attack.

They will not have known that the MP was not there for I never advised the police of my whereabouts. Professional discretion may have been suspended in the canteen, and the story may have got around . . . well, let's be realistic: I would be amazed if the entire Derbyshire Constabulary did not know it fast. And that was the smoke behind the fire which *Scallywag* was to report:

Times columnist and erstwhile MP Matthew Parris is still sorely missed by his erstwhile boyfriends and the landlady of the pub in his former constituency of Derbyshire where he held outrageous drag parties after hours.

But what remains a mystery are the names of the other MPs who took part. One, said to be from a Midlands constituency, was of middle height, tubby and balding. He regularly turned up in evening dress, high heels, stockings and suspenders, full make-up with ruby-red lips and told everyone he wanted to be called Joan.

What isn't a mystery is that Parris resigned just before the *(News of the) Screws* was about to reveal all.

It would have made an excellent chapter in this book. But I cannot remember ever entertaining another Midlands MP, tubby or otherwise, let alone at a drag party, let alone above a pub. The only minister I did entertain was Dr Rhodes Boyson, who came to speak to the Matlock Conservative branch. Afterwards we shared a whisky, then I put him in the spare room, under my Superman quilt. Delightful as the bewhiskered and Dickensian stickler for school discipline was, it is difficult to imagine Rhodes in suspenders and lipstick, asking to be called Joan. Or perhaps not. But he never did.

I should be proud to think I had the guts to give an after-hours drag party in the pub in West Derbyshire when I was its MP, or subsequently. But I am not so daring. It would be exciting to believe I later quit Parliament to avoid a scandal, but reality was duller.

Rhodes's visit to West Derbyshire was one of the few by a colleague: I did not live in the kind of style which would have made it easy to tempt other Tories to make star appearances at constituency fund-raising bunfights. But I did persuade one of my best friends, the MP for Brigg and Scunthorpe, Michael Brown, to come (and bring a friend) one weekend when I needed a speaker for a cheese-and-wine evening at the fine house of the late Lady Caroline Waterhouse: Middleton Hall. Michael turned up in good time, with a young man called Derek Laud.

I liked Derek. He was black as the ace of spades but with one of the poshest English accents imaginable, a slight drawl, and a rather grand, camp manner. He had all the mannerisms of an eighteenth-century dandy. He had the wit, too. Years later, after an unfortunate road accident in New York in which an elderly couple were injured when the car he was driving hit them, his only comment to the press was. 'One can't take one's chauffeur everywhere.'

On this occasion, while my party activists pretended to listen to Michael's graceful little speech about politics, but in fact gazed around them at the interior of Middleton Hall – which it had been their main purpose to see – Derek floated around with a glass of wine, inspecting the oil-paintings. After the speech we all mingled. I came upon Derek, surrounded by a small group of my Derbyshire farming constituents. He was talking. They were stunned.

'Do *you* ride to hounds?' he was asking. 'I simply *adore* hunting. I'm having a new riding outfit made just at present. In *green velvet*. Heavenly. It's with my tailors now.' He moved off, to circulate some more. The farmers and their wives just stood, mouths open, dumbfounded. You rarely see black people at all in rural Derbyshire; Derek was nothing like those they had seen on television.

One of the farmers broke the silence. 'Ee must 'ave eaten a very posh missionary,' he said.

Princess Margaret was nothing like as grand as Derek. She came to Matlock to open the new District Council Offices. The MP was invited. It was 10 a.m. I drank instant coffee. She drank gin and tonic. She knew I was a long-distance runner and asked if I sported those strangely revealing shorts she had noticed on television. I said one needed more to reveal if they were to be worth sporting. We both laughed and she drifted off, collecting another gin and tonic.

I was no longer with her when she journeyed to the north of the constituency to open some old people's sheltered bungalows, but her visit will not be forgotten by those responsible for the catering. A special dish of Coronation chicken had been prepared for the royal visit. 'This looks like sick,' she said.

Sir Edward Heath was more polite. He called in on West Derbyshire while campaigning for the European election in 1984. I was to accompany him to the Matlock Bath Pavilion, where he was billed to speak, and then onward into Matlock for a walkabout. Ted had his own official car, of course, with driver and bodyguard. I was still driving that Honda 250 motorbike.

I arrived noisily at the Pavilion, as Sir Edward's car drove in. He looked up startled as I removed my leather jacket. I reminded him who I was. 'And you ride that . . . *thing* in the constituency?' he said.

'I shall pursue you on it to Matlock, after you've made your speech,' I said. And I did. Laughing when we got there, he said it felt quite like the old times 'when one had motorcycle outriders while visiting banana republics'. 'Have you ever voted in the division lobby in leather?'

A few months later, travelling at top speed for this moderately powered machine, about 75 mph, in the fast lane of the M1 on my way to London, I misjudged and rammed the side of a Jaguar car. The collision was violent enough to gouge the car's side and, in the split second one has at such times to calculate the consequences, I concluded that I was about to come off and spread myself and my bike over the fast lane, to be steam-rollered by whatever traffic was thundering behind.

I am not a good balancer, at anything. I felt conscious of something

I had not hitherto experienced on a bike: the gyroscopic power of a spinning wheel, resisting alteration to the plane of spin (hence the stability of a spinning top). Amazingly, I kept my balance. The bike and I stayed upright. I pulled over, shaking, on to the hard shoulder and gave the Jag driver my address. A few hundred pounds to repair his scratch seemed a small price to pay for my good fortune. After that I scaled down the biking.

Not long before the 1983 election I was invited to a small ceremony to celebrate the opening of an extension to the refurbished Conservative Club in Matlock. These clubs have only the most tangential connection with the party and on the whole discourage politics within their doors; some are even reluctant to display posters at elections. So it was pleasing that ours in Matlock wanted to involve their MP.

Perhaps the real reason I was asked, however, was that the guest they really wanted, the president of our Conservative Association, Andrew, Duke of Devonshire, had consented to come. The MP was a courteous afterthought.

The Duke and Duchess of Devonshire (the mix-up of counties derives from an ancient clerical error) live at Chatsworth House, a sort of rural palace of mainly eighteenth-century origin but somewhat resembling Barcelona's Post Office, in glorious Chatsworth Park, near Bakewell. I think they saw less of me, and I of them, than of my predecessor, Sir James (he had now been knighted) Scott-Hopkins, but a modern Tory MP needs a broad base of support even in rural England, and I did not want to become a toff. Hundreds, perhaps thousands, of my constituents depended directly or indirectly on Chatsworth as landlord (the Duke owned three villages), employer or customer, and though the Chatsworth Estate was a model employer – a judicious mix of modernity and paternalism – and a good landlord, it would not have done for me to be thought in cahoots with them.

A certain distance was appropriate, and on both sides it was kept, though I was invited once to Chatsworth when the Devonshires were entertaining Michael Heseltine and his wife for the weekend. I remember how cold the dining room was, and that the Duchess (Deborah, one of the Mitford sisters) took a heated dinner plate and hugged it gratefully to her bosom. It was an honour to eat from crockery flattered by such an embrace.

I admired the Duchess. She was clever, shrewd and funny. ('Who'd *want* to be Prime Minister?' she sighed to me. 'But, you know, people do. It's *quite* extraordinary.') She had done much to put the estate on a sound commercial footing, she had opened shops – good shops – and a garden centre, and worked hard to popularize Chatsworth for visitors. She was also a sociable, adroit and well-informed woman – a real pro – with a clever line in self-deprecatory prose.

The Duchess ran things, including, it was believed locally, the Duke. I never found him less than perfectly sharp but people said that, as part of a reduced-alcohol regime, his wife had ordained that, if he was to have a bottle opened, this must be solely in order to share a glass with friends. Electricians or damp-proof specialists who called in pursuit of their trade during this period were apparently quite taken aback to be welcomed in like long-lost comrades.

Less forward than the Duchess, the Duke was nevertheless a kind and thoughtful man, charming in the best sense. He took his responsibilities not just as a power in the land but as a social provider unusually seriously. As with many younger brothers (King George VI, for instance), the departure of the older brother had visited upon him responsibilities, never expected, whose weight one sensed he felt keenly. Once, when a visiting minister, John Biffen, made, in a speech, a respectful reference to Devonshire's older brother, fallen in war, the Duke's eyes swam with tears. He treated all with equal courtesy and, whatever the occasion (both he and his wife were tireless patrons of good causes), would inform his hosts on leaving that 'I can't *remember* when I've enjoyed myself so much.'

At the Matlock Conservative Club, having drawn a little string to pull back a blue curtain to reveal a mini plaque commemorating his visit, and assuring the crowd gathered to watch that he couldn't remember when he had enjoyed himself so much, Andrew Devonshire took my arm to be escorted to his waiting Bentley. His eyesight was very poor (at a Conservative bring-and-buy fête in the village of Baslow I had had to steer him away from a wickerwork tailor's dummy, there to display a blouse for sale but which he had mistaken for an elaborate basket and was attempting to buy) so we walked slowly together up the steps at the back to the car park. At the top he gripped my hand and said, 'There's something you should know, Matthew, but you must keep it to yourself.' I waited.

'I'm leaving the Conservative Party. In the House of Lords I shall be taking the whip of the new Social Democratic Alliance which my friend Roy Jenkins has started. But I shall not announce this until the autumn [it was spring] and I don't want the press to find out. Tell nobody; but I thought I owed it to you as our Conservative Member to let you know.'

With that he got into the Bentley which had drawn up. I thought there was nothing I could say and it was really not my place to argue, so I bade him goodbye and returned to the club lounge, where members still excited by his visit told me how His Grace was the very best kind of Tory and a wonderful advertisement for our party.

I kept my word, except that I told the Prime Minister, asking her to respect the confidence into which the Duke had taken me. She did, and his departure never leaked and, when it came later that year, caused only a ripple nationally.

In the constituency, however, it caused a storm. Some in our Conservative Association wanted me to 'hit out' at the Duke, call him a turncoat and betrayer, or remind him which party had most consistently defended the foundations of the pile on which he sat. But I thought better of this. One could not dislike or wish to hurt so fundamentally decent a man and it was his choice what party he supported. Neither he nor (I suspect) the Duchess were very Thatcherite types and his family have a long liberal tradition; they may have thought her strident and uncaring, and that it was she who had betrayed Conservatism. Best, I decided, simply to thank him for his past support and say I thought he was making a mistake; and nothing more than that.

I felt that not only did the Duke of Devonshire have every right to switch, but that it was the more admirable because he had absolutely nothing to gain from the move: unlike others who crossed the floor, he did not want office or political prominence of any sort. He did it because he believed it was right.

My instinct not to attack proved not only the polite, but probably the politic, thing to do, for the family commanded broader and deeper personal respect in parts of my constituency than I would ever do. The storm soon passed. The Duchess remained a supporter, and at the 1983 election the lawns of Chatsworth Park – usually a sea of blue posters – sprouted a gay miscellany. The Duke and Duchess had agreed an active truce. At the next election there were no posters at all.

Al feared that the loss of so popular a figure might badly dent the Conservative vote but it hardly seemed to make a difference. In 1983, after a more relaxed campaign than 1979, my majority more than doubled. We may in our anxiety have overestimated the political impact of ducal figures on modern voters, but I think the Duchess's decision to stay neutralized the shock.

Chatsworth was not the only great house in West Derbyshire. Haddon Hall, on the other side of Bakewell, belongs to the Duke of Rutland – whose seat is Belvoir Castle in Leicestershire – and is usually occupied for part of the year by his heir. Open to the public, it is much older and (to my taste) more beautiful a house: less showy, calmer and with a strong atmosphere.

The late Duke, Charles, was another patron of our association. Locally the family were thought to be harder-nosed as employers and landlords (they own the mineral rights beneath large swathes of the Derbyshire hills, and in the dales the beds of the streams and rivers) but I was a fan from the start for a single but compelling reason. Charles Rutland often chaired local party meetings. He was a fantastically ruthless chairman. He could gallop through a long agenda almost as fast as those at the meeting could read it – indeed this was part of his tactics: we would have moved on from an item before anyone had had time to think of anything to say about it. He dispatched business with brisk courtesy and a glance of steel. He saved me hours – perhaps days – of my life.

As the MP I was invited to Haddon Hall for the coming-out party of Charles Rutland's daughter. The evening – night, really, for we stayed until dawn – was magical. It was summer. All the roses on the old walls of Haddon were in bloom. There were bands in the gardens and a small orchestra within. Couples wandered, hand in hand in the moonlight; expensive motor cars and their chauffeurs waited for them, all night if necessary, beneath the stone portals. People said Prince Charles was there, though I never checked. It was one of those nights whose passage a diarist wants to mark in some way, for fear that there will never be such a party again. Not my scene at all but, chance witness to it, unforgettable.

Kedleston was also in my constituency. This great Palladian

mansion, home of the Curzon family when Lord Curzon was Viceroy of India, was my least favourite of the area's great aristocratic houses, its cold grey-white stone adorned within by many marble figures with seashells over their genitals. The Scarsdale family, who now occupied the place, were having quite a battle with the inland revenue over death duties, I think, and one of my grander constituents took me aside and suggested that Lord Scarsdale would surely appreciate it if as his MP I could intercede on his behalf with the Chancellor of the Exchequer, but he would be unlikely to ask me himself.

I have no reason to believe the suggestion originated from Lord Scarsdale and he never approached me directly. I am no leveller but, with constituency cases cropping up weekly in which humbler citizens were unable to pay much smaller dues but could not expect the rules to be accommodated to their own personal crises, this idea stuck in my throat. I kept out of it. I never wanted to be part of, or in any way attached to, that echelon of British society.

My favourite local minor grandee I liked because he was genuinely lovable. Henry Harpur Crewe was elderly and childless – I believe the last surviving member of his family dynasty. I came to know him because as a Derbyshire MP I was invited to join the board (on which he sat) of governors of Repton, a well-regarded public school just outside West Derbyshire. Repton's school statutes required that one member of the board be appointed from the Derbyshire Members, Labour Members refused to have anything to do with it, and the board were terrified of their local MP, Edwina Currie (though when, in the end, there was no escape, they found her to be an excellent governor). So they asked me. Along with Henry and a few others I was able to argue for the admittance of girls at a time when the decision was very much in the balance; and it went our way.

The Harpur Crewes, Henry's family, were ancestral owners of Calke Abbey. Henry was its final master. Calke was not an abbey but a fine, square great house, like so many others. What distinguished it was the contents. Obsessive and rather undiscriminating collectors, the family had been pathologically unable to throw anything away. Fine tapestries, beautiful old Arab and Indian carpets, priceless silverware vied with stuffed rabbits, penguin's eggs and souvenirs from Llandudno. There was hardly space to swing a cat. There was probably a stuffed cat to try swinging, if you could find it among the heaps of memorabilia to which every Harpur Crewe, it seemed, had added his or her own life's collection. The family had become the ultimate upmarket equivalent of those old ladies trundling down the Embankment pushing prams, containing all their possessions in plastic bags. Henry, the family's last gasp before the National Trust got the lot, was a shy man. He sought me out at meetings. He would always say the same. 'Y-y-you're quite right, you know, to, er, speak up for, er, chaps who find, er, *friendship* with other chaps. D-d-don't let your critics stop you or get you down, you know. It used to be very different when I was young – t-t-terrible d-d-disgrace, you know, terrible. But it *shouldn't* be. Doesn't do anyone any harm. Private, *p-p-rivate*, you know, nobody else's business, and it helps some people to be happy. I w-w-wish I had been born later.'

People like Henry Harpur Crewe, an old man near the top of the social scale, and an anonymous correspondent from whom I only received one letter; Edward I'll call him (and I've scored out what might identify him), nerved me to face the uncomprehending silences which my work at Westminster for homosexual law reform provoked in West Derbyshire. I knew there would be many silent constituents, people who would never dream of approaching an MP, who needed me. My work was more important for them, and more meant for them, than for the brazen new breed of out queers whose anger and outrageousness showed they had won their personal battles. Edward had not, and Henry never did.

If my work gave any kind of encouragement to correspondents like this one, who wrote anonymously, then it made it worthwhile. I never forgot Edmund Burke's advice that a politician should not allow the few he will meet to deafen him to the voices of the many he never will.

Meanwhile, something unexpected was happening. I was falling gently in love with my constituency. In moments of cynical calculation I had thought of West Derbyshire as a rung on the ladder of politics. Now politics was beginning to feel like a rung on the ladder to West Derbyshire. I preferred it. It was this place, not Westminster, that meant more to me.

How to describe my small corner of England, and why it grew on me?

The English countryside is not big on majesty, but such majesty as

Dear Matthew,

I have to write to you because I have nobody
I can talk to. I think I'm gay. I've just finished
my A levels so I'm not tied down to revising.
I have wanted to write to you for ages.
I admire you so much. I wish I had the guts to
'come out'. I can't. I need my parents to pay my
university/professional bills as I'm hoping to study
~~   ~~ I would probably be 'kicked out'
if they knew. My life wouldn't be worth living. It
would destroy them. I don't want to hurt them or myself.
I've known I was gay since I was five. At first I
was sexually attracted to men but that has turned
to the more spiritual side - more love than sex.
I've had no experience. Recently I went through a
phase of thinking I was straight. To be honest,
although the coin turns up homosexual I don't know
what I am anymore. I am so confused Matthew.
I wanted to write and let you know that you keep
me going when I get depressed. I watch you reviewing

the papers on Breakfast TV and I read The Times
articles you do. I'm not literary or critical. I did science
A levels — mainly mathematical. You just have to spot
patterns & relationships. It was still tough though!
The reason I know about you is that I vaguely remember
watching you present 'Weekend World' — I got a remark.
There is so much prejudice. How can one survive?
I hope I can handle it. ^I'll follow your example. ^I can't bear the thought
of spending the rest of my life alone. Maybe I'll
find someone who I can talk to later on.
Matthew I had this letter all prepared on my
computer. I was about to print it out & the computer
broke down. It is totally busted, I couldn't believe
it. There was more to say but I have forgotten
what I typed. I'll continue to read your
articles Matthew. You have been a help to me.
I'll write again maybe and tell you my results
when I get them. You're the only person who knows.

there is you will hardly encounter in Derbyshire. You will find higher hills, wilder valleys and grander scale in the Lake District. You will find bigger woods in the south of England, wider horizons in the east, prettier stone in the Cotswolds and lovelier fields in Kent. Beyond Haddon Hall, Chatsworth and Kedleston there are some fine houses in Derbyshire, and in addition to Tideswell's there are some good churches . . . but an architectural tour of the British Isles would not start in our county. The Derbyshire dales are not on the scale of Yorkshire's, the Derbyshire moors are tame beside the North York moors, and though Dovedale is charming, our streams and rivers are for the most part simply pretty.

But there is a tenderness and a sweetness in the Derbyshire dales. The area, which is really the southern footings of the Pennines, is called the White Peak to distinguish it from the great black-brown moors of the more famous Dark Peak to the north. The White Peak is where the redbrick and hedgerows of the Midlands give way to the drystone walls and lime and gritstone houses of the north.

Driving up from Ashbourne, a country town which really looks towards the Midlands, you arrive at a village called Brassington, and all at once the hills steepen, the brick vanishes and the hedgerows stop. Behind you lie the urban terraces, the great cooling towers and the wet plains of the Trent basin – and beyond them the North Sea. Ahead of you the land is rising into a spine which, with Staffordshire, Cheshire and Lancashire dropping away to its west, and Nottingham-shire and the Humber and Tyne to its right, runs all the way to Scotland. This is the Peak District, and this is Derbyshire.

Small outcroppings of chalk and sandstone are strewn across green hills and valleys, some quite sharp. Oak, hawthorn and ash abound, and there are snowdrops and cowslips, bluebells and foxgloves, and brambles and berries in profusion. Here the Romans mined for lead, and everyone quarries for lime. The land is almost worth ploughing, and almost not; sheep and cattle do well, but not well enough to make anyone's fortune; and farming trots along, not struggling as badly as in Staffordshire or Wales nor prospering as brutally as in Lincolnshire; just about making ends meet.

There is a sort of county set, but they're not too county nor too rigidly a set. A few ride to hounds, but a bit apologetically. There's money from Manchester and Sheffield and this shows in some of the smarter villages but without the ostentation of Cheshire or the Northern Posh of South Yorkshire. Derbyshire is Derbyshire and nobody's suburb.

If you cut out Great Britain in cardboard and by hanging it from threads established the lines whose intersection marks its centre of gravity, I believe they would intersect in our county, right in the centre of West Derbyshire. In more ways than that, my former constituency was in the middle. I don't usually care for the middle, but for this middle England I did, and do.

In time I moved from my terraced cottage in the village of Elton. Training for the marathon I had often jogged down a country lane and up and over a hill on whose side sat a house alone, looking out over the valley. People called it 'The Spout' because beside it there was a copious and constant spring. It was a stone house of no great pretension, once a gamekeeper's dwelling, with a wood behind. Running by, I saw it as some kind of perfection: solitary, set back, modest, commanding. If by some extraordinary luck that place was ever to come up for sale, I said to myself, I should buy it.

One day it did. I didn't have the money but I borrowed all I could. That was Christmas 1985. I will never forget moving in: the freezing nights and the howling wind and the worry. I had paid £10,000 more than the market value of the house, for it needed work. Looking back now it would not have mattered if I had paid ten times £10,000 too much. No amount would have been too much for 'The Spout'. I hope I shall have it always.

It is a fine thing when still only in middle age to be able to say that one would never want a grander house or a grander style of life, or to live in a better place, or to have other friends or a more impressive social circle, than one has found already. I could say that then and can say it now.

Out of the blue one morning I took a telephone call from Granada Television's *World in Action* programme. Their researcher asked how I would like to try living on the dole in Newcastle for a week. Of course the idea appealed, so I asked him to explain.

It seemed the plan was to get a Tory MP to experience for himself life on benefit and film him doing it. I asked why they had chosen to invite me. I had not been their first choice by any means, the researcher said, but dozens of others had turned it down; so far only one of my colleagues had shown any interest at all – and that was in how much Granada would pay him to do it, which was nothing.

So I said yes. This was 1984 and after five years in Parliament I was not so naive as to think that *World in Action*'s hope would be anything other than to make a fool of me; but (not, perhaps, as media-wise as I believed myself to be) I felt sure that one *could* live on benefit; and that as an MP who supported a government which had established these levels of benefit, I ought to be prepared to give it a go; and that if I did, and showed the benefit was adequate, the TV documentary about my experience would honestly reflect that.

All my colleagues said I was a fool, that the programme would make me look like a monster or an idiot, and that I should not touch it.

Then I asked Mrs Thatcher. She said the same. 'They will make whatever programme they want to make.' I asked Norman Fowler, then Secretary of State for Health and Social Security, and a politician I respected. He was not quite so emphatic – I had every right to try if I wanted to, he said – but thought the best I could hope to do was fight the programme to an even draw; he too advised against.

I went ahead anyway. Truth is, I was getting nowhere in politics, and frustrated at Westminster. An exciting experiment appealed.

Quite how exciting I discovered when I began a series of hard-fought negotiations with the producer and his deputy. They played the roles for which they were typecast – hard cop, soft cop – but their strategy was clear: to whittle down the £26.70 which as a single unemployed man on housing benefit I would be due, so I had as little as possible to spend during my week. Fairly, they pointed out that there's much that you don't buy every week – shoes, toothbrush, soap, clothes – which must still be paid for. They totted up pro-rata allowances for everything they could think of; we argued over every one.

We also discussed my timetable. I had thought it a good idea to visit a library, which would be free and warm; they said that would be patronizing because unemployed Geordies didn't; instead they wanted me to visit a football match, for which I must pay. I lost most of these battles.

Still it was in optimistic mood that I arrived at Newcastle station and strode up a little grassy knoll to the rented maisonette (of a kind housing benefit would pay for) in Scotswood, a suburb of Newcastle where the male unemployment rate at the time was almost 80 per cent.

My human and political reaction is perhaps best described in an article I wrote for *The Times*, quoted below. But there was more to the experience than that. I made friends among those I met on the estates at Scotswood, some of whom became permanent friends. I was later best man at the wedding of Vicky Morgan (the daughter of a likeable and articulate unemployed shipyard worker, Harry, who in the documentary became quite a star). The couple came to live with me for some time in Derbyshire, while Kevin, Vicky's new husband, was looking for work.

A week is only a week (in fact it turned out to be five days). Everyone's immediate reaction was that one could learn little in so short a time, dipping a toe in the water but experiencing nothing of the despair and boredom which come with long-term unemployment. But a toe in the water tells you things: the emptiness and frustration I saw in that single week brought me up hard against the reality for those who could not leave on the train to London at the weekend. Perhaps the sharpest lesson I drew from the experience – and one which I did manage to get past the Granada cutting-room – was that unemployment is not only a problem of the pocket but of the spirit; and that once the spirit is broken neither money nor training can easily help.

I learned, too, how enraging it is to be blamed as the author of your own misfortune, when you are really trying. Our tone as a government was all wrong: quite incendiary, in fact.

I learned a lot about television in that week, and a certain amount about poverty in the north-east, too. About television I learned that it is not a good idea for an over-confident young Tory to let a camera crew follow him to a posh Tory fund-raising ladies' buffet in a neighbouring Tory MP's constituency, and film him mingling with the ladies as they stuff little cakes into their mouths and sip wine and nod while he pontificates about the poor having never had it so good. These were actually civilized and thoughtful women, and kind to invite me. They emerged from the documentary looking like monsters.

I learned that it takes much of a morning and an expensive hired

crane to film someone going through a door and climbing the stairs
to a bedroom. I learned that for the producers and crew the nature of
the luxury hotel to which all (except me) would repair every night
was a topic of great interest. And I was surprised when after about
five days, as I ran out of money more than a day before my week was
up, my producers sat me down for a confidential chat and suggested
that, as we had now done all we meant to do in a week, we call it a
week and pretend for the purposes of the programme that it had been
a week. Anxious to go home, I connived in this.

That said, I was impressed with my television producers. They
drove a hard bargain – but I was a cocksure Tory MP and fair game
– and at the core of their plan was a perfectly professional and not
unprincipled desire to prove, if it could be proven, that life on the
dole was tough. They cut a few corners but they (and I) did prove
that; and the programme they made was watchable television, made
a good case, and was in its essentials bullet-proof. It achieved the
largest viewing figures any *World in Action* programme had ever
attracted. In *The Times* I wrote this:

You can forget leather armchairs and Socratic dialogue: there's nothing like
physical discomfort to challenge intellectual certainty: and I'm cold.

It's snowing outside and I've just come in from dealing with the frozen
corpse of a stray cat – a kerbside victim of feline hypothermia. I had
not realized their tails went so stiff. Fumbling for a 50p coin for the gas
meter, it occurs to me that perhaps poverty is as good a test of a Tory's
commitment to Conservatism as is prosperity of a Socialist's commitment
to egalitarianism.

I run, mentally, through the tenets of the Free Market Philosophy,
repeating them to myself a little desperately, seeking (as did Saint Theresa
or Pooh Bear, in moments of spiritual or physical peril) the reassurance of a
familiar recitation.

'The Market must decide.' Yesterday's industries must be allowed to die
if room is to be made for tomorrow's. Gosh that sounds harsh, but I still
believe it. Even as I stare at the sad, empty shipyards, or talk to the
unemployed men who used to work there, I cannot waver from that, and
nor do many of them. Unrealistic though some of them are about what the
government can do, they glumly acknowledge that there is no point in
pouring billions into loss-making industries.

'Regional aid distorts the market and props up inefficiency. The state has no more business choosing the geography of investment than choosing the type.' I'm less cocksure about that than I was a few days ago. Millions of people are settled here; must they move to the jobs – or cannot industry be prodded into moving to them? No – come to think of it – no: on the economic argument it is wrong to interfere. But on the social argument? I'm less sure . . . but then so is Norman Tebbit, so I cannot be all that wet. If we cannot transform the Northeast, perhaps we can at least help let people down gently? Or do I really mean 'die with dignity'?

'People should move to where the jobs are.' It has just struck me, and struck me hard, that Adam Smith is not saying that at all. I've been muddling him up with Sir Alfred Sherman. Smith was not a moralist. Smith would say that people 'will' move to where the jobs are. Sherman would say that that they 'should'. It is the difference between the priest and the scientist and why Sherman is offensive and Smith is not. The fact is, of course, that people do move, without needing instructions from any of us. People are quitting Newcastle at a faster rate than the economy can absorb, already. There is no evidence of a shortage, anywhere in the country, of middle-aged, unemployed ship workers, created by the disinclination of these gentlemen to leave Newcastle.

I see why the moral imperative in that word 'should' is gratuitous and therefore offensive – but I see, too, why it is important to those who use it: it comforts them. It implies that the distress of the unemployed is somehow self-imposed, unnecessary – their responsibility entirely.

'We must not stifle energy and initiative.' Fear not, Prime Minister. That famous British drive and ingenuity is alive and well in Scotswood, Tyneside – and emerging in ways which are not quite what you, or I, had in mind. Curiously, I find that rather encouraging, if reprehensible. Far worse would be to see people's spirits broken . . . but one had better say no more, for fear of being thought to condone fraud or vandalism.

Less controversially, it could be put like this: I worry most about those who do not riot, or become barrack-room social-security experts, but passively accept their fate.

The outward signs are often those of passivity, even laziness, but as the manager of the job centre here told me, people do not start that way. At first, a man who has had a job all his life is sure he will find another. Gradually confidence wanes. Twice-daily visits to the job centre become twice-monthly. Eventually he stops calling.

I am meeting many such people. For those in middle life, unskilled or skilled only in the trades whose industries are declining in Newcastle (and everywhere else), the chances of a job are poor indeed. You could (my hard-line colleagues are right) push them into seeking the unskilled broom-and-shovel jobs for which school-leavers already vie, at rock-bottom wages, by reducing the family benefits which create the 'poverty trap'; but what would be the point, when unskilled work is already as sought after and as badly paid as it is in the Northeast? Alternatively you could, as more 'imaginative' politicians often argue, try to train people for new careers. We do this, for some, but to do it for all would cost the earth, produce mixed results, and offload on to the jobs market hundreds of thousands of middle-aged men to compete with apprentices and college leavers for jobs which there is already no difficulty in filling.

So what else can these men do? Is it practical to urge that they take their families and rise, like a flock of birds, heading for the Home Counties? Of course not. The government rather depends on their not doing so – not, at least, all at once. They are well and truly stuck.

What is there to say to them? When I protest that Mrs Thatcher is doing as much as anyone is able, this is met with incredulous jeers. 'Why are we being punished?' is the question I have been asked everywhere. In that sense, the residents of the estate where I am living are deeply unrealistic. I keep telling them so. But, it occurs to me, am I, too, living in a fantasy world believing that there is any way to lead them away from such delusions. What is more bitter than the thought that your problems are nobody's fault at all, but just your own bad luck – that your region is a victim of some kind of economic road accident?

Is there any way you can tell a man that his industry, his job and his family are necessary, even glorious, casualties in the battle to transform the British economy and revolutionize social attitudes – and make him feel good about it?

Five years ago, scolding a Conservative parliamentary candidate who had got into hot water for writing a rude letter to a complaining council tenant, Auberon Waugh wrote:

'. . . The truth of the matter is that something rather nasty is going to happen to the Collingwoods of this world and . . . the least we can do is imitate the Walrus:

> "I weep for you," the Walrus said.
> "I deeply sympathize."
> With sobs and tears he sorted out
> Those of the largest size."

The best idea might be genuinely to feel sorry for the things that have got to be done.'

The parliamentary candidate in question happened to be me. After five years in the House of Commons and three days in Newcastle, I rather think Mr Waugh was right.

For about two weeks after that documentary was broadcast in 1984, every kind of anger, contempt and dismissal rained down on me. Tories thought I had failed to stick up properly for the cause and fallen into a Marxist documentary-maker's trap. Left-wingers derided me for thinking I could understand anything from a week with television cameras. Social liberals laughed at me for having proved the opposite of what I had set out to prove. And cabinet ministers gazed sadly at me in the division lobbies: 'the man who thought he could outwit *World in Action*'.

But as the scorn faded I was surprised what did persist. For the eighteen years which have followed that fortnight of derision I have found myself remembered affectionately for little else – and for nothing more – than for this one episode of *World in Action*. The abiding public impression seems to have been that I was game to try, and that I tried to be honest about the failure. When someone comes up to me on a train or in a restaurant and begins: 'Weren't you the bloke who, all that time ago . . . ?' I can finish the question every time.

I'm glad I went to Newcastle. It taught me something. It made me friends. It got me (as things turned out) my next job. And it secured for me one of my very first articles for *The Times*.

12. The Prostitutes from Birmingham

'Are you the prostitutes from Birmingham?'

It had been idiotic to put the question like that – I realized this the moment I said it. But there seemed little doubt they were. Before daring to make such an inquiry in the Central Lobby of the House of Commons I had hung close by to listen in, and all these women had strong Birmingham accents. They were overdressed, mutton dressed as lamb, and more than a few appeared to have hit the lipstick with a vengeance. They had to be of doubtful virtue.

There was an awful pause. They were temporarily too affronted to reply. 'No,' said their leader. 'We're a Catholic women's group and we've come to lobby for the rights of the unborn child.'

My blunder was forgivable though. Expected precisely then was a coachload of prostitutes I had invited down to address members of the standing committee on the Criminal Justice Bill, on which I served. Along with a young Labour Member called Robert Kilroy-Silk, I had put down an amendment to abolish the penalty of imprisonment for the crime of being a 'common prostitute'. It was the best thing I ever did in Parliament.

The depth of one's irrelevance as a backbench MP takes time to sink in, especially after the build-up before getting there. Some flavour of the slow humiliation is offered in a small scene of which I was part a couple of years after being elected. An evening division was looming after a debate on overseas aid in which the Opposition were, naturally, calling for more. Few Tories are much interested in overseas aid, one way or the other, and few had attended. From the chamber, the whip on duty had sent an SOS: 'Running out of speakers on the government side: two hours left before the vote.'

This looks bad, so a posse of whips scoured the bars and tea rooms for stragglers. Having nothing else to do and no great interest in a debate on overseas aid, I was in the Members' Tea Room. 'Be a Good Samaritan,' implored the whip, 'get in there and make a speech.'

'But I haven't attended,' I protested. 'I didn't even hear the opening speeches.'

'Doesn't matter,' he said. 'We're desperate. The Speaker won't mind; he wants contributions from both sides. Needs must.'

'But I don't know anything about it.'

'Who does? Here – here's an article about aid in the *Daily Mail*,' he said, thrusting the paper into my hands. 'Read that.'

The article cast doubt on the efficacy of overseas aid. I had myself always been, in an ignorant and uninformed sort of way, a bit sceptical about handouts to poor countries, so I read and digested the article, traipsed into the chamber, listened to a speech or two, caught the Speaker's eye, and rehashed in my own words the simple argument I had just read.

Nobody raised an eyebrow, nobody commented, and the whips were grateful. And that was that – save that, a few years later, I noticed in Roth's *Parliamentary Profiles* that the potted account of my special interests and opinions included a sceptical expertise on foreign aid and overseas development. I have since been invited to make any number of speeches, join any number of symposia, write articles, and even join conferences abroad, all on aid: invitations I have always turned down, but which could easily have led to my recruiting myself to the ranks of Commons and media pundits on this issue.

Such is the nature, often enough, of backbenchers' special interests. It is desperately haphazard, lightweight, casual, insulting to the scale of the problems on which we legislate. It arises mostly from the starting assumption a backbencher makes that his opinions are unlikely to make much difference anyway.

In the chamber I was cannon-fodder like all the rest. Ignored by the press, patronized by the party's great ones and threatened by the whips, a backbencher with a safe seat will be generally left alone to paddle his slow canoe towards the twenty-year knighthood, the columnar cliché 'Knight of the Shires' and the appellation 'veteran Tory MP' – just as long as he votes as instructed and keeps out of trouble.

Anything more – any scramble to climb over the backs of his comrades in the pit and claw his way up into the sunlight of a junior ministerial post – requires a struggle. The struggle first is to be noticed;

then, once noticed, to look useful. At that later stage reliability
becomes the best-regarded asset, but to get noticed first one needs to
look either a little dangerous, or spectacularly sycophantic. Rebels
and poodles both catch a chief whip's eye.

I was neither. The guts to rebel often deserted me, but sycophancy
always stuck in my throat. I just ended up being snide.

This was not entirely through failure of resolve. Thatcherism was
approaching its noontide and I felt (and feel) genuinely ambivalent
about the period. My doubts about its central figure were growing,
but they really were that: doubts, not opposition.

I had known her first in Opposition. Then, the single-mindedness
had grated but one saw its necessity. In victory, I told myself, she
will emerge as a bigger person; she will acquire mercy; she will find
grace.

But here she was now, victorious. Soon, with the Falklands war
and then another, bigger general election victory in 1983, she would
have no serious enemy at all. Increasingly she was carrying all before
her. There were always battles of course – with the recession: won;
with Argentina: won; with the miners: won – but as the eighties
gathered pace she and we were the big guy; opponents, the trade
unions, the miners, the unemployed . . . these were the little guy, a
raggle-taggle army by turns ludicrous or pathetic. In short the boot
was now on the other foot: ours. And I didn't care for it.

At some point during this transition from underdog to top dog I
wanted a kind of magnanimity to settle upon us. To Ian Gow,
her parliamentary private secretary (later assassinated), I once said
something like this over one of his enormous bowls of sherry at his
club in Piccadilly. He looked at me with mournful humour. 'As the
Lady would put it, if you're crocodile-hunting and after a hell of a
struggle you finally drive your croc into the shallow where he's
floundering in the mud, do you help him back into the deep? No.
Hah! You stick the knife in.'

I laughed along with him, but thought she could afford not to
dance on graves now.

Still we Tories seemed to. We could surely see, I could see – and
if I had not at first seen then I had seen in Newcastle – that those of
our countrymen who were not 'one of us', 'our people', were neither
evil nor, any longer, particularly formidable, and those socialist poli-

ticians who represented and cared about them might be misguided
but they were not ill-motivated.

What we were doing had to be done but it was hurting many
people, most of them small people. Did our rhetoric have to suggest,
as it seemed to, that the poor or the unemployed were where they
were because of lack of virtue or drive? Could we not see that a vision
of society in which some trees are allowed to grow tall logically
requires that some will be smaller? Why could we not acknowledge
that luck – and inheritance – plays a great part in the division between
the successful and the failures? Why did we have to pretend to
ourselves that 'our people' were all there by deserving and merit?
Why did we have to talk as though Thatcherism was about punishing
people?

What am I saying? Not, as a Conservative, that there's an awful lot
anyone can do about the luck of the draw, except at the margins; or
that 'cycles of deprivation' are easily broken or – always – breakable
at all; or that I know any alternative to the Tory model of a society in
which people strive to do better than others and to pass on the
advantage they win to their children. I just don't think it is anything
to crow about, that's all. I think there's something sad, regrettable,
about the necessity for failure, for relative hardship and for the pain
these bring; and that those of us who escape them might not be God's
elect, but lucky; and that we might show a little grace in good fortune.
Thatcherism never found that grace.

This did not make me an anti-Thatcherite, nor did it lessen my
admiration for Thatcher's nerve, her keen brain and her steel. But it
made me feel, and it made me want to show I felt, that there was
another side. Too often I did this by taking refuge in humour.

In front of the shaving mirror I would resolve to stop making jokes
about the Prime Minister and to find opportunities to praise senior
colleagues who could help my career, but I lacked the application. A
sort of facetiousness kept breaking through. How little we change:
'Stop being clever, Matthew, it isn't funny' was my father's regular
refrain when I was small.

I failed to understand that effective sycophancy takes application
and a sort of doggedness.

Early one evening I was part of a table of Tory backbenchers in the
Strangers' cafeteria. In bustled Mrs Thatcher, alone. There was an

empty chair at our table. Too late – she spotted it and made straight for us carrying her favourite dish: what she called a 'buck rabbit' involving a fried egg on top of something or other. Everybody froze. There was a long silence. How, she inquired, by way of conversation, were things looking from our constituencies?

Things, as it happened, were not looking good from our constituencies; the government were enjoying a rather strained relationship with the populace at the time. I briefly contemplated pointing this out, but opted for silence. So did the others – all except nice, sensible John MacGregor, a well-regarded but rather low-key, apparently slightly bumbling junior whip. John seemed neither an arch-Thatcherite nor a rebel, but a man of moderate views, hardly one of the loyalist Turks.

He launched into a totally uncharacteristic hymn of praise for everything Mrs Thatcher and her ministers were doing. It was shameless. Had I wished to ingratiate myself with the Prime Minister I would have taken care to mention problems as well as successes in her government's performance, for anyone who says everything is perfect, especially in politics, surely invites questions as to his sincerity? But John allowed no hint of criticism to cloud the sunny skies he now described to Mrs Thatcher. I thought to myself, God, how embarrassing; this is toe-curling; poor John's digging his own grave in his anxiety to please. She'll despise him now.

She stared at him, her face inscrutable as ever but masking, I assumed, contempt. After she left the table there was an awkward silence. All of us just felt sad for John. A diminished man with diminished prospects now, we thought.

Within months he was made a minister. It was the beginning of an ascending career path which led him into the Cabinet. Later, as Secretary of State for Transport, he went on to privatize the railways. He's now in the Lords. I had not appreciated the need, if talent is to be unlocked, for a lubricant.

As for rebellion I was too much of a solo artist. To rebel noticeably and effectively you need to bide your time, choose one issue (pathological rebels are soon dismissed with a shrug of the whips' shoulders) and choose it carefully, gang up with others, agree tactics, and follow them through until *almost* the end – and then deal; and if ministers won't deal follow them to the very end, win (or lose), and shut up. Instead I would giggle, fret and chafe about things which bothered me, make unhelpful noises, irritating the whips, occasionally vote the wrong way, then think better of the whole thing and drop it. This achieved nothing.

Just occasionally a joker would make it through. I was in the chamber when Alan Clark, a newly appointed junior minister in the Employment Department, wound up a debate at 10 p.m. and was required to deliver a speech on equal opportunities, possibly not a cause of particular interest to him. This was the occasion on which Clare Short accused him of being drunk, and I thought at the time that he was. Certainly it is the kindest explanation (though poor Clare was slapped down by the Speaker for suggesting it). The other is that Alan was seized by a perfectly sober wish to make fun of his own speech and its subject by reading the speech in the slow, flat, schoolboy delivery of a thirteen-year-old performing in a reading-aloud class. I'm a little ashamed to say we all thought it amazingly funny.

Alan got away with this because he was handsome, charming, lived in a castle and did subtly crawl to Mrs Thatcher – but in a way he was clever enough to disguise. In his place I would have sunk.

I voted against the Assisted Places Scheme, believing that the government's job was to make state schools better for all pupils rather than winch a handful of high-achieving pupils out of state schools and into the relative advantages of a private education. I had no ideological objection to private schools – I was governor of one – but thought their profusion a sign of the failure of the state, and that it was to this failure that the state should attend. Right or wrong, it was a powerful argument and there was no reason a Conservative should not advance it.

I should have done it properly: written articles in newspapers explaining myself, trawled the Commons tea rooms for fellow-rebels, put down Early Day Motions on the Order Paper to signal our dissent, then, finally, when it became apparent the government was going to win the vote regardless, downed a tumbler of whisky with the chief whip and agreed to climb down and persuade my fellow-dissenters to climb down too.

Instead I grumbled and muttered, told my constituency chairman in West Derbyshire (who agreed with me), yielded to pressure from the whips not – at least – to make too public a fuss, then slunk, isolated and unnoticed, into the No lobby. There I found myself in the company of one other Tory loner whose like-mindedness on this issue I had not been sufficiently organized or in touch to discover beforehand. The papers did not even bother to report our stand. The whips will have marked me down as a prat. Plainly – plainly, that is, to all except myself at the time – I lacked the instincts required for a ministerial career.

It grated. Generally liked by my colleagues, I began to turn a bit sour, sharp and smart-alecky. Early in 1985, on the standing committee of the Sexual Offences Bill (an ill-drafted and knee-jerk Private Members' Bill to criminalize kerb-crawling) on which I was adopting harrying tactics, I infuriated a rising junior Home Office minister of conspicuous talent and limited patience: David Mellor. I had been exploring out loud the possibility that a lost motorist stopping to ask the way might be convicted of kerb-crawling. The minister accused his hon. Friend (me) of filibustering and 'arguing with himself'.

MR PARRIS: My hon. Friend accuses me of arguing with myself: but one needs some sort of intellectual challenge in this place.

MR BEAUMONT-DARK (C, Selly Oak): My hon. Friend is arrogant as well as wrong. I have never heard anything so disgraceful.

MR PARRIS: If my hon. Friend the Member for Solihull–

MR BEAUMONT-DARK: Selly Oak.

MRS JILL KNIGHT (C, Birmingham Edgbaston): He should have asked the way.

MR PARRIS: I am sorry. I am dragging myself deeper and deeper.

And I was.

In one standing committee I did, however, get the chance to do something I could tell myself mattered.

I had become something of a specialist on the law relating to sexual offences. As a parliamentary vice-president of the Conservative Group for Homosexual Equality I took up the cause of many gay men who were being arrested for 'importuning' in the vicinity of gay pubs or clubs. When anxious for easy arrests to boost their performance records, the Metropolitan Police had taken to dressing their officers in plain clothes and instructing them to get themselves chatted up, then effect an arrest for importuning. I had been asking questions, writing letters and articles, trying to introduce amendments to the law with the aim of reforming the rules or at least persuading the police and courts to interpret them more intelligently.

The enforcement of this law was a disgrace. 'Importuning' did not mean importuning: anything but. The courts interpreted this as making or implying a sexual invitation, more than once, however discreetly, to another person, however willing, in a public place, however unobserved. Almost anywhere outside home is a public place. Obviously a similar statute could have caught the vast majority of the adult population, in their time, but the police and the law, however, cast a net to trawl for gay men only. A conviction could be secured without difficulty because the evidence of the officer usually satisfied the magistrates, no other witnesses were needed, and the poor accused, desperate to avoid a public fuss, could be persuaded to plead guilty in hopes of being quickly and quietly dispatched.

Police and magistrates' behaviour during this period was an abuse of justice. Little has ever been said about the episode because it was hardly in the nature of the popular press to take up the cause of the accused; but thousands of men were having their lives and careers wrecked and their reputations ruined in the sort of way which never surfaces in public debate but scars the memory in a thousand family archives. A one-paragraph report on an inside page of a small local newspaper – a report which never even spells out the offence – goes beneath the radar of the national press but may devastate an individual who has no freedom to change his address, his job, his family or his friends, and get new ones.

I wanted the law to be changed so that it caught people who were harassing others rather than those who were simply chatting each other up outside home. Short of a change in the law, I wanted the existing law to be implemented more thoughtfully. The fuss many of us made did eventually help persuade the police to act more sensitively, but ministers – meaning, presumably, the Home Office – were uninterested in changing the law itself. When I was appointed to the standing committee of a new Criminal Justice Bill, I did my best to introduce amendments which would alter the law. But Government ministers were having none of it. Even Walter Harrison, Opposition deputy chief whip and an old-fashioned northern Labour man, took me quietly and kindly aside in the corridor one afternoon and told me this was not the way to advance a career in British politics. 'Take my advice, lad. Leave it alone.' I didn't, and my amendments were voted down and my hopes dashed.

When I put to ministers a different and more modest reform to the sexual offences legislation, however, they were not averse.

A Criminal Justice Bill is one of those measures which pass through their committee stages, Second and Third Readings and Lords stages like slow-moving Christmas trees on which ministers and back-benchers attempt to hang a miscellany of baubles – crimes amended, crimes abolished, new tariffs introduced and procedures changed – before the whistle blows, the royal wand is waved, and the whole thing is frozen into statute.

Usually, government backbenchers have little to do on standing committees, though they often sit for a hundred hours or more while Opposition MPs go through the motions of opposing or trying to amend the measure. Hundreds of nights of your life are whiled tediously away in mock battles, of interest to nobody, not even, except fitfully, the participants themselves. Once this system is reformed, which it will be, everybody will wonder how it was ever allowed to survive for so long.

We Tory backbenchers were discouraged from speaking, except when ministers needed to keep a debate going because they were not ready for the next; the dutiful backbencher must therefore observe long periods of Trappism punctuated by shorter periods of intense filibustering – one of the many reasons why any attempt to size up an MP from studying the entries under his name in Hansard is likely to mislead: they may come across as taciturn fellows fitfully seized by a babbling interest in a minor detail. But in whatever mode, babbling or silent, we all had to be there to vote every few hours.

An occasional opportunity did arise to propose new clauses to which ministers were not particularly hostile but which had not occurred to them – or, if they had, had been judged better-suited to backbench amendment than to government. I had tried this with my reforms to the law on homosexual importuning, and failed. So I cast my net on the other side.

A 'common' prostitute was in law a woman who could be shown to have prostituted herself more than a couple of times. On being convicted of being a common prostitute women could be imprisoned, and many were. There is no need to waste the reader's time explaining why this was a bad idea. Robert Kilroy-Silk and I thought, and most agreed, there was little to be gained and damage to be done by taking a woman away from what home and family and legitimate employment she might have and sticking her in jail for a few months.

We talked to ministers, who neither encouraged nor discouraged us in our plan to propose to the committee that a simple amendment be made to the relevant Sexual Offences Act (the descendant of a nineteenth-century measure) abolishing imprisonment in these cases. Amendments made in committee have to be endorsed afterwards by the House as a whole, but if the committee voted to make this change then, unless the government seriously tried to reverse it, we reckoned it was likely to go through; and we had the nod and wink that the government was neutral. Being humans, ministers approved but, being Tories, they did not want to say so. So it was up to Robert and me.

Our main task was to persuade a majority of the committee to support us. Robert found that almost all the Labour side would, and the Liberals would; but the government had a majority, so my job was to bring just a few of my own side over. In fact this proved easy: a few agreed, a few disagreed, and most didn't care.

Janet Fookes, a fellow-Conservative, agreed.

A word about Janet. Miss Fookes (later Dame Janet and now in the Lords) was a creature of monumental qualities, almost statuesque. The harsh lights of the Commons chamber glanced helplessly off the dignity that it seemed lèse-majesté to address merely as Miss. Nothing coarse demeaned the serenity of her countenance. Miss Fookes had smiled but she had never grinned; frowned but never scowled.

She did not, as other women do, wear dresses, but robes: rich, dark, silk-and-jade affairs. Her hair was burnished copper. The whole impression was of a minor but deeply respected Javanese sea goddess. This was reinforced by the application to sculpted cheeks of powder so pale that Miss Fookes appeared to be almost of alabaster. In repose her face was without expression. Her head, motionless, was held high. As if in a trance, Miss Fookes seemed to contemplate with dreadful tranquillity man's terrible fall from grace.

A maiden lady who somehow gave meaning to that curious phrase, she was the almost inseparable but platonic friend of Charles Irvine, the wealthy and unmarried MP for Cheltenham, a town where he had been mayor.

A word about Charles. Charles was, I judged, a homosexual of the old school: you didn't talk about it, he never mentioned the subject, and I never asked. Privately, and whenever things came to a vote in the chamber, Charles was a liberal legislator. Publicly he was discreet silence made flesh.

He was also the chairman of the Commons Catering Committee, in charge of the Refreshment Department: all the restaurants, bars and the wine-cellar. He loved the job and brought to it his sense of style. He continued until his death to send Mrs Thatcher a bouquet of fresh flowers every morning at his personal expense: he had done so from the day she became leader.

On parliamentary business in Berlin, Charles once received a phone call from a distressed Alan Roberts, the flamboyant (as the press would say) young Labour MP for Bootle, and a friend of mine.

A word about Alan. Later a Labour environment spokesman, Alan was an exotic. Drink, drugs, wild parties with strange young men . . . he seemed to lead a charmed life in his avoidance of press exposure, but it was probably because he was also warm-hearted and brave and nobody disliked him.

In Berlin, however, Alan had gone too far. He was in hospital with painful if superficial wounds incurred when visiting a gay club in which he had arranged to be fitted up with a dog's collar (and little else) and whipped around the room on all fours. The hospital wanted money from him to pay for his treatment, and Alan lacked it. Charles paid and never told the story; the hospital squealed, but only *Private Eye* reported it. Later, after he had become an Opposition front-bencher, Alan invited me round to a flat in the East End, where some seriously odd young men and an ambiguous sort of woman – but, unusually, a real woman – were drinking and smoking marijuana in industrial quantities with Alan, who was horribly stoned. He told me he hoped to marry the woman.

I was unsure, as one so often was with Alan, what this was all about. But he was a loyal man with an extravagance of nature rare in politics, which (as with Peter Ackroyd) I secretly envied. He died young (I was always doubtful about the cause); it was a pity that at his memorial service in Merseyside nobody even mentioned he was gay. He had encouraged me greatly in my small crusades within the Tory Party.

Charles Irvine was always kind to him, though it is hard to imagine two more different types of gay man.

Charles once invited me to a small party at his flat in Pimlico. Afterwards he offered his car and chauffeur, in a cap, to take me the short ride back to Westminster. The car was a white Cadillac; the interior trim, leather, was white too. In the back with me was a senior employee of the Refreshment Department. As we approached the Commons he leaned over and said, confidingly: 'Has Charles ever mentioned that, if you ever wanted a *special* sort of party – private, like – we can arrange that through the Commons Refreshment Department?'

I have often wondered what he meant, and whether my Conservative colleagues would have known at once, and I was just naive. But perhaps I misread the nuances. I sometimes do.

And I have digressed from the Criminal Justice Bill.

Charles was not on our standing committee, but told me that, if the question of the imprisonment of prostitutes came up on the floor of the House, he would vote as Janet instructed him, and help muster others. Janet told me she was sympathetic but would like to know more about the background. The English Collective of Prostitutes had written to me from Birmingham, asking if our committee would like to meet a delegation of their members. I asked them to send a busload. Janet agreed to chair the meeting, to which the committee was invited, and Charles said he would come.

After the mishap in the Central Lobby, and once I found the women who really were the prostitutes, all went smoothly. Janet, opening the meeting, declared in her crystalline tones to our West Midlands guests: 'Ladies, Mr Parris has asked you to see us so that we may learn about your circumstances. I can tell you at once that I am sympathetic to your concerns. I can tell you that I propose to vote for Mr Parris's amendment, and to urge my colleagues to do the same.'

She paused, then added, somewhat in the manner of Glenda Jackson playing Queen Elizabeth I, 'But I cannot pretend I approve. I must tell you now that' (pause) 'to do' (pause) 'what you do' (pause) 'would be' (pause) 'for me' (pause) 'a fate' (pause) '*worse than death.*'

We won our amendment, Janet voting with us. We won on the

floor of the House, Charles supporting us. The House of Lords made no alteration.

I expect many of my constituents thought I was mad to make a song and dance about this sort of thing. Briefly I appeared in the Sheffield newspapers as some kind of demon-apologist for vice. The constituency association were forbearant but bemused. Prostitution, my agent reminded me, was not a big problem in West Derbyshire, though a woman who was no better than she ought to be had once been spotted loitering outside the wine shop in Matlock and been shooed away.

Detained in committee by these clauses on prostitution, and so forced to cancel an appearance at a Conservative ladies' lunch in Derbyshire, I sent the ladies a message of apology with the explanation that I was in London, taking care of their interests. I don't *think* I had intended it to come out sounding like that, but it did. Luckily my message was greeted with hilarity rather than affront.

So maybe there are some women alive in Britain today who have not been to prison and who, were it not for Robert Kilroy-Silk and me and our supporters on that dismal committee, would have done time. But we only hastened the day. This was a reform whose day had arrived and if we had not pushed it then within a matter of years the idea would have recommended itself to somebody else.

So what can I claim? That there was a temporary vacancy in the Conservative Party for an MP who, by supporting a modest liberal reform, would help make it look bipartisan; and that I filled it. Beyond that my years on the backbenches of the House of Commons seemed without effect. Was there anything, literally anything, I said or did which materially affected any political outcome?

Perhaps this. Along with another gay Tory MP, the late Martin Stevens, a fine man whose contribution must never be written out of the record, a couple of liberal-minded Tory parliamentary colleagues of whom Sir John Wheeler and Robin Squire were among the most steadfast, and a small group of others on whose support we could often count, I think I helped keep the flag flying – a flag if not of equality then at least of understanding – at a very dark time for sexual tolerance in Tory politics in the early eighties.

Two non-parliamentarians in particular helped our small, beleaguered Conservative Group for Homosexual Equality survive: Peter

Campbell, a professor of politics at Reading University, and Ian Harvey, a former minister whose career had ended in 1958 when he was caught with a guardsman in the bushes of St James's Park. I had agreed early to be a parliamentary vice-president of the group.

With the group's support I did something which, though now forgotten (I had forgotten it myself until, trawling through old files, I found the newspaper clippings), did more to define me as a gay campaigner than my late-night speech about the Northern Ireland measure. One of the Queen's bodyguards, Commander Michael Trestrail, was forced to admit that he was gay, and resigned. There was some idiotic babble in the press about the supposed scandal of a 'blackmailable' bodyguard and the poor man was universally described as having left in disgrace.

It angered me. It was the attitude this commentary reflected which allowed the press to call him blackmailable; without that hatred he would have had no reason to make a secret of his sexuality; while the implication that the commander would in any circumstances have behaved treacherously was wounding and unfounded. What a way to end an unblemished career.

So I drafted an Early Day Motion (a written declaration couched as a motion for debate, though there is no prospect of debate) congratulating Trestrail on a lifetime of loyal service; understanding why he had had to resign; but regretting the unkindness of his dispatch by the press. I hawked this Early Day Motion round the tea rooms and bars of the Commons and managed to persuade more than thirty MPs, including a handful of Conservatives, to sign it. It was then duly printed along with its signatories in the official record of proceedings of the House. My EDM caused a good deal of clucking and sniggering reflected here by the William Hickey column in the *Daily Express* in 1983:

. . . Indeed the bachelor Parris, looked on as one of the brighter sparks in Parliament, has seen much in his young life. When Commander Michael Trestrail resigned as the Queen's bodyguard after admitting he was gay, Parris sent him a cheer-up message. And last year I recall he was among forty-nine fellows attending the Gay Tory Group's annual dinner at Bertorelli's restaurant in London – £7 a head including meringues.

It is difficult today to credit how crushing were the disapproval, disbelief and sometimes contempt we faced. But we printed a news-letter, organized regular meetings, wrote (often without reply) to ministers, and at every party conference since 1979 we ran a fringe meeting in a damp basement of a third-rate hotel some distance from the conference centre. Our annual dinners in London were sneered or tittered at in the gossip columns of newspapers. After one of these reports, more menacing than usual, two or three of our parliamen-tarian honorary members (we only had a handful) rather cravenly resigned after pressure (they said) from their constituents. They never thought of the constituents not confident enough to exert pressure.

To our meetings, even our conference event, we could rarely get more than one or two MPs to come, and never a minister. At conferences a group of twenty or thirty embarrassed-looking Tories (some of whom would have removed their identity badges) would sneak into whichever hotel Peter Campbell had managed to persuade to take us, and it always seemed to be downstairs. The hotels never liked to spell out our name, and some members were shy about it too, so the notice-cards in the foyer just said 'CGHE'.

Martin, Robin or I would often end up as guest speaker – again; and we would say – again – how encouraging the turnout was this year, and remind ourselves – again – that Margaret Thatcher had voted for the Wolfenden reforms of 1967: the partial decriminalization of homosexual behaviour in private between adults over twenty-one. Peter would report – again – on the representations he had made to the party chairman, politely acknowledged or not acknowledged at all. We would deplore – again – whatever insult Norman Tebbit or one of a number of other prominent Tory deriders had most recently offered, and I would regret that – again – the conference organizers still refused to mention our meeting in the fringe guide, and protest – again – that this was not the true spirit of Conservatism, which was a belief in individual liberty. And everyone would applaud, rather desperately. Then we would drink a glass of bad, warm white wine, grab a handful of crisps, and creep away into the night. And I would hope that that year's small delegation of representatives from the West Derbyshire Conservative Association (only one of whom ever attended any of my CGHE speeches) would understand, or at least overlook, my puzzling adherence to this cause.

A magazine called *Gay News* asked me to contribute a monthly column as one of a trio of political writers: Peter Tatchell had agreed to do the same for the Labour Party, and Simon Hughes MP for the Liberals. I enjoyed collaborating with Peter, despite the violence of his views: I had written a column for *The Times* on 19 February in 1983 in his defence, after he was outed in a by-election where his own party (among others) sabotaged his bid for the seat of Bermondsey. Simon Hughes had won. My taking on this column raised eyebrows, but I stuck to it. So did Tatchell. Simon Hughes kept promising to write something, but he never did.

I do not know whether in the final reckoning it matters that all through the eighties there always was − just − a gay campaigning group within the Conservative Party, but I am proud that there was, and proud that I played a central role in this organization, however pathetic. Sometimes I would go to a gay pub or club (I was hardly ever recognized; few young gay men took much interest in politics) and stand anonymously at the back, watching people having a good time and feeling, as the decade went on, the mood of confidence among homosexual men very gradually growing, the recourse to self-pity diminishing year by year, and be moved almost to tears by the thought that, whether they knew me or not, I was playing my part in this.

Now we are left in the dust by the gathering pace of change, sometimes even wondering if the pendulum is swinging too far towards assertiveness. I am proud to be left in the dust, proud to see my attitudes overtaken and my further efforts unnecessary. We won, and I do not believe that what we gained will ever now be lost again.

It is a fine thing to believe so strongly in a cause as not to care whether one deserves or gets any notice for the part one has played. 'Stick to your guns, dear boy!' the very Noel Coward-ish Martin Stevens said to me not long before he died. I'm glad I did.

If this is something positive in my record, there was something negative too. I was one of a small group of Tory backbench idiots who carved up the late Nicholas Ridley as he tried to explain to the House his plan for a Falklands compromise with Argentina. The idea was shelved. It was after this that Argentina despaired, and attacked. I am ashamed of our unwitting part.

Nick Ridley, Minister of State at the Foreign Office, had returned from Buenos Aires with the gist of a plan which he must have cleared both with his Secretary of State, Lord Carrington, and with Margaret Thatcher. It was a 'lease-back' arrangement involving continued British governance but the ceding of sovereignty to Argentina.

This was a sensible idea. It was brave. It was unpopular with Falklands residents. And it was howled down to Ridley's humiliation by a small number of Tories like me, most of whom had never visited either Argentina or the islands, who understood little of the background and had given the matter scant attention. We just thought 'Foreign Office defeatism versus imperial pride' and started shooting our mouths off for imperial pride.

Peter Carrington, the Foreign Secretary, should have taken us aside privately and argued us round; he was capable of that, but he never did. The idea was simply dropped. I suspect that Margaret Thatcher, for whom discretion was surprisingly often the better part of valour, had taken fright.

Nick Ridley was right. It may be too early and the wrong time for his successors in government to be hinting this, and 'no compromise' is usually the best slogan until you do compromise, but one day we must turn our thoughts again to a deal. I was an admirer and supporter of Nick Ridley throughout my time in Parliament. He was thereafter always cool towards me. He was very proud.

To say all this is to make some sort of apology to Nick, who is dead. I was wrong; but, worse than that, I was silly. My teenage squawk about the Falklands had not even sprung from any deep-rooted convictions on the subject. It was capricious. Brave little outpost of empire under threat – shame! Boo! Land of Hope and Glory, etc.

It would be truer to say that I did and do feel drawn to these far-flung places, and vaguely proud that this one was British, but had never given a moment's thought to why, or at what potential cost, or whether the arrangement was ideal or could be improved upon.

When, not much later, General Galtieri invaded and occupied the islands, my private reaction, though politically correct (a Tory would say 'sound') was dismay, naturally, but less than shock. I hoped Argentina could be repulsed and shared my colleagues' view that our country must try to do this. But the surge of fury and the astonishing wave of bellicosity which ran through, not just the Conservative benches, but every chip shop in Matlock Bath, took me quite by surprise.

It was a Friday and I had already reached West Derbyshire for the weekend, having long agreed to be the guest of honour at the Grindleford Branch's chicken-in-a-basket fund-raising dinner at the Maynard Arms Hotel. As rumblings of discontent that the Member of Parliament had been ignoring Grindleford had reached my ears, I decided to skip the emergency Saturday session of the House of Commons which the Prime Minister had immediately called, and stay up-country. What had I to add at Westminster? There would be the usual drum-banging and hear-hearing and tally-hoing, I thought, no vote, and a full report on the radio.

So I didn't bother to return. Good of me to stick with my constituents, I thought. I felt miffed when the Grindleford people looked startled and disappointed I'd chosen their company at the Maynard Arms, rather than my colleagues' at the House of Commons, at such a time.

This was a mistake, though it had no repercussions. I missed witnessing an occasion which all who were there found unforgettable. It might have taught me something about the warlike streak in our nation which from time to time takes me so much by surprise. As I found out time and again as a parliamentary sketchwriter later, there is no substitute for being there.

But I was already subliminally off-message on the Falklands affair. The whole business struck me as a regrettable blunder on both sides, to be repaired as best we could, if necessary by compromise. It struck my colleagues, my constituents and most of the country as a huge and historical affront which must at all costs, and at whatever cost, be avenged at once.

When I did return to Westminster on Monday, something seemed to have come over the whole place. All other concerns were forgotten, all other business relegated. It was as though we were fighting for our national life. And it went on for months. I became gradually and ever more alienated from the whole war business. I felt quite outside it, and saw friends and colleagues drifting away, as it were, on a strong current of patriotic anger, leaving me stranded on a sandbank and almost completely alone. Even the leader of the Labour Party, Michael Foot, a man of viscerally anti-war instinct, had the sense to shut up.

Even John Biffen, one of my yardsticks of sane detachment, slapped me down when I asked him sarcastically, as Leader of the House, whether we might find time to squeeze into a Commons business crowded with Falklands-related debate, any discussion at all of the daily administration of our own country.

Back in the constituency it was the same. Reading between the lines I had picked up the impression that the then Foreign Secretary, Francis Pym, was interested in compromise and intent, if possible, on the avoidance of war. I had already decided to nail my colours to this half-perceived mast when Al asked me to give the main speech at the Annual General Meeting of the Matlock Branch of the West Derbyshire Conservative Association.

Obviously the MP was expected to say something about the only issue in the news, and I chose my words carefully, confident that West Derbyshire Tories were a civilized bunch, hardly right-wing maniacs, who on almost every economic or industrial relations issue on which Tory opinion spread from left to right, and even on law-and-order, had felt comfortable with their MP's conciliatory instincts. So they'd be middle-of-the-road on the Falklands, too, I thought.

I told the Matlock Branch that of course we were right to send the fleet, and of course if no solution could be found we must invade; the threat was there and it was meant; but if in the shadow of such a threat Mr Pym were able to reach a negotiated solution, and if it involved a measure of compromise on both sides, then I thought he should be given a free hand to try. I paused, for dutiful applause.

I was nearly lynched. Somebody – a *member of the party* – shouted 'Boo'. One or two others hissed. There was a generalized angry growl. One man even walked out. And these were the gentle, rural folk who had always been so happy to sustain in office a series of soft-liners as their MP. I left Matlock really shaken. I had learned something about my countrymen which I will not now forget.

After that I shut up about the war. However, I sensed that I was not completely alone on the right. I saw an unexpected side of Norman Tebbit when, as guest speaker at the East Midlands Conservative AGM that year, he was invited by a questioner to underline our party's defiant attitude to Argentina. The audience settled back for a patriotic rant from their favourite ranter.

Norman said that most of the Argentine troops in occupation of the islands looked to him like callow youths, conscripts, few of them understanding why they were there and some no doubt ignorant even of where they were. These people and not their politicians were the people who would die if it came to a bloody conflict. And so it was with our men too. If a bit of argy-bargying between us and them, and a bit of willingness to negotiate, could save the lives of these Argentine kids, no less than the lives of our own men, then (said Tebbit, to a baffled and complete silence) he would be pleased to see the politicians try. Nobody had expected such an answer from Norman. I have never been able to dislike him since.

Anyway, we won.

Perhaps because the whips had identified me as a possible trouble-maker over the Falklands, I was invited, after we had won, to join a small group of parliamentarians on a 'fact-finding' trip to Port Stanley. We gathered at RAF Brize Norton on a rainy Thursday evening for our pre-flight briefing.

Here the cliché 'we were a motley crew' must serve. There was Geraint Howells, a tremendous, lumbering, ageing, wily, amiable Liberal from Wales, with huge ears. There was David Marshall, a small, gentle and almost completely silent Scottish Labour MP. There was the sarcastic, maverick, joke-cracking, secretly idealistic and thoroughly decent Labour wiseacre from Grimsby, Austin Mitchell, who could never resist playing the jackass. There was Robin Maxwell-Hyslop, the insistently bloody-minded constitutionalist Tory, for whom the word 'stickler' does inadequate duty, who had given us such trouble at the Foreign Office over his constituent Professor Pugsley. Robin was the man credited with bringing down the last Labour government's attempted nationalization of the shipbuilding industry. He had discovered that it was constitutionally 'hybrid', colleagues would say. 'Ah,' fellow-MPs would murmur knowingly, as though the interesting condition were as much within their understanding as hybridity in dogs. I myself never knew what hybridity in Bills amounted to, and showed a depressing (in Robin's ill-concealed view, for he was ever willing to explain) disinclination to find out. But we got on fine.

There was Julian Amery, once a minister, friend and confidant of unnumbered heroes from the past and of soldiers and statesmen of note in *Who Was Who*, a man who did not so much speak as gurgle and grunt, and who probably gargled Armagnac.

There was the Earl of Onslow, still in his forties, who wore a sort of cloak, carried a silver-tipped stick, and prided himself on the shockingly independent and often eccentric line he took on almost everything: an *enfant terrible* and a bit of an attention-seeker, but secretly bright and rather kind.

There was Anthony Beaumont-Dark, the Tory MP for Selly Oak. Anthony could not stop making statements. In opining mode the Birmingham stockbroker and golf-club bar philosopher was like a man possessed. There was a Beaumont-Dark response to every item of news: 'Beaumont-Dark reproves . . .', 'Beaumont-Dark lashes out . . .', 'Beaumont-Dark calls for . . .', 'Beaumont-Dark raps . . .' On the whole the Beaumont-Dark conclusion was that Something Must Be Done.

There was Anna McCurley, a breezy blonde Scots Tory with a limp. Anna was sharp and spirited, a good talker, no team player: gutsy, pretty, stroppy and rather flirtatious.

And there was me.

Such was the small band which braved the Brize Norton drizzle to board an RAF VC10, bound for the British possession of Ascension Island, south of the Atlantic equator off Africa.

Julian Amery called immediately for drinks. He had been in mellow mood already as we gathered in the airfield waiting-room, and a hospitality glass of something strong was seized upon, drained, and a refill called for.

We nearly didn't take off. As we waited, Robin Maxwell-Hyslop was arguing unstoppably about the constitutional status of the presence of the large American base which dominated Ascension. In this arrangement he seemed to have detected a new kind of hybridity, and had become excited by it. He wanted to know (and had asked) by whom we MPs would be formally greeted on arrival – not something which much bothered the rest of us as we were expected to touch down late, and would presumably head for bed.

He was told it would be the British Resident and the most senior officer among the British forces there who greeted us. That would not do, said Robin. We were MPs. The commanding officer of the US base should be among the greeters.

Robin was insistent. I seem to recall him threatening to take the matter to the Foreign Secretary unless we were properly greeted. He was unwilling to commit himself now to the earth's upper atmosphere unless the right arrangements had been made, from the constitutional point of view, to receive him back out of it and on to the ground in eight hours' time.

Phone calls were made. We were, in the event, properly greeted. Someone American, senior enough to satisfy Robin, was dragged from bed. 'It's not a matter of pride,' said Maxwell-Hyslop (who was not in fact a pompous chap, just an unbelievable stickler), 'it's a question of propriety.' Austin Mitchell could hardly conceal his impatience with the whole palaver. Anna McCurley had no view. David Marshall was silent. The Earl of Onslow made a polite show of interest.

Geraint Howells was preoccupied with a more immediate anxiety: he had been experimenting with one of the expandable ear-plugs with which we had been issued for the next, noisier, leg of our journey – rolling it between index-finger and thumb, as instructed, into a tight little sausage, and placing it inside one of his enormous ears. The theory is that the plug then gently re-expands within the ear-hole until it fits snugly. But Geraint's inner ear was so cavernous that even after the plug had resumed its full girth it was still not thick enough. It fell down inside the passage and rattled around, beyond retrieval, within his head, vexing the great Welsh parliamentarian mightily. On arrival at Ascension, medical staff had to be summoned with tweezers, to pull it out.

As a group – I in a rather strange seventies green-and-grey-flash anorak I had judged suitable for the expedition, Austin quipping and snapping (he was a compulsive photographer) as he walked, Robin quibbling, the Earl of Onslow with his silver-tipped cane, Geraint pawing at his ear, Julian Amery sniffing the wind for whisky, Anthony Beaumont-Dark delivering himself of an opinion on something or other, David silent and Anna limping prettily behind – we must have provided secret amusement to the British officials obliged to greet us on the tarmac at Ascension Island. It always used to beat me how perfectly competent people with jobs to do, people who really knew things, proved able to keep a straight face when receiving groups of MPs. They even listened respectfully to our views.

We sat outside in the warm equatorial night and drinks were served: a large one for Julian Amery, smaller for the rest of us. I noticed that

Julian summoned me to fetch him a little extra cold soda for his
whisky – something with which I had obliged at Brize Norton. Along
with Beaumont-Dark I was becoming his unofficial batman. The
job was not onerous. He preferred to rise around ten, and his first
requirement of the day – a small whisky and soda by his bed when he
awoke – could be catered for without a dawn start.

But I did rise early on Ascension Island. I was training hard for the
1985 London Marathon and needed a quick ten-miler, which
the bemused administrator mapped out for me.

We assembled on the airfield for the final lap to Port Stanley by the
next stage of our transport: an RAF Hercules. This was before
the big extended runway capable of taking jets had been built at a
new airport outside Port Stanley, and the old one right beside the
town was still in use. The aircraft's accommodation was utilitarian:
canvas seats in the fuselage. There were no windows and no
upholstery, just the huge, unadorned bare metal cigar-tube in which
we sat – or lay, if we liked, on the metal floor. I had taken a sleeping
bag and tried the floor. The moisture from my body must have
dampened the covers of the bag, which froze to the metal beneath
me, cooled to the sub-zero temperatures of the South Atlantic at high
altitude outside.

For all his bonhomie, Julian was not so mellow as not to have made
a shrewd guess about the likely discomfort of this thirteen-hour leg
of the journey. Somehow he had persuaded our military hosts that he
was the senior member of the parliamentary party (though you might
think the Earl of Onslow had some claim) and deserving of accommodation in keeping with his status. So they had fixed him up with a
proper bunk bed just behind the cockpit.

He had his whisky with him. 'Make sure before we fly that you
have sufficient supplies of soda,' he instructed me, 'and keep it cold
for me; there's a good chap.' We did. Julian was well tanked-up by
the time we took off, slept like a baby, and was refuelled on awaking.
There had been no difficulty making sure his soda was cool: our
problem was to stop it freezing.

Our own refuelling was remarkable. The distance from Ascension to
Port Stanley being too great for a Hercules to accomplish on its fuel
tanks, a second Hercules, empty of everything but fuel, had taken off
with us. Half way to the Falklands this auxiliary plane would refuel our

own in flight, then peel away and return to Ascension. Alarmingly, our RAF pilot was blind in one eye. 'Of course in the world of commercial aviation nobody would allow such a pilot to fly,' one of his colleagues told us, by way of explaining how the RAF respected competence rather than a mindless adherence to rules. It was reassuring.

We crowded into the cockpit and watched him squint forward as the second aircraft lined itself up in front of us. Sudden turbulence shook our plane as we hit the slipstream. Then a black hose not unlike the kind you pull from the pump at a filling station emerged from the leading aircraft, trailing in the wind and growing as it was fed out to a decent length. Slowly and with infinite care our pilot positioned our Hercules so that our nose was just a few yards away from the trailing end of the hose, which had a special nozzle ready to lock into a port just above the cockpit.

It worried me that, being blind in one eye, our pilot might have difficulty judging distance; but we felt the welcome clunk as we attached. The two aircraft had then to be flown carefully together in this formation until the refuelling, which took some time, was over. Then the auxiliary pulled ahead, wheeled to starboard, and disappeared into the grey Atlantic cloud.

Since the war had begun, every one of the Hercules flights to and from Stanley had had to be accomplished like this: two aircraft dispatched for every one which went through. 'What a tribute to these people,' I gushed to Austin Mitchell.

'Shows why Nick Ridley wanted to get shot of the islands in the first place,' he replied.

The journey seemed to last for ever. Even with our ear-plugs the roar of the engines, coupled with the roar of huge fan-heaters which roasted the topside of passengers while the bottom-sides were freezing fast to the fuselage, made sleeping difficult. Only Julian Amery slept – like a bottle-fed baby. Odd as our fact-finding mission must have looked on arrival at Ascension, we must have looked even odder as we stumbled across the tarmac at Port Stanley. Mrs Thatcher, we had been told, had emerged to the cheers of the assembled Falklanders unruffled, immaculately made-up and raring to go; but she had her own Portakabin, in which to arrange herself. We, who had not, were not raring to go. Only Julian, to whose VIP bunk I had delivered his morning soda, looked refreshed.

So refreshed that, finding a newspaper reporter, two local councillors and a small group of curious individuals among the reception
party in the small room resembling a bus shelter which passed as the
Port Stanley airport lounge, Julian announced that he was going to
make a speech.

A flutter of horror rose in colleagues' breasts. One or two murmured
to him that this was unnecessary – indeed might be more appropriate
after rather than before we found the facts which as a fact-finding
mission we had come to look for. The Governor, Sir Rex Hunt,
there to meet us, gently suggested that, kind as it was of Sir Julian to
offer a speech after so arduous a journey, this was a treat for the
islanders which could surely be stored up for a grander occasion and
a larger audience, later. 'I can make another then,' grunted Julian, and
was about to start when Anthony Beaumont-Dark decided to make
one of his own: 'Beaumont-Dark offers solemn pledge to islanders' –
something the backbencher was arguably in no position to do having
no gunboats in Selly Oak to back it up.

After this there was no stopping Julian. He was (always, before
supper) able to stand unassisted, and, with the local cub reporter taking
notes, he began. And, strange to say, it was a marvellous speech.
The eccentric mode of delivery, Julian's little stomach gruntings and
wheezes often replacing entire words, phrases or whole sentences
which the orator deemed obvious enough to be taken as read – a sort
of oesophageal et cetera – seemed to impress the islanders and even
the voluble Sir Rex was struck dumb.

As to the substance of the speech, I cannot remember it, which
suggests it was prudently unspecific, but I do remember he did a very
good job of persuading his audience he was on their side, without
promising them anything. Through the Falklands mist I recall phrases
like 'faith – the faith that can move mountains . . .' and 'the untold
mineral riches which may lie beyond, behind or beneath these lovely,
lonely shores . . .' and 'the confidence you have reposed in us and the
famous hospitality – may I even say trust? – you show in inviting us
here as your guests . . .'

The speech was quite short, and just right. Everyone, even Julian's
colleagues, burst into applause. The reporter put down his pencil and
applauded too. My stewardship of the cool soda bottle had been worth
the lost sleep. Austin marred the triumph of our arrival by telling the

local paper he remained to be convinced that recovering the islands had been worth the cost. My colleagues thought this bad form which perhaps it was; but a politician is at his most vulnerable when in the lap of his hosts: tempted to commit himself, as a kind of courtesy, to more than he should. Austin had resisted.

The Upland Goose Hotel was pleasant, the landscape blandly hilly, the weather much milder than the picture of howling Antarctic horror the British press had painted, and Stanley itself no better or worse than a large, scrappy Highland village by the sea in Scotland. We were taken to a hilltop fortification by helicopter and, the summit being in cloud, we landed in cloud. I saw the amazed British squaddies waiting in the grass as out of a swirling mist came Onslow in his cape with silver-tipped cane, Amery puce-faced and not at his best, having been obliged to rise at 8 a.m., Austin taking snapshots of fog, and the beaming Anna with her limp. We prodded around a bit, then reboarded our chopper and took off back into the cloud. The servicemen may have thought it was some sort of a dream.

Worse was to come at Goose Green, the place where British forces had made their first, triumphant landing to reoccupy the islands. We had already visited a British warship and been well lunched, so Julian was spluttering contentedly on all cylinders while Austin, who had spent the previous evening aboard, where the officers had tried to get him drunk, was pale. Anna was flirting mildly and in a general and perfectly proper way: a great hit.

Except that half way through the meal she stopped talking. Conversation flowed all around her and it must have been a little while before her silence was noticed. By the time it was, we could see also that her face had darkened, its colour approaching a sort of purple. Her eyes goggled and watered. All of us afterwards, ashamed, admitted to each other that none of us had had the wit to spot the classic signs of choking.

A doctor among the officers did realize. By now the entire table was silent and staring at Anna, who had begun to shake as in a fit. Nobody was doing anything. The doctor rushed at her, flung her arms around her torso and under her ribs from behind and gave a hefty tug and violent squeeze combined. The mutton bone which had stuck in Anna's throat shot out of her mouth and she breathed again.

Austin, too, had surprised the locals but differently: by making an impassioned speech to a colony of rock-hopper penguins. Irony can be misunderstood and I doubt either the islanders or the officers appreciated Austin's joke, which was to stand before the jibbering birds – a crowd of hundreds – and speak for quite some time on the theme of 'extending the flipper of friendship'. More jaundiced by the hour at his colleagues' patriotic posturings, Austin was getting pretty frustrated.

Gossip travels fast in the Falklands and by now this parliamentary mission must have been viewed as a sort of travelling circus. I hardly helped by setting out from the Upland Goose at dawn one morning in a blowing fog, in shorts, vest and training shoes, to get a bit more training for the London Marathon. In the mist I strayed into an area as yet uncleared of mines, and had to be urgently retrieved by soldiers.

Geraint did something to restore our reputation by visiting an isolated sheep farm with me, inspecting their peat-drying arrangements, and for the next half-hour talking peat with his hosts with such happy expertise that they admitted themselves amazed at his knowledge. They had not known there was peat in Wales too, they said. Geraint would have made an excellent governor of the colony.

The existing Governor, however, looked set, and happy, to stay. Sir Rex Hunt drove around in a London taxi – it was personal whimsy, I think – and had gone so native that even the mildest questions about, for instance, the cost of maintaining the garrison, would prompt him to weigh in on his familiar 'Falklands for ever!' theme. He loved the place – which made a touching contrast with the usual Foreign and Commonwealth Office career cynicism, but was slightly disconcerting in a governor. He organized a farewell dinner for our parliamentary mission when, our few days over, the eve of our departure arrived.

We gathered in the white clapboard lodge which passes in Port Stanley for Governor's mansion. Several senior island councillors had been invited by Sir Rex and Lady Mavis, and a range of officers. There was a generous buffet, and a generous drinks trolley and a generous sofa. Julian commuted unsteadily between the last two.

Some time later we became aware that the MP was trying – after many brandies – to rise from the sofa. But he had by now sunk deep back into the feather cushions and, huge brandy glass in hand, was struggling like an upturned turtle. 'A speech,' he gurgled.

Sir Rex assured him that this would be quite unnecessary, there having been a number of speeches during the visit, but Julian remembered being promised this one. So I offered an arm and he pulled himself to his feet where he stood, swaying slightly, then abruptly sat down again. We suggested he make his speech from the sofa. He did so, waving his slopping brandy glass.

I can remember only the closing remarks: 'Sir Rex, I have briefly touched on but a few of the economic possibilities – possibilities, I put it no higher than that – of these bountiful isles. I spoke of mining. I spoke of farming. I spoke of tourism. I spoke of oil. But I wish finally to say a word about fishing. Specifically, salmon ranching.'

Something seemed to have occurred to Sir Julian – to have strayed into his thoughts – and a wild look entered his eye.

'Of course, the *tragedy* of the *salmon* is that the *gentleman* salmon never actually *meets* the *lady* salmon . . .' The MP stared around the room. 'And yet they multiply. How do the fish do this? Let me delicately explain.

'It is as if . . .' He paused wickedly, 'our esteemed Governor, Sir Rex, were to have spent *Tuesday* night alone in the best bedroom in the Upland Goose Hotel, and his *delightful* wife, Lady Mavis, were to have spent *Wednesday* night in that same bed alone, and . . .'

Mercifully, a ripple of embarrassed laughter from all the Hunts' guests turned into a gale of applause as it dawned on all of us that in this way we could bring Julian's speech, and our visit, to a seemly conclusion. Though seldom as sober as he ought to have been, Julian was never quite as drunk as he appeared. He got the message, inclined his head in the slightest of bows to acknowledge us, and lapsed into silence.

For all the cloud of controlled insobriety in which he walked, Julian Amery was a deep and kindly man. Alan Glyn was not. I had first encountered Dr Alan Glyn MP years before I joined the great man in the House, at a dingy little restaurant in Clapham Junction called the Blue Room. My South Battersea Conservative Association had chosen this venue for one of our occasional series of political speaker-dinners to hear a special guest. Special guests prepared to give up their Friday evening for an indifferent meal with a struggling Tory association in a downmarket part of South London didn't come all that special; in fact, it was hard to get a real MP at all; so as secretary organizing these dinners I should have been suspicious at the ready acceptance of our invitation by Dr Glyn, whose name had been supplied to us on a list provided by Conservative Central Office. He was MP for Windsor and Maidenhead, and I was impressed. The Queen's MP!

I was not to know of Dr Glyn's long-standing bafflement that his most significant constituent never seemed to invite him to any of the innumerable banquets held at her castle for people of note; nor of the reason, hidden from the good doctor by embarrassed palace officials as they invented ever-unlikelier answers to his ever-more-pressing inquiries why. The reason was that Her Majesty had encountered the MP once, and afterwards insisted to her staff that she was never, in any circumstances, to be obliged to endure his company again.

All I knew was that a real, senior, veteran and surely distinguished Conservative MP had consented to be our guest at South Battersea. He duly turned up – late, as is the custom among MPs. He looked a little like Adolf Hitler, but greyer and droopier, with an ill-cut walrus moustache. Unfortunately he lacked the great dictator's gaiety and charm.

Conversation flagged from the start. My fellow-association members began to look despondent as the tomato soup arrived – and left, much of it, when it did, on Dr Glyn's moustache. He had not got off to a very good start by announcing on arrival that he was quite delighted to be back in Brixton, a part of London he knew well from earlier canvassing experiences. I dare say to much of the world the difference between Brixton and Clapham is only a mile or two and of no account; but to a bunch of exclusively white and emphatically middle-class Tories who had chosen to invest their life's savings in a terraced home in Clapham, where there are trees, rather than, for instance, Brixton, where there are not, the difference was very important indeed.

Dr Glyn congratulated us for 'keeping the blue flag flying' in an area where obviously no Tory had a snowball's chance in hell of winning. He had neglected to find out that his hosts' constituency was in fact a key marginal in which they were within sight of winning. Beyond this he had no conversation except hanging, of which he was in favour, very much so. I later looked up one of his many Commons speeches on the subject – no parliamentary debate on capital punishment being complete without a speech from Dr Glyn. It was a tradition, the Glyn Speech, part of the pomp and pageantry of an event which itself was a kind of parliamentary ceremony in twentieth-century British parliaments. In one of these he offered the Home Secretary his own services as a GP, to witness the execution and pronounce death.

In fact Dr Glyn was 'veteran' and 'senior' only in terms of age. He had entered the Commons in 1959. Nobody can account for his selection as candidate for Windsor and Maiden-head, the only credi-table explanation being the forceful impression given by his wife, the Lady Rosula Glyn, who had not accompanied her husband to Clap-ham but was by all accounts a most determined and effective political spouse, if slightly intimidating.

Not that Dr Glyn lacked opinions, he had oodles of them, all forceful; it was just that his choice of subjects on which to have a forceful opinion was haphazard.

Prawns, for instance. Our guest at the Blue Room glared at me through the huge smeared lenses of spectacles more in need of a window-cleaner than a wipe, as I peeled the shells from the large prawns which we had both ordered as our second course. 'You don't remove the shells of prawns,' he rasped, 'you eat them whole. Only people who don't know remove the shells. Best part.' He proceeded to stuff two whole prawns into his mouth, shut his thin lips over the crustaceans, and began crunching. Bits of prawn – shell, eyes, feelers – emerged briefly from his mouth as he chewed. I remember especially the feelers poking through his moustache and waving wildly as his yellowed teeth chomped the heads.

It was a dreadful evening. Nobody even wanted to ask him any questions after his speech, which was about 'the greatest weapon in the Conservatives' electoral arsenal: capital punishment'. I sensed then what I confirmed later as a colleague: Glyn was a figure of horrified amusement in the House. I should however record that some have kinder memories of his earlier days.

He became a standing joke among the whips. One of them told me of a story which became a legend: the day Dr Sir Alan Glyn (as the Queen's MP they knighted him in the end) went canvassing.

It was a general election, nobody could remember which. Apparently Glyn's constituency association, along with any who had his best interests at heart, did all they could to prevent their candidate actually meeting voters, but on this bright morning Dr Sir Alan had expressed his absolute determination to 'give a lead to his men' (they were mostly women). The Lady Rosula Glyn, a brisk and able campaigner who understood very well what a liability her husband was, was with him as he spruced himself up for the battle. Some say that, gloved, hatted and ready, she was making for the front door – others, more mischievously than credibly, say she was still in the room – when Dr Sir Alan stepped into a large walk-in wardrobe to find the canvassing jacket he required.

He stepped too violently. He collided with something and lost his balance. His fall, within the wardrobe, destabilized the wardrobe itself. It too fell – forwards, apparently, on to its face. Its door was in its face. Dr Sir Alan Glyn was on his face, on the floor, inside the wardrobe, which had become a kind of coffin-shaped wooden hut on top of him, too low for him to get up. He bellowed for help. Nobody heard.

The Lady Rosula had set off, ignorant – or careless – of her husband, the candidate's, fate. Perhaps she thought he had been detained by some detail of his dressing. She was in any case used to handling these constituency canvasses by herself. She did not seem, during the morning's door-knocking which followed, to have been too troubled by the absence of the candidate himself. Dr Sir Alan, meanwhile, had found he lacked the strength from the prostrate position to heave the wardrobe upright, or over, or at all.

By the time the Lady Rosula returned, accompanied by her fellow canvassers, for a spot of coffee, Glyn's cries were feeble; but this time they were heard. He was retrieved from the wardrobe. That was the end of Dr Sir Alan Glyn's canvassing in general elections.

The Tory Party contains a pretty wide range of types – from Alan Glyn to Edwina Currie. Edwina, not Alan, became a friend. But that was later. On one of my first encounters with her I made her cry. It came as such a shock.

I had already been an MP for nearly five years and she for less than one when she invaded my constituency. Edwina represented South Derbyshire, which bordered my West Derbyshire just south of an open prison called Sudbury, near Derby. Open prisons, no less than closed ones, are not popular with local residents. The villagers of Sudbury and Doveridge in my constituency had always been uneasy about this one.

The idea persisted that absconding murderers and rapists would be trampling across their vegetable garden in the night, and no amount of reasoned argument about the overwhelming incentive a serious offender has to behave, would change their minds. If he is in an open prison he will be on the very last lap of his time in custody; to abscond then would put him straight back inside. Time and again I would reply to anxious villagers along these lines. With Home Office briefing I had done my best to pacify meetings in village halls. Still the suspicion lingered that I was being feeble, taking the civil servants' line, and failing to stand up for my constituents as an independent backbencher should. But at least we were keeping the lid on local anxiety.

In barged Edwina. Bang. All my carefully assembled confidence-building efforts smashed.

There is a convention that an MP does not invade or comment on another's patch without warning and consultation at least. Edwina ignored it. One could understand her wish to visit the prison: many of its closest environs lay in South Derbyshire and her villagers too were troubled. But she should have asked me first. More particularly, she should not have told the *Derby Evening Telegraph*, in terms which allowed the paper to suggest that brave Edwina was 'hitting out' and daring to speak the truth: that Sudbury open prison was an accident waiting to happen, a powder keg.

The breaking of convention incensed me less than the destruction of years of patient work to build a fragile acquiescence to the prison's existence among the residents of Sudbury and Doveridge. All at once I was the Home Office poodle, she the gutsy independent who put her constituents' lives first.

My habitual timidity about remonstrating with people fled. I cornered Edwina in the Members' Smoking Room and ranted at her at length and with real ferocity. I did not spare her feelings because I assumed her to be insensitive: the thick-skinned publicity-junkie of media fable who was already so enraging her parliamentary colleagues. She could take it, I thought.

And then she began to cry. She did not blub uncontrollably, but tears began rolling down her cheeks.

In mid-flow I stopped. This was awful. I began to understand then what I have learned well since, that Edwina Currie is super-sensitive as well as brave and clever. She had made a mistake and let her love of publicity cloud her better judgement – had I not sometimes done the same? – but she was not an empty self-publicist after all.

One day, responding to an invitation from a largely black Christian group in the city of Derby (in neither Edwina's nor my constituency) to attend one of their services, I thought, I bet no Tory MP is going to bother; someone should. So on a cold winter's night I went along. And at the back of the church hall, warmly wrapped in artificial fur, was Edwina, all alone. I doubt she is a Christian and I knew, as she will have, that there were few votes there for her.

Over the years that followed I came to know her better. Edwina Currie was often ill-judged, and maybe Parliament was not the best place for her. It wasn't for me. But she's worth a thousand Dr Sir Alan Glyns and it is a shame that a man like that could flourish so long in a place whose members never really seemed able to accept her.

We became friends later. Once I visited the curious windmill in which she and her then husband, Ray, lived near Derby. It was an open house, 'at home' sort of do, with tables of food and drink and music playing. With a glass of wine in one hand, I passed a sweet-looking little girl and, wanting to say something nice, remarked to her, 'What pretty music!'

She cast me a withering glance. 'It's the "Dance of the Sugar Plum Fairy", by the Russian composer Peter Ilyich Tchaikovsky, played here by the London Symphony Orchestra,' she said, severely. I was talking to Edwina's daughter.

Her mother was not the only curiosity surrounding West Derbyshire. Bordering another flank of my constituency was Derby North, represented by Greg Knight. Greg kept monkeys as pets. His mother looked after them when he was down in London at the House. Next around my constituency border came Amber Valley, represented by the noisy, brutal, sometimes rowdy, secretly clever Phillip Oppenheim (whose mother Sally I had once seen voting in the division lobby in a dressing-gown: it was an unexpected late-night vote, and Sally was rich enough to live within division bell distance).

Along my eastern flank prowled the Beast of Bolsover, Dennis Skinner. The swivel-eyed Tony Benn arrived later, to represent

Chesterfield, next door. Further round the border the incomprehensible Spencer le Marchant inhabited the High Peak. Nicholas Winterton, the megaphone-populist maverick, touched West Derbyshire along the Cheshire border. Representing the neighbouring Staffordshire Moorlands was David Knox, a wild-eyed if mild-spoken Scot, who was so much a pro-European wet that he seemed at times virtually to have detached himself from the Conservative Party.

And in the middle of all these obsessives, eccentrics and lunatics, there was me. Perhaps there was something in the water in the North Midlands?

Not much further from my seat was a parliamentary couple whom I helped out by speaking at their constituency dinner.

Neil and Christine Hamilton met me at Macclesfield station and drove me to their Tatton seat in a big white Mercedes car, Neil at the wheel, Christine telling him to hurry up because we were late – something which, stuck in a traffic jam, Neil was unable to do. We called at their house first. It was imposing without being tasteless and had a peaceful, almost lonely feeling. The Tatton Tories, when I spoke to them, may not all have been huge fans, but I had the impression they viewed the noisy couple affectionately and that the Hamiltons worked hard. Even at the time the couple's attention-seeking was well known, but not regarded as a particular fault in an MP.

Though I did not know them well, or particularly want to, but I did not have the impression that Neil and Christine were false or that they were wicked. They had energy, humour and tolerance, and they had fun. They were fun. They drank a bit, I think, and were greedy. Greed was at the root of the deceptions and the errors of judgement. Later I spent time as a writer researching and assessing the parliamentary scandal which engulfed them. The task was dispiriting and I never felt confident of untangling the affair in my own mind – but neither did I get the whiff of any serious evil: just rapacity, and silly impropriety, and evasion. Their outrage at how the world has used them may not be reasonable, but it is real. They were unlucky to become symbols – for that is what they were – of a political era.

Another speaking engagement on a colleague's behalf proved baffling. In the constituency of Michael Grylls MP I had sat down to the usual polite applause. His wife Sally rose and made a little speech of her own, containing at the start a word of thanks to me, and a bit about her husband and politics, and the dreadful Labour Party, and the needs of the constituency – the usual stuff.

Then she started talking about water filters. This move from one to another section of her speech was hardly seamless. All at once she just launched into water filters and the merits of a particular brand. I had a sense among her audience of weary familiarity with this turn in her remarks. It dawned on me that she was promoting these filters herself, and looking for expressions of interest from the audience. It was a sales-pitch. She had a contract with the company. I sat bemused on the train home to Waterloo.

As a constituency visit, however, this was at least orderly. Spectacularly less so was one I paid to another colleague's seat for the weekend, to speak to his Tory ladies' group and then to stay as his guest. Let us call him Tom: he was youthful-middle-aged. I took a friend (only a friend, and not an MP: let us call him Ian) with me. Ian was younger than Tom or me, and rather a quiet sort of chap. Staying with Tom, my parliamentary colleague, was a man who, I realized, was more than a friend. He was in his thirties and rather camp in manner; we shall call him Hugh.

After a good meal which Tom cooked himself (his wife was away) and a little too much wine, he sat the three of us down by the fire with coffee and returned to the kitchen, refusing to let us help with the washing-up.

My fellow-guest, Ian, left the room. I remained at the fireside, talking to Hugh. After about twenty minutes we both began to wonder what had happened to our host; his friend wandered off kitchenwards to look for him.

Moments later came an almighty shriek, and then a banging and a crashing, as of a bar-room brawl. A brawl it was. Ian ran in from the kitchen: 'Tom and Hugh are fighting,' he said. Terrible screams followed. I was worried: other houses were quite close to ours, and we were in the middle of our host's constituency. What if anxious neighbours called the police?

Our host ran through the sitting room, chased by his lover Hugh, who rugby-tackled him on the stairs and, gripping him by the hair on his head, began shaking him. Then the MP broke free and rushed out into the garden, hotly pursued. Ian and I stood terrified within as blood-curdling shouts and thumps ripped through the air outside. We had just decided to run out and try to break the pair up when I heard the sound of Tom's car revved hard, a great scattering of gravel from his drive as the wheels span, and then a crash as he hit the gatepost. Undeterred he reversed, roared out of the gate, and off into the night. Hugh staggered in, sobbing.

I calmed him, satisfied myself that he was all right, then said to Ian: 'Come on. We're going. Before the police get here. Or think of the headlines on Monday.' We grabbed our weekend luggage, jumped into my Land-Rover, and sped away. I interrupted the dazed silence in which we drove to ask Ian if he had the least idea what had caused this.

'I did,' he said.

He and Tom had been discovered kissing and cuddling on the kitchen floor by Hugh. I later found out that my parliamentary colleague had driven all the way up to London that night, with the wing of his car stove in and one headlight missing. He was not stopped.

I was luckier taking a friend on a weekend visit to a colleague's constituency in Kent. The constituency was in Thanet and the MP was Jonathan Aitken. He had not invited me to make a speech or grace a dinner, but to run with him in a Thanet half-marathon, raising funds for charity. I had asked to bring a fellow-runner with me. 'Sure,' said Jonathan, 'stay the night beforehand and we'll all have a healthy pre-race meal.'

The healthy pre-race meal turned out to be caviar and vodka in large quantities, and nothing else. Jonathan said this was much to be recommended before a race — and I finished the half-marathon the next day in near-record time. Jonathan ran well too. He had been the best of company: relaxed, interesting, funny and quite deep, a good listener as well as talker.

He told us about a fortnight when as a young journalist he became temporary astrologer for the London *Evening Standard*, their regular astrologer being on holiday. He had a date one night with a young woman he fancied, and whom he knew to be a regular reader of the *Standard*. In his 'Your Stars' column for the newspaper on the after-noon before their evening together, he wrote (under her star sign) that a tall and darkly handsome young man might take her out this evening. She should trust him and give herself to him. She did.

George Foulkes (later a minister in Tony Blair's government) was to fare better in political life. In his company and that of the Liberal MP Bill Pitt I visited the haunts of the Polisario Front in the Western Sahara. It was a bizarre trip.

I supported and sympathized with the Polisario. They were fighting for the independence of their homeland which was once a Spanish possession but, in the era of decolonization, was simply handed over by General Franco to King Hassan II of Morocco and has been occupied by Morocco since. I had arranged an informal meeting in a private house between the Polisario's then deputy Prime Minister (whom I met at Heathrow in my old Land-Rover) and officials at the Foreign Office. The Polisario invited me and my two parliamentary colleagues to fly out to Algeria and visit their refugee camps near Tindouf in the west. We were driven through Algiers in a small convoy with sirens.

The camps were orderly, the heat intense. We were driven further, over the frontier into the disputed territory itself and saw the site of an old battle with the Moroccans. The skeletons of their soldiers lay where they had fallen in the sand, one partly mummified youth lying just a few feet from a home-knitted beret in bright colours – perhaps made for him, I thought, by his mother before he left for battle. Bill Pitt was sick.

We were shown the shards of huge explosions. '*Dans le parti Liberal,*' said Bill, still pale, to our French-speaking hosts, '*nous n'aimons pas les bombes.*'

That night a feast of roast camel and chips was laid on in our honour, under the desert stars. Only water was available by way of refreshments. 'In Scotland where I come from,' an incredulous but permanently good-humoured George Foulkes explained to our hosts, 'water is not considered a social drink.' But the evening soon became animated as a choir of Saharawi schoolgirls with shrieky voices began to sing while the boys thumped drums. Quite unaccountably, but in a spirit of British–Saharawi concord, George decided to dance. He leaped on to the improvised wooden stage and swayed to the rhythm in a strangely statuesque manner – his body facing us, his face in profile, his hands held forward in a pose influenced, I think, by Ancient Egyptian drawings. We begged him to desist, but the girls screamed with delight at his dance and it took some time for him to finish. It was hard in later years to take George quite seriously as a new Labour minister. He's a privy councillor now.

I have a similar difficulty with Michael Cocks. Michael was the Opposition chief whip and had been in and out of the Labour whips' office for a decade or more. One day I strode into the Members' Changing Room to shower after running in from South London, to find Michael standing in the middle of the carpet, stark naked, and towelling himself down vigorously. A big man with a moustache and furry chest, he looked like a Mexican bandit at his ablutions. He was singing at the top of his voice. I found his merriment surprising. Neil Kinnock's Labour Party was floundering badly.

'You sound a happy man, Michael,' I said.

'I am,' he replied, 'and you know why?' He gave himself another rub. 'I've been a whip in a Government with no direction, a whip in a Government with no majority, a whip in an Opposition with policies but no leader, and a whip in an Opposition with a leader but no policies. Now my Constituency Association in Bristol are trying to de-select me.' (Another towelling.) 'And you know what? I just don't give a fuck any more.'

He resumed his song. If later Alastair Campbell were to have given his briefings in this condition it might be easier for journalists to remember that they are off-the-record.

Less likeable or candid was a senior Tory colleague in whose very existence I had serious difficulty in believing. The Members' Smoking Room nickname, 'the one-armed bandit', for Billy Rees-Davies was apt, and not only because he had only one arm and was a lawyer. Cold, rude, repellent of aspect, rapacious and smelly, he was also quite often drunk. The sight of Billy's car lurching through the Carriage Gates as the monster-like MP in the driver's seat tugged and pawed at the steering wheel with his one arm was truly frightening. When you were crushed up against him in the division lobby, the smell was pretty awesome too.

One evening, eating in the Members' Dining Room, I encountered Rees-Davies on an adjacent table lunging at his meal, dandruff cascading down his collar, flanked by two gorgeous, pouting blondes in T-shirts so tight it was a wonder the head waiter had let them in. Under the table, his leg was hard against the thigh of one of the blondes. Other, younger and less ugly Members were staring across at them with expressions suggestive of George Formby's refrain: 'If Girls Like That Like Men Like That Then Why Don't Women Like Me?' Perhaps it was the scent of power.

Or money. The MP used to let his Kent home to American tourists in the summer. Some years after he retired news reached the papers of a court case in which a couple of his unlucky guests were at loggerheads in court with Rees-Davies over the fact that they had found the house to be full of vermin.

Billy had once, it was said, been involved in an accident in which he had run over and killed a pedestrian, for which, bafflingly, he had never been prosecuted. The truth of this I have never been able to establish. Easier to verify, however, was the story of another colleague who, for his many children's sake, I would rather leave unnamed, but who was involved in a road accident late one night in London in which there was some suspicion that alcohol was involved. Equally worryingly, the young black woman with him on the front seat when he crashed was not his wife. Worse was said of her, which I shall not repeat. The police became involved and decided to charge him.

It is a fallacy to suppose (though many an anxious MP has supposed it) that, once a prosecution has been brought, the government whips can cause it to be withdrawn. They know the limits of their powers. They knew these limits in this situation. My colleague's case was heard in the normal way at a magistrates' court, all the proprieties were observed, and he was convicted, fined and suspended from driving.

As, however, the case was heard at 8 a.m. – before the court would normally have opened – and as it was heard in a room in which cases were never normally tried, there were no reporters present. Not, of course, that they would have been barred if they had sought access. No report ever reached the newspapers. Years later this colleague retired, full of honour.

I suppose I might have done the same, leaving someone else to write about my own follies. All I needed was the patience to wait for the knighthood, and the resignation to accept that this, and returning furtively to Clapham Common from time to time until I got too old for that sort of game, was all there would be to life.

It was not an intolerable idea and I would hardly have been the first to adopt it. Cruising on Clapham Common I had once encountered a parliamentary colleague, each of us beating a hasty and embarrassed retreat. I do not know which of us had been more shocked and neither has ever mentioned it to the other again.

I can see the obituary now: 'Sir Matthew Parris, senior Tory MP and Chairman of the Committee of Selection . . . good constituency MP . . . tireless campaigner for rural transport . . . never happier than in the company of the young hopefuls to whom he was a friend and mentor, he never married.' Yuk. Not the life for me. Already I was becoming frustrated. I must have been, or I would not during those years have run myself almost into the ground.

Literally. Ever since the London Marathon in 1980 I had run this race, year on year. Being a backbench MP does not sit ill with serious training – to and from the House, between divisions and in the constituency at weekends, where I had joined the Matlock Athletic Club for whom I was running quite seriously – and my form was improving. From a more-than-four-hour marathon in Boston when I was twenty-one I had steadily cut my time. I had joined the Herne Hill Harriers when I first moved into Clapham and enjoyed the companionship as well as the racing. By the early eighties I was often part of the leading pack in five- and ten-mile races, and had my marathon times down to something approaching three hours. Each London Marathon I had run as an MP was completed faster than the year before, and I had always beaten all the other Members. Few if any could better four hours and by 1984 I was hovering below three.

I resolved to give it a really good push for my fifth, in 1985. I laid out for myself a training programme which built gradually to eighty, then ninety, and finally a hundred miles a week during the last months of 1984 and the first months of 1985. Between the autumn of 1984 and April 1985 I ran a couple of thousand miles, almost all on London roads or Derbyshire lanes. Serious running is not good for your health and I was tired, drawn and as scrawny as a Third World. But I was beginning to hit my stride. Fifteen-milers and eighteen-milers at weekends were becoming easy. Training on hills in sleet in Derbyshire over that winter I gave myself a mild dose of pneumonia, but recovered fast and soon hit the road again.

One evening in March, after a visit to the Anthony Gell school in Wirksworth in my constituency to talk to the headmaster, I had arranged to change into running gear at his house and run the seven miles by road home. This involved a short uphill, a longer downhill, then a very long and gradual climb up an empty, wooded valley.

It was a cool, moist night. The trees dripped. As I pulled into the long but gentle uphill stretch a quite sublime feeling of rhythm came over me. Notching my pace up a jot I found myself running harder but in a more sustained way than I could ever remember doing. This was overdrive: controlled power delivered at a rate I reckoned I could maintain indefinitely, a fantastic feeling, unstoppable, almost drugged. I remember that night because it was then that something clicked inside my body and I understood that I was ready. I slept that night with confidence boosted.

Not many weeks later in the London Marathon I ran the best race I had ever run in my life, or ever will.

It is, for anyone, a nervy feeling, pacing Blackheath too early on a cold Sunday morning, seeing the crowds and yet blind to them, hearing the loudspeakers and yet somehow miles away, wondering why you ever entered and – worse – why you ever told everyone you were entering. For an MP the 'everyone' you told includes 69,000 constituents, 649 critical fellow-MPs, twenty-five newspapers, four television channels and the Prime Minister. A sort of misery, a wretchedness, invades the runner's soul in the moments before the Off in an important race. You wish you hadn't entered. You promise yourself that if you can just get through this one without disgrace you'll pack it in. Shaking your head in regret at your own folly, you eye the starting paddocks.

These are a game in themselves. The faster you have predicted your time the further forward you start. So everybody cheats. The extra yards are immaterial but what counts is the speed of the pack. You don't want to be held back for the first few miles. But what if they check your time on their records? It might be raised in the chamber, and the Liberals are sure to put out a leaflet in the constituency.

Then the cannon, and you're off. Wave at the cameras, just in case. It's a human traffic jam. Why didn't I cheat more? Then the road clears and – hey – this is OK! What's wrong? Why am I going so fast? Surely I can't keep this up? Look – somebody's recognized me – they're all waving and cheering . . . a frenzy of applause – surely I can't be that famous? I'm not. It's Jimmy Savile in a gold lamé tracksuit, in front.

Tower Bridge and it still felt fine. I was running much faster than I had trained. Could I keep it up? Checking the clocks I saw I was several important seconds-per-mile inside the average I had set myself for the first half. Logic told me I would burn out but it just didn't feel like that. It felt easy. Could it last?

It didn't. A sudden stitch knotted my stomach. I gritted my teeth and kept going – but was this where it would all start to go wrong? I faltered. A stitch. There I was, only half way round, and already in trouble. Was this burn-out? Would I even finish? Morale swung wildly from over-confidence to despair, and back.

How, I groaned to myself, had I even thought I could carry this off? Obviously I was too old. At thirty-six I should have bowed out with dignity the previous year . . . all that training wasted . . . thousands of miles . . . 2 a.m. sessions down the Wandsworth Road after a late sitting in Parliament . . . the policeman who thought I was a midnight smash-and-grab raider until I showed him my MP's pass. I waved wearily at the many people who didn't know me in E14.

They cheered back, a huge cheer. And a band was playing. And that stitch – where was it? Gone. Disappeared while my mind was off it. I sped up a bit and checked the time. If I could only keep this up . . . No, I said, stop thinking about it. Just run. My pace quickened after that. People in front of me were wobbling into the arms of spectators. Good, I thought. Let them.

They say the marathon's a friendly race: 'all in it together', they say. Together? Can there be any other occasion when so many thousands gather to do the same thing, in the same place at the same time, yet each entirely alone, each in his or her own world, each with so different an idea of why he or she is there? Each conscious of a sympathetic fellow-feeling for every other runner in trouble . . . and yet – he's fading, I'm still here; one down, ten thousand to go. Hah.

The miles around the Isle of Dogs melted and I was feeling fine. The carbohydrate-loaded diet really did work. All that stuff about 'hitting the wall' at eighteen miles was just old wives' tales, I told myself, powering past the nineteen-mile marker.

Seven to go. Nothing could stop me now, I thought, why, I was virtually there. 'Keep it up, Matt,' yelled a fellow-Herne Hill Harrier, spectating. 'Dave Glasborrow's just ahead of you.' *Dave?* Dave was miles better than me. Now I was flying.

Then the wall did hit me. It was awful. People around me began dropping like flies, and all at once I sympathized and knew what they were going through. I too was ready to drop. Narrow Street passed in a grim haze. Five miles left – could I keep any kind of a pace going? I slackened speed but ground on. This really hurt.

As I ran under Tower Bridge I saw Gary Waller, MP for Keighley, crossing it above, still on the first leg of his marathon. There was no mistaking the silhouette of an amiable bumble-bee. Brave sod. He had three hours still to suffer, I only a few minutes. Which of us was the bigger hero? But then again, wouldn't it be nice to finish in exactly half Waller's time? I cheered up – better, sped up – and ran alongside a woman entrant, savouring the roars of the crowd – for her. I was up with the female winners. And I was doing well.

Big Ben at last. The last mile had been torture. A House of Commons policeman on duty, called, 'Nearly there, Mr Parris!' as I ran past and I was literally too tired even to raise my eyes from the road to acknowledge him. Tomorrow, Matthew, I recall thinking, you'll remember this and you won't understand how it was possible to be too tired to raise your head. But you understand now.

2.32.55–2.32.56 . . . And I came in at 2.32.57: fastest MP ever, again, and 385th out of 20,000. I limped into the Hercules pub where Herne Hill runners used to gather for the post-race drink. 'OK, Matt?' someone asked. 'You finished then? Did you hear Dave Glasborrow's time? Club record. We're celebrating.' Serious runners are not interested in parliamentarians as a field. I bought Dave a drink.

But what a feeling, inside. I resolved never to enter another London Marathon. This result was so much better than I had expected, so much better than I deserved. Not for me the slow decline as year succeeds year and you enter the veterans' section and begin comparing yourself not with the generality but with fellow-members of a sub-group you redefine every year to make it small enough to hold your head up in. Then at sixty the knee troubles hit. No, I resolved, this is the best I'll ever do so I'll quit while I'm ahead; and I did. Sixteen years later I quit the Commons sketch in the same spirit.

'I won't cling,' said Mrs Thatcher the following week. 'I'll know when the time has come to go.' I did, anyway. It is still the case that I ran every one of my five marathons as an MP faster than any MP has ever run any marathon then or since, and my best nearly an hour faster.

I had arranged to go on after the race and the post-race drink to a meal with friends at a hamburger joint, Maxwell's, to celebrate. But they meant Maxwell's at Covent Garden, and I thought they meant Maxwell's in Hampstead. So I sat at a table for one, in my tracksuit, at Maxwell's in Hampstead, savouring my triumph alone.

My hunger to travel, always strong, was growing. And for me every parliamentary recess was inevitably a time to travel because, even if I went home to my parents, brothers and sisters, home was now northern Spain – or, to be precise, Catalonia. From Jamaica my father had been posted there to run a Spanish cable factory.

These visits were wonderful times, not only for the warmth of my family, but for the chill of the Pyrenean mists and for the sharp sunlight on the cliffs as I walked, often for hours, in the empty oak- and beech-covered foothills of the range.

A favourite walk was from one small stone-built Catalan village, Tavertet, to another, Rupit. Between them was a waste of cliff-systems from whose edge, along which my sisters Deborah and Belinda and I would sometimes ramble with our little brother Mark, the views were staggering. Across the great gorge of the river Ter you could see another mountain range, the Montseny. Far over the plain at the foot of the gorge lay the city of Girona, and beyond it the Mediterranean.

Nobody lived where we walked, but there was one great, isolated and ruined house, 'l'Avenc'. What was such a place doing here, Belinda and I asked ourselves when first we rounded a bend in the track to see the house standing tall, proud and abandoned in the cold sunlight of a windy spring day. We were exploring the path and had no idea there would be a house in such a place – and such a fine house! Above one window was a family crest – it looked like a single thread, weaving between strings – and a date, IHS Maria, 1559. We managed to squeeze in past a broken door.

It was clear that half the house was even older. The new part, finished presumably in 1559, was the first stage of an operation designed to rebuild on ancient foundations. Lines of stone teeth jutted from its rear walls, ready to key into rooms which had never been built. The older back half had delicate stone arches of Gothic design and a sort of minstrels' gallery, in wood, above its hall, beneath which a great but crude fireplace was surrounded by stone flags and wood benches.

This felt medieval. The new part was refined, its stone doorways carved with intricate designs, and the mitred head of a bishop, cut into a wall above a stone washing basin. The rooms were enormous. Who had lived here? The place looked long abandoned, but cattle had been quartered recently in the downstairs rooms. People had camped and built fires, but the interior was more or less intact.

Not for much longer, I thought. The floors and stairs were rotting and in places had fallen through. The terracotta-tiled roof was leaking. The ridge support to the roof – a single great wooden beam – had cracked. Someone had jammed a vertical pole under it for support, but rested it only on the rotten wooden third floor beneath. When this went, the roof would fall. I gave it a few years more.

The house, Belinda later discovered, was well known locally. The oldest part was Gothic. A bishop was born there in the fourteenth century. This was one of just a handful of great houses which survived a huge earthquake in 1428, and another at the beginning of the seventeenth century. L'Avenc, too far from the beaten track to be interesting to modern farmers and their families, had fallen into disrepair. The house had finally been abandoned to cattle in the 1950s.

Thereafter, whenever in Catalonia I would always try to visit l'Avenc. The day would come, though I did not know it, when our association with this magical house would deepen. Already l'Avenc had cast its spell on us as it stood so fine and sad and solitary and facing the end.

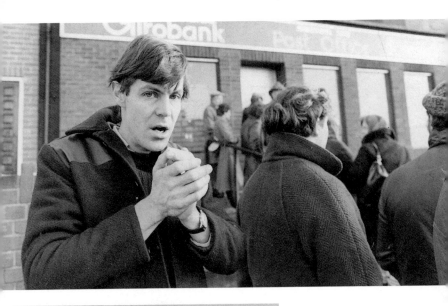

It was my week on the dole in Newcastle for Granada's *World in Action* which caught the eye of London Weekend Television. My job with LWT, as presenter of *Weekend World*, followed

Photoshoot for the *Daily Mail*. Only the serious correspondents got shelter from the rain. They include, back row, left to right: Melanie Phillips, Peregrine Worsthorne, Andrew Rawnsley, Steve Richards, Michael Brunson, Anne Applebaum, Don Macintyre, Peter Dobbie, Elinor Goodman. Sitting, left to right: Petronella Wyatt, myself, Michael White, Jon Snow

Michael Fabricant, Tory candidate for Lichfield.
MPs will do anything at general elections, and sketchwriters will follow

Avoiding the Labour conference on the Pepsi-Max Big One at Blackpool, with the *Guardian*'s sketchwriter Simon Hoggart (left) and cartoonist Steve Bell (bottom left)

Time off in Catalonia. L'Avenc was a ruin when I first saw it. Now we are restoring this part sixteenth- and part twelfth-century house. *The Times* calls it my 'castle in Spain'

For the cameras we are all smiles. In reality, John Prescott bitterly resented sketchwriters' mockery of his grammar

Below: While Tony Blair launches the 2001 general election at St Olave's and St Saviour's Grammar School in South London, Alastair Campbell (centre) worries about what sketchwriters will make of it

Moonlighting as a television pundit during the 1997 Conservative leadership election. The outgoing leader, William Hague, once joked, as he and I applied our own powder, that we had 'only one puff between us'

Above: The moment when Jeremy
Paxman's jaw dropped

My jaw dropped later when I saw
the critical reaction to my remarks
about Peter Mandelson on
Newsnight

Skydiving over Hawaii, strapped to
an Arizonan, for fun. I was nearly sick

FIRST PARACHUTE JUMP
CERTIFICATE
Presented To
Matthew Parris
On 1.3.03, after jumping from a C-206
Aircraft, at an altitude of 10,000 feet above
the Hawaiian Island of Oahu, at Dillingham
Airfield; then Free-Falling for 40 seconds
in tandem with:
Tandem Master
SKYDIVE HAWAII
D 02752

Enjoying the fear: being chased by bloodhounds, for *The Times*, in Suffolk

For the publicity shoot, I shaved and removed the horns

With my llamas, by the *Times* cartoonist Richard Willson

On top of Mount Illimani in Bolivia, at 21,000 feet

On the Plateau du Vent in Kerguelen, or Desolation Island, where I spent four months in 2000

With Julian Glover on the frontier between Bolivia and Chile, at 14,000 feet

In my flat in London, planning the next adventure

13. Ducking Out

I have never until now written about leaving Parliament. It was too painful, painful not because I had greatly loved or would miss the place but because I was letting my constituency down, and they had trusted me. I felt ashamed. But it is possible to know that what you are doing is at the same time indefensible and right. West Derbyshire could find another MP and would soon forget me. I could not find a useful career in politics.

It took me seven years to despair.

Perhaps only actors possess to a greater degree than politicians the ability to keep believing that, despite all the evidence, success is just around the corner. A price is paid for this faith: at times of unclouded success a politician (and actor, I think) secretly suspects a brewing storm. First, when he is succeeding, to know that his success is hollow, a politician can be the last to see he is failing when anyone around him could tell him so. There are so many ways you can persuade yourself that the best is yet to come.

An absurd self-belief is, as I suggest in an earlier chapter, almost a prerequisite for the job. What other human type would spurn more secure career-paths and opt for a candidature in the first place – which any kindergarten actuary could tell you has only a limited chance of leading to a seat in the House?

Say you get that seat. Your great achievement attracts no more than a modest income, terrible hours, no clear sense of doing a proper job, no proper work schedule, nagging anxiety that your imperfections may at any moment become the subject of national media attention, no sensible demarcation between what time is your own and what is claimed by career, and splits between two places of work and two separate homes which gnaw cruelly at leisure and social life, human partnerships, marriages and families.

Nor is this job even secure. In all but the minority of seats which may be called 'safe' (where confidence is regularly dashed) you may be out on your ear after four, fourteen or forty years without explanation or apology and with only modest compensation – for reasons which are for the most part wholly beyond your control. Even MPs with seats as safe as mine live in irrational fear of some kind of electoral ambush.

Having arrived full of pride and hope, you find yourself within a year swinging around in a vast mock-Gothic folly, knowing only that you must be there at all sorts of extraordinary times, persistently confused as to why.

Party discipline belittles you. Your secretary tolerates you. Your constituents pester you. Journalists deride you. Even your local paper ignores you. Your senior colleagues patronize you, your junior colleagues resent you and your equals mistrust you. The parliamentary clerks despise you and the Speaker fails to recognize you.

I recite these truths not to invite sympathy for an MP's lot. You might as well feel sorry for the man who invests his whole fortune on lottery tickets but does not win the jackpot. He gambles and he loses. So it is with the man who intends to reach the top in politics. He freely chooses to put himself up for election, often against stiff competition. He chooses it because he believes there is something so special about him that his career will defy probability and prove the exception. A glance at his curriculum vitae will confirm that he has no good reason for this belief, but he entertains it in the comical hope that it may lead to greater things, though a glance at the arithmetic shows him the unlikelihood of that. In both senses of 'vain' he stumbles vainly on, teased and buoyed between bouts of despair by the strange subterranean conviction that destiny has singled him out.

He needs help. I did. Drowning in shallow water is a horribly pointless thing to do but, shallow as the water at Westminster is, better men and women than I have come to grief there, and I too was sinking.

Failing, however gently, is the only word, but failing in the lower reaches of the House of Commons is a very comfortable experience. Nobody (except the sketchwriters) laughs at you to your face, your constituency association carry on believing in you, some of them revere you, and for the regrettable lack of any outward sign that your great talents have been rewarded with any useful position in the governance of the country there is never a shortage of explanations.

You were too clever. You were too independent. You were too irreverent. You were too impatient. You were too nice. You had too great a sense of humour. You were gay.

All these thoughts had comforted me at different times as, while seven years slipped by, I noticed first the ablest, then the more average and finally the undeniably idiotic among my contemporaries tiptoeing past me up the political stairs at whose foot I still waited, asking earnest questions about bus services. It would have helped to have been too stupid to notice. Or too mad, like Dr Sir Alan Glyn. But slowly I realized.

The realization that one is failing in politics comes, if it comes, very gradually, and to some it never comes at all. There is no single career path, no timetable for promotion and chance really does play an important part; so you can carry on for years – decades – believing that one fine day luck may come your way. To one or two it finally does. Their example encourages the rest, and above the parliamentary harbour a score of Madam Butterflies are keeping watch through the long, dark night of an obscure Commons career, waiting for their ship to come in.

You have been an MP for a couple of years and already some of those elected with you have their feet on the bottom rung, as bag-carriers (or parliamentary private secretaries) to the Great Ones? Ah, not every hare wins the race, you tell yourself. Then a couple of palpable tortoises go lumbering past you into the whips' office, and still you're nowhere.

Ah, you tell yourself, quality will out, in the end. And you throw yourself with redoubled energy into your work in the constituency where at least (you comfort yourself) your goodwill and intelligence are recognized. A whip makes an encouraging remark about that speech you made on the bus deregulation Bill. Aha! They've spotted me, perhaps.

Four years pass and a general election looms. 'We're so glad you're not a minister,' a constituency stalwart tells you gamely. 'We have you all to ourselves and with your hard work here you've really built up a good base in the constituency now. It's going to stand us in good stead in the General.' You congratulate yourself on what you now realize was your game-plan all along: to spend the early years taming the natives and securing your electoral base, so that when you are a minister the whole constituency thing will be sewn up, tickety-boo – running itself, almost.

The election comes and, sure enough, you do rather better than the nationally averaged swing. You return, heartened, to London. Now for your career.

More of your backbencher cohort are promoted. You are now in a distinct minority. 'What we admire about you,' your constituency chairman says, 'is the way you don't see the Commons as just a ladder to a ministerial limousine. Whatever happened to the independent backbencher for whom the Commons itself was reward enough? And aren't there the revamped select committees now? I was reading in the *Telegraph* that these are the new power-base for MPs who don't even want to be ministers . . .'

Your heart sinks. You aren't on a select committee. And you did want to be a minister. Two years into your second term a couple of your cohort who were made ministers two years into their first, make it into the Cabinet. Hmm. More staying-power than might have been expected – from hares. In your constituency ignorant people start assuming that you *are* a minister by now, and you have to explain.

'Our Member's too principled to be lobby-fodder,' your kindly constituency chairman, introducing you at a meeting, tells the audience, to polite applause. 'The whips want sheep, but our MP votes with his conscience' (more applause) 'and I know you'd all much rather have a representative who speaks his mind and stands up for us, than a Minister for Paper Clips.' More applause as you smile in what you hope is a modestly principled manner. Truth is, your voting record has been distinguished less by courage than caprice. Truth is, there were backbench colleagues who did take a defiant stand, stuck to their guns – and are junior ministers now.

Truth is, if they offered you Paper Clips you'd fall on the chief whip's neck and weep with gratitude. But nobody has.

You soldier on. Nearly seven years down, now: and thirteen to go before the knighthood. 'Knight of the Shires' is something to be, isn't it? Soon the *Daily Mail* will be calling you 'senior', 'seasoned' – and, in time, 'veteran'. You ask the Commons Library to compile for you the lengths of time each one of your constituency's MPs over the last century has served. How long until you're the longest-serving? That would be something to be, wouldn't it?

How many of your cohort, you muse, will still be in the House in forty years? You were, after all, one of the youngest of that crop, and you have one of the safest seats. 'Father of the House' – that would be something to be, wouldn't it?

In the night you catch yourself wondering at what point in a backbencher's Commons career the length of your Commons experience ceases to count as a plus on your CV (supposing, just supposing, you were to seek a new career) and turns to a minus as potential employers ask why the political career never took off.

I had told the West Derbyshire selection committee that my ambition was to be Home Secretary because Prime Minister would have sounded pretentious. It had not taken long to scale down my ambitions to something more modest: *any* Cabinet post would be an honour, and if I climbed no higher peak, that was altitude enough, wasn't it? Later I had started to think that 'Minister of State' had a certain ring – and this breed were often made privy councillors near the end of their careers, to walk off into the sunset as Right Honourables.

Then I started to think it was perhaps pointless to aim for anything at all, except the nearest hilltop, from which a better view of the terrain might inform my choice of mountain. So I would just like to be a junior minister. Of anything – though transport had become my overriding interest and I had at last been placed on the Transport Select Committee and offered a chance to join a fact-finding trip to the Humber Bridge, and later a bus garage in Toronto.

No offer came. I now know it nearly did. Times were changing even in the Tory Party and homosexuality was no longer a complete bar. Peter Lloyd, a good man and then a whip, told me later that I had been under consideration just at the point when I had defied a three-line whip and wrecked my chances. That this act of defiance must have arisen from some mulish whim rather than long consideration and an agonized conscience, is suggested by the fact that I have not the faintest recollection of what the rebellion concerned – nor recollection of rebelling at all.

It is tempting to submit that at this point, or some point, I concluded that it was more honourable to be my own man, stay my own man, and stop sniffing around for a pair of ministerial boots to lick; but the truth is so much cloudier. I did keep vaguely hoping for something;

but, believing less and less that it would come, I grew careless in what I said or how I conducted myself as a Thatcherite foot-soldier. I wrote an article for the *Guardian* which was critical of our certitude and stridency as a government. I organized resistance to the arrival of the heavier kind of lorries which European directives threatened to send into rural England; I ganged up with others to make a rude noise about cuts in funding for the World Service of the BBC. I wish I could believe (as my friends believed, and still believe, many of them) that this truculence arose from principle; but really it arose at least as much from despair, and from a failure to apply myself in a focused way to a plan for my career. I was drifting away, just as I had in the Foreign Office, just as I had at Yale, just as I had in Southern Rhodesia.

Drift, however, seldom seems so pronounced to the drifter as it might to the eye of the lighthouse. I might have drifted in politics for forty years. I might by degrees have subsided into the role of 'maverick' backbencher, generally liked, even respected, penning the occasional piece (as by now I was beginning to do) for *The Times* and *Sunday Telegraph*. I had been pleased with the amusement caused by my letter to the *Times Business News* suggesting that Industry should take a leaf from the Common Agricultural Policy's book, set an intervention price for new British motor cars, and stockpile those unsold at this price on Canvey Island. Some colleagues did realize it was meant to be a joke, though I was never sure whether the letters editor had. It's not brave to be a maverick, it's lazy, but the self-indulgence is fun.

I was heading for a tolerable niche.

To refresh my own memory of what I actually did as an MP between 1979 and 1986, I have called up on a website called Parlianet an abstract of my parliamentary career. Here, on a chillingly geometric grid with subtitles and neat boxes, is marked, against every subject a named MP has raised, the number of times he has raised it. *Agricultural products – 1. Argentina – 1. Bicycles – 1. Bus services – 4 . . .* and so on. From this emerges a picture of a backbencher who lived and breathed bus deregulation, lorry weights and railway services, roads and public transport, the arrest of gay men for importuning, and whirling disease in trout. It is sobering, it is cruel, to see all those years of bobbing up and down trying to catch the Speaker's eye, all those long nights on standing committees ticking off clauses and sub-clauses and agonizing about words, and all those meetings being sleeve-tugged by the mad or importunate, reduced to a small spreadsheet of mostly dead issues, set against them a casual scatter of numbers.

I did and do care greatly about transport policy and know and have thought quite a lot about it – if you're interested. But you are not. Nor was anybody much else in my party. Here, unlike with health or social services, was an area where the state really could spend money and get big results; here . . .

No, what's the point. Nobody's listening and, anyway, if what I say is true, then sooner or later people better equipped than me to take the argument forward will make it their cause. 'Remember,' as an acquaintance of mine, a stage entertainer, was once advised by an old hand, 'you can't tell 'em everything you know.' So let us quietly close the door on my Commons career. It was achieving not much, and I was lucky to realize this in time.

For I honestly think John Major would have made me a junior minister. And I would have cocked it up with some smart-assed remark which would have had the press on my back; and John would have held on to me loyally for a few weeks insisting it had been out of character and just a silly mistake; and eventually would have had to let me drop. Oh yes, it was predictable, as predictable as my long twilight after that as a loose-tongued old maverick Tory. 'Likeable eccentric,' they would say, and I could have lived with that. 'Come now, Sir Matthew, you're only teasing us, surely, when you say pensioners with not too long to live should be put to work clearing blue asbestos from building sites?' I could have dwindled into something like this and half expected to.

When Eileen Wright, my long-serving secretary, told me a man from London Weekend Television had telephoned and wanted a chat, I assumed it would be about some programme they were planning on transport. Perhaps if I was lucky they wanted to interview me.

I returned the call. The man from LWT asked if I was familiar with their Sunday morning political interview programme, anchored by the famous Brian Walden, called *Weekend World*.

I've never watched much serious television: it bores me, it's slow. Singing and dancing, comedy, cartoons, soap opera and light entertainment work well on TV; documentaries where the pictures are what counts are well suited to the medium; and television drama can be powerful. TV can popularize an argument, tell a story or dramatize a case. But as a way of getting information across or advancing human understanding, of pushing forward reasoning or knowledge, television is unwieldy; it plonks along, for ever in need of pictures, and pictures are seldom central to the argument.

But everyone had heard of Brian Walden. He was the man who had persuaded Mrs Thatcher to agree with him that she was in favour of Victorian values. I told the man from LWT I was familiar with his programme.

'Would you like to present it?'

I asked myself, as he explained that Brian was quitting to withdraw to the Channel Islands, whether there had been some mistake. I asked him why me.

'You weren't – I must be honest – our first choice,' he said. He explained that they had asked Bryan Gould (a prominent Labour frontbencher who was later to bid for the Labour leadership), who had turned them down; after which they had asked Chris Patten, who had also declined. LWT bosses had been impressed by my (*my?*) *World in Action* documentary, living on the dole for a week in Newcastle; and by some columns I had written in the newspapers. They were offering a two-year contract, with no security beyond that, but for those two years at least double the salary a backbench MP earned. So was I interested?

The salary was of no consequence to me. The media career was.

I recall a short pause following his question, after which I remember being startled by the sound of my own voice saying yes. I am unsure whether I understood at that point that this would entail (as the broadcasting rules then required) resigning my seat in Parliament; but I know that when this was explained it made no difference to my decision. Nor did the money.

I think big decisions are often made – or drafted – over long periods in the unconscious mind, where evidence accumulates and the arguments are weighed without the conscious man knowing what's going on. In time, everything is ready for the flick of the switch, and it is only of that final flick that we are conscious.

I told my constituency agent – John Smith, who had replaced Al. This meant a by-election, a huge financial blow, a mountain of work for him and his wife, Vivienne, and the possible loss of their livelihoods at the end of it, should the Conservatives lose. John and Vivienne could have gone crazy at me, or gone sour. Instead, and without recrimination, they calmly discussed how I should go about things. This was deeply professional.

I told the chief whip, by then John Wakeham, who took the news without comment and did not try to talk me out of it. We agreed I would delay my resignation until it suited the party to have a by-election, probably not until the early summer. It was then March 1986. I had been an MP for just short of seven years.

John Smith advised me to head straight for the constituency and drive round visiting every member of the association who needed early warning before LWT, who were impatient to manage the announcement in the press, made it official. John and I made a list, not only of committee chairmen and others who had to know, but of stalwarts, supporters and personal friends in the association who deserved to know. West Derbyshire is two hours' drive from end to end, and the melancholy tour was a major undertaking. John telephoned ahead and set up each house call.

Everybody – bar none – was nice about it. The late Andrew George, then chairman of the association and a person of real stature, was calm, regretful, but pleasant. For one or two it was a real shock; for all of them it meant a tremendous burden of work and thousands of pounds to raise. And all this because they had entrusted one of the safest seats in the country to a young man who had had no previous connection with the area, who had been almost unknown to them, but who had promised to adopt the constituency and serve them – the undertaking was implicit – for life. With many of them the penny had long dropped that I would never marry and they had understood and accepted the reason why. Almost all of them had borne without complaint or murmur the (to them) exotic and irrelevant causes I had so embarrassingly championed down in London, and defended me when necessary.

And now I had come to tell them I was ratting on them. Mrs Thatcher, I had just heard, was furious and regarded this as an act of total betrayal. She had told colleagues that the electorate would forgive death as an excuse for a by-election, but not ambition. It would almost have been a relief if my friends and constituency officials in West

Derbyshire had been similarly angry. Instead each one of them, to a woman and man, sadly wished me well. I felt a complete shit.

The first person I had told had been my secretary, Mrs Eileen Wright.

Eileen must have thought to herself that a warning she had been given many years before was being proved right. She had been advised not to work for me when she had first been considering doing so. At the time she was the secretary of my predecessor, James Scott-Hopkins. She had worked at the Commons for forty years (she works there for me still). She was twenty years my senior, and the question was whether she would take me on, rather than the other way round.

The warning not to do so came from someone inside politics and connected with the Home Office and, I suspect, via Scott-Hopkins. I think Eileen knows more about this but, respecting confidences, has never told me. All I know was that she was told I was not a suitable person and that there were reasons I would go nowhere.

Autobiographies are not the place for lists of names of those who need to be thanked. I could write a book about Eileen; I won't. She could write her own book, if she chose to, about the changing Commons over the last half century, but she's far too discreet.

She mends my clothes, buys me second-hand jackets for £1 in Oxfam shops, and occasionally hands me bits of cheese or cake in plastic bags, surplus to her own requirements. Her late mother, Lily Hoad (at ninety), knitted me a green wool beret to wear on an expedition to the Andes. As Lily's sight was fading, the occasional stitch had been missed and the hat was regarded as quite a curiosity by the Indians, but I wore it with pride.

Eileen would do anything for me except take me at my own estimation. After a particularly bad week in which I had forgotten diary commitments, missed one important Commons division and misunderstood innumerable assignments, she began (as was her habit) writing out on a stack of little cards my constituency engagements for the weekend. Finishing the series, she took a final card and wrote 'Matthew Parris MP' on it, placing it last. 'Why are you writing my name?' I asked.

'For when you forget it.'

On another occasion I had to telephone her from Paddington station to ask where I was going (Exeter) and then later from Exeter to ask why I was going there.

To those she suspects of sleeve-tugging or wasting my time, she can be ferocious. More than once I've turned up at her desk to be informed that 'someone claiming to be a friend telephoned – sounded like one of those homos to me. I dare say you met him on a train or somewhere. I asked him which bit of the woodwork he had crawled from. He seemed to take offence, and put the phone down.'

Long after I had ceased to be an MP, and as a *Times* columnist had written something which the then Foreign Secretary thought daft, Douglas Hurd wanted to put me right and invited me over to the Foreign Office for a chat. The engagement was entered in my diary by Eileen. Before the date arrived, Douglas left office, to be replaced by Malcolm Rifkind, whose private secretary rang Eileen to maintain the arrangement, Malcolm and I being on friendly terms.

'Oh no,' Eileen told the private secretary, 'I don't think that would be a good idea at all. Mr Hurd had been Foreign Secretary for a long time and knew all about it, so Mr Parris would have wanted to listen to what he had to say. But your Mr Rifkind has only just arrived in the job and it would be a waste of Mr Parris's time to discuss the Balkans, or anywhere else, with him. I suggest Mr Rifkind waits until he's got his feet properly under the desk and learned all about the job. Then he and Mr Parris can have a useful cup of tea.'

Eileen greeted me later that day. 'I've just got you out of a tiresome engagement next week,' she said with pride.

We reinstated it. When we met I apologized to Malcolm Rifkind for the misunderstanding. 'Indeed no,' he said, 'it was really very good of you to see me.'

Thank God (in whom Eileen at least believes; she prays for parking spaces) she ignored the warning. We have agreed that she can retire when I, if I live, reach sixty-five and she is eighty-four. I have been lucky in Eileen. Can anyone be more blessed than by the care of someone who loves and knows them well, without ever quite understanding them?

Kevin Storey acted as my chauffeur for that wretched day and night when I had to tell my party I was leaving. Kevin was the new son-in-law of the unemployed Geordie, Harry Morgan, who had given me grief so articulately in Newcastle in front of the *World in Action* cameras all those years back, and whose family had since become my friends. Television had set me up, television had knocked me down and now television was taking me away. It was fitting that Kevin should drive.

Months later I lay in my bed, alone in my isolated stone cottage above a green valley – the farmhouse I had jogged past so many times as I pounded the lanes training for five London marathons, had finally been able to buy and have never left – and listened to the by-election result. It was not long before dawn. There had been many recounts. My former majority of more than 15,000 had evaporated. The Conservative candidate, Patrick McLoughlin, had just, and only just, beaten a strong Liberal challenger, Chris Walmsley. His majority was 100 votes. Had I not made the train journey that afternoon, it would have been 99.

And had I not lied in an interview with the late Vincent Hanna, a BBC pollster carrying out a rogue poll which most improbably suggested that Labour and not the Liberal Democrats could be the challengers in this by-election, Chris Walmsley would have won. Vincent and I both knew that poll was well adrift (Labour came nowhere) but I helped him stand it up by saying it rang true.

It was my only intervention in a campaign where I had refused every interview and all comment. I broke my silence knowing that this would make a splash. I knew it would propel the poll into the news. I knew what I said was false. I knew that Labour would trade on it, printing (as they did) thousands of last-minute leaflets for floating non-Tories. I had no regrets and no doubt at all that it made the critical difference. For the Liberals – shameless poll-twisters whom I love dearly – it was a taste of their own medicine. For the Conservatives it was one last and decisive act of helpfulness from a man who had seriously let them down.

In Ryedale, another Conservative seat where a by-election was held on the same day, this one caused by the death of the sitting Member, the Tories lost. The swing against us there had been even greater. Margaret Thatcher had remarked, as I've said, that the British electorate will not forgive their MP for leaving them for another job. It now appeared that in Ryedale they would not forgive him for dying. I turned over in bed and smiled with relief at our success, however narrow. So much for Margaret Thatcher's electoral wisdom. Now for my next career.

I should perhaps have realized, but did not, that in this she was to have the last laugh.

After I had told the chief whip of my resolve to quit the Commons to present *Weekend World*, and after the date of my resignation and the by-election had been agreed, but before I finally left, I thought I really ought to take my leave of the leader of my party and the woman without whom I would never have got that far.

Whatever her private anger, she was prepared to see me. Her office proposed ten minutes and a cup of tea during the afternoon. I travelled in from Clapham on the number 77 bus for this, sitting on the top deck and rehearsing in my mind, again and again, what I would say. It was my last chance.

I was shown in to her room behind the Speaker's chair at the Commons. Her then parliamentary private secretary, Michael Alison, a cold, churchy fish, stayed for the interview. In her mother-hen way she poured the tea and made much of giving me the right amount of milk and sugar. She began to talk.

It was one of those one-sided conversations in which intervention proved all but impossible: as though she did not especially care for this meeting but wished me no ill and did not want to be unkind. I got no word in edgeways as she talked non-stop about this or that . . .

'You'll need to keep in touch with what's happening *here* of course do keep in touch with our colleagues I know you have friends and then naturally you'll need to see politics from another standpoint now do read the *columnists* some of them are very good you know read Hugo Young I try to do you? – '

During the tiny pause this interrogative required I decided to take my courage in my hands and leap. She had been talking at me for the whole interview, which I realized she was now steering towards its conclusion. 'There was just one thing I did want to say, Mrs Thatcher,' I ventured.

She stopped and looked at me not unkindly. 'Oh I'm so sorry, dear,' she said, 'I've just been talking all the time and you haven't had the chance to chip in at all, and perhaps there was something *you* wanted to say?'

'Well yes, there was, really.' I swallowed. This was the bit I had been practising on the bus. 'As I'm sure you know, I'm homosexual, and as I suppose you know too a number of our colleagues in the parliamentary party are also. And hundreds of thousands of people in the world outside, in Britain, voters, are; and many of them are very much the Conservative way in outlook and would be natural supporters of our party, but they feel put off. They think we hate them. I think we should try to make them feel more at home. This would also lessen the anxiety felt by some MPs you and I know . . .'

I faltered, having more or less said what I had resolved to. She looked at me, as she had throughout my little speech, in quite an intense way. There was a longish pause. Then she leaned across the table and placed her hand on mine.

'There, dear,' she breathed. 'That must have been very hard to say.'

That was all she said. As I left, Michael Alison followed me into the outer office. 'It would be most helpful if you could give me the names of these colleagues,' he said. 'It would be useful to know. We might be able to . . . er, help them.' It struck me he must have thought I was very stupid.

14. A Star is Not Born

London Weekend Television took me to a studio in Wandsworth to learn the use of Autocue. They took me to Gieves & Hawkes to buy shirts, ties and three classy suits. They took me to a speech therapist to learn how not to pop my p's or sss my s's. They frog-marched me to a cosmetic dentist to remove my beloved crooked front teeth and replace them with capped ones. They took me to a chic hairdresser in South Kensington for an expensive haircut. They took me to an aural technician to measure my left ear passage for a custom-made earpiece for insertion there. They rehearsed me in interview using an obliging Michael Portillo as my guinea pig.

Then, all dressed up in blue pinstripe and a silk tie, smiling for the first time in my life a straight-toothed smile, muffling my p's, reining back on my s's and with my hair just so, I was marched into the big LWT studio. They sat me down in front of the cameras and whispered commands into my little earpiece. Leaving the *Weekend World* team as I arrived was a young man with a moustache. His name was Peter Mandelson but his team-mates had nicknamed him 'the Snake'. I remembered my own old nickname: 'Judas'.

The newspapers, however, dubbed me the 'new Brian Walden'. After my first programme my old supporter and counsellor, Sir Peter Tapsell MP, sent me a message: 'A STAR IS BORN'. More presciently, Jonathan Aitken said, 'Television won't be where you end up, but it will be a stepping stone for you into the world of the media.' And it was no good. I couldn't do it.

You've got to be reasonably bright to succeed in television, and I was. You've got to know your onions if you are to be an ace interviewer of politicians, and I did. You've got to have a nice clear voice and a passable appearance, and I had. But you've got to have something more than all these things: there must be some kind of magic about you. About me there just wasn't. I was, in the end, so forgettable. I led *Weekend World* to an early grave.

Brian Walden had been special. This was not due only to his funny voice and Midlands accent, his good mind, his quick wit, his sharp memory, his aptitude for the memorable phrase and his dogged insistence on hammering a message home a dozen times if necessary until every one of his audience had got the point and could congratulate themselves on their grasp and perception. All these caricaturable qualities fitted him well for TV stardom but he had something beyond this, too. He radiated self-belief. His whole demeanour winked at the viewer: 'You, clever viewer, and I, know that this politician is trying to wriggle out from under; and we – *we* – are not going to let him get away, are we?' Walden's intelligence flattered his audience's.

As I came to know more about him I understood that this huge apparent certitude was an act; but this was something few of his viewers and none of his interviewees ever suspected.

I lacked such confidence. It was more than a matter of first-night nerves and not something mere habituation was ever going to cure. It went deeper. The truth is, I have never quite felt comfortable in my own skin and, on television especially, this shows. Viewers saw a nice young man, perfectly articulate, with a pleasant voice and a neutral accent; but they sensed no ability to soar and no readiness to kick; no swagger; no finesse; no twinkle. Interviews were almost always live – even my reading the Autocue voice-over to the recorded pictures was, for some eccentric reason, live. If you had been in the studio you would have seen my knuckles, knotted and gripping at the side of my chair, just out of shot. This came through, I fear.

It never got much better. I hoped it would but I started tense and stayed tense. I was never cut out to be a physical presence and have always had a hankering to be invisible. This is not helpful in an on-screen television career. I can grin cheesily for a stills photograph, and that's about the limit of it. TV is all about physical presence, about visibility, about movement and animation, about the light. I prefer the dark, and when I want to think I shut my eyes and stay still. The term which best describes the quality needed for televisibility is 'in your face'. I've never cared to be in anybody's face. Even when we recorded rather than broadcast live, this unease came through: it was not just a matter of nerves.

There were more things wrong with *Weekend World* than its new presenter. This was an old-fashioned programme whose format was to spend more than half the show on a sort of Open-University-style introduction to the subject under discussion, leaving twenty minutes or so for the big interview. The idea was that the interviewer would explore with the interviewee, as aggressively as necessary, the key questions which (the viewer was to have concluded from the long introduction) needed asking.

Nigerian night-school students loved it. They were always coming up to me shyly on the Tube to say so. Few white people ever recognized me, except for sixth-formers studying A-level politics, whose teachers used to recommend the programme.

The problem with the format was twofold. First, it must be open to question whether television of any sort is well suited to the *exploration* of an argument. The medium is such a delicately balanced hybrid of words and pictures, some of them necessarily pre-packaged, that a TV show really needs to know where it is going before it starts.

This led to *Weekend World*'s second problem. Each show undoubtedly did know where it was going. Days before we were on air, our team, led by our editor, would have pondered, decided, then imposed an iron-clad line of reasoning upon the programme; pundits would be bullied into saying what we wanted them to say (in one case this took twenty-seven takes) or discarded if they failed to. Expert witnesses would be carefully selected. The interview itself would then be mapped out with absurd attempted precision – 'If he says A then we move to B; but if he says C then we revert to Q . . .' and so on – calculated to obtain the required confession from the interviewee, signed along a dotted line already set down in the presenter's head. Editor or producer would be in the control room, linked up to my specially moulded earpiece, whispering (or barking, depending on their personal styles) instructions and suggestions to steer the questioning.

Not that intricacy was always needed. One interview planned with a Tory minister – it was probably Health but I cannot be sure – was mapped out in advance in rather broad terms, followed by the instruction (in square brackets). 'Whatever he says he'll do, say it's surely too little, too late; whatever sum he promises to spend, ask why it isn't more.'

Sometimes I felt we became so absorbed in the course we intended the interview to take that we overlooked more interesting detours which arose as we went along. So determined might we be (for example) to get Edward Heath to say that he did or did not support the European Community's latest directive about this or that, that if Ted had suddenly roared, 'I've come to the end of my tether with that bitch Thatcher and I shall tomorrow be crossing the floor and joining the Liberals' my editor might have breathed anxiously into my earpiece, 'He's straying; bring the subject back to the directive.'

On one occasion, while I was interviewing Norman Tebbit, our deputy editor, sitting in for the editor, so disliked the line of questioning I had veered off into that, while I was still talking to Norman, he started shouting in my earpiece, 'That was a stupid question. Why in God's name did you ask that?' This did not make my job any easier – not least because Tebbit was a wicked interviewee at the best of times.

Nothing conspired to build my confidence. Only the faithful telephone calls from my mother, wherever she was, every Sunday morning as I faced another show, buoyed my spirits. My friend Peter would come afterwards to collect me, which cheered.

One Sunday I stared – like a frightened rabbit, as usual – into the Autocue to read (live) a long and very technical introduction to a programme about the spread of HIV and Aids. The passage I was reading described the means by which the Aids virus takes hold in the immune system. I became vaguely, then substantially, then acutely aware that I had already read the passage about blood cells which I was reading now. My Autocue had gone into some kind of loop.

I stopped and as good as said so, while an assistant rushed on to give me a script, which I promptly began to read in the wrong place. It was awful. I went home to Derbyshire covered in shame, though it had not been my fault.

At that time my friend Carl, a kindly soul, had been visiting an old lady who had survived all her friends and relatives and had nobody left. In the old people's home where she lived she was, Carl told me, my greatest fan. She insisted that I actually knew all the things I said, and was not reading from a script. The other old ladies laughed at her and told her about Autocue, but she believed in me and refused to listen. What, I thought, would they say to her now?

I rang Carl. She had died the day before that programme. In the circumstances, I accompanied him to her cremation. We were the only mourners.

I did improve a bit as the series went on. At first I had asked myself whether stomach-knotting tension would go on for ever, and of course it doesn't. You learn. You learn not just about interviewing but about being interviewed – for sitting in the interviewer's chair teaches, as nothing else could, how you can most easily be thrown.

Most politicians never seem to notice or learn that a short answer will throw the interviewer off balance where a long one almost never does. A short answer is the thing an interviewer fears most, for the more his interviewee rambles the less convincing he sounds to the public and the more time the interviewer has to choose, frame and point his next question. 'Yes', 'no', 'no comment', or 'I haven't the least idea' are, to a TV interviewer for whom a blank silence is the cardinal sin, truly terrifying replies. Another unsettling tactic is for the interviewee to turn the tables and start asking questions.

Norman Tebbit understood this better than most. Always terse, he interrupted me half way through a waffling question about elections, and said, apropos of very little, 'When is the next Irish general election?'

Of course I did not know and had to say so. And when Norman managed to come straight back at me with a supplementary question related to Irish electoral politics I was made to look ill-briefed and slow-witted: quick to ask smart-assed questions, not so hot at answering them.

I am a persistent admirer of Norman Tebbit, subversive a politician though he can be. When, years later, he wrote to the Letters page of *The Times* taking issue with me (as he always has) over homosexual law reform, I was keen that his letter be published. It began by describing me as 'the swivel-bottomed Matthew Parris'. The letters editor rejected it as an unseemly way to describe one of *The Times*'s regular columnists. I thought it fair enough.

Edward Heath was mischievous in a less elegant way. Booked as my star interviewee for a programme about Europe, he submitted grumpily to the researcher's lengthy pre-interview interview which broadcasters have a habit of inflicting on a guest (they call it 'picking your brains', which means, 'finding out what you will say, because we don't want any surprises on our programme') and gave her a clear idea of the line he would take. We prepared our interview tactics on the basis of this: testing, probing and questioning Heath's view. When he came on (live) he took the diametrically opposite line from the one he had put to my researcher. I was completely thrown.

What disappointed me most about television was the degree to which (if my programme was anything to go by) even good minds in television seem to become captured by current thinking on any subject. The medium prides itself on being bold, brash and fearless, and in some ways it can be; but morally and intellectually it tends towards timidity, even cravenness. Those at LWT who had chosen me as a star presenter had done so partly, I think, because I had not toed any lines and had a reputation (insofar as I was known at all) for taking risks with arguments. But once I was in my presenter's chair, I found their instincts were against giving me my head, while my own diffidence and the TV L-plates I somehow never shed held me back from insisting.

One week, for example, our programme was centred on the aggressive stance which Israel was taking on some now-forgotten middle-eastern issue. That country's behaviour was thought hard to defend. In one of the weekly brainstorming sessions our *Weekend World* team would conduct to decide what to do and how to do it, I suggested that most of the rest of the media would be taking a square-on look at this controversy, and it might be more interesting to turn our camera, so to speak, back on the United Kingdom, and that in pursuit of the question 'Is Zionism squandering the reserve of goodwill and sympathy upon which, ever since the Holocaust, Jewish causes and Jewish people have been able to rely?' we should interview a range of gentiles and Jews in Britain. Everyone nodded interestedly. Nothing more was said of my suggestion.

Once, when we had decided to make a programme about the underclass (a term only just beginning to gain currency) I queried the idea that this should be a harrowing documentary about the excluded poor which would conclude that unless society took action we should all be murdered in our beds. Why not, I suggested, explore the opposite conclusion: that a developed country like ours could coexist for ever with a minority within, who just kept failing and reproducing failure in their children? Modern Britain could surround, fence, feed, police and otherwise effectively ignore such a class. They would be a perpetual but manageable nuisance – stealing, brawling and drug-dealing but, even then, mostly among themselves: a leg-ulcer, not a cancer. The problem *behind* the problem of social exclusion, *Weekend World* would suggest, was not that it was a pressing problem we must confront – but that it was not.

The team nodded interestedly. Nothing more was said of it. We made a beautifully shot, harrowing documentary about the time-bomb ticking away on our council estates, with grainy pictures and wailing babies. I remember standing on a particularly nasty piece of waste ground near Finchley Road Tube station to talk over our establishing shots of dereliction on Merseyside. We were short of time and it would have been expensive to take the presenter to Liverpool. Every time a Metropolitan Line train passed along the skyline we had to re-take.

Do not let me paint a picture of a young TV star, his amazing ideas stifled by organizational deadbeats. My production team (which Peter Mandelson had not long left) were of high quality, many (David Aaronovich among them) going on later to fame in their own right; my editor, Hugh Pile, was scholarly and thoughtful. I did not bubble over with brilliant ideas each week and, when I did have a brainwave, then if I had stuck to my guns those around me would have listened, and I might have shaped the programme.

I did not, it did not work out, and you can probably hear a note of bitterness creeping in. In some measure this is because I failed. A presenter with the personal and professional authority of (say) Jonathan Dimbleby, a man of at least as much independence and brain as I might boast, could have put his stamp on such a programme. In my heart I knew I should refuse to accept 'talkback' (guidance through the earpiece), and take a stand from time to time on the direction of individual shows. But I lack natural arrogance and was a television novice: I felt very much in the hands of my clever, nice and hardwork-ing team, all of whom were tremendously loyal to me; and I felt that LWT had, in some curious way, done me a favour by choosing me at all.

Paradoxically, this feeling of indebtedness hindered me from repay-ing the debt, which I could only have done by proving a success, which in turn could only have come through being myself. People who are themselves often succeed in television, yet television does not encourage independence of spirit. The medium militates against the very thing it wants. LWT had chosen me for my quirkiness, then stamped on it. They capture the wild birds because their wildness appeals, and then they put them in cages and wonder why they fail to sing.

Had this not been the problem with my Commons career? A feeling of being in hock had stopped me even from doing my best for those to whom I was in hock.

Had I the confidence either to soar or to creep, to lead the mutinies or to march proudly behind my officers, I might have made my mark. But at key moments a sort of sheepishness has let me down. I could have been a one-off, a maverick interviewer who exuded a sense of danger, and won a career like that. I could have been a shameless hack, reading his Autocue in a mindless, exaggerated broadcasting voice and slavishly following instructions from the voice in his earpiece, and won a career like that. But, shrinking from being quite my own man, and balking at the role of dumbbell, I fell between. *Weekend World* made no bad programmes, and few very good ones. Our ratings sunk gradually.

While they were doing so I was outed in the *News of the World*.

For all I knew I was out already. Truths about B-list celebrities are not available for inspection at the Public Records Office and we do not apply for certification that aspects of our personalities have officially entered the public domain, so it is possible to mistake one's status – a mistake I was to make a few years later about Peter Mandelson's. Vincent Hanna (a celebrated, mainstream, yet always faintly rogue interviewer) had interviewed me for a BBC radio programme shortly after I had accepted the *Weekend World* job, and asked me off-air, before we started, if I minded him inquiring whether I was gay. If I minded, he said, he would not ask. 'Do by all means ask,' I had replied, 'I don't mind at all. And I will reply that my private life is private and you should mind your own business.' This seemed to me a good route towards indicating that I was gay without flaunting it in a way which might have looked like a sort of two-fingered salute at all the friends in the West Derbyshire Conservative Association who had been so loyal and kind when I as good as shafted them by resigning and making them fight a by-election.

So Vincent had asked the question, and I had answered, in so many words, as promised. At the time, which was the mid-eighties, I thought my response to this situation both shrewd and bold. In retrospect it just looks prissy. It certainly sounded prissy when somebody dug it up after I had mentioned Peter Mandelson's homosexuality on *Newsnight*, and re-broadcast the exchange. Were I a listener I would have formed the view that here was a hypocrite whose advice to questioners to mind their own business might usefully be directed back at himself. Oh, I could defend myself with a little lecture on the difference between attitudes to homosexuality in politics in 1986, and a decade later, but if I am honest with myself the better response would be, 'Fair cop – served me right' – not for mentioning the truth about Peter, but for taking umbrage when Vincent Hanna tried to prise it out of me. That interview with Vincent, however, did embolden the *News of the World*.

The paper's story about me appeared in an edition which splashed rather more prominently the 'revelation' that Roy Hattersley kept a mistress, and was about as little a secret. But the Hattersley story was more interesting and I remember falling on it that Sunday morning in the company of some of my *Weekend World* team, ignorant of what was in store for me and giggling with them at the details about Mr Hattersley. We paged on to see what other delights the paper offered. As I flipped through the inside pages I seemed to see my own photograph staring out from a corner. My heart stopped. By now the page had been turned so I turned it back. There I was.

Either out of some sheepish sense of the unrevelatory nature of this revelation (they could not even find a news-peg to hang it on) or because I was hardly an A-list celebrity, the report was short and less than breathless. My team were indignant but I was not. The *News of the World* claimed to be reporting some kind of an interview they had had with me 'last night' and of course there had been no such thing, last night or any night, but – what the heck – the substance was true. There are worse circumstances in which to be exposed as gay and I had courted them recklessly for years. I was lucky, and knew it. I felt no resentment against the tabloid.

Unlike an inexplicably large number of my countrymen, I have never been able to work up much indignation about the publication of something which is in fact the case, and this was not even embarrassing. For a not-quite-proclaimed homosexual, I thought, the *News of the World* was surely the equivalent of a coming-out ball for a society debutante. Though friends commiserated I reflected that as ceremonies go, a Sunday tabloid with a circulation of millions seemed adequate as a rite of passage. So now the deed was done. It was a small relief.

These were the years in which the government was pushing into law a small legislative measure which came to be known as Clause 28, which reached Royal Assent in 1988. Its purpose was to stop schools and local authorities 'promoting' homosexuality: the measure was a right-wing reaction to a handful of loopy left-wing authorities (the usual suspects) which had dreamed up provocative ideas for combating anti-gay prejudice.

Clause 28 did not start as a government measure or with any government help: it was a Tory Private Member's folly which Mrs Thatcher's ministers somehow got panicked into supporting at a later stage. It was ill-drafted, its intent anyway difficult in principle to enforce through legislation. Perhaps it should just have been laughed into oblivion. It was not as if many of us on the Conservative side in politics actually supported the use of public money to 'promote' homosexuality, or indeed heterosexuality, or any sexuality, or a million other things which we do not imagine we elect local councillors to fill their heads with.

But there was something profoundly offensive about placing on the statute book a law which singled out, from the infinite range of inappropriate causes a local authority might try to promote, one group in society, and prohibit teachers in state schools from talking positively about this group. Right across that city of the imagination known as the 'gay community', from left to right, there was a deep and spontaneous sense of outrage about this. We found (and still find) the incomprehension among some which our anger met, itself incomprehensible. Few people, for example, would think it was any business of a local council to promote Judaism, but a law specifically aimed to prohibit the promotion of Judaism in schools, a statute in which that faith alone was named, would be offensive for reasons it is hardly necessary to spell out.

The anger against Clause 28 was not synthetic, not restricted to the left and not just another buzz from another bee in the bonnets of the politically correct. It went very deep, and it was a serious misjudgement by Conservative ministers at the time to brush it aside as they did. As far as the attitudes towards the Conservative Party of huge numbers of homosexual people were concerned, this measure poisoned the well for many years. Foot-dragging in reforming the law we could understand, but this was not foot-dragging, it was a positive new piece of discriminatory legislation which the government had been under no serious pressure to sponsor.

We were gripped by a kind of collective rage. I was, anyway. A man called Nicholas de Jongh, then the *Guardian*'s theatre critic, approached me as he had approached a number of others, with a view to organizing some kind of a crusade against the proposals, centred upon but not restricted to our own industry: the media.

With Nick and the actor Ian McKellen as our principal ringleaders, we agreed to meet regularly at a mostly gay club called Heaven (under the arches at Charing Cross station in London) owned by Richard Branson, who had agreed to let us borrow a room – one of the bars – in which to meet.

Peter Mandelson, who was by now thought a well-informed and influential link with the Kinnockite Labour Party, agreed to come along to as many of our meetings as he could, to help us in our plans. We were in no sense a secret group but our aim was not to promote ourselves as an outfit, but our campaign. This quickly found focus in a plan to take out a full-page advertisement in a national broadsheet newspaper, to draft a short statement to head this page, explaining the principle of our opposition to Clause 28, and beneath it to print the names of as many men and women in public life as we could persuade to join our list of opponents of the measure. In effect it was a big, signed letter to Parliament from a host of people thought to command respect.

With help from all the gang I (I think) drafted the statement and we set about collecting names, and the money to buy a page in the *Independent*, the paper which made us the best offer. We did assemble an impressive list of some 200 eminent, famous or respected supporters (I remember Cilla Black refusing to sign), and we found the money too. It was time-consuming and hard work. The advertisement was duly published, it made no discernible difference, and the Bill passed easily through both Houses. I remember the night it passed the Lords: the only political event which has ever made me cry.

I was not a leading member of our Heaven team, just a regular attender. This was the time when Ian McKellen really got the bit between his teeth, and I watched him grow in determination and confidence, and in political sophistication as a campaigner – and saw his stature grow within the group. Ian was a natural leader: calm, good-humoured, attentive to every member of the team, and very slightly other-worldly. He made a shrewd virtue of political naivety. Surprisingly for an actor there was no apparent attempt to grab attention or credit for himself. For a gay group the whole endeavour was astonishingly unbitchy, unedgy, undefensive. It was comradely, moving and fun.

Peter Mandelson, conspiratorial at the best of times, seemed especially so in the black-walled and windowless upstairs bar of Heaven, where we sat on big leather sofas trying not to be distracted by the gorgeous and minimally clad barmen who would flit in with refreshments for the gang. Before Peter Mandelson joined us, Nick de Jongh did explain something about the exact status of Peter's attendance according to Peter's explicit instructions – his presence not secret but not official: not to be hidden but not advertised; not representing the Labour Party but there *from* the Labour Party to guide us as himself, as it were, and yet not *as* himself – not as a public name himself . . . or something. It was all too complicated for me. I just thought it was good of him to come. Obviously he was gay.

That self-recruited, self-appointed group in Heaven, with no rules, no constitution, no name, no agenda, no minutes, no agreed procedure and no institutional form at all, was really the core upon which the Stonewall Group for Homosexual Equality was afterwards founded. I was a founder and board member of Stonewall, staying for a few years until a loathing of committee meetings drove me away to support (as Lord Melbourne said he did the Church of England) not as a pillar but as a bulwark: from the outside.

This, during my short time as presenter of *Weekend World*, was the most positive thing I did. But my programme was slipping.

Nobody ever took me aside to talk about this. Failing in television, like failing in politics, was a foggy business with few opportunities to climb above the cloud and assess your progress. People congratulate you when things go well and, when they don't, say you were 'fine', the programme was fine, everything's fine. It is a wretched business being a none-too-brilliant television presenter. They pay you like royalty and treat you like shit. My own team were super-loyal but there was no hiding the pecking-order. On any questions of programme policy the presenter was to be consulted, no more, if there was time. In terms of personal convenience the presenter, along

with all those of his team concerned with what you might call the
intellectual content of the show – from the editor down to the
researchers and PAs – took second place behind the technical people.
We waited on their convenience.

There are plausible and practical arguments why those who actually
produce the pictures and the sound may sometimes have to call the
shots, but in television it goes deeper than that. The hierarchy has its
roots in more than the need to coordinate efforts within a sensible
flow-chart. The whole philosophy of the medium is centred upon
what they call actuality. Everybody in TV, from the top to the
bottom, senses this truth: that first and last comes the moving picture
and the soundtrack to go with it. If viewers don't get this, they will
notice. If the *argument* doesn't flow, or indeed simply isn't there, that
is not a hanging offence.

You cannot decide which way a programme's going to go, without
knowing whether you can get the pictures. Often the words are
written around the pictures, not the other way round.

Say an African leader in your mini-documentary was killed in an
air crash. Do you have pictures of the wreckage? Do you have pictures
of him getting into the plane? Do you have pictures of him getting
into *a* plane, any plane? Do you have pictures of a plane of the same
type as that into which he got, to be screened along with a voice-over:
'It was in a single-engined Cessna like this . . .'? Depending on the
answers to such questions, the death of the African in question will
occupy a larger, smaller, or perhaps no part in your documentary.

In this respect radio, though it is usually bracketed with television
as another broadcast medium, is quite unlike television, and more like
newspapers. In radio and print journalism the direct quote – the
ambient sounds, the 'actuality' – is to be preferred where available,
and of course in a newspaper a good photograph can rescue a marginal
story; but if the argument or story is strong enough and true – but,
there being nothing on-the-spot available to illustrate it, would simply
have to be recounted in reported speech – you tell it anyway.

There is therefore a sense in which television *must* dumb down:
the whole mechanics of the medium drives it down. *Weekend World*
was less afflicted by such considerations than almost any programme
of its type in the current affairs output of the era: we were a high-
minded lot. But in the end, we too were slaves to pictures. I was

never comfortable with this. Blind people make their way quite easily in the world so vision cannot be in any vital way irreplaceable. Deaf people are critically disabled. Vision is the least important, though the most immediate, of our three principal senses.

Apart, then, from my general lack of physical presence or aptitude for performance, I was never quite in sympathy with the medium as a medium. Perhaps that was a reason I should not have taken the job in the first place, but I had hardly watched television and think I just assumed I could busk it, like everything else. I was not busking well.

We were not helped, however – and that's an understatement – by the Prime Minister's consistent refusal ever to appear on the programme while I presented it.

This was never made explicit. No refusal in principle was ever suggested. But whenever she was asked it was not convenient and, as one year succeeded another and it had still not proved convenient, and as I remembered her former willingness to appear on the programme when presented by Brian Walden, noticed her appearing on every other mainstream interview show, and reflected that my reputation for savagery in interview was hardly such that I could comfort myself that her press advisers were scared of me, the conclusion was hard to escape: I was being punished for deserting the Conservative Party between elections and causing a by-election. I knew she took a dim view of this and understood why. Quite how dim, however, I was now being forced to recognize.

It was a major blow to *Weekend World* as LWT's prime claim to serious political programme-making that we could not get the Prime Minister. A new controller of programmes came in at LWT, and slowly the understanding grew that at the end of my two-year contract, the offer would not be renewed. The whole programme was to be axed.

The spirit among us on the *Weekend World* team was always good. But it's odd how, among a large and friendly group working together in some common purpose, the really important things – like whether any of you will be in a job in six months' time – are sidled around, never properly discussed. Most – as it turned out, all – of my team could be assured that television work would be found somewhere, but this was not the case with me and I think they felt a bit sorry for me and preferred to avoid the subject.

Someone said I should pursue my employment rights with LWT,

and that the fact that my contract was only for the two years I had served, did not negate these. But in my mind it did. My job, and our programme, had gone because we were not good enough. I had doubled my salary and taken my chances with a short-term contract. There was no point in whimpering about rights, now that the two years were up. If I was any good, I would find another job; if not, not. Why should this be my former employer's problem?

Instead I threw myself into more writing. Penny Perrick, then the literary editor of the *Sunday Times*, had taken me on as a regular book-reviewer, and my fortnightly review of an extravagantly varied range of books – from a republication of Malthus, to a biography of Gladstone, to a dictionary of opposites – had proved fun for me. Peregrine Worsthorne, when editor of the *Sunday Telegraph*, had commissioned columns from me. I was learning the ropes.

Early in 1988 there was a terrible fire underground at King's Cross. Among the many who died was a young man called Lawrence Newcombe, a nurse, who had run back into the fire with incredible courage to rescue others. Examining his blackened body they had discovered he was HIV positive. The *Daily Mail*'s front-page headline had splashed the scare that the firemen who rescued him might have been (they were not, of course) under threat of infection. Nothing was said about his heroism.

A mood of huge anger – I cannot explain it – settled on me and stayed for weeks. I resolved to find out all I could about Lawrence. I walked the streets near where he had lived, near King's Cross, asked in pubs, found friends and interviewed them. Then I wrote a column about him for the *Sunday Telegraph*.

I spent more time and more care on that column than on anything I had ever written before or have since. I don't know why. The story, the photograph of Lawrence, even the tape of his music (he was a talented man) possessed me for a while.

The LWT studios were in a high-rise modern slab on the south bank of the Thames, a little way downstream from Westminster Bridge. Walking along by the river from that building one evening in the spring of 1988, as *Weekend World* neared its end, I passed the riverside parapet where, ten years earlier, I had rescued Jason the mongrel, and the stone steps up which they had pulled us out.

I stopped, leaning against the stone balustrade, to look again at the scene. All of that had led to all of this. I had made it to Westminster with Jason's help, to be a famous Cabinet minister, but it had not worked out. And then I had turned my back on Westminster and crossed the river to be a television star, but it had not worked out. Now, in a few weeks, I must creep away, tail between my legs.

I reflected on all the opportunities which had come my way and which had not worked out. My fellowship to Yale: wasted. Too much bourbon, too much hanging around at Peter Ackroyd's parties, too little patience with the academic approach, no real originality as a scholar, no talent as a postgraduate. My time as a trainee diplomat: fruitless. Too little sense of method, too careless an attitude to office politics and career, no talent as a courtier.

I had failed: failed as a scholar, failed in Whitehall, failed at Westminster and failed on the South Bank: failed comprehensively on both sides of Westminster Bridge. I had no idea what to do next.

15. Looking Down on Politics

To the parliamentary sketchwriter of *The Times*, the bald patch on the back of the head of the leader of the Opposition is not ten yards beneath. Opposite and on the other side is the Prime Minister, whose every frown the sketchwriter can directly read. He sees the fear in the Prime Minister's eyes.

He watches the Opposition leader's bald patch grow as the years roll on. Between 1988 and 2001 I saw Neil Kinnock's comb-over forced to bridge a widening gap, John Smith's monkish saucer become a soup plate, Tony Blair's tufts thin, William Hague lose most of what was left of his encircling fuzz, and Iain Duncan Smith trying (we suspected) powder to soften the shine. Being leader of the Opposition is bad for your hair.

The Commons Press Gallery is a dress circle, cradling one end of the long chamber it overlooks. From its leather seats we peer at the dusty top of the canopy over the Speaker's chair a few feet beneath us, as passengers on a double-decker see the beer-can-strewn roof of a bus shelter. I have yet to see a beer can on the canopy, but a piece of discarded trailing cable has lain there for a couple of decades now, and once a workman left his pliers behind. Of this shabbiness on top the Speaker is presumably unaware. Dressed as decorously as the oak and leather around him, he faces – as do we journalists and Hansard reporters above – a long chamber with government benches to the right, Opposition to the left.

This was the perch to which, as *The Times*'s new sketchwriter, I was introduced in the autumn of that year, 1988.

Sketchwriters are a strange breed and one which it had never so much as crossed my mind I might ever join. They and their product are something of an anachronism. For as long as accounts of Commons proceedings have been printed, the practice has existed of writing the occasional 'colour' story to accompany the factual report. People have been curious to know more than what was said: how it was said, what the atmosphere in the chamber was like. They want to know about moods, behaviour, appearance, eccentricity, comedy, even dress. They want to know about hair.

Writing in the nineteenth century, the Irish nationalist MP and sketchwriter T.P. O'Connor, explained:

The reporting columns of a newspaper do not always give an accurate and rarely a vivid picture of what really takes place in a legislative body. Columns appear of speeches which have been delivered to empty benches, and which, therefore, have influenced the fortunes of debate little, if at all . . . The speech that reads convincing and eloquent, may, owing to the physical defects of the orator have not been listened to at all. Equally a speech which appears dull and cold in print may have produced wild outbursts of enthusiasm or of anger. It is assuredly as important that there should be some record of how the speeches influence the assemblies to which they were addressed as of the mere words of the speeches themselves. Nor can any account of the speech be entirely complete which does not convey some idea of the man who makes it, his manner of speaking, his appearance, his character, his career.

Charles Dickens worked as a young parliamentary reporter, and later published as *Sketches by Boz* a collection of some of his more colourful columns in the *Morning Chronicle* where he had worked from 1834 to 1836. He knew the importance of colour:

There he stands, leaning on his stick; looking at the throng of Exquisites around him with the most profound contempt; and conjuring up before his mind's eye, the scenes he beheld in the old House, in days gone by, when his own feelings were fresher and brighter, and when, as he imagines, wit, talent, and patriotism flourished more brightly too.

I would stare down from my gallery seat, pen poised above the Commons Order Paper on whose margins all my notes were scrawled (I never learned shorthand or bought a notebook) in barely legible abbreviations, by turns amused, appalled, absorbed or bored, and think of Dickens sitting there a century and a half before. My mother's literary idol much of whose vast work she had read to me in boyhood, chapter by chapter before bed, was one of my predecessor sketch-writers. I kept my scrawled-over Order Papers, every one, in a growing pile by my bed.

I was thirty-nine when I started, and it was the first thing I did well. Yet unlike most of the positions in which I had failed, this one started with no roll of drums. Every previous appointment – Yale Fellow, Foreign Office, Conservative Research Department, Member of Parliament, presenter of *Weekend World* – had seemed a triumph in its way, a step on an imaginary ladder which in my mind would lead to some sort of glory. But this, this trudging back, a mere reporter, into a place I had quit as a Member with head held high to be a television star, was a kind of defeat. How could I return except with my tail between my legs? The job seemed a come-down. It was to be my making.

Charles Wilson, then editor of *The Times* and the man who had taken the paper through its long strike, recruited me. The call came out of the blue by telephone. I had never met him. He sounded an unlikely *Times* editor. I heard a Glaswegian Billy-goat-gruff voice ask, in a let's-get-to-the-point way, if I wanted to take over from Craig Brown as *The Times*'s parliamentary sketchwriter.

I wasn't at all sure I did. Could I do the job? I had never written a sketch in my life. What of my thin portfolio of published work might Charles have seen? My book reviews for the *Sunday Times*? My scattering of eccentric columns for Peregrine Worsthorne? My account in the *Spectator* of being ambushed by bandits in Peru? My rant (in favour of road-pricing) in the London *Evening Standard* or (in the *Sheffield Morning Telegraph*) bus deregulation? My report of desert life among the Polisario Front for the *Derby Evening Telegraph*? My defence of gay rights, as a Tory MP, writing in the *Sun*?

I had written perhaps three pieces of which I was proud: that 'Stop being beastly to Tatchell' piece in *The Times*; a eulogy in *The Times* to Fred Hill, an old man who, serving his thirty-second prison sentence for refusing to wear a crash helmet, had died in Pentonville Gaol; and the column in the *Sunday Telegraph* about Lawrence Newcombe, killed in the King's Cross fire.

Did any of this add up to the wry and relentless daily column a parliamentary sketchwriter had to churn out? I asked Charles Wilson, why me? Besides, I said, Craig Brown was brilliant: if this meant doing a budding genius out of a job, the answer was no. Charles said that a year had been enough for Brown, who wanted to pack it in.

I rang Craig to check this, and it was true. I rang Charles back. He said he thought I could write, and knew I understood Parliament from the inside, so why not give it a try? And would I also write a weekly column for the side or bottom of the page opposite the leading articles and letters in *The Times*: something of a generally humorous or at least light nature. And could we talk about a contract?

Mentally, I took a deep breath. Was this really me at all? On the other hand, I needed money. I could sell my Derbyshire house or my Clapham house, pay off the mortgage on the other, and live for a while – but for how long without an income? More important, I was nearly forty and I had never met with conspicuous success in any job I'd done. What was I good for? Would I ever find something I could do?

Did I panic? I ought to have. Unable to recall, I recently asked a friend who was a lodger in London at the time. This was his reply: 'I've never told you this . . . I remember seeing you very worried in the living room at Bramfield Road one Sunday afternoon. I felt too young and unworldly to say anything that would be helpful. We all admired you and thought you were amazing (even as a TV presenter) – so my seeing you doubting yourself was a little difficult to deal with. I still regret saying nothing.'

Sometimes periods of deep anxiety are wiped from the memory, and I remember nothing of this – nothing of the self-doubt – but only some calculations about the mortgage. It was the need for money which clinched it. I told Charles I would try.

I said I didn't want a contract as I was not confident of being any good at the job, so why did he not take me on trial, as it were, pay me whatever he thought appropriate, and see where we both stood a year later? I doubted, I said, if I would want to carry on for more than a year, or whether he would want me to, but it would be fun to try twelve months at *The Times*.

Charles sounded surprised. Fine by him, he said: what about my job security, though? Was I sure I wanted no contract? But I stuck to the idea, and, fourteen years later, still do. Nobody should keep a job a minute longer than his employers want him for it or he wants to do it. Unsure I could do this one I certainly did not want to be retained or compensated if I could not.

So, on that basis, I started. Charles asked me to go up to the Liberal and Social Democratic Party Alliance conference, the first of the three big party conferences, in Blackpool that September.

I checked into the hotel where the *Times* team were staying. They were all friendly, did not regard me as a proper journalist, and left me alone except when I asked for help or advice, which was always generously given. I had only the sketchiest of ideas what they were doing, what their job entailed, what 'the desk', 'the late', 'the back-bench at Wapping' or 'the subs' were – or how a newspaper ever really comes to appear on the streets at all: always a mystery to me (and, I sometimes suspect, its editor). But I had the impression that the responsibilities of a professional reporter – a creature I could never be and should on no account pretend to be – were more thankless and more exacting than mine, and was grateful providence had never pointed me that way.

So it started and so it stayed: 585 words by 7 p.m., and the happiest of relationships, born of amity, cooperation and a mutual sense of the separation of provinces. Strange to relate, I worked for thirteen years right at the hub of a great newspaper's political reporting – the *Times* room at Westminster is little more than a Portakabin on the Commons roof – in a tiny, busy, noisy office, in the midst of the process and the people that turn politics into the pages of a newspaper, and never really got the hang of their job, or tried to. I was in my own world.

On the first day of the first conference I had attended as a journalist, the assembled party members spent most of the morning arguing about what to call themselves: 'Liberal Democrat' was the proposal. For as self-absorbed a party as this, a whole session spent discussing their own name was a gift for a sketchwriter, and easy to send up.

Re-reading that sketch, my first, one is struck by how little my style has improved, deteriorated, changed or developed in any way in the thirteen years of sketchwriting which followed. Any success I have had must be due to readers having got used to it.

On my second day I wandered into the conference centre after breakfast and listened to the debates. But they were without interest so I went back to the hotel. Just before seven in the evening a call came from that mysterious place, 'the desk', at Wapping. Where was my sketch? 'There wasn't anything worth writing about,' I said.

Baffled silence at the other end. 'There wouldn't be,' said the voice, 'it's a Liberal Party conference. But where's your sketch?' This time the baffled silence was mine. 'We need one every day,' said the voice.

'Every day? Even from the Liberals? I hadn't realized . . .'

'Never mind.'

I had the impression of the momentary exertion in Wapping of near-superhuman powers of self-control. 'A sketch tomorrow, then,' said the voice. 'And thereafter.'

And thereafter there always was.

16. In Bed with the Bottomleys

Nowhere is a kick-start more important in getting a career going than in the media. My own as a sketchwriter was given a lucky boost within a few months of the first Queen's Speech I watched as a journalist.

I had entered the Press Gallery one day when nothing much was happening. Staring idly down I noticed in the chamber beneath, two newish ministers, both of whom I knew (and liked) from my old days as an MP. They were young, they were popular, and they happened to be married to each other. That afternoon it fell to the one (a junior minister in one department) to answer a parliamentary question put down by the other (a junior minister in another).

I daydreamed up a minor fantasy for my sketch:

There is about Mrs Virginia Bottomley MP something of the blue-stocking, something of the glamorous air-hostess, and something of the hockey team.

Were she Sister on night-duty, unusual would be the patient who did not require his fevered brow to be gently mopped. Even a reprimand, from her, would be sweet. If she were Assistant English Mistress, could there be a single spotty youth in the Lower Sixth in whom she did not kindle a longing to know more of Milton?

Mrs Bottomley's evident ability only adds spice. Like those soft-core movies whose plots unfold in a dimly lit corner of a public library (non-fiction section), one sees the camera panning from the lady-librarian's desktop, up to her crisp white Quaker-collar and sensible glasses and then slowly down, to reveal, beneath the desk, fishnet stockings, stiletto heels and a split skirt.

Not I hasten to add that Mrs Bottomley, Under Secretary in the Department of the Environment (with special responsibility for the National Parks) is anything but a model of modest propriety. Besides, she is married to the Under Secretary of State in the Department of Transport, Mr Bottomley.

And how remarkable a partnership. For Mr Peter Bottomley MP is just the kind of man who would have organized a protest outside the cinema where our blue movie was playing, parading a placard: 'This Film Insults Women'. Tall, pale and thin, with Trotsky-spectacles and a crusading ambition to extinguish sin, transport is his special interest, and he regards every drink-driver dragged weeping from the court as a personal victory.

Readers versed in French history will recognize a Robespierre in Mr Bottomley. Younger readers will recognize a Richard Dreyfus.

Both partners in this unlikely match featured in Environment questions yesterday. Mrs Bottomley was at the dispatch box answering a question on rats.

Harry Greenway (C, Ealing N) was worried about 'dog mess and the extermination of rats and other rodents', especially in Ealing; and this led Davyhulme's Winston Churchill to complain too: about litter on motorways.

Mrs Bottomley's eyes shone with a tender inward flame. Ah, this was a matter for Someone Else. Someone very wonderful.

'I shall have to pass that on to my . . .' and she paused, lovingly '. . . My close, and honourable friend,' she murmured. The House chuckled, indulgently.

Readers, let us, so far as is possible without impropriety, picture the Bottomleys' marital bed, in a peaceful home at the end of a crunchy gravel drive in a leafy part of Surrey. The children are asleep. Peter and Virginia, too, have retired, after an evening at work on their ministerial red boxes: she sipping orange juice; he, an alcohol-free riesling. The silence, now, is broken only by the hoot of an owl and the night breeze whispering in the laburnum tree.

But someone is awake.

'Darling?'

'Yes darling?'

'Litter on the M18, darling . . .'

'What about it, darling?'

'It's piling up, darling. All over the central reservation. Mr Churchill's worried about it . . .'

'Set your mind at rest, Virginia. I'll get them: every motorist who drops a crisp packet: every last one of them: I'll destroy them: I'll have them dragged in open ox-carts down the hard shoulder and spat at by the travelling public. Just you see.'

'Oh Peter! Thank heaven.'

'As you well know, Virginia, I do not believe in the afterlife.'

'Sorry, darling.' And quiet returns to the scene. But not for long.

'Virginia, darling?'

'Yes, darling?'

'There's something I ought to tell you, Virginia. It's been bothering me.'

'What is it, Peter?'

'I want . . . well . . . it's hard to say, darling.'

'Try, darling.'

'I want to drive a six-lane motorway across one of your National Parks.'

'Oh Peter . . .' (long pause) 'Which one?'

Hush, readers: let us steal away before they hear.

It looks a slight enough piece of work now, but it hit the spot. The joke amused two important audiences. Insiders – members of the press and insider-Tory MPs, who mostly liked Peter and Virginia – thought the sketch fun, teasing a couple they knew. Outsiders – my ordinary readers to many of whom the Bottomleys were unfamiliar – enjoyed a faintly saucy mix of domesticity, sex and politics.

After I filed my copy, terror gripped me. What would Peter and Virginia think? What I had written had seemed harmless fun while I was writing it but as I lay in my own bed that night – no owls hooting nor night breeze whispering in the laburnum – parts of it now seemed rather smutty. Had I lost two friends? Had I been cheap? It was a restless night.

Needlessly. They were, apparently, quite chuffed. This couple are anyway good sports, but I had overlooked what I was quickly to discover: that most MPs just want to be written about. If they cannot be praised they are happy enough to be teased. Even vulgar abuse is, for many, preferable to being ignored. Over the years which followed I learned that most MPs do accept with a pretty good grace that if you dish it out you must take it too. Peers are different and can be quite pompous, too grand to complain directly but likely to get their friends to write sad little notes regretting your discourtesy.

The response to my Bottomley sketch, in comments, readers' letters and phone calls, was striking: good for my standing and, just as important, for my morale. It helped set me up as an insider-outsider: one who knew these people as friends, knew their little foibles, and was able to write about them for a wider audience. It set a knowing tone of irreverent affection which became rather my trademark over the years. An unkind but accurate critic once likened me to the young Anglican curate in cycle-clips who can make respectable ladies laugh with his cheeky *double entendres* but steers clear of anything interesting enough to be seriously rude.

Still, readers liked it. Having been an MP I could trade on a personal acquaintance with the jungle and the beasts who lived there. It was a familiarity I sometimes exaggerated: colleagues such as Robin Oakley and Phil Webster and later Peter Riddell often understood better than many MPs how the place works, and I relied on them constantly. Some of my knowingness was bluff, but being a gamekeeper-turned-poacher seemed to distinguish me from other sketchwriters.

Denied to me, though, was the pen of an aghast onlooker which a colleague such as Simon Hoggart of the *Guardian* could wield so well. Simon was always unequivocally on the readers' side. I could be suspected of complicity with the politicians. Complicity is a two-edged sword in political journalism and when readers wanted to squawk in amused horror, Simon had the edge over me: he was simply funnier. But when a sketch could usefully invite readers into a weird world they didn't know, and show them round, I was sometimes well placed to do this.

That Bottomley sketch was Plasti-tacked to quite a few readers' fridge doors. I think it established me.

Soon after came a sketch which really wrote itself: the occasion made it. Heading for probable defeat at the next general election and challenged for the leadership, Margaret Thatcher fell, and then the party which had toppled her cut down her most prominent enemy, Michael Heseltine, too. For a while the whole Conservative Party was seized by huge internal violence. On 28 November 1990 I wrote:

There will be people who will portray what has passed in recent days as an embarrassing lapse. Such people speak of chaos and confusion, of panic and self-destructive anger. Soon they will be referring to these past few weeks as an awkward wobble, when the Tory Party temporarily took leave of its senses, then recovered its nerve.

Nothing could be further from the truth. As in some tribal folk-mystery, the Conservative Party has suffered a great internal convulsion, triggered as much by the collective unconscious of the tribe as by any conscious plan to contrive its survival. They have not, as individual men and women, known what they were doing, but the tribe has known what it was doing, and has done it with ruthless efficiency. The instinct to survive has triumphed. Not that they were aware of that. All they knew was that they were heading for disaster. Each had his own opinion as to why. What they concurred upon was the imminence of danger; and when they concurred on that, the convulsion began.

At their conference in Bournemouth, a strange, flat despair gripped the occasion. We all noticed it; none of us understood it. Then they began to fight. They lashed out at the media, they lashed out at Europe, they lashed out at the Opposition, and they lashed out at each other. The tribe was in turmoil.

Michael Heseltine as much, by now, a totem of dissent as a person found members of the tribe dancing around him and chanting. He responded. The media took up the chant. Michael Heseltine started a teasing dance: was it a war-dance? Nobody knew. He did not know himself.

At this point their leader took on a dervish character. Saddam Hussein said she was 'possessed'. In a series of sustained rants she stunned the chamber, alienated half her party and scared the hell out of most of us.

There followed a short silence, and then the murmurs began. They grew until an extraordinary thing happened. One of the elders of the tribe, Sir Geoffrey Howe, began to speak. He spoke almost in tongues: he spoke as he had never spoken. He poured down imprecations upon the head of the leader.

Around Mr Heseltine the dance now reached a pitch of excitement that demanded answer. He rose, took the dagger and stabbed her.

What happened next is folklore. With the leader now wounded, but still alive, her own senior tribesmen drew back with one accord and left her. Suddenly alone, she hesitated, then staggered from the stage.

The tribe mourned her departure. Not falsely or without feeling, they wept. Then, last night, the final twist occurred. The tribe fell upon her assailant, Michael Heseltine, and slew him, too, with many shouts of anger. Real anger.

It could have been done as a ballet. It had all the elements of a classical drama. Like Chinese opera or Greek tragedy, the rules required that certain human types be represented; certain ambitions be portrayed; certain actions punished. Every convention was obeyed: every actor played out his role. The dramatic unities of time, place, and action were fulfilled. It started in

autumn 1990, and ended in the same season; it started in committee room
12 at Westminster, and ended there.

It started with an old leader, who was assassinated as she deserved; then
her assassin was assassinated, as he deserved. Then the new leader stepped
forward; and here the ballet ended.

Nobody who had been, as had I, a Tory MP, and had so often
heard the rumbling, anonymous thunder of thumped desks as the
1922 Committee of the whole backbench party cheered on whoever
would do their dirty work for them, and cheered off whomever their
dirty work had been done to, could have seen it differently. Many
former colleagues and many fellow-journalists and *Times* readers too
recognized the picture.

Next came a fillip I did not wholly deserve. At the 1992 general
election I appeared to predict (on Thursday 2 April) Neil Kinnock's
unexpected defeat seven days later. And not only did I appear to
predict it, but to explain it too. The truth was slightly different.

It happened like this. Close to eve-of-poll, when the Labour
Opposition seemed from the opinion surveys to be heading for a small
but decisive overall majority, Labour organized a pre-election rally at
the Sheffield Arena. It was billed in celebratory terms. *The Times* asked
me to produce a sketch.

This was hardly possible as the rally proper did not begin until just
before 7 p.m. The deadline for my sketch was about half an hour later
minus the fifteen minutes needed to dictate it down the telephone to
the copytakers. I've learned, though – and it's good advice for any
young writer or reporter – that if an editor wants to commission you
to cover an event, just say yes; work out later whether you can do
what is envisaged, and if you cannot, dream up a way of writing about
it anyway.

That is what I did. I took a train up to Sheffield, arriving mid-
afternoon and hoping for the best. The media were not permitted to
hang around the arena while final preparations were made, but instead
were asked to gather at a venue with conference facilities some
distance away, to be briefed, and await a signal to be bussed to the
stadium for the start.

There was the usual milling around, crisp-eating and sandwich-
nibbling. We were handed a printed battle-plan for the rally, a chron-

ology of events, if this sort of glitzy pap can be called events. Idly I half listened to the briefing: the usual self-serving puffery dished out by humourless apparatchiks whose whole purpose is to tell you nothing new, and who do it with all the insolence of office. Then I wandered away and chomped a sandwich and studied the printed programme.

The whole thing – the mixture of triumphalism, trumpets, helicopters, hollowness and image control – jarred. They hadn't even won yet and they had nothing in particular to say beyond 'look at us, we're the champions'. A young *Times* photographer, Chris Harris, came over and told me he had been following Neil Kinnock on an afternoon primary-school visit, and that the pushy way in which Labour enforcers had made sure their leader was photographed only against a background of smiling kids had been sickening.

I decided this would do for my sketch. It had to: my deadline was approaching, still we were not being ferried to the arena, and anything involving helicopters tends to run late. So I took a taxi back to Sheffield railway station and, squatting on my haunches on the London platform because there were no seats, while balancing my unwieldy laptop on my knees (this was the Stone Age of laptops), dashed off this sketch about the planned happenings, telephoning it through from the train phone as we rattled across the East Midlands:

It is at times of retreat that an army's strengths can best be observed. It is in moments of triumphalism that we first see the seeds of its downfall. It was when Margaret Thatcher employed a train-bearer to carry her gown that we knew her day was done. And it was in the slick, sick, cynical image-manipulation of Labour's spectacular at Sheffield last night that we first sensed the contempt into which they too must come.

'Any dream will do,' sang the children, as Neil Kinnock played king of the kids in a Leeds school yesterday. He was preparing for the Sheffield Arena. He took their song to heart. Any dream would do.

Something about the very instructions printed for backstage operators last night chilled the soul. It was entitled 'Running order for Mega Rally'.

'*17.30: Doors open; party bus; band, etc., arrive. Street entertainers will be working the audience outside.*'

The days when candidates would have worked the audience themselves, treading the streets in person, are gone. The candidates were in helicopters.

'*18.00: Dave Blunkett does welcome. DB to Royal Box.*'

'Will Mr Blunkett sing?' asked a reporter. 'And is it true his guide dog's gone sick? Will he sing "How Much is That Doggy in the Window?"'

'*Regional contingents with banners & bands. 18.42: Neil Kinnock arrival in helicopter shown on video screen.*'

After speeches by Roy Hattersley and John Smith came the '*first endorsement, 2 mins*'. 'That's Mick Hucknall of Simply Red,' said the aide. 'No, he won't actually be there. He's in Marseilles working on his next LP. He'll be signing his postal vote and singing "Something's Got Me Started" and this will be intertwined with his message. The message will say (and she began to dictate): "On April 9 I'll be voting Labour . . ." (she paused for us to take this down). "It's time for a government that invests in skills . . ."'

And we were promised '*Sarah Jane Morris, ex-of the Communards*'. Now of the Democratic Socialards, I expect. This item was to appear in the '*Top-Slot, 15 mins*' preceding the '*second endorsement*' after which came '*Opera-Slot, 15 mins*', except that it wasn't opera, but a lady singing 'Summertime'. Normally, as John Cole observed, 'You know it's over when the fat lady sings,' but this was a thin lady and it was far from over: for next came '*20.05: NK speech*'. This was printed in advance. It was entirely devoid of content.

'*20.35: NK finishes; 20.40: "Jerusalem"; 20.45: finale, NK & Shad Cab leave. 20.55: All out, "Goodbye" music.*'

I spoke to a press photographer who has been following the Kinnock campaign. Photographers are normally mute and I have no reason to think this one was a Tory: his frustration was professional. 'The manipulation has been crushingly successful,' he said. 'This has all been done for television: it goes against a video cameraman's instincts to show the props holding things up and all the minders marshalling the crowds.

'All we're shown is Kinnock with smiling kids, Kinnock in hospitals, happy faces, young children . . . the image control has been total. The TV bosses need a few minutes of Kinnock every day to balance their few minutes of Major and if all he gives them is sanitized pap, that's all they can use. That's all anyone sees.'

As an ideal matures into a crusade and a crusade translates into a government, there comes a point when, throttled by the very apparatus set up to project it, the ideal begins to choke. This point has come early with Labour. Last night in Sheffield, image throttled intellect and a quiet voice in every reporter present whispered that there was something disgusting about the occasion. Those voices will grow. Peter Mandelson has created this Labour Party and, on last night's showing, Peter Mandelson will destroy it.

'We will govern,' Neil Kinnock said, opening his speech, 'as we have campaigned.'

Oh I do hope not.

One or two people liked the sketch, but it had been almost forgotten by polling day a week later. Then, against all forecasts, Labour lost. Columnists and pundits began casting around for clever reasons – not least to rescue their own reputations.

When media predictions have failed there is a commentators' appetite for explanations which point to things that happened after their predictions were made and which they could not therefore be expected to have taken into account. 'Premature triumphalism' was one; at its centre was the theory that the prospect of an imminent Labour victory with Neil Kinnock air-punching had frightened doubtful Tory voters to the polls. That rally was said to have scorched this prospect into the public imagination. My sketch was quickly dug up and I was credited with having foreseen everything. The phrase 'Sheffield rally' began to be used as a shorthand to describe Kinnock's mistake. The word 'triumphalism' (which had until then not been used much) was flogged almost to death. I heard myself quoted again and again as having analysed, in a sketch written after witnessing the Sheffield rally, the fatal flaw in Labour's approach.

It may have been, but I had not said so and I had not witnessed the rally. I had been writing not about the prospects for the imminent general election (which it never occurred to me could be lost by Labour) but for the incoming Labour Government towards which I was then looking. It was as a government, not as a would-be government, that I believed they would be throttled by their own image-manipulators. That sketch has more application to New Labour now than it did to Neil Kinnock then.

Still, it was nice to be hailed as an election clairvoyant. My reputation as a sketchwriter received another boost.

One or two other papers began inquiring whether I would be interested in coming over from *The Times*, but I valued the total freedom given me by successive *Times* editors (I have by now worked under five) and, though other editors offered more money, *The Times* paid me well and, whenever I had asked for more, granted it: any ceiling which existed on my income was self-imposed by my desire not to be greedy. I know what proper journalists – who work harder, have to learn shorthand and get horribly pushed around – earn; already I was earning twice that: it was enough. And besides, I had grown fond of my readers. *Times* readers are a predictably educated but unpredictably diverse bunch, of all ages and opinions and many walks of life. I felt secure at *The Times*.

There was a moment, however, when my carelessness could have compromised this security. I took two of Rupert Murdoch's children, one of them under-age, parachuting. I did so without asking my proprietor's permission. It all happened by mistake.

I had recruited a shy, polite, thoughtful youth called Lachlan, doing work-experience in our *Times* office at Westminster, to join a group of my friends on a charity parachute jump near Nottingham. It was his idea. He had overheard me on the telephone making plans and asked if he could be included in them. He had always wanted to try parachuting, he said. I knew nothing about this youth – we had work-study people in and out of our office all the time at Westminster – except that he sounded American.

Fine, I said, and gave him a form to fill in.

I liked this Lachlan. He was unusually respectful to senior colleagues, and called us all sir. When it came to signing the form *in loco parentis* because he was not yet twenty-one ('My father isn't around at the moment,' he explained) I signed in place of his father. Then he asked if his older sister, Elisabeth, could come too. I said sure, and got the forms for her. She joined our group.

It was only later, when I had a moment to review our documentation, that I noticed the surname of the young siblings: Murdoch. It struck me that Lachlan and Elisabeth were the names of our proprietor's children. Nobody in the office had mentioned this. Everybody else knew, of course, and assumed I had twigged. But I thought, what the hell – I don't expect their parents would mind. And parachuting's pretty safe.

I was on the ground, my own jump over, when the young man and his sister jumped.

You know when a parachutist is leaving an aeroplane because the pilot cuts the engine. For a second all noise stops, and you look up. I watched as a tiny ant-like black dot dropped from the small plane high above me. That would be Lachlan. Then another. That would be Elisabeth.

Now a twinge of anxiety surfaced. This – the moment of engine cut-out – had been the moment after which, on my previous (and first) jump as a young MP, for charity, near Bristol, I had watched from the ground as one of my Tory parliamentary colleagues tumbled awkwardly, drifted badly, narrowly missed a power line, landed far from the appointed place, rigid with terror, and broke his back. He was in hospital for weeks and disabled for life.

What if Elisabeth's or Lachlan's chute failed to open? What if they panicked and drifted away over Nottinghamshire? But above each, five seconds later, the full canopy spread. Silence ended, engine whine resumed. Both steered correctly down on to the target-patch. Both landed without mishap.

I told Lachlan that I had not known his surname when first he asked to join our charity jump and, on learning it, had become anxious lest his or Elisabeth's parachute fail. Lachlan asked mildly whether it was only because his father was Rupert that I was anxious for his chute to open.

Many years later I dared mention this to his father, at a supper party at Claridge's for Peter Stothard who was retiring as editor of *The Times*.

'I know about it,' said Rupert Murdoch, his lips, I thought, slightly pursed. 'They didn't dare tell me for months.' I hadn't dared tell him for twelve years.

When the newish editor of the *Daily Mail*, Paul Dacre, telephoned and in a conspiratorial voice invited me for a drink, I accepted, though I realized he might want me to write for his paper. He chose a dimly lit bar in a discreetly posh hotel off the Embankment. I arrived at the appointed time. Mr Dacre lunged at me out of a dark corner like a bear. He was not over-smooth or garrulous and I liked him and his directness. We chatted for a while. I said I was happy at *The Times*.

'I happen to know that in Derbyshire you drive an ancient Land-Rover,' he said. Surprised that he should be so well informed, I began an enthusiastic description of my classic and cherished 1959 Series II long wheel-base cab-and-canopy Land-Rover.

He cut me short. 'Yes,' he said, with a hint of impatience, 'but that vehicle's *ancient*. How about a new one? On top of whatever *The Times* pay you per sketch, and a flat "introductory" fee of £50,000, the *Mail* would arrange to have a brand-new, top-of-the-range Range-Rover – petrol or diesel, any accessories you care to name – waiting for you at your Derbyshire home.'

I respect the *Daily Mail* very much as a journalistic enterprise: it is (someone has remarked) a brilliant paper with a distinct, and disturbed, personality. But I declined the offer and have declined every inducement to desert since. I stuck with *The Times*. Even the dullest day would yield something, while just occasionally – what follows was at the general election of 1997 – I would find myself chance witness to the unforgettable . . .

For the Baroness Thatcher, another Friday, another walkabout. For Shirley Taylor, Tesco till-operator, a nightmare. Lady Thatcher had no cheque guarantee card.

All had gone so swimmingly well. It was British Week at Tesco's in Maldon, Essex, and Union Jacks decorated the merchandise. The baroness, in stunning blue with a gold English rose brooch, swept in from her blue Daimler. She looked a million dollars. Senior staff stood in line, as if for inspection. Several Tory women swooned, one so excited that her knees gave way.

The former Prime Minister surveyed the huge store. 'It makes shopping so much easier,' she breathed. Her hair was perfect. 'How are you dear?' she gushed to randomly selected cheese operatives and shelf-packers. 'One does have to be careful one doesn't spend too much,' she confided to a female fan. 'I named my Dobermann Margaret, after her,' the fan later told me.

A shopper asked, nervously: 'You are going to support Mr Major, aren't you, Lady Thatcher?'

'Of course, dear.' And she began to shop. After a nasty brush with a French apple at the fresh produce counter, her eye lighted on a massive carrot. 'British carrots?' she inquired, with bayonet glance. 'From Norfolk, Lady Thatcher.' Phew.

'Is Friday your busy day?' she demanded of an awe-struck young member of Tesco's staff called Gareth. 'No, I expect it's Saturday. Good thing I'm here on Friday, then.' Gareth was quite overcome.

Pausing for a terrifying instant by the Danish Speckle Bread, she plunged on towards the Selected Crusty White. Bakery staff hovered. 'In my day,' she told them, 'bread grew hard on the shelf.'

Lady Thatcher was hitting her stride. She had bought an orange and two lemons and made for the cheese and pâté counter. Eyeing the full fat soft French brie as though the cat had just been sick, she lighted on the England's Choice selection, and selected. A journalist recommended the Brussels Pâté. 'I can't stand garlic,' she snorted, and selected a chicken, mushroom and white wine cream pâté – British.

We made for the beef. 'I bought this,' she declared, brandishing a bloody piece of Scottish rump, 'because it's £1.50 off.' A tub of Tesco's own-brand strawberry yoghurt was chosen. Cress and Essex lettuce were tossed into the basket. Battered cod was rejected in favour of Tesco's own-brand British bacon, as the baroness made for the checkout counter, to ripples of applause and admiration.

Lady Thatcher took this as a call for an encore. Breaking from her arranged plan, she decided to do a reprise shop: a quick twirl through the fruit and vegetables again for tomatoes and conference pears. Then she was headed off by the soft toiletries and diverted to counter 19.

Ah, fateful day for Shirley Taylor! Looking only slightly tense, the operative at counter 19 did everything right. Each purchase was rung on the till, and Shirley remembered to offer her Special Customer a Tesco Clubcard, which the baroness, unconvinced, signed and popped into her handbag. Then she took out her Midland chequebook. The till said £21.44, a sum Shirley Taylor will never forget.

'And your cheque guarantee card?' she asked the baroness pleasantly.

Lady Thatcher looked blank. Panic entered the eyes of her staff. Lady Thatcher, suddenly shaky, offered Shirley the Clubcard she had just been given.

'No, a cheque guarantee card,' said Shirley, firmly but politely. 'It's an awful nuisance, but it's the rules. I can't put it through without it.' Disbelieve me if you like, but it looked as though Lady Thatcher did not know what a cheque guarantee card was. Plastic has not entered this baroness's life. A minder said, desperately, to Shirley, 'I promise you there won't be any problems,' but Shirley knew the rules.

'Well, I'll have to go round putting everything back,' said Lady Thatcher. Tesco executives groaned inwardly. Then, recovering herself, and in Lady Bracknell tones, the baroness declared: 'Something will have to be done!'

But what? Ah, cash! She opened a purse. It contained £25 and no cards. Shirley Taylor's relief was palpable. Panic over. They presented Lady Thatcher with flowers. She presented her shopping to a minder, and swept away, to applause.

Margaret Thatcher was always good for a colourful sketch. A pantomime figure such as she presented – whether it was Fairy Godmother, Wicked Witch or Widow Twankey, and on a good day she could do all three – had two enormous advantages over lesser members of the Commons cast. First, and obviously, she was colourful, larger-than-life, a walking caricature. Some politicians, and she was one, do regularly deliver the goods.

Just as important, her presence would spice up a column even if she did nothing. The slightest sketch must tell a story; your Thatchers, your Kinnocks, your Enoch Powells or Dennis Skinners have only to walk on to your stage for what it is now fashionable to call a narrative to take shape. Readers know these characters and will react mentally with the appropriate oohs and aahs, 'look-behind-you', 'oh-no-she-isn't' and 'oh yes she is'. As a sketchwriter you buy into a long-running soap opera with whose cast and expected storyline your audience is already familiar. That is one of the reasons why journalism tends to confirm stereotypes (it's easier) and why public figures tend to grow into them (there's no point in confusing people).

My last Commons sketch about Mrs Thatcher was less knockabout than the generality, and I was not unmoved in writing it. It appeared under the headline 'The lady sails proudly away', and again it was just lucky that I happened to be present as she left the Commons for the last time.

Parliament had galloped through remaining business. To watch 170 clauses pass in the twinkling of an eye was breathtaking. The sitting was then suspended while the Lords passed what the Commons had sent, and sent it back. Mrs Thatcher walked alone into the Chamber.

After years of making personal remarks about the former Prime Minister, perhaps I am permitted to say that yesterday she looked lovely. She wore very dark green with black collars and a diamond star on one lapel. She seemed quite composed. John Major was absent. Mrs Thatcher made for the government front bench, which was empty. What, we wondered rather nervously, had she in mind?

The table on which the dispatch box sits where she had stood so many thousands of times was littered with papers. Mrs Thatcher walked up and tidied the mess. She put the documents together into neat little piles, glanced at her handiwork, and left . . .

I quit the *Times* sketch at the end of 2001. After more than thirteen years I was keen not to court the danger of getting into a rut. One does not want to become stale, and I was still enjoying sketchwriting when I stopped: the right time to move.

But it was sad to leave the *Times* room. Parliament doesn't matter these days so much that the parliamentary sketch can be thought secure in a modern newspaper. I had been proud to join the small gang who have kept this anachronism going, and going strong. It is like sailing an old ketch and keeping her shipshape. To whomever you finally hand her over, you want her, and therefore her skipper, to fare well.

So I told myself I did not want my successor to falter, and was surprised to find that I meant it. For a competitive person it was unusual to find no part of me hoping to hear that the next man was not as good; and unusual now to find no part of me less than overjoyed to watch him becoming a success.

17. The Blue Chips

On my wall in London is a big, framed colour print of a portrait of the Blue Chip Supper Club, seated in Tristan Garel-Jones's dining room near Westminster. It is a portrait of my friends in politics. Most I came to know while I was still their colleague in the House. After I left and while I sketched them for *The Times*, they took power. They kept it for seven years. For a while my friends were the governing ascendancy. Then they were thrown out angrily by a country impatient for the era they had done much to arrange. Though large, this then is a portrait in miniature of a political era, a short and transitional time, and the men who shaped it. Many are forgotten already. But at least none is in prison.

I had not long joined the club – a late entrant – when that picture was painted. If I seem to be smiling it is perhaps at the invitation we had just received from our parliamentary colleague Alan Clark, then MP for Plymouth Sutton, to visit him ('in the club charabanc', he suggested) at his home in Saltwood Castle. This was easy to find, said his note, which Tristan read out. The gate was easy to spot, and we would immediately see that the drive up to his castle had at the appointed time been lined in our honour with naked black eunuchs, their heads shaven bare, each inclining towards the road an outstretched palm on which there would be a line of cocaine of the finest quality, to sniff as we passed.

'Blue Chip Supper Club'. It sounds so smug now. The very name breathes the breezy confidence our cohort of young MPs was able to feel in its talents and its prospects in the early eighties. We were not really Thatcherites, a type we thought obsessive, dim or rather naff. Nor were most of us rabid anti-Thatcherites: these, fronted by pre-1979 'wet' grandees such as Ian Gilmour or clever jokers such as Julian Critchley, seemed to us to lack any firm footing in the future.

So we were not really her enemies either. Even those of us most sympathetic to the Thatcher enterprise thought it smart neither to deplore nor worship, but display a faintly amused regard for the fierce, blinkered little woman who was doing the necessary dirty work. Heavens, somebody had to.

Her rank certainties appalled us. Were we to occupy her position, we felt, we would do it with an apologetic grin. We saw the joke in politics. She had no sense of humour at all. We saw the ambivalences in life. To her it was all so simple. We met unpleasant duty with a polite handshake, ready to wash hands afterwards. She met it in a furious embrace.

We did not assume our opponents were mad or bad, nor our allies sane or good. She saw politics as total war on all fronts against the forces of evil and folly. We saw allegiances as shifting, ambivalent things. For her, in a world where people were for or against you and all but the feeble or infirm of purpose took sides, loyalty, absolute loyalty, was the highest virtue.

Among us it was uncool to view our own voters and workers with more than paternal affection or less than shudder. She disapproved of that. We frankly distrusted the mob. To her it was the final court of appeal.

It wasn't that we didn't think her clever, but we thought her unreflective. She led, we were sure, an unexamined life. To her things were right or wrong. To us they were agreeable or otherwise – or often something in between. To us duties sometimes conflicted even in the breasts of the strong. To her only the weak would agonize.

The smirk I described hovering over Chris Patten's Conservative Research Department while she was Opposition leader had not quite vanished. It was very faint, slowly fading and as insubstantial as the Cheshire Cat's smile, and you might just have caught it in a corner by the ceiling in the red-walled dining room of Tristan Garel-Jones's elegant townhouse at Catherine Place, SW1.

Robert (Lord) Cranborne's artist sister, Rose Cecil, captured us wonderfully as a group in that picture. The portrait was painted in the early eighties, not long after John Major (as well as I) had been invited to join: afterthoughts on the part of the founder members, neither as rich nor as distinguished nor as well born as many of the others. I have rolled-up sleeves. The others have cuff-links. My shirt (cotton-polyester mix) has a pocket. Gentlemen's shirts do not have pockets. What would they put in them – bus tickets?

Each of us sat for Rose separately for an afternoon in her riverside flat near Rotherhithe, where I first conceived the ambition to buy a place by the Thames myself, and later did. Then she grouped us together in the imagination, at Tristan's. And it is true that Tristan's house was our haunt.

On the extreme left in the foreground is her brother. Robert Cranborne was heir to the title of his aged father Lord Salisbury, and to Hatfield House, and then MP for the constituency where the village of Cranborne is situated: Dorset South. John Major himself put in for the parliamentary candidature there but said he realized he hadn't a chance when Robert, also applying, walked into the room and all present stood up.

Clever, interested, proud, restless, suddenly and eccentrically principled, Robert was capable of tormenting himself – and the whips – with fierce attachments to ancient obligations. He gave that convincing impression of carelessness of status which a perch on the top rung can lend, and it may have been genuine, but I think he craved instrumentality. Confident that he already was somebody who mattered, he wanted to do things which mattered. His ancestors had been advisers to Tudor monarchs, and Robert loved smoky rooms and conspiratorial conversations – perhaps too much, for he was Machiavellian only by turns, but with a strong sense of honour and the occasional terrible, career-wrecking access of idealism. He would have done well as one of the Afghan warlords he used to admire and visit.

Robert was to become a whip then quit in protest at Margaret Thatcher's Northern Ireland policy which he thought sold out the Unionists; then a doubting ally of John Major, then leader and finally shadow leader of the House of Lords. Major's successor, William Hague, sacked him while Tony Blair was reforming the Upper Chamber, for secretly negotiating terms. He was an architect of the compromise which followed, allowing a body of hereditary peers to stay on indefinitely, but he chose not to join them.

Standing behind Robert is Michael Ancram, in reality the Earl of Ancram (a Scottish title), but at that time Scottish Tory MP too. Nearly twenty years later he was to throw his hat into the ring for the party leadership and if Kenneth Clarke had not entered the race I would have supported him. Moderate and affable yet somehow exuding a sense of belief, he belonged to the humane rather than the cynical school of middle-of-the-roaders. He could play the guitar and sing 'Blowing in the Wind' – an ability which within the parliamentary Conservative Party made him almost unique.

Some of the press said Michael was no great brain but I always thought him too deft to be stupid, though as a platform speaker he did fortissimo like an impassioned guinea pig. He ended up in the next century as Shadow Foreign Secretary, deputy leader of Iain Duncan Smith's Conservative Party, and token of its sanity. I remember standing at the Institute of Directors as Ken Clarke, also pitching for the leadership, took a gratuitous sideswipe at Michael. Silly arse, I thought. There goes your best potential lieutenant.

For some of us, Michael serves the same function in the twenty-first-century Tory Party as those pit canaries sent down coal mines to keel over at the first whiff of poison-gas. As long as such coves can still breathe in the shadow Cabinet, the old party remains habitable by humans.

Standing in his shirtsleeves next to Michael is Peter Fraser, now Lord Fraser of Carmyllie, then – for those were the days when there used to be many Scottish Conservative MPs – the Member for South Angus. Peter was quiet, clever and nice. Mrs Thatcher made him Solicitor General for Scotland, then Lord Advocate. Major made him Minister for Energy. He was a background man: Rose Cecil's positioning of us all was shrewd – or lucky.

She has made William Waldegrave, lounging in front of John Major, look positively Byronic – but then he sometimes did. William was the kind of young man whom a certain type of society hostess would describe as 'frightfully clever' – but who really was. It is even claimed he thought up the poll tax.

Others have found William edgy and proud, but I never did. He was more than a brain: he was a mind. On the upward part of his trajectory William reached Minister of State in the Foreign Office in Thatcher's final years; for Major he served as Secretary of State for Health, Minister of Agriculture and Chief Secretary.

He became associated in the media's imagination – and it was mostly imagination – with the arms-to-Iraq scandal, a scandal which was about as big a scandal as the Cats-have-fleas! scandal, rating about 10,000 pages in the popular journalism of the time, and about ten words in any history which may one day be written of the age; and associated, too, with having told the Scott Enquiry into the affair that ministers sometimes lie.

This blindingly obvious truth was then seized upon by the news-papers as a revelatory 'gaffe' indicative of the slipperiness of politicians generally and William in particular. Of course it was evidence for the opposite: that competent ministers do have to lie sometimes, and that William Waldegrave was an unusually honest one because he admitted it. Something I have noticed about people of high intelligence and personal honour is that they are more unguarded than the rest.

When Scott reported, more blue chip reputations than William's were on the line. Nicholas Lyell (standing in front of the curtain, to the right of Major) was to find himself first in the firing line beside Waldegrave. He was a legal minister and it fell to him to instruct Michael Heseltine to sign what the press came to call a 'gagging order' in the trial which became central to the arms-to-Iraq story. As a barrister, Nick was a smooth-talking man, too smooth-talking for his own good.

A lawyer's skill is – must be – to impress other lawyers, for judges are lawyers too. That they raise the hackles of the generality does not seem to have occurred to team selectors in the sport of politics. Nick seemed to me a decent and affable person, doomed to sound like a lawyer. As with his fellow-barrister Michael Howard (no blue chipper he, but a passionate moral conservative), his merits as a human being were horribly obscured by the patina of paid advocacy which no former barrister can shake off. It isn't clever to look clever in British politics.

Seated at Major's back in the picture is Robert Atkins (or Ratkins, as we liked to call him), who was anything but silky. A former London local councillor, then a Lancashire MP, he finally became, under Major, a minister of state. Ratkins seemed to be an eternal parliamen-tary private secretary: acting as a sort of appointed but unpaid bag-carrier for a minister, a curious British custom dubbed by one appalled political scientist as 'fagging at forty'.

Everybody liked him and he could take a joke, though he did once look peeved when I asked if he would mind my describing him in a *Times* sketch as a brilliantined stick-insect. His enthusiastically matey if sometimes clumsy conversational manner concealed his pleasant art:

to be one of nature's golf-caddies. This is an important breed in parliamentary life. There was a time when Ratkins was one of the few colleagues with whom Major felt relaxed.

Beside Robert, wearing a pink shirt, sits our artist's only mistake. Not that John Watson was not a good and capable fellow – one of the nicest in the club – but that the ethereal spotlight which seems to fall on him in Rose's fairytale picture, never fell on him in real politics. MP for Skipton, he left Parliament for business. I don't think his elbows were sharp enough, or that he cared to sharpen them. He genuinely chose to go. People who quit before it is evident they are going nowhere are more convincing than those who do not discern the family they want to spend more time with until career failure has blown the fog away, and suddenly they notice their wife.

Alex Pollock (standing behind John Watson with a coffee mug) was assisted in his decision to leave Westminster by the electorate of Moray. His nice, loose fawn jumper, which will have been 100 per cent Scottish lambswool, seems to say everything about him. A gentle, courteous Scot and good listener who could exude an air of learning without saying anything learned – indeed without saying anything at all – Alex had the knack of staring thoughtfully at his shoes and appearing considered. I think he probably was.

To the right of William Waldegrave sits Chris Patten. Some of the people in this portrait were to be rather surprised by the success that came their way, not least John Major; but Chris would have been surprised if it had not, and so would we. He was not notably vain and not pompous at all, but after so much experience shaping policy in Opposition, Chris spoke at dictation speed and as though teams of craftsmen were chiselling his words into stone even as he uttered them. 'There is no such thing,' I noted him declaring over the soup at Tristan's, 'as a' (pause) '*voteless*' (pause) '*economic*' (pause) '*recovery*'. *Chisel-chisel*. We all, including John Major, nodded wisely. When, at the general election of 1997, an electorate enjoying a whopper of an economic recovery carelessly dispatched Major, did the outgoing Prime Minister remember?

A decade and a half later I visited Chris for Christmas in Hong Kong, almost his last as Governor. He was under something close to a siege of resentment from the British business community there. They thought his late moves to encourage democracy in the colony, which infuriated Beijing, threatened confidence in the territory's future. About Margaret Thatcher Chris was now warm – his old boss had been firm in his support – much warmer than John Major was able to be about her. But towards Ted Heath Chris could not conceal his bitterness, though he tried. Thatcher's predecessor used Government House and its hospitality as a luxurious stopping-off point for his business trips to Beijing; then he would join the Communist Chinese leadership in denouncing the Governor. One of Chris's staff told me of an occasion when, after the London-to-Hong Kong leg of his flight (no doubt from the dizzying effect of the long flight and high altitude), Ted had had to be literally carried by detectives into the waiting government Daimler.

There was something wrong with Government House in Hong Kong, some kind of a bad spell cast on it. The building was of low, long and cold design (a Japanese architect, apparently), set in generous grounds like a small park, bordered by towering skyscrapers which poked their sides into this green handkerchief of imperial history.

I slept in a splendid bedroom – Prince Charles had stayed there – and everything was . . . well, 'gracious' is the ghastly word. But sorrow and anger hung in the air. I do not know if Chris was personally unhappy – his friend and patron's government back in London was teetering in tragi-comic fashion towards its doom – or whether sorrow just went with a last Governor's job. Chris's rage at the British expatriate community seemed to be gnawing at his inside, though they were only behaving as British expatriates always do: selfishly. He arranged for me to visit various English big-wheels in the business community. They all told me how they hated him and everything he stood for, particularly the prospect of a diminution in their own incomes.

My memory will be for ever of small, disconsolate Chinese people, the Governor's domestic staff, their own futures uncertain, on all fours scraping and cleaning the patches on the immense cold white oriental hall carpet where Chris and his wife Lavender's famous little dogs, Whisky and Soda, had left their tiny heaps of dogshit; and of Chris looking tense, and being jolly, and rather desperately soliciting the friendly handshakes and wellwishes which Chinese passers-by in the street (but not his own countrymen in their grand Hong Kong boardrooms and exclusive clubs) pressed upon him.

Everything about Hong Kong seemed to dash the spirits, though Chris's work and achievement there were almost noble.

Beside Chris in the picture sits Douglas Hogg in red braces, looking rather sleeker than in real life this little wart-hog of a politician usually did. The beaming smile is also untypical. A sort of chippy disgruntlement was more characteristic. Like his father, the late Lord Hailsham (better known as Quintin Hogg), Douglas was hard to place on the left or right in politics but was more decidedly his own man than anybody else in the picture.

When I first encountered Douglas I took an instant dislike to him. I had been asked by some West Derbyshire Tories (who I think had worshipped his father) whether I would invite him to come up and speak in the constituency, his Lincolnshire constituency being only a couple of hours' drive away and part of our East Midlands region. I approached Douglas rather hesitantly in a division lobby while we were voting, and asked.

'What's your main town?' he grunted.

'Matlock,' I said. His jaw jutted.

'Not bloody likely. Too bloody far.'

This response upset me. But in time I realized that Douglas always reacted like this: honestly, you could say.

Some years later I encountered the same traits in his late father, who had just ceased to be Lord Chancellor, and, an old man and very lame, was hobbling down a Westminster corridor some way behind me when I passed through swing doors and checked before letting them shut, in case anyone was coming. I waited, holding the door open. He took a long time getting there – time enough for me to think up what I thought was a smart but respectful remark from a smart but respectful young man. 'Never mind, sir,' I said, as, apologizing for his lameness, he hobbled through the door, 'what you lose in speed, you gain in dignity.'

He stopped dead in his tracks and swung round on his stick, glaring at me. 'I don't think,' he barked, 'anyone. Has ever. Called. *Me*. Dignified. Thank *God*.' And he hobbled on.

The son was no different. Douglas never calculated whether his response would dismay or flatter and, though from a morally conservative background, a man who delighted in quibbling and a born lawyer, he was astonishingly open-minded and seemed able to approach any question absolutely straight-on. From the press gallery nearly twenty years later I saw the Tory jaws all round him drop as he declared – as though it were simply obvious – that if the requirement on a new MP's part to declare an oath of loyalty to the Queen was disbarring the Sinn Fein men whom voters in Northern Ireland had elected from taking their seats and representing their constituents, then the requirement should be dropped. He didn't see what it had to do with anything, he said.

Douglas was no revolutionary, nor by disposition any kind of liberal. He simply refused to approach discussion as a team game. He listened to the arguments, careless how it might be thought he would or should jump. This is surprisingly rare in politics, and in Douglas was born of a tremendous intellectual self-confidence and an alarming tendency to produce snap judgements, even when he was wrong. I found it admirable, and his honesty admirable, and his brusqueness – once one learned not to take it personally – tolerable.

But he talked and looked and sounded like a caricature of an out-of-touch and arrogant Tory, and Labour MPs dislike him until they study him and his record more carefully. Journalists have generally seen only the apparent, and disregarded him. Major was to make him, in time, Minister of Agriculture; but he had often had a hard time in the House and at public meetings, and a thin time in the press, and it's rather a pity. As I write he's still an MP; his wife Sarah, who became a key adviser to John Major, is in the House of Lords.

Next to Douglas behind the table, sitting with head in hand, is Ian Lang.

Years later, John Major, as Prime Minister, with William Waldegrave and Nick Lyell, faced a stormy Commons with their survival uncertain as the Scott Enquiry into the arms-for-Iraq affair reported. Ian was then President of the Board of Trade: a fancy title for Secretary of State for Trade and Industry. To Ian fell the task of making the statement outlining the Scott Report, just published – and in the hands of Robin Cook, leading for the Opposition, for a few hours beforehand.

Cook had skimmed the report at speed for every rock he could chuck. He was brilliant, ostentatiously brilliant. Ian was quietly masterful. Drawing every drop of comfort he could, and some he couldn't, from the report, he smoothed, downplayed, soothed and steadied the Government benches, confounded the press and helped cheat the Labour Party of the Tory débâcle for which they had hoped.

Had you asked me, as I sat for that portrait, to choose from its ranks a Prime Minister, it would have been Lang, though I've never been a close friend. Classy without a hint of class in the way that an educated Scot can be, a good and undogmatic brain and calm hand, and in some indefinable sense a *modern* man (he had been a scriptwriter for the iconoclastic sixties TV satire series *That Was The Week That Was*, was a talented stage mimic and understood broadcasting), Ian had everything, I suppose, except pizazz.

Behind Ian stands Richard Needham, bewilderingly a Jewish MP with an Irish peerage (he is sixth earl of Kilmorey) and an English seat: Chippenham. We all loved him and his noisily good-natured bounce, though his volubility and his enthusiasm could be staggering and his language blister the wallpaper. Richard was one of nature's salesmen. It could have been vacuum cleaners, but instead he turned his talents to the economic prospects of Northern Ireland when he was made a minister there by Margaret Thatcher, whom he was embarrassed to be overheard calling 'the old cow' on a mobile telephone. (She took it well, telling journalists she was lucky 'if that's the worst they're calling me'.)

On form, Needham is a nonpareil raconteur. He described to us over dinner how he had been entertained as an English gentleman in the grand house of the German parents of his bride-to-be. Asked whether he minded his daughter marrying a foreigner, Richard's intended's father replied, 'At least he is not a Jew.'

To hear Richard talk about Ulster at Tristan's house, you might have thought he had stumbled upon El Dorado. Anyway, he stumbled finally upon the board of GEC, a privy councillorship and a knighthood.

Behind Richard – half way out of the door, it seems (and it is said Rose Cecil was punishing him for being unhelpful about his sittings) – stands John Patten, looking, as ever and as the parliamentary sketchwriters had it, like an outraged hairdresser, but in fact a geography don from Oxford. He was known affectionately by Chris Patten as John No-Relation and in those early days seemed thoughtful, teasing and funny. Ambition – or office – soured him. Major made him Education Minister, a post in which he became a puffed, thin-skinned and angry figure. Of all my colleagues and blue chip comrades, John Patten was the one made unhappiest by politics.

Seated in the bottom right-hand corner, smoking as he endlessly did, is Tristan. Of those sitting round that table Tristan is the most moving writer, though his entire literary output would not fill one *Spectator* magazine. He thought of himself as a Machiavellian schemer when, really, he was a Welsh dreamer.

In Thornton Wilder's *The Merchant of Yonkers* (adapted into the musical *Hello Dolly*) Dolly Levy, matchmaker extraordinaire, declares that 'I've always been a woman who arranges things.' Tristan's great ambition was to be the Dolly Levy of a Tory government. He it was, really, who had arranged the Blue Chip Supper Club, kept it going, fed and watered it and stocked its cellars with good wine in which he took great pride and of which he drank not a drop. His wife, Catali, was a well-born Spanish lady and a devout Catholic. Tristan was a Welsh, atheist, nonconformist, teetotal chain-smoker. On the cornerstone of the chapel he caused to be built for his wife on their estate in Spain, he had engraved (I translate) 'From TGJ, an unbeliever, to Catali, a believer in whom he believes'.

He was forever drawing hearers off into a conspiratorial huddle. John made him, finally, deputy chief whip. He rendered good service to Major's administration, and one should not overlook (as historians will) his deft work in cheering, consoling and jollying people along; but as an *éminence grise* Tristan was an excess of *éminence* and not enough *grise*: there was a flash of scarlet in the lining of his grey cloak. Like Peter Mandelson, Tristan wanted too much to be known for his role as insider-fixer. To be a wholly convincing fixer you need to be genuinely dull; Tristan was secretly exotic. But he did act as an effective lightning-conductor: with his fondness for Europe and undivided (if often sorely tested) loyalty to John Major, he became the anti-European Tories' favourite demon.

And then there was Jocelyn. Jocelyn Cadbury is pictured in the portrait as himself a portrait on the wall (though in reality there is no picture there) because he was by then dead.

From among a bunch not short of promise, one of the most promising, and one to whom I always felt drawn, was Jocelyn Cadbury. The youngest son of the famous Birmingham chocolate-making family, and like his family a Quaker, Jocelyn was about my age when elected for the marginal seat of Birmingham Northfield, where his family home stood. He and I were among the youngest. He was a handsome man: bright-eyed, fair, spare and fit. He had everything going for him, including the sense not to draw attention to that; only the hint of intellectual impatience and an intolerance of the morally second-rate betrayed the brittleness I later detected.

But he was not rude or unkind. If he was rich, he never made anything of it. If he was clever, he never wore his scholarship on his sleeve. If he was idealistic, this was betrayed only by quiet intensity in the causes he took up. One of the earliest of these was the plight of the Banaban islanders.

This is not the place for a background to that dispute which involved Britain's treatment of a remote Pacific community whose phosphate-rich land was more useful to Britain than its inhabitants. It was a story I never wholly mastered. But Jocelyn, whose undergraduate subject at Cambridge and whose abiding interest was anthropology, knew it inside out. He led a Commons rebellion against the Government's plans, at its core a group of us in the 1979 intake. We thought it stirring stuff, and ourselves wonderfully brave, at the time – the whips enlarging our pretensions by acting as though the very survival of a new Conservative government was being undermined, and issuing dark threats about what we were doing to our career prospects.

I admired Jocelyn's leadership of this campaign and we became, not close friends, but friendly. He and I shared a three-backbencher office at Westminster and he would laugh at some of my constituency cases, and reprove me for struggling (sometimes and for whole evenings drafting speeches and articles, never made or published) to reconcile my declared support for capital punishment in principle with my objections to it in practice. He, being a Quaker, was an abolitionist and thought I should cease quibbling and join him.

I went to visit him in his family's imposing but strangely faded mansion in what looked like a municipal park in Northfield – until you realized it was enclosed and contained the Cadburys' house. Within, the air was musty. Jocelyn's father was very, very old and was wheeled around by a nurse. In her seventies, his mother was much younger. Around the walls were trophies of his father's youth, including, I remember, a stuffed Kodiak bear's head, shot by a Cadbury in the Aleutian Islands near the beginning of the twentieth century. In the grounds – 'garden' would be too suburban – were many cannons, placed in odd positions on the grass and pointing in all directions under the trees. Jocelyn said his father had collected them.

One summer, when I was with my family in Spain, he diverted from an Iberian tour to stay with us in the Pyrenees where by then my family lived. On a cloudless day he and I climbed a high hill called Taga, had a picnic, and stared long and silently at the stupendous view. It is one of those happy, peaceful moments which for some reason lodges itself in recollection. We drove down to the Costa Brava at Pals where my family have a seaside flat and stayed there a night. The next morning we went swimming, deciding to strike quite far out to sea.

As we swam together Jocelyn confided (it is sometimes easier for two people to talk – as in a car, driving – when both pairs of eyes are occupied by some external focus) that he had just spent an awkward week with his girlfriend. It seemed they had been staying in a fairly grand home, in north-western England I think, with bedrooms off corridors, he in one, she in another. After making love in her bed, he had made his way back down the corridor to his own room, and she had found this unromantic and been hurt. This was troubling him. I cannot remember making any kind of comment but sometimes I, too, find it hard to sleep peacefully with anyone else in the bed, so I probably said so.

After swimming we showered, changed and set out by car back inland to the mountains. I was driving. We needed petrol and I pulled off the road into a wayside filling station and filled up. Driving back out on to the road I failed to notice a car speeding towards us from my left and there was nearly an accident. I was surprised how much this threw Jocelyn, who yelled at me for my inattention. 'You could have killed me,' he shouted.

Not so very long after, he killed himself. He walked out into the grounds of his house at Northfield and shot himself. I thought of all his father's cannons.

Nobody knew why, and I do not. 'Shock' is always expressed at untimely death, but Jocelyn's really was shocking. Some people said he had been over-conscientious, having taken the strains and conflicts of political life, and his own responsibilities, more to heart than most. His workload, too, was greater than mine – this I realized while sharing an office. Northfield had its quota of social and economic problems, Jocelyn used to pitch in regularly on constituents' behalf, and he knew that at the end of all this he might anyway lose the seat at a future general election, and have to start all over again.

But these are difficulties with which scores of MPs struggle, and they do not kill themselves. Some friends spoke of an earlier break-down and severe depression at Cambridge, about which I had not been aware when I knew him, and not suspected. I cannot say I saw anything unbalanced in his behaviour during the years we knew each other. He struck me as a rational man.

A memorial service was held for Jocelyn at Bourneville. I decided to struggle up by train, changing at Birmingham New Street for a suburban service, which involved more than an hour's wait.

It was lunchtime. I walked out of New Street station, turned right and, looking for a sandwich and drink, resolved to take the first pub I encountered. This was called (as I remember) the Railway – or some such – and was a shabby place. I walked over to the bar, bought a pint of bitter and a none-too-fresh cheese sandwich, and sat down near the window. A couple of middle-aged men at a nearby table struck up conversation with me.

Having left the street, vision and hearing, blunted outside by the noise and glare, resharpen and accustom themselves to the gloom inside and, as the mind stops racing you awaken to the place you have just entered. Its atmosphere, its own quieter sights and sounds, swell and impinge on your consciousness. I realized that this was a gay pub. It was not a very gay gay pub – pretty sad, really – but dress and speech and conversations around me, including the one I was now in, betrayed its type.

'What brings you here?' asked one of the men. I told them I was an MP, a former colleague of Jocelyn Cadbury and a friend, and that I was on my way to his memorial service. His suicide had been a mystery, I said.

'Not a mystery to us,' said one of the men. They went on to claim that Jocelyn was thought to be gay by some in the gay community there, and that he had been seen more than once in the sorts of places which suggested it. 'Everybody knows,' a man said (as 'everybody' always seems to) that the Birmingham newspapers were on to it, and had been asking him questions.

I finished the sandwich and left the pub in time to reach the memorial service, about which I remember nothing, absolutely nothing, except that the conversation I had just been party to was not the tenor of the eulogy.

I know what passes as the gay community well enough to realize that 'everybody knows' all sorts of things, some of which turn out to be true, some to contain an element of truth and a fair few to be absolutely without foundation. And there can sometimes be an element of wishful thinking, too, about the names of those attractive individuals, apparently straight, who are pronounced to be secretly queer as coots. About a good-looking bachelor, much in the public eye, who takes his own life, speculation would arise even if there were no cause for it, and I neither know nor assume that any of what I heard was true. Jocelyn never gave me reason to think it.

Perhaps there was wishful thinking in the interest I felt in that pub conversation. But I hope it was true. I prefer not to believe Jocelyn's life ended in madness or chaos or stupidity, but instead in a desperate but rational resort. What I had just heard seemed to explain something which badly needed explaining – gave, in my eyes, a sort of dignity to Jocelyn's last actions. It made me feel more tenderly towards him. I added his name to my broken ribs on Clapham Common, as reasons to be braver.

We had stuck together, some of us, we who were from the 1979 intake. Part of the glue was a confidence that we were rather a bright bunch, and some of us were. Tristan believed that, there being no opposition worthy of the name, the Tory Party would have to produce its own tough questioners: us. William Waldegrave had said in his maiden speech that there were some things in politics which you did not because they conformed with any ideology or strategy but because they seemed the right thing to do. This remark, made in heady Thatcherite days thick with the smoke of ideological battle, was thought faintly shocking. Gradually our sense of collective danger-ousness faded.

Now the Blue Chip Club has not met for years. As John Major's premiership rolled on, differences arose. There were no grand rows –

we were too civilized for that – but some among us felt John had let them down, and John probably felt some among us had let him down, and I am really not sure whether Chris is a Conservative at all any more, or how wedded Tristan feels to the twenty-first-century Tory Party. I am fairly sure, though, that even today few of us can look at that portrait without feeling a general affection for the whole gang, and for the hopes we had, not just for our own careers, but for Conservative government.

As the gang's fortunes rose (and they were already on the rise when Rose painted) our dinner meetings began to change. When I first joined, the conversation would be boisterous but earnest. It was rather like a turbulent symposium in which every tenth word was 'fuckpig' but whose participants were genuinely trying to think their way through to answers and didn't care what they said. Those were heady days. So much seemed doable. Nothing was unthinkable. We Blue Chips were not in power.

One by one the members accepted office – in time Cabinet office – until half the Club seemed to be in the Cabinet and half the Cabinet seemed to be in the Club; and one of us was Prime Minister. I, meanwhile, had left the House and become a journalist, though I carried on attending the dinners and never leaked.

Conversation began to degenerate. The ribaldry and joshing and the violent language remained, but the underlying seriousness, the sense of honest inquiry, grew weaker. We were in power now. Egos and rivalries jostled, ideas took a back seat. Less and less were the big questions about compass bearings for the long term asked. Members of the group were preoccupied with how to get through to the end of the month, let alone the century, and it all felt so much less easy. Problems loomed larger and events felt more compelling. Constraints and dangers filled our thoughts. Who had time for theory now? Survival was the watchword. People who published pamphlets were nerds. Blue sky thinking was no longer for Blue Chips. My friends were the government.

And so the Blue Chip Supper Club died.

18. Lampooner of My Friends' Woes

Though lazily we talk of John Major as rising without trace, his competence and discretion registered early but in the corner of the eye. Rose Cecil's portrait places him off-centre yet dominant; noticed yet turning away from the light. And so at first he was though I was late to notice. As luck would have it my job would be to watch him move into the light and then out. I was meant to be funny about it.

Never be the hired lampooner of a friend's woes. You will finish by pulling your punches or worse. You will struggle to get the tone right. As *The Times*'s parliamentary sketchwriter I struggled often painfully for most of the seven years of John Major's premiership to be honest and funny about his travails – I owed that to my readers – without forsaking a wish to be fair to a friend. It was a curious position, mine up there above their heads. There I was, my gang in power, chronicling their noontide, their late afternoon, their internal mutinies and finally their sunset and night. At one point I even found myself sketching the delivery of a leader's conference speech, a passage of which I had written myself.

John Major was a friend, never a close friend. I am unsure whether he has close friends, though I know optimists who claim that status. His reputation among the caricaturists as ordinary is shockingly off-target. John is a strange, strange man. As a stage performance, perhaps, grey: but there are shades of grey (three words I almost succeeded in persuading him to make the title of his autobiography) and their tortured combination can produce a bizarre and fractured picture.

The first time I met John Major properly I altogether failed to notice him. In the early eighties he was one of the small cast of characters in a weekend farce at Cranborne in Dorset. I used often to entertain friends by describing the farce. Years later, someone who was there pointed out that my account left out the most interesting fact of all: that among the weekend party had been the next Prime Minister. His presence had entirely slipped my mind.

The weekend had been organized by Robert Cranborne and his

wife, Hannah. The house party consisted of a small group of youngish MPs. One was Tristan. Another was Virginia Bottomley, later Major's Health Secretary. She had not long been returned in a recent by-election and was still a backbencher, though PPS to Chris Patten. On her arrival at Westminster she had aroused immediate interest in the Members' Smoking Room, not all of it on account of her political promise.

Virginia's husband, the junior minister Peter Bottomley, was invited to Cranborne too. And of course there was the one who I always forgot in subsequent accounts had been there.

Robert was the local MP. The catch behind our invitation was that on the first evening we must sing for our supper: Robert's guests were to form a panel at an amateur *Any Questions?* session for his local Conservative Association members, to be held in the village hall at a small place called Wool.

The team travelled down on the Friday. Robert drove us from Westminster to Wool in the afternoon in his Range-Rover. We were late. Robert hit the road to Dorset as though he were in the Dakar rally. It was lucky Virginia's husband joined us only later. He was the minister for road safety.

To keep our spirits up on the perilous journey to Wool, somebody proposed a game for our secret entertainment during the *Any Questions?* which Robert was to chair. At first it was a joke, but in the end we all dared one another to go ahead. The idea was that each of us would be allocated one 'silly fact', the challenge being to introduce the fact into our *Any Questions?* reply. This was to be done deadpan and inconspicuously. Wool was to suspect nothing.

The silly facts were these: (1) Anne Boleyn had six fingers on one hand; (2) 18 per cent of the British public regularly share a bath; (3) frogs eat with their eyes shut; (4) Upper Volta has been renamed Burkina Faso, 'the land of wise men'.

By the time we filed in, to applause (the entire hall rising respectfully as their MP, Lord Cranborne, entered), and sat down at a long table on the hall's small stage, the whip was already having trouble keeping a straight face.

The first question, 'What does the panel think of women's lib?', was from a lady in the audience and was given to me for reply. I went straight over the wire. Unlike some countries, I said, Upper Volta, for example, renamed Burkina Faso, or 'country of wise men', we British did admit the existence of wise women . . . Margaret Thatcher . . . courage and determination, etc . . . Tristan's shoulders began to heave.

Virginia came next. Asked her opinion on the safety of nuclear power, she said she distrusted the doomsday theorists who predicted we should all end up with horrifying deformities or six fingers, like Anne Boleyn. Tristan's eyes were watering. Members of the audience remarked afterwards on the strange levity of the panel that night.

I now remember, but for years forgot, that it was John Major, then a junior DHSS minister, who came next. Frogs shutting their eyes when eating was his challenge. I have not the least recollection of what he said, but the challenge was successfully met, without even raising an eyebrow in the audience. The frogs must have slipped in unnoticed, as he had.

I remember only that Tristan appeared to be choking. When his turn came he was barely able to speak. He says he dared not bring the bathing habits of Britons into his reply or he would have cracked up. We just about accepted this. Robert, however, placed a white feather on his plate at breakfast next morning. By then Peter Bottomley had joined us. We had to explain the feather to him. He was sorry to have missed the game.

Though the surroundings at Cranborne were grand the company was relaxed. Hannah kept a pet cockatiel free-range at Cranborne Lodge (source of the feather). Something about my hair appealed to this bird. Try expatiating earnestly at dinner on the state of the economy with a cockatiel sitting on your head and digging in its claws.

Some days later, Peter was at the dispatch box answering a question on public transport. I have the Hansard before me as I write: column ten. Alf Dubs (Lab, Battersea) complained that the bus lane in Park Lane was clogged . . .

MR PETER BOTTOMLEY: I have been down Park Lane on a bus. I took a sandwich. It was unfinished when I reached the other end. Unlike frogs, which eat with their eyes closed, I had mine open. Neither the bus nor other traffic was held up.

In the two next questions the minister wondered, with the wise men of Burkina Faso, why his department had taken powers over bus lanes. To Labour's Tony Banks, who quoted statistics, Bottomley despaired of figures such as the number of fingers Anne Boleyn possessed, or the percentage of the population sharing a bath and proposed that we examine problems case by case.

To suggest that future generations will read old Hansards at all is pushing it a bit. But if anyone should, and wonders just what possessed the Transport Minister on that particular afternoon, the explanation lies in this story.

Dared by John Major to tell Mrs Thatcher about Bottomley's amazing *tour de force*, Tristan redeemed himself by doing so. 'It's the best thing I've ever heard about him,' she replied sadly.

By the time I started *The Times* parliamentary sketch in 1988, John Major was a heavyweight and we Blue Chips were sensing, in an overblown empress who as Prime Minister was lashing increasingly wildly about, a regime approaching its last years. I think we sensed, too, that our time was coming.

When I had left the Commons for the media two years earlier our club was still only a tributary to the mainstream. I had offered to quit and members had discussed whether membership was for life, and whether, if it was, there might be dinners set aside for 'country members' who were no longer in active politics, so that the real politicians could sometimes meet without us. But the feeling had been strong that there should be only one kind of member and one kind of dinner. Potential conflicts of interest were only dimly sensed. After all, I (for instance) was not then directly covering Parliament in my work and none of us was Prime Minister.

Gradually, as Blue Chips rose, a feeling that we needed to be careful about each other rose too. Not only did nobody ever ask me explicitly to go easy on them but I never detected any hint that this was expected. However, I would have thought twice before putting the boot in.

One day, early in his dispatch box career, John Major, as minister with responsibility for the elderly, had got into difficulties in the press when his department's Cold Weather Payment scheme proved ill-adapted to deliver quick help in a sudden cold snap. The press thought he, a reluctant accountant, was being pressured by a more political Prime Minister to alter the scheme. In fact it was the other way round. When the scheme was made more generous, he was, I thought, disconsolate about the bad publicity: 'Maggie steps in'. Not long in the media I asked if he would like me to see the truth was put quietly about. He had been wronged and people should know it.

I was taken aback by his response. That he thought the issue best left unstirred would not have surprised me but the violence with which he hammered this home did. He was not rude, just very, very emphatic, returning again to the point to make sure I had got it: absolutely no spinning in his favour, please – was that quite clear? Not a word against her, not a word supporting him; not a word; nothing.

Wiser than then, I now see why: she, the arch-briefer, might think she was being briefed against. This he knew she could not abide. The very hint of it infuriated her. He knew his best strategy lay in being thought safe, and silent. I was thinking of his immediate interests; he was thinking of his long-term prospects. He knew his face must for the moment remain, as in that portrait, turned from the light.

After that I never tried to guess what my friends would want me to say and, when the scene I was sketching included them, erred always on the side of reticence. Never once did I write that John Major had performed well when I thought otherwise; but sometimes, when a performance had flopped, I wrote less gleefully about a frontbencher's misadventure than I would otherwise have done; or simply wrote about something else.

I think John was underrated as a political leader by critics who overlooked the ball and chain that circumstance, and the Conservative parliamentary party, tied to his ankles. I think his treatment by the press was downright nasty, unprecedented in its ferocity and deeply unfair. I think he had the makings of a political philosophy which was decent, workable and prophetic – and much more marketable than timid and unoriginal advisers, and perhaps he, ever realized. I think that in another situation, as his biographer Anthony Seldon has said, the man and his ideas might have presided over the growth of the new understanding between a modern Conservative Party and the British people for which his successors still cast vainly around. I think that within his Citizen's Charter, much mocked, were the seeds of what later became a ruling idea of the age. And I think his dignity and politeness in the face of adversity and mockery were heroic.

I also think something which I struggle to express, even now, in a way which will not hurt him. A journalist colleague of mine (not a particular critic of Major) once remarked to me that John had some of the qualities of a confidence trickster. I disagreed, and disagree, strongly because a confidence trickster sets out to deceive, and John never set out to deceive. But I see how that view might form. A natural comforter (he could have sold life assurance in spades) his instinct to reassure often outpaced his capacity to deliver.

He had an uncanny ability of implying, as much by listening sympathetically as by anything he said, that he shared your concern. He was softly expert at insinuating that your fears – well understood – could be allayed. I am not sure the question *how* always pushed itself urgently enough to the front of his mind. In the soft glow of the lamplight, private persuasiveness was his great talent, but in the unforgiving glare of the following morning's sun, and *Sun*, and *Daily Telegraph*, indecision was his flaw. Private petulance disfigured him, and a fatal disinclination to turn and face problems undermined all his efforts.

John Major's failures were marked by avoidance, but his two greatest achievements – to keep a Conservative administration in office for seven years beyond its natural life and to reserve indefinitely Britain's position on monetary union – were also a kind of avoidance and (I would argue) a valuable one. Avoidance can be sold in politics (look at Appeasement) but it must be sold with conviction or it will be taken for weakness.

In truth, with John it sometimes was weakness. No platform orator, he had a wonderful ability, one-to-one, to persuade. At meetings of the sympathetic or speaking after dinner, he was and is an almost charismatic speaker. His technique (which I think was unwitting) was more soft soap than hard sell, and depended on eye contact and quite often, even with other men, touch. His shoulder squeeze became famous.

John Major's body language said, 'Trust me: I like you', whereas Tony Blair's says, 'Trust me: you like me'. I doubt he ever knowingly lied, but where the outward impression was of quiet solidity, the reality was inner despair and a panicky slalom down a steepening slope. Yet he lacked neither idealism nor ideas, and never spoke truer than when he recognized candidly in his autobiography that he had something to say in politics but never found his voice.

I think I once found it for him. One of his assistants, Nick True, had asked me if I would put together some thoughts for his conference speech in 1994, and I did. Much of what I wrote – a couple of pages – he used in Bournemouth a few weeks later.

I tried, as I had with Foreign Secretary Jim Callaghan twenty years before, to get inside the mind of the man, to feel its temper. John could be the last to grasp the strength of his own beliefs and my aim was to be truer to his thoughts than he was himself. The speech asked the Conservative Party and the country to 'look for achievements not always in bold plans or crude conflict' but sometimes in small, incremental steps, in conflicts avoided, and in detail – for the devil was often in the detail – because this was also what government entailed. The speech spoke of the need for steadiness, and for grown-up politics.

. . . No windy rhetoric, no facile phrases, no pious cliché, no mock-honest, mock-familiar, adman's speak can conceal the infinite complexity of government . . . the glib phrases, the sound-bites, the ritual conflicts – all these may be the daily stuff of life for the upper one thousand of politics, but to fifty million other people in this country they are utterly irrelevant. My interest is with them.

. . . My trade has never been in adjectives. I shall be patient. I shall be realistic. I shall ask for patience and realism in others. And I shall put my trust in results.

It was strange to watch from the conference floor as John delivered the lines I had written for him. 'Very statesmanlike,' a Tory lady in front of me nodded. I could have kissed her. The speech, designed to reassure rather than enrapture, achieved its purpose and aroused more interest than usual among commentators, some of whom quoted from the passages I had written.

I told nobody. I steered clear of my own bits when sketching the speech for *The Times* and described it as a modest success, which is what it was. Hugo Young in the *Guardian* was intrigued by the passage I had written, calling it 'the ultimate in anti-speeches', which pleased me, for if John Major was to make his mark it must be as an anti-political politician. Some years later I was pleased to see Anthony Seldon's biography describe my passage, which John used in his peroration, as 'written by Major himself, and peculiarly personal to him', and I make no dig at Seldon in mentioning it, because I think he is right: that peroration *was* peculiarly personal to John. It's just that it was written by me.

The man I came to know slightly round Tristan Garel-Jones's table differs from the man he came to appear in a number of respects. Ideologically he was never, in Tory terms, remotely a Thatcherite or even a centrist. More than once, when the argument was about state spending and state intervention, John was way to the left of many of us, and certainly me, in his belief in the role of the state. He saw this role as that of protector of the weak, empowerer of merit where merit lacked muscle, and preserver and promoter of social balance. I never heard him express strong views (and rarely heard him express any views) about defence, foreign affairs or Europe, but his general outlook was marked by mild scepticism about any adventure or international plan. I only ever noticed real passion over welfare, social inequality, cricket – and racism, which he absolutely loathed.

It is not true, as the Tory Europhobes persuaded themselves, that Major was a closet Europeanist. I don't believe he was ever confident that the single European currency could work, even for its early entrants. If in conversation anyone tried to congratulate him for keeping alive at least the possibility of joining the euro – and did it on the assumption that Major believed Britain's joining one day was both inevitable and desirable – he would come down hard against the idea. I remember exchanges in which he and Chris Patten were divided on this. As Prime Minister later he never struck me as very interested in the European Union – just desperately anxious about what European controversy was doing to his government.

John was not among the noisier at our table in Catherine Place, but he was a player. We stayed in touch, at his instigation, he being Prime Minister, after our dinners there became less frequent and big round-table discussions became trickier. But our private meetings and conversations were not regular and hardly amounted to more than a cup of tea or a few glasses of wine in his room.

One afternoon in May 1995 he called me in. I was hard at work up in *The Times*'s roof hut of a room at Westminster, sketching – but this was, after all, the Prime Minister, and the government were going through a particularly bloody time. Commons divisions on

Europe loomed in which defeat was all too possible. Mutinies abounded.

John knew Tristan's view on how to deal with mutineers (or mutants, as Tristan called them). To express it in characteristic Garel-Jones style, the advice of his former Minister for Europe (and former deputy chief whip) was that at the first hint of insubordination a ringleader should be identified, given one chance to make a humiliating public climbdown and, if he failed to make it, thrown from the parliamentary party, his constituency chairman and quite possibly his wife and children summoned, and all informed that the Prime Minister knew better than anybody – and better certainly than the offending Member – that Europe was a fuckpig organization but that the test of a Tory backbencher's right to exist was his preparedness to defend fuckpig ideas if that was what the survival of the government depended upon, and this fuckpig MP had now failed that test. Suicide would not be inappropriate and, if this was his preference, provision would be made from party funds for the widow.

But there was – Tristan Garel-Jones would have liked to add – *perhaps* an alternative. If, after three months or the next score of whipped votes on important matters, whichever came first, there had been not a single further abstention from the offending MP, let alone a rebellion, if he had made a series of speeches in the chamber and his constituency deeply helpful to the government on unpopular causes and framed them in language which was grovelling to the point of comicality, and followed this up with a string of loyal letters to the *Daily Telegraph*, and if the chief whip's currently limitless rage had by then begun to subside, then his constituency association – for the time being blacklisted – would be removed from Conservative Central Office's roll of dishonour, while the Member himself, on all fours and (if practicable) naked, tarred and white-feathered, with a rolled-up copy of the Hansard recording his unspeakable division lobby mutiny stuck up his own arse and a spray of white roses clenched between his teeth, would be admitted into the presence of the chief whip, to beg for forgiveness and the return of the Tory whip.

Tristan would not have put it so colourlessly but you get the gist.

John had another idea, and over a cup of tea in the Prime Minister's room behind the Speaker's chair he explained. I sat wordless as he outlined a plan forming (he said) in his mind. He would like me to say whether I thought it far-fetched. He would resign, he said, not as Prime Minister, but as leader of the Conservative Party. Tory MPs would then be forced to hold an election to choose a leader. He would stand.

Perhaps John saw my jaw drop, but he carried on. This would put his rivals on the spot, he explained. Did they have the guts to put up against him, or would they shut up? It would also put the parliamentary party on the spot: did they want him as their leader or did they not? It would be their choice. He started to become angry. 'For three ha'pence I'd do it,' he said. He would hope to win but if he couldn't then 'I'd rather we had it out in the open; they'd have rejected me fair and square. Rather that than limping on like this with everyone complaining behind my back.' He asked for my reaction.

I said I doubted it was wise; it wasn't as simple as 'put up or shut up'. He hoped nobody would put up but somebody well might ('a Vulcan', I thought: Michael Portillo or John Redwood). And, having put up – and though the Europhobes would probably lose badly – this would be unlikely to silence them. 'Or the worst of all outcomes might result,' I continued. 'You win, but by a disappointing margin, then you have to limp on – or limp out.' He nodded. 'But for three ha'pence I'd do it,' he repeated. Yet again he emphasized that he was not proposing this out of any confidence he would win, but a longing for clarity. 'Win or lose, that would settle it.' He meant that.

An optimistic view, I thought, but John was in an emotional mood so I said nothing more. I had the strong impression that he was serious.

Like many on the fringes of public life, I've never felt confident of the rules governing what's on and what's off the record. What was the status of this conversation? Why had the Prime Minister consulted me? Did he really want my views, was he just sounding off and weeping on a friendly shoulder, did he expect me to speculate in print and help him fly a kite? Or was he doing me a favour as an old friend, tipping me off so I could get the credit for predicting this bizarre turn of events? I suppose I could have telephoned and asked him, but I felt he would then have to say I should not use what he had told me. I felt sheepish that as a professional journalist I had not understood the code.

So I asked an old and trusted friend in journalism, a man with much better connections than I had. 'Don't say anything,' he said, 'I'll check it out.' A few days later he came back to me. 'I checked it out,' he said, 'there's nothing in it.'

But I could not quite forget my conversation with the Prime Minister. At that time I wrote a weekly column for the *Investors Chronicle*, so I floated Major's idea there – not as a plan, but as my reading of his state of mind – ready for three ha'pence to throw in the towel, even challenge his rivals to put up or shut up. No doubt because the idea sounded so weird my column elicited no notice at all, not a single comment: not from readers, not from colleagues, not from the editor, not from anyone. And when, a few weeks later, John did exactly what he had said he would, I must have been one of the least astonished people in Britain.

I fervently wanted him to win but was not surprised a rival came forward to challenge him, as he had hoped none would; and not surprised it was John Redwood though it should have been Portillo. That episode, not his later and inevitable failure to secure the leadership, was the real end of Michael Portillo. I expect he recognizes this.

I had noticed Redwood some years earlier, on the front bench. I liked his intellectual honesty, his dry refusal to fudge and his uncompromisingly rationalist approach to political theory. He was an ideologue and we are short of those for they rarely thrive in the British establishment. Redwood did that unforgivable thing: followed arguments to their logical conclusions.

This was seldom good politics. He looked puzzled by the incomprehension which greeted his responses in the chamber and, later, when he became Secretary of State for Wales, baffled at the hostility excited by his reluctance to cuddle people. Redwood, daffodils and choral singing never mixed; he looked as though he would be happier playing computer games. From the start he seemed to be, though I believe is not, cold.

In my *Times* sketch I had christened him (along with Michael Portillo, though this is now forgotten) a Vulcan. Like the famous half-human, half-Vulcan Mr Spock, hero of *Star Trek*, my Redwood character was being controlled, according to the *Times* sketch, from another planet and running into difficulty because, though superbrainy and unrelentingly logical, he was unable to understand human emotions.

The Vulcan caricature had stuck – sub-editors liked it and pulled it up into my sketches' headlines. Other sketchwriters were doing Vulcan sketches too.

And now here was my Vulcan, on the front page of *The Times*, flanked by Teresa Gorman looking wide-eyed and loopy, and a range of apparently demented characters.

My sketch was headlined: 'Vulcan launches from slopes of Gorman'.

Television viewers yesterday watched the first Tory leadership campaign in history to be launched from the bosom of Teresa Gorman. Viewers were startled by the strange green-clad torso behind John Redwood as he spoke at his press conference yesterday. No head was visible in the frame.

I can reveal that it belonged to Mrs Gorman. We would recognize that bust anywhere. Once, as Redwood parried, a hand could be seen tugging at her lapels, drawing them together like green curtains across the cleavage. We trust the hand belonged to Mrs Gorman.

With such a launching pad, how can a campaign fail? Mrs Gorman was joined in a little claque of MPs in what television producers call a 'doughnut' around their hero: surely the whackiest doughnut in history.

Behind her, bullet-headed blond rightwinger Tony Marlow (his mates call him 'Von Marloff') wore a ludicrous striped blazer. Beside him, Bill 'Biggles' Walker had not opted for the kilt he often sports in the chamber. Norman Lamont (every day more like Badger in *Wind in the Willows*) joined Christopher Gill, a suitable extra for *Dad's Army*; and ex-minister Edward Leigh, to whom *Some Mothers Do 'Ave 'Em* could offer a role.

From time to time this bizarre claque would interrupt their master's flow with a raucous little chorus of 'hya, hya', 'hearrr, hearr' (from the Scot) and 'yeah! yeah!' from Mrs Gorman. It sounded like *The Goon Show*, but which of us can choose his claque?

And John Redwood did himself no harm. He achieved a tactical master-stroke by excluding from the room the observer who first recognized he was not human. It is five years since I uncovered Redwood's Vulcan origins, and the revelation has damaged him.

Reaching the conference twenty minutes early, I was told the room was full. Journalists with me were similarly barred. Watching the Vulcan's performance on Sky (where else but on satellite?) I saw no journalist I recognized. The room was 'full'. But not with humans. Redwood had packed it with alien clones. Reading aloud his letter to Mr Major, Redwood remembered his voice-teachers had told him to inject 'passion'. Vulcans

cannot feel this emotion but know that Earthlings often shout when passionate. So he shouted every eighth word ('. . . to regain the TRUST of the
British people!'). It produced a weird effect.

How did he view Wales? 'It-is-a-beautiful-country,' said the Vulcan,
because that is what Earthlings say about Wales. Instructed by his minders
to display humour, Redwood told us he was a 'jobseeker'. He followed this
with the smile he has now learned to do very nicely: a triumph of muscular
control.

Most sinister of all was a Vulcan triple-bluff. Mr Redwood made a joke
about a Vulcan being unable to see the joke about Vulcan jokes. There was
a danger that his microchips might fuse at the fiendish internal logic of this
inferential sequence, but, though his eyes bulged for a moment, all was well.

Few, however, will have failed to notice that, asked point-blank whether
he was a Vulcan, Redwood replied that many people had seen his parents.
He did not answer the question.

All in all, it was a successful performance. His claque of Earthling riff-raff
cheering, he wound up the meeting. What, we wondered, would be his
final word?

'No extra charge!' he declared. Mr Redwood must have seen this in a
supermarket, recorded it as a useful idiomatic phrase, and inputted it on to
the wrong disk-drive in his logic system.

It made a pretty readable parliamentary sketch. The paper put it on
the front page. John Redwood, fighting from the first a rearguard
action not to be seen as part of his party's lunatic fringe (which he is
not), was dismayed that his campaign should start with this. Teresa
Gorman, whom I've never been able to help liking, and who had told
me she wanted to pack me in her suitcase and take me with her to the
Algarve (she who sang 'You're the Tops' down the telephone to a
horrified accommodations whip after he allocated her a luxurious
new office, probably by mistake), was full of remorse lest she and
Tony Marlow had inadvertently ruined Redwood's campaign launch.
They had. Teresa still regrets this very much, believing, as I do, that
a few fewer votes would have seen Major quit.

The *Sun*, supporting John Redwood, printed an edition of the
tabloid with cut-out Vulcan ears for like-minded readers to strap on.
John Redwood, years later when we were together on a *Question
Time* programme on BBC TV in Norwich, sounded so angry when

I made an on-air joke about Vulcans, that I afterwards asked, incredulous, if he really minded.

'Of course I do,' he said (and I could tell he meant it). 'It wasn't so bad when you had Portillo as one too, so I was just one of many Vulcans, but then you dropped Portillo and singled me out, and I hate it, *hate* it when you do.' There was something close to a lump in his throat – proof, indeed, that he must be human. So I promised not to write any new Vulcan sketches, and kept to my promise. I hope this does not count as a reprise.

Unlike John Major, who hates him, I still like Redwood and respect those rare politicians who don't think being a vanilla-flavoured splodge is what clever politics is all about. But I wanted Major to win. Redwood would have been a disastrous party leader, the section of the Conservative Party in which he was anchored was mad and, anyway, John Major was my friend. When he did win, by a less than wholly convincing margin which his friends all pretended (not least to him) was a smashing victory, I was content.

I always wanted to believe in John's chances. Perhaps that is why I was slow to accept that, even with his leadership reaffirmed, it was all over for him. For me the moment of realization came during a European summit in Greece. Under pressure beforehand from the Tory parliamentary right, the Prime Minister had declared at the dispatch box that Britain would not back down on the issue of 'qualified majority voting' – a term which meant giving up the national veto in certain areas of decision-making.

I was dining in the West End with one of John's last remaining supporters in Fleet Street, a vigorous columnist, when the news came through from Greece that Britain was, after all, prepared to concede an extension of qualified majority voting. Douglas Hurd, the Foreign Secretary, was executing the necessary climbdown. Even I was forced in my mind to confront a dismaying question. The question was not 'Why are we climbing down?' but 'Why did John say we wouldn't?' I was quietly disappointed.

My dinner companion was incandescent. Though it was late, he had telephoned the Prime Minister's press office, said he was on the point of denouncing John, and demanded to speak to his press secretary. This was arranged, but still my friend was seething.

I remained on Major's side. Once my friend had calmed down I pointed out to him forcefully, over several brandies, that it was now too late for Majorites in the press to quit our man. If we were ever going to do so, I said, we should have done it years ago. Even if Major did sink there would be a resignation honours list. Prime ministers can and do reward friendly journalists. John would not have a big field to choose from. Why quit a market in which my friend was a preferential bidder? He listened in silence and I have no reason to think this weighed with him but by the end of the evening he had thought better of switching loyalties, and he never did, sticking with John to the last. To John's everlasting credit, there were no resignation honours for journalists. No political journalist or newspaper editor, serving or retired, should ever accept an honour, and no politician should offer one. I should have thought that was obvious.

Years later at a dinner at Claridge's for Rupert Murdoch I rashly said, 'Promise us you'll never take a title.' The newspaper proprietor broke the sudden quiet this seemed to cause. 'No,' he replied, 'I would not.'

John's gesture in neither rewarding journalists nor taking any title himself was hardly remarked upon, but struck me as quietly magnificent. Quite how unusual a Tory John was, I doubt most people noticed.

His election defeat a few years further on was inevitable but it was better for the Conservative Party that when they went down, as they did, very hard, as they would have under any leader, there was still a kind of dignity in the way John Major was able to lead them off the stage. It meant, and still means, that the phrase 'the last Conservative government', though it recalls a pretty sad collapse, also recalls a leader – the last Conservative Prime Minister – who retains respect and some sympathy across Britain.

When he went, the *Today* programme asked me to record a short essay for broadcast on a Saturday morning, 26 May 1997. I only got round to writing it on the London Underground between Whitechapel and Temple stations on the District Line, and galloped into a recording studio at Bush House in the Strand breathless, with a piece of paper covered in a just legible scrawl in my hand. Perhaps it was the better for being fresh. Hundreds wrote to me and to the BBC asking for copies afterwards so my secretary Eileen made a transcript. It reads a bit lushly now, a bit over-the-top, but it did reach and touch many listeners then, after his defeat on 3 May 1997:

My friend John Major would almost certainly rather I didn't describe him thus. I hardly see him often. Since we were both elected to Parliament seventeen years ago, our paths have sometimes run together, sometimes apart, but I do not know him well. Perhaps it would be fairer to call myself a friendly observer of the man, but still I will say 'friend', because I feel so strongly that John Major is so much more capable a leader than it has been fashionable to allow, that there are moments when I'd shout it from the rooftops. This is one of them.

Almost everything, you see, that they say about the character of the Prime Minister is completely wrong. Almost everything, that is, except that he is – as people say – a decent man. He has a hatred of bullies and snobs, of bigots and cheats, of greed, so fierce as to make his relationship with as worldly a party as his always an uneasy accommodation. He also has a near-crippling inability – I would say unwillingness – to articulate any of this. That is why people say he lacks 'vision'. He does not lack vision. He hates talking about vision. He is very English.

They say he is too nice. He isn't actually, not in the saccharine sense. He is quite prickly and vindictive on occasions, not so much to opponents as to those he thinks have tricked or misjudged him. They say he is even-tempered. He isn't: he is controlled. He is also moody and secretly irritable. John Major handles opposition to his plans very, very well: with patience, with cajolery, with cunning and with charm. He does not, however, handle hostility towards his own person well. Whole mountains blocking his way do not dismay him. One small personal slight can.

They say he is easily pushed around. This is the greatest of the mistakes people make in assessment of the Prime Minister. He is a man of steel will and unending, cat-like persistence. When one route is blocked he will try another. He will duck, dive and ride the punches. He will dodge, burrow, play dead, wait, yield, pounce – he can be surprisingly devious – but he will not give up. It is fair to say that this is no general to blast his way across history, taking no prisoners and occupying all he surveys.

But where guerrilla tactics are called for – where the game is defensive – nobody is more skilled at preserving his position, confounding fate and extracting what advantage can be found, than John Major. He is at his best when all seems lost.

They say, finally, that he is a cautious man. Wrong, quite wrong. He is a careful man, which is different. But, so far from being timid, this so-called grey man is capable of breathtaking nerve, of risking all, of leaping into

space, where to hesitate is more perilous than to leap. In such leaps he has
never yet failed.

My friend John Major is a pretty quirky individual, a maverick in accountant's clothing. This Prime Minister is a more dangerous enemy than his
opponents realize, and a more formidable friend.

In the end in politics we are all unlucky. We go by defeat, by death, by
accident, by incapacity, by exhaustion or disgrace. We go, all of us, the
question is only how. John Major, you could have gone betraying your own
principles: you never did.

You could have failed the country, failed the unemployed; you never
did. Abroad, you could have let slip those patiently won advantages we have
still to appreciate. You held on to them. You could have won easy cheers
with megaphone language and stupid gestures; you never did. All the
pressures, all the temptations of your time in office were to save yourself by
selling short what you knew to be the interests of your country. You never
did. By being strong you were called weak, but you would never have
behaved weakly to be called strong. You never did what you knew would
be cowardly, in order to be called by the shallow or ignorant 'brave'.

With a momentarily sour smile, perhaps, you hear some of those voices
who mocked and undermined you when you needed friends, praising your
dignity and good humour in the defeat they helped to engineer. You must
know what John Clare meant when, in his lament to a fallen elm, he wrote:

> Thou'st sheltered hypocrites in many a shower,
> That when in power would never shelter thee.

Everyone, the whole of Britain, has seen the example set in courtesy and
good grace during this campaign. Few have failed to notice the stature with
which you conducted yourself in defeat.

Is it a small thing to end some seven years in power, still kindly regarded,
still liked, still personally admired? Is it any disgrace to lose an election when
the whole campaign only added to the respect people feel for you?

Five years ago you saved Britain: you alone could have done it – from
government by a party which, as its present leader knows, was all at sea.
That defeat transformed that party. You then guided us through some most
difficult transitional years. In the most real sense, the hopes and opportunities
with which a new government now begins, are your own work.

It is the fate of those who form a bridge between eras to be distrusted by those unwilling to cross, and disregarded by those who make the crossing. It is the fate of those who hold the line between two equally dangerous and opposite extremes to be called indecisive from both fringes. But it is they who form the bridge; they who hold the line – who are the decisive ones. It is they who are brave. If the price of being steadfast is to be mocked as timid, and if, despite the mockery, they hold the line, we owe them our thanks. We owe you our thanks, John. The party does: the country does.

Already some appreciation of that is stirring. In time it will be commonplace to acknowledge it. And you, John, will be entitled to a rueful grin.

Someone once said that all newspaper editors ever do is wait until the battle is over, then come down from the hills and bayonet the wounded. So don't read the papers for a few weeks, John. Wait for a few months. By then you will know that we are missing you.

I cannot say I was proved triumphantly right in that last prediction. Still, it was a nice sentiment.

All that John Major's triumph against John Redwood had meant for him was two years more torment. It was a torment in which I had felt badly torn between personal friendship and professional . . . well, 'duty' is a bit pompous for a journalist, but the fact was that the Prime Minister cut a beleaguered and forlorn figure, his party were sinking with all hands and the nation, and my readers, could see it. When a leader is being humiliated by his times while his party disintegrates, the public do not see a satirist's job as being to soften the blows. They expect a satirist to satirize.

I did my best, but too often pulling punches. The *Guardian*'s Simon Hoggart had more fun and so, I fear, did his readers. I made no jokes about John tucking his shirt into his underpants because Norma told me it wasn't true, it wasn't funny, and that she couldn't even bear to watch the satirical television puppet-show, *Spitting Image*, because its depiction of her husband as a grey puppet pushing his peas around his plate hurt her too much. 'He doesn't even like peas, particularly,' she told me. This was immaterial, but not to her. I did not want to hurt her.

It is easy for me to protest that mocking the afflicted isn't funny, and that calling Mrs Thatcher (for instance) a cross between Widow

Twankey and Lucretia Borgia *was* funny because that is what she was: comical but formidable and therefore a fair target for lampoonery. Or I could insist that you cannot prick a deflated balloon. Well, maybe you cannot, but you can kick it around a bit in the dirt. And the truth is that I had been pretty mocking about Neil Kinnock and, along with the rest of the media, did hit him when he was down. And the reason was that, unlike John, he was no particular friend of mine.

I had merrily joined in all the Welsh Windbag jokes when Mr Kinnock was floundering as leader of the Opposition. Kinnock was irritating. Thatcher was appalling. But she could look after herself, and he in the end could not, and sank. In Kinnock I had seen the posturing but not the principle, a failure of insight on my part. At least, though, I was being as rude about the Prime Minister, Mrs Thatcher, who had become a pantomime dame, with Kinnock playing the village idiot. It made a good sketch.

But the other day I was listening to one of Kinnock's old speeches and found myself moved almost to tears by its power. 'Why was I closed to that when I heard it the first time?' I wondered.

It is clear to me now that Kinnock was a better man than his newspaper critics or political foes, or even his friends in Parliament, allowed; and not just a better man, but a force for reason in his party, someone who changed British politics. I had never allowed myself to see that, just as I held back from relishing and ridiculing John Major's plight, some of it of his own making. Friendship was the problem.

When we who write about politics are simply partisan, we can acknowledge that. We can remind our readers and let them take what we write with a pinch of salt; or we can remind *ourselves* where we are coming from and try extra hard to be balanced.

As for naked corruption we know that to be wrong: threats and bribes wear their impropriety on their sleeve and we can arm ourselves against such weakness. But friendship is more insidious. Loyalty to a friend comes bonneted as a virtue – and it is, in a friend. In a journalist it is not. Friend and journalist can conflict within the same man and if you soften the blow for a friend, congratulating yourself for allowing humanity to triumph over career, even thinking yourself brave to compromise career for the sake of decency, you forget that to spare your embarrassment with someone you do know you are cheating thousands you do not: your readers. You call it friendship but you have begun to spin.

Often enough it is chance which releases a journalist from the bonds of friendship. Unreasonably but frequently a friend will take exception to something you have written about him which is perfectly fair and not unkind – for some people prove unexpectedly touchy about anything published which fails to eulogize. When that happens, when a jokey or teasing column triggers a declaration of hostilities, the journalist should not fret but breathe a sigh of relief. You were not unfair, you were not unmindful of your friendship, you did not start this. Strike the guy from your address book, cut the strings and let go. This is what happened to me with John Patten and with Alan Clark, both of whom were once friends, one of whom is now disliking me from the House of Lords, and the other from a less earthly assembly (and in Alan's case a more fiery chamber).

After his exit from the front bench I accepted a commission to review John Patten's autobiography for a newspaper. Unwisely, finding it not as good as I had expected (for John is a thoughtful and interesting man), I did not ask to relinquish my commission but struggled hard in the review to praise what I honestly could, and offer distinctly faint praise for the rest. It was not a good review but it was a much better review than the book would have attracted had its author not been my friend. If John Patten had known what an effort I made to tone down criticism for friendship's sake he would not subsequently have stormed past me in the street without acknowledging my greeting, face like thunder. I think we are not speaking. Ah me.

With Alan Clark came a more violent rift. Every word of the parliamentary sketch I devoted to his falling asleep during Questions to the Member representing the Church Commissioners, was true – and I took the precaution of checking my impression with a colleague, then and there. Parliamentary journalists are well advised never to spell out the word 'sleep' (or 'drunk') when describing a Member in his place in the chamber, and I did not. Unfortunately the sub-editor who devised the headline 'Clark sleeps through divine thunder and saintly sermon' did.

I was more oblique. Nothing, I said, not even a clap of afternoon thunder, had seemed to rouse the MP for Kensington and Chelsea, 'sunk in what was presumably deep thought for most of the Questions to Defence ministers that preceded those to the Church Commissioners'.

His eyes were shut, his head had dropped forward and one hand spread across his famously chiselled jaw, covering his mouth. Mr Clark looked profoundly at peace. Even the mention of Clark's constituency's name failed to jolt him from his meditations. When the Defence Secretary mentioned him, 'all eyes moved to Mr Clark, but his own remained at rest, head sunk – if anything – deeper on his chest'. A colleague beside him turned to gauge his reaction, noted the Zen-like calm, and looked hastily away.

Any sketchwriter will find himself writing such a sketch more than once, about more Members than Alan Clark. Years before I had devoted much of a column to the privilege we, who had never slept with Hugh Dykes MP, had now shared with Mrs Dykes: that of seeing the loveliness of her husband when insensible, comatose, eyes shut, head lolled, mouth agape and breathing gently. Mr Dykes had not complained and carried on behaving in a friendly way towards me.

So I expected no complaint from Clark, who loved to be written about and could quote by heart long passages of an admiring sketch I had once written, comparing him with an eagle. But now he went crazy. The attendants in the Press Gallery told me he had come up the very next morning and demanded to sit where I sit, so he could establish for himself how much of his expression I could really have seen. He overlooked the fact that sketchwriters rove around when they want a better look, and a friend across the gallery (one of my witnesses) had actually beckoned me over in this case. I understand he made complaints to the Speaker.

Then came a furious tirade at me over the telephone. I stuck to my guns. He had been asleep. He denied it so indignantly that I suspected he had genuinely forgotten that he had dozed off – but that was not the point. The point was that the whole thing was trivial; MPs nod off all the time. So do sketchwriters, and I had got more than one sketch out of my own somnolence.

Next Alan tried to intervene with *The Times* itself. There were calls to the editor's office. It would not surprise me if there were calls to Rupert Murdoch in New York, too. This was absurd. Alan Clark dished it out without compunction: it was one of his charms. I was amazed not so much that he was vain and had a thin skin, which I knew, but that he was silly enough to let it show like this.

Later that year I bumped into him at *The Times*'s champagne reception at the Tory Party Conference. His tough and capable wife, Jane, was with him, but even Jane was having trouble handling him. He marched up to me and stood, swaying slightly. 'Oh,' he said with heavy stage-sarcasm, 'it's the great Matthew Parris, sketchwriter extraordinaire. *How* we all adore him. How we worship at his feet. What words of wisdom have you for us today, oh prophet . . .' and so on. Jane Clark was tugging at him to go. I grinned and shrugged my shoulders and soon managed to extricate myself and leave. My assistant, however, and a *Times* colleague, remained in his circle; he did not realize his audience now included informers. 'Wanker. *Wanker.* Fucking wanker. Fucking cunt. Wankerish, cuntish fucker . . .' Finally Jane managed to steer him to the door.

There is a twist to this tale. *Times* colleagues with the technical know-how have been helping me write this book by finding from the newspaper's archives, on disc, the old columns I want to quote or consult. They are comprehensively available from 1985. But not the Clark sketch. I know the date, I know the page and I know the edition – I keep an index of my own on paper and was eventually able to track it down manually in my own files – but the whole column is absent, wiped, from *The Times*'s electronic records.

Wary of falling into the paranoid speculation which my old friend at Cambridge, Ahmed, taught me to watch out for, I shall not speculate on the reasons for this.

It is sad that Alan is dead. He would have been a worthy combatant in a lifelong feud. Released from the bonds of friendship, I should have enjoyed the duel. Friendship brings paralysis. Enmity liberates a journalist. Trainee paratroopers are – it is said – ordered to adopt, feed and care for a fluffy white rabbit, stroke it, then shoot it point-blank to teach them to harden their hearts in the course of duty. Trainee journalists should be made to foster a sweet old granny, gain her confidence, then tear her to shreds in what they write.

Fitfully, however, and not too unprofessionally, I did lampoon the rise of my Blue Chip friends to power, and their fall. It would have been an absorbing time for any sketchwriter. For me it had all the morbid fascination of a snuff movie.

19. Sketching the Dog's Bollocks

I first met the Blairs long before Tony Blair looked like the next Labour leader, at a small supper party given by a *Times* colleague. I recall it clearly. I can remember where we were sitting, the decor of the room, some of the conversation – and of course I recall the special guest.

It was Cherie: indisputably Cherie. She made a tremendous impression: prettier than she looks in the press photographs, lively, funny, slightly scary, directed, crusading, forceful, clever, opinionated, interesting and interested. I made a mental note that she would go far: was going far already.

And then there was her husband. I remember noting him down as a pleasant, bright, new Labour prototype, with a sense of humour and a nice silk tie: probably ambitious. He dressed well, looked good and spoke nicely. But Cherie stole the show; Tony was part of the supporting cast. I cannot remember a word he said about politics. He sounded modern, that's all – the type you realize could have tossed a coin at university and joined either main party.

It was not quite the first time I had noticed him. That had been before John Major won the 1992 election. In July the previous year, looking down from the *Times* sketchwriter's perch, I spotted the new MP for Sedgefield who had intervened in debate. 'A likeable young swell,' I wrote. It is not a judgement I have ever needed to revise.

The likeable young swell I had noted from the gallery and met later, re-entered my life in 1994 when I interviewed him as a contender for the Labour leadership. As one of a small stable of commentators, I was in those days writing and presenting a regular, light review of the morning newspapers for BBC television's *Breakfast News* programme. I did this for nearly ten years (fun once you got stuck into it but made a chore by the need to get up at four o'clock in the morning). One of the perks was to be asked from time to time to help *Breakfast News* with little extras, performed at a more civilized hour, and one such was to interview all the candidates for the Labour leadership after the death of John Smith in 1994. We cross-examined each in turn, on succeeding mornings. One of my fellow-interviewers was an assistant editor at the now defunct newspaper, *Today*: Alastair Campbell. We now know (I did not then) that he was also working for Blair's election team.

On the morning we were to interview Tony Blair, Alastair shared my BBC car to their Westminster studio at Millbank. For much of the journey he was on the mobile phone to someone, obviously in the Labour Party, discussing the imminent interview, the questions likely to come up and the questions he was thinking of asking. It did sound as though it was his interviewee he was talking to, but nothing in the conversation offered firm proof of that so I banished the thought. He spoke to this person more than once from the car.

Alastair turned to me between calls and asked, chattily, what I had it in mind to ask. I said I was wondering whether to ask about the fact that Tony Blair planned to send his son to a selective school (the Oratory) on the other side of London, rather than one of the state schools within the catchment area of Islington where the Blairs lived. I might ask (I suggested to Alastair) how he squared this with a bid to lead a party which did not believe in selective schools. What did Alastair think, I inquired.

'Ask that if you want,' he replied, chummily but in the manner of a senior chum, 'but as a colleague I would warn you off it. Most people are going to think that's pretty offside.' It was not, he said, as if the Oratory were a private school. It was a Church school. I was in danger of getting my argument muddled, which would be misleading and unfair and make me look a fool. Viewers, he advised me, as well as my professional colleagues, would see questioning about Tony Blair's family and his children's schooling as 'below the belt'.

As a result I altered that line of questioning, avoiding any personal enquiry. Alastair had brutally undermined my confidence in the idea of tackling Tony Blair in what was to become, had I known it, one of the most persistent and damaging areas of personal criticism he has had to face.

Whatever my questions, they cannot have been devastating. A few weeks later, Blair was the leader of his party. Alastair became his press secretary.

His methods never changed. When in the advance serialization of the first edition of this book *The Times* included the story just recounted, Campbell spotted an error: a silly but immaterial mistake, rectified by substituting the words used a couple of paragraphs back – 'planned to send his son to a selective school' – for the words I had originally used: 'sent his son to a selective school'.

Without revealing that those schooling plans had been well-trailed in advance, and seizing on the fact that my words had implied Blair's son was at the Oratory school when he was not, Campbell bombarded *The Times* (a personal fax to the editor), its letters editor and the managing director of Penguin Books, with angry letters. All used the Royal-crested notepaper of the Prime Minister's office, 10 Downing Street, though Campbell had not been in Mr Blair's employ at the point in his career under scrutiny. All impugned my own professionalism, *The Times* letter suggesting that the rest of my book should now be under suspicion of being made up.

He said he had no recollection we had shared a car then or ever. For good measure he defended himself against an accusation I had not made (that his questioning of the candidates had been biased). Of Penguin he demanded damages, then when he did not get that, he said if there was no correction he would take legal advice on how to prevent publication until a change was made.

Luckily I was able to establish that the Oratory story had been splashed in the press before the *Breakfast News* interviews. Being deeply embarrassing to Mr Blair the story had been much talked about of course, but I suppose it possible that Alastair had simply forgotten this and that, with all the resources of Downing Street at his disposal, he had neglected to make the easy checks necessary, before spraying out accusations about my own integrity.

Penguin robustly decided to take no notice of him. *The Times* felt (rightly) obliged to publish his letter. After that we all gave him no further response. He went away. But it is fair to say he seriously frightened me, and would have frightened a weaker-kneed publisher. And all with the intention of blocking the suggestion that Campbell is a ruthless operator: something his behaviour was in this case demonstrating.

Alastair will have been deeply involved in one of Mr Blair's first media engagements after being chosen as leader: a kind of coronation address held in a lecture hall in Bloomsbury – an event which coincided with a comet hitting Jupiter. Mr Blair laid before the press, television and members of the Labour Party his hopes and dreams for the party he had just inherited. *The Times* had sent me to write about it. So I was there at the start. Allow me to pause here and linger over that occasion for it was there in Bloomsbury that my suspicions about Tony Blair hardened and the iron entered my Tory soul.

Sometimes you can know, at the start. Straight away I noted the void. I noticed his infatuation with abstract nouns. Straight away I heard the engaging light tenor of the second male lead in a light operetta. My reaction was immediate and strong. My whole being rose up in revolt against this: in revolt, not against the likeable young swell, but against his and his mission's pretence to be anything more. This, which appeared on 22 July 1994 under the headline 'Word-pollution alert as Comet Tony falls to Earth', is what I wrote:

As fragments of Shoemaker Levy-9 thudded into the surface of Jupiter, Tony Blair stood up in Bloomsbury yesterday and released a barrage of abstract nouns of unprecedented duration and ferocity.

It was awesome. Grown men – hardened journalists – rocked against the walls in disbelief; camera crews, unable to cope with exposure to such sustained levels of intellectualism, staggered from the hall; Tories ran for cover. Even Liberal Democrats winced. Across the nation TV viewers watching the event live shielded themselves as honour, pride, humility, community, excitement, conviction, trepidation, passion, aspiration, gratitude, courage and determination – and that's only the first page and a half – rocketed out of television sets and across their living rooms, thudding into a million sofas.

Devices tracking earth from Jupiter will have blown their fuses at the sheer philosophical energy unleashed. Never, even in Islington, have so many generalities been uttered with such passion by a single politician within one lunchtime.

For those inclined to doodle it was interesting to take keynote phrases ('the power of all for the good of each,' 'ours is a passion allied to reason') and try swapping their constituent elements, to see whether it made any difference: 'the power of each for the good of all,' 'ours is a reason allied to passion,' or even 'the power and passion of each, allied to reason, for the good of all'.

The show was well executed: stagey without being vulgar, media-friendly, cunningly lit, pre-scripted, press-released, sound-enhanced, Autocue-supported, video-assisted and cheap. Seating in the hall was divided into the three sections eligible to choose the Labour leader: one third BBC, one third print journalists and one third Labour Party. The trade unions had disappeared: something called 'affiliated organizations' figured in the videographics. There were no comrades either. Those present were addressed by loudspeakers as 'colleagues'. Next year we will be ladies and gentlemen. Blue was the predominant colour.

And another Tory feature is creeping into Labour occasions: incessant, fatuous applause. Tony Blair's speech was prefaced by some fifteen seconds of applause, interrupted by twenty-seven separate bursts of mostly polite clapping, each lasting about ten seconds, and concluded with some two minutes' clapping.

Blair delighted most journalists. His skills would serve in those amusement-arcade 'Grand Prix' screen games. His own screen the Autocue screen, and his gaze rigid with concentration, Mr Blair drove at gathering velocity round a track littered with the death-traps of policy commitments, swerving to avoid every one, fuelled by a tankful of abstract nouns.

Meanwhile, in an event which cannot be unrelated to the discovery of Tony Blair, a team of scientists in a remote mountain range in New Guinea have discovered a species of whistling tree-kangaroo: the bondegezou. These kangaroos, held in huge affection by local tribesmen, are soft, furry, and completely unthreatening. They sit amiably on their branches and when they see a human being walking below, they whistle a friendly greeting.

It remains to teach the bondegezou to intersperse its song with words like 'honour, pride, conviction' and 'passion', and to teach Mr Blair to climb trees. Then British political life may become interchangeable with that of the New Guinea cloud forests.

Getting on for nine years and two massive new Labour election victories later, I would make only one change to that: in the word 'intellectualism' I would italicize the *ism*.

Re-reading this, and the polemic which follows, I am aware as an autobiographer that in the interests of my own good name I ought to leave it out. It makes me sound mean-spirited, vengeful and almost obsessed by an irritable dislike of a politician who, whatever his faults or virtues, is hardly a monster and has never claimed to be a saint.

But it is what I feel. It is how I have felt from the start. Expressed or unexpressed, this has animated much of my writing about Tony Blair and new Labour. Writing which harps on the writer's pet hates can be unlikeable, but more so is the style which affects even-handedness while hiding a stone in one clasped hand: a false generosity in which, the animosity being cloaked, a writer pretends to be a disinterested party with an objective view. It is better we wear our prejudice on our sleeves. I declare mine. I am not disposed to see the best in Tony Blair's politics. I decided it was hollow there and then in Bloomsbury, and I will always tend to interpret new evidence in that light.

The revulsion was not at the man. In Bloomsbury Tony Blair seemed genuinely personable, and still does. He had charm. He had an apparent earnestness of purpose which, for at least as long as a purpose inhabits him, I'm still inclined to think genuine. When later he was to say he was 'a pretty straight sort of a guy', I did not doubt it and never have. This is not a villain, showing a contrived face to the world then sniggering up his sleeve. I did not then and have not since seen him as aiming at anything less than to do good in the world, though he will not scruple to cut moral corners as he travels. His achievement – even should he achieve nothing more than make his party electable then bow out – cannot be denied.

What repelled me, apart from the tendency (like Peter Pan's) to crow, was his mind. There was a sloppiness which, coming from the top, later infected the whole new Labour project. He showed no sense of the importance of ideas. He had no respect for rigour in language or thought. Arguments were simply *used*, never entered: there to achieve a purpose, not to settle purposes. Purposes were short-term. Aspirations were so long-term as to be almost without meaning. Reason was of little consequence: an appearance of reason-ableness being all.

How people use words tells you so much. The aim of language for Tony Blair was to impress, inspire and fudge, all at the same time. Cunningness in words is something almost everybody can sense without knowing how we do. We make a small mental note: not so much hostile as a reserving of position.

In that speech in Bloomsbury there were ambitions, but no plan. Of high-minded waffle this politician had no monopoly but what I found unusually repellent about Mr Blair's was that it came across unaccompanied by even the slightest wink. All politics involves a measure of sham, and a little sheepishness befits those who make it their career. The disjunction between a largeness of gesture and a timidity of intent can be redeemed by humour or by apology, but Mr Blair did not think he was funny and showed no potential for contrition. It was very American, very televangelist and most unBritish.

You don't need to be a political analyst to sense this man grasping at happy thoughts and high-minded concepts as a weak swimmer grasps at a passing log. He does not master an argument, but hitches a ride on someone else's as a going concern. In Tony Blair's philosophy there are dreams for a better world and schemes for getting through to the end of the summer, but between next autumn and the next generation, a howling void, no explanation, no apology, no shrug, no embarrassed smile and no joke. Graced with however beguiling a lightness of touch, he remains one of life's buskers. I could see that in Bloomsbury all those years ago.

In many minds these small reservations have been registered. They have not yet come home to roost but when they do – if he does not get out in time – they will darken the sky.

Rant over.

I should have found my sometimes lonely Blairoscepticism easier to maintain if hostilities had ever been returned by Downing Street. But Alastair Campbell has always denied me the bludgeonings or withering asides he can direct at other unhelpful journalists, and which help them feel big. He looks at me with the amiable forbearance one might direct towards a person of unsound mind. And my two most recent encounters with the Blairs have left me uncertain whether they might be muddling me up with another journalist.

At English's restaurant during a Labour Party conference at Brighton, I was sitting with friends at the bar downstairs when a group none of us had expected turned up at the door. It was the Prime Minister, and a posse of aides and journalists. It seems they had booked a room and a meal upstairs.

I cowered at the bar and tried to look fixedly the other way. I had that week been writing the usual disobliging stuff about him. I hoped he might not see me. But he did. Mr Blair turned on the stairs, bounced back down again, came over, and said, 'Ah, Matthew. How *are* you? Enjoying the conference?' Then he made for the first floor.

I wish I could report that it was said sarcastically, but the tone was genuine and friendly. It made me feel a total heel.

As did Cherie during the 2001 election when she spotted me in the media crush outside the Labour Club in Sedgefield as she and her husband went in. An apparently delighted smile lit her face. 'Matthew!' she called, as though she had spotted an angel in the throng. Easily flattered, I could not help liking her, as I did the first time we met.

At the funeral of a friend whose long and wasting disease has been followed by years of dementia before death, we may comfort each other with the thought that in our minds we already lost and mourned him long ago. So it was with the Conservative Party at the general election of 1997. From three years before at Bloomsbury, and as John Major's demise looked ever less avoidable, I had been readjusting. The brief ascendancy of my friends was over. John Major's government had died years before Tony Blair buried it.

Covering that election for *The Times*, I was sketching more than a change of government; I was sketching the ruin and fall of the house of my friends. It was inevitable and deserved, but as it came I toyed briefly with the idea of quitting my own post when John Major quit his. Had I done the parliamentary sketch for long enough? While writing about a Tory Parliament I had been able to rely on inside knowledge and, more important, a personal feel for what these people were all about. I could sniff the breeze and tell what was going on. I understood them.

I did not understand New Labour. It still feels alien – somehow Soviet – to me. The Tories could be an appalling bunch of shits but they were my shits, and all too human. The new crowd were a very different kind of shit, and behind the warm words I sensed a coldness and a sort of vacuum. Could I talk usefully to my readers about these people?

I trotted along to a post-election photo-call at Church House – the one which became famous for its image of the newly massed ranks of Labour women posing with their Prime Minister . . .

So many purple suits! So much hairspray! The mood teetered between a fashionable charity première of a star-studded new show and the head-master's First Day address to new boys and girls.

Or should we say new girls and boys? The pastel and primary colours of the hundred-odd women present turned their male counterparts into backdrop.

'You are all ambassadors!' declared Tony Blair. Four hundred eager faces, gathered for this first prime ministerial address to the new Labour MPs, looked up in rapture. All ambassadors? Not in their wildest dreams had they thought Cabinet patronage extended this far.

The occasion was staged at Church House whose circular hall permits journalists to peer over the rim, as into a goldfish bowl. In the bowl, 400 new MPs had milled around, waiting. Cries of 'Darling!', 'Well done!' and 'I just can't believe it!' surfaced through the hubbub. Grunts and snuffles of a thousand little hugs and mwah! mwah! kisses rose ceilingwards.

Somewhat removed from all this, Tony Benn sat near the back, sucking his cheeks. Dennis Skinner strode in, a man unchanged. In the same jacket, the same tie and the same jaundiced expression he always wears, Skinner looked adrift: a castaway on a sea of bright eyes, expensive haircuts, southern accents and soft suiting.

He marched up to the new Cabinet. He began shaking their hands. Had the Beast of Bolsover been tamed?

He had not. Skinner sat down in the seat kept empty for the Chancellor and stayed there, beaming. Everyone looked embarrassed. Jack Straw looked terrified. A hatchet-faced apparatchik herded him away to an outer circle, not far from Barbara Follett, power-dressed creator of New Labour Woman. The irony was delicious.

Peter Mandelson, Minister without Portfolio (did ever so vacant a title belie so occupied a plot?), ambled palely down the aisle. When Mr Mandelson appears, something is about to happen. It was. John Prescott was about to happen. Unable to suppress glee, the Deputy Prime Minister belted out his curtain-raiser for the Real Thing. 'I don't want to say some of the surprising constituencies we won in!' roared the great butcher of Tory government, and English prose.

The doors opened and in strode the Prime Minister, to roars of applause. Two doorkeepers must have been ready behind the doors, one assigned to each, to open both in a synchronized movement.

Blair looked relaxed. He stared around the hall. What a spectacle! The scene resembled a high-school dance. Most of the girls sat together in clumps. The boys laughed extra loud, to show how confident they were. The Prime Minister spoke like a headmaster exhorting new pupils to uphold the highest standards – and never to eat on buses, in uniform.

Around the ceiling a huge, devotional frieze proclaimed in gold leaf 'Holy is the true light and passing wonderful, lending radiance to them that endured in the heat of conflict . . .' His conflict over, Mr Blair looked radiant. The parliamentary Labour Party looked passing wonderful. I glanced around Church House. '. . . wherein they rejoice with gladness, evermore.'

No mistaking the gladness and rejoicing. Evermore? Time will tell.

. . . and decided that, stranger though I was to this world, I would find my themes.

And I did, fast, and stuck to them. Nine days later, as the new Commons assembled and under the headline 'Enter the First Poodles', I was writing:

Boring. That was the verdict after the new, improved, extra-length super-constructive Prime Minister's Questions, unveiled amidst much excitement yesterday. Within days Tony Blair has experienced a sensation it took Margaret Thatcher years to organize: scores of little wet backbench tongues caressing the prime ministerial boot; a sea of moist, adoring eyes around him; and the sound of orchestrated panting from those desirous of office.

As most of Britain, including millions who were not natural Labour supporters, wished the best for this fresh administration, and a sincere feeling of hope and of new beginnings suffused the nation, something about the vanity and the essential hollowness of the new Labour project infuriated me. As a satirist I wanted to expose that, while as a serious columnist on Saturdays (my column had now been moved from the side-bars and basements to centre-page, and could be as serious as I liked) I wanted to warn readers of the bubble-nature of the whole enterprise – of the spectacular suddenness with which I think it could implode.

I was, in the event, consistently wrong about the timing. In the *Sun*, where I had also started a weekly column, I advised readers as Major fell and Blair rose, to cut out and keep my page and dig it out in a year's time, when (I said) Blair would be one of the most unpopular politicians in recent British history. That prophecy was timed for about 1998, at which point he was one of the most popular Prime Ministers of all time.

I watched him at his second party conference as Labour leader, in 1995. Unlike almost all my News International colleagues in the press room, who loved it, I felt ambivalent. There was something brilliant, and something offputting, about this:

Before Tony Blair's speech, a chap near me growled: ''E thinks 'e's the dog's bollocks.' Well he's entitled to. It was a commanding speech: a real dog's bollocks of an oration.

Echoing John F. Kennedy, Newt Gingrich and Jesus Christ, and interrupted by thirteen minutes (in total) of mid-speech applause, the Labour leader came as close as a politician can to offering a glimpse of the Promised Land. We can identify six key elements to this: new Britain, new Labour, new technology, New Testament, new audience and old Tony.

Before this week new Britain was a sun-drenched dependency in the Pacific. But as Blair himself said, picturing the future: 'Virtual reality tourism allows you anywhere in the world.' Thrilling to his picture of a classless, crime-free, brotherly, sisterly nation, delegates filed out into a grey sky and spitting wind. It spoilt a Britain where we half-thought (though he never quite promised) there would be no more rain.

What, then, is new Labour? Tony Blair has discovered what other socialists have missed. That a Tory speech goes down well in Britain. He therefore gave one. There were even cries – non-ironic – of 'hyah, hyah!' during his passage on law and order. But the British enjoy a frisson of modernism too. So with Mary Wilson sitting proudly behind him, Blair treated us to a 1990s rerun of Harold Wilson's sixties dream about the technological revolution.

Few understood much of this but we knew it was terrifically important probably for the young. But there was something for older voters too. Blair offered the New Testament. Within moments he was quoting Christ. Near the end he declared (twice): 'Be strong and of good courage.' The tone was positively messianic. Mr Blair has yet to declare: 'As God said, and rightly . . .' but he will.

'Discipline! Courage! Determination! Honesty!' Caught on a cusp somewhere between Florence Nightingale and Che Guevara, Mr Blair's peroration approached the phrasing they embroider on school caps. We loved it.

Commentators will say he is winning his audience round, but I think he is winning a new audience. There are missing faces this year and many unfamiliar ones.

Politicians used to think that if the audience didn't like the message, you changed the message. Mr Blair has changed the audience.

So was it new Britain? Or the old Britain that Labour never noticed? New Labour? Or old Harold repolished? New Testament? Or old-time religion?

Perhaps Professor Hawking is right: Blair has fused the funnels between black holes and is taking us time travelling. Old Tony stays as fresh as each succeeding dawn.

On Tuesday this sketch suggested that, like Dorian Gray, Tony Blair keeps a likeness somewhere, absorbing his sins and ageing for him. A friend has sent the quote from Wilde:

Now wherever you go you charm the world. Will it always be so? . . . You have a wonderfully beautiful face Mr Gray. Don't frown. You have. And Beauty is a form of genius, is higher, indeed, than Genius because it needs no explanation . . . it cannot be questioned. It has its divine right of sovereignty. It makes princes of those who have it. You smile? Ah! When you have lost you won't smile.

Yesterday Tony Blair made a beautiful speech and made it beautifully. It will not stand question but does not need to. As Wilde says: 'Beauty is the wonder of wonders. It is only shallow people who do not judge by appearances.'

Yesterday Dorian Blair was the dog's bollocks.

I doubted it could last. Six years later, with Blair at Downing Street and still on a massive personal roll, I remained convinced the wave must break soon. His speech at a South London girls' school, with which Tony Blair kicked off his triumphant 2001 general election campaign had convinced me that such hubris must shortly meet its nemesis:

Tony Blair, who last year ran into trouble with women at the WI, yesterday chose girls of a more gullible age.

With a Cross behind him, sacred stained glass above him, the upturned faces of 500 schoolgirls in pink-and-blue gingham before him, and to the strains of a choir singing 'I who make the skies of light/I will make the darkness bright/Here I am', Mr Blair launched his campaign at the St Olave's and St Saviour's church school in Southwark.

In these dark days, life remains bearable by grace only of the conviction that one day this kind of thing will surely be swept away on a great wave of national revulsion. Yesterday that conviction faltered.

It was nauseating. It was breathtakingly, toe-curlingly, hog-whimperingly tasteless. It was unbelievably ill-judged. Just when one is teased by the thought that Blair might not be all bad, he does something which nobody with a grain of sense or sensibility could even contemplate.

If the PM sanctioned the arrangements for this dire event, and if there is a hell, he will go there.

To prepare for his entry, the choir sang an ethnic song whose predominating lyric was wa-wa-wa. In new Labour this passes for an argument. The wa-wa-was increased. Cameras swivelled.

Wild rumours swept the audience that Phoenix the calf was coming on with Blair. Then, to girlish screams normally reserved for adolescent pop idols, Tony Blair strode calfless on to the chapel stage, positioned himself between the Cross and the cameras and beneath the motto 'Heirs of the past, makers of the future', flung off his jacket to further screams, and sat down in shirtsleeves, legs apart, arms spread like a sumo-wrestler. A girls' choir sang 'We are the children of the future', which was not the case.

Blair grinned soupily. Mobile phones trilled. Flashguns popped. I moved closer. A Labour aide warned me off. 'You will end up in the cutaways, Matthew,' she hissed.

> 'A time to love, a time to share,
> A time to show how much we care,'

sang the girls. Alastair Campbell clapped caringly.

Of Mr Blair's speech, the less said the better. We are not used to seeing a Prime Minister, with a Cross behind him, preaching to an audience of children in their own school chapel, attacking the Opposition. 'What did you think of that?' my *Daily Mail* colleague said to a small black girl after the speech.

'Pack o' lies,' said the perceptive child.

Something amiss with the chapel sound-amplification caused Mr Blair's voice to sound as though he had just inhaled from a helium tap. Listening to it made us feel as though we had. But the speech was for television. Few of the children looked riveted by his thoughts on negative equity.

Most did not try. When the Prime Minister told them he had come to win not just votes but hearts, one girl, drawing her blouse up at the midriffs, placed the collar over her head. It was an eloquent response. The speech was vapid. Seldom have so many clichés of sound, vision and song been dragooned together in so dismal a cause.

'What I say to my country,' said Mr Blair, extemporizing in monarchical fashion from a speech we were told was not a speech but 'remarks' – but which was pre-released to the press. Even the remarks are scripted.

Beside me, and before the closing hymn – yes, hymn – Alastair Campbell sneezed. I tried to say 'Bless you.' The words stuck in my throat.

He won the election, as expected, easily. My prophecy of nemesis would have to be postponed yet again. I began to feel rather like those old men in Oxford Street carrying sandwich-boards proclaiming that the end of the world is nigh. Plainly for Mr Blair it was not. But by then my cynicism had come to be quite widely shared. At the end of that year I watched his party conference performance:

Snakes alive. Talk about 'mission-creep' – this was mission-lurch, mission-leap. At his party's Brighton conference yesterday Tony Blair left the runway on a limited strike to remove one individual from a hillside in Afghanistan – and veered off on a neo-imperial mission to save the entire planet. Such was the Prime Minister's resolve that even the grey had miraculously fled his hair.

His ambitions left Kipling looking wimpish.

First a government was to be removed. The Taliban must 'surrender'.

Then all terrorism was to be wiped off the face of the earth: 'We will take action at every level.' Then all who give succour to terrorists would be zapped, being 'every bit as guilty'.

This 'force for good' was something Britain was to 'take pride in leading'.

And he had hardly started. To his audience's astonishment, after tipping his wings over the Balkans ('we won'), Blair threw the prime-ministerial VC10 into a steep starboard bank and headed for Africa.

Far below, Rwanda caught his eye. If the slaughter of millions that happened there eight years ago should be repeated, 'we would have a moral duty to act there also'. As the skies above Rwanda filled with British parachutes, Blair roared northwest to Sierra Leone. 'We were there,' he declared.

Actually, we still are. By page 5 of his speech, the greater part of Britain's armed forces was earmarked for battle across the globe.

National conscription loomed. Peering from the cockpit Blair shrugged off such details – for what was below? An immense, impenetrable jungle cut by a vast river stretching half way across Africa.

Engines roar. He wheels south. We must 'sort out', he said, the Congo.

Crikey. The cockpit radio crackles as Blair speaks. 'Hello, Aldershot, are you receiving me? Fifty thousand more troops – with parachutes, submersibles, Zodiacs, malaria pills and jungle survival kits . . .

'. . . Hello? Hello? There aren't any left? Damn. Get me Gordon Brown.'

He flies on. Zambia slips beneath him, mercifully, in a moment of inattention. Sudan, Eritrea, Somalia, Kenya, Zanzibar, are hidden below the horizon behind, thank God. But what's this? Oops. Zimbabwe.

'No excuses!' Blair cries, 'no tolerance of' . . . the activities of Mr Mugabe's henchmen. 'Proper commercial, legal and financial systems! The will . . . to broker agreements for peace and provide troops to police them!' Locked into the aircraft loo the Defence Secretary, Geoff Hoon, was softly weeping.

'Africa is a scar,' Blair declared. 'We could heal it.'

Nor was there limit to the great healer's optimism. As cloudbanks roll beneath his rhetorical journey – now to create a Palestinian homeland, secure the state of Israel and – hey presto! – sort out the Middle East – Mr Blair's thoughts turn to meteorology. 'We could defeat climate change if we chose to. Kyoto is right!

'But it's only a start!' Cripes. The Prime Minister then vowed to 'create energy without destroying our planet; we could provide work and trade without deforestation'.

Time to head home, via a gushing transatlantic tribute to American values. Land rises in the east. Uh-oh. Ireland. 'The Unionists must accept . . . the Republicans must show.' Musts, shoulds and wills peppered his text like bulletholes in a Kabul ceiling.

As the PM brought his oratorical jetliner into land at Brighton yesterday, he looked exhausted. His audience looked exhausted. The Chancellor looked inscrutable.

Tony Blair had done superlatively what he does best. Talked. He had marched his troops to the top of the hill and must hope Fate does not finish the couplet. And – what the hell – it was only a speech. *C'était magnifique mais ce n'était pas la guerre.*

Both this sketch and the sketch about the election launch at St Olave's and St Saviour's school were placed on the *Times* front page. More and more, I was finding that these assessments struck a chord at least with some. Instead of seeming out on a limb and perversely unappreciative of new Labour's appeal, I found readers and colleagues chuckling in agreement.

But they carried on voting for the enterprise I held in such scorn. There is a limit to the number of times a columnist can warn of an impending implosion and as the century turned I was aware that I was approaching it.

To myself I explained this, and still do, with the thought that, like rubble tipped into a lake, doubts about a party in government sink into the collective unconscious of a nation and settle below the surface. Over time the sub-aquatic heap grows, but until it breaks the surface the lake appears untroubled. One day, however – and one rock too many – the tip of this hidden mountain breaks through. The collective conscious has been forced to take account of what has long been forming the collective unconscious. Something perhaps in itself quite small becomes horribly prominent in the public imagination. We call it a 'turning point' or 'the end of the affair' but in reality the change has been incremental and slow.

This, I tell myself, is why everything we know about our present governors seems still to make no impact on voting intentions. Besides, the times are good, the economy's strong, the Tories are weird, and people are not yet ready to tell themselves out loud what silently they have known for many years.

Well, perhaps. But I may be deluding myself. As likely is that adulation for New Labour will subside gently into qualified appreci-ation, followed by mild doubt, followed, a couple of general elections down the line, by an inclination to give another party its turn in government; but that throughout and subsequently new Labour will be appreciated as a serious and positive force, a transformed political party led by a man who made the centre-left grow up, and thus left his country stronger and safer than he found it. And, honoured and respected, he will retire.

Oddly enough, I find that second account to be not just as likely an outcome but as fair a picture as the account coloured by my own personal irritation at the man. Maybe I'm jealous. Maybe I'm tilting against a hated part of my own nature for which poor Mr Blair has become the surrogate target. In some lights he resembles a better-looking version of me: we both have oversized ears and we both tend to preach.

Anyway, he can take it. But I would not have dished it out with such relish these last ten years had Tony Blair behaved, whatever his faults, with more generosity in victory. Crowing is an ugly sound.

Triumphalism is simply bad form. That, at least – from Neil Kinnock's Sheffield rally in 1992 right through to Tony Blair's conference rants as the century turned – I did see clearly as Labour modernized. I may be wrong, but I think I know what to make of him.

What to make of Gordon Brown I have not the least idea. Focused as a sketchwriter must be on performance, I noticed from the start the shadow Chancellor's leaden delivery. It was a form of verbal heavy-shelling, accompanied (until he learned to stop the habit) with a thumping fist on the lectern or dispatch box.

The leadenness seemed more than a matter of delivery: it inhabited the man, and the word really is 'leaden' rather than 'wooden' for it was not lifeless but heavy, full of force, and, I sensed, touched by anger. Even the argument came in bullet-points, and I noted in one sketch how, where most of us bring the pitch of our voice in to land on the last syllable of a sentence, Gordon Brown would hit the runway two or three words from the end, then bounce – bang, bang, bang – along the bottom to the finish.

These were the obvious points to make. Less obvious but, once spotted, more intriguing, was something which seemed at odds with the unforgiving tenor of Mr Brown's speech and refusal, as it were, to sing: he really was keen to perform more prettily. I never noticed any conscious attempt at self-improvement or sign of coaching in Tony Blair's delivery: Blair was a natural and always the same. Gordon Brown was not a natural, knew it, and slowly altered his delivery in an attempt to become more audience-friendly and better at pleasing the crowd. At the end of the year in which he first became Chancellor, I noted this:

Gordon Brown's presentational skills have been transformed over the past year. He used to be boring and deafening. Now he is just boring. He used to thunder; now he just rumbles. He used to sound positively suicidal; now he just sounds faintly grumpy. He used to seem gripped by some black and fathomless internal rage; now he just looks cross.

Joking apart, the Chancellor's delivery is more deft than once it was. He has learned a lighter touch and stopped thumping the table. Most important, he sounds confident and sure of his ground.

I had little doubt the effort to change had been conscious, perhaps even systematic. Because these things interest me I had lighted upon and read carefully a report which appeared in *The Times* a few months earlier. It summarized the findings of an academic who had studied the interrelationship between politicians' speeches and crowd applause, and concluded that a wickedly effective technique among speakers who wanted to give the impression of wowing an audience was to angle for applause, then interrupt it, as if impatient to go on. The impression would be given of a demagogue struggling to make progress against his own followers' adoration. Speakers who did this were judged as being among the best orators.

Not many weeks later, I observed Gordon Brown doing precisely this, at a party conference. I could not recall that it had ever been his habit before. And it worked. I think he had read that article and altered his own technique to produce the desired effect. This, I concluded, was a man who, aware that he was not one of nature's orators, was working on it. This was a politician doggedly intent on turning himself into a leader.

I saw a different facet of the same picture in 2001, after clambering aboard the quasi-royal special train which conveyed Gordon Brown, Tony Blair and a wagonload of journalists to Birmingham where Blair was to unveil his party's general election manifesto. I noticed that Blair and Brown had been seated facing each other, Blair facing forward in the direction of travel, and thought, ho-hum.

Sure enough, within minutes of the train pulling out of Euston station in London Gordon Brown was out of that seat like a scalded cat. Bursting from the prime ministerial carriage, and for what seemed like hours (and was certainly the better part of the journey), the Chancellor paced the section of the train where we journalists sat, working the carriages like minor royalty, asking people how they were, sharing little jokes and often laboured conversations with each. We couldn't get rid of him.

This was not the behaviour of a man careless of appearances and above stooping to soft-soap the media. The impression did not sit easily with his other image: of lofty disregard for politicking.

A few weeks later, at the end of the campaign, I followed him to a school near Nottingham where he was to speak. The speech hardly yielded a sketch so I approached the aide accompanying him and asked for details of his day's itinerary after that, so I could try to keep up by train or plane. His aide gave me the schedule but (perfectly politely) doubted I could travel as fast as the Chancellor and regretted that there was no space in his car (I had not asked for or expected this). I decided to make the best of what I had already seen, sketch that and go home.

En route my mobile telephone rang. It was the Chancellor's aide, travelling with him. He wanted to tell me he was sorry he had not been able to be more helpful; was there anything more Mr Brown could do to make sure I got my sketch? Would I like to try to get to Scotland where that day's campaigning would end?

I am not a lobby correspondent, a top-flight financial journalist or any kind of financial journalist. Nor am I a Fleet Street heavyweight commentator. I'm just a capering sketchwriter with a reputation for being consistently horrid about Tony Blair. The aide's behaviour, which I think may well have been prompted by his boss, struck me as interesting. Gordon Brown, I thought, is a very odd man indeed. I was relieved to think he did not hate me.

John Prescott, on the other hand, did.

An important plank of my whole sketchwriting career has consisted in lampooning Mr Prescott's long and inconclusive war with the English language, and it is true that from my (and fellow-sketchwriters') many columns describing his tangles with words and fist-fights with grammar, he emerges as a figure of fun. But he does not emerge as an unlikeable figure nor necessarily a lightweight one. Any reader will have drawn from my pictures the consistent impression of a politician with something to say who never fails to get it across, even if the words are in the wrong order. This we may contrast with the generality of his colleagues, whose words are in the right order but who have nothing to say.

In short, I do not think I ever did John Prescott's career the slightest damage. I did, however, hurt him, though without meaning to.

There is never any mistaking real hurt; there had not been when John Redwood looked so obviously wounded by my Vulcan sketches. John Prescott spotted me at a *Times* reception at the Reform Club in the late nineties and stormed straight at me. I backed. He raised a clenched fist and applied it so gently as to be just touching, to my face. I wish there had been a camera present. A photographer bounded over but by then Prescott was contriving a grin. There was no thought of actually landing a blow – but it had not been a joke. He told me it was all very well for stuck-up, smart-arsed grammar-school boys like me to mock the grammar of a self-made man, but some people did not think it was funny and he resented it very much. I said that sketchwriters would be just as hard on an upper-class twit. I doubt we will ever be friends.

Whether I shall ever be friends with . . . well, why name him? His rudeness was not intended, just indicative.

We met, introduced by a mutual friend, at a Labour Party Conference at Blackpool during the early years of Tony Blair's leadership. A young, fair-haired and slightly intense former theologian, he seemed pleasant, and the three of us formed a plan to find supper together. We walked along the promenade on a dark, windy evening, towards the town centre.

Tony Blair had made his leader's speech that day, and the three of us talked about it; I was taking my habitual sceptical view. I began to laugh about Blair's hand-gestures which this year had been particularly demagogic. I illustrated one, stalking along and throwing out an outstretched palm as if in appeal to some divinity.

Our young companion stopped dead in his tracks on the promenade. 'I'm sorry,' he said, 'but I cannot eat with you.' He wanted no part, even as witness, in tomfoolery about the leader and took personal offence, he said, at the implied criticism. He walked off. The next day when we passed he refused to look at me, whether on principle or in embarrassment I cannot say.

I was taken aback. It was creepy. Nobody in the political world I
shared and lived in took themselves, their party or their leader that
seriously. Even at the height of her ascendancy it was always acceptable
among Tories to giggle at Mrs Thatcher. This young Puritan's reaction
was an early warning of the Orwellian/Cromwellian flavour to the
ascendancy which was now coming in.

He's an MP now.

Over a glass of wine one afternoon, John Major had told me there
was one among his ministers of whom Britain would be seeing a great
deal more in the years to come: a first-rate man the press had not
much noticed yet, but would. Did I know about whom he was
talking?

I guessed the name right, and did not disagree.

I had first met William Hague when I, who had ceased to be an
MP, went round for supper at the new flat of a friend who was on
the verge of becoming one. Alan Duncan and I had known each other
since my Blue Chip days when he had worked for my fellow-Blue
Chip, John Patten. A former President of the Oxford Union and a
sort of bonsai Michael Heseltine known among friends as Hunky
Dunky, Alan Duncan had been an oil-trader and returned from
Singapore to start looking for a seat. He was a capable liberal of a
politically unsentimental kind with a good understanding of global
economics.

I had helped Alan secure an interview – and written him a reference
for Conservative Central Office (a friendly duty of which I am prouder
than of that performed for Ivan Massow, the gay financial services
entrepreneur, to whose party loyalty I testified in the following words:
'Ivan could never be anything other than a Conservative.' He later
defected to the Labour Party. Fond as I am of Ivan, I should have
thought twice before trusting a man who, when at his housewarming
party an expensively suited guest fell into Ivan's new pond, could hiss
'Is my fish hurt? I paid fifty quid for that carp.'

With Alan my faith was well placed: he is a Tory frontbencher
now. But long before he entered Parliament I gave him the use of my
barn in Derbyshire, to store two huge wooden containers of his
belongings from Singapore. When, after more than a year, he bought
his flat in south-west London and was able to unpack them, rats had

unfortunately got into the crate containing his clothes, and gnawed them. Alan suggested we throw away his gnawed shirts but they were good shirts so I decided to wash and keep them. To this day I wear a couple of (for me) untypically expensive shirts with rat-holes bitten into their shoulder-seams. It's just a matter of keeping your jacket on. I hate wasting things.

Alan had taken as a lodger his old friend from Oxford Union days: William Hague.

William turned up only at the end of that evening at Alan's. He had not joined us for dinner, at which Alan's other guest was Andrew Sullivan, another Oxford friend. Now a magazine editor in the United States and an acknowledged writer and thoughtful right-wing publicist for gay emancipation, Andrew is one of the first generation of HIV-positive men who are not going to die young, do not need to make a big thing of it and can get on with their lives. I did not know then he was gay. He was a slight, pale, teasing, alluring, strangely assured young man. Now he's pumping iron.

William came bounding up the stairs just before midnight like an enthusiastic retriever puppy, full of intelligence and goodwill and a sense of fun. He was direct, sharp and blunt all at the same time – the best sort of Yorkshireman. We sat around over coffee, attempting mimicry of the Tory great and good, not least Margaret Thatcher.

I took to William immediately, as most people do, and never altered that judgement. He was certainly a no-nonsense kind of Conservative and loved to mock the liberal, the weasely and the politically correct, but there was nothing bitter or hateful in his Conservatism.

Years later I found it hard to recognize the divisive and sour caricature he had attracted, and temporarily invited, as a rightward-lurching Tory leader.

I think it was a mixture of opportunism and cock-up. It was certainly not William, nor was it ever true that he is without beliefs and instincts of his own; he was just too young to become Opposition leader – his mother Stella was right, as mothers tend to be – and wanted it too much, then panicked and let judgements inferior to his own prevail.

The William I saw is better expressed in an unexpected moment a few years later, when both Alan and he had become Members of Parliament while I was now a journalist. Hague and I were to join a

TV discussion on the politics of the moment. The studio was a cramped affair on Charlotte Street, and there was no changing room and no make-up assistant. We were both hot and sweaty, my eternal six o'clock shadow was more Desperate Dannish than ever, and William's bald head was shining. 'You'll have to use the gents' loo,' said an apologetic production assistant. 'Here's a make-up compact you could share.'

Neither Hague nor I knew much about make-up but the box contained a single powder-puff and powder and we thought we could make do with that. He powdered his pate, then I powdered my chin. William looked at me with laughing eyes. 'Well, who would have thought it, eh, Matthew?' he said. 'That it should come to this. Together in the gents' lavatory and only one puff between us.' After that it would have been impossible to dislike him.

When he became Tory leader I was determined not to make the mistake I had arguably made as a result of my soft spot for John Major. I was very hard on William Hague both as a sketchwriter and as a columnist, though I think my sketches did, with those of other sketchwriters, establish him early as the brilliant Commons performer he was. But I mocked his voice, his harangues, his soap-box anti-euro hard sell, his baldness and his gimmickry; and the picture I painted of the last days of the gruesome general election campaign which finished him was cruel – because the spectacle was cruel. I wrote what follows on the day after the Deputy Prime Minister, John Prescott, hit a man who threw an egg at him . . .

'Have you got any eggs?' asked William Hague in the rain yesterday. He was descending from his helicopter, *Common Sense*, in one of those car-coats they advertise in the *Sunday Times Magazine* at £39.95. Ffion was with him.

Egg-throwing? It was a forlorn hope. Arriving out of a grey cloud the Tory leader was struggling to be interesting enough for anyone to want to hit him.

The touchdown of *Common Sense* on a waste of wet grass somewhere near the A1 was not auspicious. The helicopter flew in confidently enough, but seemed to hesitate about where to land. It hovered over what seemed like a likely patch of grass, then changed its mind and hovered somewhere else. Finally it hovered back to where it had started and, very tentatively, settled in a puddle. A metaphor for Mr Hague's leadership.

Undaunted the pair sped to St Albans for a rally in the square. The weather turned icy. The rain bucketed down. The rally was cancelled and a meet-the-party-workers in the Town Hall hastily arranged. A claque of supporters were spooked by protestors with pillowcases over their heads. Ffion ignored them and looked overjoyed as shivering Tories attempted an ecstatic cheer in the rain. Upstairs the couple staged Britain's first centrally heated, indoor walkabout in a half-empty hall. Hague threw himself at his speech like a *Just a Minute* contestant – a marriage of energy with passionlessness – the candidate, Charles Elphincke, nodding and grinning like a zombie.

William and Ffion left, for all the world as though they were having a perfectly lovely time – to brave cheers and a group outside shouting, 'You're not welcome here!'

This campaign was to be William Hague's finest hour, the journey he has been planning for twenty years. It must be scary to grab the wheel, hit the gas pedal, and feel no response. Alone in the dark with Ffion in the small hours, does he weep?

In return for the rude reception I gave his leadership, William Hague was never anything but kind, good-humoured, hospitable and warm towards me. He is a big man who seized too early what he mistakenly thought to be his moment. His moment will come. I think that if he stays in politics he will occupy more than one of the great offices of state as the most substantial Tory figure of his political generation.

Not so long ago I found myself by chance at the performance of *The Rivals* which, I later read, Tony and Cherie Blair also attended. Tony Blair had by then already been Prime Minister for many years. I wonder whether he noted, as I did, this line of Richard Sheridan's: '. . . While Hope pictures to us a flattering scene of future bliss, let us deny its pencil those colours which are too bright to be lasting.'

I had come full circle. In a small sleight of hand cynically dispatched over a mobile telephone in that BBC car by Alastair Campbell, I had seen the worm in the apple. I had watched these hermit crab politicians, sharp-clawed but pliable, scuttling beneath the carapaces of other men's ideas. And in a lecture theatre in Bloomsbury as the new Opposition leader crayoned our imaginations with his dreams, I had been dazzled then disgusted for the first time by colours too bright to be lasting.

20. Peter, Jeremy, *Newsnight* and Me

To some extent a television or radio programme matters because people think it matters. Serious viewers listen, serious journalists report, so serious pundits and politicians appear – and the 'mattering thing' becomes self-reinforcing. Invited on to BBC television's *Newsnight* programme, people tend to accept, because *Newsnight* matters. A taxi across town after 10 p.m. is fast and you're home by midnight. All you have to remember is not to drink too much beforehand.

I had limited myself to a Becks lager at Chilli's Mexican restaurant at Canary Wharf when on the evening of 27 October 1998 I tore into the BBC Television Centre at White City in a taxi from London Docklands, late: so late I almost missed my *Newsnight* interview slot. I wish I had.

A researcher had telephoned me that morning to ask if I would appear around eleven to talk to the programme's interviewer and anchor, Jeremy Paxman, about homosexuality and politics. Specifically they wanted to discuss Ron Davies.

Ron Davies, the Secretary of State for Wales, had found himself in difficulty after meeting a man late at night on Clapham Common – for what purpose the nation remained uncertain – after which he had been robbed. He described the episode as 'a moment of madness' and was quickly forced to resign from the Cabinet. The whole affair, a lucky blend in confused and half-informed minds of sex (possibly), drugs (possibly), politics (undoubtedly) and crime (allegedly) lacked only a royal dimension to make it the perfect tabloid and broadsheet feast. It was at any event a ripping good story.

Primarily out of sympathy for Mr Davies, but not without an element of calculation, I had chosen the moment a few days previously to write in *The Times* for the first time about my own experience on Clapham Common: about being beaten up there.

It was not a column I ever wanted to write. My failure to tell the truth about this assault had never been (to me) wholly excusable, but for as long as I was an MP I could comfort myself that the truth might have destroyed me. After leaving Parliament I told myself that serious television presenters, too, have appearances to keep up, so this was not the moment to say more. And the incident receded into the past, with every passing year less important. There was now no reason to come out with it, apropos of nothing. I had told a lie many years ago and in circumstances when disclosure might have been self-destructive – well, so what?

But it nagged at my conscience. Could I not afford to set the record straight? I had thought and worried about it for years. Not that anybody else cared – I had told almost nobody – but for the sake of my own self-respect, it would be good to get it off my chest.

It would make a good story. That was important. Most of the personal stories a journalist tells, however painful, are related because he thinks they will engage his readers. This would. But, though I had always known as much – known it was a cracker of a tale, better than many which, week by week, I was choosing – still I had shrunk from writing about it. Some people enjoy cataloguing their own disgrace, others are careless about what they confess, but on the most personal sorts of things I have always felt stupidly but incurably on my dignity. For me to admit I had hung around in the dark, under trees, for sex, wounded my pride. There was also the embarrassment of friends, the disapproval of the censorious and the disillusionment of kind people who thought better of me. This last weighed most heavily.

I was not sure that my paper, its editor, and its proprietor, Rupert Murdoch, would think such reminiscence – unprompted, years after the event – quite fitted the dignity of *The Times*. Only once in more than a decade had an editor ever asked me to reconsider a word I had written, and that was when I had submitted a lively column describing Mr Amateur Strip Night at the White Swan (a gay pub near where I lived in Limehouse) and discussing male stripping as an art. The page editor had gently suggested that, as Rupert Murdoch was in town that week, and as it was not known what view he took of these sorts of frolic, I should resubmit it later. I did, and *The Times* published it.

As strongly as doubt and inertia kept me from writing about Clapham Common, something pulled the other way. To have done these – to many – quite disgraceful things, and to have persisted in such risky behaviour for some time at a period in my life when the truth would have ruined me, and never since to have breathed a word of it, was neither candid nor brave.

I had been writing regularly about morality and homosexuality and, as an MP, urging reform of the law (for instance) on soliciting; yet here was a direct interest I had never declared. And if a columnist has a habit of writing in a personal way, seeming to reveal himself as a flesh-and-blood human being to his readers, taking them into his confidence and implicitly asking for their understanding or approval, should he leave something so big out of the account?

'Why now, in particular?' had always settled it. This time, however, that 'why now?' was squared. Ron Davies had been caught where I had not, and ruined where I was not.

I wrote the column and it was well received. I felt incredibly tense about the whole thing, but there had been no repercussions. This was the background to *Newsnight*'s request that I join a discussion about Ron Davies's fate.

I knew what I wanted to say: that Mr Davies may have been foolish but that I knew the temptations; that trying to deny things often got you into more stupid behaviour than being relaxed about them would; that it was a pity for anyone's Cabinet career to founder on their sexuality these days because the whole atmosphere had changed and being gay was no bar to a political career; that the country and the Prime Minister had already accepted openly gay Cabinet ministers; that even the Tories would; and that Davies was probably one of the last of a passing generation for whom these things had been taken as grave impediments to office.

My car, which had failed to find me for twenty minutes at Canary Wharf, swept into the BBC Television Centre minutes before this discussion was due. An anxious researcher was waiting at reception. We hurried through empty corridors. The White City complex seems almost deserted late at night, and *Newsnight* is such a laid-back programme that in the unpeopled quiet of the night I felt a sense of the *Marie Celeste*, a great, empty ship, broadcasting live, with just a relaxed Jeremy Paxman and my fellow-guest, Dr Liam Fox, the Opposition health spokesman, rattling around in a little pool of light in a huge, mostly dark studio, a couple of unspeaking cameramen wheeling their machines silently around, and a few operatives, no doubt, in a control room somewhere flicking switches.

It was possible to forget that though there were only a million or so people out there watching, they included many of the nation's political journalists; and that the deadline for the late editions of the next morning's papers had not yet passed.

Jeremy asked me about homosexuality and politics. Making the point that being gay was no longer a bar to office, I said, 'There are at least two gay members of the Cabinet.' In fact I knew of three, but no story about the sexuality of the former government chief whip and by then Minister of Agriculture, Nick Brown, had, as far as I knew, ever been published.

JEREMY PAXMAN: *Are* there two gay members of the Cabinet?
MYSELF: Well, Chris Smith is openly gay and I think Peter Mandelson is certainly gay.
PAXMAN: I think we will just move on from there. I am not quite sure where he is on this.

Jeremy Paxman's jaw dropping was my first warning of the row which was to follow.

For all the regret which I have expressed ever since, and repeat here, for saying what I did, when, where and in the way I did, I must say too that I think the whole fuss was perfectly absurd.

One must not be disingenuous. As the 'I think' which jumped in (awkwardly, introducing as it did the word 'certainly') betrays, I must have realized I had lurched on to tricky terrain. But were one to choose a word to describe the territory I thought we were in, 'cheeky' is that word.

For as long as I had known him Peter Mandelson had scolded people who discussed his homosexuality – but in the way we might scold someone for talking about politics or religion in the pub. I had absolutely no idea anybody would seriously maintain that Peter Mandelson's homosexuality was a secret. It never occurred to me.

I had smiled at Rory Bremner's 'you can come out now sketch' of Mandelson. I knew that Edwina Currie had said he was gay on her radio programme. I had read quite recently a leading article in the *Independent* newspaper saying so, and I knew that the same paper had published articles, one by a psychologist and one by their gay columnist John Lyttle, mentioning Peter's homosexuality. The Lyttle column had revealed that if you typed 'gay' and 'Mandelson' into a database, 111 newspaper stories were referenced.

I knew Peter Kellner in the London *Evening Standard* had said so: he had made it one of the key points of a column. I knew the *News of the World*, years previously, had devoted its front-page splash to Mandelson's living with a boyfriend. I had seen the fact reported so often, heard it discussed so regularly and in such a matter-of-fact way that I assumed that Peter Mandelson's homosexuality was a matter of public record, often alluded to, uncontested and beyond contention.

I did know that all mention of his private life riled him. I knew that mention of David Mellor's or Cecil Parkinson's private lives riled *them*. What I thought I was doing in adding Peter Mandelson explicitly to my list of two gay MPs (Chris Smith's sexuality was even more famous) was twitting him, in a not entirely unaffectionate way, with something he rather grandly thought he could banish from conversation. I have since watched the interviewer Michael Parkinson broach with Nicole Kidman her former marriage to Tom Cruise, to her evident irritation. This is just the sort of thing I had in mind for Peter: to prod, not to wound, and not to reveal.

Inasmuch as I thought about it at all, then, I suspected that this reference would irk the Secretary of State for Trade and Industry – the sort of remark that evokes a fiery glance, a too hearty chuckle, and an 'Oh not that nonsense again, Matthew. Have you nothing new to tell us?'

But Paxman looked stunned. Liam Fox looked aghast and said not a word. Slight anxiety – the first rustling of leaves hinting at the impending storm – ruffled my composure, but we carried on. At the end of the interview, Jeremy shook my hand – odd, I thought – and disappeared. I now know that he headed off to compose a handwritten letter of apology to Mandelson, which he personally delivered at dawn the following day.

There was a reason for this. That summer, Jeremy had (Peter believed) told friends, though not maliciously, about a man he had seen Peter going out with socially. Mandelson and Paxman were friends; an account of this chatter had reached Mandelson's ears and he had let Jeremy know of his irritation. And now Mandelson switched on his television and saw Jeremy asking me to name the Cabinet ministers I thought were gay. One can guess how Mandelson would have interpreted this. Jeremy Paxman must have made just such a guess as his jaw dropped.

The handwritten note was not just to apologize but to make clear that he, Jeremy, had had nothing to do with it. And I know that he had not, for there had been no talk preliminary to the interview, there or elsewhere, and he and I had never discussed Mandelson. Unless he was psychic, Jeremy can have had no inkling what I was going to say. But for Peter to suppose otherwise was, though mistaken, not so paranoid as many, hearing about it later, thought.

I as yet knew nothing of any of this when my BBC car ferried me, tired and only slightly unsettled, back to Narrow Street. I was in a hurry as I had a half-hour stint down the line from home with BBC Radio 5 Live lined up for midnight. (I have a home microphone and an ISDN link-up.)

I was in place just in time. I forget what it was about – certainly not Mandelson – but will never forget the discussion because after ten uneventful minutes my line suddenly went dead. I was left at dead of night calling 'Hello? Hello?' into a dead microphone. I put down the phone.

Immediately it rang. It was my friend and assistant, Julian Glover, who had said he would watch the *Newsnight* interview. He sounded terrified. He had only one question: 'Did you mean to say that?'

'What?'

'About Mandelson.'

'Yes, I did. No secret – is it?'

'Don't say anything more. We'll talk tomorrow. Unplug your telephone and get some sleep.' Deluged by calls, he had had to unplug his.

I left my telephone plugged in. Within minutes, newspapers were ringing. I took Julian's advice. When I reconnected the phone early the next morning the calls resumed at once. The *Daily Mail* offered me £10,000 for a single column.

I disconnected the telephone again, and realized fully and for the first time the enormity of my error on *Newsnight*. Half the world, it seemed, didn't know anybody who didn't know Peter Mandelson was gay. Half the world didn't know anybody who did. I had breached the wall between those two halves.

★

There followed a pretty bloody week. It was hard to know who dismayed me more: gay campaigners on the left who tore into me for betraying a fellow-homosexual or Tory stalwarts who congratulated me for 'telling the truth about that furtive little . . .' – and then they would stop, embarrassed at the realization that 'queer' would not be my favourite word.

Neither response was the worst of my woes. Though it was politic to appear mortified that I might have hurt Peter Mandelson – and I do regret hurting anybody – the truth is that squeamishness on Peter's behalf is not called for: he can look after himself and has seldom hesitated to crush, by fair means or foul, those who get in his way. What troubled me most was the sympathetic silence of colleagues who knew, as I knew, that what had happened was simply a blunder. It's fine in journalism to wound someone on purpose, but unprofessional to do it by mistake.

The possibility opened up, I suppose, of yanking my career off in a tabloid direction and taking the *Daily Mail*'s silver: to become Parris, the Man They Couldn't Gag, but I did not care for such a role nor would I have been good at it. The idea that I had been 'brave' on *Newsnight* was wrong. For a writer and broadcaster who remained hopeful of commanding some respect, this particular career – in my series of careers – shipwreck was nearer than it ever had been before. In retrospect I have no doubt that it was at this point – this quiet, sickening realization that I had behaved in a way that would be seen as unprofessional and dishonourable – and not in the thick of battle as I was attacked later, that my future came closest to being knocked totally off course.

The battle saved me, and Peter started it. Unwittingly, Peter Mandelson rescued me, I have no doubt of that.

He should have retreated hurt. This would have been the best means of attack. Few in Britain can resist an injured party, and if he had expressed his sense of offence once and in a clear and dignified way, and then said nothing more in public and done nothing more in private, but accepted in a generous though wounded way the apologies which had already started coming (for instance) from Jeremy and would quickly have come from me too, then the chapter would have closed and there could only have been one lesson the world would have drawn from it.

Parris would have been the aggressor. I would have been judged to have spoken in a way which was uncalled for, ungentlemanly, uncivilized, unprovoked, attention-seeking and cheap. To rub my face in it people could have replayed time and again that eighties interview with Vincent Hanna in which, to Vincent's question about my sexuality, I had cordially told him to mind his own business.

As victim Peter would have been undamaged by the episode; on a tide of sympathy his stock would actually have risen. Also achieved would have been the reconciliation of his private life with his public profile without any effort on his part: everything out in the open, no more anxiety, and no possible breath of complaint that he had tried to draw attention to himself in any way. It would all have been that wicked Parris. No gay politician could hope for a more cost-free route from A to B than by way of an uncalled-for disclosure by an unkind journalist. It is the journalist who will get the opprobrium.

And at first I did. The immediate reaction, almost unmitigatedly pro-Peter and anti-me, knocked me for six. Four distinct conspiracy theories quickly formed. They were of varying plausibility and all untrue.

The first was that I had cooked this up alone as a means of getting publicity for myself and for my (largely historical) book on Church scandal which was by coincidence just on the verge of publication at the time of the Ron Davies affair; in short a career move by a journalist prepared to betray anyone for a newspaper splash.

That would have been a good idea – for a more single-minded publicist than myself. In fact I had forgotten all about my new book when I entered the *Newsnight* studio. I thought bitterly when I heard this suggestion of all the stories with which I could have made a splash, were I so minded: of my days at the Conservative Research Department; of an evening not so long before when, leaving from the English National Opera, I had encountered a married Labour Party frontbencher emerging from a gay bar on St Martin's Lane, Brief Encounter – a place below street-level where rent-boys ply. I thought of the former Tory MP I had bumped into in the West End, all in leather and chains. What stories these would have made. But such journalism is not my trade.

The second conspiracy was that Jeremy Paxman and I had cooked this up together as a means of advancing both our careers, the well-publicized hand-delivered letter of apology a fiendish ploy to add to its appeal while distracting the media from Jeremy's complicity. This might have been a good idea too, had Jeremy needed to raise his profile and been the kind of man to stoop in this way. He didn't and isn't.

The third conspiracy was that Rupert Murdoch, the proprietor of News International and my biggest ultimate employer, had cooked this up with me. His Sky television network were bidding at the time for Manchester United Football Club, a bid which would come before the Industry Secretary for approval. The *Newsnight* episode was a way of putting a warning shot across Peter's bows.

This, I thought (and I heard it repeatedly), was plausible but would have been poor psychology for anyone who knew Peter. When I was later sacked from the *Sun*, the Murdoch conspiracy ran again on new legs, now as a bid by Mr Murdoch for Mandelson's forgiveness. This too was plausible, but would have been poor psychology on the part of anyone who knew Rupert Murdoch. Both versions ran into one difficulty: Rupert Murdoch was uninvolved. I had at that time spoken to him only once in my life, many years previously.

The fourth conspiracy was that Peter Mandelson and I had cooked this up as a means of getting his sexuality definitively into the public domain by the least embarrassing means possible – and before the tabloids took another lunge. This was in my view the most plausible explanation of all and would have been a very good idea on Peter's part. But as the next turn of events was to show, it cannot have appealed to him.

The BBC banned all mention of Peter Mandelson's private life. The memo, issued hard on the heels of the *Newsnight* interview, could not be couched in general terms, banning mention of any public figure's private life, because that would have ruled out much of the media report and commentary on the previous eighteen years of Tory misdemeanours, not to mention the story of the hour: Ron Davies. So the memo said this: 'Please will all programmes note that under no circumstances whatsoever should allegations about the private life of Peter Mandelson be repeated on any broadcast.'

Some said Peter had himself demanded it, having made a direct or indirect approach at a high level in the corporation. He was a friend of, among others, the director-general, John Birt. Others said a twitch of his eyebrow was enough: middle-ranking BBC executives had reacted as they supposed Mr Mandelson would have wished. I have never bothered to find out because it is immaterial who initiated the ban: as soon as Mandelson got wind of it he could have had it rescinded. A thirty-second telephone call would have sufficed.

Much to my good fortune, he cannot have made it. The impact was immediate. The ban at once became a bigger story than the *Newsnight* interview. Panellists on the *Question Time* political discussion programme on BBC television were warned beforehand by their chairman, Jonathan Dimbleby, not to mention Mandelson – prompting one of his Cabinet colleagues, Mo Mowlam, to say, on air, that it was insulting to be gagged in this way. There was a tremendous fuss in the newspapers, which dragged out the story for weeks. The story was revived when, during a BBC interview with the gay actor Nigel Hawthorne, the interviewer repeatedly interrupted and finally silenced Hawthorne, who was trying to talk about media curiosity about Mandelson. (The interview was about the unveiling of the first public statue of Oscar Wilde to appear in Britain. As it happened, and though nobody mentioned it, I had been a member of the committee which had planned and commissioned this work.)

Then I was sacked from the *Sun*.

I had been writing a weekly page – a magazinish mixture of politics and current affairs – for about a year. I was never happy I was achieving quite the right tone but was pleased at the chance to try writing for a tabloid and would have liked to continue. It ended a couple of days after *Newsnight*. Sitting at my desk at the *Times* room at Westminster I answered a telephone call from the *Sun*'s editor, David Yelland, with whom I was on friendly terms, but hardly really knew.

'What did you think of Prime Minister's Questions this week?' he asked – an odd inquiry from a tabloid editor out of the blue, especially since this was the first time he had ever rung for a chat. We maintained the pretence of a conversation for a minute or so before I decided to end it. 'Have you rung to fire me?' I asked.

He said he had. He sounded embarrassed. 'Is this because of Mandelson?' I asked.

'Yes,' he said. He explained that the paper wanted to take a clear stand, demonstrating that it would have nothing to do with homophobia. As I was, as far as anyone knew, the paper's only gay columnist, ever, the logic here was tortured. When a few days later the paper ran a lead story entitled 'Is Britain being run by a gay mafia?', I gave up trying to work out what they were up to. It is always a mistake to suppose that a thread of consciousness runs through the psyche of a popular newspaper.

I did hear gossip that Rupert Murdoch's daughter, Elisabeth (whom I took parachuting all those years ago), was a friend of David Yelland '. . . and you know Peter's a chum of Elisabeth's, and Elisabeth is an influence on David, and . . .' and so on; but people always talk like this and, having learned to discount the many conspiracy stories I heard about myself, I was equally wary of those I heard about Peter. Lots of people speculated about who was up to what but, though at the centre of the whole thing, I was uninterested. I've never seen the point of whodunnits; you have to care who did it. Life is short and the truth usually turns out to be an inconclusive mess.

Besides I was not too cast down about the *Sun*. I was never meant to be a tabloid journalist. But might this be a first shot in a Murdoch-led programme of removing me from all of his newspapers? Sky Television had already sacked me (I used to deliver a weekly commentary) after I had written a column in *The Times* criticizing the concept of rolling twenty-four hour news on television – a column directed mostly at BBC *News 24*, who have merrily continued to use me since then.

I could do without Sky and the *Sun*, but I loved *The Times* and loved my place in it.

It was not by then a matter of having nowhere else to turn. As my parliamentary sketching had continued, more and more opportunities to work in broadcasting and journalism had been coming in; more television than I wanted to accept, and a great deal of radio too, which I did accept as I enjoy it. Collaborating with a friend, David Prosser, who ran an independent production company called All Out and with whom over many years I had done some of my best radio and book-researching work, a series of programmes for BBC Radio 5 Live on a variety of subjects had gone well. I could do more.

And as soon as the *Newsnight* affair had blown up, and especially after the BBC ban, editors of other newspapers had been in touch suggesting that I might want (or need) to leave *The Times*, and inviting me to talk about switching. I would not starve. But to leave *The Times* would have hurt. You get fond of a paper and feel loyal to it, abstraction though it is. You develop a relationship with your readers, or think you do. *Times* readers are a special breed.

So, after my conversation with David Yelland, I rang *The Times*'s editor, then Peter Stothard. I trusted him. He stood back most of the time but would always come forward when support was needed. I admitted feeling insecure. He said my worries were unfounded, but that I had better hear this from the proprietor. One telephone call from Rupert Murdoch in New York gave me the reassurance I needed. He said he had not known about David Yelland's decision, which was up to David Yelland, that he had no intention of sacrificing me and wanted to strengthen my bond with *The Times* (an undertaking he made good). After that I never looked back with the paper.

Slowly the reverberations from the *Newsnight* affair died away. But I found I was more famous than before, thought more controversial, and seen by some as braver and by others as more disgraceful than before. I was even treated as risky and asked anxiously by programme-makers what sort of thing I was going to say, as though I might at any point explode into the airwaves with some new and shocking revelation.

Gay friends and acquaintances in particular were split, but predominantly they did not approve. Peter had not been admired for his reticence, but I was not admired for (as they saw it) exposing him. Most gay men have had to agonize over the question of how and when to come out, and few would thank a journalist for making the decision for them. And I would agree with them – if that were what I had done, or meant to do.

A gay newspaper, the *Pink Paper*, filled the whole of its front page with my face, part-covered by a demon mask over the eyes, under the caption 'Is this the most dangerous gay man in Britain?' I felt secretly flattered. Before this my reputation wore bicycle clips; now they had been replaced by spurs and a riding whip. The episode had sharpened up my image in a way I did not entirely welcome, though in career terms it would have to be called helpful. When I make speeches or write books I still find people hoping for and half expecting saucy revelations. Sadly, I have few to offer.

If I could re-run that *Newsnight* interview, knowing what I know

now, I would not do it again. In his sympathetic political biography, *Mandelson — and the making of New Labour*, the *Independent* journalist Donald Macintyre gives the fullest account I have seen of this episode, and I do not quarrel with a word of it.

Mr Macintyre's implied conclusion is that neither Paxman nor Mandelson nor I should count this our finest hour. I do not quarrel with that either.

Because people expect contrition and it is generally best in my profession to give people what they want, I have been contrite. I have repeated that I would never have said what I did if I had thought it would cause Peter Mandelson anything like the trouble it did. This statement is true. I have said that I had not realized that discussion of his sexuality wounded rather than simply irked him. That too is true. I have added that my mistake was to overlook the difference between, for instance, the *News of the World*, Talk Radio, an editorial in the *Independent* — and *Newsnight*. All this is true. I evidently did overlook it.

I have rounded off my apology by conceding that it was stupid to overlook these obvious truths. Well, an oversight which wounds another and causes a huge row must, I suppose, be stupid. I went badly wrong. But you would be optimistic to conclude that even today I really understand how.

Were I to awake tomorrow morning and, rubbing my eyes, realize that all that business about the media going wild had been a bad dream; and, were I, as I drew my bedroom curtains and reality came flooding back, to recall that what really did happen was precisely nothing: just a knowing chuckle from a colleague at work the next day — 'You little stirrer, Matthew!'; and later one of those notelets so many of us have received in Peter's spidery hand scolding us for something disobliging we've said and vowing never to speak to us again — until next week; and a continuation of the occasional media asides about Peter being gay . . . Were I, in short, to pinch myself awake and realize the *Newsnight* interview had caused nothing like the nightmare from which I had just awoken, then on such a morning I would set out for work more confident than I am now that I understood the world into which I have fallen.

Peter is fond of explanations by conspiracy. I generally am not, but here's one, and it's an unwitting conspiracy . . .

It is true that most of the world did not know that Mandelson was gay, but in the sense that – as no doubt a poll could demonstrate – most of the world does not know that the former Transport Secretary, Stephen Byers, is not married to his partner. Most of the world has never thought to inquire.

Most of the world will take something to be a shock revelation if the media tell them it is a shock revelation. But if the media tell them that it is already well known, they will take it to be already known, though they may not have known it themselves.

Peter Mandelson, about whose private life there was plenty of published material on every file, was not liked in the media and had offended many. Whenever any colleague – for instance, Peter Kellner of the *Evening Standard* – had mentioned Mandelson's homo-sexuality in print, there had been (I now know) an intimidatory private reaction. This irritated people, not least because the minister had himself been part (at least by association) of a sustained new Labour campaign to talk up the private misdemeanours of Tories. Peter was therefore, as tabloid thugs like to put it, 'cruising for a bruising' by the press.

No journalist conspired with any other to talk up my *Newsnight* remarks, but, encouraged by Jeremy Paxman's dropped jaw, the appeal of this mischief as a good news story for those looking for mischief occurred simultaneously to many. Peter's furious overreaction to the story then played into their hands, and it took off. Thus was a tempest whipped up from the fluttering of a butterfly's wing in the forest. I was the butterfly.

I am not sure this analysis is right. It is not easily reconciled with the apparent spontaneity of the reaction to the interview. But there might be something in it. I remained, like a child who does not quite understand what he has done wrong, puzzled: a bystander to the storm, witness to my own confusion.

I had learned at least this: that once the press decides to call something a revelation, there is no point in arguing. When in the summer of 2002 my friend Alan Duncan, by now an Opposition spokesman on foreign affairs, decided it was time to acknowledge in public what we who knew him had assumed, along with much of the press, for years – that he was gay – there was absolutely no way of knowing where, on a scale from 'So what?' to 'Top Tory tells all', the press reaction would register. I knew of no sexual skeletons in Alan's cupboard, so he was well-placed to lead rather than react to the news.

It was Alan's decision but I helped him plot its management. We met at a small Greek restaurant in Marylebone after a *Today* programme party on a hot July evening in the middle of a Tube strike. I had walked in from Limehouse. We agreed that *The Times* would be best, and that if there was one thing Tory colleagues and members could not stomach it was the volunteering of uncalled-for, breast-beating, confessional statements about sex. Alan should therefore answer a question, not make a speech. I agreed to act as go-between, snaffled a plate of Turkish Delight, and tore off to St Pancras station for the last train to Derby.

Next morning I rang the editor of *The Times*, Robert Thomson, who I knew would deal straight. I mentioned that a journalist colleague, Tom Baldwin, was someone Alan trusted. We agreed to keep the whole thing under our hats.

Alan and I spoke again that weekend. From having been hesitant, he was now almost exhilarated and I recognized from personal experience the sense of release which comes from honesty. He was also subject, I think, to a small rush of idealism (it happens even to Tory frontbenchers): he felt angry about the prejudice which still existed and almost excited that by acknowledging his own homosexuality he was standing up for others. Idealism in adolescents is as unremarkable as acne; when it breaks the surface in middle age among the careworn and cynical, it is strangely moving.

When on the last Monday in July the front page of *The Times* was dominated by a lead story – 'Senior Tory's gay revelation to test party' – written in a wholly positive way, and the pages within carried a friendly interview with Tom and a leading article praising Alan, I too felt a sense of elation. Alan had secured a good, supportive statement from Iain Duncan Smith, and even Ann Widdecombe had obliged by being cross.

By sheer coincidence the episode happened when the Tories were in one of their agonizing bouts of internal bickering (the leader had just sacked the chairman of the party) and it was being said that Duncan Smith's 'inclusive' brand of Conservatism was under test. It followed that Alan's story was helpful to the leadership, allowing it to show off its new, tolerant face, while the party's troubles were helpful to Alan, guaranteeing that only a few lunatics would choose such a time for a bout of queer-bashing. So of course everyone assumed that Alan's interview had been hastily arranged to take the heat off Duncan Smith. I know that must have been untrue because I was helping arrange it before the heat came on. There is nothing like being involved in events subject to conspiracy theories for an insight into how very plausible such theories can seem, and how false.

I decided to keep off television – my grinning chops popping up all over the place might be counterproductive, I thought – but did a series of radio interviews all day, while writing 2,000 words about the Conservative Party's strange relationship with homosexuality for the cover story in *The Times*'s second section. It had struck me that the new mood of which Alan had been able to take advantage was a change not in his party's attitude to homosexuality – with which, privately, Tories had always been as comfortable as they are, privately, with adultery – but to openness. I thought of the chief whip's advice to handle my sexuality as he handled his atheism ('You don't have to shout about it') and smiled.

I thought of my own botched attempts to come out, too, and my failure of courage in admittedly less favourable times, and felt a tinge of envy for Alan. It was easier for him than it would have been for me, but still he was brave: the first sitting Conservative MP in history to volunteer the fact that he was gay.

And as for Peter Mandelson I saw him some months after the *Newsnight* episode, surrounded by networkers, at a large reception given by the Canadian newspaper proprietor, Conrad Black, and his wife, Barbara Amiel. Peter saw me. We both looked away. This is silly, I thought, one must not shrink from these things. So, steeling myself, I walked up, drink in hand. People talking to him melted away, receding into a ragged circle, hushed, as around a brewing streetfight.

'I would never have said what I did on *Newsnight* if I had known the trouble it would cause you,' I said. 'I'm sorry.' There was silence among the spectators.

In a friendly way Peter replied that there was nothing to apologize for. He said that this had forced him to deal with something he should already have dealt with. In doing so it had done him some service. I do not know whether he really believes this but it was a generous thing to say.

21. 'You'd Better Not Look Down'

In the dead of night I awoke suddenly and for no reason. I had been working perhaps a little too hard and sleeping fitfully. It was pitch dark and I was wide awake: two hours still before dawn.

Annoying, because sleep is precious. I was thirsty. You know where everything is in your own flat, so without switching on the light, I padded gingerly to the bathroom, filled a cup with water, and sat on the edge of the bath to drink. Sleep fell away.

Blind people don't miss much. The immediacy of vision crowds out components of our perception which are more important. When the light comes on, an invisible monitor turns down the volume of our other senses; but sound, touch, and smell go very deep, and we think best with eyes screwed up.

Sit in the dark for a while and the deeper elements of our sentience begin to swell.

I did so, on the edge of the bath. I became aware of new noises, as though someone was turning up all the sound knobs. All at once I could hear the faint, low, continuous rumble of London in the night: the blurring of a million distant noises: factories, trains, and cars. Now I could hear the very slightest of hums from my stereo in the sitting room; I must have left it on stand-by.

The compressor working in my fridge was just audible from the kitchen, and so amazingly was the gentle, unfocused tick-tick of the quartz kitchen clock. From outside I could hear the Thames at high tide, whispering on the wall beneath.

And I could hear what you might call the central nervous system of my apartment block: a swish of water in the pipes, an electrical singing in the wires, the whirr of the central-heating pump upstairs, and a creak here and there as small temperature changes triggered tiny movements in the building's structure. Every sound, every growl, every little murmur, spoke (as Hardy put it) to my intelligence.

I swallowed a gulp of water. Loud within my head was the swish of the liquid, the pop and crackle as the air passage to the inner ear temporarily closed, and the sound of moving muscles in my throat. Turning my head, I heard two sharp cracks in the vertebrae, and a low grinding as the head moved. My stomach rumbled as the water went down. Breathing, I listened to each breath: the air supply whistling up and down.

I replaced the cup. Ever since smashing my right elbow when I was six, that joint, when flexed, has made a muffled wrenching sound. Usually, it can't be heard; now it seemed loud. 'It must have been doing this all day, every day, for the past thirty-nine years,' I thought. I flexed both elbows and felt, beneath the scars on my right elbow, the minimal, usually unnoticeable resistance as compared with the left. The scars seemed to rise to my fingers, impostors on the skin, silky to the touch.

Running my fingertips up towards my shoulders, I could feel the beginnings of a flabbiness around the top of the arms, such as comes with middle age; and that slight paperiness of the skin. I swung one knee, then the other, and listened to the barely audible grinding in both joints. All those marathons I have run, all those thousands of miles of training, and never a failure in either delicate, complicated joint.

I sat absolutely still in the blackness. All at once I was aware of a sound louder than these others. It had been there all along, but I had not focused upon it. It was a singing in my head: that weird, discordant electrical noise as of transformers in a sub-station or a high-voltage overhead power cable. White noise.

As I concentrated, it seemed to swell, to become almost deafening, yet I knew there was no change in the volume, just an uncharacteristic tuning in to a perception we usually screen out, but which is always with us. I was eavesdropping, as it were, on my own central nervous system, my own heating, my ventilation and power supply.

I was listening to the white noise generated by my own electronics. And now I could hear my blood, too, coursing through the artery near each ear. I could hear my heart, strong and regular: each smooth, powerful pulse followed by a gush past the ears.

What a piece of work is man. I would have rejected the design outright. I would have called for something solid and straightforward to fix. 'Too clever by half,' I would have said. 'All of that "black box" technology, that super-sophisticated electronics, those eggshell-delicate parts. Sacrifice sophistication. Design me something durable, robust.'

Yet the machine sitting on that bath's edge was both. Man is an almost miraculous combination of fragility with resilience. It doesn't bear thinking about. 'You'd better not look down if you want to keep on flying,' B. B. King used to sing.

It seems to me that human viability is an impossibility sustained by inattention. We must not eavesdrop on those noises too often or for too long. That singing in the wires should stay, mostly, a secret. I switched on the light and it fled.

This I wrote for *The Times* in March 1995. By then I had been sketching Parliament for more than six years. At the same time (and almost from the start) Charles Wilson had asked me to write a weekly side-column for the 'op-ed' page of *The Times*. Op-ed means opposite the leading articles and letters page, and is dominated by a large opinion piece on a major issue of the day by one of the paper's principal columnists. My side-column, however, was meant to be more whimsical – sometimes funny, sometimes sad: about 1,000 words and not too heavy. I wrote this for many years, for Mondays. These columns would themselves fill a book and many of them are, on re-reading, ephemeral, but this one struck a chord. Simon Jenkins, who followed Charles Wilson as editor of *The Times* and remains a columnist on the paper, wrote me a note saying so, and quoting me a passage from George Eliot's *Middlemarch* which I loved so much I have it now almost by heart:

. . . we do not expect people to be deeply moved by what is not unusual. That element of tragedy which lies in the very fact of frequency, has not yet wrought itself into the coarse emotion of mankind; and perhaps our frames could hardly bear much of it. If we had a keen vision and feeling of all ordinary human life, it would be like hearing the grass grow and the squirrel's heart beat, and we should die of that roar which lies on the other side of silence. As it is, the quickest of us walk about well wadded with stupidity.

When Peter Stothard, by then editor, asked me to move from my side-column to writing the main comment column for the op-ed page, every Saturday, I was reluctant. I know people who throw their hats into the ring for any big job always protest that they have done so unwillingly, on the insistence of friends, but so it was in this case. I did not think I was up to heavyweight commentary every week. I asked Peter if I could do it less frequently but he said it must be weekly or nothing. So I complied. I have written this column since, for many years. These would fill about two books.

As would my travel writing. Peru, Bolivia, Paraguay, Eritrea, Kilimanjaro, Desolation Island . . . I thought hard about describing some of my travels in this book, for they have occupied a quarter of my life and half my imagination, but they are separate, another life.

I keep everything I write – some 3,000 articles since I started – and the ring-bound files already fill a shelf. The books in all their editions fill a small shelf too: none dearer to my heart than the first I wrote – *Inca-Kola – A Traveller's Tale of Peru* – after some hair-raising and unforgettable journeys in the Andes in the 1980s. It is like a favourite child. Every year since then its persistence in paperback lifts my spirits.

Harder to do (and helped by friends) I wrote a book, *Great Parliamentary Scandals*, on the history, modern and ancient, of this subject, and based a radio series on later interviews not with the central figures but with some of the people peripheral to the story whose lives had been touched, often blighted, by these affairs. This we followed up with an anthology of church scandal: *The Great Unfrocked*. In both books I attempted a balance of humour, curiosity, information and sympathy.

As these aims are at war with each other (most sympathetic of all can be to write nothing) the balance is uneasy, and caused some abashed pauses on the author's part. True, my own brushes with the world I was writing about gave me a useful view of that strange, broken, disputed frontier between the personal and the public. I do believe we need to experience for ourselves, if we can, those things on which we are to be free with our opinions, and made myself very sick once by trying to become addicted to nicotine through wearing the patches smokers use as route to a cure.

But my own guilty former secrets were not research, and there was an element of hypocrisy in choosing as my subject stories which, but for the world's itch to tut-tut, would never have been famous. I had been lucky not to be a chapter in one of my own books, for by the skin of my teeth I had escaped the disgrace I now wrote about in others. Only in my thirties and forties, and only with a good deal of wrenching, and only in the nick of time, had I brought my real and my acknowledged life back into some kind of accord. I am inexpressibly glad and relieved that I did.

The gap had caused strain. I am not by nature an honest person, but one who is unhappy with dishonesty; and the two are not the same. Forty years before in the night at Vumba Heights School when Bill was sick and afraid to leave his bed alone, I had resolved that courage which was not spontaneous might come by application and I would become brave by acting bravely. Now and likewise I was trying to become honest by saying what was true. I remember in the early 1980s determinedly reading *Gay News* on a bus – because I thought nobody should be afraid to. But I was afraid to. How much better to be someone like Peter Ackroyd, and just not care.

My own nocturnal prowls on Clapham Common had long ceased. No young man today should take my example. These follies – though I cannot say I would not repeat them – were an act of desperation and inseparable from an era in which there seemed for many of us no other way. Now there are better ways. Coming out remains, for many, at best awkward and at worst horribly difficult, but there are few for whom with a bit of courage it is impossible.

Sometimes these days I stand in gay bars, often unrecognized, and watch people laughing and talking, or dancing, or drinking – so much more confident and relaxed, so much more straightforward than it ever was for me – and I think how times have changed, and try to persuade myself that, in however marginal a way, the Commons speech or two I made, and all the letters I wrote, and all the university debates I spoke at, all those bleak and awkward meetings which nobody came to, the embarrassment and strain of it all, made some difference. If so, then there is no need for those people laughing and talking, with lives of their own to lead, to know it or see me. I would rather be invisible and watch them all unknowing: my tribe.

Men and women who tried to be bridges between the attitudes of the world in which we grew up and the world we believed should come, tend to end up overlooked by both worlds. As a gay campaigner I used to support an age of consent of eighteen – a view many gay men would now think shocking – because I believed this was the best achievable. I am still unsure about same-sex marriage. People like me have been left behind. Some of us may reflect that we risked more and made our stands at more personal cost than the apparently bolder campaigners who have followed us in an easier world, and feel bitter or unrecognized because of that. But I simply rejoice at the change. I am glad to be left behind. I never liked campaigning. It always felt so awkward yet I couldn't let it go.

For me there would be a kind of honour in finding that what I *was* had been eclipsed by what I had helped to do. Some years ago the obituary appeared in the *Independent* of Douglas Scott, the man who designed London Transport's Routemaster bus, possibly the last bus it will be possible to love. Unusually the obituary featured a photograph not of the designer, but of the bus. I thought of Mr Scott relaxing in the canteen of some celestial bus garage, smiling with pride that the newspapers had replaced his own crumpled features with a portrait of his bus.

When I was a little boy I wanted to be a famous explorer. Later I wanted to be a famous doctor, then a famous governor, after that a famous diplomat and finally a prime minister: a wide range of careers with one common feature. But at fifty something began to change. Some intimation of this came when at a dinner party I overheard someone repeat (she did not know where she had heard it) a clever observation which I recognized (no one else did) as originally my own.

I felt not the slightest desire to inform the company of my link with this remark. No, pleasure was given edge by the knowledge that my remark had entered the currency of intelligent conversation, its authorship forgotten and of no account. Could anything better lift the heart of a composer than to hear, years after the composition of his song, someone who did not even know he existed whistling the melody in a park?

To be famous is something and I enjoy my limited 'B-list' status. I cannot say that fame and fortune mean nothing to me: I love both. But to make something worthwhile in itself is something more. To make something so enduringly worthwhile that one's own umbilical link with the artefact withers and drops away and the work lives in its own right – celebrated, loved or depended upon for itself – is surely the greatest thing of all. My brother Roger is an artist who does not even seek exhibitions for his wonderful paintings. To paint them is enough.

Just occasionally I wish I were invisible. And if as a ghost I found evidence that anything I had done had worked out well – was proving useful, giving pleasure, offering shelter or protection – it would be an immeasurable delight. This is not humility; it is a vanity greater even than the wish for attention. It is the wish to play God, invisible to your creation.

Anyway, I reckon I escaped coming a terminal cropper by the narrowest of squeaks.

For others it has been harder. Harvey Proctor was and remains a friend, but his tortured relationship with the hard right hugely complicated things for him. In Basildon, which he won in 1979, his populist support for Powellite opinions kept him in the good books of an awkward constituency association but lost him almost all the sympathy he was to need from the liberal press when the tabloid newspapers, in an unforgivable and professionally unethical sting, framed him (using a rent-boy wired for sound), exposed him and pilloried him week after week.

The trouble for Harvey, who is not a Nazi, was that he looked like one. Tall, pale-eyed, pale and blond and possessed of a faintly ominous manner, his secret (but in the House widely guessed at) homosexuality coupled with his Poujadist opinions on matters such as immigration, made him an easy target and a difficult friend. He joined me for a kitchen supper in my house in Clapham on the eve of the trial for indecency which followed his exposure in the newspapers in 1986.

At supper he told me about the time his hotel room in Morocco had been besieged by journalists from a British Sunday tabloid who had tracked him down there and bullied the hotel manager into forcing his way in. As the hammering on the door intensified, his guest, a young Arab man, had with Harvey's help squeezed himself under the bed. Unfortunately it was a low bed and the Arab could not breathe without lifting it a few inches off its legs. The manager came in and after a while the Arab had to breathe. In our merriment over the story we forgot for half an hour that the next morning Harvey was to plead guilty to gross indecency. He had anyway seemed resigned to his fate; he knew his political career was over. He avoided prison – just – and stood down as an MP.

In the late nineties I went to a bizarre party in his Putney mansion block flat, thrown for the oldest son of the Duke of Rutland, the Marquis of Granby, who had just become engaged. The Marquis and

Harvey had known each other for years, and Harvey knew his friend was fascinated by the story of the sinking of the *Titanic*, and an expert on it. To celebrate this betrothal, Harvey and his close friend Terry therefore laid on a meal which was the exact replica of that enjoyed by the first-class passengers on the *Titanic*, their last before she sank. I hope the later-to-be Duchess of Rutland enjoyed the joke.

At this party I was monopolized by a guest I had never met before. She was sitting on the sofa by the door, in a mock leopard-skin trouser suit. She was slightly drunk and a lot of fun. I like blowzy women. She pulled me on to the sofa, threw an arm around my neck and started a stream of hilarious banter.

That was all there was to our encounter. Before leaving she scrawled out her address and telephone number and took mine. I thought no more of her.

Some days later some friends were round for a takeaway pizza in my flat in East London when the telephone rang. 'It's—,' said a theatrical voice at the other end of the line. 'Come to dinner.'

'I can't,' I said, unable to put a face to the name. 'I have friends round.'

'Your gay-boy lovers, no doubt. Bring them. I don't care. I'm at—' When she barked out her address, it came to me who she was. 'Or come tomorrow,' she said.

A warning bell was ringing. I pleaded another engagement. She suggested another date. I told her there was just too much work on at present, and could we leave it for a few months? She rang off.

Five minutes later she rang again, insisting. Still polite, I said no. She waited only moments before redialling. I took half a dozen calls within twenty minutes. Finally she refused to hang up. 'I can't come to dinner,' I said, 'and you can't keep on like this, and I'm just going to have to hang up.'

She rang again and I took the receiver off the hook. When my friends left I replaced it. The phone rang immediately: it was her. I unplugged the phone for the night.

And that began a long, strange time for me. It seems funny now, but then it was not.

She just kept telephoning. Every evening – all through the night until I would unplug the phone; and as soon as I plugged it in again next day. It was a siege.

A couple of strange letters came, too. These stopped, but the telephoning intensified.

Early in the siege I started hanging up as soon as I heard her voice. She would cackle delightedly if I showed signs of irritation. When once I lost my temper and shouted it was noticeable that this seemed to excite her, for she began calling almost feverishly immediately afterwards. I had learned one lesson.

Another was that if anyone other than I answered she would, if it was a man, speak until convinced that I was not there. If it was a woman she would hang up at once. Much later I asked a female friend to re-record my answering-machine message, which seemed to help.

Silly as you think this, I did not know that you can limit the time a telephone answering-machine allows a caller, so she would talk for hours into mine while I was out. I would have to listen to it all (fast-forwarding in jumps) in case a genuine message from someone else was among hers. When I did work out how to limit the length of her calls she began leaving scores of short messages, ringing again and again, then waiting a while to trap me into answering, before she rang again. These short calls were maddening. The long messages, however, were unforgettable.

She was an actress – a rather talented actress. Sometimes she would leave soliloquies, occasionally obscene, fantasizing about what she and I might do together. Sometimes she would recount stories (whether true I never knew) about the celebrities she knew or had been intimate with or in one case (she claimed) had been married to. I could have checked with them, I suppose, but it somehow seemed best to leave it alone. Harvey was mortified but was unable to help.

On a message she left one morning, a doorbell rang while she was speaking. Leaving the phone off the hook, she admitted a plumber and electrician. Recorded on my machine, her exchanges with them made me realize how drunk she was, and that this was part of the problem.

Weirder even than this were her dialogues. She would play herself, and me. Sometimes I would be angry, sometimes seductive. 'Our' dialogues were of a courtly kind and she called me sir. Usually I would consent to make love to her.

It is odd to come home late at night, let yourself into a dark flat to see, with sinking heart, the red light flashing on the answering-machine, and to sit there alone after midnight as these creepy dialogues between 'me' and a crazy woman echoed round the flat.

I was never really scared. Spooked, yes, but not scared. I simply hated it. Often I became quite angry, and sometimes unsettled. I lost sleep when, catching me unawares after a few days' lull in which it seemed the calls had stopped, she would throw herself at the telephone for a night.

Despite everyone's advice to do so, I never once considered reporting her to the police. The tragedy seemed more hers than mine, and not a matter for the police. Nor (again despite advice) would I change my telephone number. If she were half as well connected as she claimed (I thought) she would quickly discover the new number and hours of work alerting all my friends to the change would be wasted.

Besides, why let her win? This had become a battle of wills. Yet when she became drunker and drunker, and the calls less frequent, I began to worry about her. I did not want her to call again – please God, not that! – yet I was concerned that she might have drunk herself to death. What if she tried to hang herself from a lamppost outside my front door, as one of the late Sir Nicholas Fairbairn's mistresses was reported to have done? I checked the lamppost – I really did – for easy hitching-points. To my relief there were none.

I had by now been able to discover a little about her, and that at least not all her stories were invented. Her brother was in the media world, although I had never made his acquaintance. One morning, after a bad night with her, I got through to him on his mobile phone. He said that I was in exalted company: she had plagued Sir John Gielgud before me and no, there was nothing he could do.

Slowly, the calls subsided. When they stopped altogether I began to worry whether she was all right. If they ever resume I shall deal with them as I dealt with the last, and I certainly never want to speak to her again. But, oddly enough, I wish her happiness and no longer feel aggrieved.

Some years later her brother wrote an unpleasant and fairly personal attack on me in the *News of the World*, after the *Newsnight*–Peter Mandelson affair. He must have been counting on my sense of honour not to retaliate. It was obliquely flattering.

As for Harvey, who introduced me to my stalker, he is forgotten now, as he probably prefers. He was less lucky than me.

My telephone stalker was an oddity, a one-off. But a columnist develops a sort of relationship with tens of thousands of people who think they know him and partly do. Every year, a few thousand make contact direct, or try, by letter or (now) e-mail. Some fellow-journalists are dismissive about such readers and acknowledging every message can be a chore, but I find the contacts useful and good. They teach you, and remind you when you forget, that the public does not exist: there are only people. When I gave up my whimsical Monday side-column to begin the more central commentary, I wrote this:

Newspaper columns are a long-distance relay, the runner the columnist, the page his track. It was there before he started and remains when he goes, but around his allotted laps he trots or powers his way, sometimes flagging, sometimes finding new energy.

By this columnist, on this page, the baton was taken up nearly nine years ago. Not for me, then, the 100-yard sprint or the special commentary from the celebrity outside-contributor. Instead a certain gentle stamina has been required: but for a journey which is not gruelling, but rather a kind of odyssey.

As any distance runner knows, in our event there is time to observe the observers. The sprinter is the spectacle: the crowd looks in – at him. But the marathoner looks out. He can scrutinize the faces as he passes – even exchange a little banter with his audience. For me the most surprising pleasure of writing this column has been to make the acquaintance of tens of thousands of readers, who have written to contribute thoughts, criticism, encouragement – and even, just occasionally, abuse.

The pleasure was unexpected. I receive between twenty and 100 letters a week. To my dear secretary Eileen Wright has fallen the task of typing and sending out my replies, and for me there has usually been time to do little more than read each letter and thank its sender. I thought that with the years, a columnist would grow cynical about this task. Instead, my interest in my readers, and my respect for them, has grown.

They are such good, nice people. The news media subject us to a daily bombardment of horrible stories about the misdoings of our countrymen: it can lead us to despair of fellow Britons. If you want an antidote, read the daily postbag from his readers of a *Times* columnist. You will find that far from being alone in a nation of thugs, yobs and cheats, you are surrounded out there in the dark by millions of intelligent, kindly, lively souls astonishingly various in their habits and opinions but united by a civilizing tolerance and tremendous goodwill.

If it was ever the case that the *Times* reader was a predictable type – rich, stuffy, 'establishment' and almost certainly male – then my postbag tells me that it is emphatically not the case now. Every human type is there. Some are rich, most strike me as neither rich nor poor, and a notable group are of above average education and below average income: young people and old (especially elderly ladies), who in material terms have quite a struggle and for whom an intelligent newspaper represents a vantage point from which to survey the world of ideas, research and the arts. Perhaps my correspondents are untypical, but I am struck by how unmaterialistic most who write to me are: life to them is about more than money. There are millions of such people. I do not recognize them in the picture of my countrymen the popular media portray.

If I were to name, from among these letters, one reaction running like a thread through many, it could be represented by a phrase so tempting that columnists must ban it from their repertoire. 'Am I alone in thinking . . . ?' I suspect that millions in modern Britain are bewildered and irritated by media assumptions about what 'people' think or 'people' do. They search for reassurance that their own doubts about received opinion and popular behaviour are not eccentric or absurd; that they are not mad.

That the average Briton has 2.4 children, when no Briton actually has 2.4 children points us to a profound error in the current fashion for constructing our supposed countrymen from the results of polls. It is perfectly possible to paint, from data about the opinion and practice of the many, a picture of a 'typical' citizen with which no living creature actually accords. I think this is what the mass media do.

Especially that is true of television. A good broadsheet newspaper has time and space for many voices. They may be a cacophony, not a chorus.

Broadcasting, by its very nature, tends to assume a single voice, a single 'sound'. The assumption grows that 'we' as a nation think this, do that, approve of the other. 'We' take on a distinctive aspect. My dismayed correspondents do not recognize themselves in this portrait. Have they been left behind like the little lame boy, as the Pied Piper and his band surge towards some magic mountain? If they could read all the letters that arrive with theirs, they would know that the little lame boys are in the majority.

It is important to the very idea of democracy that such a thing as public opinion exists. The ghastly possibility that among a population there may be diverse and contradictory opinions and no 'democratic' way of satisfying them all is brushed uneasily aside. The unease explains fevered attempts throughout this century to find ways – by 'proportional representation' or 'consultation' for instance – to pretend to ourselves that irreconcilable desires can be blended into unified decisions. They cannot.

Give me the cacophony. Give me my readers, a band who have in common only the quality that each one is original, and to whom, as I move to another space and a different day, I offer an affectionate thank you.

At the beginning of 1993 I had accepted a new job and one which it proved difficult, but just possible, to fit in with all the others. For the next five years I became a member of the Broadcasting Standards Council, a government quango. I had been David Mellor's last appointment before a toe-sucking actress toppled him in his Chelsea strip (of the three ingredients in this famous story – toe-sucking, actress, Chelsea strip – only the actress was true: the media and its suppliers made up the rest). Our remit on the BSC was 'taste and decency' and our job was to view or hear every item on radio or television over which we had received a complaint from the public, and offer a judgement, which was only advisory. We had no teeth.

I cannot justify the existence of such a body except as a sop to those who, were they not offered this apology for censorship, would demand real censorship. Its work was hilarious. We would sit around for mornings at a time, in a well-appointed darkened basement opposite Westminster Abbey, about twelve of us – vicars, psychiatrists, ladies from the Welsh WI – chaired by a grandee such as Lord Rees-Mogg, Lady Howe or Dame Jocelyn Barrow, watching smut, dirt, gratuitous violence and TV commercials for home insurance in the making of which real budgies may or may not have suffered distress.

Given that a very substantial part of the British population believes that someone is trying to poison them, pervert them, insult them, mock their gods, frighten their goldfish or sell their souls to the devil in a black mass at midnight on Hampstead Heath, you can imagine the variety of the alarms we had to consider and adjudicate. It fell to me as the youngest member of the council (I was forty-nine when my term expired) to explain to Dame Jocelyn Barrow what the word 'shag' meant and how and with what propriety Chris Evans might have used it between the hours of six and seven a.m. on BBC Radio One.

'It means "make love"', I said to Dame Jocelyn.

'Nothing wrong with that, is there?'

'But it's ruder than that.'

'How rude?'

'Well, say a word, Jocelyn, and I'll say if "shag" is ruder or less rude than that.'

'Fuck.'

'Less rude.'

'Bonk.'

'Ruder.'

And so we proceeded. Elspeth Howe got the bit between her teeth over 'shag' but the council was divided and my vote swung it for giving the green light to 'shag' before breakfast. Finally, at a meeting from which I was absent, Elspeth had her way. Chris Evans was censured. The council moved on to debate whether a 'twat' is a silly person or a vagina.

We all liked the energetic Elspeth, who was married to Geoffrey Howe, the former Foreign Secretary. She was wilful, but a terrifically good sport and not easily bruised. Still, there were only just suppressed titters as the whole council, chaired by Lady Howe, sat watching a controversial scene in the televised version of one of Michael Dobbs's political novels, *The Final Cut*. A woman of a certain age was naked astride an equally naked Cabinet minister, he passive, she bouncing vigorously up and down, as he moaned, 'I only ever wanted to be Foreign Secretary.' None of us dared catch another's eye.

Membership of the BSC involved homework too. Part of our job was to keep watch over the hard-core porn channels then beaming in from Europe, the most notorious of which was Red Hot Dutch. Our office staff made videos of some twenty hours of this stuff and we were each given a couple to watch, viewing the entire footage and marking with ticks on specially prepared forms our answers to multiple-choice questions. Thus:

Nudity: male: full frontal   Yes No
Male erection   Full Partial None
Explicit sexual intercourse   Real Simulated Vaginal Anal

I have never been a great expert at sex and it was often hard to tell which boxes to tick. The dog position is favoured over the missionary position by pornographic film-makers, for reasons of camera-angle, and a general shot of a man on top of a woman in this position offers an amateur like me few clues as to whether the action is real or simulated. Friends told me, however, that close scrutiny of the position and angle of the two pelvises could determine whether the sex was anal or vaginal, and we would all sit round of an evening in Derbyshire, operating the freeze-frame video function at critical moments and arguing about which box to tick. These sequences were at least more interesting than the many hours spent viewing lesbians writhing on fur rugs, and nothing happening at all.

I was paid £12,000 a year for these public services. It was embarrassing that during the time I did this job I came briefly to tabloid attention under the headline 'Tory ex-MP in Commons Nipples Storm'. Perhaps as a result of my BSC training I had noticed from my sketch-writer's seat that one lady backbench MP suffered from involuntary nipple-erection whenever she rose to ask the Prime Minister a question and had the full attention of the House. Because her blouses were sometimes of flimsy cloth, and because the nipples stood out like chapel hat-pegs, this could be spotted from thirty yards.

Unfortunately I had not thought I might not be alone in noticing this. I, of course, did not name the MP in the sketch I wrote which was a mostly but not entirely humorous discussion of the links between public performance and sexual arousal. But the *Sun* did name her – and, what's worse, offered a photograph of her in exactly the condition I had described, taken from the live television feed.

I wrote to her at once, and to the Speaker, Betty Boothroyd, apologizing, but there are some things for which an apology is pretty futile. Elspeth Howe, a great crusader on women's issues, never mentioned the episode, which had failed to reach the broadsheet newspapers and had not, I prayed, reached her attention either. It quickly blew over.

★

From the top of the cliff, as the track turned a corner, we could see the whole Mediterranean coast of northern Catalonia – all the lights of the towns – up to the French border where the Pyrenees topple into the sea. It was midnight, cold and clear with a yellow moon rising. Across the valley the summits of the Montseny mountains, dusted in a March snowfall, shone in the starlight. We paused to look, then drove on. L'Avenc would be just round the next bend.

With my sister Belinda and her husband and his brother, I had decided to buy l'Avenc. A fine and public-spirited local builder had acquired the house, hoping to raise the funds to rescue it from ruin, but had despaired of the attempt. He sold it to us with its land for 40 million pesetas – a little less than £160,000. We knew that in the end we shall spend ten times that, over as many years as it took us to raise it, to restore the house: but the urgent task was to renew the roof before it fell in.

With two friends, I had slept there on a cold March night in 1998. Superstitious to say so, but Belinda and I had provisionally made the decision to buy, and first I wanted to make l'Avenc's acquaintance. Sleeping in a place creates a tie which cannot be made in any other way. So we drove into the night with a bottle of wine, some sleeping bags, a boxer dog Tana, candles and enough wood for a fire.

We forgot matches. We spent an hour trying to light newspaper from a hired car's cigarette lighter (you can't), then stumbled with our sleeping bags up to the top floor. A bat flitted out. The wind hissed in the rafters but there was never a creak all night. We drank the wine and turned in. It was very cold, way below freezing.

We were not afraid. L'Avenc had a solid, sheltering feel; nothing bad. All slept well, and when my mother arrived with coffee and warm bread from the village, and matches, the dawn had crept past the boarded-up windows, bathing each floor with soft, dim light. We made a fire and sat talking, the youngest nephews and nieces (I now have ten) playing at being scared.

But the moment of loneliness had passed. The loneliness had been earlier, in the dead of night, with a full moon outside. Have you ever lain in a ruined building with holes in the stonework and gaps in the rotting wood, when there is a full moon? Outside was moonlight and within, vague and unfocused, I could just discern the outlines of the room, and see the chinks in the roof. Wind sighed without, leaves and paper rustled within.

Why do they speak of the soft light of the moon? Moonlight is harder than the sun, crueller. Sun shines – moon stares. Our world becomes shadowy, insubstantial – shapes unsolid like scissored card, moonlight the reality. The moon shone through the great arched and broken door, searchlight through black lace, skeleton of wood flimsy against the light, filigreed like a rotted leaf. Where the moon penetrated the holes in the stone, even the wall became a torn fabric, pricked through with light. Moon becomes the foreground. What is in front of you becomes background in the presence of some great celestial mainbeam.

A ruin is lovely in itself. It has a character of its own and the ruination is part of the character. When you restore a ruin something dies. All these years l'Avenc had had herself to herself; and we had come now not only as rebuilders but, in a way, as destroyers of her solitude and abandon, come to wreck the wreck. Strange to report, but with the others asleep I experienced that moment in the still of the night as a sort of saying goodbye.

Not long after came another farewell, of a kind.

Court and Social columns are not my metier, but the guest list at the Foyle's seventieth anniversary literary luncheon in 2001 was so extraordinary, so gilded, so melancholy as to be a period piece in itself. A last snapshot of a departing time, you might say; except that the time had already departed. Only the people were left behind.

I had returned some months before from my great expedition, finally brought off in the year 2000, to Kerguelen – the Desolation Island of which I had told Lady Thatcher and with which she had advised me not to bother. I had lived there in the sub-Antarctic for four months among a small group of Frenchmen – scientists and technicians – in the station established by the French government there. My sojourn on Kerguelen had been one of the most intense periods of my life, its strangeness and poignancy added to by the terrible accident of a shooting: a hunting accident in which our doctor killed our radio officer, and had to stay with us, and his awful feelings of guilt, until months later the government ship could bring a replacement. Surrounded by thousands of miles of the icy Southern

Ocean, and sharing a great, wild, gale-lashed archipelago with only albatrosses and elephant seals, I had been 10,000 miles not only in geography but in my mind from the scene which now confronted me at the Foyle's literary lunch.

I had for some years been writing a fortnightly column – 'Another Voice' – for the *Spectator* magazine. I went home and wrote this:

I am no Samuel Pepys, but public moments that seem indelible in a thousand minds fade quickly if nobody writes them down. There must have been almost a thousand people, of whom nearly 250 were 'guests of honour'. So much honour. Honour's battalions extended across six top tables: a 'top' top table, and beneath it a sort of tournament of top tables.

The seating plan on which I rely charts the field of contest. On paper, the line-up emerges peppered by a hailstorm of decorations. Just a couple for Sir Nicholas Henderson, GCMG, KCVO; a modest three for General Sir Peter de la Billière, KCB, KBE, DSO. At four, the Rt Hon. The Lord Carrington, KG, GCMG, CH, MC was numerically honours–even with Field-Marshal the Rt Hon. Lord Carver, GCB, CBE, DSO, KCVO; yet in this war of acronyms, both were outgunned by Marshal of the RAF Sir Michael Beetham, GCB, CBE, DFC, AFC, DL, FRAeS.

On the 'top' top table, James Callaghan's last Chancellor sat almost next to Margaret Thatcher's first Foreign Secretary. The Rt Hon. The Lord Healey of Riddlesden, CH, MBE and Lord Carrington found themselves to the left of the principal guest speaker, Mr Ned Sherrin, CBE. The Baroness Thatcher herself was to Mr Sherrin's right. Lord Tebbit had been mischievously seated between Lady Thatcher and the German ambassador.

Lady Thatcher has never been one for staring around. But had she looked along the seats to her right, her eye – lighting briefly on Lord (Kenneth) Baker and lingering perhaps a moment longer on Lord (Cecil) Parkinson – would have passed three ambassadors, the New Zealand High Commissioner and five peers, as well as her husband and Penelope Keith, before reaching her host, Christopher Foyle, and his wife. Glancing now to her left, she would have noticed two more ambassadors and the Australian High Commissioner – if she were not distracted by Lord (Bill) Deedes, the Duke of Devonshire, Lord Snowdon, Lady (Barbara) Castle, Sir Hardy Amies, Sir Ludovic Kennedy, and others equally illustrious.

And that was just her side of the table. Across it, Katie Boyle, Nigel Nicolson, Dame Norma Major, Sir David Frost, the Lords Cranborne,

McAlpine, Biffen, Carr (Robert), Rawlinson (Peter), Mackay of Clashfern, Fellowes . . . oh, where shall we linger? Not by the barons alone, but by the court jesters, troubadours and travelling players too: Harry Secombe, Alan Whicker, Robert Robinson, Thora Hird. Many of the surviving members of the Thatcher, Callaghan, Heath and even Wilson Cabinets were there.

Lady (Mary) Wilson herself was seated between Norris McWhirter and Lord Ryder. Richard Ryder was once Mrs Thatcher's private secretary, later John Major's chief whip, and now sat not far from Uri Geller, looking across at Chapman Pincher. The Thatcher-impersonator, Janet Brown, and Lord Saatchi were close by.

'I've recently become a surrealist,' said Ms Zsu-Zsi Roboz, an artist beside me, and I think I knew what she meant.

Further up the table, Lady Thatcher's head of the civil service, Lord (Robert) Armstrong, was within her direct eyeline, though it was Sir Bernard Ingham who will have had the full force. Peering past them (and past Ann Leslie's mischievous eyes), she may have noticed two former editors of *The Times*. Except that she looked a little tired.

A certain ennui seemed to dog Denis Healey too, though when he spoke he gallantly kissed her hand. By the seventh speech it was nearly four o'clock and a number of noble guests were nodding off. It didn't matter. They had nowhere to go. Little that anyone here said mattered any more. Little that anyone here thought was any longer of much account.

In private conversation Ned Sherrin seemed to get on well with Lady Thatcher, though when the jokes in his speech bordered on the risqué, she fixed Norman Tebbit in determined small talk. As Gyles Brandreth began a joke about marijuana, the small talk became quite intense.

But she sang along when Larry Adler played the mouth-organ. Nothing in Auberon Waugh's short speech upset her; Frederick Forsyth's thoughts seemed to please; and Christopher Foyle was heard with the respect due to our host.

I found the occasion strangely moving. Strangely sad. There was almost nobody there representing the new Labour dispensation. Apart from Lord Bragg, seated opposite Lord Mishcon, Tony's cronies do not do the literary lunch. This was the old guard, the *ancien régime*. One bomb could have taken out most of what's left of the 1970s, almost all of the 1980s and most of the 1990s, too. Whole lives must have scrolled before that eminent throng as they surveyed their fellow diners in the vast ornate, yet indefinably tatty dining-hall. Every one had mattered once, very few did now. Thus it must be to die and find oneself in some Elysian field among all the great and the good from the era in which one had spent one's prime. These our actors were all spirits, projected out of air, out of thin air. Their revels were ended. They would soon vanish.

These people had done so much, meant so much. We owed them – I owed them – so much. On the original canvas their portraits radiated such potency. Now, cut out and glued flat on to the baseless card of a bookseller's fantasy seating plan, the montage was unreal. Elbowed into a new era which they had helped to create but which was not their era, they looked displaced, faded, insubstantial. Bric-à-brac. These were people who could now lunch until tea. They had nothing else to do. The next time many would meet again would be at each others' funerals. I was put in mind of those Russian émigrés in 1920s Paris, still toasting the Tsar.

Every age has its monarchs and their courts. Around Margaret Thatcher sat the courtiers, viziers, inquisitors, propagandists, scribblers, soldiers, philosophers, jesters, hairdressers and spies who had once dominated their epoch. But the Queen is dead – long live the King! It was a very twentieth-century lunch: one of the most glittering, perhaps the saddest, maybe the last.

22. Chance Witness

A good leg will fall, a straight back will stoop, a black beard will turn
white, a curled pate will grow bald, a fair face will wither, a full eye
will wax hollow, but a good heart, Kate, is the sun and the moon: or,
rather, the sun and not the moon: for it shines bright, and never
changes, but keeps his course truly.

Henry V, Act 5, scene 2

How to end a book? Not here with any kind of resolution for little is
resolved and an impression grows of sensory overload. Nor in this
case at the end of a life, I hope. There could be much to come, or
nothing. But who knows? Any guess – ten, twenty, forty years ago –
would have been adrift. As expected, the future has not worked out
as expected.

The past has not worked out as expected either. No less than a
biographer, an autobiographer may fall a little out of love with his
subject as he proceeds. This one appears to himself neither as likeable
nor as interesting as at first he thought.

We are each of us two people, observer and observed, but for the
most part nobody is taking notes. With autobiography a reporter
enters the room, the couple are themselves observed, and we become
three. Two has been company these last fifty years but over many
months now three has been a crowd. I looked through the eyes of a
writer, and often to my sorrow the view was messy and unremarkable.

A life is not a story, any more than a yew tree is a bird. Topiary can
make a yew tree into a bird, and a determined editor's shears can clip
a shapeless history into apparent significance; but the meaning is as
illusory as a yew peacock.

Looking inward the man I met seemed calculating, preachy, too
anxious about how something might play. I wanted to show a good
heart but doubt the record proves it. And as the book progressed I
saw with dismaying clarity that of greater interest than who I was,

which is unexceptional, or what I did, which is negligible, was what I stumbled upon; what I saw. Some of this has perhaps been worth recounting. Better then to look out than in.

Still one frowns at what is missed here. Where are my llamas, Llesley, Imp and Knapp, part of my weekends in Derbyshire for years now? Not mentioned. Where is the Wild Camel Protection Foundation, where Peru, Kilimanjaro, deserts, islands, car mechanics, tadpoles? They do matter but they don't fit. Where are my tree-nurseries, my Bolivian music? Where are my friends?

You write a book about your life, then you re-read it and find that if by 'life' we mean the way we live, the book is about almost everything but a life. Mostly your life is commonplace, or odd in an inconsequential sort of way: small joys and trivial anxieties; a tangle of cotton waste, coloured glass and bits of string. Such things, though they were the centre of your daily round, are crowded out to the margins of your book.

For now you are an autobiographer. Big word. What should have concerned you, what others think matters, elbows aside what did. Pride of place is given to noises only fitfully heard in a daily diary loud with irrelevance. There was no time, I recall, to go down to Portsmouth to join the crowds greeting HMS *Invincible*'s triumphant return from the Falklands campaign – I had friends for lunch.

Dreaming, too, writes no diary. So many years of our lives are spent in the hallucination called sleep, and these dark hours can be strange, shocking, perhaps significant; but there is nothing here about the night. Even our waking hours are marked by daydreaming and – who knows? – whimsy may define us. So much that defines us escapes autobiography. Boredom, anticipation, disappointment, irritation, sudden delight and pointless doubt, petulance and caprice, fatigue and routine – small pleasures, long habits, nagging worries – these, not the elements of Greek tragedy or modern romance, are the dominant passions. Being human is so distracting.

How much of my nervous energy is wasted on worry, unrepresented here, about being untidy, unbriefed or late? How much squandered thinking fruitlessly about people I would like to help, or punish, or sleep with, or forget? How much attention frittered away in sudden concern about my fingernails, or glancing restlessly around at people in railway carriages? How do you put that into a book?

Once with time to kill I stationed myself by the ticket barrier at St Pancras railway station to make a pencilled tally of the sum total of all passengers passing through; and beside it a tally of those to whom at a pinch I would make love. My aim was scientific: to establish what proportion of the general population the smaller tally comprised. The figure hovered between 2 and 3 per cent. What a waste of time, to be distracted by 3 per cent of everyone you see. So many thoughts never carried into action.

There is nothing here about relationships. I have had lovers but with my lips to theirs would find my gaze wandering. Call this selfishness if you like but I have never wanted anyone to lose themselves in me, and I don't call that selfishness. One day I should like to look back and remember loving and being loved along the way. But along the way. Look into your lover's eyes or refocus on the starry sky behind: which is the distraction? A matter of opinion. I know my own.

As for sex, I was a young man during the first Aids epidemic. If I had been more handsome I would be dead now. Like the lame boy limping too far behind the pied piper, I was thwarted and thus saved. It didn't always feel like salvation.

How wearying is restlessness. How much nervous energy, how much anxiety, how much hope and intelligence – how much of one's life force – flares through the night like a fire blazing unwatched under the cold stars, illuminating nothing, warming no one: profligate, wanton, red smouldering to grey as energy is tipped upwards into the unreflecting dark. Flames leap but they are earthbound.

We burn on the earth as a fire burns orange. We burn as a tree burns green, spreading from the spark of its seed and blazing for a few years, its leaves a flickering, seasonal combustion: green flames hovering above their roots, licking the oxygen for a few summers, then gone. Who has seen this green fire? What has it done, but lived and burned and burned itself out?

The burning is everything but it is not memorable, not interesting to you. Ten thousand constituency letters answered, 10,000 miles training for long-distance running-races, 3,000 newspaper columns written, 2,000 parliamentary sketches, 2,000 Commons afternoons, 200 reviews of morning papers on TV, 100 hours of interviews on *Weekend World*, fifty party conferences, nine books, seven general elections, countless journeys in six continents, great mountains climbed – all done, gone, knocked off, ticked and finished, each the centre of my whole being for an hour or two, a day or two, a month or two, few remembered now.

I've lived since university at a dozen addresses and barely bothered to mention them, though each was a home and there were landlords and tenants and lodgers and lovers and walls to paint and leaks to fix and gardens to tend. I've counted as friends better men and women than me, spent years of my life eating and drinking and working and talking with them, and hardly touched on any of it here. Half my passion and much of my wealth has been directed to my house in the Derbyshire hills and our magical crumbling mansion, l'Avenc, in the Pyrenees, months of pleasure spent on my balcony in London watching the Thames flow – and these places, anchors to my life, consumers of my energies, holes in my pocket, all but escape mention here.

What has this book told you of my five brothers and sisters and their husbands, wives and children? Almost nothing, yet I love and would do anything for each.

Instead, painted here are scenes to which the author has usually been only chance witness, hardly involved, seldom instrumental.

If in my life I had been able to think up just one important thing – one musical phrase from a song, the wing of an aeroplane, Prospero's eight-line farewell to magic – it would have been better than all my years of churning, the whole damn plod, though it might have taken only an hour. Then I could be happy in anonymity. My idea, poem, machine, tune would be me, giving ease, pleasure, illumination or shelter: and there would be no need for others to know.

Sometimes you meet someone who has seen the light: accepted a compass-bearing, a vocation to build or destroy. But if I knew what had to be done I would have done it. I think only that there is no God and that life and man are good – a conviction from which little instruction flows. Priests exhort us to do what is right as though the path were clear and all we lacked was the will to stick to it. But I could keep to any mark. I have never been shown the mark.

Missing vocation, impatient with love and untouched by genius, I have taken refuge in assiduity and enlivened it by caprice. 'No talent, darling,' Peter Ackroyd said, and he was right, but I've seen a lot and sometimes understood; and been a good critic, helped some good causes, and stuck to my guns. Amused, I have learned through journalism to share the joke and sometimes to explain. Always I wanted to understand.

Too often I seemed to be barking at the wheels of history: 'The dogs bark,' as William Waldegrave used to say at our Blue Chip dinners, 'but the caravan moves on.' It would have been nice to lead a camel for a while.

And then again no. I'd soon have bored of stately progress and gone haring off after some dry mountain. I lack patience and, though politics always seemed to me less worthwhile than public administration, I could not administer the tying of my own bow-tie.

But I have struggled to be honest, meant to be brave, and want to be judged to have had a good heart and a prosecuting intellect; and, missing instrumentality, to have seen my times as an outsider who happened to get in: a chance witness.

Epilogue to the 2013 Edition

They say you don't know what the future holds. But I do. I'm writing in the future: the future that lay ahead of this story as I signed it off more than ten years ago. Now, for a second edition, I have the luxury of epilogue. I can look back, knowing how things worked out.

The last chapter of that first edition ends in rather melancholy voice; as though I thought the best of my life were over. Why did I suppose any such thing? I've tried to put myself back into my frame of mind then; but though I could picture and describe my lunch companions on any day for which my diary shows an entry, I'm at a loss to remember or describe myself. Who was I, then? Where did I think I was going?

We think we know ourselves because we're on immediate terms with the identity we woke up with this morning, but the person we were even ten years ago has become a stranger. He signed off at the end of the last edition of this book. He's gone.

Memory, wrote an old friend of mine, the late John Peyton, in his hardly remembered autobiography of a cabinet minister,

loses much that was important and yet clings on to and preserves quite small things which, like stray, unconnected footprints, have escaped erosion by the winds and tides of time. [Much is] lost beyond recovery: of the remainder, some, glimpsed for a moment like a fish in clear, still water, vanish as you move towards them; the outstretched hand comes back empty save for some bits of unmemorable debris from the bed of the stream . . .

I quoted this beginning my introduction to the first edition of this book. Reaching the epilogue I am more sure than ever of its truth. But looking back I do know this: that in the event my race was by no means almost run. I see and write this with the eyes of a man whose life, instead of slackening from a trot to a walk as he probably expected, quickened into a canter; and is cantering all the faster through the second decade of a new century that has turned out to be curiously different from the old one.

A llama peers over the fence and through my kitchen window as I write but he (Knapp) was youthful then; now he carries himself with the slightly ceremonious dignity of an elderly gentleman mindful of his responsibilities and accustomed to respect. He doesn't run much any more. But I'm running harder than ever.

I write now from the Derbyshire home described in earlier pages, but a home now brighter, less spartan and (literally) warmer than when I first met Julian. Of him a little more (but only a little) later. The revolution in attitudes towards homosexuality that I thought more or less complete a decade ago had so much further to go; and as this manuscript heads for the publishers it looks likely that *Chance Witness* will be reprinted in a Britain where people of the same sex can marry. When that day comes Julian and I will do so.

I write now as *The Times*'s parliamentary sketchwriter no longer, but instead as a full-time, regular columnist and broadcaster, a little better known than I was ten years ago. The personal story has been, as ever, tangled with bigger stories, national stories, and the story, too, of l'Avenc: the great ruined house in the mountains of Spanish Catalonia whose rescue my family and I had just begun when I described the place in the chapter 'You'd Better Not Look Down'. That great project – so much higher a hill to climb than we ever envisaged when we started – was finally completed this year, 2013. The restoration became a book in its own right, *A Castle in Spain*, written by myself and my sister Belinda; and the story that ended in triumph. And debt. Now we have to pay for l'Avenc, or make it pay for itself.

Because I am a columnist and because I don't know (though I'd love to know) how to disengage from the outside world and the future of our country, the personal story is tangled, too, with a decade in which I've watched that country puff itself into a state of preposterous hubris, only a hint of which was evident in 2002 when this book closed; a Britain that thought it had transcended what Gordon Brown called 'Tory boom and bust'. A Britain that Mr Brown's successor as Prime Minister, David Cameron, had assumed could look forward to the luxury of spending ever-increasing wealth on ever more compassionate, 'green' and caring government. That dream proved only ever a dream.

A Britain that would walk tall in the world righting wrongs, top-pling totalitarian regimes alongside the United States and in Tony Blair's words 'healing the scars' of Africa; a Britain best pictured in my own mind by those 2002 photographs of our then Prime Minister and George W. Bush strolling together on the lawns at Camp David; Mr Blair in trousers that were altogether too tight, and Mr Bush with a swagger that was altogether too loose. Many were reminded of Batman and Robin. I was more reminded of George Eliot's prelude to *Middlemarch* – if you can picture, as I so vividly can, Tony Blair as the infant Santa Teresa '... holding her brother's hand, to go and seek martyrdom in the country of the Moors. Out they toddled from rugged Avila, wide-eyed and helpless-looking as two fawns, but with human hearts, already beating to a national idea; until domestic reality met them in the shape of uncles, and turned them back from their great resolve'.

Truly, we British have met our uncles, though we'll never know if Mr Blair recognizes his. Whether his early morning expedition to West-minster Catholic Cathedral to touch a casket containing the touring relics of Saint Theresa of Lisieux provided an epiphany for him, it did for me – chance witness in every sense to private devotions. It was pure coincidence I spotted him outside, and confronted the appalling possi-bility that he might be sincere. In 2002 all this was still to come.

The story of a man is, to some degree at least, a story about his relationships: his relationships with people; his relationships with places; his relationships with events. In the decade past, I found a partner, and lost a father.

And so to my partner, Julian. I said in an earlier chapter that I didn't want to write about relationships. I still don't. Had I any talent for such literature I would have tried my hand at writing slushy novels. Had I any interest in it I would have read some. As it is, *Pride and Prejudice* is about the limit of my incursions into romantic litera-ture, enjoyed mainly for its catty asides; and were a storm at sea to cast me naked onto a desert shore, bereft of everything but a novel by Charlotte Brontë, I would have been washed ashore with one book too many, and blessed the tempest for sweeping away my read-ing glasses too. No book, not even any of George Eliot's, ever gave me more pleasure than *Swiss Family Robinson*.

But suffice it to say that for me, and I'm sure for millions more, whirlwinds have not proved the best analogy for romance. I always wanted a best friend for life, and at a point in my own life when I'd probably despaired of finding one and wasn't even looking, Julian appeared, and he and I became closer and closer friends, until I started to miss him when he wasn't there, and to feel happy when he was happy, and find it hard not to feel sad when he was feeling sad. As that Lerner and Loewe lyric in *My Fair Lady* runs, 'I was serenely independent and content before we met/Surely I could always be that way again, and yet . . .' I grew accustomed to his face.

And who says that this kind of love is any less strong than the whirlwind kind? When Eliot writes 'some inclinations become manifest slowly, like the sunward creeping of plants,' for me she says it all.

We had already known each other for more than a decade when in 2006 we called into Bakewell Town Hall for the obligatory interview in advance of the civil partnership ceremony, and the registrar asked me Julian's age and birthday, and I could remember neither. As he's twenty-two years younger than me, and looks younger still, I understood how it would feel to be suspected of importing a takeaway Thai child-bride; but the registrar overlooked my lapse.

All my life I've had a particular horror of any occasion where women wear hats. I'm proud of never once having been the cause of such an event. Another horror is cake, the point of which is entirely lost on me. But the greatest horror of all is dancing. I simply won't. It follows that any occasion that involves cake, dancing and women in hats bundles together my principal nightmares. Such, then, is a wedding.

I intend to keep my record clear. If one could die knowing that however little positive good one had done in the world, one had at least taken care not to add to the sum total in human history of cake-eating, dancing or hat-wearing, one could die with a thin smile on one's lips.

So Julian and I didn't have a civil partnership celebration: just the bare minimum legal folderol. A party? As I get older it's borne in on me that there are only so many Saturdays left in life; and that friends of my own generation are running out of Saturdays too. I wouldn't visit upon them the expenditure of a whole Saturday attending my tedious nuptials. We avoided a party. I hope Julian agreed; he said he did. I told literally nobody. Rashly Julian told his mother and one or two people then told one or two others. But the outcome was pleasant:

after the civil partnership ceremony at Bakewell in August 2006 (apparently only the second to take place there), two good friends organized a half-hour champagne-sip in the sunshine, attended by about nine friends and relations. Outdoors on the grass. No marquee. No cake. No speeches. No hats. No dancing. Just right.

A less welcome consequence was that someone threw confetti at us in the street. I shudder at the memory.

Later that day, as we queued at the check-in desk for our flight abroad, my mobile phone rang. A voice said, 'Hello, I'm from the *Daily Mail* and we'd like to join your well-wishers': two assertions so inherently incompatible as to be almost an offence against grammar. But the diary column which followed was anodyne – though its declaration that Julian 'was Matthew's first love' required some swift text-messages to a few old flames, to calm them down. A little-known feature of our laws on libel is that you can make things up as long as they don't damage anyone's reputation. The Diary piece also reported that I was 'whisking Julian away on a dream holiday'. My new civil partner pointed out rather mournfully to me that, as we were in a Ryanair queue at Luton airport when the *Mail* called and as he had arranged and paid for the flight himself, this was far from the truth.

Hard to believe that that was nearly seven years ago, the year after my father died. He went in the middle of May 2005. Dad had not long celebrated his eighty-second birthday, and he and Mum were ten days short of their fifty-eighth wedding anniversary.

Leslie, my father, lived three or four years too long, and it's a mistake I'm now resolved not to repeat. He had been struggling against ill-health with ever greater difficulty. His heart and lungs were weakened by forty years of smoking thirty cigarettes a day, until his first heart attack finally broke the habit. His last years became ever more wretched for him; and hard for those around him too, especially my mother who was becoming a full-time nurse in her late seventies. Dad was not born to be useless and he always hated society, conviviality, family gatherings – almost everything except work, driving and walking alone by the sea. He could no longer work, and the seaside trips became more and more of a strain. He carried on driving, refusing my mother's entreaties to stop; but he did laugh when I repeated to him the old joke about the chap who declared, 'When I

die I want it to be peacefully in my sleep, like my father; not screaming in terror like his passengers.' It was only luck that never happened
to my father.

Dad no longer wanted to live, and said so, but seemed afraid to die.

I had always loved Dad's honesty about things. We suggested he
accompany my mother to French lessons, but he said, 'Why? What's
the point of improving my French? I'll be dead soon.' When the
nuclear reactor at Chernobyl blew apart and workers later risked
radiation by trying to stabilize the ruin, Dad said they should have
sent old people like him in to do the job, having less life left to spoil.
He meant it. I would speak to him on the phone from England on
the rare occasions when he could be persuaded to come to the phone.
In our last such conversation I asked, in a ritual sort of way, how he
was doing; and he replied, in a non-ritual sort of way: 'I'm finished.'

He was. When news of his collapse reached me I flew at once
from England and got to the state hospital in Vic just in time. My
father died in the small hours of a cool, wet Saturday morning, my
sister Belinda, my mother and I sitting by him holding his hand and
talking to him, with rain falling softly outside and dripping from the
trees. The hospital asked if they could have the eyes; Dad's sight had
remained keen. Of course they could. The corpse wasn't Dad.

I thought of a night when I had driven out in my Land-Rover
from England to visit l'Avenc – and Dad's chuckled warning about
the project, then in full restoration mode: '*pozo sin fondo*' – bottomless pit. To return to England I had needed to depart my parents'
house in the small hours to catch a ferry from Bilbao. I was in my
ancient 1959 Land-Rover, which had been proving difficult to start
and whose headlights had been faulty. Dad, who taught me car
mechanics, had helped fix them.

He had woken up and dressed to see me off, and to make sure the
Land-Rover started and check again its lights. It did start, the lights
worked and, waving goodbye to both parents, I set off, climbing in
first gear up the long hill at the end of l'Hostalot's drive. I was heavily
loaded with olive oil, tiles, wine, saplings and shrubs, and garden pots.

Half way up the hill I noticed there was a car behind me, keeping
its distance and making no attempt to overtake. I recognized my
father's headlights. He was following for a while, to see I was all right:
knowing him I knew this at once. He followed to the end of the

rural road and onto the main road; and he followed still, about five miles further, down into a little valley.

As I crossed the bridge and pulled away up the hill, heading west towards the Atlantic, I saw his headlights dwindle in the rear-view mirror. He had stopped, assured that I was OK, and would return to l'Hostalot and his bed. He did not flash his lights, or hoot, or want any kind of goodbye conversation. The support was wordless, at a distance, without show, and careless whether I knew. It always was, with Dad.

I was alone on my long drive west. Continuing through the Catalan night I had felt a momentary pang of loneliness now that his headlights were no longer with me, and my rear-view mirror was empty and dark.

I felt it again outside the church in Pruit after Dad's funeral, as the red tail-lights of his hearse disappeared into the rain.

Death is strange. Not frightening, not particularly painful or hard to behold or 'accept', not even (for me) 'tragic'. Just very strange. I was not knocked to the ground by grief. Instead I felt disoriented, forgetful, fretful . . . I guess 'distracted' is the word. A world which had always had my father in it no longer did; and he had not wanted to go, not at all. Waves more of melancholy and depression than of grief would sweep over me quite briefly, then seem to pass.

All through the days that followed before the funeral, people kept arriving at my parents' house, though it is twenty miles from almost anywhere, and down the end of a long track. On the occasions Mum was temporarily out, people went away and came back again later. She and I lost track of the numbers who came, sat with her, sometimes awkwardly, for a while, and then departed – usually as yet another car came down the hill towards us. People she hardly knew – people like the trade-union convenor from the days Dad had been general manager at the cable factory in Manlleu – turned up with wife and often family. Dad had retired after his heart attack almost twenty-five years earlier, but still they remembered him, and came.

We arranged the funeral at the small, ancient church at Pruit: once the centre of a parish, now just a sentinel on a hill with a couple of houses attached. The church was completely packed: standing-room only. About 200 people came – again, how they all knew is a mystery to me – including many of the workers at Dad's factory all those years ago, whom nobody else in my family knew, but who seemed to have found their way to the little church out in the wilds.

Julian had joined me. My family stood at the door of the church when the service was over, every mourner bidding leave of us all as they left. As it is the custom to kiss twice – to left and right – on greeting or leaving, this meant about 400 kisses for each of us and threatened to end in seriously cricked necks, but the kindness was overwhelming.

The emergence out of what seemed to be nowhere of this legion of people, most of them strangers but whose lives Dad's life had touched, gave rise in my mind to an idea that so fired my imagination that it has been burning stronger ever since.

After the death of a friend or when anticipating my own, I imagine that everyone the departed soul has ever helped, or who has loved him or admired him, or whose life his own life has brushed against – even if only briefly or incidentally – in some act of consideration towards them, gathers to see him off into oblivion. The son to whom you patiently explained calculus in his teens; the daughter you dandled on your knee as a toddler; the beggar you tossed a shilling to; the girl with a baby to whom you impulsively gave a £5 note; the admirer you let down gently; the street musician you stopped to hear for a while and thanked; the youth you gave a job to; the debtor whose small debt you forgave; the lunatic on the bus that you didn't shun but politely heard out; the friend to whom you gave an honest, hard opinion instead of fobbing him off with false encouragement; the cold-canvasser from a telephone call centre you resisted the temptation to insult; the person whose whole life you changed by some great act of generosity and the person whose hunt for a street address you foreshortened by walking twenty yards to point the way ... all of them, every one, beneficiaries massive or slight, will be there, massed on the shore as your boat pushes away into the dark, calling and waving you goodbye. A reserved and unsociable man who expressed himself through practical help, my father would have cast off from the shore to the fond goodbyes of thousands.

Years later, I wrote this, in the *Spectator*:

It is five years since my father died. I thought I would get over it, but I haven't. This is not a plea for sympathy – I'm fine, all's well – but simply an observation, a report. Unusually for a man of 55 I had never, before Dad's death, lost anyone close; and I had no idea what to expect.

I guessed, though, that the experience would not differ from other violent emotional traumas: first the shock, then a blank aftershock; then busy-ness – displacement activity; then perhaps a relapsing into grief. And after that and over many years a slow but steady process of what sensitive people might call 'healing' and the rest of us would call getting over it.

The shock, it turned out, though expected, was the phone-call. At the bedside of a dying man I expected no theatre, and found none. Just as I'd supposed, the immediate feeling was only bleak, banal – no trumpets or violins, no wailing or floods of tears, but a kind of blankness, a grey hour in a grey dawn. And so it proved: the rain coming down softly (I remember) outside in Catalonia. Blank.

Then (I thought) might follow a few weeks' false-normality: still numb, but with arrangements of a practical nature to busy myself with. One would have too much to do to mope.

And so this proved, too: there's plenty to fill close relatives' days when somebody dies, and hardly time to miss the deceased. And it rained at the funeral too, and there were hundreds of Catalan and Spanish mourners to air-kiss at the door of the little church before Dad's coffin was borne away in the hearse: red tail-lights in the rain. And I still wasn't feeling much.

But waiting, I suppose, for the lapse into grief: a month or two of wallowing.

This never came. I went back to England and back to work. Ordinary service was resumed. There was no time of quiet, after-the-event confrontation with what I had lost, no delayed grief once I had, as they say, 'time to grieve'. There we are, then, I thought. One down – and how many more to go? The waters had closed over my father's head and the ripples subsided. I missed him, of course, but from now on, with each month that passed, I would surely miss him a little less. Time heals all wounds, etc. So now, I thought, begins that famous healing process.

I thought wrong. At least a year after Dad had gone, I started waking up in the night, missing him. Silly, because it's not as though we were together much after I'd left home, and anyway Dad found all of us – all mankind – intermittently irritating. But I'd lie there and think of the things I might have organised for him; the ways in which his last years might have been made more comfortable. Should he have moved to the seaside, which he loved? Should I have taken him to the opera again? Should I have tried harder to persuade him to accompany me on one of Concorde's last flights?

It took me perhaps a couple of years to begin fully to understand, with an intensity that grew, that the world had changed when he died; that there was still a big gap where he had been; and that it was not closing over.

And now, five years later, I see clearly that it never will. Now never a week passes – hardly a day – when I do not remember him: see a shoreline and think how he would have liked to walk there; hear some Brahms and remember that he liked Brahms; spot an ocean liner and recall how he would have wanted to take a pointless photograph of it; read an item of news about technological innovation or some new advance in engineering, and think how interested he would be to know of it. Not only in the night, now, but during the day, even at busy times, and at happy times, he enters my imagination, a welcome guest.

Quite simply, he has left a space that will never be filled; therefore he is, paradoxically, still here because the space is still here, and I can feel it all the time. The gap Dad left is not a vacuum, a void, a soft area of low pressure to be filled. The gap is hard-edged, chiselled by him into my life, measured by his worth, and ineradicable.

With this realisation has come another: that this sorrow is not itself a cause for sorrow. Regret is not a cause for regret. We ought to be sorry. We ought to regret. Death is not a 'wound' to be 'healed' or a 'scar' to 'fade'. Once someone has been in the world, they have always been in the world; and once they have gone their absence will be in the world forever, part of the world; in Dad's case part of mine. This is a good thing.

How foolish, then, is all this talk of 'getting over' death. How empty, how wrong-headed the exhortations we make to those who love us that they should try not to miss us when we're gone. Why not? You do miss someone you love, don't you, when they're gone? How self-negating is the wish that others should not feel sad when they remember us. Of course they should feel sad! They can't talk to us any more.

It is right that we make an imprint on the minds and lives of others, right that we should be needed while still alive; and therefore right that the imprint remains and the loss hurts, and continues hurting.

So I've decided that I don't want to 'come to terms' with Dad's death. It's bloody awful that he isn't here. It still cuts me up, and this is a fact of love. I'm perfectly capable of keeping things in proportion, as Dad always did, but I don't want to 'get things into perspective', if by that one means wanting them to grow smaller. It's a fact; his life is a fact; the gap now is a fact; it's not getting any smaller; I'm sad, but I'm happy that I'm sad.

I was taken by surprise by the response among *Spectator* readers. It was immediate, positive and – in many letters – so heartfelt. It seems those thoughts chimed with feelings and the reflections of many. When the magazine temporarily lifted its 'paywall' for online readership, the article became the magazine's most-read column. More people wrote to me, and I had a couple of approaches proposing I might write a book collecting or expanding on such thoughts and experiences.

I could see that such a book might achieve a wide circulation. Among the reasons I rejected the suggestion, the foremost was that my father would have hated the very thought. I remembered again the way – on hearing an orchestra repeating, *appassionato*, in a second encore, the theme from Handel's lovely *Largo* in *Xerxes* – Dad's doing the motions of wringing the last drops from a wet tea-towel.

Human relationships can be with teams, tribes or institutions too. Since the first edition of my story was published, my bond with my old party – which with age, and since it's now twenty-seven years since I quit as a Conservative MP you might expect to have loosened – has grown more intense. I choose the word 'intense' rather than 'close' or even 'affectionate' because I do feel the most intense loyalty to the party as an abstraction, while being driven almost to distraction by its neurotic and self-defeating behaviour. I write as a Conservative-led government that has achieved much, totters, tearing intermittently at its own entrails, towards an uncertain result in a general election in a couple of years' time.

I respected and liked David Cameron from the day I first met him. I met him by mistake. Lizzie (then) Pitman, who had been the Tories' valiant candidate against Tony Blair in his Sedgefield seat, asked later if I would come and speak for her in Oxfordshire. Supposing she was the candidate, I at once agreed. But she wasn't. At a very grand dinner in the Witney constituency I quickly realized that Lizzie was a friend and supporter of the candidate; and the candidate was a young man called David Cameron. This happened not long before he was elected in 2001 but you will find no reference to the evening in the first edition of my book because nobody at the time – certainly including me – had any idea of how high Mr Cameron was headed.

I remember only a pleasant evening in fairly sumptuous surroundings at a fine house among some very rich people, and a smooth young candidate who seemed genuinely pleasant, and was obviously a moderate and sensible kind of Tory. I was more concerned to cover my embarrassment at having mistaken the purpose of my visit, and speech, than to observe him closely. You do meet rather a lot of bright and mildly affable people with good connections and considerable means, in Conservative politics.

But I kept an eye on Cameron, still with what I can only call a vaguely good feeling about him. Julian and I met for a talk with him in his Commons office not long before he formally threw his hat into the ring for the party leadership. I remember his exact words as we chatted: 'I think I might have a pop at it.'

I've got to know him a little since, though hardly well. Julian and I have stayed at Chequers once. I remain impressed not only by his polish but by the basically nice man to be found, I believe, beneath the polish. I became a supporter in print of his bid for the leadership, and a strong supporter of his decision to lead his party into coalition after the 2010 general election. In Derbyshire I got to know his friend and fellow-warrior George Osborne, too, whose Cheshire seat virtually adjoins what was mine, and whose constituency home is not far away.

The two men complement each other: Mr Osborne (I'd judge) with the sharper-edged mind and the deeper interest in ideas and argument; and Cameron better able to communicate what it's fashionable to call emotional intelligence and a general impression of being the good egg I think he is. I haven't sensed that Cameron likes arguments very much: neither entertaining them nor having them. At dinner with him I wouldn't suppose that to raise the issue of electronic road-pricing over pudding, hopeful of kicking around both the practical and the philosophical implications, would be greeted with enthusiasm by my host. Margaret Thatcher would have dived with intense relief into such a conversation, not least as an escape from small-talk.

But Cameron is much, much quicker-minded than the sometimes bland impression he gives might suggest; and shrewd; and privately quite hard in his judgements. And I sense that Osborne is more tolerant, kinder, more loyal, and more passionate about ideas of liberty and justice, than the rather eighteenth-century cynic that he may appear (and like to appear) to be.

I've never had a moment's doubt about David Cameron's instincts. When you see him with his wife, Samantha, and their children, you know you are with nice people, perhaps at times too nice. Nor do I worry about collisions between Mr Cameron and events. He's very good with events: suddenly decisive, suddenly incisive, suddenly communicative; suddenly sure. The collisions that worry me are with his party – my party. This is no place for yet another column on the Tories; I'll limit myself to saying that both within Parliament and without, the party contains a small but poisonous quotient of dangerous zealots on the right, and a much larger minority of fearful shits. The two groups can blend, merge and combine: the shits tending, like a pack of dogs, to follow the scent of blood. In a collision with Cameron he'd see them off, but he tends to avoid collisions, and perhaps shouldn't. I wrote this in my weekly diary in *The Times* in the summer of 2012, and it sums up the worry:

There's a little parking space opposite my flat in London. From my window I watch the litter build up there until, once there's enough, I clear it. I observe a pattern in the litter's distribution; you'd think it would be random but it isn't.

If an object can blow in the wind and lacks means of self-propulsion or anchorage, then once entered into this zone it will eddy in the end towards one quite small and identifiable patch. Here it will rest, twirling a little in the gusts but essentially trapped. Hugely complicated aerodynamics arising from the interplay of wind, street furniture, kerbs and walls determine with fierce but invisible precision the resting place of every sweet-wrapper or tissue.

Being Prime Minister of the United Kingdom is a bit like this. Unless you're absolutely sure where you will and won't go, you'll end up where most of the rest, for most of the time, went.

Making threatening noises about Europe but never quite kicking over the traces. Promising to do something some day about the House of Lords but never finding a majority for anything in particular. Growling about immigration but concluding that grumbling is about the limit of it. Snarling at 'shirkers' (as David Cameron did in PM's Questions yesterday) and slipping into the British-jobs-for-British-workers language of the populist meanies, but without follow-up. Taking verbal pot-shots at greedy businessmen but, on the whole, leaving it at that. Talking big on defence but snipping furtively away at what we spend on it. Promising to simplify, while adding on complexity, item by item, as you respond to the daily news agenda and the cries of 'something must be done'.

So now Mr Cameron loses a Lords reform he probably didn't really want anyway but had sort of promised, and it's all been put off again. Euro referendum – sort of, someday, maybe. And he comes into the Commons and takes a verbal kick at shirkers (hear! hear!): feigning moral horror at the discovery that if you offer people money they'll take it. Oh, spare us. It wasn't going to be like this, was it? Is this where it's all going, is this where every Prime Minister must go, eddying with the litter, floating as free as paper in the wind – and as confined?

Those paragraphs end with a question: is this where it's going? The question was not rhetorical. This needn't be where it goes. I have seen and still see Cameron as a leader capable of setting his own direction. But he'll have to want to. On balance, but only on balance, I think he will.

At the beginning of this Epilogue I remarked that a man's story threads together relationships with people, with places and with events. A columnist's story is particularly heavily threaded with events. What is called the 'news agenda' has been the bread and butter of my column writing, but in my philosophy (which Julian says is essentially Marxist) events often have less significance than the deeper currents on which they may simply be bobbing up and down. The events are news; the news is fast-moving and visible; the currents are slower-moving and often unseen; but it is the currents that interest me most.

In November 2008, after the banking crash and during a briefing by academics at the London School of Economics on turmoil on the international markets, the Queen is reported to have asked: 'Why didn't anybody see it coming?' But I have believed from the start that at the deepest level many, perhaps most, people did half-see it coming. Throughout the late 1990s and first years of the twenty-first century I noticed a quiet but persistent undercurrent of public doubt about the solidity of the foundations for the growth in our prosperity. Most of us seemed to be getting richer without working proportionately harder; taxes were staying low yet government spending seemed to be splurging. It didn't add up. I believed that on some level millions sensed this.

But, being no economist and hardly able even to read a balance sheet, I hesitated to rush in. Hesitated, and then did. In 2004 I earned myself a journalistic slapping from a fellow-writer and economic commentator on *The Times*, Anatole Kaletsky, who devoted two articles of his own to shooting down a column I had written whose headline, 'Beneath our wave of optimism an anxious foreboding lurks' pretty well summed up my case.

We are, reported *The Times* this week, 'blithely optimistic' about our country's economy [according to a Populus poll]. Three in four of us think Britain as a whole will prosper in the year ahead. Net optimism has improved thirteen points in the past five months.

. . . Yet unless my own antennae are picking up rogue signals, a worry lurks beneath the good cheer in the public mood. A darker melody in a minor key is faintly audible beneath the oompah-pah of economic optimism: a persistent, puzzled, inquisitive counterpoint. Why? Why does there seem to be all this money sloshing around?

Taking the closest large town to our Derbyshire home, Chesterfield, I described its (to many) remarkable turnaround after the death of nearly all the mining-based and steel-based industries on which it had relied. Its whole reason for existence had gone, yet driving most weeks to the railway station there I had observed the many signs of prosperity, the 4x4s, the private housing estates under construction, the clubs, the shopping centres, 'even what is every formerly working-class town's ultimate social trophy: a Liberal Democrat MP'. So many people I spoke to wondered, as did I, where this new prosperity was coming from:

There is a feeling that we are living beyond our means and beyond our deserts. It feeds into, and is fed by, worry about the world's oil supplies and reserves. It feeds into, and is fed by, concern about global warming, and a suspicion that mankind is playing fast and loose with the environment and that we or our descendants will somehow have to 'pay' for all that we are enjoying now.

. . . the fear that nemesis will follow hubris has always lurked in the collective unconscious of mankind, and in my own country that anxiety seems to me as close to the surface now – just when things really do look so rosy – as in my short lifetime I can remember.

... So where is all the money coming from? Applied more widely, I think this is an unspoken question in millions of British minds. There is a feeling that somehow it cannot all add up. It is as though we have looked at our bank account as a nation and found ourselves significantly better off than we had guessed. We seem to have more than we have earned. Someone must surely have made a mistake in the calculations? When will we get the notice of error? When will we get the bill?

Maybe it is all to do with invisible earnings and the City of London. Maybe the growing wealth so many of us feel conscious of (and borrow against) simply because each of us is prepared every year to set a higher valuation on our fellow citizens' houses, is not a chimera. But I cannot but share with many of my countrymen this nagging feeling that a nation of homeowners energetically bidding up the value of each other's property, borrowing on the basis of the inflating figures, then spending the money in hypermarkets every weekend buying Chinese power-tools, Brazilian hardwood, Swedish furniture and Australian wine, and jetting back and forth across the Continent ... such a country is somehow riding for a fall.

The very wave which that Populus poll described carries with it an underlying national anxiety lest the wave break. Were it to do so I can already hear the voices of millions confiding that they always did think our prosperity was built upon the sand.

In a version of Euripides's brutal, simple play, *Hecuba* ... Hecuba describes her sense of unfocused foreboding: 'By day, by night, by light and darkness/Why am I tortured?/Why do I see things? ... Something is going to happen.'

Something is going to happen. In a less theatrical way I sense that same worry beneath the surface of these fat times for modern Britain.

After Anatole's clear and persuasive columns politely explaining why that analysis was ignorant and wrong, a friend and fellow-columnist, Mike White of the *Guardian*, remarked to my partner Julian: 'I see Mr Kaletsky has put our young Matthew in his place.'

But I stuck to my opinion – or, rather, instinct – and never doubted that many shared it. And in my mind grew a picture of a country secretly troubled by a sense of national undeserving, a fear of national nemesis, and an increasing resentment and irritation towards the unthinking politicians and the media that led us all into this candy mountain.

When, one morning, I listened to Gordon Brown (still Chancellor) being grilled on the radio, I heard no depth or courage, originality or independence of thought. He just seemed to be ducking and avoiding all the time – and inelegantly too. This was a period when it was fashionable among political commentators to nod wisely and say 'never underestimate Gordon Brown'. I wrote a column in *The Times* remarking on that and asking where all these people were who were underestimating Gordon Brown, as I'd like to join them. He didn't speak to me much after that.

Six years after I'd written my column about Chesterfield, and two years after the financial turmoil in 2008 and the economic depression that has followed it, the underlying resentment and insecurity that I thought I'd sensed had well and truly broken the surface. But in different places and under different guises.

My theory was (and remains) that the particular and apparent causes of the great waves of public indignation that have been sweeping Britain in recent years, are not, in fact, the real causes. In 2012, under the headline 'Sure, we're angry. But are we sure what about?' I wrote about it in *The Times*. Below I reprint much of that column. I have not removed, explained or refreshed readers' memories on those references to individuals and scandals that may now seem rather obscure. It was only last year! Their very descent into obscurity so soon after they had seemed to be on everybody's lips, serves to reinforce my argument ...

Do you know what Libor is? Be honest. Can you unblushingly claim not just to have furrowed a studious brow over the little potted summaries in this week's newspapers, but to have a well-founded understanding of what the London Interbank Offered Rate means in the world of the City?

How grounded are you in the business culture surrounding such matters? Have you made any calculation of what Libor-rigging might have cost (or indeed benefited) you yourself? Have you any real feel for how much it matters?

I haven't. And so I surprised myself by the depth and spontaneity of my fury on learning this week that Barclays has been manipulating Libor. My indignation felt genuine but I confess that had I read that it was the Robil rate – or indeed the Brilo or Orbil rate – I would have been just as cross. Incandescent, in fact.

Barclays are bankers. We hate bankers. Whatever it is they're said to have done, we're pretty sure it was dreadful and they're undoubtedly guilty of doing it. The whole lot of them. We started being angry with them even before the exact nature of their dark deeds was revealed.

For all of us, press and public, the sequence is becoming a habit. First the anger. Then a scramble to find out what precisely it is we're going to be angry about. And finally a bit of hasty cramming so we can express the anger with fluency and apparent authority. Again and again, that has been the story for the past four or five years. We seize upon an abuse, rip it out of context, kick aside the caveats and explanations, stamp our feet, pucker our faces with rage, do a little homework on Wikipedia – and shout. Somebody must swing for this!

God knows, I've no brief for Bob Diamond. He can go to blazes for all I care and take his minions and his millions with him. I no more make the case for amoral banking or greedy hedge-fund managers than I would for expense-cheating MPs, conniving police officers, grasping public utility companies or phone-hacking journalists. Or indeed for pig-ignorant and grotesquely overpaid sportsmen, were the public in a mood to drag soccer stars off to the media tumbrils – which it isn't.

But when I look at the suddenness and intensity of each succeeding squall, the arbitrary way in which groups of offenders are plucked from context and skinned alive as public enemies, and – this is very telling – the careless shrug of shoulders when it subsequently turns out an accusation was false or unfair (it's by no means certain that the *News of the World* deleted Milly Dowler's messages), I see something deeper is at work.

This is the Age of Disenchantment. We're all going to hell in a handcart and it wasn't meant to be like this; it wasn't what we were promised. We're furious, but we don't quite know about what. We've been robbed, but we're not quite sure how. We want to settle scores, but we can't decide with whom.

Destiny has dumped on us and we don't know why. We secretly wonder whether it might be a little bit our fault and that makes us even angrier.

So any demon will do. Bob Diamond. Fred the Shred. Anyone called Murdoch. The Chinese. Rebekah Brooks. Greek hairdressers. Geek traders. Andy Coulson. Some poor, obscure Labour MP who claimed a bit more in expenses than the others and is now in prison and, ahem, we don't quite recall the name but his shame was big in the headlines then. Sir Philip Hampton, ah, he'd slipped your mind. But, boy, did you see red about his bonus (declined) at the time! And who was that other bank chief, the one in hunt attire on a horse? Some of these people may deserve their violent public opprobrium. Others may be innocent. All alike are carted down the media street in a hail of stones and bottles.

Don't you see? The anger is real, the indignation is genuine, the feeling is high – and the culprit is random. In a wicked world there are so many to choose from.

But the world always was wicked and there always were culprits. What's slightly disturbing about the second decade of the 21st century is the sense of national and media hunger to find a whole class of people to cast as co-conspirators in a villainous plot against the public interest.

... It's a long, long road from the public humiliation of bankers, newspapermen and MPs to the concentration camps; and I'm not for a second suggesting that we'll go anything like that far. But the compass bearing is the same and it's not hard to see why.

... I'm sure that bankers are playing foul, but then I'm sure they always did. I'm far less sure that it's bankers who stole our future. I believe we may have been under a misapprehension about our future. Maybe bankers have been complicit – with us – in helping us buy time against an inevitable reckoning with an oncoming truth.

We have been living beyond our means. We have been paying ourselves more than our efforts were earning. We sought political leaders who would assure us that the good times would never end and that the centuries of boom and bust were over; and we voted for those who offered that assurance. We sought credit for which we had no security and we gave our business to the banks that advertised it.

We wanted higher exam grades for our children and were rewarded with politicians prepared to supply them by lowering exam standards. We wanted free and better health care and demanded chancellors who paid for it without putting up our taxes. We wanted salacious stories in our newspapers and bought the papers that broke the rules to provide them.

And now we whimper and snarl at MPs, bankers and journalists. Fair enough, my friends, but, you know, we really are all in this together.

I could now, a year later, add to that list the recent media fever for identifying elderly figures who were well-known thirty or forty years ago, and are now accused of improper sexual behaviour. Of course if you so much as raise an eyebrow at the national neuralgia about sexual impropriety, people will accuse you of condoning it or, worse, having something to hide. I don't. I merely wonder whether in thirty years' time the issue will seem to have merited the central place it achieved on our front pages, in broadcast bulletins and in commentary. The news is not always the news: or, rather, our relationship with the news is often what makes the news the news. My own relationship with the news has been difficult and prickly. I've always found the psychology of what lies beneath it more interesting. The entire hoo-hah about Lord Justice Leveson's enquiry into the press, for instance, has struck me as a major spasm triggered by nothing big or new; and I've nothing to add beyond the observation that it will all fizzle out and future generations will wonder why it ever fizzled in.

Thus I was gripped by a book published in 2010 by David Willetts who later that year became Universities Minister. *The Pinch: How the Baby Boomers Stole Their Children's Future* argued that our generation had been storing up debt for future generations but was in denial about what we were doing. The argument made a deep impression on me. As signs appeared in the spring of 2013 that the depression was beginning to ease I started to fear we had not really learned the lessons. I see government (effectively) printing money to get us out of this depression, and shuffling taxes and tax breaks around to keep house prices buoyant and stop the property bubble from bursting – or bursting yet. All this, I suspect, is unconsciously designed to keep the boat afloat until some great tide of pan-European recovery comes in to lift us all out of trouble. But what if that tide never comes in? What if we never resume the levels of growth that forecasts continue to treat as a kind of baseline for normality?

Then, one way or another, the next generation will pay. I doubt we've fixed things. I suspect we're just buying time again. I do not believe this financial crisis is over.

Meanwhile, we cultivate our garden. The third of my trilogy of relationships in a man's life – relationship with place – sees me renewing friendships with places I used to know, and making new ones.

Over the last decade life became materially very comfortable for me. I was paid well by publishers and newspaper proprietors, I made speeches, and my earnings grew. Julian – who, if he had chosen, could have become the world's best professional travel planner – organized voyages of discovery into Colombia, where we became part of the first wave of visitors to find out that the bad old days have gone from that country, and that its mountains, forests, rivers and beaches, and its warm and civilized population, rival anything you will find anywhere in the New World.

To stand in the warm rain in the remote interior Tierradentro region of Colombia, where beneath dripping trees giant and menacing stone bird-man statues grip their prey of human babies in their beaks, the statues guarding the entrances to vertical shafts down into hollowed-out subterranean halls where wait the skeletons of the dead, surrounded by all they'll need for the next life ... these were travels I never expected might still lie ahead when I put down my manuscript for the first edition of this book.

And, just as unpredicted, an appetite grew to rediscover the country of my boyhood, Rhodesia, now Zimbabwe. Returning there, we did not find the chaos or collapse that one would expect from reading British newspapers. Instead we found a country materially surprisingly unchanged from the old days; the infrastructure still largely intact, the railways more or less running, the potholes more numerous and deeper, the towns and cities much as they were but a bit shabbier – and Zimbabwe's rather diminished population the same gentle, friendly, tolerant, kindly, slightly too passive people that they always were: often astonishingly well educated.

Climbing Mount Binga in the Chimanimani mountains on the eastern border of the country I looked out over the granite domes and crumbling quartzite of the Eastern Highlands and reflected that this was an ascent I always wanted to try as a boy, but could find nobody to come with me. Now Julian had. Zimbabwe is a breathtakingly beautiful country, with a beautiful soul.

South Africa's soul is darker, more troubled. I was never optimistic about South Africa and am still not. I was always optimistic about Zimbabwe and still am, though I cannot know how soon real stability will return. Africa will be resurgent – is already, however unsteadily and however patchily, resurgent. Born in Africa, I am still an African. If there ever seems a fair prospect of security for white people and their property in Zimbabwe, I shall return. It would be wonderful to have a place there.

★

Meanwhile, the columns keep pouring out, while my biographical BBC radio series, *Great Lives*, gets more and more fun. Politics absorbs me and always will, but ideas and social observation occupy more of my thoughts than when I was younger. An example is a column I wrote for *The Times* on bisexuality, which became one of the most commented upon I've ever written. A man like me doesn't have many big ideas or theories in his life, just a few, but they keep recurring, and one about which I'm absolutely sure is that the division of humans into basically two camps, heterosexual and homosexual, is a twentieth-century mistake which will be looked upon with scorn and incredulity by the time our succeeding century ends. We're all scattered across a wide range, with clusters towards the two poles. That's obvious, and has been apparent to me (sometimes rather directly) throughout my adult life – however close to the homosexual end of the spectrum I may be myself.

And, though a columnist must not just keep repeating himself, he makes a mistake if he assumes he was necessarily heard the first time. It's more like being a bat: you just keep emitting the same range of squeaks until sooner or later they bounce off something solid in the lives or thoughts of your readers.

So I'll squeak on for a few years more. In 2011 I think I was sounded out (you're never quite sure, this being the British way) for a possible seat in the House of Lords. I indicated, I hope politely, that honorifics mean nothing to be, they rather appal me, and unless it was to do something rather than be something, then I'd rather not. 'Mr' was good enough for my father, and it's good enough for me.

I'm sixty-four this year. And in my sixties I'm learning something entirely new to me, but surely the experience of so many throughout history: the experience of having clawed your way to a position of influence but reached it almost too late, when some of the edge you'd need to use it well has blunted. The idea that the human animal reaches the height of its powers at a particular age, peaks, and having peaked, gently declines, is a great truth but a horrible over-simplification. I realize now that some powers arrive, and some power arrives, after others have gone.

I learned as a marathon runner that raw prowess – muscular strength, heart–lung capacity, the physical things a long-distance runner must call upon – decline very noticeably from our late twenties onwards, and probably earlier. But what – rather misleadingly – we are accustomed to call 'stamina' carries on building as we get older. I say 'misleadingly' because I think what we call stamina is in fact more a moral or mental quality than a physical one, and arises from the mastery of the body by willpower, of the flesh by the spirit. Stamina can to a great degree be acquired by instruction, repetition and intensive training: plus, importantly, the gaining of self-belief. It follows that with the increasing professionalization of athletics I would expect the record-holders in long-distance events to be younger and younger as the century proceeds.

To achieve optimal times you would want to bring the peak in 'stamina' as close as possible to coinciding with the peak in prowess. For marathons this could be as young as eighteen, but at present champions are much older. In marathon running we do not teach adolescents to aim for the top before they are twenty. If we did we might be surprised at the results. I got my best result at the age of thirty-five. Had I brought to my twenty-five-year-old body the self-discipline in training (and self-belief in winning) that I'd acquired by thirty-five I have no doubt my personal best would have been faster. At thirty-five I was already wearing out, but fuelled by huge determination and the experience of heavy, sustained training.

As for marathons, so for career and for life itself. It is entirely true that our strengths and capabilities ebb inexorably away, usually earlier and faster than we think, and to deny this to ourselves is pure folly. But different strengths, different facilities and different potencies peak at different times – very different times – and the interplay of the accretion of some capabilities with the diminution of others makes for an exceedingly complicated dynamic.

Prowess of most kinds, physical and mental, does probably peak even earlier than we think. It might be as early as sixteen. The ability to learn peaks even earlier, probably in the toddler. At sixty-three my capacity (say) to learn a language is literally a fraction of what it was when I was learning the language I speak best, English, at two.

But not all learning is a matter of raw capacity. Much is mediated by having learned how to learn; and learned to want to learn; and acquired already the knowledge without which no further learning can proceed – a foundation which takes time to build, time during which the raw capacity is already starting to slacken.

And then there is moral knowledge. Without it, other strengths will be misdirected, or stunted, or wasted, or self-defeated. The acquisition of moral knowledge continues lifelong. So by definition does the acquisition of experience, lacking which – again – other capacities will be misdirected or under-employed. These are the sorts of thing we like to call 'wisdom' – and of course old men and women will make much of telling you they are what count most. Yes, up to a point they do, but only up to a point; and there's a point past which acres of experience and any amount of shrewd understanding of mankind and life in general will not compensate for having become so slow on the uptake that you simply cannot keep up, keep abreast or – on occasions – keep awake.

But there's something more, and of this I've learned much in the last few years in a relatively short space of time. It's the growth of reputation. It's the acquisition of command, the gathering of respect, the collecting of friends and contacts, the getting of attention. These can come with age and career progress, and as they come they elevate essentially the same man – or even a gradually deteriorating version of the man – to a position where he will be seen, heard and believed, where he was not before. Experiencing this elevation will help him, in turn, to believe in himself: sometimes excessively.

At twenty-nine I would sit on the Commons benches during speeches by or even simple questions from Enoch Powell, and note the total silence that fell upon the chamber as he rose. If it was a speech he was to make then you'd see scores of Members hurrying in to crowd around the doorway and listen. Mr Powell could choose his own pace. He could pause for what seemed like an age between sentences. He could fall silent and stare with a kind of theatrical gloom around the chamber: balefulness made flesh. Nobody would heckle, giggle or even cough. The slower he spoke and the longer his pauses the more attentive we would become, our brows furrowed, our own intelligences furiously following, trying to understand and weigh his argument.

And I remember thinking, yes, great, splendid, a fine sight. But I could be an orator like that if my speeches were heard with such reverence. If the esteem were there I could rise to it. If people didn't talk among themselves when I paused then I too could acquire Enoch's 'timing'. And I too have great arguments I long to put across. But it's only me, and no one would consider my words or weigh my thoughts, and the audience would walk away.

In a minor way at a lower elevation I have in my fifties and sixties gained the platform I longed for. I revel in this, yet am not comfortable with it. Composing a column these days I can understate a rebuke, and in the very understatement some people will think they see gravity and authority. When I was thirty I had to overstate to get anyone so much as to listen. Now I can fail to write a column about something at the centre of the news and be asked why I didn't, as if the answer might be interesting. When I was thirty nobody would have wondered why Parris hadn't spoken. On Tuesdays at *The Times* we have a meeting with the editor to talk about the political news and I'm sometimes horrified when, if I begin to venture a thought, probably nonsensical, my younger colleagues shut up and listen. They know much more than me, these days, and react and analyse with greater speed and skill. When I join a knot of them talking, quickfire, about the day's events, it's often all I can do to keep up.

Yet – I cannot deny it – the sense that people are listening when I speak or write, gives me confidence that this might be worth saying. It might, however, be rubbish. I've been wrong or silly about no end of things in my time, and doubtless still am. And I'm terribly ignorant – always have been. As Julian once candidly replied when I asked him my greatest fault: 'You don't know much.'

So the score-card at sixty-three is roughly as follows. Physical prowess: about 40 per cent of former capacity. Learning ability: about 15 per cent. Acquired knowledge: declining as I forget faster than I absorb and old stuff goes out of date. Wisdom, etc.: probably on plateau. Powers of reasoning: about 65 per cent of former capacity. Drive/hunger/ambition: still strong, but sights lowered; governor of small colony now the limit. Command/respect: still creeping up but probably near peak. In due course they'll begin to giggle.

Such are the differently peaking and variously declining powers with whose interplay I wrestle, and will have to judge before deciding when to throw in the towel. But I dread – and any man or woman who has reached my stage in life and career must know and dread – that chilling sensation which begins already to tug at the corners of my self-confidence: the sensation of being thought still worth listening to, when your own suspicion grows that, frankly, you're past it and you haven't anything useful left to say.

Index